GREENS
SHERIFF COURT RULES
2010/2011

Reprinted from the *Parliament House Book*, published in looseleaf form
and updated five times a year by W. Green, the Scottish Law Publisher

The following paperback titles are also available in the series:
Annotated Rules of the Court of Session 2010/2011
Solicitors Professional Handbook 2010/2011

Parliament House Book consists of the following Divisions:
A Fees and Stamps
B Courts, Upper
C Court of Session Practice
D Courts, Lower
E Licensing
F Solicitors
G Legal Aid
H Bankruptcy and other Mercantile Statutes
I Companies
J Conveyancing, Land Tenure and Registration
K Family Law
L Landlord and Tenant
M Succession, Trusts, Liferents and Judicial Factors

GREENS
SHERIFF COURT RULES
2010/2011

Reprinted from
Division D (Courts, Lower)
of the *Parliament House Book*

W. GREEN   THOMSON REUTERS

Published in 2010 by
Thomson Reuters (Legal) Limited
(Registered in England and Wales,
Company No 1679046.
Registered office and address for service
100 Avenue Road, Swiss Cottage,
London, NW3 3PF) trading as W. Green

Printed in the UK by CPI William Clowes Ltd, Beccles, NR34 7TL

No natural forests were destroyed to make this product;
only farmed timber was used and replanted

A CIP catalogue record for this book is available from the British Library

ISBN 9780414018082

© 2010 Thomson Reuters (Legal) Limited

Thomson Reuters and the Thomson Reuters Logo
are trademarks of Thomson Reuters.

DIVISION D

Courts, Lower

Statutes

Acts of Sederunt, etc.

2

[1] **Sheriff Courts (Scotland) Act 1907**

(7 Edw. 7 c. 51)

An Act to regulate and amend the laws and practice relating to the civil procedure in sheriff courts in Scotland, and for other purposes. [28th August 1907]

NOTE
[1] As amended by the Sheriff Courts (Scotland) Act 1913 (2 & 3 Geo. V, c. 28). Applied by the Agricultural Holdings (Scotland) Act 1991 (c.55), s.21(4), (5).

For the interpretation of the terms "sheriff" and "sheriff-substitute" throughout this Act, see now the Sheriff Courts (Scotland) Act 1971 (c.58), s.4, and the Interpretation Act 1978 (c.30), Sched. 1.

PRELIMINARY

Short title
1. This Act may be cited for all purposes as the Sheriff Courts (Scotland) Act 1907.

2. [*Repealed by the Statute Law Revision Act 1927, (c.42).*]

Interpretation
3. In construing this Act (unless where the context is repugnant to such construction)—
[1] (a) "Sheriff principal" includes sheriff;
   (b) "Tenant" includes sub-tenant;
   (c) "Lease" includes sub-lease;
[2] (d) "Action" or "cause" includes every civil proceeding competent in the ordinary sheriff court;
   (e) "Person" includes company, corporation, or association and firm of any description nominate or descriptive, or any Board corporate or unincorporate;
   (f) "Sheriff-clerk" includes sheriff-clerk depute;
   (g) "Agent" means a law-agent enrolled in terms of the Law Agents (Scotland) Act 1873;
   (h) "Final judgment" means an interlocutor which, by itself, or taken along with previous interlocutors, disposes of the subject-matter of the cause, notwithstanding that judgment may not have been pronounced on every question raised, and that the expenses found due may not have been modified, taxed or decerned for;
   (i) [*Repealed by the Sheriff Courts (Scotland) Act 1971 (c.58), Sch. 2.*]
   (j) "Small Debt Acts" means and includes the Small Debt (Scotland) Acts 1887 to 1889, and Acts explaining or amending the same;
   (k) "Initial writ" means the statement of claim, petition, note of appeal, or other document by which the action is initiated;
   (l) "Procurator-Fiscal" means procurator-fiscal in the sheriff court;
   (m) [*Repealed by the Statute Law (Repeals) Act 1989 (c.43), Sch.1, Pt I.*]
   (n) "Pursuer" means and includes any person making a claim or demand, or seeking any warrant or order competent in the sheriff court;
   (o) "Defender" means and includes any person who is required to be called in any action;
[3] (p) "Summary application" means and includes all applications of a summary nature brought under the common law jurisdiction of the sheriff principal, and all applications, whether by appeal or

otherwise, brought under any Act of Parliament which provides, or, according to any practice in the sheriff court, which allows that the same shall be disposed of in a summary manner, but which does not more particularly define in what form the same shall be heard, tried, and determined;

(q) [*Repealed by the Law Reform (Miscellaneous Provisions) (Scotland) Act 1980 (c.55), Sch.3.*]

NOTES

[1] As substituted by the Sheriff Courts (Scotland) Act 1971 (c.58), s.4.
[2] As amended by the Sheriff Courts (Scotland) Act 1913 (c.28), Sch.1.
[3] As substituted by the Sheriff Courts (Scotland) Act 1971 (c.58), s.4.

JURISDICTION

Jurisdiction

[1,2] **4.** The jurisdiction of the sheriffs principal, within their respective sheriffdoms, shall extend to and include all navigable rivers, ports, harbours, creeks, shores, and anchoring grounds in or adjoining such sheriffdoms. And the powers and jurisdictions formerly competent to the High Court of Admiralty in Scotland in all maritime causes and proceedings, civil and criminal, including such as may apply to persons furth of Scotland, shall be competent to the sheriffs principal, provided the defender shall upon any legal ground of jurisdiction be amenable to the jurisdiction of the sheriff principal before whom such cause or proceeding may be raised, and provided also that it shall not be competent to the sheriffs principal to try any crime committed on the seas which it would not be competent for him to try if the crime had been committed on land: Provided always that where sheriffdoms are separated by a river, firth, or estuary, the sheriffs on either side shall have concurrent jurisdictions over the intervening space occupied by water.

NOTES

[1] Repealed, so far as relating to criminal proceedings, by the Criminal Procedure (Scotland) Act 1975 (c.21), Sch.10.
[2] As substituted by the Sheriff Courts (Scotland) Act 1971 (c.58), s.4.

Extension of jurisdiction

[1] **5.** Nothing herein contained shall derogate from any jurisdiction, powers, or authority presently possessed or in use to be exercised by the sheriffs of Scotland, and such jurisdiction shall extend to and include—

[2,6] (1) Actions of declarator;

(1A) [Repealed by the Law Reform (Parent and Child) (Scotland) Act 1986 (c.9), Sch.2.]

[3] (2) Actions for aliment or separation (other than any action mentioned in subsection (2A) below):

[4] (2A) Actions, arising out of an application under section 31(1) of the Maintenance Orders (Reciprocal Enforcement) Act 1972, for the recovery of maintenance:

[5] (2B) Actions for divorce:

(2C) [*Repealed by the Children (Scotland) Act 1995 (c.36), Sch.5.*]

(3) Actions of division of commonty and of division or division and sale of common property, in which cases the Act of 1695 concerning the division of commonties shall be read and construed as if it conferred jurisdiction upon the sheriff court in the same manner as upon the Court of Session:

(4) Actions relating to questions of heritable right or title (except actions of adjudication save in so far as now competent and actions of reduction) including all actions of declarator of irritancy and removing, whether at the instance of a superior against a vassal or of a landlord against a tenant:

(5) Suspension of charges or threatened charges upon the decrees of court

granted by the sheriff or upon decrees of registration proceeding upon bonds, bills, contracts or other obligations registered in the books of the sheriff court, the books of council and session, or any others competent.

NOTES
[1] Explained (legal aid): see SI 1958/1872, r.2(2). Excluded by the Land Registration (Scotland) Act 1979 (c.33), ss.21(6) and 22(7). As amended by the Law Reform (Miscellaneous Provisions) (Scotland) Act 1980 (c.55), s.15(a) and Sch.3, and the Civil Jurisdiction and Judgments Act 1982 (c.27), Sch.14.
[2] As amended by the Law Reform (Parent and Child) (Scotland) Act 1986 (c.9), Sch.2.
[3] As substituted by the Family Law (Scotland) Act 1985 (c.37), Sch.1, para.1. As amended by the Law Reform (Parent and Child) (Scotland) Act 1986 (c.9), Sch.2. See the Domicile and Matrimonial Proceedings Act 1973 (c.45), Sch.2.
[4] As inserted by the Domestic Proceedings and Magistrates' Courts Act 1978 (c.22), Sch.2.
[5] As inserted by the Divorce Jurisdiction, Court Fees and Legal Aid (Scotland) Act 1983 (c.12), s.1.
[6] As amended by the Family Law (Scotland) Act 2006 (asp 2), s.4 (effective May 4, 2006 (SSI 2006/212)).

Power of sheriff to order sheriff clerk to execute deeds relating to heritage
[1] **5A.**—(1) This section applies where—
 (a) an action relating to heritable property is before the sheriff; or
 (b) it appears to the sheriff that an order under this section is necessary to implement a decree of a sheriff relating to heritable property.
(2) Where the grantor of any deed relating to the heritable property cannot be found or refuses or is unable or otherwise fails to execute the deed, the sheriff may—
 (a) where subsection (1)(a) above applies, on application;
 (b) where subsection (1)(b) above applies, on summary application,
by the grantee, make an order dispensing with the execution of the deed by the grantor and directing the sheriff clerk to execute the deed.
(3) Where in pursuance of an order under this section a deed is executed by the sheriff clerk, it shall have the like force and effect as if it had been executed by the grantor.
(4) In this section—
 "grantor" means a person who is under an obligation to execute the deed; and
 "grantee" means the person to whom that obligation is owed.

NOTE
[1] As inserted by the Law Reform (Miscellaneous Provisions) (Scotland) Act 1985 (c.73), s.17.

Action competent in sheriff court
[1,3] **6.** Subject to section 8 of the Domicile and Matrimonial Proceedings Act 1973 and Chapter III of Part I of the Family Law Act 1986 any action competent in the sheriff court may be brought within the jurisdiction of the sheriff principal—
 [4] (a) Where the defender (or when there are several defenders over each of whom a sheriff court has jurisdiction in terms of this Act, where one of them) resides within the jurisdiction, or having resided there for at least forty days has ceased to reside there for less than forty days and has no known residence in Scotland:
 [5] (b) Where a defender carries on business, and has a place of business within the jurisdiction, and is cited either personally or at such place of business:
 (c) Where the defender is a person not otherwise subject to the jurisdiction of the courts of Scotland, and a ship or vessel of which he is the owner or part owner or master, or goods, debts, money, or other moveable property belonging to him, have been arrested within the jurisdiction:

(d) Where the defender is the owner or part owner or tenant or joint tenant, whether individually or as a trustee of heritable property within the jurisdiction, and the action relates to such property or to his interest therein:

(e) Where the action is for interdict against an alleged wrong being committed or threatened to be committed within the jurisdiction:

(f) Where the action relates to a contract the place of execution or performance of which is within the jurisdiction, and the defender is personally cited there:

(g) Where in an action of furthcoming or multiplepoinding the fund or subject *in medio* is situated within the jurisdiction; or the arrestee or holder of the fund is subject to the jurisdiction of the court:

(h) Where the party sued is the pursuer in any action pending within the jurisdiction against the party suing:

[2] (i) Where the action is founded on delict, and the delict forming the cause of action was committed within the jurisdiction:

(j) Where the defender prorogates the jurisdiction of the court.

NOTES

[1] Excluded by the Civil Jurisdiction and Judgments Act 1982, s.20(3). This section ceases to have effect in relation to actions to which s.45 of the Administration of Justice Act 1956 applies; *ibid.* s.45(6).

As amended by the Domicile and Matrimonial Proceedings Act 1973, Sch.4 and by the Family Law Act 1986, Sch.1, para.3.

[2] As substituted by the Law Reform (Jurisdiction in Delict) (Scotland) Act 1971, s.1(2).

[3] As substituted by the Sheriff Courts (Scotland) Act 1971 (c.58), s.4.

[4] As amended by the Sheriff Courts (Scotland) Act 1913 (c.28), Sch.1.

[5] As substituted by the Sheriff Courts (Scotland) Act 1913 (c.28), Sch.1.

Privative jurisdiction in causes under one thousand five hundred pounds value

[1] **7.** All causes not exceeding £5000 in value exclusive of interest and expenses competent in the sheriff court shall be brought and followed forth in the sheriff court only, and shall not be subject to review by the Court of Session: Provided that nothing herein contained shall affect any right of appeal competent under any Act of Parliament in force for the time being.

NOTE

[1] As amended by the Sheriff Courts (Scotland) Act 1971 (c.58), Pt III, s.31. The figure is substituted subject to savings specified in SSI 2007/507 by the Sheriff Courts (Scotland) Act 1971 (Privative Jurisdiction and Summary Cause) Order (SSI 2007/507) art.2 (effective January 14, 2008).

8. [*Repealed by the Sheriff Courts (Scotland) Act 1971 (c.58), Sch.2.*]

9. [*Repealed by the Sheriff Courts (Scotland) Act 1971 (c.58), Sch.2.*]

Privilege not to exempt from jurisdiction

10. No person shall be exempt from the jurisdiction of the sheriff court on account of privilege by reason of being a member of the College of Justice.

SHERIFFS

Appointment of sheriffs and salaried sheriffs-substitute

[1] **11.** The right of appointing to the salaried offices of sheriff principal and salaried sheriff shall be vested in His Majesty, and shall be exercised on the recommendation of the Secretary of State.

NOTE

[1] As substituted by the Sheriff Courts (Scotland) Act 1971 (c.58), s.4 and the Secretaries of State Act 1926 (c.18), s.1(3).

12, 13. [*Repealed by the Sheriff Courts (Scotland) Act 1971 (c.58), Sch.2.*]

Salaries of sheriffs and sheriffs-substitute

[1] **14.** It shall be lawful to grant to any sheriff principal or sheriff such salary as to the Treasury may seem meet, and every such salary shall be paid quarterly or otherwise in every year as the Treasury may determine, and shall be charged upon and be payable out of the Consolidated Fund.

NOTE
[1] As substituted by the Sheriff Courts (Scotland) Act 1971 (c.58), s.4 and amended by the Sheriffs' Pensions (Scotland) Act 1961 (c.42), Sch.1.

15, 16. [*Repealed by the Sheriff Courts (Scotland) Act 1971 (c.58), Sch.2.*]

Honorary sheriff-substitute

[1] **17.** The sheriff principal may by writing under his hand appoint such persons as he thinks proper to hold the office of honorary sheriff within his sheriffdom during his pleasure, and for whom he shall be answerable. An honorary sheriff, during the subsistence of his commission, shall be entitled to exercise the powers and duties appertaining to the office of sheriff. An honorary sheriff shall hold office, notwithstanding the death, resignation, or removal of the sheriff principal, until his commission shall be recalled by a succeeding sheriff principal. In this section "sheriff principal" does not include sheriff.

NOTE
[1] As substituted by the Sheriff Courts (Scotland) Act 1971 (c.58), s.4.

18, 19. [*Repealed by the Sheriff Courts (Scotland) Act 1971 (c.58), Sch.2.*]

20. [*Repealed by the Sheriffs' Pensions (Scotland) Act 1961 (c.42), Sch.2.*]

21. [*Repealed by the Sheriff Courts (Scotland) Act 1971 (c.58), Sch.2.*]

22–24. [*Repealed by the Sheriff Courts and Legal Officers (Scotland) Act 1927 (c.35), Sch.*]

25, 26. [*Repealed by the Sheriff Courts (Scotland) Act 1971 (c.58), Sch.2.*]

APPEALS

Appeal to sheriff

[1] **27.** Subject to the provisions of this Act an appeal to the sheriff principal shall be competent against all final judgments of the sheriff and also against interlocutors—
    (a) Granting or refusing interdict, interim or final;
    (b) Granting interim decree for payment of money other than a decree for expenses, or making an order *ad factum praestandum*;
    (c) Sisting an action;
    (d) Allowing or refusing or limiting the mode of proof;
    (e) Refusing a reponing note; or
    (f) Against which the sheriff either *ex proprio motu* or on the motion of any party grants leave to appeal;
Provided always that notwithstanding the death, resignation, or removal of a sheriff principal, appeals may be taken from the judgment of the sheriff, which appeals shall be heard by the succeeding sheriff principal when he shall enter upon office. It shall be competent for the sheriff principal, when the action is before him on appeal on any point, to open the record *ex*

proprio motu if the record shall appear to him not to have been properly made up, or to allow further proof.

NOTE
[1] As substituted by the Sheriff Courts (Scotland) Act 1971 (c.58), s.4 and amended by the Law Reform (Miscellaneous Provisions) (Scotland) Act 1980 (c.55), Sch.3.

Appeal to the Court of Session
[1] **28.**—(1) Subject to the provisions of this Act, it shall be competent to appeal to the Court of Session against a judgment either of a sheriff principal or of a sheriff if the interlocutor appealed against is a final judgment; or is an interlocutor—
  (a) Granting interim decree for payment of money other than a decree for expenses; or
  (b) Sisting an action; or
  (c) Refusing a reponing note; or
  (d) Against which the sheriff principal or sheriff, either *ex proprio motu* or on the motion of any party, grants leave to appeal.
(2) Nothing in this section nor in section 27 of this Act contained shall affect any right of appeal or exclusion of such right provided by any Act of Parliament in force for the time being.

NOTE
[1] See SI 1949/2062. As substituted by the Sheriff Courts (Scotland) Act 1913 (c.28), s.2 and the Sheriff Courts (Scotland) Act 1971 (c.58), s.4 and amended by the Sheriff Courts (Scotland) Act 1971 (c.58), Sch.2.

Effect of appeal
[1] **29.** An appeal shall be effectual to submit to review the whole of the interlocutors pronounced in the cause, and shall be available to and may be insisted in by all other parties in the cause notwithstanding they may not have noted separate appeals. An appeal shall not prevent immediate execution of warrants to take inventories, or place effects in custody *ad interim*, or warrants for interim preservation, and an interim interdict, although appealed against, shall be binding till recalled.

NOTE
[1] As amended by the Bankruptcy and Diligence etc. (Scotland) Act 2007 (asp 3) Sch.6(1) para.1 (effective April 22, 2009).

30. [*Repealed by the Law Reform (Miscellaneous Provisions) (Scotland) Act 1980 (c.55), Sch.3.*]

31. [*Repealed by the Law Reform (Miscellaneous Provisions) (Scotland) Act 1980 (c.55), s.11 and Sch.3.*]

32. [*Repealed by the Sheriff Courts (Scotland) Act 1913 (2 & 3 Geo. V, c.28), s.1.*]

33. [*Repealed by the Juries Act 1949 (c.27), Sch.3.*]

[1] REMOVINGS

NOTE
[1] The provisions of this Act relating to removings are, in the case of an agricultural holding, subject to the Agricultural Holdings (Scotland) Act 1991 (c.55), s.21: see subs. (4).

Removings
[1] **34.** Where lands exceeding two acres in extent are held under a probative lease specifying a term of endurance, and whether such lease contains an

obligation upon the tenant to remove without warning or not, such lease, or an extract thereof from the books of any court of record shall have the same force and effect as an extract decree of removing obtained in an ordinary action at the instance of the lessor, or any one in his right, against the lessee or any party in possession, and such lease or extract shall along with authority in writing signed by the lessor or any one in his right or by his factor or law agent be sufficient warrant to any sheriff-officer or messenger-at-arms of the sheriffdom within which such lands or heritages are situated to eject such party in possession, his family, sub-tenants, cottars, and dependants, with their goods, gear, and effects, at the expiry of the term or terms of endurance of the lease: Provided that previous notice in writing to remove shall have been given—

(a) When the lease is for three years and upwards not less than one year and not more than two years before the termination of the lease; and

(b) In the case of leases from year to year (including lands occupied by tacit relocation) or for any other period less than three years, not less than six months before the termination of the lease (or where there is a separate ish as regards land and houses or otherwise before that ish which is first in date):

Provided that if such written notice as aforesaid shall not be given the lease shall be held to be renewed by tacit relocation for another year, and thereafter from year to year: Provided further that nothing contained in this section shall affect the right of the landlord to remove a tenant who has been sequestrated under the Bankruptcy (Scotland) Act 1913, or against whom a decree of cessio has been pronounced under the Debtors (Scotland) Act 1880, or who by failure to pay rent has incurred any irritancy of his lease or other liability to removal: Provided further that removal or ejectment in virtue of this section shall not be competent after six weeks from the date of the ish last in date: Provided further that nothing herein contained shall be construed to prevent proceedings under any lease in common form; and that the foregoing provisions as to notice shall not apply to any stipulations in a lease entitling the landlord to resume land for building, planting, feuing, or other purposes or to subjects let for any period less than a year.

NOTE
[1] Reference to the Bankruptcy (Scotland) Act 1913 inserted by virtue of the Interpretation Act 1889 (c.63), s.38 (1). The 1913 Act was repealed by the Bankruptcy (Scotland) Act 1985 (c.66): see s.5(1) and Sch.8.

Letter of removal
[1] **35.** Where any tenant in possession of any lands exceeding two acres in extent (whether with or without a written lease) shall, either at the date of entering upon the lease or at any other time, have granted a letter of removal, such letter of removal shall have the same force and effect as an extract decree of removing, and shall be a sufficient warrant for ejection to the like effect as is provided in regard to a lease or extract thereof, and shall be operative against the granter of such letter of removal or any party in his right within the same time and in the same manner after the like previous notice to remove: Provided always that where such letter is dated and signed within twelve months before the date of removal or before the first ish, if there be more than one ish, it shall not be necessary that any notice of any kind shall be given by either party to the other.

NOTE
[1] As amended by the Requirements of Writing (Scotland) Act 1995 (c.7) Sch.5 (effective August 1, 1995: s.15(2)).

Notice to remove
36. Where lands exceeding two acres in extent are occupied by a tenant without any written lease, and the tenant has given to the proprietor or his

agent no letter of removal, the lease shall terminate on written notice being given to the tenant by or on behalf of the proprietor, or to the proprietor by or on behalf of the tenant not less than six months before the determination of the tenancy, and such notice shall entitle the proprietor, in the event of the tenant failing to remove, to apply for and obtain a summary warrant of ejection against the tenant and every one deriving right from him.

Notice of termination of tenancy
[1] **37.** In all cases where houses, with or without land attached, not exceeding two acres in extent, lands not exceeding two acres in extent let without houses, mills, fishings, shootings, and all other heritable subjects (excepting land exceeding two acres in extent) are let for a year or more, notice of termination of tenancy shall be given in writing to the tenant by or on behalf of the proprietor or to the proprietor by or on behalf of the tenant: Provided always that notice under this section shall not warrant summary ejection from the subjects let to a tenant, but such notice, whether given to or by or on behalf of the tenant, shall entitle the proprietor to apply to the sheriff principal for a warrant for summary ejection in common form against the tenant and every one deriving right from him: Provided further that the notice provided for by this section shall be given at least forty days before the fifteenth day of May when the termination of the tenancy is the term of Whit-sunday, and at least forty days before the eleventh day of November when the termination of the tenancy is the term of Martinmas.

NOTE
[1] As substituted by the Sheriff Courts (Scotland) Act 1971 (c.58), s.4.

Exception for certain tenancies
[1] **37A.** The provisions of this Act relating to removings (including summary removings) shall not apply to or in relation to short limited duration tenancies or limited duration tenancies within the meaning of the Agricultural Holdings (Scotland) Act 2003 (asp 11).

NOTE
[1] As inserted by the Agricultural Holdings (Scotland) Act 2003 (asp 11), Sch., para.1 and brought into force by the Agricultural Holdings (Scotland) Act 2003 (Commencement No.3, Transitional and Savings Provisions) Order 2003 (SSI 2003/548), reg.2(i) (effective November 23, 2003).

SUMMARY REMOVINGS

Summary removing
[1,2] **38.** Where houses or other heritable subjects are let for a shorter period than a year, any person by law authorised may present to the sheriff principal a summary application for removing, and a decree pronounced in such summary cause shall have the full force and effect of a decree of removing and warrant of ejection. Where such a let is for a period not exceeding four months, notice of removal therefrom shall, in the absence of express stipulation, be given as many days before the ish as shall be equivalent to at least one-third of the full period of the duration of the let; and where the let exceeds four months, notice of removal shall, in the absence of express stipulation, be given at least forty days before the expiry of the said period. Provided that in no case shall notice of removal be given less than twenty-eight days before the date on which it is to take effect.

NOTE
[1] Proviso added by the Rent (Scotland) Act 1971 (c.28), Sch.18.
[2] As substituted by the Sheriff Courts (Scotland) Act 1971 (c.58) s.4. In terms of s.3(a) of the 1907 Act, the meaning of the term "sheriff principal" includes "sheriff".

Notice of termination in respect of dwelling-houses
[1] **38A.** Any notice of termination of tenancy or notice of removal given under sections 37 and 38 above in respect of a dwelling-house, on or after the date of the coming into operation of section 123 of the Housing Act 1974, shall be in writing and shall contain such information as may be prescribed by virtue of section 131 of the Rent (Scotland) Act 1971, and Rule 112 of Schedule 1 to this Act shall no longer apply to any such notice under section 37 above.

NOTE
[1] As inserted by the Housing Act 1974 (c.44), Sch.13, para.1. For rule 112 read rule 105 of the rules substituted by SI 1983/747, and rule 34.7 of the rules substituted by SI 1993/1956.

Lord Advocate as party to action for divorce
38B. [*Repealed by the Family Law (Scotland) Act 2006 (asp.2), Sch.3 (effective May 4, 2006).*]

38C. [*Repealed by the Children (Scotland) Act 1995 (c.36), Sch.5 (effective November 1, 1996).*]

PROCEDURE RULES

Procedure rules
39. Subject to the provisions of any Act of Parliament in force after the passing of this Act, the procedure in all civil causes shall be conform to the rules of procedure set forth in Schedule 1 hereto annexed. Such rules shall be construed and have effect as part of this Act.

Court of Session to regulate fees, etc.
[1] **40.** The Court of Session may from time to time, by act of sederunt, make such regulations for regulating the fees of agents (other than such of the fees of agents as the Secretary of State may regulate under or by virtue of section 14A of the Legal Aid (Scotland) Act 1967), officers, shorthand writers, and others. Provided that every such act of sederunt shall, within one week from the date thereof, be transmitted by the Lord President of the Court of Session to the Secretary of State, in order that it may be laid before the Houses of Parliament; and, if either of the Houses of Parliament shall within 36 days after it has been laid before them resolve that the whole or any part of such act of sederunt ought not to continue in force, the whole or such part thereof as shall be included in such resolution shall from and after the date of the passing of such resolution cease to be binding.

NOTE
[1] As amended by the Sheriff Courts (Scotland) Act 1913 (c.28), Sch.1, the Administration of Justice (Scotland) Act 1933 (c.41), Sch, the Divorce Jurisdiction, Court Fees and Legal Aid (Scotland) Act 1983 (c.12), Sch.1, para.7 and Sch.2, and substituted by the Secretaries of State Act 1926 (c.18), s.1(3).

POSTAL CHARGE

41. [*Repealed by the Administration of Justice (Scotland) Act 1933 (c.41), Sch.*]

SMALL DEBTS ACTS

42–48. [*Repealed by the Sheriff Courts (Scotland) Act 1971 (c.58), Sch.2.*]

49. [*Repealed by the Execution of Diligence (Scotland) Act 1926 (c.16), s.7.*]

SUMMARY APPLICATIONS

Summary applications
[1] **50.** In summary applications (where a hearing is necessary) the sheriff principal shall appoint the application to be heard at a diet to be fixed by him, and at that or any subsequent diet (without record of evidence unless the sheriff principal shall order a record) shall summarily dispose of the matter and give his judgment in writing: Provided that wherever in any Act of Parliament an application is directed to be heard, tried, and determined summarily or in the manner provided by section 52 of the Sheriff Courts (Scotland) Act 1876, such direction shall be read and construed as if it referred to this section of this Act: Provided also that nothing contained in this Act shall affect any right of appeal provided by any Act of Parliament under which a summary application is brought.

NOTE
[1] As substituted by the Sheriff Courts (Scotland) Act 1971 (c.58) s.4. In terms of s.3(a) of the 1907 Act, the meaning of the term "sheriff principal" includes "sheriff".

THE POOR'S ROLL

51. [*Repealed by the Statute Law (Repeals) Act 1973 (c.39).*]

REPEAL

52. [*Repealed by the Statute Law Revision Act 1927 (c.42).*]

SCHEDULES

FIRST SCHEDULE

[1] ORDINARY CAUSE RULES 1993

[1] The Ordinary Cause Rules were amended *inter alia* by SI 1996/2445, effective November 1, 1996. The amendments made thereby apply equally to causes commenced before that date: see SI 1996/2586

ARRANGEMENT OF ORDINARY CAUSE RULES

INITIATION AND PROGRESS OF CAUSES

Chapter 1

Citation, Interpretation, Representation and Forms

Rule
1.1 Citation.
1.2 Interpretation.
1.3 Representation.
1.4 Forms.

Chapter 2

Relief from Compliance with Rules

2.1 Relief from failure to comply with rules.

Chapter 3

Commencement of Causes

3.1 Form of initial writ.
3.2 Actions relating to heritable property.

Chapter 4

Caveats

[omitted by SSI 2006/198]

Chapter 5

Citation, Service and Intimation

Chapter 6

Arrestment

Chapter 7

Undefended Causes

Chapter 8

Reponing

Chapter 9

Standard Procedure in Defended Causes

Chapter 9A

Documents and Witnesses

Chapter 10

Additional Procedure

Chapter 11

The Process

Chapter 12

Interlocutors

Chapter 13

Party Minuter Procedure

Chapter 13A

Interventions by the Commission for Equality and Human Rights

Part II

Undefended Family Actions

Part III

Defended Family Actions

Part IV

Applications and Orders Relating to Children in Certain Actions

Part II

Undefended Civil Partnership Actions

Part III

Defended Civil Partnership Actions

Part IV

Applications And Orders Relating To Children In Certain Actions

Part V

Orders Relating To Financial Provisions

Part VI

Applications Relating To Avoidance Transactions

Part VII

Financial Provision After Overseas Proceedings

Part VIII

Actions In Respect Of Aliment

Part IX

Applications For Orders Under Section 11 Of The Children (Scotland) Act 1995

Part X

Actions Relating To Occupancy Rights And Tenancies

Part XI

Simplified Dissolution Of Civil Partnership Applications

Part XII

Referrals To Principal Reporter

Part XIII

Sisting Of Civil Partnership Actions

Chapter 33B

Financial Provision for Former Cohabitants

Chapter 34

Actions Relating to Heritable Property

Part I

Sequestration for Rent

Part II

Removing

Chapter 35

Actions of Multiplepoinding

Chapter 36

Actions of Damages

Part I

Intimation to Connected Persons in Certain Actions of Damages

Part II

Interim Payments of Damages

Part III

Provisional Damages for Personal Injuries

Part IV

Management of Damages Payable to Persons under Legal Disability

Part IV A

Productions in Certain Actions of Damages

Part V

Sex Discrimination Act 1975

Chapter 37

Causes under the Presumption of Death (Scotland) Act 1977

Chapter 38

European Court

Chapter 39

Provisions in Relation to Curators Ad Litem

Chapter 46

Companies Act 2006

INITIATION AND PROGRESS OF CAUSES

CHAPTER 1

CITATION, INTERPRETATION, REPRESENTATION AND FORMS

Citation
1.1. These Rules may be cited as the Ordinary Cause Rules 1993.

Interpretation
1.2.—(1) In these Rules, unless the context otherwise requires—
"document" has the meaning assigned to it in section 9 of the Civil Evidence (Scotland) Act 1988;
[1] "enactment" includes an enactment comprised in, or in an instrument made under, an Act of the Scottish Parliament;
"period of notice" means the period determined under rule 3.6 (period of notice after citation).
[2] "the Act of 2004" means the Vulnerable Witnesses (Scotland) Act 2004.
(2) For the purposes of these Rules—
(a) "affidavit" includes an affirmation and a statutory or other declaration; and
(b) an affidavit shall be sworn or affirmed before a notary public or any other competent authority.
(3) Where a provision in these Rules requires a party to intimate or send a document to another party, it shall be sufficient compliance with that provision if the document is intimated or sent to the solicitor acting in the cause for that party.
(4) Unless the context otherwise requires, anything done or required to be done under a provision in these Rules by a party may be done by the agent for that party acting on his behalf.
(5) Unless the context otherwise requires, a reference to a specified Chapter, Part, rule or form, is a reference to the Chapter, Part, rule, or form in Appendix 1, so specified in these Rules; and a reference to a specified paragraph, sub-paragraph or head is a reference to that paragraph of the rule or form, that sub-paragraph of the paragraph or that head of the sub-paragraph, in which the reference occurs.
[3] (6) In these Rules, references to a solicitor include a reference to a member of a body which has made a successful application under section 25 of the Law Reform (Miscellaneous Provisions) (Scotland) Act 1990 but only to the extent that the member is exercising rights acquired by virtue of section 27 of that Act.

NOTES
[1] As inserted by the Act of Sederunt (Ordinary Cause, Summary Application, Summary Cause and Small Claim Rules) Amendment (Miscellaneous) 2007 (SSI 2007/6), para.2(2) (effective January 29, 2007).
[2] As inserted by the Act of Sederunt (Ordinary Cause, Summary Application, Summary Cause and Small Claim Rules) Amendment (Vulnerable Witnesses (Scotland) Act 2004) 2007 (SSI 2007/463), r.2(2) (effective November 1, 2007).
[3] As inserted by the Act of Sederunt (Sheriff Court Rules Amendment) (Sections 25 to 29 of the Law Reform (Miscellaneous Provisions) (Scotland) Act 1990) 2009 (SSI 2009/164) r.2 (effective May 20, 2009).

Representation
1.3.—(1) Subject to paragraph (2), a party to any proceedings arising solely under the provisions of the Debtors (Scotland) Act 1987 shall be entitled to be represented by a person other than a solicitor or an advocate provided that the sheriff is satisfied that such person is a suitable representative and is duly authorised to represent that party.

(2) Paragraph (1) shall not apply to an appeal to the Sheriff Principal.

[1] (3) A party may be represented by any person authorised under any enactment to conduct proceedings in the sheriff court in accordance with the terms of that enactment.

[1] (4) The person referred to in paragraph (3) may do everything for the preparation and conduct of an action as may have been done by an individual conducting his own action.

NOTE
[1] As inserted by the Act of Sederunt (Ordinary Cause, Summary Application, Summary Cause and Small Claim Rules) Amendment (Miscellaneous) 2007 (SSI 2007/6), para.2(3) (effective January 29, 2007).

Forms
1.4. Where there is a reference to the use of a form in these Rules, that form in Appendix 1 or Appendix 2, as the case may be, to these Rules, or a form substantially to the same effect, shall be used with such variation as circumstances may require.

CHAPTER 2

RELIEF FROM COMPLIANCE WITH RULES

Relief from failure to comply with rules
2.1.—(1) The sheriff may relieve a party from the consequences of failure to comply with a provision in these Rules which is shown to be due to mistake, oversight or other excusable cause, on such conditions as he thinks fit.

(2) Where the sheriff relieves a party from the consequences of a failure to comply with a provision in these Rules under paragraph (1), he may make such order as he thinks fit to enable the cause to proceed as if the failure to comply with the provision had not occurred.

CHAPTER 3

COMMENCEMENT OF CAUSES

Form of initial writ
3.1.—[1] (1) A cause shall be commenced—
   (a) in the case of an ordinary cause, by initial writ in Form G1; or
   (b) in the case of a commercial action within the meaning of Chapter 40, by initial writ in Form G1A.
   or
[2] (c) in the case of a personal injuries action within the meaning of Part AI of Chapter 36, by initial writ in Form PI1.

(2) The initial writ shall be written, typed or printed on A4 size paper of durable quality and shall not be backed.

(3) Where the pursuer has reason to believe that an agreement exists prorogating jurisdiction over the subject matter of the cause to another court, the initial writ shall contain details of that agreement.

(4) Where the pursuer has reason to believe that proceedings are pending before another court involving the same cause of action and between the same parties as those named in the instance of the initial writ, the initial writ shall contain details of those proceedings.

(5) An article of condescendence shall be included in the initial writ averring—
   (a) the ground of jurisdiction; and
   (b) the facts upon which the ground of jurisdiction is based.

(6) Where the residence, registered office or place of business, as the case may be, of the defender is not known and cannot reasonably be ascertained, the pursuer shall set out in the instance that the whereabouts of the defender are not known and aver in the condescendence what steps have been taken to ascertain his present whereabouts.

(7) The initial writ shall be signed by the pursuer or his solicitor (if any) and the name and address of that solicitor shall be stated on the back of every service copy of that writ.

NOTES

[1] As inserted by the Act of Sederunt (Ordinary Cause Rules) Amendment (Commercial Actions) 2001 (SSI 2001/8) (effective March 1, 2001).

[2] As inserted by the Act of Sederunt (Ordinary Cause Rules Amendment) (Personal Injuries Actions) 2009 (SSI 2009/285) r.2 (effective November 2, 2009).

Actions relating to heritable property

3.2.—(1) In an action relating to heritable property, it shall not be necessary to call as a defender any person by reason only of any interest he may have as the holder of a heritable security over the heritable property.

(2) Intimation of such an action shall be made to the holder of the heritable security referred to in paragraph (1)—

    (a) where the action relates to any heritable right or title; and

    (b) in any other case, where the sheriff so orders.

[1] (3) In an action falling within section 1(1)(b) or (c) of the Mortgage Rights (Scotland) Act 2001, the initial writ shall include averments about those persons who appear to the pursuer to be entitled to apply for an order under section 2 of that Act and such persons shall, so far as known to the pursuer, be called as defenders for their interest.

NOTE

[1] As inserted by the Act of Sederunt (Amendment of Ordinary Cause Rules and Summary Applications, Statutory Applications and Appeals etc. Rules) (Applications under the Mortgage Rights (Scotland) Act 2001) 2002 (SSI 2002/7), para.2(2).

Actions relating to regulated agreements

[1] **3.2A.** In an action which relates to a regulated agreement within the meaning given by section 189(1) of the Consumer Credit Act 1974 the initial writ shall include an averment that such an agreement exists and details of that agreement.

NOTE

[1] As inserted by the Act of Sederunt (Sheriff Court Rules) (Miscellaneous Amendments) 2009 (SSI 2009/294) r.2 (effective December 1, 2009) as substituted by the Act of Sederunt (Amendment of the Act of Sederunt (Sheriff Court Rules) (Miscellaneous Amendments) 2009) 2009 (SSI 2009/402) (effective November 30, 2009).

Warrants of citation

[1,3] **3.3.**—(1) The warrant of citation in any cause other than—

    (a) a family action within the meaning of rule 33.1(1),

    (b) an action of multiplepoinding,

    (c) an action in which a time to pay direction under the Debtors (Scotland) Act 1987 or a time order under the Consumer Credit Act 1974 may be applied for by the defender,

    (d) an action to which rule 3.2(3) applies,

[2]   (e) a civil partnership action within the meaning of rule 33A.1(1)

shall be in Form O1.

(2) In a cause in which a time to pay direction under the Debtors (Scotland) Act 1987 or a time order under the Consumer Credit Act 1974 may be applied for by the defender, the warrant of citation shall be in Form O2.

(3) In a cause in which a warrant for citation in accordance with Form O2 is appropriate, there shall be served on the defender (with the initial writ and warrant) a notice in Form O3.

(4) In an action to which rule 3.2(3) applies, the warrant of citation shall be in Form O2A.

NOTES

[1] Inserted by the Act of Sederunt (Amendment of Ordinary Cause Rules and Summary Applications, Statutory Applications and Appeals etc. Rules) (Applications under the Mortgage Rights (Scotland) Act 2001) 2002 (SSI 2002/7), para.2(3).

[2] As amended by Act of Sederunt (Ordinary Cause Rules) Amendment (Family Law (Scotland) Act 2006 etc.) 2006 (SSI 2006/207), para.2 (effective May 4, 2006).

[3] As amended by the Act of Sederunt (Ordinary Cause, Summary Application, Summary Cause and Small Claim Rules) Amendment (Miscellaneous) 2007 (SSI 2007/6), para.2(4) (effective January 29, 2007).

Warrants for arrestment to found jurisdiction

3.4.—(1) Where an application for a warrant for arrestment to found jurisdiction may be made, it shall be made in the crave of the initial writ.

(2) Averments to justify the granting of such a warrant shall be included in the condescendence.

Warrants and precepts for arrestment on dependence

3.5. [*Repealed by the Act of Sederunt (Sheriff Court Rules Amendment) (Diligence) 2008 (SSI 2008/121) r.5(2) (effective April 1, 2008).*]

Period of notice after citation

3.6.—(1) Subject to rule 5.6(1) (service where address of person is not known) and to paragraph (2) of this rule, a cause shall proceed after one of the following periods of notice has been given to the defender:—

    (a) where the defender is resident or has a place of business within Europe, 21 days after the date of execution of service; or

    (b) where the defender is resident or has a place of business outside Europe, 42 days after the date of execution of service.

(2) Subject to paragraph (3), the sheriff may, on cause shown, shorten or extend the period of notice on such conditions as to the method or manner of service as he thinks fit.

(3) A period of notice may not be reduced to a period of less than 2 days.

(4) Where a period of notice expires on a Saturday, Sunday, or public or court holiday, the period of notice shall be deemed to expire on the next day on which the sheriff clerk's office is open for civil court business.

Chapter 4

Caveats

[*Omitted by Act of Sederunt (Sheriff Court Caveat Rules) 2006 (SI 2006/198), effective April 28, 2006*]

Chapter 5

Citation, Service and Intimation

Signature of warrants

5.1.—[1](1) Subject to paragraph (2), a warrant for citation or intimation may be signed by the sheriff or sheriff clerk.

(2) The following warrants shall be signed by the sheriff:—

    (a) a warrant containing an order shortening or extending the period of notice or any other order other than a warrant which the sheriff clerk may sign;

[1] (b) a warrant for arrestment to found jurisdiction;

[1,2] (b-

    a)

    a warrant for arrestment on the dependence;

    (c) a warrant for intimation ordered under rule 33.8 (intimation where alleged association).

[3] (d) a warrant for intimation ordered under rule 33A.8 (intimation where alleged association).

(3) Where the sheriff clerk refuses to sign a warrant which he may sign, the party presenting the initial writ may apply to the sheriff for the warrant.

NOTES

[1] As inserted by the Act of Sederunt (Ordinary Cause, Summary Application and Small Claim Rules) Amendment (Miscellaneous) 2004 (SSI 2004/197) para.2(3) (effective May 21, 2004).

[2] As amended by Act of Sederunt (Ordinary Cause Rules) Amendment (Family Law (Scotland) Act 2006 etc.) 2006 (SSI 2006/207) para.2 (effective May 4, 2006).

[3] As inserted by Act of Sederunt (Ordinary Cause Rules) Amendment (Family Law (Scotland) Act 2006 etc.) 2006 (SSI 2006/207) para.2 (effective May 4, 2006).

Form of citation and certificate

[1,3] **5.2.**—(1) Subject to rule 5.6 (service where address of person is not known), in any cause other than—

    (a) a family action within the meaning of rule 33.1(1),

[2] (aa) a civil partnership action within the meaning of rule 33A.1(1);

(b) an action of multiplepoinding,

(c) an action in which a time to pay direction under the Debtors (Scotland) Act 1987 or a time order under the Consumer Credit Act 1974 may be applied for by the defender, or

(d) an action to which rule 3.2(3) applies,

citation by any person shall be in Form O4 which shall be attached to a copy of the initial writ and warrant of citation and shall have appended to it a notice of intention to defend in Form O7.

(2) In a cause in which a time to pay direction under the Debtors (Scotland) Act 1987 or a time order under the Consumer Credit Act 1974 may be applied for by the defender, citation shall be in Form O5 which shall be attached to a copy of the initial writ and warrant of citation and shall have appended to it a notice of intention to defend in Form O7.

(2A) In an action to which rule 3.2(3) applies, citation shall be in Form O5A which shall be attached to a copy of the initial writ and warrant of citation and shall have appended to it a notice of intention to defend in Form O7.

(3) The certificate of citation in any cause other than a family action within the meaning of rule 33.1(1) or an action of multiplepoinding shall be in Form O6 which shall be attached to the initial writ.

(4) Where citation is by a sheriff officer, one witness shall be sufficient for the execution of citation.

(5) Where citation is by a sheriff officer, the certificate of citation shall be signed by the sheriff officer and the witness and shall state—

(a) the method of citation; and

(b) where the method of citation was other than personal or postal citation, the full name and designation of any person to whom the citation was delivered.

(6) Where citation is executed under paragraph (3) of rule 5.4 (depositing or affixing by sheriff officer), the certificate shall include a statement—

(a) of the method of service previously attempted;

(b) of the circumstances which prevented such service being executed; and

(c) that a copy was sent in accordance with the provisions of paragraph (4) of that rule.

NOTES

[1] As amended by SI 1996/2445 (effective November 1, 1996) (clerical error) and further amended by the Act of Sederunt (Amendment of Ordinary Cause Rules and Summary Applications, Statutory Applications and Appeals etc. Rules) (Applications under the Mortgage Rights (Scotland) Act 2001) 2002 (SSI 2002/7), para.2(4).

[2] As inserted by Act of Sederunt (Ordinary Cause Rules) Amendment (Family Law (Scotland) Act 2006 etc.) 2006, para.2 (SSI 2006/207) (effective May 4, 2006).

[3] As amended by the Act of Sederunt (Ordinary Cause, Summary Application, Summary Cause and Small Claim Rules) Amendment (Miscellaneous) 2007 (SSI 2007/6), para.2(5) (effective January 29, 2007).

Postal service or intimation

5.3.—(1) In any cause in which service or intimation of any document or citation of any person may be by recorded delivery, such service, intimation or citation shall be by the first class recorded delivery service.

(2) Notwithstanding the terms of section 4(2) of the Citation Amendment (Scotland) Act 1882 (time from which period of notice reckoned), where service or intimation is by post, the period of notice shall run from the beginning of the day after the date of posting.

(3) On the face of the envelope used for postal service or intimation under this rule there shall be written or printed the following notice:—

"This envelope contains a citation to or intimation from (*specify the court*). If delivery cannot be made at the address shown it is to be returned immediately to:— The Sheriff Clerk (*insert address of sheriff clerk's office*)".

(4) The certificate of citation or intimation in the case of postal service shall have attached to it any relevant postal receipts.

Service within Scotland by sheriff officer

5.4.—(1) An initial writ, decree, charge, warrant or any other order or writ following upon such initial writ or decree served by a sheriff officer on any person shall be served—

(a) personally; or

(b) by being left in the hands of a resident at the person's dwelling place or an employee at his place of business.

(2) Where service is executed under paragraph (1)(b), the certificate of citation or service shall contain the full name and designation of any person in whose hands the initial writ, decree, charge, warrant or other order or writ, as the case may be, was left.

(3) Where a sheriff officer has been unsuccessful in executing service in accordance with paragraph (1), he may, after making diligent enquiries, serve the document in question—
    (a) by depositing it in that person's dwelling place or place of business; or
    (b) by affixing it to the door of that person's dwelling place or place of business.

(4) Subject to rule 6.1 (service of schedule of arrestment), where service is executed under paragraph (3), the sheriff officer shall, as soon as possible after such service, send a letter containing a copy of the document by ordinary first class post to the address at which he thinks it most likely that the person on whom service has been executed may be found.

[1] (5) Where the firm which employs the sheriff officer has in its possession—
    (a) the document or a copy of it certified as correct by the pursuer's solicitor, the sheriff officer may serve the document upon the defender without having the document or certified copy in his possession, in which case he shall if required to do so by the person on whom service is executed and within a reasonable time of being so required, show the document or certified copy to the person; or
    (b) a certified copy of the interlocutor pronounced allowing service of the document, the sheriff officer may serve the document without having in his possession the certified copy interlocutor if he has in his possession a facsimile copy of the certified copy interlocutor (which he shall show, if required, to the person on whom service is executed).

NOTE
[1] As inserted by the Act of Sederunt (Ordinary Cause, Summary Application, Summary Cause and Small Claim Rules) Amendment (Miscellaneous) 2003 (SSI 2003/26), para.2(3) (effective January 24, 2003).

Service on persons furth of Scotland
[1] **5.5.**—(1) Subject to the following provisions of this rule, an initial writ, decree, charge, warrant or any other order or writ following upon such initial writ or decree on a person furth of Scotland shall be served—
    (a) at a known residence or place of business in England, Wales, Northern Ireland, the Isle of Man, the Channel Islands or any country with which the United Kingdom does not have a convention providing for service of writs in that country—
        (i) in accordance with the rules for personal service under the domestic law of the place in which service is to be executed; or
        (ii) by posting in Scotland a copy of the document in question in a registered letter addressed to the person at his residence or place of business;
[2] (b) in a country which is a party to the Hague Convention on the Service Abroad of Judicial and Extra-Judicial Documents in Civil and Commercial Matters dated 15th November 1965 or the Convention in Schedule 1 or 3C to the Civil Jurisdiction and Judgments Act 1982—
        (i) by a method prescribed by the internal law of the country where service is to be executed for the service of documents in domestic actions upon persons who are within its territory;
        (ii) by or through the central, or other appropriate, authority in the country where service is to be executed at the request of the Secretary of State for Foreign and Commonwealth Affairs;
        (iii) by or through a British Consular Office in the country where service is to be executed at the request of the Secretary of State for Foreign and Commonwealth Affairs;
        (iv) where the law of the country in which the person resides permits, by posting in Scotland a copy of the document in a registered letter addressed to the person at his residence; or
        (v) where the law of the country in which service is to be executed permits, service by an huissier, other judicial officer or competent official of the country where service is to be executed; or
    (c) in a country with which the United Kingdom has a convention on the service of writs in that country other than the conventions mentioned in sub-paragraph (b), by one of the methods approved in the relevant convention.
    (d) [*Repealed by the Act of Sederunt (Ordinary Cause, Summary Application, Summary Cause and Small Claim Rules) Amendment (Miscellaneous) 2004 (SSI 2004/197) r.24(a) (effective May 21, 2004).*]
[3,4] (1A) In a country to which the EC Service Regulation applies, service—
    (a) may be effected by the methods prescribed in paragraph (1)(b)(ii) and (iii) only in exceptional circumstances; and
    (b) is effected only if the receiving agency has informed the person that acceptance of

service may be refused on the ground that the document has not been translated in accordance with paragraph (6).

(2) Any document which requires to be posted in Scotland for the purposes of this rule shall be posted by a solicitor or a sheriff officer; and on the face of the envelope there shall be written or printed the notice set out in rule 5.3(3).

(3) In the case of service by a method referred to in paragraph (1)(b)(ii) and (iii), the pursuer shall—

(a) send a copy of the writ and warrant for service with citation attached, or other document, as the case may be, with a request for service by the method indicated in the request to the Secretary of State for Foreign and Commonwealth Affairs; and

(b) lodge in process a certificate signed by the authority which executed service stating that it has been, and the manner in which it was, served.

(4) In the case of service by a method referred to in paragraph (1)(b)(v), the pursuer or the sheriff officer, shall—

(a) send a copy of the writ and warrant for service with citation attached, or other document, as the case may be, with a request for service by the method indicated in the request to the official in the country in which service is to be executed; and

(b) lodge in process a certificate of the official who executed service stating that it has been, and the method in which it was, served.

(5) Where service is executed in accordance with paragraph (1)(a)(i) or (1)(b)(i) other than on another party in the United Kingdom, the Isle of Man or the Channel Islands, the party executing service shall lodge a certificate by a person who is conversant with the law of the country concerned and who practises or has practised law in that country or is a duly accredited representative of the Government of that country, stating that the method of service employed is in accordance with the law of the place where service was executed.

(6) Every writ, document, citation or notice on the face of the envelope mentioned in rule 5.3(3) shall be accompanied by a translation in—

³ (a) an official language of the country in which service is to be executed; or

⁴ (b) in a country to which the EC Service Regulation applies, a language of the member state of transmission that is understood by the person on whom service is being executed.

(7) A translation referred to in paragraph (6) shall be certified as correct by the person making it; and the certificate shall—

(a) include his full name, address and qualifications; and

(b) be lodged with the execution of citation or service.

⁴ (8) In this rule "the EC Service Regulation" means Regulation (EC) No. 1393/2007 of the European Parliament and of the Council of 13th November 2007 on the service in the Member States of judicial and extrajudicial documents in civil or commercial matters (service of documents), and repealing Council Regulation (EC) No. 1348/2000, as amended from time to time.

NOTES

¹ As amended by SI 1996/2445 (effective November 1, 1996) and the Act of Sederunt (Ordinary Cause, Summary Application, Summary Cause and Small Claim Rules) Amendment (Miscellaneous) 2003 (SSI 2003/26), para.2(4) (effective January 24, 2003).

² As amended by the Act of Sederunt (Ordinary Cause, Summary Application and Small Claim Rules) Amendment (Miscellaneous) 2004 (SSI 2004/197) (effective May 21, 2004), para.2(4).

³ As inserted by the Act of Sederunt (Ordinary Cause, Summary Application and Small Claim Rules) Amendment (Miscellaneous) 2004 (SSI 2004/197) (effective May 21, 2004), para.2(4) and substituted by the Act of Sederunt (Sheriff Court Ordinary Cause, Summary Application, Summary Cause and Small Claims Rules) Amendment (Council Regulation (EC) No. 1348 of 2000 Extension to Denmark) 2007 (SSI 2007/440) r.2(2) (effective October 9, 2007).

⁴ As substituted by the Act of Sederunt (Sheriff Court Rules) (Miscellaneous Amendments) (No.2) 2008 (SSI 2008/365) r.7 (effective November 13, 2008).

Service where address of person is not known

5.6.—¹ (A1) Subject to rule 6.A7 this rule applies to service where the address of a person is not known.

(1) Where the address of a person to be cited or served with a document is not known and cannot reasonably be ascertained, the sheriff shall grant warrant for citation or service upon that person—

(a) by the publication of an advertisement in Form G3 in a specified newspaper circulating in the area of the last known address of that person, or

(b) by displaying on the walls of court a copy of the instance and crave of the initial writ, warrant of citation and a notice in Form G4;

and the period of notice fixed by the sheriff shall run from the date of publication of the advertisement or display on the walls of court, as the case may be.

(2) Where service requires to be executed under paragraph (1), the pursuer shall lodge a service copy of the initial writ and a copy of any warrant of citation with the sheriff clerk from whom they may be uplifted by the person for whom they are intended.

(3) Where a person has been cited or served in accordance with paragraph (1) and, after the cause has commenced, his address becomes known, the sheriff may allow the initial writ to be amended subject to such conditions as to re-service, intimation, expenses, or transfer of the cause as he thinks fit.

(4) Where advertisement in a newspaper is required for the purpose of citation or service under this rule, a copy of the newspaper containing the advertisement shall be lodged with the sheriff clerk by the pursuer.

(5) Where display on the walls of court is required under paragraph (1)(b), the pursuer shall supply to the sheriff clerk for that purpose a certified copy of the instance and crave of the initial writ and any warrant of citation.

NOTE

[1] As inserted by the Act of Sederunt (Sheriff Court Rules Amendment) (Diligence) 2008 (SSI 2008/121) r.5(3) (effective April 1, 2008).

Persons carrying on business under trading or descriptive name

[1] **5.7.**—(1) A person carrying on a business under a trading or descriptive name may sue or be sued in such trading or descriptive name alone; and an extract—

(a) of a decree pronounced in the sheriff court, or

(b) of a decree proceeding upon any deed, decree arbitral, bond, protest of a bill, promissory note or banker's note or upon any other obligation or document on which execution may proceed, recorded in the sheriff court books,

against such person under such trading or descriptive name shall be a valid warrant for diligence against such person.

(2) An initial writ, decree, charge, warrant or any other order or writ following upon such initial writ or decree in a cause in which a person carrying on business under a trading or descriptive name sues or is sued in that name may be served—

(a) at any place of business or office at which such business is carried on within the sheriffdom of the sheriff court in which the cause is brought; or

(b) where there is no place of business within that sheriffdom, at any place where such business is carried on (including the place of business or office of the clerk or secretary of any company, corporation or association or firm).

NOTE

[1] As amended by SI 1996/2445 (effective November 1, 1996).

Endorsation unnecessary

5.8. An initial writ, decree, charge, warrant or any other order or writ following upon such initial writ or decree may be served, enforced or otherwise lawfully executed anywhere in Scotland without endorsation by a sheriff clerk; and, if executed by a sheriff officer, may be so executed by a sheriff officer of the court which granted it or by a sheriff officer of the sheriff court district in which it is to be executed.

Re-service

5.9. Where it appears to the sheriff that there has been any failure or irregularity in citation or service on a person, he may order the pursuer to re-serve the initial writ on such conditions as he thinks fit.

No objection to regularity of citation, service or intimation

5.10.—(1) A person who appears in a cause shall not be entitled to state any objection to the regularity of the execution of citation, service or intimation on him; and his appearance shall remedy any defect in such citation, service or intimation.

(2) Nothing in paragraph (1) shall preclude a party from pleading that the court has no jurisdiction.

CHAPTER 6

[1] INTERIM DILIGENCE

NOTE
[1] Chapter renamed by the Act of Sederunt (Sheriff Court Rules Amendment) (Diligence) 2008 (SSI 2008/121) r.5(4) (effective April 1, 2008).

Annotations to Chapter 6 are by Tim Edward.

Interpretation
[1] **6.A1.** In this Chapter—
    "the 1987 Act" means the Debtors (Scotland) Act 1987; and
    "the 2002 Act" means the Debt Arrangement and Attachment (Scotland) Act 2002.

NOTE
[1] As inserted by the Act of Sederunt (Sheriff Court Rules Amendment) (Diligence) 2008 (SSI 2008/121) r.5(5) (effective April 1, 2008).

Application for interim diligence
[1] **6.A2.**—(1) The following shall be made by motion—
    (a) an application under section 15D(1) of the 1987 Act for warrant for diligence by arrestment or inhibition on the dependence of an action or warrant for arrestment on the dependence of an admiralty action;
    (b) an application under section 9C of the 2002 Act for warrant for interim attachment.
    (2) Such an application must be accompanied by a statement in Form G4A.
    (3) A certified copy of an interlocutor granting a motion under paragraph (1) shall be sufficient authority for the execution of the diligence concerned.

NOTE
[1] As inserted by the Act of Sederunt (Sheriff Court Rules Amendment) (Diligence) 2008 (SSI 2008/121) r.5(5) (effective April 1, 2008).

Effect of authority for inhibition on the dependence
[1] **6.A3.**—(1) Where a person has been granted authority for inhibition on the dependence of an action, a certified copy of the interlocutor granting the motion may be registered with a certificate of execution in the Register of Inhibitions and Adjudications.
[2] (2) A notice of a certified copy of an interlocutor granting authority for inhibition under rule 6.A2 may be registered in the Register of Inhibitions and Adjudications; and such registration is to have the same effect as registration of a notice of inhibition under section 155(2) of the Titles to Land Consolidation (Scotland) Act 1868.

NOTES
[1] As inserted by the Act of Sederunt (Sheriff Court Rules Amendment) (Diligence) 2008 (SSI 2008/121) r.5(5) (effective April 1, 2008).
[2] As substituted by the Act of Sederunt (Sheriff Court Rules Amendment) (Diligence) 2009 (SSI 2009/107) r.3 (effective April 22, 2009).

Recall etc. of arrestment or inhibition
[1] **6.A4.** An application by any person having an interest—
    (a) to loose, restrict, vary or recall an arrestment or an interim attachment; or
    (b) to recall, in whole or in part, or vary, an inhibition,
shall be made by motion.

NOTE
[1] As inserted by the Act of Sederunt (Sheriff Court Rules Amendment) (Diligence) 2008 (SSI 2008/121) r.5(5) (effective April 1, 2008).

Incidental applications in relation to interim diligence, etc
[1] **6.A5.** An application under Part 1A of the 1987 Act or Part 1A of the 2002 Act other than mentioned above shall be made by motion.

NOTE

[1] As inserted by the Act of Sederunt (Sheriff Court Rules Amendment) (Diligence) 2008 (SSI 2008/121) r.5(5) (effective April 1, 2008).

Form of schedule of inhibition on the dependence

6.A6. [*Revoked by the Act of Sederunt (Sheriff Court Rules Amendment) (Diligence) 2009 (SSI 2009/107) r.3 (effective April 22, 2009).*]

Service of inhibition on the dependence where address of defender not known

[1] **6.A7.**—(1) Where the address of a defender is not known to the pursuer, an inhibition on the dependence shall be deemed to have been served on the defender if the schedule of inhibition is left with or deposited at the office of the sheriff clerk of the sheriff court district where the defender's last known address is located.

(2) Where service of an inhibition on the dependence is executed under paragraph (1), a copy of the schedule of inhibition shall be sent by the sheriff officer by first class post to the defender's last known address.

NOTE

[1] As inserted by the Act of Sederunt (Sheriff Court Rules Amendment) (Diligence) 2008 (SSI 2008/121) r.5(5) (effective April 1, 2008).

[1] *Form of schedule of arrestment on the dependence*

6.A8.—(1) An arrestment on the dependence shall be served by serving the schedule of arrestment on the arrestee in Form G4B.

(2) A certificate of execution shall be lodged with the sheriff clerk in Form G4C.

NOTE

[1] As inserted by the Act of Sederunt (Sheriff Court Rules Amendment) (Diligence) 2009 (SSI 2009/107) r.3 (effective April 22, 2009).

Service of schedule of arrestment

6.1 If a schedule of arrestment has not been personally served on an arrestee, the arrestment shall have effect only if a copy of the schedule is also sent by registered post or the first class recorded delivery service to—

(a) the last known place of residence of the arrestee, or

(b) if such place of residence is not known, or if the arrestee is a firm or corporation, to the arrestee's principal place of business if known, or, if not known, to any known place of business of the arrestee;

and the sheriff officer shall, on the certificate of execution, certify that this has been done and specify the address to which the copy of the schedule was sent.

Arrestment on dependence before service

[1] **6.2.**—(1) An arrestment on the dependence of a cause used before service shall cease to have effect unless—

(a) the initial writ is served within 20 days from the date of arrestment; and

(b) in the case of an undefended cause, decree in absence has been pronounced within 20 days after the expiry of the period of notice.

(2) After such an arrestment has been executed, the party who executed it shall forthwith report the execution to the sheriff clerk.

NOTE

[1] As amended by the Act of Sederunt (Sheriff Court Rules Amendment) (Diligence) 2008 (SSI 2008/121) r.5(6) (effective April 1, 2008).

Movement of arrested property

6.3.—(1) Any person having an interest may apply by motion for a warrant authorising the movement of a vessel or cargo which are the subject of an arrestment to found jurisdiction or on the dependence of a cause.

(2) Where the court grants a warrant sought under paragraph (1), it may make such further order as it thinks fit to give effect to that warrant.

CHAPTER 7

UNDEFENDED CAUSES

Application of this Chapter
7.1. This Chapter applies to any cause other than an action in which the sheriff may not grant decree without evidence.

Minute for granting of decree without attendance
7.2.—[2] (1) Subject to the following paragraphs, where the defender—
  (a) does not lodge a notice of intention to defend,
  (b) does not lodge an application for a time to pay direction under the Debtors (Scotland) Act 1987 or a time order under the Consumer Credit Act 1974,
  (c) has lodged such an application for a time to pay direction or time order and the pursuer does not object to the application or to any recall or restriction of an arrestment sought in the application,
the sheriff may, on the pursuer endorsing a minute for decree on the initial writ, at any time after the expiry of the period for lodging that notice or application, grant decree in absence or other order in terms of the minute so endorsed without requiring the attendance of the pursuer in court.
(2) The sheriff shall not grant decree under paragraph (1)—
  (a) unless it appears *ex facie* of the initial writ that a ground of jurisdiction exists under the Civil Jurisdiction and Judgments Act 1982; and
  (b) the cause is not a cause—
    (i) in which decree may not be granted without evidence;
    (ii) to which paragraph (4) applies; or
  [1] (iii) to which rule 33.31 (procedure in undefended family action for a section 11 order) applies.
(3) Where a defender is domiciled in another part of the United Kingdom or in another Contracting State, the sheriff shall not grant decree in absence until it has been shown that the defender has been able to receive the initial writ in sufficient time to arrange for his defence or that all necessary steps have been taken to that end; and for the purposes of this paragraph—
  (a) the question whether a person is domiciled in another part of the United Kingdom shall be determined in accordance with sections 41 and 42 of the Civil Jurisdiction and Judgments Act 1982;
  (b) the question whether a person is domiciled in another Contracting State shall be determined in accordance with Article 52 of the Convention in Schedule 1 or 3C to that Act; and
  (c) the term "Contracting State" has the meaning assigned in section 1 of that Act.
(4) Where an initial writ has been served in a country to which the Hague Convention on the Service Abroad of Judicial and Extra-Judicial Documents in Civil or Commercial Matters dated 15th November 1965 applies, decree shall not be granted until it is established to the satisfaction of the sheriff that the requirements of Article 15 of that Convention have been complied with.

NOTES
[1] As amended by SI 1996/2167 (effective November 1, 1996) and SI 1996/2445 (effective November 1, 1996).
[2] As amended by the Act of Sederunt (Ordinary Cause, Summary Application, Summary Cause and Small Claim Rules) Amendment (Miscellaneous) 2007 (SSI 2007/6) r.2(6) (effective January 29, 2007).

Applications for time to pay directions or time orders in undefended causes
7.3.—(1) This rule applies to a cause in which—
  [1] (a) a time to pay direction may be applied for under the Debtors (Scotland) Act 1987; or
  (b) a time order may be applied for under the Consumer Credit Act 1974.
(2) A defender in a cause which is otherwise undefended, who wishes to apply for a time to pay direction or time order, and where appropriate, to have an arrestment recalled or restricted, shall complete and lodge with the sheriff clerk the appropriate part of Form O3 before the expiry of the period of notice.
[2] (2A) As soon as possible after the application of the defender is lodged, the sheriff clerk shall send a copy of it to the pursuer by first class ordinary post.
(3) Where the pursuer does not object to the application of the defender made in accordance with paragraph (2), he shall minute for decree in accordance with rule 7.2; and the sheriff may grant decree or other order in terms of the application and minute.

[3] (4) Where the pursuer objects to the application of the defender made in accordance with paragraph (2) he shall on the same date—
 (a) complete and lodge with the sheriff clerk Form O3A;
 (b) minute for decree in accordance with rule 7.2; and
 (c) send a copy of Form O3A to the defender.

[3] (4A) The sheriff clerk shall then fix a hearing on the application of the defender and intimate the hearing to the pursuer and the defender.

[3] (4B) The hearing must be fixed for a date within 28 days of the date on which the Form O3A and the minute for decree are lodged.

(5) The sheriff may determine an application in which a hearing has been fixed under paragraph (4) whether or not any of the parties appear.

NOTES
[1] As amended by the Act of Sederunt (Ordinary Cause, Summary Application, Summary Cause and Small Claim Rules) Amendment (Miscellaneous) 2007 (SSI 2007/6) r.2(7) (effective January 29, 2007).
[2] As inserted by the Act of Sederunt (Sheriff Court Rules) (Miscellaneous Amendments) 2009 (SSI 2009/294) r.2 (effective December 1, 2009).
[3] Para.(4) substituted for paras (4)–(4B) by the Act of Sederunt (Sheriff Court Rules) (Miscellaneous Amendments) 2009 (SSI 2009/294) r.2 (effective December 1, 2009).

Decree for expenses
7.4. On granting decree in absence or thereafter, the sheriff may grant decree for expenses.

Finality of decree in absence
[1] **7.5.** Subject to section 9(7) of the Land Tenure Reform (Scotland) Act 1974 (decree in action of removing for breach of condition of long lease to be final when extract recorded in Register of Sasines), a decree in absence which has not been recalled or brought under review by suspension or by reduction shall become final and shall have effect as a decree *in foro contentioso*—
 (a) on the expiry of six months from the date of the decree or from the date of a charge made under it, as the case may be, where the service of the initial writ or of the charge has been personal; and
 (b) in any event, on the expiry of 20 years from the date of the decree.

NOTE
[1] As amended by SI 1996/2445 (effective November 1, 1996).

Amendment of initial writ
7.6.—(1) In an undefended cause, the sheriff may—
 (a) allow the pursuer to amend the initial writ in any way permitted by rule 18.2 (powers of sheriff to allow amendment); and
 (b) order the amended initial writ to be re-served on the defender on such period of notice as he thinks fit.

(2) The defender shall not be liable for the expense occasioned by any such amendment unless the sheriff so orders.

(3) Where an amendment has been allowed under paragraph (1), the amendment—
 (a) shall not validate diligence used on the dependence of a cause so as to prejudice the rights of creditors of the party against whom the diligence has been executed who are interested in defeating such diligence; and
 (b) shall preclude any objection to such diligence stated by a party or any person by virtue of a title acquired or in right of a debt contracted by him subsequent to the execution of such diligence.

Disapplication of certain rules
[1] **7.7** The following rules in Chapter 15 (motions) shall not apply to an action in which no notice of intention to defend has been lodged or to any action in so far as it proceeds as undefended—
 rule 15.2 (intimation of motions),
 rule 15.3 (opposition to motions),
 rule 15.5 (hearing of motions).

NOTE
[1] Inserted by SI 1996/2445 (effective November 1, 1996).

CHAPTER 8

REPONING

Reponing
8.1.—(1) In any cause other than—
³ (a) a cause mentioned in rule 33.1(1)(a) to (h) (n) or (o), (certain family actions), or
⁴ (aa) a cause mentioned in rule 33A.1(a), (b) or (f) (certain civil partnership actions);
   (b) a cause to which Chapter 37 (causes under the Presumption of Death (Scotland) Act 1977) applies,
the defender or any party with a statutory title or interest may apply to be reponed by lodging with the sheriff clerk, before implement in full of a decree in absence, a reponing note setting out his proposed defence or the proposed order or direction and explaining his failure to appear.
   (2) A copy of the note lodged under paragraph (1) shall be served on the pursuer and any other party—
   (3) The sheriff may, on considering the reponing note, recall the decree so far as not implemented subject to such order as to expenses as he thinks fit; and the cause shall thereafter proceed as if—
      (a) the defender had lodged a notice of intention to defend and the period of notice had expired on the date on which the decree in absence was recalled; or
   ² (b) the party seeking the order or direction had lodged the appropriate application on the date when the decree was recalled.
   (4) A reponing note, when duly lodged with the sheriff clerk and served upon the pursuer, shall have effect to sist diligence.
   ¹ (4A) Where an initial writ has been served on a defender furth of the United Kingdom under rule 5.5(1)(b) (service on persons furth of Scotland) and decree in absence has been pronounced against him as a result of his failure to enter appearance, the court may, on the defender applying to be reponed in accordance with paragraph (1) above, recall the decree and allow defences to be received if—
      (a) without fault on his part, he did not have knowledge of the initial writ in sufficient time to defend;
      (b) he has disclosed a prima facie defence to the action on the merits; and
      (c) the reponing note is lodged within a reasonable time after he had knowledge of the decree or in any event before the expiry of one year from the date of decree.
   (5) Any interlocutor or order recalling, or incidental to the recall of, a decree in absence shall be final and not subject to appeal.

NOTES
   ¹ Inserted by SSI 2000/239 (effective October 2, 2000).
   ² Inserted by the Act of Sederunt (Ordinary Cause, Summary Application and Small Claim Rules) Amendment (Miscellaneous) 2004 (SSI 2004/197) r.2(5) (effective May 21, 2004).
   ³ As amended by Act of Sederunt (Ordinary Cause Rules) Amendment (Family Law (Scotland) Act 2006 etc.) 2006 (SSI 2006/207) r.2 (effective May 4, 2006).
   ⁴ Inserted by Act of Sederunt (Ordinary Cause Rules) Amendment (Family Law (Scotland) Act 2006 etc.) 2006 (SSI 2006/207) r.2 (effective May 4, 2006).

CHAPTER 9

STANDARD PROCEDURE IN DEFENDED CAUSES

Notice of intention to defend
9.1.—¹,³ (1) Subject to rules 33.34 (notice of intention to defend and defences in family action) 33A.34 (notice of intention to defend and defences in civil partnership action) and 35.8 (lodging of notice of appearance in action of multiplepoinding), where the defender intends to—
   (a) challenge the jurisdiction of the court,
   (b) state a defence, or
   (c) make a counterclaim,
he shall, before the expiry of the period of notice, lodge with the sheriff clerk a notice of intention to defend in Form O7 and, at the same time, send a copy to the pursuer.
   (2) The lodging of a notice of intention to defend shall not imply acceptance of the jurisdiction of the court.
   ² (3) This Chapter shall not apply to a commercial action within the meaning of Chapter 40.

NOTES

[1] As amended by the Act of Sederunt (Family Proceedings in the Sheriff Court) 1996 (SI 1996/2167) (effective November 1, 2000).

[2] Inserted by the Act of Sederunt (Ordinary Cause Rules) Amendment (Commercial Actions) 2001 (SSI 2001/8) (effective March 1, 2001).

[3] As amended by Act of Sederunt (Ordinary Cause Rules) Amendment (Family Law (Scotland) Act 2006 etc.) 2006 (SSI 2006/207) r.2 (effective May 4, 2006).

Fixing date for Options Hearing

9.2.—[1] (1) Subject to paragraph (1A), on the lodging of a notice of intention to defend, the sheriff clerk shall fix a date and time for an Options Hearing which date shall be on the first suitable court day occurring not sooner than 10 weeks after the expiry of the period of notice.

[2,4] (1A) Where in a family action or a civil partnership action—

    (i) the only matters in dispute are an order in terms of section 11 of the Children (Scotland) Act 1995 (court orders relating to parental responsibilities etc.); or

    (ii) the matters in dispute include an order in terms of section 11 of that Act,

there shall be no requirement to fix an Options Hearing in terms of paragraph (1) above insofar as the matters in dispute relate to an order in terms of section 11(2) of the Children (Scotland) Act 1995.

[5] (1B) In paragraph (1A) above—

    (a) "family action" has the meaning given in rule 33.1(1); and

    (b) "civil partnership action" has the meaning given in rule 33A.1(1).

(2) On fixing the date for the Options Hearing, the sheriff clerk shall-

    (a) forthwith intimate to the parties in Form G5-

      (i) the last date for lodging defences;

      (ii) the last date for adjustment; and

      (iii) the date of the Options hearing; and

    (b) prepare and sign an interlocutor recording those dates.

[3] (3) The fixing of the date for the Options Hearing shall not affect the right of a party to make any incidental application to the court.

NOTES

[1] As amended by the Act of Sederunt (Sheriff Court Ordinary Cause Rules Amendment) (Miscellaneous) 2000 (SSI 2000/239) (effective October 2, 2000).

[2] Added by the Act of Sederunt (Sheriff Court Ordinary Cause Rules Amendment) (Miscellaneous) 2000 (SSI 2000/239) (effective October 2, 2000).

[3] As amended by the Act of Sederunt (Sheriff Court Ordinary Cause Rules Amendment) (Miscellaneous) 1996 (SI 1996/2445) (effective November 1, 1996).

[4] As amended by Act of Sederunt (Ordinary Cause Rules) Amendment (Family Law (Scotland) Act 2006 etc.) 2006 (SSI 2006/207) (effective May 4, 2006).

[5] Inserted by Act of Sederunt (Ordinary Cause Rules) Amendment (Family Law (Scotland) Act 2006 etc.) 2006 (SSI 2006/207) (effective May 4, 2006).

Alteration of date for Options Hearing

9.2A.—(1) Subject to paragraph (2), at any time before the date and time fixed under rule 9.2 (fixing date for Options Hearing) or under this rule, the sheriff—

    (a) may, of his own motion or on the motion of any party—

      (i) discharge the Options Hearing; and

      (ii) fix a new date and time for the Options Hearing; or

    (b) shall, on the joint motion of the parties—

      (i) discharge the Options Hearing; and

      (ii) fix a new date and time for the Options Hearing.

(2) The date and time to be fixed—

    (a) under paragraph (1)(a)(ii) may be earlier or later than the date and time fixed for the discharged Options Hearing;

    (b) under paragraph (1)(b)(ii) shall be earlier than the date and time fixed for the discharged Options Hearing.

(3) Where the sheriff is considering making an order under paragraph (1)(a) of his own motion and in the absence of the parties, the sheriff clerk shall—

    (a) fix a date, time and place for the parties to be heard; and

    (b) inform the parties of that date, time and place.

(4) The sheriff may discharge a hearing fixed under paragraph (3) on the joint motion of the parties.

(5) On the discharge of the Options Hearing under paragraph (1), the sheriff clerk shall forthwith intimate to all parties—

(a) that the Options Hearing has been discharged under paragraph (1)(a) or (b), as the case may be;
(b) the last date for lodging defences, if appropriate;
(c) the last date for adjustment, if appropriate; and
(d) the new date and time fixed for the Options Hearing under paragraph (1)(a) or (b), as the case may be.

(6) Any reference in these Rules to the Options Hearing or a continuation of it shall include a reference to an Options Hearing for which a date and time has been fixed under this rule.

NOTE
[1] Inserted by the Act of Sederunt (Sheriff Court Ordinary Cause Rules Amendment) (Miscellaneous) 1996 (SI 1996/2445) (effective November 1, 1996) and substituted by the Act of Sederunt (Ordinary Cause and Summary Application Rules) Amendment (Miscellaneous) 2006 (SI 2006/410) (effective August 18, 2006).

Return of initial writ
9.3. Subject to rule 9.4 (lodging of pleadings before Options Hearing), the pursuer shall return the initial writ, unbacked and unfolded, to the sheriff clerk within 7 days after the expiry of the period of notice.

Lodging of pleadings before Options Hearing
9.4. Where any hearing, whether by motion or otherwise, is fixed before the Options Hearing, each party shall lodge in process a copy of his pleadings, or, where the pleadings have been adjusted, the pleadings as adjusted, not later than 2 days before the hearing.

Process folder
9.5.—(1) On receipt of the notice of intention to defend, the sheriff clerk shall prepare a process folder which shall include—
(a) interlocutor sheets;
(b) duplicate interlocutor sheets;
(c) a production file;
(d) a motion file; and
(e) an inventory of process.

(2) Any production or part of process lodged in a cause shall be placed in the process folder.

Defences
9.6.—(1) Where a notice of intention to defend has been lodged, the defender shall (subject to paragraph (3)) lodge defences within 14 days after the expiry of the period of notice.

(2) Subject to rule 19.1(3) (form of defences where counterclaim included), defences shall be in the form of answers in numbered paragraphs corresponding to the articles of the condescendence, and shall have appended a note of the pleas-in-law of the defender.

[1,2] (3) In a family action (within the meaning of rule 33.1(1)) or a civil partnership action (within the meaning of rule 33A.1(1)), neither a crave nor averments need be made in the defences which relate to any order under section 11 of the Children (Scotland) Act 1995.

NOTES
[1] Inserted by the Act of Sederunt (Family Proceedings in the Sheriff Court) 1996 (SI 1996/2167) (effective November 1, 2000).
[2] As amended by Act of Sederunt (Ordinary Cause Rules) Amendment (Family Law (Scotland) Act 2006 etc.) 2006 (SSI 2006/207) (effective May 4, 2006).

Implied admissions
9.7. Every statement of fact made by a party shall be answered by every other party, and if such a statement by one party within the knowledge of another party is not denied by that other party, that other party shall be deemed to have admitted that statement of fact.

Adjustment of pleadings
9.8.—(1) Parties may adjust their pleadings until 14 days before the date of the Options Hearing or any continuation of it.

(2) Any adjustments shall be exchanged between parties and not lodged in process.

(3) Parties shall be responsible for maintaining a record of adjustments made during the period for adjustment.

(4) No adjustments shall be permitted after the period mentioned in paragraph (1) except with leave of the sheriff.

Effect of sist on adjustment

9.9.—(1) Where a cause has been sisted, any period for adjustment before the sist shall be reckoned as a part of the period for adjustment.

(2) On recall of the sist of a cause, the sheriff clerk shall—

  (a) fix a new date for the Options Hearing;

  (b) prepare and sign an interlocutor recording that date; and

  (c) intimate that date to each party.

Open record

9.10. The sheriff may, at any time before the closing of the record in a cause to which this Chapter applies, of his own motion or on the motion of a party, order any party to lodge a copy of the pleadings in the form of an open record containing any adjustments and amendments made as at the date of the order.

Record for Options Hearing

9.11.—(1) The pursuer shall, at the end of the period for adjustment referred to in rule 9.8(1), and before the Options Hearing, make a copy of the pleadings and any adjustments and amendments in the form of a record.

(2) Not later than 2 days before the Options Hearing, the pursuer shall lodge a certified copy of the record in process.

[1] (3) Where the Options Hearing is continued under rule 9.12(5), and further adjustment or amendment is made to the pleadings, a copy of the pleadings as adjusted or amended, certified by the pursuer, shall be lodged in process not later than 2 days before the Options Hearing so continued.

NOTE

[1] Inserted by SI 1996/2445 (effective November 1, 1996).

Options Hearing

9.12.—(1) At the Options Hearing the sheriff shall seek to secure the expeditious progress of the cause by ascertaining from parties the matters in dispute and information about any other matter referred to in paragraph (3).

(2) It shall be the duty of parties to provide the sheriff with sufficient information to enable him to conduct the hearing as provided for in this rule.

(3) At the Options Hearing the sheriff shall, except where the cause is ordered to proceed under the procedure in Chapter 10 (additional procedure), close the record and—

  (a) appoint the cause to a proof and make such orders as to the extent of proof, the lodging of a joint minute of admissions or agreement, or such other matter as he thinks fit;

  (b) after having heard parties and considered any note lodged under rule 22.1 (note of basis of preliminary plea), appoint the cause to a proof before answer and make such orders as to the extent of proof, the lodging of a joint minute of admissions or agreement, or such other matter as he thinks fit; or

  [1] (c) after having heard parties and considered any note lodged under rule 22.1, appoint the cause to debate if satisfied that there is a preliminary matter of law which if established following debate would lead to decree in favour of any party, or to limitation of proof to any substantial degree.

  [4] (d) consider any child witness notice or vulnerable witness application that has been lodged where no order has been made, or

  [4] (e) ascertain whether there is or is likely to be a vulnerable witness within the meaning of section 11(1) of the Act of 2004 who is to give evidence at any proof or hearing and whether any order under section 12(1) of the Act of 2004 requires to be made.

(4) At the Options Hearing the sheriff may, having heard parties—

  (a) of his own motion or on the motion of any party, and

  (b) on being satisfied that the difficulty or complexity of the cause makes it unsuitable for the procedure under this Chapter,

order that the cause proceed under the procedure in Chapter 10 (additional procedure).

(5) The sheriff may, on cause shown, of his own motion or on the motion of any party, allow a continuation of the Options Hearing on one occasion only for a period not exceeding 28 days or to the first suitable court day thereafter.

(6) On closing the record—

  (a) where there are no adjustments made since the lodging of the record under rule 9.11(2), that record shall become the closed record; and

  (b) where there are such adjustments, the sheriff may order that a closed record including such adjustments be lodged within 7 days after the date of the interlocutor closing the record.

[2] (7) For the purposes of rules 16.2 (decrees where party in default), 33.37 (decree by default in family action) and 33A.37 (decree by default in civil partnership action), an Options Hearing shall be a diet in accordance with those rules.

[3] (8) Where the cause is appointed, under paragraph (3), to a proof or proof before answer, the sheriff shall consider whether a pre-proof hearing should be fixed under rule 28A.1.

NOTES

[1] As amended by the Act of Sederunt (Ordinary Cause, Summary Application and Small Claim Rules) Amendment (Miscellaneous) 2004 (SSI 2004/197) (effective May 21, 2004).

[2] As amended by Act of Sederunt (Ordinary Cause Rules) Amendment (Family Law (Scotland) Act 2006 etc.) 2006 (SSI 2006/207) (effective May 4, 2006).

[3] Inserted by the Act of Sederunt (Ordinary Cause and Summary Application Rules) Amendment (Miscellaneous) 2006 (SSI 2006/410) (effective August 18, 2006).

[4] As inserted by the Act of Sederunt (Ordinary Cause, Summary Application, Summary Cause and Small Claim Rules) Amendment (Vulnerable Witnesses (Scotland) Act 2004) 2007 (SSI 2007/463) r.2(3) (effective November 1, 2007).

9.13.–9.15. [*Omitted by the Act of Sederunt (Ordinary Cause, Summary Application and Small Claim Rules) Amendment (Miscellaneous) 2004 (SSI 2004/197) (effective May 21, 2004), r.2(7).*]

[1] CHAPTER 9A

DOCUMENTS AND WITNESSES

NOTE

[1] Inserted by the Act of Sederunt (Ordinary Cause, Summary Application and Small Claim Rules) Amendment (Miscellaneous) 2004 (SSI 2004/197) (effective May 21, 2004) and substituted by the Act of Sederunt (Ordinary Cause, Summary Application, Summary Cause and Small Claim Rules) Amendment (Miscellaneous) 2007 (SSI 2007/6) (effective January 29, 2007).

Application of this Chapter

9A.1. This Chapter applies to any cause proceeding under Chapters 9 and 10.

Inspection and recovery of documents

9A.2.—(1) Each party shall, within 14 days after the date of the interlocutor allowing proof or proof before answer, intimate to every other party a list of the documents, which are or have been in his possession or control and which he intends to use or put in evidence at the proof, including the whereabouts of those documents.

(2) A party who has received a list of documents from another party under paragraph (1) may inspect those documents which are in the possession or control of the party intimating the list at a time and place fixed by that party which is reasonable to both parties.

(3) A party who seeks to use or put in evidence at a proof a document not on his list intimated under paragraph (1) shall, if any other party objects to such document being used or put in evidence, seek leave of the sheriff to do so; and such leave may be granted on such conditions, if any, as the sheriff thinks fit.

(4) Nothing in this rule shall affect—

(a) the law relating, or the right of a party to object, to the inspection of a document on the ground of privilege or confidentiality; or

(b) the right of a party to apply under rule 28.2 for a commission and diligence for recovery of documents or an order under section 1 of the Administration of Justice (Scotland) Act 1972.

Exchange of lists of witnesses

9A.3.—(1) Within 28 days after the date of the interlocutor allowing a proof or proof before answer, each party shall—

(a) intimate to every other party a list of witnesses, including any skilled witnesses, on whose evidence he intends to rely at proof; and

(b) lodge a copy of that list in process.

(2) A party who seeks to rely on the evidence of a person not on his list intimated under paragraph (1) shall, if any other party objects to such evidence being admitted, seek leave of the

sheriff to admit that evidence whether it is to be given orally or not; and such leave may be granted on such conditions, if any, as the sheriff thinks fit.

[1] (3) The list of witnesses intimated under paragraph (1) shall include the name, occupation (where known) and address of each intended witness and indicate whether the witness is considered to be a vulnerable witness within the meaning of section 11(1) of the Act of 2004 and whether any child witness notice or vulnerable witness application has been lodged in respect of that witness.

NOTE
[1] As amended by the Act of Sederunt (Ordinary Cause, Summary Application, Summary Cause and Small Claim Rules) Amendment (Vulnerable Witnesses (Scotland) Act 2004) 2007 (SSI 2007/463) r.2(4) (effective November 1, 2007).

Applications in respect of time to pay directions, arrestments and time orders
9A.4. An application for—
    (a) a time to pay direction under section 1(1) of the Debtors (Scotland) Act 1987;
    (b) the recall or restriction of an arrestment under section 2(3) or 3(1) of that Act; or
    (c) a time order under section 129 of the Consumer Credit Act 1974,
in a cause which is defended, shall be made by motion lodged before the sheriff grants decree.

CHAPTER 10

ADDITIONAL PROCEDURE

Additional period for adjustment
10.1.—(1) Where, under rule 9.12(4) (order at Options Hearing to proceed under Chapter 10), the sheriff orders that a cause shall proceed in accordance with the procedure in this Chapter, he shall continue the cause for adjustment for a period of 8 weeks.

(2) Paragraphs (2) and (3) of rule 9.8 (exchange and record of adjustments) shall apply to a cause in which a period for adjustment under paragraph (1) of this rule has been allowed as they apply to the period for adjustment under that rule.

Effect of sist on adjustment period
10.2. Where a cause has been sisted, any period for adjustment before the sist shall be reckoned as part of the period for adjustment.

Variation of adjustment period
10.3.—(1) At any time before the expiry of the period for adjustment the sheriff may close the record if parties, of consent or jointly, lodge a motion seeking such an order.

(2) The sheriff may, if satisfied that there is sufficient reason for doing so, extend the period for adjustment for such period as he thinks fit, if any party—
    (a) lodges a motion seeking such an order; and
    (b) lodges a copy of the record adjusted to the date of lodging of the motion.
(3) A motion lodged under paragraph (2) shall set out—
    (a) the reasons for seeking an extension of the period for adjustment; and
    (b) the period for adjustment sought.

Order for open record
10.4. The sheriff may, at any time before the closing of the record in a cause to which this Chapter applies, of his own motion or on the motion of a party, order any party to lodge a copy of the pleadings in the form of an open record containing any adjustments and amendments made as at the date of the order.

Closing record
10.5.—(1) On the expiry of the period for adjustment, the record shall be closed and, without the attendance of parties, the sheriff clerk shall forthwith—
    (a) prepare and sign an interlocutor recording the closing of the record and fixing the date of the Procedural Hearing under rule 10.6, which date shall be on the first suitable court day occurring not sooner than 21 days after the closing of the record; and
    (b) intimate the date of the hearing to each party.
(2) The pursuer shall, within 14 days after the date of the interlocutor closing the record, lodge a certified copy of the closed record in process.
(3) The closed record shall contain only the pleadings of the parties.

Procedural Hearing

10.6.—(1) At the Procedural Hearing, the sheriff shall seek to secure the expeditious progress of the cause by ascertaining from parties the matters in dispute and information about any other matter referred to in paragraph (3).

(2) It shall be the duty of parties to provide the sheriff with sufficient information to enable him to conduct the hearing as provided for in this rule.

(3) At the Procedural Hearing the sheriff shall—

(a) appoint the cause to a proof and make such orders as to the extent of proof, the lodging of a joint minute of admissions or agreement, or such other matter as he thinks fit;

(b) after having heard the parties and considered any note lodged under rule 22.1 (note of basis of preliminary plea), appoint the cause to a proof before answer and make such orders as to the extent of proof, the lodging of a joint minute of admissions or agreement, or such other matter as he thinks fit; or

[1] (c) after having heard parties and considered any note lodged under rule 22.1, appoint the cause to a debate if satisfied that there is a preliminary matter of law which if established following debate would lead to decree in favour of any party, or to limitation of proof to any substantial degree.

[4] (d) consider any child witness notice or vulnerable witness application that has been lodged where no order has been made, or

[4] (e) ascertain whether there is or is likely to be a vulnerable witness within the meaning of section 11(1) of the Act of 2004 who is to give evidence at any proof or hearing and whether any order under section 12(1) of the Act of 2004 requires to be made.

[2] (4) For the purposes of rules 16.2 (decrees where party in default), 33.37 (decree by default in family action) and 33A.37 (decree by default in civil partnership action), a Procedural Hearing shall be a diet in accordance with those rules.

[3] (5) Where the cause is appointed, under paragraph (3), to a proof or proof before answer, the sheriff shall consider whether a pre-proof hearing should be fixed under rule 28A.1.

NOTES

[1] As amended by the Act of Sederunt (Ordinary Cause, Summary Application and Small Claim Rules) Amendment (Miscellaneous) 2004 (SSI 2004/197) r.2(9) (effective May 21, 2004).

[2] As amended by the Act of Sederunt (Ordinary Cause and Summary Application Rules) Amendment (Miscellaneous) 2006 (SSI 2006/410) (effective August 18, 2006).

[3] Inserted by the Act of Sederunt (Ordinary Cause and Summary Application Rules) Amendment (Miscellaneous) 2006 (SSI 2006/410) (effective August 18, 2006).

[4] As inserted by the Act of Sederunt (Ordinary Cause, Summary Application, Summary Cause and Small Claim Rules) Amendment (Vulnerable Witnesses (Scotland) Act 2004) 2007 (SSI 2007/463) r.2(5) (effective November 1, 2007).

CHAPTER 11

THE PROCESS

Form and lodging of parts of process

11.1. All parts of process shall be written, typed or printed on A4 size paper of durable quality and shall be lodged, unbacked and unfolded, with the sheriff clerk.

Custody of process

11.2.—(1) The initial writ, and all other parts of process lodged in a cause, shall be placed by the sheriff clerk in the process folder.

(2) The initial writ, interlocutor sheets, borrowing receipts and the process folder shall remain in the custody of the sheriff clerk.

(3) The sheriff clerk may, on cause shown, authorise the initial writ to be borrowed by the pursuer, his solicitor or the solicitor's authorised clerk.

Borrowing and returning of process

11.3.—(1) Subject to paragraph (3), a process, or any part of a process which may be borrowed, may be borrowed only by a solicitor or by his authorised clerk.

(2) All remedies competent to enforce the return of a borrowed process may proceed on the warrant of the court from the custody of which the process was obtained.

(3) A party litigant—

(a) may borrow a process only—

(i) with leave of the sheriff; and

    (ii) subject to such conditions as the sheriff may impose; or

  (b) may inspect a process and obtain copies, where practicable, from the sheriff clerk.

(4) The sheriff may, on the motion of any party, ordain any other party who has borrowed a part of process to return it within such time as the sheriff thinks fit.

Failure to return parts of process

11.4.—(1) Where a solicitor or party litigant has borrowed any part of process and fails to return it for any diet or hearing at which it is required, the sheriff may impose on such solicitor or party litigant a fine not exceeding £50, which shall be payable to the sheriff clerk; but an order imposing a fine may, on cause shown, be recalled by the sheriff.

(2) An order made under this rule shall not be subject to appeal.

Replacement of lost documents

11.5. Where any part of process is lost or destroyed, a copy of it, authenticated in such manner as the sheriff thinks fit, may be substituted for and shall, for the purposes of the cause to which the process relates, be treated as having the same force and effect as the original.

Intimation of parts of process and adjustments

[1] **11.6.**—(1) After a notice of intention to defend has been lodged, any party lodging a part of process or making an adjustment to his pleadings shall, at the same time, intimate such lodging or adjustment to every other party who has entered the process by delivering to every other party a copy of each part of process or adjustment, including, where practicable, copies of any documentary production.

(2) Unless otherwise provided in these Rules, the party required to give intimation under paragraph (1) shall deliver to every other party who has entered the process a copy of the part of process or adjustment or other document, as the case may be, by—

  (a) any of the methods of service provided for in Chapter 5 (citation, service and intimation); or

  (b) where intimation is to a party represented by a solicitor—

    (i) personal delivery,

    (ii) facsimile transmission,

    (iii) first class ordinary post,

    (iv) delivery to a document exchange,

    to that solicitor.

(3) Subject to paragraph (4), where intimation is given under—

  (a) paragraph (2)(b)(i) or (ii), it shall be deemed to have been given—

    (i) on the day of transmission or delivery where it is given before 5.00 p.m. on any day; or

    (ii) on the day after transmission or delivery where it is given after 5.00 p.m. on any day; or

  (b) paragraph (2)(b)(iii) or (iv), it shall be deemed to have been given on the day after posting or delivery.

(4) Where intimation is given or, but for this paragraph, would be deemed to be given on a Saturday, Sunday or public or court holiday, it shall be deemed to have been given on the next day on which the sheriff clerk's office is open for civil court business.

NOTE

[1] As amended by SI 1996/2445 (effective November 1, 1996).

Retention and disposal of parts of process by sheriff clerk

11.7.—(1) Where any cause has been finally determined and the period for marking an appeal has expired without an appeal having been marked, the sheriff clerk shall—

  (a) retain—

    (i) the initial writ;

    (ii) any closed record;

    (iii) the interlocutor sheets;

    (iv) any joint minute;

    (v) any offer and acceptance of tender;

    (vi) any report from a person of skill;

    (vii) any affidavit; and

    (viii) any extended shorthand notes of the proof; and

  (b) dispose of all other parts of process (except productions) in such a manner as seems appropriate.

(2) Where an appeal has been marked on the final determination of the cause, the sheriff clerk

shall exercise his duties mentioned in paragraph (1) after the final disposal of the appeal and any subsequent procedure.

Uplifting of productions from process
11.8.—(1) Each party who has lodged productions in a cause shall—
    (a) within 14 days after the final determination of the cause, where no subsequent appeal has been marked, or
    (b) within 14 days after the disposal of any appeal marked on the final determination of the cause,
uplift the productions from process.
    (2) Where any production has not been uplifted as required by paragraph (1), the sheriff clerk shall intimate to—
    (a) the solicitor who lodged the production, or
    (b) where no solicitor is acting, the party himself or such other party as seems appropriate,
that if he fails to uplift the production within 28 days after the date of such intimation, it will be disposed of in such a manner as the sheriff directs.

CHAPTER 12

INTERLOCUTORS

Signature of interlocutors by sheriff clerk
12.1. In accordance with any directions given by the Sheriff Principal, any interlocutor other than a final interlocutor may be written and signed by the sheriff clerk and—
    (a) any interlocutor written and signed by a sheriff clerk shall be treated for all purposes as if it had been written and signed by the sheriff; and
    (b) any extract of such an interlocutor shall not be invalid by reason only of its being written and signed by a sheriff clerk.

Further provisions in relation to interlocutors
12.2.—(1) The sheriff may sign an interlocutor when furth of his sheriffdom.
    (2) At any time before extract, the sheriff may correct any clerical or incidental error in an interlocutor or note attached to it.
    [1,2] (3) In any cause, other than a family action within the meaning of rule 33.1(1) or a civil partnership action within the meaning of rule 33A.1(1) which has proceeded as undefended, where at any stage evidence has been led, the sheriff shall—
    (a) in the interlocutor, make findings in fact and law; and
    (b) append to that interlocutor a note setting out the reasons for his decision.
    [1] (4) In any other interlocutor, the sheriff may, and shall when requested by a party, append a note setting out the reasons for his decision.
    (5) Where the sheriff reserves his decision and gives his decision at a date later than the date of the hearing outwith the presence of the parties—
    (a) the date of the interlocutor of the sheriff shall be the date on which it is received by the sheriff clerk; and
    (b) the sheriff clerk shall—
        (i) enter that date in the interlocutor; and
        (ii) forthwith send a copy of the interlocutor and any note attached to it free of charge to each party.

NOTES
[1] Substituted by SI 1996/2445 (effective November 1, 1996).
[2] As amended by Act of Sederunt (Ordinary Cause Rules) Amendment (Family Law (Scotland) Act 2006 etc.) 2006 (SSI 2006/207) r.2 (effective May 4, 2006).

CHAPTER 13

PARTY MINUTER PROCEDURE

Person claiming title and interest to enter process as defender
13.1.—(1) A person who has not been called as a defender or third party may apply by minute for leave to enter a process as a party minuter and to lodge defences.
    (2) A minute under paragraph (1) shall specify—
    (a) the applicant's title and interest to enter the process; and
    (b) the grounds of the defence he proposes to state.

(3) Subject to paragraph (4), after hearing the applicant and any party, the sheriff may—

    (a) if he is satisfied that the applicant has shown title and interest to enter the process, grant the applicant leave to enter the process as a party minuter and to lodge defences; and

    (b) make such order as to expenses or otherwise as he thinks fit.

[1] (4) Where an application under paragraph (1) is made after the closing of the record or in a personal injuries action subject to personal injuries procedure after the date upon which the record is required to be lodged, the sheriff shall only grant leave under paragraph (3) if he is satisfied as to the reason why earlier application was not made.

NOTE

[1] As amended by the Act of Sederunt (Ordinary Cause Rules Amendment) (Personal Injuries Actions) 2009 (SSI 2009/285) r.2 (effective November 2, 2009).

Procedure following leave to enter process

13.2.—[1] (1) Where a party minuter lodges answers, the sheriff clerk shall fix a date and time under rule 9.2 for a hearing under rule 9.12 (Options Hearing) as if the party minuter had lodged a notice of intention to defend and the period of notice had expired on the date for lodging defences.

(2) At the Options Hearing, or at any time thereafter, the sheriff may grant such decree or other order as he thinks fit.

(3) A decree or other order against the party minuter shall have effect and be extractable in the same way as a decree or other order against a defender.

[2] (4) Paragraphs (1), (2) and (3) shall not apply to a personal injuries action which is subject to personal injuries procedure.

[2] (5) Where the sheriff grants an application under rule 13.1 in a personal injuries action which is subject to personal injuries procedure, the sheriff may make such further order as he thinks fit.

NOTES

[1] As amended by SI 1996/2445 (effective November 1, 1996).

[2] As inserted by the Act of Sederunt (Ordinary Cause Rules Amendment) (Personal Injuries Actions) 2009 (SSI 2009/285) r.2 (effective November 2, 2009).

[1] CHAPTER 13A

INTERVENTIONS BY THE COMMISSION FOR EQUALITY AND HUMAN RIGHTS

NOTE

[1] As inserted by the Act of Sederunt (Sheriff Court Rules) (Miscellaneous Amendments) 2008 (SSI 2008/223) r.4(2) (effective July 1, 2008).

Interpretation

13A.1. In this Chapter "the CEHR" means the Commission for Equality and Human Rights.

Interventions by the CEHR

13A.2.—(1) The CEHR may apply to the sheriff for leave to intervene in any cause in accordance with this Chapter.

(2) This Chapter is without prejudice to any other entitlement of the CEHR by virtue of having title and interest in relation to the subject matter of any proceedings by virtue of section 30(2) of the Equality Act 2006 or any other enactment to seek to be sisted as a party in those proceedings.

(3) Nothing in this Chapter shall affect the power of the sheriff to make such other direction as he considers appropriate in the interests of justice.

(4) Any decision of the sheriff in proceedings under this Chapter shall be final and not subject to appeal.

Applications to intervene

13A.3.—(1) An application for leave to intervene shall be by way of minute of intervention in Form O7A and the CEHR shall—

    (a) send a copy of it to all the parties; and

    (b) lodge it in process, certifying that subparagraph (a) has been complied with.

(2) A minute of intervention shall set out briefly—

    (a) the CEHR's reasons for believing that the proceedings are relevant to a matter in connection with which the CEHR has a function;

    (b) the issue in the proceedings which the CEHR wishes to address; and

    (c) the propositions to be advanced by the CEHR and the CEHR's reasons for believing that they are relevant to the proceedings and that they will assist the sheriff.

(3) The sheriff may—

    (a) refuse leave without a hearing;

    (b) grant leave without a hearing unless a hearing is requested under paragraph (4);

    (c) refuse or grant leave after such a hearing.

(4) A hearing, at which the applicant and the parties may address the court on the matters referred to in paragraph (6)(c), may be held if, within 14 days of the minute of intervention being lodged, any of the parties lodges a request for a hearing.

(5) Any diet in pursuance of paragraph (4) shall be fixed by the sheriff clerk who shall give written intimation of the diet to the CEHR and all the parties.

(6) The sheriff may grant leave only if satisfied that–

    (a) the proceedings are relevant to a matter in connection with which the CEHR has a function;

    (b) the propositions to be advanced by the CEHR are relevant to the proceedings and are likely to assist him; and

    (c) the intervention will not unduly delay or otherwise prejudice the rights of the parties, including their potential liability for expenses.

(7) In granting leave the sheriff may impose such terms and conditions as he considers desirable in the interests of justice, including making provision in respect of any additional expenses incurred by the parties as a result of the intervention.

(8) The sheriff clerk shall give written intimation of a grant or refusal of leave to the CEHR and all the parties.

Form of intervention

    13A.4.—(1) An intervention shall be by way of a written submission which (including any appendices) shall not exceed 5000 words.

(2) The CEHR shall lodge the submission and send a copy of it to all the parties by such time as the sheriff may direct.

(3) The sheriff may in exceptional circumstances–

    (a) allow a longer written submission to be made;

    (b) direct that an oral submission is to be made.

(4) Any diet in pursuance of paragraph (3)(b) shall be fixed by the sheriff clerk who shall give written intimation of the diet to the CEHR and all the parties.

[1] Chapter 13B

INTERVENTIONS BY THE SCOTTISH COMMISSION FOR HUMAN RIGHTS

NOTE
[1] As inserted by the Act of Sederunt (Sheriff Court Rules) (Miscellaneous Amendments) 2008 (SSI 2008/223) r.4(2) (effective July 1, 2008).

Interpretation

    13B.1. In this Chapter—

    "the Act of 2006" means the Scottish Commission for Human Rights Act 2006; and

    "the SCHR" means the Scottish Commission for Human Rights.

Application to intervene

    13B.2.—(1) An application for leave to intervene under section 14(2)(a) of the Act of 2006 shall be by way of minute of intervention in Form O7B and the SCHR shall—

    (a) send a copy of it to all the parties; and

    (b) lodge it in process, certifying that subparagraph (a) has been complied with.

(2) In granting leave the sheriff may impose such terms and conditions as he considers desirable in the interests of justice, including making provision in respect of any additional expenses incurred by the parties as a result of the intervention.

(3) The sheriff clerk shall give written intimation of a grant or refusal of leave to the SCHR and all the parties.

(4) Any decision of the sheriff in proceedings under this Chapter shall be final and not subject to appeal.

Invitation to intervene

13B.3.—(1) An invitation to intervene under section 14(2)(b) of the Act of 2006 shall be in Form O7C and the sheriff clerk shall send a copy of it to the SCHR and all the parties.

(2) An invitation under paragraph (1) shall be accompanied by—

(a) a copy of the pleadings in the proceedings; and

(b) such other documents relating to those proceedings as the sheriff thinks relevant.

(3) In issuing an invitation under section 14(2)(b) of the Act of 2006, the sheriff may impose such terms and conditions as he considers desirable in the interests of justice, including making provision in respect of any additional expenses incurred by the parties as a result of the intervention.

Form of intervention

13B.4.—(1) An intervention shall be by way of a written submission which (including any appendices) shall not exceed 5000 words.

(2) The SCHR shall lodge the submission and send a copy of it to all the parties by such time as the sheriff may direct.

(3) The sheriff may in exceptional circumstances—

(a) allow a longer written submission to be made;

(b) direct that an oral submission is to be made.

(4) Any diet in pursuance of paragraph (3)(b) shall be fixed by the sheriff clerk who shall give written intimation of the diet to the SCHR and all the parties.

CHAPTER 14

APPLICATIONS BY MINUTE

Application of this Chapter

14.1.—(1) Where an application may be made by minute, the form of the minute and the procedure to be adopted shall, unless otherwise provided in these Rules, be in accordance with this Chapter.

[1] (2) This Chapter shall not apply to—

(a) a minute of amendment;

(b) a minute of abandonment; or

(c) a joint minute.

NOTE

[1] As amended by SI 1996/2445 (effective November 1, 1996).

Form of minute

14.2. A minute to which this Chapter applies shall contain—

(a) a crave;

(b) where appropriate, a condescendence in the form of a statement of facts supporting the crave; and

(c) where appropriate, pleas-in-law.

Lodging of minutes

[1] **14.3.**—(1) Before intimating any minute, the minuter shall lodge the minute in process.

(2) On the lodging of a minute, and any document under rule 21.1(1)(b) (lodging documents founded on or adopted), the sheriff—

(a) may make an order for answers to be lodged;

(b) may order intimation of the minute without making an order for answers; or

(c) where he considers it appropriate for the expeditious disposal of the minute or for any other specified reason, may fix a hearing.

(3) Any answers ordered to be lodged under paragraph (2)(a) shall, unless otherwise ordered by the sheriff, be lodged within 14 days after the date of intimation of the minute.

(4) Where the sheriff fixes a hearing under paragraph (2)(c), the interlocutor fixing that hearing shall specify whether—

(a) answers are to be lodged;

(b) the sheriff will hear evidence at that hearing; and

(c) the sheriff will allow evidence by affidavit.

(5) Any answers or affidavit evidence ordered to be lodged under paragraph (4) shall be lodged within such time as shall be specified in the interlocutor of the sheriff.

(6) The following rules shall not apply to any hearing fixed under paragraph (2)(c):—

rule 14.7 (opposition where no order for answers made),

rule 14.8 (hearing of minutes where no opposition or no answers lodged),

rule 14.10 (notice of opposition or answers lodged).

(7) The sheriff clerk shall forthwith return the minute to the minuter with any interlocutor pronounced by the sheriff.

NOTE
[1] Substituted by SI 1996/2445 (effective November 1, 1996).

Intimation of minutes
[1] **14.4.**—(1) The party lodging a minute shall, on receipt from the sheriff clerk of the minute, intimate to every other party including any person referred to in rule 14.13(1)—
(a) a notice in Form G7A, G7B or G7C, as the case may be, by any of the methods provided for in rule 14.5 (methods of intimation); and
(b) a copy of—
(i) the minute;
(ii) any interlocutor; and
(iii) any document referred to in the minute.
(2) The sheriff may, on cause shown, dispense with intimation.

NOTE
[1] Inserted by SI 1996/2445 (effective November 1, 1996).

Methods of intimation
[1] **14.5.**—(1) Intimation of a minute may be given by—
(a) any of the methods of service provided for in Chapter 5 (citation, service and intimation); or
(b) where intimation is to a party represented by a solicitor, by—
(i) personal delivery,
(ii) facsimile transmission,
(iii) first class ordinary post, or
(iv) delivery to a document exchange,
to that solicitor.
(2) Where intimation is given—
(a) under paragraph (1)(b)(i) or (ii), it shall be deemed to have been given—
(i) on the day of transmission or delivery where it is given before 5.00 p.m. on any day; or
(ii) on the day after transmission or delivery where it is given after 5.00 p.m. on any day; or
(b) under paragraph 1(b)(iii) or (iv), it shall be deemed to have been given on the day after the date of posting or delivery.

NOTE
[1] Inserted by SI 1996/2445 (effective November 1, 1996).

Return of minute with evidence of intimation
[1] **14.6.** Where intimation of any minute has been given, the minute and a certificate of intimation in Form G8 shall be returned to the sheriff clerk within 5 days after the date of intimation.

NOTE
[1] Inserted by SI 1996/2445 (effective November 1, 1996).

Opposition where no order for answers made
[1] **14.7.**—(1) Where a party seeks to oppose a minute lodged under rule 14.3 (lodging of minutes) in which no order for answers has been made under paragraph (2)(a) of that rule, that party shall, within 14 days after the date of intimation of the minute to him—
(a) complete a notice of opposition in Form G9;
(b) lodge the notice with the sheriff clerk; and
(c) intimate a copy of that notice to every other party.
(2) Rule 14.5 (methods of intimation) and rule 14.6 (return of minute with evidence of intimation) shall apply to intimation of opposition to a minute under paragraph (1)(c) of this rule as they apply to intimation of a minute.
(3) The sheriff may, on cause shown, reduce or dispense with the period for lodging the notice mentioned in paragraph (1)(b).

NOTE
  [1] Inserted by SI 1996/2445 (effective November 1, 1996).

Hearing of minutes where no opposition or no answers lodged
  [1] **14.8.**—(1) Where no notice of opposition is lodged or where no answers have been lodged to the minute within the time allowed, the minute shall be determined by the sheriff in chambers without the attendance of parties, unless the sheriff otherwise directs.
  (2) Where the sheriff requires to hear a party on a minute, the sheriff clerk shall—
    (a) fix a date, time and place for the party to be heard; and
    (b) inform that party—
        (i) of that date, time and place; and
        (ii) of the reasons for the sheriff wishing to hear him.

NOTE
  [1] Inserted by SI 1996/2445 (effective November 1, 1996).

Intimation of interlocutor
  [1] **14.9.** Where a minute has been determined in accordance with rule 14.8 (hearing of minutes where no opposition or no answers lodged), the sheriff clerk shall intimate the interlocutor determining that minute to the parties forthwith.

NOTE
  [1] Inserted by SI 1996/2445 (effective November 1, 1996).

Notice of opposition or answers lodged
  [1] **14.10.**—(1) Where a notice of opposition has, or answers have, been lodged to the minute, the sheriff clerk shall—
    (a) assign a date, time and place for a hearing on the first suitable court day after the date of the lodging of the notice of opposition or answers, as the case may be; and
    (b) intimate that date, time and place to the parties.
  (2) The interlocutor fixing a hearing under paragraph (1) shall specify whether the sheriff will hear evidence at the hearing or receive evidence by affidavit.

NOTE
  [1] Inserted by SI 1996/2445 (effective November 1, 1996).

Procedure for hearing
  [1] **14.11.**—(1) A certified copy of the interlocutor assigning a hearing under this Chapter and requiring evidence to be led shall be sufficient warrant to a sheriff officer to cite a witness on behalf of a party.
  (2) At the hearing, the sheriff shall hear parties on the minute and any answers lodged, and may determine the minute or may appoint such further procedure as he considers necessary.

NOTE
  [1] Inserted by SI 1996/2445 (effective November 1, 1996).

Consent to minute
  [1] **14.12.** Subject to paragraph (2) of rule 14.8 (hearing of minutes where no opposition or no answers lodged), where all parties to the action indicate to the sheriff, by endorsement of the minute or otherwise in writing, their intention to consent to the minute, the sheriff may forthwith determine the minute in chambers without the appearance of parties.

NOTE
  [1] Inserted by SI 1996/2445 (effective November 1, 1996).

Procedure following grant of minute
  [1] **14.13.**—(1) Where the minute includes a crave seeking leave—
    (a) for a person—
        (i) to be sisted as a party to the action, or
        (ii) to appear in the proceedings, or
    (b) for the cause to be transferred against the representatives of a party who has died or is under a legal incapacity,
the sheriff, on granting the minute, may order a hearing under rule 9.12 (Options Hearing) to be fixed or may appoint such further procedure as he thinks fit.

(2) Where an Options Hearing is ordered under paragraph (1), the sheriff clerk shall—
    (a) fix a date and time for such hearing, which date, unless the sheriff otherwise directs, shall be on the first suitable court day occurring not sooner than 10 weeks after the date of the interlocutor of the sheriff ordering such hearing be fixed;
    (b) forthwith intimate to the parties in Form G5—
        (i) where appropriate, the last date for lodging defences;
        (ii) where appropriate, the last date for adjustment; and
        (iii) the date of the Options Hearing; and
    (c) prepare and sign an interlocutor recording those dates.
(3) For the purpose of fixing the date for the Options Hearing referred to in paragraph (1), the date of granting the minute shall be deemed to be the date of expiry of the period of notice.

NOTE
[1] Inserted by SI 1996/2445 (effective November 1, 1996).

[1] CHAPTER 15

NOTE
[1] Substituted by SI 1996/2445 (effective November 1, 1996).

MOTIONS

Lodging of motions
15.1.—(1) A motion may be made—
    (a) orally with leave of the court during any hearing of a cause; or
    (b) by lodging a written motion in Form G6.
(2) Subject to paragraph (3), a written motion shall be lodged with the sheriff clerk within 5 days after the date of intimation of the motion required by rule 15.2 (intimation of motions) with—
    (a) a certificate of intimation in Form G8; and
    (b) so far as practicable any document referred to in the written motion and not already lodged in process.
(3) Where the period for lodging opposition to the motion is varied under rule 15.2(4) (variation of and dispensing with period of intimation) to a period of 5 days or less, the written motion and certificate to be lodged in terms of paragraph (2) shall be lodged no later than the day on which the period for lodging opposition expires.

Intimation of motions
15.2.—(1) Subject to paragraphs (4) and (7), a party intending to lodge a motion in accordance with rule 15.1(1)(b) (lodging written motion) shall intimate the motion in Form G7, and a copy of any document referred to in the motion, to every other party.
(2) Intimation of a motion may be given by—
    (a) any of the methods of service provided for in Chapter 5 (citation, service and intimation); or
    (b) where intimation is to a party represented by a solicitor, by—
        (i) personal delivery,
        (ii) facsimile transmission,
        (iii) first class ordinary post, or
        (iv) delivery to a document exchange,
        to that solicitor.
(3) Where intimation is given—
    (a) under paragraph (2)(b)(i) or (ii), it shall be deemed to have been given—
        (i) on the day of transmission or delivery where it is given before 5.00 p.m. on any day; or
        (ii) on the day after transmission or delivery where it is given after 5.00 p.m. on any day; or
    (b) under paragraph (2)(b)(iii) or (iv), it shall be deemed to have been given on the day after posting or delivery.
(4) The sheriff may, on the application of a party intending to lodge a written motion, vary the period of 7 days specified in rule 15.3(1)(c) for lodging opposition to the motion or dispense with intimation.
(5) An application under paragraph (4) shall be made in the written motion, giving reasons for such variation or dispensation.
(6) Where the sheriff varies the period within which notice of opposition is to be lodged under

rule 15.3(1)(c), the form of intimation required under rule 15.2(1) (intimation of motion in Form G7) shall state the date by which such notice requires to be lodged.

(7) A joint motion by all parties lodged in Form G6 need not be intimated.

Opposition to motions

15.3.—(1) Where a party seeks to oppose a motion made in accordance with rule 15.1(1)(b) (written motion), he shall—

    (a) complete a notice of opposition in Form G9;

    (b) intimate a copy of that notice to every other party; and

    (c) lodge the notice with the sheriff clerk within 7 days after the date of intimation of the motion or such other period as the sheriff may have determined under rule 15.2(6).

(2) Paragraphs (2) and (3) of rule 15.2 (methods and time of intimation of motions) shall apply to the intimation of opposition to a motion under paragraph (1)(b) of this rule as they apply to intimation under that rule.

Consent to motions

15.4. Where a party consents to a written motion, he shall endorse the motion, or give notice to the sheriff clerk in writing, of his consent.

Hearing of motions

15.5.—(1) Subject to paragraph (2), where no notice of opposition is lodged with the sheriff clerk within the period specified in rule 15.3(1)(c), or ordered by virtue of rule 15.2(4), the motion shall be determined by the sheriff in chambers without the appearance of parties, unless the sheriff otherwise directs.

(2) In accordance with any directions given by the sheriff principal, the sheriff clerk may determine any motion other than a motion which seeks a final interlocutor.

(3) Where the sheriff clerk considers that a motion dealt with by him under paragraph (2) should not be granted, he shall refer that motion to the sheriff who shall deal with it in accordance with paragraph (1).

(4) Where the sheriff requires to hear a party on a motion which is not opposed, the sheriff clerk shall—

    (a) fix a date, time and place for the party to be heard, and

    (b) inform that party—

        (i) of that date, time and place; and

        (ii) of the reasons for the sheriff wishing to hear him.

(5) Where a notice of opposition is lodged in accordance with rule 15.3(1), the sheriff clerk shall—

    (a) assign a date, time and place, on the first suitable court day after the lodging of the notice of opposition, for the motion to be heard; and

    (b) intimate that date, time and place to the parties.

(6) Where a motion has been determined under paragraph (1) or (2), the sheriff clerk shall intimate the interlocutor determining that motion to all parties forthwith.

(7) Where the sheriff, under paragraph (4) of rule 15.2, dispenses with intimation required by paragraph (1) of that rule, he shall make such order as he thinks fit for intimation of his determination of the motion to every party to the action in respect of whom intimation has been so dispensed with.

(8) Subject to paragraph (4), where all parties consent to a written motion, the sheriff may determine the motion in chambers without the appearance of parties.

(9) Subject to paragraph (4) where a joint motion of all parties in Form G6 is lodged with the sheriff clerk, the sheriff may determine the motion in chambers without the appearance of parties.

Motions to sist

[1] **15.6.**—(1) Where a motion to sist is made, either orally or in writing in accordance with rule 15.1(1)(a) or (b)—

    (a) the reason for the sist shall be stated by the party seeking the sist; and

    (b) that reason shall be recorded in the interlocutor.

(2) Where a cause has been sisted, the sheriff may, after giving parties an opportunity to be heard, recall the sist.

NOTE

[1] Inserted by SSI 2000/239 (effective October 2, 2000).

Dismissal of action due to delay

[1] **15.7.**—(1) Any party to an action may, while that action is depending before the court,

apply by written motion for the court to dismiss the action due to inordinate and inexcusable delay by another party or another party's agent in progressing the action, resulting in unfairness.

(2) A motion under paragraph (1) shall—

[2] (a) include a statement of the grounds on which it is proposed that the motion should be allowed; and

(b) be lodged in accordance with rule 15.1.

(3) A notice of opposition to the motion in Form G9 shall include a statement of the grounds of opposition to the motion.

(4) In determining an application made under this rule, the court may dismiss the action if it appears to the court that—

(a) there has been an inordinate and inexcusable delay on the part of any party or any party's agent in progressing the action; and

(b) such delay results in unfairness specific to the factual circumstances, including the procedural circumstances, of that action.

(5) In determining whether or not to dismiss an action under paragraph (4), the court shall take account of the procedural consequences, both for the parties and for the work of the court, of allowing the action to proceed.

NOTES

[1] As inserted by the Act of Sederunt (Sheriff Court Rules) (Miscellaneous Amendments) 2009 (SSI 2009/294) r.14 (effective October 1, 2009).

[2] As amended by the Act of Sederunt (Sheriff Court Rules) (Miscellaneous Amendments) 2010 (SSI 2010/279) para.7 (effective July 29, 2010).

CHAPTER 16

DECREES BY DEFAULT

Application of this Chapter

[1] **16.1.** This Chapter applies to any cause other than—

(a) an action to which rule 33.37 (decree by default in family action) applies;

[2] (aa) an action to which rule 33A.37 (decree by default in a civil partnership action) applies;

(b) an action of multiplepoinding;

(c) a cause under the Presumption of Death (Scotland) Act 1977; or

(d) a commercial action within the meaning of Chapter 40.

NOTES

[1] As amended by SSI 2001/8 (effective March 1, 2001).

[2] Inserted by Act of Sederunt (Ordinary Cause Rules) Amendment (Family Law (Scotland) Act 2006 etc.) 2006 (SSI 2006/207) (effective May 4, 2006).

Decrees where party in default

16.2.—(1) In a cause to which this Chapter applies, where a party fails—

(a) to lodge, or intimate the lodging of, any production or part of process within the period required under a provision in these Rules or an order of the sheriff,

(b) to implement an order of the sheriff within a specified period,

(c) to appear or be represented at any diet, or

[1] (d) otherwise to comply with any requirement imposed upon that party by these Rules;

that party shall be in default.

[2] (2) Where a party is in default the sheriff may, as the case may be—

(a) grant decree as craved with expenses;

(b) grant decree of absolvitor with expenses;

(c) dismiss the cause with expenses; or

(d) make such other order as he thinks fit to secure the expeditious progress of the cause.

(3) Where no party appears at a diet, the sheriff may dismiss the cause.

(4) In this rule, "diet" includes—

(a) a hearing under rule 9.12 (Options Hearing);

(b) a hearing under rule 10.6 (Procedural Hearing);

(c) a proof or proof before answer; and

(d) a debate.

NOTES

[1] Inserted by the Act of Sederunt (Ordinary Cause and Summary Application Rules) Amendment (Miscellaneous) 2006 (SSI 2006/410) (effective August 18, 2006).

[2] As amended by the Act of Sederunt (Ordinary Cause and Summary Application Rules) Amendment (Miscellaneous) 2006 (SSI 2006/410) (effective August 18, 2006).

Prorogation of time where party in default

16.3. In an action to which this Chapter applies, the sheriff may, on cause shown, prorogate the time for lodging any production or part of process or for giving intimation or for implementing any order.

CHAPTER 17

SUMMARY DECREES

Application of this Chapter

17.1. This Chapter applies to any action other than—
    (a) a family action within the meaning of rule 33.1(1);
[1] (aa) a civil partnership action within the meaning of rule 33A.1(1);
    (b) an action of multiplepoinding; or
    (c) an action under the Presumption of Death (Scotland) Act 1977.

NOTE

[1] Inserted by Act of Sederunt (Ordinary Cause Rules) Amendment (Family Law (Scotland) Act 2006 etc.) 2006 (SSI 2006/207) r.2 (effective May 4, 2006).

Applications for summary decree

17.2.—(1) Subject to paragraphs (2) to (5) of this rule, a pursuer may, at any time after a defender has lodged defences, apply by motion for summary decree against that defender on the ground that there is no defence to the action, or part of it, disclosed in the defences.

(2) In applying for summary decree, the pursuer may move the sheriff—
    (a) to grant decree in terms of all or any of the craves of the initial writ;
    (b) to pronounce an interlocutor sustaining or repelling a plea-in-law; or
    (c) to dispose of the whole or part of the subject-matter of the cause.

(3) [*Repealed by SSI 2000/239 (effective October 2, 2000).*]

(4) On a motion under paragraph (1), the sheriff may—
    (a) if satisfied that there is no defence to the action or to any part of it to which the motion relates, grant the motion for summary decree in whole or in part, as the case may be; or
    (b) ordain any party, or a partner, director, officer or office-bearer of, any party—
        (i) to produce any relevant document or article; or
        (ii) to lodge an affidavit in support of any assertion of fact made in the pleadings or at the hearing of the motion.

(5) Notwithstanding the refusal of all or part of a motion for summary decree, a subsequent motion may be made where there has been a change of circumstances.

Application of summary decree to counterclaims, etc.

17.3.—(1) Where a defender has lodged a counterclaim—
    (a) he may apply by motion for summary decree against the pursuer on that counterclaim on the ground that there is no defence to the counterclaim, or a part of it, disclosed in the answers to it; and
    (b) paragraphs (2) to (5) of rule 17.2 shall, with the necessary modifications, apply to a motion by a defender under this paragraph as they apply to a motion by a pursuer under paragraph (1) of that rule.

(2) Where a defender or third party has made a claim against another defender or third party who has lodged defences or answers, as the case may be—
    (a) he may apply by motion for summary decree against that other defender or third party on the ground that there is no defence to his claim, or a part of it, disclosed in the defences or answers, as the case may be; and
    (b) paragraphs (2) to (5) of rule 17.2 shall, with the necessary modifications, apply to a motion by a defender or third party under this paragraph as they apply to a motion by a pursuer under paragraph (1) of that rule.

CHAPTER 18

AMENDMENT OF PLEADINGS

Alteration of sum sued for
18.1.—[1] (1) In a cause in which all other parties have lodged defences or answers, the pursuer may, before the closing of the record, alter any sum sued for by amending the crave of the initial writ, and any record.

(2) The pursuer shall forthwith intimate any such amendment in writing to every other party.

NOTE
[1] As amended by SI 1996/2445 (effective November 1, 1996).

Powers of sheriff to allow amendment
18.2.—(1) The sheriff may, at any time before final judgment, allow an amendment mentioned in paragraph (2).

(2) Paragraph (1) applies to the following amendments:—
  (a) an amendment of the initial writ which may be necessary for the purpose of determining the real question in controversy between the parties, notwithstanding that in consequence of such amendment—
      (i) the sum sued for is increased or restricted after the closing of the record; or
      (ii) a different remedy from that originally craved is sought;
  (b) an amendment which may be necessary—
      (i) to correct or supplement the designation of a party to the cause;
      (ii) to enable a party who has sued or has been sued in his own right to sue or be sued in a representative capacity;
      (iii) to enable a party who has sued or has been sued in a representative capacity to sue or be sued in his own right or in a different representative capacity;
      (iv) to add the name of an additional pursuer or person whose concurrence is necessary;
      (v) where the cause has been commenced or presented in the name of the wrong person, or it is doubtful whether it has been commenced or presented in the name of the right person, to allow any other person to be sisted in substitution for, or in addition to, the original person; or
      (vi) to direct a crave against a third party brought into an action under Chapter 20 (third party procedure);
  (c) an amendment of a condescendence, defences, answers, pleas-in-law or other pleadings which may be necessary for determining the real question in controversy between the parties; and
  (d) where it appears that all parties having an interest have not been called or that the cause has been directed against the wrong person, an amendment inserting in the initial writ an additional or substitute party and directing existing or additional craves, averments and pleas-in-law against that party.

Applications to amend
18.3.—(1) A party seeking to amend shall lodge a minute of amendment in process setting out his proposed amendment and, at the same time, lodge a motion—
  (a) to allow the minute of amendment to be received; and
  (b) to allow—
      (i) amendment in terms of the minute of amendment and, where appropriate, to grant an order under rule 18.5(1)(a) (service of amendment for additional or substitute party); or
      (ii) where the minute of amendment may require to be answered, any other person to lodge answers within a specified period.

(2) Where the sheriff has pronounced an interlocutor allowing a minute of amendment to be received and answered, he may allow a period of adjustment of the minute of amendment and answers and, on so doing, shall fix a date for parties to be heard on the minute of amendment and answers as adjusted.

[1] (3) Any adjustment to any minute of amendment or answers shall be exchanged between parties and not lodged in process.

[1] (4) Parties shall be responsible for maintaining a record of adjustment made and the date of their intimation.

[1] (5) No adjustments shall be permitted after the period of adjustment allowed, except with leave of the sheriff.

[1] (6) Each party shall, no later than 2 days before the hearing fixed in terms of paragraph (2),

lodge in process a copy of their minute of amendment or answers with all adjustments made thereto in italic or bold type, or underlined.

NOTE
[1] Inserted by SSI 2000/239 (effective October 2, 2000).

Applications for diligence on amendment
18.4.—(1) Where a minute of amendment is lodged by a pursuer under rule 18.2(2)(d) (all parties not, or wrong person, called), he may apply by motion for warrant to use any form of diligence which could be used on the dependence of a separate action.

(2) A copy certified by the sheriff clerk of the interlocutor granting warrant for diligence on the dependence applied for under paragraph (1) shall be sufficient authority for the execution of that diligence.

Service of amended pleadings
18.5.—[1] (1) Where an amendment under rule 18.2(2)(b)(iv), (v) or (vi) (additional or substitute defenders added by amendment) or rule 18.2(2)(d) (all parties not, or wrong person, called) has been made—
  (a) the sheriff shall order that a copy of the initial writ or record, as the case may be, as so amended be served by the party who made the amendment on that additional or substitute party with—
    [2] (i) in a cause in which a time to pay direction under the Debtors (Scotland) Act 1987 or a time order under the Consumer Credit Act 1974 may be applied for, a notice in Form O8 specifying the date by which a notice of intention must be lodged in process, a notice in Form O3 and a notice of intention to defend in Form O7; or
    (ii) in any other cause, a notice in Form O9 specifying the date by which a notice of intention to defend must be lodged in process and a notice of intention to defend in Form O7; and
  (b) the party who made the amendment shall lodge in process—
    (i) a copy of the initial writ or record as amended;
    (ii) a copy of the notice sent in Form O8 or Form O9; and
    (iii) a certificate of service.

(2) When paragraph (1) has been complied with, the cause as so amended shall proceed in every respect as if that party had originally been made a party to the cause.

(3) Where a notice of intention to defend is lodged by virtue of paragraph (1)(a), the sheriff clerk shall fix a date for a hearing under rule 9.12 (Options Hearing).

NOTES
[1] As amended by SI 1996/2445 (effective November 1, 1996).
[2] As amended by the Act of Sederunt (Ordinary Cause, Summary Application, Summary Cause and Small Claim Rules) Amendment (Miscellaneous) 2007 (SSI 2007/6), para.2(9) (effective January 29, 2007).

Expenses and conditions of amendment
18.6. The sheriff shall find the party making an amendment liable in the expenses occasioned by the amendment unless it is shown that it is just and equitable that the expenses occasioned by the amendment should be otherwise dealt with, and may attach such other conditions as he thinks fit.

Effect of amendment on diligence
18.7. Where an amendment has been allowed, the amendment—
  (a) shall not validate diligence used on the dependence of a cause so as to prejudice the rights of creditors of the party against whom the diligence has been executed who are interested in defeating such diligence; and
  (b) shall preclude any objection to such diligence stated by a party or any person by virtue of a title acquired or in right of a debt contracted by him subsequent to the execution of such diligence.

Preliminary pleas inserted on amendment
18.8.—(1) Where a party seeks to add a preliminary plea by amendment or answers to an amendment, or by adjustment thereto, a note of the basis for the plea shall be lodged at the same time as the minute, answers or adjustment, as the case may be.

(2) If a party fails to comply with paragraph (1), that party shall be deemed to be no longer insisting on the preliminary plea and the plea shall be repelled by the sheriff.

If the minute of amendment or answers thereto seeks to add a preliminary plea, a note of the basis of that plea must be lodged at the same time as the minute, answers or adjustments thereto which introduces the plea (OCR 18.8(1))

CHAPTER 19

COUNTERCLAIMS

Counterclaims
   19.1.—(1) In any action other than a family action within the meaning of rule 33.1(1), a civil partnership action within the meaning of rule 33A.1(1) or an action of multiplepoinding, a defender may counterclaim against a pursuer—
   (a) where the counterclaim might have been made in a separate action in which it would not have been necessary to call as defender any person other than the pursuer; and
   (b) in respect of any matter—
      (i) forming part, or arising out of the grounds, of the action by the pursuer;
      (ii) the decision of which is necessary for the determination of the question in controversy between the parties; or
      (iii) which, if the pursuer had been a person not otherwise subject to the jurisdiction of the court, might have been the subject-matter of an action against that pursuer in which jurisdiction would have arisen by reconvention.
   (2) A counterclaim shall be made in the defences—
   (a) when the defences are lodged or during the period for adjustment;
   (b) by amendment at any other stage, with the leave of the sheriff and subject to such conditions, if any, as to expenses or otherwise as the sheriff thinks fit.
   (3) Defences which include a counterclaim shall commence with a crave setting out the counterclaim in such form as, if the counterclaim had been made in a separate action, would have been appropriate in the initial writ in that separate action and shall include—
   (a) answers to the condescendence of the initial writ as required by rule 9.6(2) (form of defences);
   (b) a statement of facts in numbered paragraphs setting out the facts on which the counterclaim is founded, incorporating by reference, if necessary, any matter contained in the defences; and
   (c) appropriate pleas-in-law.

NOTE
   [1] As amended by Act of Sederunt (Ordinary Cause Rules) Amendment (Family Law (Scotland) Act 2006 etc.) 2006 (SSI 2006/207) r.2 (effective May 4, 2006).

Warrants for diligence on counterclaims
   [1] **19.2.**—(1) A defender who makes a counterclaim may apply for a warrant for interim diligence which would have been permitted had the warrant been sought in an initial writ in a separate action.
   (2)–(4) [*Repealed by the Act of Sederunt (Sheriff Court Rules) (Miscellaneous Amendments) 2009 (SSI 2009/294) r.10 (effective October 1, 2009).*]

NOTE
   [1] As amended by the Act of Sederunt (Sheriff Court Rules) (Miscellaneous Amendments) 2009 (SSI 2009/294) r.10 (effective October 1, 2009).

Form of record where counterclaim lodged
   [1] **19.2A.** Where, under rule 9.10 (open record), 9.11 (record for Options Hearing), 10.4 (open record), or 10.5 (closed record), a record requires to be lodged in an action in which a counterclaim is included in the defences, the pleadings of the parties shall be set out in the record in the following order:—
   (a) the crave of the initial writ;
   (b) the condescendence and answers relating to the initial writ;
   (c) the pleas-in-law of the parties relating to the crave of the initial writ;
   (d) the crave of the counterclaim;
   (e) the statement of facts and answers relating to the counterclaim; and
   (f) the pleas-in-law of the parties relating to the counterclaim.

NOTE
   [1] Inserted by SI 1996/2445 (effective November 1, 1996).

Effect of abandonment of cause

19.3.—(1) The right of a pursuer to abandon a cause under rule 23.1 shall not be affected by a counterclaim; and any expenses for which the pursuer is found liable as a condition of, or in consequence of, such abandonment shall not include the expenses of the counterclaim.

(2) Notwithstanding abandonment by the pursuer, a defender may insist in his counterclaim; and the proceedings in the counterclaim shall continue in dependence as if the counterclaim were a separate action.

Disposal of counterclaims

19.4. The sheriff may—
- (a) deal with a counterclaim as if it had been stated in a separate action;
- (b) regulate the procedure in relation to the counterclaim as he thinks fit; and
- (c) grant decree for the counterclaim in whole or in part or for the difference between it and the sum sued for by the pursuer.

CHAPTER 20

THIRD PARTY PROCEDURE

Applications for third party notice

20.1.—(1) Where, in an action, a defender claims that—
- (a) he has in respect of the subject-matter of the action a right of contribution, relief or indemnity against any person who is not a party to the action, or
- (b) a person whom the pursuer is not bound to call as a defender should be made a party to the action along with the defender in respect that such person is—
  - (i) solely liable, or jointly or jointly and severally liable with the defender, to the pursuer in respect of the subject-matter of the action, or
  - (ii) liable to the defender in respect of a claim arising from or in connection with the liability, if any, of the defender to the pursuer,

he may apply by motion for an order for service of a third party notice upon that other person in Form O10 for the purpose of convening that other person as a third party to the action.

[1] (2) Where—
- (a) a pursuer against whom a counterclaim has been made, or
- (b) a third party convened in the action,

seeks, in relation to the claim against him, to make against a person who is not a party, a claim mentioned in paragraph (1) as a claim which could be made by a defender against a third party, he shall apply by motion for an order for service of a third party notice in Form O10 in the same manner as a defender under that paragraph; and rules 20.2 to 20.6 shall, with the necessary modifications, apply to such a claim as they apply in relation to such a claim by a defender.

NOTE

[1] As amended by SI 1996/2445 (effective November 1, 1996).

Averments where order for service of third party notice sought

20.2.—(1) Where a defender intends to apply by motion for an order for service of a third party notice before the closing of the record, he shall, before lodging the motion, set out in his defences, by adjustment to those defences, or in a separate statement of facts annexed to those defences—
- (a) averments setting out the grounds on which he maintains that the proposed third party is liable to him by contribution, relief or indemnity or should be made a party to the action; and
- (b) appropriate pleas-in-law.

(2) Where a defender applies by motion for an order for service of a third party notice after the closing of the record, he shall, on lodging the motion, lodge a minute of amendment containing—
- (a) averments setting out the grounds on which he maintains that the proposed third party is liable to him by contribution, relief or indemnity or should be made a party to the action, and
- (b) appropriate pleas-in-law,

unless those grounds and pleas-in-law have been set out in the defences in the closed record.

(3) A motion for an order for service of a third party notice shall be lodged before the commencement of the hearing of the merits of the cause.

Warrants for diligence on third party notice

20.3.—(1) A defender who applies for an order for service of a third party notice may apply for—

    (a) a warrant for arrestment to found jurisdiction;

    (b) a warrant for interim diligence,

which would have been permitted had the warrant been sought in an initial writ in a separate action.

(2) Averments in support of the application for a warrant under paragraph (1)(a) shall be included in the defences or the separate statement of facts referred to in rule 20.2(1).

(3) An application for a warrant under paragraph (1)(a) shall be made by motion—

    (a) at the time of applying for the third party notice; or

    (b) if not applied for at that time, at any stage of the cause thereafter.

(4) A certified copy of the interlocutor granting warrant for diligence applied for under paragraph (2) shall be sufficient authority for execution of the diligence.

NOTE

[1] As amended by the Act of Sederunt (Sheriff Court Rules) (Miscellaneous Amendments) 2009 (SSI 2009/294) r.10 (effective October 1, 2009).

Service on third party

20.4.—(1) A third party notice shall be served on the third party within 14 days after the date of the interlocutor allowing service of that notice.

(2) Where service of a third party notice has not been made within the period specified in paragraph (1), the order for service of it shall cease to have effect; and no service of the notice may be made unless a further order for service of it has been applied for and granted.

[1] (3) There shall be served with a third party notice—

    (a) a copy of the pleadings (including any adjustments and amendments); and

    (b) where the pleadings have not been amended in accordance with the minute of amendment referred to in rule 20.2, a copy of that minute.

(4) A copy of the third party notice, with a certificate of service attached to it, shall be lodged in process by the defender.

NOTE

[1] As amended by SSI 2003/26, r.2 (effective from January 24, 2003).

Answers to third party notice

20.5.—(1) An order for service of a third party notice shall specify 28 days, or such other period as the sheriff on cause shown may specify, as the period within which the third party may lodge answers.

(2) Answers for a third party shall be headed "Answers for [E.F.], Third Party in the action at the instance of [A.B.], Pursuer against [C.D.], Defender" and shall include—

    (a) answers to the averments of the defender against him in the form of numbered paragraphs corresponding to the numbered articles of the condescendence annexed to the summons and incorporating, if the third party so wishes, answers to the averments of the pursuer; or

    (b) where a separate statement of facts has been lodged by the defender under rule 20.2(1), answers to the statement of facts in the form of numbered paragraphs corresponding to the numbered paragraphs of the statement of facts; and

    (c) appropriate pleas-in-law.

Consequences of failure to amend pleadings

[1] **20.5A.** Where the pleadings have not been amended in accordance with the minute of amendment referred to in rule 20.2, no motion for a finding, order or decree against a third party may be enrolled by the defender unless, at or before the date on which he enrols the motion, he enrols a motion to amend the pleadings in accordance with that minute.

NOTE

[1] As inserted by SSI 2003/26 r.2 (effective January 24, 2003).

Procedure following answers

20.6.—(1) Where a third party lodges answers, the sheriff clerk shall fix a date and time under rule 9.2 for a hearing under rule 9.12 (Options Hearing) as if the third party had lodged a notice of intention to defend and the period of notice had expired on the date for lodging answers.

(2) At the Options Hearing, or at any time thereafter, the sheriff may grant such decree or other order as he thinks fit.

(3) A decree or other order against the third party shall have effect and be extractable in the same way as a decree or other order against a defender.

CHAPTER 21

DOCUMENTS FOUNDED ON OR ADOPTED IN PLEADINGS

Lodging documents founded on or adopted

21.1.—(1) Subject to any other provision in these Rules, any document founded on by a party, or adopted as incorporated, in his pleadings shall, so far as in his possession or within his control, be lodged in process as a production by him—

[1] (a) when founded on or adopted in an initial writ, at the time of returning the initial writ under rule 9.3 or, in the case of a personal injuries action raised under Part AI of Chapter 36, when the initial writ is presented for warranting in accordance with rule 5.1;

(b) when founded on or adopted in a minute, defences, counterclaim or answers, at the time of lodging that part of process; and

(c) when founded on or adopted in an adjustment to any pleadings, at the time when such adjustment is intimated to any other party.

(2) Paragraph (1) shall be without prejudice to any power of the sheriff to order the production of any document or grant a commission and diligence for recovery of it.

NOTE
[1] As amended by the Act of Sederunt (Ordinary Cause Rules Amendment) (Personal Injuries Actions) 2009 (SSI 2009/285) r.2 (effective November 2, 2009).

Consequences of failure to lodge documents founded on or adopted

21.2. Where a party fails to lodge a document in accordance with rule 21.1(1), he may be found liable in the expenses of any order for production or recovery of it obtained by any other party.

Objection to documents founded on

21.3.—(1) Where a deed or writing is founded on by a party, any objection to it by any other party may be stated and maintained by exception without its being reduced.

(2) Where an objection is stated under paragraph (1) and an action of reduction would otherwise have been competent, the sheriff may order the party stating the objection to find caution or give such other security as he thinks fit.

CHAPTER 22

PRELIMINARY PLEAS

Note of basis of preliminary plea

22.1.—(1) A party intending to insist on a preliminary plea shall, not later than 3 days before the Options Hearing under rule 9.12 or the Procedural Hearing under rule 10.6—

(a) lodge in process a note of the basis for the plea; and

(b) intimate a copy of it to every other party.

[1] (2) Where the Options Hearing is continued under rule 9.12(5) and a preliminary plea is added by adjustment, a party intending to insist on that plea shall, not later than 3 days before the date of the Options Hearing so continued—

(a) lodge in process a note of the basis for the plea; and

(b) intimate a copy of it to every other party.

(3) If a party fails to comply with paragraph (1) or (2), he shall be deemed to be no longer insisting on the preliminary plea; and the plea shall be repelled by the sheriff at the Options Hearing or Procedural Hearing.

[2] (4) At any proof before answer or debate, parties may on cause shown raise matters in addition to those set out in the note mentioned in paragraph (1) or (2).

[1] (5) Where a note of the basis of a preliminary plea has been lodged under paragraph (1), and the Options Hearing is continued under rule 9.12(5), unless the basis of the plea has changed following further adjustment, it shall not be necessary for a party who is insisting on the plea to lodge a further note before the Options Hearing so continued.

NOTES

[1] As inserted by the Act of Sederunt (Sheriff Court Ordinary Cause Rules Amendment) (Miscellaneous) 1996 (SI 1996/2445) (effective November 1, 1996).

[2] As amended by the Act of Sederunt (Sheriff Court Ordinary Cause Rules Amendment) (Miscellaneous) 2000 (SSI 2000/239) (effective October 2, 2000).

CHAPTER 23

ABANDONMENT

Abandonment of causes

23.1.—(1) A pursuer may abandon a cause at any time before decree of absolvitor or dismissal by lodging a minute of abandonment and—

    (a) consenting to decree of absolvitor; or

    (b) seeking decree of dismissal.

[1] (2) The sheriff shall not grant decree of dismissal under paragraph (1)(b) unless full judicial expenses have been paid to the defender, and any third party against whom the pursuer has directed any crave, within 28 days after the date of taxation.

(3) If the pursuer fails to pay the expenses referred to in paragraph (2) to the party to whom they are due within the period specified in that paragraph, that party shall be entitled to decree of absolvitor with expenses.

NOTE

[1] As amended by SSI 2003/26, reg. 2 (effective from January 24, 2003).

Application of abandonment to counterclaims

23.2. Rule 23.1 shall, with the necessary modifications, apply to the abandonment by a defender of his counterclaim as it applies to the abandonment of a cause.

CHAPTER 24

WITHDRAWAL OF SOLICITORS

Intimation of withdrawal to court

24.1.—[1] (1) Subject to paragraph (3), where a solicitor withdraws from acting on behalf of a party, he shall intimate his withdrawal by letter to the sheriff clerk and to every other party.

[1] (2) The sheriff clerk shall forthwith lodge such letter in process.

[2] (3) Where a solicitor withdraws from acting on behalf of a party in open court and in the presence of the other parties to the action or their representatives, paragraph (1) shall not apply.

NOTES

[1] As amended by the Act of Sederunt (Sheriff Court Ordinary Cause Rules Amendment) (Miscellaneous) 2000 (SSI 2000/239) (effective October 2, 2000).

[2] Inserted by the Act of Sederunt (Sheriff Court Ordinary Cause Rules Amendment) (Miscellaneous) 2000 (SSI 2000/239) (effective October 2, 2000).

Intimation to party whose solicitor has withdrawn

24.2.—[1] (1) Subject to paragraph (1A), the sheriff shall, of his own motion, or on the motion of any other party, pronounce an interlocutor ordaining the party whose solicitor has withdrawn from acting to appear or be represented at a specified diet fixed by the sheriff to state whether or not he intends to proceed, under certification that if he fails to do so the sheriff may grant decree or make such other order or finding as he thinks fit.

[2] (1A) Where any previously fixed diet is to occur within 14 days from the date when the sheriff first considers the solicitor's withdrawal, the sheriff may either—

    (a) pronounce an interlocutor in accordance with paragraph (1);

    or

    (b) consider the matter at the previously fixed diet.

(2) The diet fixed in the interlocutor under paragraph (1) shall not be less than 14 days after the date of the interlocutor unless the sheriff otherwise orders.

(3) The party who has lodged the motion under paragraph (1), or any other party appointed by the sheriff, shall forthwith serve on the party whose solicitor has withdrawn a copy of the interlocutor and a notice in Form G10; and a certificate of service shall be lodged in process.

NOTES

[1] As amended by the Act of Sederunt (Sheriff Court Ordinary Cause Rules Amendment) (Miscellaneous) 2000 (SSI 2000/239) (effective October 2, 2000).

[2] Inserted by the Act of Sederunt (Sheriff Court Ordinary Cause Rules Amendment) (Miscellaneous) 2000 (SSI 2000/239) (effective October 2, 2000).

Consequences of failure to intimate intention to proceed

24.3. Where a party on whom a notice and interlocutor has been served under rule 24.2(2) fails to appear or be represented at a diet fixed under rule 24.2(1) and to state his intention as required by that paragraph, the sheriff may grant decree or make such other order or finding as he thinks fit.

CHAPTER 25

MINUTES OF SIST AND TRANSFERENCE

Minutes of sist

25.1. Where a party dies or comes under legal incapacity while a cause is depending, any person claiming to represent that party or his estate may apply by minute to be sisted as a party to the cause.

Minutes of transference

[1] **25.2.** Where a party dies or comes under legal incapacity while a cause is depending and the provisions of rule 25.1 are not invoked, any other party may apply by minute to have the cause transferred in favour of or against, as the case may be, any person who represents that party or his estate.

NOTE

[1]As amended by the Act of Sederunt (Sheriff Court Ordinary Cause Rules Amendment) (Miscellaneous) 1996 (SI 1996/2445) (effective November 1, 1996).

CHAPTER 26

TRANSFER AND REMIT OF CAUSES

Transfer to another sheriff court

26.1.—(1) The sheriff may, on cause shown, remit any cause to another sheriff court.

(2) Subject to paragraph (4), where a cause in which there are two or more defenders has been brought in the sheriff court of the residence or place of business of one of them, the sheriff may transfer the cause to any other sheriff court which has jurisdiction over any of the defenders.

(3) Subject to paragraph (4), where a plea of no jurisdiction is sustained, the sheriff may transfer the cause to the sheriff court before which it appears to him the cause ought to have been brought.

(4) The sheriff shall not transfer a cause to another sheriff court under paragraph (2) or (3) except—

    (a) on the motion of a party; and

    (b) where he considers it expedient to do so having regard to the convenience of the parties and their witnesses.

(5) On making an order under paragraph (1), (2) or (3), the sheriff—

    (a) shall state his reasons for doing so in the interlocutor; and

    (b) may make the order on such conditions as to expenses or otherwise as he thinks fit.

(6) The court to which a cause is transferred under paragraph (1), (2) or (3) shall accept the cause.

(7) A transferred cause shall proceed in all respects as if it had been originally brought in the court to which it is transferred.

(8) An interlocutor transferring a cause may, with leave of the sheriff, be appealed to the sheriff principal but shall not be subject to appeal to the Court of Session.

Remit to Court of Session

26.2.—(1) The sheriff clerk shall, within four days after the sheriff has pronounced an interlocutor remitting a cause to the Court of Session, transmit the process to the Deputy Principal Clerk of Session.

(2) The sheriff clerk shall, within the period specified in paragraph (1), send written notice of the remit to each party and certify on the interlocutor sheet that he has done so.

(3) Failure by a Sheriff Clerk to comply with paragraph (2) shall not affect the validity of a remit made under paragraph (1).

Remit from Court of Session
26.3. On receipt of the process in an action which has been remitted from the Court of Session under section 14 of the Law Reform (Miscellaneous Provisions) (Scotland) Act 1985, the sheriff clerk shall—
   (a) record the date of receipt on the interlocutor sheet;
   (b) fix a hearing to determine further procedure on the first court day occurring not earlier than 14 days after the date of receipt of the process; and
   (c) forthwith send written notice of the date of the hearing fixed under sub-paragraph (b) to each party.

CHAPTER 27

CAUTION AND SECURITY

Application of this Chapter
27.1. This Chapter applies to—
   (a) any cause in which the sheriff has power to order a person to find caution or give other security; and
   (b) security for expenses ordered to be given by the election court or the sheriff under section 136(2)(i) of the Representation of the People Act 1983 in an election petition.

Form of applications
27.2.—(1) An application for an order for caution or other security or for variation or recall of such an order, shall be made by motion.
   (2) The grounds on which such an application is made shall be set out in the motion.

Orders
27.3. Subject to section 726(2) of the Companies Act 1985 (expenses by certain limited companies), an order to find caution or give other security shall specify the period within which such caution is to be found or such security given.

Methods of finding caution or giving security
27.4.—(1) A person ordered—
   (a) to find caution, shall do so by obtaining a bond of caution; or
   (b) to consign a sum of money into court, shall do so by consignation under the Sheriff Court Consignations (Scotland) Act 1893 in the name of the sheriff clerk.
   (2) The sheriff may approve a method of security other than one mentioned in paragraph (1), including a combination of two or more methods of security.
   (3) Subject to paragraph (4), any document by which an order to find caution or give other security is satisfied shall be lodged in process.
   (4) Where the sheriff approves a security in the form of a deposit of a sum of money in the joint names of the agents of parties, a copy of the deposit receipt, and not the principal, shall be lodged in process.
   (5) Any document lodged in process, by which an order to find caution or give other security is satisfied, shall not be borrowed from process.

Cautioners and guarantors
[1] **27.5.** A bond of caution or other security shall be given only by a person who is an "authorised person" within the meaning of section 31 of the Financial Services and Markets Act 2000.

NOTE
[1] As amended by the Act of Sederunt (Ordinary Cause Rules) Amendment (Caution and Security) 2005 (SSI 2005/20) r.2(2) (effective February 1, 2005).

Form of bonds of caution and other securities
27.6.—(1) A bond of caution shall oblige the cautioner, his heirs and executors to make payment of the sums for which he has become cautioner to the party to whom he is bound, as validly and in the same manner as the party, his heirs and successors, for whom he is cautioner, are obliged.
[1] (2) A bond of caution or other security document given by a person shall state whether that

person is an "authorised person" within the meaning of section 31 of the Financial Services and Markets Act 2000.

NOTE
[1] As amended by the Act of Sederunt (Ordinary Cause Rules) Amendment (Caution and Security) 2005 (SSI 2005/20) r.2(3) (effective February 1, 2005).

Sufficiency of caution or security and objections
27.7.—(1) The sheriff clerk shall satisfy himself that any bond of caution, or other document lodged in process under rule 27.4(3), is in proper form.

(2) A party who is dissatisfied with the sufficiency or form of the caution or other security offered in obedience to an order of the court may apply by motion for an order under rule 27.9 (failure to find caution or give security).

Insolvency or death of cautioner or guarantor
27.8. Where caution has been found by bond of caution or security has been given by guarantee and the cautioner or guarantor, as the case may be—
  (a) becomes apparently insolvent within the meaning assigned by section 7 of the Bankruptcy (Scotland) Act 1985 (constitution of apparent insolvency),
  (b) calls a meeting of his creditors to consider the state of his affairs,
  (c) dies unrepresented, or
  (d) is a company and—
       [1] (i) an administration, bank administration or building society special administration order or a winding up, bank insolvency or building society insolvency order has been made, or a resolution for a voluntary winding up has been passed, with respect to it,
       (ii) a receiver of all or any part of its undertaking has been appointed, or
       (iii) a voluntary arrangement (within the meaning assigned by section 1(1) of the Insolvency Act 1986) has been approved under Part I of that Act,
the party entitled to benefit from the caution or guarantee may apply by motion for a new security or further security to be given.

NOTE
[1] As substituted by the Act of Sederunt (Sheriff Court Rules) (Miscellaneous Amendments) 2009 (SSI 2009/294) r.16 (effective October 1, 2009).

Failure to find caution or give security
27.9. Where a party fails to find caution or give other security (in this rule referred to as "the party in default") any other party may apply by motion—
  (a) where he party in default is a pursuer, for decree of absolvitor; or
  (b) where the party in default is a defender or a third party, for decree by default or for such other finding or order as the sheriff thinks fit.

CHAPTER 28

RECOVERY OF EVIDENCE

Application and interpretation of this Chapter
28.1.—(1) This Chapter applies to the recovery of any evidence in a cause depending before the sheriff.

(2) In this Chapter, "the Act of 1972" means the Administration of Justice (Scotland) Act 1972.

Applications for commission and diligence for recovery of documents or for orders under section 1 of the Act of 1972
28.2.—(1) An application by a party for—
  (a) a commission and diligence for the recovery of a document, or
  (b) an order under section 1 of the Act of 1972,
shall be made by motion.

(2) At the time of lodging a motion under paragraph (1), a specification of—
  (a) the document or other property sought to be inspected, photographed, preserved, taken into custody, detained, produced, recovered, sampled or experimented with or upon, as the case may be, or

(b) the matter in respect of which information is sought as to the identity of a person who might be a witness or a defender,

shall be lodged in process.

[1] (3) A copy of the specification lodged under paragraph (2) and the motion made under paragraph (1) shall be intimated by the applicant to—

(a) every other party;

(b) in respect of an application under section 1(1) of the Act of 1972, any third party haver; and

[2] (c) where necessary—

(i) the Advocate General for Scotland (in a case where the document or other property sought is in the possession of either a public authority exercising functions in relation to reserved matters within the meaning of Schedule 5 to the Scotland Act 1998, or a cross-border public authority within the meaning of section 88(5) of that Act); or

(ii) the Lord Advocate (in any other case),

and, if there is any doubt, both.

(4) Where the sheriff grants a motion under paragraph (1) in whole or in part, he may order the applicant to find such caution or give such other security as he thinks fit.

[2] (5) The Advocate General for Scotland or the Lord Advocate or both, as appropriate, may appear at the hearing of any motion under paragraph (1).

NOTES

[1] As substituted by SI 1996/2445 (effective November 1, 1996).

[2] As substituted by the Act of Sederunt (Ordinary Cause, Summary Application, Summary Cause and Small Claim Rules) Amendment (Miscellaneous) 2007 (SSI 2007/6) r.2(10) (effective January 29, 2007).

Optional procedure before executing commission and diligence

28.3.—(1) The party who has obtained a commission and diligence for the recovery of a document under rule 28.2(1)(a) may, at any time before executing it against a haver, serve on the haver an order in Form G11 (in this rule referred to as "the order"); and if so, the provisions of this rule shall apply.

[1] (2) The order and a copy of the specification referred to in rule 28.2(2) as approved by the court shall be served on the haver or his known solicitor and shall be complied with by the haver in the manner and within the period specified in the order.

[1] (3) Not later than the day after the date on which the order, the certificate appended to Form G11 and any document is received by the sheriff clerk from a haver, he shall intimate that to each party.

(4) No party, other than the party who served the order, may uplift such a document until after the expiry of 7 days after the date of intimation under paragraph (3).

(5) Where the party who served the order fails to uplift such a document within 7 days after the date of intimation under paragraph (3), the sheriff clerk shall intimate that failure to every other party.

(6) Where no party has uplifted such a document within 14 days after the date of intimation under paragraph (5), the sheriff clerk shall return it to the haver who delivered it to him.

(7) Where a party who has uplifted such a document does not wish to lodge it, he shall return it to the sheriff clerk who shall—

(a) intimate the return of the document to every other party; and

(b) if no other party uplifts the document within 14 days of the date of intimation, return it to the haver.

(8) If the party who served the order is not satisfied—

(a) that full compliance has been made with the order, or

(b) that adequate reasons for non-compliance have been given,

he may execute the commission and diligence under rule 28.4.

(9) Where an extract from a book of any description (whether the extract is certified or not) is produced under the order, the sheriff may, on the motion of the party who served the order, order that that party shall be allowed to inspect the book and take copies of any entries falling within the specification.

(10) Where any question of confidentiality arises in relation to a book ordered to be inspected under paragraph (9), the inspection shall be made, and any copies shall be taken, at the sight of the commissioner appointed in the interlocutor granting the commission and diligence.

[1] (11) The sheriff may, on cause shown, order the production of any book (not being a banker's book or book of public record) containing entries falling under a specification, notwithstanding the production of a certified extract from that book.

NOTE
[1]As amended by SI 1996/2445 (effective November 1, 1996).

Execution of commission and diligence for recovery of documents
  28.4.—(1) The party who seeks to execute a commission and diligence for recovery of a document obtained under rule 28.2(1)(a) shall—
  (a) provide the commissioner with a copy of the specification, a copy of the pleadings (including any adjustments and amendments) and a certified copy of the interlocutor of his appointment; and
  (b) instruct the clerk and any shorthand writer considered necessary by the commissioner or any party; and
  (c) be responsible for the fees of the commissioner and his clerk, and of any shorthand writer.
  (2) The Commissioner shall, in consultation with the parties, fix a diet for the execution of the commission.
  (3) The interlocutor granting such a commission and diligence shall be sufficient authority for citing a haver to appear before the commissioner.
  [1] (4) A citation in Form G13 shall be served on the haver with a copy of the specification and, where necessary for a proper understanding of the specification, a copy of the pleadings (including any adjustments and amendments) and the party citing the haver shall lodge a certificate of citation in Form G12.
  (5) The parties and the haver shall be entitled to be represented by a solicitor or person having a right of audience before the sheriff at the execution of the commission.
  [1] (6) At the commission, the commissioner shall—
  (a) administer the oath *de fideli administratione* to any clerk and any shorthand writer appointed for the commission; and
  (b) administer to the haver the oath in Form G14, or, where the haver elects to affirm, the affirmation in Form G15.
  (7) The report of the execution of the commission and diligence, any document recovered and an inventory of that document, shall be sent by the commissioner to the sheriff clerk.
  (8) Not later than the day after the date on which such a report, document and inventory, if any, are received by the sheriff clerk, he shall intimate to the parties that he has received them.
  (9) No party, other than the party who served the order, may uplift such a document until after the expiry of 7 days after the date of intimation under paragraph (8).
  (10) Where the party who served the order fails to uplift such a document within 7 days after the date of intimation under paragraph (8), the sheriff clerk shall intimate that failure to every other party.
  (11) Where no party has uplifted such a document within 14 days after the date of intimation under paragraph (10), the sheriff clerk shall return it to the haver.
  (12) Where a party who has uplifted such a document does not wish to lodge it, he shall return it to the sheriff clerk who shall—
  (a) intimate the return of the document to every other party; and
  (b) if no other party uplifts the document within 14 days of the date of intimation, return it to the haver.

NOTE
[1]As amended by SI 1996/2445 (effective November 1, 1996).

Execution of orders for production or recovery of documents or other property under section 1(1) of the Act of 1972
  28.5.—(1) An order under section 1(1) of the Act of 1972 for the production or recovery of a document or other property shall grant a commission and diligence for the production or recovery of that document or other property.
  (2) Rules 28.3 (optional procedure before executing commission and diligence) and 28.4 (execution of commission and diligence for recovery of documents) shall apply to an order to which paragraph (1) applies as they apply to a commission and diligence for the recovery of a document.

Execution of orders for inspection etc. of documents or other property under section 1(1) of the Act of 1972
  28.6.—(1) An order under section 1(1) of the Act of 1972 for the inspection or photographing of a document or other property, the taking of samples or the carrying out of any experiment thereon or therewith, shall authorise and appoint a specified person to photograph, inspect, take samples of, or carry out any experiment on or with, any such document or other property, as the case may be, subject to such conditions, if any, as the sheriff thinks fit.

(2) A certified copy of the interlocutor granting such an order shall be sufficient authority for the person specified to execute the order.

(3) When such an order is executed, the party who obtained the order shall serve on the haver a copy of the interlocutor granting it, a copy of the specification and, where necessary for a proper understanding of the specification, a copy of the pleadings (including any adjustments and amendments).

Execution of orders for preservation etc. of documents or other property under section 1(1) of the Act of 1972
[1] **28.7.**—(1) An order under section 1(1) of the Act of 1972 for the preservation, custody and detention of a document or other property shall grant a commission and diligence for the detention and custody of that document or other property.

(2) The party who has obtained an order under paragraph (1) shall—
- (a) provide the commissioner with a copy of the specification, a copy of the pleadings (including any adjustments and amendments) and a certified copy of the interlocutor of his appointment;
- (b) be responsible for the fees of the commissioner and his clerk; and
- (c) serve a copy of the order on the haver.

(3) The report of the execution of the commission and diligence, any document or other property taken by the commissioner and an inventory of such property, shall be sent by the commissioner to the sheriff clerk for the further order of the sheriff.

NOTE
[1] As amended by SI 1996/2445 (effective November 1, 1996).

Confidentiality
[1] **28.8.**—(1) Where confidentiality is claimed for any evidence sought to be recovered under any of the following rules, such evidence shall, where practicable, be enclosed in a sealed packet:—
28.3 (optional procedure before executing commission and diligence),
28.4 (execution of commission and diligence for recovery of documents),
28.5 (execution of orders for production or recovery of documents or other property under section 1(1) of the Act of 1972),
28.7 (execution of orders for preservation etc. of documents or other property under section 1(1) of the Act of 1972).

(2) A motion to have such a sealed packet opened up or such recovery allowed may be lodged by—
- (a) the party who obtained the commission and diligence; or
- (b) any other party after the date of intimation by the sheriff clerk under rule 28.3(5) or 28.4(10) (intimation of failure to uplift documents).

(3) In addition to complying with rule 15.2 (intimation of motions), the party lodging such a motion shall intimate the terms of the motion to the haver by post by the first class recorded delivery service.

(4) The person claiming confidentiality may oppose a motion made under paragraph (2).

NOTE
[1] As amended by SI 1996/2445 (effective November 1, 1996).

Warrants for production of original documents from public records
28.9.—(1) Where a party seeks to obtain from the keeper of any public record production of the original of any register or deed in his custody for the purposes of a cause, he shall apply to the sheriff by motion.

(2) Intimation of a motion under paragraph (1) shall be given to the keeper of the public record concerned at least 7 days before the motion is lodged.

(3) In relation to a public record kept by the Keeper of the Registers of Scotland or the Keeper of the Records of Scotland, where it appears to the sheriff that it is necessary for the ends of justice that a motion under this rule should be granted, he shall pronounce an interlocutor containing a certificate to that effect; and the party applying for production may apply by letter (enclosing a copy of the interlocutor duly certified by the sheriff clerk), addressed to the Deputy Principal Clerk of Session, for an order from the Court of Session authorising the Keeper of the Registers or the Keeper of the Records, as the case may be, to exhibit the original of any register or deed to the sheriff.

(4) The Deputy Principal Clerk of Session shall submit the application sent to him under paragraph (3) to the Lord Ordinary in chambers who, if satisfied, shall grant a warrant for production or exhibition of the original register or deed sought.

(5) A certified copy of the warrant granted under paragraph (4) shall be served on the keeper of the public record concerned.

(6) The expense of the production or exhibition of such an original register or deed shall be met, in the first instance, by the party who applied by motion under paragraph (1).

Commissions for examination of witnesses

28.10.—[1] (1) This rule applies to a commission—
- (a) to take the evidence of a witness who—
  - (i) is resident beyond the jurisdiction of the court;
  - (ii) although resident within the jurisdiction of the court, resides at some place remote from that court; or
  - (iii) by reason of age, infirmity or sickness, is unable to attend the diet of proof;
- (b) in respect of the evidence of a witness which is in danger of being lost, to take the evidence to lie *in retentis*; or
- (c) on special cause shown, to take evidence of a witness on a ground other than one mentioned in sub-paragraph (a) or (b).

(2) An application by a party for a commission to examine a witness shall be made by motion; and that party shall specify in the motion the name and address of at least one proposed commissioner for approval and appointment by the sheriff.

[2] (2A) A motion under paragraph (2) may include an application for authority to record the proceedings before the commissioner by video recorder.

(3) The interlocutor granting such a commission shall be sufficient authority for citing the witness to appear before the commissioner.

[1] (4) At the commission, the commissioner shall—
- (a) administer the oath *de fideli administratione* to any clerk and any shorthand writer appointed for the commission; and
- (b) administer to the witness the oath in Form G14, or where the witness elects to affirm, the affirmation in Form G15.

(5) Where a commission is granted for the examination of a witness, the commission shall proceed without interrogatories unless, on cause shown, the sheriff otherwise directs.

NOTES

[1] As amended by SI 1996/2445 (effective November 1, 1996).

[2] As inserted by the Act of Sederunt (Sheriff Court Rules) (Miscellaneous Amendments) 2008 (SSI 2008/223) para.11 (effective July 1, 2008).

Commissions on interrogatories

28.11.—(1) Where interrogatories have not been dispensed with, the party who obtained the commission to examine a witness under rule 28.10 shall lodge draft interrogatories in process.

(2) Any other party may lodge cross-interrogatories.

(3) The interrogatories and any cross-interrogatories, when adjusted, shall be extended and returned to the sheriff clerk for approval and the settlement of any dispute as to their contents by the sheriff.

(4) The party who has obtained the commission shall—
- (a) provide the commissioner with a copy of the pleadings (including any adjustments and amendments), the approved interrogatories and any cross-interrogatories and a certified copy of the interlocutor of his appointment;
- (b) instruct the clerk; and
- (c) be responsible, in the first instance, for the fee of the commissioner and his clerk.

(5) The commissioner shall, in consultation with the parties, fix a diet for the execution of the commission to examine the witness.

(6) The executed interrogatories, any document produced by the witness and an inventory of that document, shall be sent by the commissioner to the sheriff clerk.

(7) Not later than the day after the date on which the executed interrogatories, any document and an inventory of that document, are received by the sheriff clerk, he shall intimate to each party that he has received them.

(8) The party who obtained the commission to examine the witness shall lodge in process—
- (a) the report of the commission; and
- (b) the executed interrogatories and any cross-interrogatories.

Commissions without interrogatories

28.12.—(1) Where interrogatories have been dispensed with, the party who has obtained a commission to examine a witness under rule 28.10 shall—
- (a) provide the commissioner with a copy of the pleadings (including any adjustments and amendments) and a certified copy of the interlocutor of his appointment;

(b) fix a diet for the execution of the commission in consultation with the commissioner and every other party;

(c) instruct the clerk and any shorthand writer; and

[1] (d) be responsible in the first instance for the fees of the commissioner, his clerk and any shorthand writer.

(2) All parties shall be entitled to be present and represented at the execution of the commission.

(3) The report of the execution of the commission, any document produced by the witness and an inventory of that document, shall be sent by the commissioner to the sheriff clerk.

(4) Not later than the day after the date on which such a report, any document and an inventory of that document are received by the sheriff clerk, he shall intimate to each party that he has received them.

(5) The party who obtained the commission to examine the witness shall lodge the report in process.

NOTE

[1]As amended by the Act of Sederunt (Ordinary Cause, Summary Application, Summary Cause and Small Claim Rules) Amendment (Vulnerable Witnesses (Scotland) Act 2004) 2007, r.2(7) (effective November 1, 2007).

Evidence taken on commission

28.13.—(1) Subject to the following paragraphs of this rule and to all questions of relevancy and admissibility, evidence taken on commission under rule 28.11 or 28.12 may be used as evidence at any proof of the cause.

(2) Any party may object to the use of such evidence at a proof; and the objection shall be determined by the sheriff.

(3) Such evidence shall not be used at a proof if the witness becomes available to attend the diet of proof.

(4) A party may use such evidence in accordance with the preceding paragraphs of this rule notwithstanding that it was obtained at the instance of another party.

Letters of request

[2] **28.14.**—(1) Subject to paragraph (7), this rule applies to an application for a letter of request to a court or tribunal outside Scotland to obtain evidence of the kind specified in paragraph (2), being evidence obtainable within the jurisdiction of that court or tribunal, for the purposes of a cause depending before the sheriff.

[1] (2) An application to which paragraph (1) applies may be made in relation to a request—

(a) for the examination of a witness,

(b) for the inspection, photographing, preservation, custody, detention, production or recovery of, or the taking of samples of, or the carrying out of any experiment on or with, a document or other property, as the case may be,

(c) for the medical examination of any person,

(d) for the taking and testing of samples of blood from any person, or

(e) for any other order for obtaining evidence,

for which an order could be obtained from the sheriff.

(3) Such an application shall be made by minute in Form G16 together with a proposed letter of request in Form G17.

[1] (4) It shall be a condition of granting a letter of request that any solicitor for the applicant, or a party litigant, as the case may be, shall be personally liable, in the first instance, for the whole expenses which may become due and payable in respect of the letter of request to the court or tribunal obtaining the evidence and to any witness who may be examined for the purpose; and he shall consign into court such sum in respect of such expenses as the sheriff thinks fit.

(5) Unless the court or tribunal to which a letter of request is addressed is a court or tribunal in a country or territory—

(a) where English is an official language, or

(b) in relation to which the sheriff clerk certifies that no translation is required,

then the applicant shall, before the issue of the letter of request, lodge in process a translation of that letter and any interrogatories and cross-interrogatories into the official language of that court or tribunal.

(6) The letter of request when issued; any interrogatories and cross-interrogatories adjusted as required by rule 28.11 and the translations (if any), shall be forwarded by the sheriff clerk to the Foreign and Commonwealth Office or to such person and in such manner as the sheriff may direct.

(7) This rule does not apply to any request for the taking of evidence under Council

Regulation (EC) No. 1206/2001 of 28th May 2001 on cooperation between the courts of the Member States in the taking of evidence in civil or commercial matters.

NOTE
[1] As amended by SI 1996/2445 (effective November 1, 1996).
[2] As amended by the Act of Sederunt (Taking of Evidence in the European Community) 2003 (SSI 2003/601).

Taking of evidence in the European Community
[1] **28.14A.**—(1) This rule applies to any request—
   (a) for the competent court of another Member State to take evidence under Article 1.1(a) of the Council Regulation; or
   (b) that the court shall take evidence directly in another Member State under Article 1.1(b) of the Council Regulation.
(2) An application for a request under paragraph (1) shall be made by minute in Form G16, together with the proposed request in form A or I (as the case may be) in the Annex to the Council Regulation.
(3) In this rule, "the Council Regulation" means Council Regulation (EC) No. 1206/2001 of 28th May 2001 on cooperation between the courts of the Member States in the taking of evidence in civil or commercial matters.

NOTE
[1] As amended by the Act of Sederunt (Taking of Evidence in the European Community) 2003 (SSI 2003/601).

Citation of witnesses and havers
28.15. The following rules shall apply to the citation of a witness or haver to a commission under this Chapter as they apply to the citation of a witness for a proof:—
rule 29.7 (citation of witnesses) except paragraph 4,
rule 29.9 (second diligence against a witness,
rule 29.10 (failure of witness to attend).

[1] CHAPTER 28A

PRE-PROOF HEARING

NOTE
[1] Inserted by the Act of Sederunt (Ordinary Cause and Summary Application Rules) Amendment (Miscellaneous) 2006 (SSI 2006/410) (effective August 18, 2006).

Pre-proof hearing
28A.1.—(1) On the appointment of a cause to a proof or proof before answer or thereafter on the motion of any party or of his own motion, the sheriff may appoint the cause to a pre-proof hearing.
(2) It shall be the duty of the parties to provide the sheriff with sufficient information to enable him to conduct the hearing as provided for in this rule.
(3) At a pre-proof hearing the sheriff shall ascertain, so far as is reasonably practicable, whether the cause is likely to proceed to proof on the date fixed for that purpose and, in particular—
   (a) the state of preparation of the parties; and
[1] (b) the extent to which the parties have complied with their duties under rules 9A.2, 9A.3, 29.11 and 29.15 and any orders made by the sheriff under rules 9.12(3)(a), (b), (d), or (e) or 10.6(3)(a) or (b); and
[2] (c) consider any child witness notice or vulnerable witness application that has been lodged where no order has been made, or ascertain whether there is or is likely to be a vulnerable witness within the meaning of section 11(1) of the 2004 Act who is to give evidence at any proof or hearing and whether any order under section 12(1) of the Act of 2004 requires to be made.
(4) At a pre-proof hearing the sheriff may—
   (a) discharge the proof or proof before answer and fix a new date for such proof or proof before answer;
   (b) adjourn the pre-proof hearing; or
   (c) make such other order as he thinks fit to secure the expeditious progress of the cause.
(5) For the purposes of rules 16.2 (decrees where party in default), 33.37 (decree by default in

family action) and 33A.37 (decree by default in civil partnership action), a pre-proof hearing shall be a diet in accordance with those rules.

NOTES
¹ As amended by the Act of Sederunt (Ordinary Cause, Summary Application, Summary Cause and Small Claim Rules) Amendment (Vulnerable Witnesses (Scotland) Act 2004) 2007, r.2(6)(a) (effective November 1, 2007).
² As inserted by the Act of Sederunt (Ordinary Cause, Summary Application, Summary Cause and Small Claim Rules) Amendment (Vulnerable Witnesses (Scotland) Act 2004) 2007, r.2(6)(b) (effective November 1, 2007).

CHAPTER 29

PROOF

Reference to oath
29.1.—(1) Where a party intends to refer any matter to the oath of his opponent he shall lodge a motion to that effect.
(2) If a party fails to appear at the diet for taking his deposition on the reference to his oath, the sheriff may hold him as confessed and grant decree accordingly.

Remit to person of skill
29.2.—(1) The sheriff may, on a motion by any party or on a joint motion, remit to any person of skill, or other person, to report on any matter of fact.
(2) Where a remit under paragraph (1) is made by joint motion or of consent of all parties, the report of such person shall be final and conclusive with respect to the subject-matter of the remit.
(3) Where a remit under paragraph (1) is made—
  (a) on the motion of one of the parties, the expenses of its execution shall, in the first instance, be met by that party; and
  (b) on a joint motion or of consent of all parties, the expenses shall, in the first instance, be met by the parties equally, unless the sheriff otherwise orders.

Written statements
¹ **29.3.** Where a statement in a document is admissible under section 2(1)(b) of the Civil Evidence (Scotland) Act 1988, any party who wishes to have that statement received in evidence shall—
  (a) docquet that document as follows:—
      "(*Place and date*)
      This document contains a statement admissible under section 2(1)(b) of the Civil Evidence (Scotland) Act 1988.
      (*Signed*)
      (*Designation and address*)";
  (b) lodge that document in process; and
  (c) provide all other parties with a copy of that document.

NOTE
¹ Inserted by the Act of Sederunt (Ordinary Cause, Summary Application and Small Claim Rules) Amendment (Miscellaneous) 2004 (SSI 2004/197) (effective May 21, 2004), para.2(11).

Renouncing probation
¹ **29.4.**—(1) Where, at any time, the parties seek to renounce probation, they shall lodge in process a joint minute to that effect with or without a statement of admitted facts and any productions.
(2) On the lodging of a joint minute under paragraph (1), the sheriff may make such order as he thinks fit to secure the expeditious progress of the cause.

NOTE
¹ As amended by the Act of Sederunt (Ordinary Cause and Summary Application Rules) Amendment (Miscellaneous) 2006 (SI 2006/410) (effective August 18, 2006).

Orders for proof
29.5. Where proof is necessary in any cause, the sheriff shall fix a date for taking the proof and may limit the mode of proof.

Hearing parts of proof separately
29.6.—[1] (1) In any cause, the sheriff may—
  (a) of his own motion, or
  (b) on the motion of any party,
order that proof on liability or any specified issue be heard separately from proof on the question of the amount for which decree may be pronounced and determine the order in which the proofs shall be heard.

(2) The sheriff shall pronounce such interlocutor as he thinks fit at the conclusion of the first proof of any cause ordered to be heard in separate parts under paragraph (1).

NOTE
[1] As amended by SI 1996/2445 (effective November 1, 1996).

Citation of witnesses
29.7.—(1) A witness shall be cited for a proof—
  (a) by registered post or the first class recorded delivery service by the solicitor for the party on whose behalf he is cited; or
  (b) by a sheriff officer—
    (i) personally;
    (ii) by a citation being left with a resident at the person's dwelling place or an employee at his place of business;
    (iii) by depositing it in that person's dwelling place or place of business;
    (iv) by affixing it to the door of that person's dwelling place or place of business; or
    (v) by registered post or the first class recorded delivery service.

(2) Where service is executed under paragraph (1)(b)(iii) or (iv), the sheriff officer shall, as soon as possible after such service, send, by ordinary post to the address at which he thinks it most likely that the person may be found, a letter containing a copy of the citation.

(3) A certified copy of the interlocutor allowing a proof shall be sufficient warrant to a sheriff officer to cite a witness on behalf of a party.

(4) A witness shall be cited on a period of notice of 7 days in Form G13 and the party citing the witness shall lodge a certificate of citation in Form G12.

(5) A solicitor who cites a witness shall be personally liable for his fees and expenses.

(6) In the event of a solicitor intimating to a witness that his citation is cancelled, the solicitor shall advise him that the cancellation is not to affect any other citation which he may have received from another party.

Citation of witnesses by party litigants
29.8.—(1) Where a party to a cause is a party litigant, he shall—
  (a) not later than 4 weeks before the diet of proof, apply to the sheriff by motion to fix caution in such sum as the sheriff considers reasonable having regard to the number of witnesses he proposes to cite and the period for which they may be required to attend court; and
  (b) before instructing a sheriff officer to cite a witness, find caution for such expenses as can reasonably be anticipated to be incurred by the witness in answering the citation.

(2) A party litigant who does not intend to cite all the witnesses referred to in his application under paragraph (1)(a), may apply by motion for variation of the amount of caution.

Second diligence against a witness
29.9.—(1) The sheriff may, on the motion of a party, grant a second diligence to compel the attendance of a witness under pain of arrest and imprisonment until caution can be found for his due attendance.

(2) The warrant for a second diligence shall be effective without endorsation and the expenses of such a motion and diligence may be decerned for against the witness.

Failure of witness to attend
29.10.—(1) Where a witness fails to answer a citation after having been duly cited, the sheriff may, on the motion of a party and on production of a certificate of citation, grant warrant for the apprehension of the witness and for bringing him to court; and the expenses of such a motion and apprehension may be decerned for against the witness.

(2) Where a witness duly cited and after having demanded and been paid his travelling expenses, fails to attend a diet, either before the sheriff or before a commissioner, the sheriff may—
  (a) ordain the witness to forfeit and pay a penalty not exceeding £250 unless a reasonable excuse be offered and sustained; and

(b) grant decree for that penalty in favour of the party on whose behalf the witness was cited.

Lodging productions
29.11.—[1,2] (1) Where a proof has been allowed, all productions and affidavits which are intended to be used at the proof shall be lodged in process not later than 28 days before the diet of proof.

(2) A production which is not lodged in accordance with paragraph (1) shall not be used or put in evidence at a proof unless—
(a) by consent of parties; or
(b) with leave of the sheriff on cause shown and on such conditions, if any, as to expenses or otherwise as the sheriff thinks fit.

NOTES
[1] As amended by SSI 2000/239 (effective October 2, 2000).
[2] As amended by the Act of Sederunt (Ordinary Cause and Summary Application Rules) Amendment (Miscellaneous) 2006 (SSI 2006/410) (effective August 18, 2006).

Copy productions
29.12.—[1] (1) A copy of every documentary production, marked with the appropriate number of process of the principal production, shall be lodged for the use of the sheriff at a proof not later than 48 hours before the diet of proof.

(2) Each copy production consisting of more than one sheet shall be securely fastened together by the party lodging it.

NOTE
[1] As amended by SSI 2000/239 (effective October 2, 2000).

Returning borrowed parts of process and productions before proof
29.13. All parts of process and productions which have been borrowed shall be returned to process before 12.30 pm on the day preceding the diet of proof.

Notices to admit and notices of non-admission
29.14.—[1] (1) At any time after the record has closed, a party may intimate to any other party a notice or notices calling on him to admit for the purposes of that cause only—
(a) such facts relating to an issue averred in the pleadings as may be specified in the notice;
(b) that a particular document lodged in process and specified in the notice is—
(i) an original and properly authenticated document; or
(ii) a true copy of an original and properly authenticated document.
(2) Where a party on whom a notice is intimated under paragraph (1)—
(a) does not admit a fact specified in the notice, or
(b) does not admit, or seeks to challenge, the authenticity of a document specified in the notice,
he shall, within 21 days after the date of intimation of the notice under paragraph (1), intimate a notice of non-admission to the party intimating the notice to him under paragraph (1) stating that he does not admit the fact or document specified.

(3) A party who fails to intimate a notice of non-admission under paragraph (2) shall be deemed to have admitted the fact or document specified in the notice intimated to him under paragraph (1); and such fact or document may be used in evidence at a proof if otherwise admissible in evidence, unless the sheriff, on special cause shown, otherwise directs.

(4) A party who fails to intimate a notice of non-admission under paragraph (2) within 14 days after the notice to admit intimated to him under paragraph (1) shall be liable to the party intimating the notice to admit for the expenses of proving the fact or document specified in that notice unless the sheriff, on special cause shown, otherwise directs.

(5) The party serving a notice under paragraph (1) or (2) shall lodge a copy of it in process.

(6) A deemed admission under paragraph (3) shall not be used against the party by whom it was deemed to be made other than in the cause for the purpose for which it was deemed to be made or in favour of any person other than the party by whom the notice was given under paragraph (1).

[2] (7) The sheriff may, at any time, allow a party to amend or withdraw an admission made by him on such conditions, if any, as he thinks fit.

[2] (8) A party may, at any time, withdraw in whole or in part a notice of non admission by intimating a notice of withdrawal.

NOTES
[1] As amended by SSI 2000/239 (effective October 2, 2000).
[2] Inserted by SSI 2000/239 (effective October 2, 2000).

Instruction of shorthand writer
29.15. Where a shorthand writer is to record evidence at a proof, the responsibility for instructing a shorthand writer shall lie with the pursuer.

Administration of oath or affirmation to witnesses
29.16. The sheriff shall administer the oath to a witness in Form G14 or, where the witness elects to affirm, the affirmation in Form G15.

Proof to be taken continuously
29.17. A proof shall be taken continuously so far as possible; but the sheriff may adjourn the diet from time to time.

Recording of evidence
[1] **29.18.**—(1) Evidence in a cause shall be recorded by—
  (a) a shorthand writer, to whom the oath *de fideli administratione* in connection with the sheriff court service generally shall have been administered, or
  (b) tape recording or other mechanical means approved by the court,
unless the parties, by agreement and with the approval of the sheriff, dispense with the recording of evidence.
  (2) Where a shorthand writer is employed to record evidence, he shall, in the first instance, be paid by the parties equally.
  (3) Where evidence is recorded by tape recording or other mechanical means, any fee payable shall, in the first instance, be paid by the parties equally.
  (4) The solicitors for the parties shall be personally liable for the fees payable under paragraph (2) or (3), and the sheriff may make an order directing payment to be made.
  (5) The record of the evidence at a proof shall include—
  (a) any objection taken to a question or to the line of evidence;
  (b) any submission made in relation to such an objection; and
  (c) the ruling of the court in relation to the objection and submission.
  (6) A transcript of the record of the evidence shall be made only on the direction of the sheriff; and the cost shall, in the first instance, be borne—
  (a) in an undefended cause, by the solicitor for the pursuer; and
  (b) in a defended cause, by the solicitors for the parties in equal proportions.
  (7) The transcript of the record of the evidence provided for the use of the court shall be certified as a faithful record of the evidence by—
  (a) the shorthand writer who recorded the evidence; or
  (b) where the evidence was recorded by tape recording or other mechanical means, by the person who transcribed the record.
  (8) The sheriff may make such alterations to the transcript of the record of the evidence as appear to him to be necessary after hearing the parties; and, where such alterations are made, the sheriff shall authenticate the alterations.
  (9) Where a transcript of the record of the evidence has been made for the use of the sheriff, copies of it may be obtained by any party from the person who transcribed the record on payment of his fee.
  (10) Except with leave of the sheriff, the transcript of the record of the evidence may be borrowed from process only for the purpose of enabling a party to consider whether to appeal against the interlocutor of the sheriff on the proof.
  (11) Where a transcript of the record of the evidence is required for the purpose of an appeal but has not been directed to be transcribed under paragraph (6), the appellant—
  (a) may request such a transcript from the shorthand writer or as the case may be, the cost of the transcript being borne by the solicitor for the appellant in the first instance; and
  (b) shall lodge the transcript in process;
and copies of it may be obtained by any party from the shorthand writer or as the case may be, on payment of his fee.
  (12) Where the recording of evidence has been dispensed with under paragraph (1), the sheriff, if called upon to do so, shall—
  (a) in the case of an objection to—
    (i) the admissibility of evidence on the ground of confidentiality, or
    (ii) the production of a document on any ground,
    note the terms in writing of such objections and his decision on the objection; and

    (b) in the case of any other objection, record, in the note to his interlocutor disposing of
        the merits of the cause, the terms of the objection and his decision on the objection.

  (13) This rule shall, with the necessary modifications, apply to the recording of evidence at a
commission as it applies to the recording of evidence at a proof.

NOTE

[1]As amended by SI 1996/2445 (effective November 1, 1996).

Incidental appeal against rulings on confidentiality of evidence and production of documents

    29.19.—(1) Where a party or any other person objects to the admissibility of oral or
documentary evidence on the ground of confidentiality or to the production of a document on
any ground, he may, if dissatisfied with the ruling of the sheriff on the objection, express
immediately his formal dissatisfaction with the ruling and, with leave of the sheriff, appeal to
the sheriff principal.

    (2) The sheriff principal shall dispose of an appeal under paragraph (1) with the least possible
delay.

    (3) Except as provided in paragraph (1), no appeal may be made during a proof against any
decision of the sheriff as to the admissibility of evidence or the production of documents.

    (4) The appeal referred to in paragraph (1) shall not remove the cause from the sheriff who
may proceed with the cause in relation to any issue which is not dependent on the ruling
appealed against.

Parties to be heard at close of proof

    29.20. At the close of the proof, or at an adjourned diet if for any reason the sheriff has
postponed the hearing, the sheriff shall hear parties on the evidence and thereafter shall
pronounce judgment with the least possible delay.

Chapter 30

Decrees, Extracts and Execution

Interpretation of this Chapter

    30.1. In this Chapter, "decree" includes any judgment, deliverance, interlocutor, act, order,
finding or authority which may be extracted.

Taxes on funds under control of the court

    30.2.—(1) Subject to paragraph (2), in a cause in which money has been consigned into court
under the Sheriff Court Consignations (Scotland) Act 1893, no decree, warrant or order for
payment to any person shall be granted until there has been lodged with the sheriff clerk a
certificate by an authorised officer of the Inland Revenue stating that all taxes or duties payable
to the Commissioners of Inland Revenue have been paid or satisfied.

    (2) In an action of multiplepoinding, it shall not be necessary for the grant of a decree,
warrant or order for payment under paragraph (1) that all of the taxes or duties payable on the
estate of a deceased claimant have been paid or satisfied.

Decrees for payment in foreign currency

    30.3.—(1) Where decree has been granted for payment of a sum of money in a foreign
currency or the sterling equivalent, a party requesting extract of the decree shall do so by minute
endorsed on or annexed to the initial writ stating the rate of exchange prevailing on the date of
the decree sought to be extracted or the date, or within 3 days before the date, on which the
extract is ordered, and the sterling equivalent at that rate for the principal sum and interest
decerned for.

    (2) A certificate in Form G18, from the Bank of England or a bank which is an institution
authorised under the Banking Act 1987 certifying the rate of exchange and the sterling
equivalent shall be lodged with the minute requesting extract of the decree.

    (3) The extract decree issued by the sheriff clerk shall mention any certificate referred to in
paragraph (2).

When decrees extractable

    30.4.—[1] (1) Subject to the following paragraphs:—

    (a) subject to sub-paragraph (c), a decree in absence may be extracted after the expiry of
        14 days from the date of decree;

    (b) subject to sub-paragraph (c), any decree pronounced in a defended cause may be
        extracted at any time after whichever is the later of the following:—

    (i) the expiry of the period within which an application for leave to appeal may be made and no such application has been made;

    (ii) the date on which leave to appeal has been refused and there is no right of appeal from such refusal;

    (iii) the expiry of the period within which an appeal may be marked and no appeal has been marked; or

    (iv) the date on which an appeal has been finally disposed of; and

  (c) where, the sheriff has, in pronouncing decree, reserved any question of expenses, extract of that decree may be issued only after the expiry of 14 days from the date of the interlocutor disposing of the question of expenses unless the sheriff otherwise directs.

(2) The sheriff may, on cause shown, grant a motion to allow extract to be applied for and issued earlier than a date referred to in paragraph (1).

(3) In relation to a decree referred to in paragraph (1)(b) or (c), paragraph (2) shall not apply unless—

  (a) the motion under that paragraph is made in the presence of parties; or

  (b) the sheriff is satisfied that proper intimation of the motion has been made in writing to every party not present at the hearing of the motion.

(4) Nothing in this rule shall affect the power of the sheriff to supersede extract.

NOTE
[1] As amended by SI 1996/2445 (effective November 1, 1996).

Extract of certain awards notwithstanding appeal

30.5. The sheriff clerk may issue an extract of an award of custody, access or aliment notwithstanding that an appeal had been made against an interlocutor containing such an award unless an order under rule 31.5 (appeals in connection with custody, access or aliment) has been made excusing obedience to or implement of that interlocutor.

Form of extract decree

30.6.—(1) The extract of a decree mentioned in Appendix 2 shall be in the appropriate form for that decree in Appendix 2.

(2) In the case of a decree not mentioned in Appendix 2, the extract of the decree shall be modelled on a form in that Appendix with such variation as circumstances may require.

Form of warrant for execution

30.7. An extract of a decree on which execution may proceed shall include a warrant for execution in the following terms:— "This extract is warrant for all lawful execution hereon.".

Date of decree in extract

30.8.—(1) Where the sheriff principal has adhered to the decision of the sheriff following an appeal, the date to be inserted in the extract decree as the date of decree shall be the date of the decision of the sheriff principal.

(2) Where a decree has more than one date it shall not be necessary to specify in an extract what was done on each date.

Service of charge where address of defender not known

30.9.—(1) Where the address of a defender is not known to the pursuer, a charge shall be deemed to have been served on the defender if it is—

  (a) served on the sheriff clerk of the sheriff court district where the defender's last known address is located; and

  (b) displayed by the sheriff clerk on the walls of court for the period of the charge.

(2) On receipt of such a charge, the sheriff clerk shall display it on the walls of court and it shall remain displayed for the period of the charge.

(3) The period specified in the charge shall run from the first date on which it was displayed on the walls of court.

(4) On the expiry of the period of charge, the sheriff clerk shall endorse a certificate on the charge certifying that it has been displayed in accordance with this rule and shall thereafter return it to the sheriff officer by whom service was executed.

Expenses

[1] **30.10.** A party who—

  (a) is or has been represented by a person authorised under any enactment to conduct proceedings in the sheriff court; and

(b) would have been found entitled to expenses if he had been represented by a solicitor or an advocate,

may be awarded any expenses or outlays to which a party litigant may be found entitled under the Litigants in Person (Costs and Expenses) Act 1975 or any enactment under that Act.

NOTE

[1] As inserted by the Act of Sederunt (Ordinary Cause, Summary Application, Summary Cause and Small Claim Rules) Amendment (Miscellaneous) 2007 (SSI 2007/6), para.2(11) (effective January 29, 2007).

CHAPTER 31

APPEALS

Time limit for appeal

31.1. Subject to the provisions of any other enactment, an interlocutor which may be appealed against may be appealed within 14 days after the date of the interlocutor unless it has been extracted following a motion under rule 30.4(2) (early extract).

Applications for leave to appeal

31.2.—(1) Where leave to appeal is required, applications for leave to appeal against an interlocutor of a sheriff shall be made within 7 days after the date of the interlocutor against which it is sought to appeal unless the interlocutor has been extracted following a motion under rule 30.4(2) (early extract).

(2) Subject to the provisions of any other enactment, where leave to appeal has been granted, an appeal shall be made within 7 days after the date when leave was granted.

[1] (3) An application for leave to appeal from a decision in relation to—

(a) a time to pay direction under section 1 of the Debtors (Scotland) Act 1987;

(b) the recall or restriction of an arrestment made under section 3(4) of that Act; or

(c) a time order under section 129 of the Consumer Credit Act 1974,

shall specify the question of law on which the appeal is made.

NOTE

[1] As substituted by the Act of Sederunt (Ordinary Cause, Summary Application, Summary Cause and Small Claim Rules) Amendment (Miscellaneous) 2007 (SSI 2007/6), para.2(12) (effective January 29, 2007).

Form of appeal to Court of Session

[1] **31.3.**—(1) An appeal to the Court of Session shall be marked by writing a note of appeal—

(a) on the interlocutor sheet or other written record containing the interlocutor appealed against, or

(b) where the decision appealed against is not available or the proceedings appealed against are recorded in an official book, on a separate sheet lodged with the sheriff clerk,

in the following terms:—"The pursuer [*or* defender *or as the case may be*] appeals to the Court of Session.".

(2) A note of appeal under paragraph (1) shall—

(a) be signed by the appellant or his solicitor;

(b) bear the date on which it is signed; and

(c) where the appellant is represented, specify the name and address of the solicitor or other agent who will be acting for him in the appeal.

NOTE

[1] Substituted by SI 1996/2445 (effective November 1, 1996).

Form of appeal to the sheriff principal

[1] **31.4.**—(1) An appeal to the sheriff principal shall be marked by lodging a note of appeal in Form A1.

(2) A note of appeal under paragraph (1) shall—

(a) be signed by the appellant or his solicitor;

(b) bear the date on which it is signed;

(c) where the appellant is represented, specify the name and address of the solicitor or other agent who will be acting for him in the appeal; and

(d) where a note has not been provided by the sheriff, request that the sheriff write a note setting out the reasons for his decision.

(3) The grounds of appeal in a note of appeal shall consist of brief specific numbered propositions stating the grounds on which it is proposed to submit that the appeal should be allowed or as the case may be.

(4) On making or lodging a note of appeal, the appellant shall send a copy of the note of appeal to every other party.

(5) An appellant—
(a) may amend the grounds of appeal at any time up to 14 days before the date assigned for the hearing of the appeal; and
(b) shall at the same time send or deliver a copy of such amendment to every other party.

(6) Where any party wishes to cross-appeal, he shall—
(a) lodge a note of the grounds of appeal in accordance with paragraph (1) not less than 7 days before the date assigned for the hearing of the appeal; and
(b) at the same time send a copy of the note to every other party.

(7) The sheriff principal may, on cause shown, shorten or dispense with the time limits mentioned in paragraphs (5) and (6).

(8) On a note of appeal being lodged, the sheriff clerk shall note on the interlocutor sheet that an appeal has been marked and the date of the appeal.

NOTE
[1] Substituted by SI 1996/2445 (effective November 1, 1996).

Transmission of process and notice to parties
[1] **31.5.**—(1) Where an appeal is marked in terms of rule 31.3 (appeal to Court of Session) or 31.4 (appeal to sheriff principal), the sheriff clerk shall transmit the process of the cause—
(a) in an appeal to the sheriff principal, to him; or
(b) in an appeal to the Court of Session, to the Deputy Principal Clerk of Session, within the period specified in rule 40.6 of the Rules of the Court of Session 1994.

(2) On transmitting the process in terms of paragraph (1), the sheriff clerk shall—
(a) send written notice of the appeal to every party; and
(b) certify on the interlocutor sheet that he has done so.

(3) Failure of the sheriff clerk to comply with paragraph (2) shall not invalidate the appeal.

NOTE
[1] Substituted by SI 1996/2445 (effective November 1, 1996).

Record of pleadings etc.
[1] **31.6** In an appeal to him, the sheriff principal may order the appellant to lodge a record of the pleadings containing all adjustments made in the cause with—
(a) a copy of all relevant interlocutors;
(b) any other document lodged in process by any party or produced by order of the sheriff, whether or not pursuant to the commission and diligence for its recovery; and
(c) any other document to which reference is intended to be made in the appeal, by any party.

NOTE
[1] Substituted by SI 1996/2445 (effective November 1, 1996).

Determination of appeal
[1] **31.7.** In an appeal to him, the sheriff principal shall—
(a) hear parties at an oral hearing; or
(b) on the motion of the parties, and if he thinks fit, dispose of the appeal without ordering an oral hearing.

NOTE
[1] Substituted by SI 1996/2445 (effective November 1, 1996).

Fixing of Options Hearing or making other order following appeal
[1] **31.8.** On determination of an appeal from a decision of the sheriff made before or at an Options Hearing or any contribution of it, the sheriff principal may order the sheriff clerk to fix a new date for a hearing under rule 9.12 (options hearing) or may make such other order as he thinks fit.

NOTE
[1] Inserted by SI 1996/2445 (effective November 1, 1996).

Appeals in connection with orders under section 11 of the Children (Scotland) Act 1995 or aliment
[1] **31.9.** Where an appeal is marked against an interlocutor making an order under section 11 of the Children (Scotland) Act 1995 (court orders relating to parental responsibilities etc.) or in respect of aliment, the marking of that appeal shall not excuse obedience to or implement of that order unless by order of the sheriff, the sheriff principal or the Court of Session, as the case may be.

NOTE
[1] Inserted by SI 1996/2445 (effective November 1, 1996).

Interim possession etc. pending appeal
[1] **31.10.**—(1) Notwithstanding an appeal, the sheriff or sheriff principal from whose decision an appeal has been taken shall have power—
    (a) to regulate all matters relating to interim possession;
    (b) to make any order for the preservation of any property to which the action relates or for its sale if perishable;
    (c) to make provision for the preservation of evidence; or
    (d) to make any interim order which a due regard to the interests of the parties may require.
  (2) An order made under paragraph (1) may be reviewed—
    (a) by the sheriff principal, on an appeal to him; or
    (b) the Court of Session, on an appeal to it.

NOTE
[1] Former rule 31.6 renumbered by SI 1996/2445 (effective November 1, 1996).

Abandonment of appeal
[1] **31.11.** After an appeal to the sheriff principal has been marked, the appellant shall not be entitled to abandon his appeal unless—
    (a) of consent of all other parties; or
    (b) with leave of the sheriff principal.

NOTE
[1] Former rule 31.7 renumbered by SI 1996/2445 (effective November 1, 1996).

CHAPTER 32

TAXATION OF EXPENSES

Taxation before decree for expenses
32.1. Expenses allowed in any cause, whether in absence or *in foro contentioso*, unless modified at a fixed amount, shall be taxed before decree is granted for them.

Order to lodge account of expenses
[1] **32.1A.** A party found liable in expenses may from 4 months after the date of the interlocutor finding him so liable apply by motion for an order ordaining the party entitled to expenses to lodge an account of those expenses in process.

NOTE
[1] Inserted by the Act of Sederunt (Ordinary Cause, Summary Application and Small Claim Rules) Amendment (Miscellaneous) 2004 (SSI 2004/197) (effective May 21, 2004), para.2(12).

Decree for expenses in name of solicitor
32.2. The sheriff may allow a decree for expenses to be extracted in the name of the solicitor who conducted the cause.

Procedure for taxation
32.3.—(1) Where an account of expenses awarded in a cause is lodged for taxation, the account and process shall be transmitted by the sheriff clerk to the auditor of court.
  (2) The auditor of court shall—

(a) assign a diet of taxation not earlier than 7 days from the date he receives the account from the sheriff clerk; and

(b) intimate that diet forthwith to the party who lodged the account.

(3) The party who lodged the account of expenses shall, on receiving intimation from the auditor of court under paragraph (2)—

(a) send a copy of the account, and

(b) intimate the date, time and place of the diet of taxation,

to every other party.

(4) After the account has been taxed, the auditor of court shall transmit the process with the account and his report to the sheriff clerk.

(5) Where the auditor of court has reserved consideration of the account at the date of the taxation, he shall intimate his decision to the parties who attended the taxation.

(6) Where no objections are lodged under rule 32.4 (objections to auditor's report), the sheriff may grant decree for the expenses as taxed.

Objections to auditor's report

32.4.—(1) A party may lodge a note of objections to an account as taxed only where he attended the diet of taxation.

(2) Such a note shall be lodged within 7 days after—

(a) the diet of taxation; or

(b) where the auditor of court reserved consideration of the account under paragraph (5) of rule 32.3, the date on which the auditor of court intimates his decision under that paragraph.

(3) The sheriff shall dispose of the objection in a summary manner, with or without answers.

[1] CHAPTER 32A

LIVE LINKS

NOTE

[1] As inserted by the Act of Sederunt (Ordinary Cause, Summary Application, Summary Cause and Small Claim Rules) Amendment (Miscellaneous) 2007 (SSI 2007/6) r.2(12) (effective January 29, 2007).

32A.1.—(1) On cause shown, a party may apply by motion for authority for the whole or part of—

(a) the evidence of a witness or the party to be given; or

(b) a submission to be made,

through a live link.

(2) In paragraph (1)—

[1] "witness" means a person who has been or may be cited to appear before the court as a witness, except a vulnerable witness within the meaning of section 11(1) of the Act of 2004;

"submission" means any oral submission which would otherwise be made to the court by the party or his representative in person including an oral submission in support of a motion; and

"live link" means a live television link or such other arrangement as may be specified in the motion by which the witness, party or representative, as the case may be, is able to be seen and heard in the proceedings or heard in the proceedings and is able to see and hear or hear the proceedings while at a place which is outside the courtroom.

NOTE

[1] As amended by the Act of Sederunt (Ordinary Cause, Summary Application, Summary Cause and Small Claim Rules) Amendment (Vulnerable Witnesses (Scotland) Act 2004) 2007 (SSI 2007/463) r.2(8) (effective November 1, 2007).

CHAPTER 33

FAMILY ACTIONS

PART I

GENERAL PROVISIONS

Interpretation of this Chapter
[1] **33.1.**—(1) In this Chapter, "family action" means—
(a) an action of divorce;
(b) an action of separation;
(c) an action of declarator of legitimacy;
(d) an action of declarator of illegitimacy;
(e) an action of declarator of parentage;
(f) an action of declarator of non-parentage;
(g) an action of declarator of legitimation;
(h) an action or application for, or in respect of, an order under section 11 of the Children (Scotland) Act 1995 (court orders relating to parental responsibilities etc.), except—
　(i) an application for the appointment of a judicial factor mentioned in section 11(2)(g) of the Act of 1995 to which Part I of the Act of Sederunt (Judicial Factors Rules) 1992 applies; and
　(ii) an application for the appointment or removal of a person as a guardian mentioned in section 11(2)(h) of the Act of 1995 to which paragraph 4 of the Act of Sederunt (Family Proceedings in the Sheriff Court) 1996 applies;
(i) an action of affiliation and aliment;
(j) an action of, or application for or in respect of, aliment;
(k) an action or application for financial provision after a divorce or annulment in an overseas country within the meaning of Part IV of the Matrimonial and Family Proceedings Act 1984;
(l) an action or application for an order under the Act of 1981;
(m) an application for the variation or recall of an order mentioned in section 8(1) of the Law Reform (Miscellaneous Provisions) (Scotland) Act 1966.
[3] (n) an action of declarator of marriage;
[3] (o) an action of declarator of nullity of marriage.
(2) In this Chapter, unless the context otherwise requires—
　"the Act of 1975" means the Children Act 1975;
　"the Act of 1976" means the Divorce (Scotland) Act 1976;
　"the Act of 1981" means the Matrimonial Homes (Family Protection) (Scotland) Act 1981;
　"the Act of 1985" means the Family Law (Scotland) Act 1985;
　"the Act of 1995" means the Children (Scotland) Act 1995;
　"contact order" has the meaning assigned in section 11(2)(d) of the Act of 1995;
　[2] "full gender recognition certificate" and "interim gender recognition certificate" mean the certificates issued as such under section 4 or 5 of the Gender Recognition Act 2004;
　[2] "Gender Recognition Panel" is to be construed in accordance with Schedule 1 to the Gender Recognition Act 2004;
　"local authority" means a council constituted under section 2 of the Local Government etc. (Scotland) Act 1994;
　[3] "mental disorder" has the meaning assigned in section 328 of the Mental Health (Care and Treatment) (Scotland) Act 2003;
　"order for financial provision" means, except in Part VII of this Chapter (financial provision after overseas divorce or annulment), an order mentioned in section 8(1) of the Act of 1985;
　"parental responsibilities" has the meaning assigned in section 1(3) of the Act 1995;
　"parental rights" has the meaning assigned in section 2(4) of the Act of 1995;
　"residence order" has the meaning assigned in section 11(2)(c) of the Act of 1995;
　"section 11 order" means an order under section 11 of the Act of 1995.
(3) For the purposes of rules 33.2 (averments in actions of divorce or separation about other proceedings) and 33.3 (averments where section 11 order sought) and, in relation to proceedings in another jurisdiction, Schedule 3 to the Domicile and Matrimonial Proceedings Act 1973

(sisting of consistorial actions in Scotland), proceedings are continuing at any time after they have commenced and before they are finally disposed of.

NOTES

[1] As amended by SI 1996/2167 (effective November 1, 1996).

[2] Inserted by the Act of Sederunt (Ordinary Cause Rules) Amendment (Gender Recognition Act 2004) 2005 (SSI 2005/189) (effective April 4, 2005).

[3] Inserted or substituted by Act of Sederunt (Ordinary Cause Rules) Amendment (Family Law (Scotland) Act 2006 etc.) 2006 (SSI 2006/207) (effective May 4, 2006).

[2] *Averments in certain family actions about other proceedings*

[1] **33.2.**—[2] (1) This rule applies to an action of divorce, separation, declarator of marriage or declarator of nullity of marriage.

(2) In an action to which this rule applies, the pursuer shall state in the condescendence of the initial writ—

    (a) whether to his knowledge any proceedings are continuing in Scotland or in any other country in respect of the marriage to which the initial writ relates or are capable of affecting its validity or subsistence; and

    (b) where such proceedings are continuing—

        (i) the court, tribunal or authority before which the proceedings have been commenced;

        (ii) the date of commencement;

        (iii) the names of the parties;

        (iv) the date, or expected date of any proof (or its equivalent) in the proceedings; and

        [2] (v) such other facts as may be relevant to the question of whether or not the action before the sheriff should be sisted under Schedule 3 to the Domicile and Matrimonial Proceedings Act 1973 or Council Regulation (E.C.) No. 2201/2003 of 27th November 2003 concerning jurisdiction and the recognition and enforcement of judgments in matrimonial matters and matters of parental responsibility.

(3) Where—

    (a) such proceedings are continuing;

    (b) the action before the sheriff is defended; and

    (c) either—

        (i) the initial writ does not contain the statement referred to in paragraph (2)(a), or

        (ii) the particulars mentioned in paragraph (2)(b) as set out in the initial writ are incomplete or incorrect,

any defences or minute, as the case may be, lodged by any person to the action shall include that statement and, where appropriate, the further or correct particulars mentioned in paragraph (2)(b).

NOTES

[1] As amended by Act of Sederunt (Ordinary Cause Rules) Amendment (European Matrimonial and Parental Responsibility Jurisdiction and Judgments) 2001 (SSI 2001/144) (effective April 2, 2001).

[2] As amended by Act of Sederunt (Ordinary Cause Rules) Amendment (Family Law (Scotland) Act 2006 etc.) 2006 (SSI 2006/207) (effective May 4, 2006).

Averments where section 11 order sought

[1] **33.3.**—(1) A party to a family action, who makes an application in that action for a section 11 order in respect of a child shall include in his pleadings—

    [2] (a) where that action is an action of divorce, separation or declarator of nullity of marriage, averments giving particulars of any other proceedings known to him, whether in Scotland or elsewhere and whether concluded or not, which relate to the child in respect of whom the section 11 order is sought;

    (b) in any other family action—

        (i) the averments mentioned in paragraph (a); and

        (ii) averments giving particulars of any proceedings known to him which are continuing, whether in Scotland or elsewhere, and which relate to the marriage of the parents of that child.

    [3] (c) where the party seeks an order such as is mentioned in any of paragraphs (a) to (e) of subsection (2) of that section, an averment that no permanence order (as defined in section 80(2) of the Adoption and Children (Scotland) Act 2007) is in force in respect of the child.

(2) Where such other proceedings are continuing or have taken place and the averments of the applicant for such a section 11 order—

    (a) do not contain particulars of the other proceedings, or

    (b) contain particulars which are incomplete or incorrect,

any defences or minute, as the case may be, lodged by any party to the family action shall include such particulars or such further or correct particulars as are known to him.

(3) In paragraph (1)(b)(ii), "child" includes a child of the family within the meaning assigned in section 42(4) of the Family Law Act 1986.

NOTES

[1] As amended by SI 1996/2167 (effective November 1, 1996) and SI 1996/2445 (effective November 1, 1996) (clerical error).

[2] As amended by Act of Sederunt (Ordinary Cause Rules) Amendment (Family Law (Scotland) Act 2006 etc.) 2006 (SSI 2006/207) (effective May 4, 2006).

[3] As inserted by the Act of Sederunt (Sheriff Court Rules Amendment) (Adoption and Children (Scotland) Act 2007) 2009 (SSI 2009/284) (effective September 28, 2009).

Averments where identity or address of person not known

33.4. In a family action, where the identity or address of any person referred to in rule 33.7 as a person in respect of whom a warrant for intimation requires to be applied for is not known and cannot reasonably be ascertained, the party required to apply for the warrant shall include in his pleadings an averment of that fact and averments setting out what steps have been taken to ascertain the identity or address, as the case may be, of that person.

Averments about maintenance orders

33.5. In a family action in which an order for aliment or periodical allowance is sought, or is sought to be varied or recalled, by any party, the pleadings of that party shall contain an averment stating whether and, if so, when and by whom, a maintenance order (within the meaning of section 106 of the Debtors (Scotland) Act 1987) has been granted in favour of or against that party or of any other person in respect of whom the order is sought.

Averments where aliment or financial provision sought

[1] **33.6.**—(1) In this rule—

    "the Act of 1991" means the Child Support Act 1991;

    "child" has the meaning assigned in section 55 of the Act of 1991;

    "crave relating to aliment" means—

        (a) for the purposes of paragraph (2), a crave for decree of aliment in relation to a child or for recall or variation of such a decree; and

        (b) for the purposes of paragraph (3), a crave for decree of aliment in relation to a child or for recall or variation of such a decree or for the variation or termination of an agreement on aliment in relation to a child;

    "maintenance calculation" has the meaning assigned in section 54 of the Act of 1991.

(2) A family action containing a crave relating to aliment and to which section 8(6), (7), (8) or (10) of the Act of 1991 (top up maintenance orders) applies shall—

    (a) include averments stating, where appropriate—

        (i) that a maintenance calculation under section 11 of that Act (maintenance calculations) is in force;

        (ii) the date of the maintenance calculation;

        (iii) the amount and frequency of periodical payments of child support maintenance fixed by the maintenance calculation; and

        (iv) the grounds on which the sheriff retains jurisdiction under section 8(6), (7), (8) or (10) of that Act; and

    (b) unless the sheriff on cause shown otherwise directs, be accompanied by any document issued by the Secretary of State to the party intimating the making of the maintenance calculation referred to in sub-paragraph (a).

(3) A family action containing a crave relating to aliment, and to which section 8(6), (7), (8) or (10) of the Act of 1991 does not apply, shall include averments stating—

    (a) that the habitual residence of the absent parent, person with care or qualifying child, within the meaning of section 3 of that Act, is furth of the United Kingdom;

    (b) that the child is not a child within the meaning of section 55 of that Act; or

    (c) where the action is lodged for warranting before 7th April 1997, the grounds on which the sheriff retains jurisdiction.

(4) In an action for declarator of non-parentage or illegitimacy—

    (a) the initial writ shall include an article of condescendence stating whether the pursuer previously has been alleged to be the parent in an application for a maintenance calculation under section 4, 6 or 7 of the Act of 1991 (applications for maintenance calculation); and

(b) where an allegation of paternity has been made against the pursuer, the Secretary of State shall be named as a defender in the action.

(5) A family action involving parties in respect of whom a decision has been made in any application, review or appeal under the Act of 1991 relating to any child of those parties, shall—

(a) include averments stating that such a decision has been made and giving details of that decision; and

(b) unless the sheriff on cause shown otherwise directs, be accompanied by any document issued by the Secretary of State to the parties intimating that decision.

NOTE

[1] As amended by the Act of Sederunt (Ordinary Cause, Summary Application, Summary Cause and Small Claim Rules) Amendment (Miscellaneous) 2003 (SSI 2003/26) r.2(8) (effective January 24, 2003).

Warrants and forms for intimation

[1] **33.7.**—(1) Subject to paragraphs (5) and (7), in the initial writ in a family action, the pursuer shall include a crave for a warrant for intimation—

(a) in an action where the address of the defender is not known to the pursuer and cannot reasonably be ascertained, to—

(i) every child of the marriage between the parties who has reached the age of 16 years; and

(ii) one of the next-of-kin of the defender who has reached that age,

unless the address of such a person is not known to the pursuer and cannot reasonably be ascertained, and a notice of intimation in Form F1 shall be attached to the copy of the initial writ intimated to any such person;

(b) in an action where the pursuer alleges that the defender has committed adultery with another person, to that person, unless—

(i) that person is not named in the initial writ and, if the adultery is relied on for the purposes of section 1(2)(a) of the Act of 1976 (irretrievable breakdown of marriage by reason of adultery), the initial writ contains an averment that his or her identity is not known to the pursuer and cannot reasonably be ascertained; or

(ii) the pursuer alleges that the defender has been guilty of rape upon or incest with, that named person,

and a notice of intimation in Form F2 shall be attached to the copy of the initial writ intimated to any such person;

(c) in an action where the defender is a person who is suffering from a mental disorder, to—

[3] (i) those persons mentioned in sub-paragraph (a)(i) and (ii), unless the address of such person is not known to the pursuer and cannot reasonably be ascertained;

(ii) the *curator bonis* to the defender, if one has been appointed,

and a notice of intimation in Form F3 shall be attached to the copy of the initial writ intimated to any such person;

[4] (iii) any person holding the office of guardian or continuing or welfare attorney to the defender under or by virtue of the Adults with Incapacity (Scotland) Act 2000,

(d) in an action relating to a marriage which was entered into under a law which permits polygamy where—

(i) one of the decrees specified in section 2(2) of the Matrimonial Proceedings (Polygamous Marriages) Act 1972 is sought; and

(ii) either party to the marriage in question has any spouse additional to the other party,

to any such additional spouse, and a notice of intimation in Form F4 shall be attached to the initial writ intimated to any such person;

[3] (e) in an action of divorce, separation or declarator of nullity of marriage where the sheriff may make a section 11 order in respect of a child—

(i) who is in the care of a local authority, to that authority and a notice of intimation in Form F5 shall be attached to the initial writ intimated to that authority;

(ii) who, being a child of one party to the marriage, has been accepted as a child of the family by the other party to the marriage and who is liable to be maintained by a third party, to that third party, and a notice of intimation in Form F5 shall be attached to the initial writ intimated to that third party; or

(iii) in respect of whom a third party in fact exercises care and control, to that third party, and a notice of intimation in Form F6 shall be attached to the initial writ intimated to that third party;

(f) in an action where the pursuer craves a section 11 order, to any parent or guardian of the child who is not a party to the action, and a notice of intimation in Form F7 shall be attached to the initial writ intimated to any such parent or guardian;

(g) in an action where the pursuer craves a residence order in respect of a child and he is—
   (i) not a parent of that child; and
   (ii) resident in Scotland when the initial writ is lodged,
   to the local authority within which area the pursuer resides, and a notice of intimation in Form F8 shall be attached to the initial writ intimated to that authority;

(h) in an action which includes a crave for a section 11 order, to the child to whom such an order would relate if not a party to the action, and a notice of intimation in Form F9 shall be intimated to that child;

(i) in an action where the pursuer makes an application for an order under section 8(1)(aa) of the Act of 1985 (transfer of property) and—
   (i) the consent of a third party to such a transfer is necessary by virtue of an obligation, enactment or rule of law, or
   (ii) the property is subject to a security,
   to the third party or creditor, as the case may be, and a notice of intimation in Form F10 shall be attached to the initial writ intimated to any such person;

(j) in an action where the pursuer makes an application for an order under section 18 of the Act of 1985 (which relates to avoidance transactions), to—
   (i) any third party in whose favour the transfer of, or transaction involving, the property is to be or was made, and
   (ii) any other person having an interest in the transfer of, or transaction involving, the property,
   and a notice of intimation in Form F11 shall be attached to the initial writ intimated to any such person;

(k) in an action where the pursuer makes an application for an order under the Act of 1981—
   (i) where he is a non-entitled partner and the entitled partner has a spouse, to that spouse; or
   (ii) where the application is under section 2(1)(e), 2(4)(a), 3(1), 3(2), 4, 7, 13 or 18 of that Act, and the entitled spouse or entitled partner is a tenant or occupies the matrimonial home by permission of a third party, to the landlord or the third party, as the case may be,
   and a notice of intimation in Form F12 shall be attached to the initial writ intimated to any such person;

(l) in an action where the pursuer makes an application for an order under section 8(1)(ba) of the Act of 1985 (orders under section 12A of the Act of 1985 for pension lump sum), to the person responsible for the pension arrangement, and a notice of intimation in Form F12A shall be attached to the initial writ intimated to any such person; and

[2] (m) in an action where a pursuer makes an application for an order under section 8(1)(baa) of the Act of 1985 (pension sharing orders), to the person responsible for the pension arrangement and a notice of intimation in Form F12B shall be attached to the initial writ intimated to any such person.

(2) Expressions used in paragraph (1)(k) which are also used in the Act of 1981 have the same meaning as in that Act.

(3) A notice of intimation under paragraph (1) shall be on a period of notice of 21 days unless the sheriff otherwise orders; but the sheriff shall not order a period of notice of less than 2 days.

(4) In a family action, where the pursuer—
   (a) craves a residence order in respect of a child,
   (b) is not a parent of the child, and
   (c) is not resident in Scotland when the initial writ is lodged for warranting,
he shall include a crave for an order for intimation in Form F8 to such local authority as the sheriff thinks fit.

[3] (5) Where the address of a person mentioned in paragraph (1)(b), (d), (e), (f), (h), (i), (j), (k), (l) or (m) is not known and cannot reasonably be ascertained, the pursuer shall include a crave in the initial writ to dispense with intimation; and the sheriff may grant that crave or make such other order as he thinks fit.

(6) Where the identity or address of a person to whom intimation of a family action is required becomes known during the course of the action, the party who would have been required to insert a warrant for intimation to that person shall lodge a motion for a warrant for intimation to that person or to dispense with such intimation.

(7) Where a pursuer considers that to order intimation to a child under paragraph (1)(h) is inappropriate, he shall—

    (a) include a crave in the initial writ to dispense with intimation to that child, and

    (b) include in the initial writ averments setting out the reasons why such intimation is inappropriate;

and the sheriff may dispense with such intimation or make such other order as he thinks fit.

NOTES

[1] As amended by SI 1996/2167 (effective November 1, 1996) and SI 1996/2445 (effective November 1, 1996).

[2] Inserted by the Act of Sederunt (Ordinary Cause Rules) Amendment (No.2) (Pension Sharing on Divorce etc.) 2000 (SSI 2000/408) r.2(2)(b)(ii).

[3] As amended by Act of Sederunt (Ordinary Cause Rules) Amendment (Family Law (Scotland) Act 2006 etc.) 2006 (SSI 2006/207) r.2 (effective May 4, 2006).

[4] Inserted or substituted by Act of Sederunt (Ordinary Cause Rules) Amendment (Family Law (Scotland) Act 2006 etc.) 2006 (SSI 2006/207) r.2 (effective May 4, 2006).

[1] *Intimation where alleged association*

33.8.—[1] (1) In a family action where the pursuer founds upon an association between the defender and another named person, the pursuer shall, immediately after the expiry of the period of notice, lodge a motion for an order for intimation to that person or to dispense with such intimation.

(2) In determining a motion under paragraph (1), the sheriff may—

    (a) make such order for intimation as he thinks fit; or

    (b) dispense with intimation; and

    (c) where he dispenses with intimation, order that the name of that person be deleted from the condescendence of the initial writ.

(3) Where intimation is ordered under paragraph (2), a copy of the initial writ and an intimation in Form F13 shall be intimated to the named person.

[1] (4) In paragraph (1), "association" means sodomy, incest or any homosexual relationship.

NOTE

[1] As amended by Act of Sederunt (Ordinary Cause Rules) Amendment (Family Law (Scotland) Act 2006 etc.) 2006 (SSI 2006/207) r.2 (effective May 4, 2006).

Productions in action of divorce or where section 11 order may be made

[1] **33.9.** Unless the sheriff otherwise directs—

[2] (a) in an action of divorce or declarator of nullity of marriage, a warrant for citation shall not be granted without there being produced with the initial writ an extract of the relevant entry in the register of marriages or an equivalent document; and

    (b) in an action which includes a crave for a section 11 order, a warrant for citation shall not be granted without there being produced with the initial writ an extract of the relevant entry in the register of births or an equivalent document.

NOTES

[1] As amended by SI 1996/2167 (effective November 1, 1996).

[2] As amended by Act of Sederunt (Ordinary Cause Rules) Amendment (Family Law (Scotland) Act 2006 etc.) 2006 (SSI 2006/207) (effective May 4, 2006).

Productions in action of divorce on ground of issue of interim gender recognition certificate

[1] **33.9A.**—(1) This rule applies where, in an action of divorce, the ground on which decree of divorce may be granted is that an interim gender recognition certificate has, after the date of the marriage, been issued to either party to the marriage.

(2) Unless the sheriff otherwise directs, a warrant for citation shall not be granted without there being produced with the initial writ—

    (a) where the pursuer is the subject of the interim gender recognition certificate, the interim gender recognition certificate or, failing that, a certified copy of the interim gender recognition certificate; or

    (b) where the pursuer is the spouse of the person who is the subject of the interim gender recognition certificate, a certified copy of the interim gender recognition certificate.

(3) For the purposes of this rule, a certified copy of an interim gender recognition certificate shall be a copy of that certificate sealed with the seal of the Gender Recognition Panels and certified to be a true copy by an officer authorised by the President of Gender Recognition Panels.

Application for corrected gender recognition certificate
[1] **33.9B.** An application for a corrected gender recognition certificate under section 6 of the Gender Recognition Act 2004 by—

(a) the person to whom a full gender recognition certificate has been issued; or

(b) the Secretary of State,

shall be made by minute in the process of the action pursuant to which the full gender recognition certificate was issued.

NOTE
[1] Inserted by the Act of Sederunt (Ordinary Cause Rules) Amendment (Gender Recognition Act 2004) 2005 (SSI 2005/189) r.2 (effective April 4, 2005).

Warrant of citation
33.10. The warrant of citation in a family action shall be in Form F14.

Form of citation and certificate
33.11.—(1) Subject to rule 5.6 (service where address of person is not known), citation of a defender shall be in Form F15, which shall be attached to a copy of the initial writ and warrant of citation and shall have appended to it a notice of intention to defend in Form F26.

(2) The certificate of citation shall be in Form F16 which shall be attached to the initial writ.

Execution of service on, or intimation to, local authority
[1] **33.12.**—(1) Where a local authority referred to in rule 33.7(1)(g) (residence order sought by non-parent resident in Scotland) or 33.7(4) (residence order sought by pursuer not resident in Scotland) is named as a defender in an initial writ at the time it is lodged, service of the initial writ on that local authority shall be executed within 7 days after the date of granting of the warrant of citation.

(2) Where in a family action—

(a) to which rule 33.7(1)(g) applies, or

[2] (b) in which a crave under rule 33.7(4) is required,

the local authority referred to in that provision is named as a defender in the initial writ at the time it is lodged, a notice in Form F8 shall be attached to the copy of the initial writ served on that local authority.

(3) In any family action, the sheriff may, if he thinks fit, order intimation to a local authority; and such intimation shall be in Form F8.

(4) Where, by virtue of paragraph 3 of this rule or rule 33.7(1)(g) or 33.7(4), intimation of an application for a residence order is to be made to a local authority, intimation to that local authority shall be given within 7 days after the date on which a warrant for citation, or an order for intimation, as the case may be, has been granted.

NOTES
[1] As amended by SI 1996/2167 (effective November 1, 1996).
[2] As amended by Act of Sederunt (Ordinary Cause Rules) Amendment (Family Law (Scotland) Act 2006 etc.) 2006 (SSI 2006/207) r.2 effective May 4, 2006.

Service in cases of mental disorder of defender
33.13.—(1) In a family action where the defender suffers or appears to suffer from mental disorder and is resident in a hospital or other similar institution, citation shall be executed by registered post or the first class recorded delivery service addressed to the medical officer in charge of that hospital or institution; and there shall be included with the copy of the initial writ—

(a) a citation in Form F15;

(b) any notice required by rule 33.14(1);

(c) a request in Form F17;

(d) a form of certificate in Form F18 requesting the medical officer to—

(i) deliver and explain the initial writ, citation and any notice or form of notice of consent required under rule 33.14(1) personally to the defender; or

(ii) certify that such delivery or explanation would be dangerous to the health or mental condition of the defender; and

(e) a stamped envelope addressed for return of that certificate to the pursuer or his solicitor, if he has one.

(2) The medical officer referred to in paragraph (1) shall send the certificate in Form F18 duly completed to the pursuer or his solicitor, as the case may be.

(3) The certificate mentioned in paragraph (2) shall be attached to the certificate of citation.

(4) Where such a certificate bears that the initial writ has not been delivered to the defender, the sheriff may, at any time before decree—

    (a) order such further medical inquiry, and

    (b) make such order for further service or intimation,

as he thinks fit.

Notices in certain actions of divorce or separation

33.14.—(1) In the following actions of divorce or separation there shall be attached to the copy of the initial writ served on the defender—

    [2] (a) in an action relying on section 1(2)(d) of the Act of 1976 (no cohabitation for one year with consent of defender to decree)—

        (i) which is an action of divorce, a notice in Form F19 and a notice of consent in Form F20;

        (ii) which is an action of separation, a notice in Form F21 and a form of notice of consent in Form F22;

    [2] (b) in an action relying on section 1(2)(e) of the Act of 1976 (no cohabitation for two years)—

        (i) which is an action of divorce, a notice in Form F23;

        (ii) which is an action of separation, a notice in Form F24.

    [3] (c) in an action relying on section 1(1)(b) of the Act of 1976 (grounds for divorce: interim gender recognition certificate), a notice in Form F24A

  [1] (2) The certificate of citation of an initial writ in an action mentioned in paragraph (1) shall state which notice or form mentioned in paragraph (1) has been attached to the initial writ.

NOTES

[1] As amended by SI 1996/2445 (effective November 1, 1996).

[2] As amended by Act of Sederunt (Ordinary Cause Rules) Amendment (Family Law (Scotland) Act 2006 etc.) 2006 (SSI 2006/207) r.2 (effective May 4, 2006).

[3] Inserted or substituted by Act of Sederunt (Ordinary Cause Rules) Amendment (Family Law (Scotland) Act 2006 etc.) 2006 (SSI 2006/207) r.2 (effective May 4, 2006).

Orders for intimation

33.15.—(1) In any family action, the sheriff may, at any time—

    (a) subject to paragraph (2), order intimation to be made on such person as he thinks fit;

    (b) postpone intimation, where he considers that such postponement is appropriate and, in that case, the sheriff shall make such order in respect of postponement of intimation as he thinks fit; or

    (c) dispense with intimation, where he considers that such dispensation is appropriate.

(2) Where the sheriff is considering whether to make a section 11 order by virtue of section 12 of the Act of 1995 (restrictions on decrees for divorce, separation or annulment affecting children), he shall, subject to paragraph (1)(c) and without prejudice to paragraph (1)(b) of this rule, order intimation in Form F9 to the child to whom the section 11 order would relate unless—

    (a) intimation has been given to the child under rule 33.7(1)(h); or

    (b) the sheriff considers that the child is not of sufficient age or maturity to express his views.

(3) Where a party makes a crave or averment in a family action which, had it been made in an initial writ, would have required a warrant for intimation under rule 33.7, that party shall include a crave in his writ for a warrant for intimation or to dispense with such intimation; and rule 33.7 shall, with the necessary modifications, apply to a crave for a warrant under this paragraph as it applies to a crave for a warrant under that rule.

Appointment of curators ad litem *to defenders*

33.16.—[2] (1) This rule applies to an action of divorce, separation or declarator of nullity of marriage where it appears to the court that the defender is suffering from a mental disorder.

(2) In an action to which this rule applies, the sheriff shall—

    (a) appoint a curator *ad litem* to the defender;

    [2] (b) where the facts set out in section 1(2)(d) of the Act of 1976 (no cohabitation for one year with consent of defender to decree) are relied on—

        (i) make an order for intimation of the ground of the action to the Mental Welfare Commission for Scotland; and

        (ii) include in such an order a requirement that the Commission sends to the sheriff clerk a report indicating whether in its opinion the defender is capable of deciding whether or not to give consent to the granting of decree.

[1] (3) Within 7 days after the appointment of a curator *ad litem* under paragraph (2)(a), the pursuer shall send to him—

(a) a copy of the initial writ and any defences (including any adjustments and amendments) lodged; and

(b) a copy of any notice in Form G5 sent to him by the sheriff clerk.

(4) On receipt of a report required under paragraph (2)(b)(ii), the sheriff clerk shall—

(a) lodge the report in process; and

(b) intimate that this has been done to—

(i) the pursuer;

(ii) the solicitor for the defender, if known; and

(iii) the curator *ad litem*.

(5) The curator *ad litem* shall lodge in process one of the writs mentioned in paragraph (6)—

(a) within 14 days after the report required under paragraph (2)(b)(ii) has been lodged in process; or

(b) where no such report is required, within 21 days after the date of his appointment under paragraph (2)(a).

(6) The writs referred to in paragraph (5) are—

(a) a notice of intention to defend;

(b) defences to the action;

(c) a minute adopting defences already lodged; and

(d) a minute stating that the curator *ad litem* does not intend to lodge defences.

(7) Notwithstanding that he has lodged a minute stating that he does not intend to lodge defences, a curator *ad litem* may appear at any stage of the action to protect the interests of the defender.

(8) If, at any time, it appears to the curator *ad litem* that the defender is not suffering from mental disorder, he may report that fact to the court and seek his own discharge.

(9) The pursuer shall be responsible, in the first instance, for payment of the fees and outlays of the curator *ad litem* incurred during the period from his appointment until—

(a) he lodges a minute stating that he does not intend to lodge defences;

(b) he decides to instruct the lodging of defences or a minute adopting defences already lodged; or

(c) being satisfied after investigation that the defender is not suffering from mental disorder, he is discharged.

NOTES

[1] As amended by SI 1996/2445 (effective November 1, 1996).

[2] As amended by Act of Sederunt (Ordinary Cause Rules) Amendment (Family Law (Scotland) Act 2006 etc.) 2006 (SSI 2006/207) r.2 (effective May 4, 2006).

Applications for sist

33.17. An application for a sist, or the recall of a sist, under Schedule 3 to the Domicile and Matrimonial Proceedings Act 1973 shall be made by written motion.

Notices of consent to divorce or separation

33.18.—[1] (1) Where, in an action of divorce or separation in which the facts in section 1(2)(d) of the Act of 1976 (no cohabitation for one year with consent of defender to decree) are relied on, the defender wishes to consent to the grant of decree of divorce or separation he shall do so by giving notice in writing in Form F20 (divorce) or Form F22 (separation), as the case may be, to the sheriff clerk.

(2) The evidence of one witness shall be sufficient for the purpose of establishing that the signature on a notice of consent under paragraph (1) is that of the defender.

(3) In an action of divorce or separation where the initial writ includes, for the purposes of section 1(2)(d) of the Act of 1976, an averment that the defender consents to the grant of decree, the defender may give notice by letter sent to the sheriff clerk stating that he has not so consented or that he withdraws any consent which he has already given.

(4) On receipt of a letter under paragraph (3), the sheriff clerk shall intimate the terms of the letter to the pursuer.

(5) On receipt of any intimation under paragraph (4), the pursuer may, within 14 days after the date of the intimation, if none of the other facts mentioned in section 1(2) of the Act of 1976 is averred in the initial writ, lodge a motion for the action to be sisted.

(6) If no such motion is lodged, the pursuer shall be deemed to have abandoned the action and the action shall be dismissed.

(7) If a motion under paragraph (5) is granted and the sist is not recalled or renewed within a period of 6 months from the date of the interlocutor granting the sist, the pursuer shall be deemed to have abandoned the action and the action shall be dismissed.

NOTE
[1] As amended by Act of Sederunt (Ordinary Cause Rules) Amendment (Family Law (Scotland) Act 2006 etc.) 2006 (SSI 2006/207) r.2 (effective May 4, 2006).

Procedure in respect of children
[1] **33.19.**—(1) In a family action, in relation to any matter affecting a child, where that child has—

    (a) returned to the sheriff clerk Form F9, or

    (b) otherwise indicated to the court a wish to express views on a matter affecting him,

the sheriff shall not grant any order unless an opportunity has been given for the views of that child to be obtained or heard.

  (2) Where a child has indicated his wish to express his views, the sheriff shall order such steps to be taken as he considers appropriate to ascertain the views of that child.

  (3) The sheriff shall not grant an order in a family action, in relation to any matter affecting a child who has indicated his wish to express his views, unless due weight has been given by the sheriff to the views expressed by that child, having due regard to his age and maturity.

NOTE
[1] As substituted by SI 1996/2167 (effective November 1, 1996).

Recording of views of the child
[1] **33.20**—(1) This rule applies where a child expresses a view on a matter affecting him whether expressed personally to the sheriff or to a person appointed by the sheriff for that purpose or provided by the child in writing.

  (2) The sheriff, or the person appointed by the sheriff, shall record the views of the child in writing; and the sheriff may direct that such views, and any written views, given by a child shall—

    (a) be sealed in an envelope marked "Views of the child—confidential";

    (b) be kept in the court process without being recorded in the inventory of process;

    (c) be available to a sheriff only;

    (d) not be opened by any person other than a sheriff; and

    (e) not form a borrowable part of the process.

NOTE
[1] As substituted by SI 1996/2167 (effective November 1, 1996).

Appointment of local authority or reporter to report on a child
[1] **33.21.**—(1) This rule applies where, at any stage of a family action, the sheriff appoints—

    (a) a local authority under section 11(1) of the Matrimonial Proceedings (Children) Act 1958 (reports as to arrangements for future care and upbringing of children) or otherwise, or

    (b) another person (referred to in this rule as a "reporter"), whether under a provision mentioned in sub-paragraph (a) or otherwise,

to investigate and report to the court on the circumstances of a child and on proposed arrangements for the care and upbringing of the child.

  (2) On making an appointment referred to in paragraph (1), the sheriff shall direct that the party who sought the appointment or, where the court makes the appointment of its own motion, the pursuer or minuter, as the case may be, shall—

    (a) instruct the local authority or reporter; and

    (b) be responsible, in the first instance, for the fees and outlays of the local authority or reporter appointed.

  (3) Where a local authority or reporter is appointed—

    (a) the party who sought the appointment, or

    (b) where the sheriff makes the appointment of his own motion, the pursuer or minuter, as the case may be,

shall, within 7 days after the date of the appointment, intimate the name and address of the local authority or reporter to any local authority to which intimation of the family action has been made.

  (4) On completion of a report referred to in paragraph (1), the local authority or reporter, as the case may be, shall send the report, with a copy of it for each party, to the sheriff clerk.

  (5) On receipt of such a report, the sheriff clerk shall send a copy of the report to each party.

  (6) Where a local authority or reporter has been appointed to investigate and report in respect of a child, an application for a section 11 order in respect of that child shall not be determined until the report of the local authority or reporter, as the case may be, has been lodged.

NOTE
[1] As amended by SI 1996/2167 (effective November 1, 1996).

Referral to family mediation
[1] **33.22.** In any family action in which an order in relation to parental responsibilities or parental rights is in issue, the sheriff may, at any stage of the action, where he considers it appropriate to do so, refer that issue to a mediator accredited to a specified family mediation organisation.

NOTE
[1] As substituted by SI 1996/2167 (effective November 1, 1996).

Child Welfare Hearing
[1] **33.22A.**—(1) Where—
    (a) on the lodging of a notice of intention to defend in a family action in which the initial writ seeks or includes a crave for a section 11 order, a defender wishes to oppose any such crave or order, or seeks the same order as that craved by the pursuer,
    (b) on the lodging of a notice of intention to defend in a family action, the defender seeks a section 11 order which is not craved by the pursuer, or
    (c) in any other circumstances in a family action, the sheriff considers that a Child Welfare Hearing should be fixed and makes an order (whether at his own instance or on the motion of a party) that such a hearing shall be fixed,
the sheriff clerk shall fix a date and time for a Child Welfare Hearing on the first suitable court date occurring not sooner than 21 days after the lodging of such notice of intention to defend, unless the sheriff directs the hearing to be held on an earlier date.

(2) On fixing the date for the Child Welfare Hearing, the sheriff clerk shall intimate the date of the Child Welfare Hearing to the parties in Form F41.

(3) The fixing of the date of the Child Welfare Hearing shall not affect the right of a party to make any other application to the court whether by motion or otherwise.

[2] (4) At the Child Welfare Hearing (which may be held in private), the sheriff shall seek to secure the expeditious resolution of disputes in relation to the child by ascertaining from the parties the matters in dispute and any information relevant to that dispute, and may—
    (a) order such steps to be taken, make such order, if any, or order further procedure, as he thinks fit, and
    (b) ascertain whether there is or is likely to be a vulnerable witness within the meaning of section 11(1) of the Act of 2004 who is to give evidence at any proof or hearing and whether any order under section 12(1) of the Act of 2004 requires to be made.

(5) All parties (including a child who has indicated his wish to attend) shall, except on cause shown, attend the Child Welfare Hearing personally.

(6) It shall be the duty of the parties to provide the sheriff with sufficient information to enable him to conduct the Child Welfare Hearing.

NOTES
[1] As inserted by SI 1996/2167 (effective November 1, 1996).
[2] As substituted by the Act of Sederunt (Ordinary Cause, Summary Application, Summary Cause and Small Claim Rules) Amendment (Vulnerable Witnesses (Scotland) Act 2004) 2007 (SSI 2007/463) r.2(9) (effective November 1, 2007).

Applications for orders to disclose whereabouts of children
33.23.—(1) An application for an order under section 33(1) of the Family Law Act 1986 (which relates to the disclosure of the whereabouts of a child) shall be made by motion.

(2) Where the sheriff makes an order under section 33(1) of the Family Law Act 1986, he may ordain the person against whom the order has been made to appear before him or to lodge an affidavit.

Applications in relation to removal of children
[1] **33.24.**—(1) An application for leave under section 51(1) of the Act of 1975 (authority to remove a child from the care and possession of the applicant for a residence order) or for an order under section 35(3) of the Family Law Act 1986 (application for interdict or interim interdict prohibiting removal of child from jurisdiction) shall be made—
    (a) by a party to the action, by motion; or
    (b) by a person who is not a party to the action, by minute.

(2) An application under section 35(3) of the Family Law Act 1986 need not be served or intimated.

(3) An application under section 23(2) of the Child Abduction and Custody Act 1985 (declarator that removal of child from United Kingdom was unlawful) shall be made—
- (a) in an action depending before the sheriff—
  - (i) by a party, in the initial writ, defences or minute, as the case may be, or by motion; or
  - (ii) by any other person, by minute; or
- (b) after final decree, by minute in the process of the action to which the application relates.

NOTE
[1] As amended by SI 1996/2167 (effective November 1, 1996).

Intimation to local authority before supervised contact order

33.25. Where the sheriff, at his own instance or on the motion of a party, is considering making a contact order or an interim contact order subject to supervision by the social work department of a local authority, he shall ordain the party moving for such an order to intimate to the Chief Executive of that local authority (where not already a party to the action and represented at the hearing at which the issue arises)—
- (a) the terms of any relevant motion;
- (b) the intention of the sheriff to order that the contact order be supervised by the social work department of that local authority; and
- (c) that the local authority shall, within such period as the sheriff has determined—
  - (i) notify the sheriff clerk whether it intends to make representations to the sheriff; and
  - [2] (ii) where it intends to make representations in writing, do so within that period.

NOTES
[1] As amended by SI 1996/2167 (effective November 1, 1996).
[2] As amended by Act of Sederunt (Ordinary Cause Rules) Amendment (Family Law (Scotland) Act 2006 etc.) 2006 (SSI 2006/207) r.2 (effective May 4, 2006).

Joint minutes

[1] **33.26.** Where any parties have reached agreement in relation to—
- (a) a section 11 order,
- (b) aliment for a child, or
- (c) an order for financial provision,

a joint minute may be entered into expressing that agreement; and, subject to rule 33.19(3) (no order before views of child expressed), the sheriff may grant decree in respect of those parts of the joint minute in relation to which he could otherwise make an order, whether or not such a decree would include a matter for which there was no crave.

NOTE
[1] As amended by SI 1996/2167 (effective November 1, 1996).

Affidavits

33.27. The sheriff may accept evidence by affidavit at any hearing for an order or interim order.

Applications for postponement of decree under section 3A of the Act of 1976

[1] **33.27A.** An application under section 3A(1) (application for postponement of decree where impediment to religious marriage exists) or section 3A(4) (application for recall of postponement) of the Act of 1976 shall be made by minute in the process of the action to which the application relates.

NOTE
[1] Substituted by Act of Sederunt (Ordinary Cause Rules) Amendment (Family Law (Scotland) Act 2006 etc.) 2006 (SSI 2006/207) r.2 (effective May 4, 2006) and amended by the Act of Sederunt (Ordinary Cause, Summary Application, Summary Cause and Small Claim Rules) Amendment (Miscellaneous) 2007 (SSI 2007/6) r.2(14) (effective February 26, 2007).

Part II

Undefended Family Actions

Evidence in certain undefended family actions
[1] **33.28.**—(1) This rule—
    (a) subject to sub-paragraph (b), applies to all family actions in which no notice of intention to defend has been lodged, other than a family action—
        (i) for a section 11 order or for aliment;
        (ii) of affiliation and aliment;
        (iii) for financial provision after an overseas divorce or annulment within the meaning of Part IV of the Matrimonial and Family Proceedings Act 1984; or
        (iv) for an order under the Act of 1981;
    (b) applies to a family action in which a curator *ad litem* has been appointed under rule 33.16 where the curator *ad litem* to the defender has lodged a minute intimating that he does not intend to lodge defences;
    (c) applies to any family action which proceeds at any stage as undefended where the sheriff so directs;
    (d) applies to the merits of a family action which is undefended on the merits where the sheriff so directs, notwithstanding that the action is defended on an ancillary matter.
  (2) Unless the sheriff otherwise directs, evidence shall be given by affidavits.
  (3) Unless the sheriff otherwise directs, evidence relating to the welfare of a child shall be given by affidavit, at least one affidavit being emitted by a person other than a parent or party to the action.
  (4) Evidence in the form of a written statement bearing to be the professional opinion of a duly qualified medical practitioner, which has been signed by him and lodged in process, shall be admissible in place of parole evidence by him.

NOTE
[1] As amended by SI 1996/2167 (effective November 1, 1996).

Procedure for decree in actions under rule 33.28
  33.29.—(1) In an action to which rule 33.28 (evidence in certain undefended family actions) applies, the pursuer shall at any time after the expiry of the period for lodging a notice of intention to defend—
    (a) lodge in process the affidavit evidence; and
    (b) endorse a minute in Form F27 on the initial writ.
  (2) The sheriff may, at any time after the pursuer has complied with paragraph (1), without requiring the appearance of parties—
    (a) grant decree in terms of the motion for decree; or
    (b) remit the cause for such further procedure, if any, including proof by parole evidence, as the sheriff thinks fit.

Extracts of undefended decree
[1] **33.30.** In an action to which rule 33.28 (evidence in certain undefended family actions) applies, the sheriff clerk shall, after the expiry of 14 days after the grant of decree under rule 33.29 (procedure for decree in cases under rule 33.28), issue to the pursuer and the defender an extract decree.

NOTE
[1] As amended by Act of Sederunt (Ordinary Cause Rules) Amendment (Family Law (Scotland) Act 2006 etc.) 2006 (SSI 2006/207) r.2 (effective May 4, 2006).

Procedure in undefended family action for section 11 order
[1] **33.31.**—(1) Where no notice of intention to defend has been lodged in a family action for a section 11 order, any proceedings in the cause shall be dealt with by the sheriff in chambers.
  (2) In an action to which paragraph (1) applies, decree may be pronounced after such inquiry as the sheriff thinks fit.

NOTE
[1] As amended by SI 1996/2167 (effective November 1, 1996).

No recording of evidence
33.32. It shall not be necessary to record the evidence in any proof in a family action which is not defended.

Disapplication of Chapter 15
[1] **33.33.** Other than rule 15.1(1), Chapter 15 (motions) shall not apply to a family action in which no notice of intention to defend has been lodged, or to a family action in so far as it proceeds as undefended.

NOTE
[1] As amended by SI 1996/2445 (effective November 1, 1996).

Late appearance and application for recall by defenders
[1] **33.33A.**—(1) In a cause mentioned in rule 33.1(a) to (h), (n) or (o), the sheriff may, at any stage of the action before the granting of final decree, make an order with such conditions, if any, as he thinks fit—

    (a) directing that a defender who has not lodged a notice of intention to defend be treated as if he had lodged such a notice and the period of notice had expired on the date on which the order was made; or

    (b) allowing a defender who has not lodged a notice of intention to defend to appear and be heard at a diet of proof although he has not lodged defences, but he shall not, in that event, be allowed to lead evidence without the pursuer's consent.

(2) Where the sheriff makes an order under paragraph (1), the pursuer may recall a witness already examined or lead other evidence whether or not he closed his proof before that order was made.

(3) Where no order under paragraph (1) has been sought by a defender who has not lodged a notice of intention to defend and decree is granted against him, the sheriff may, on an application made within 14 days of the date of the decree, and with such conditions, if any, as he thinks fit, make an order recalling the decree.

(4) Where the sheriff makes an order under paragraph (3), the cause shall thereafter proceed as if the defender had lodged a notice of intention to defend and the period of notice had expired on the date on which the decree was recalled.

(5) An application under paragraph (1) or (3) shall be made by note setting out the proposed defence and explaining the defender's failure to appear.

(6) An application under paragraph (1) or (3) shall not affect any right of appeal the defender may otherwise have.

(7) A note lodged in an application under paragraph (1) or (3) shall be served on the pursuer and any other party.

NOTE
[1] As inserted by the Act of Sederunt (Sheriff Court Rules) (Miscellaneous Amendments) 2008 (SSI 2008/223) r.2(2) (effective July 1, 2008).

PART III

DEFENDED FAMILY ACTIONS

Notice of intention to defend and defences
[1] **33.34.**—(1) This rule applies where the defender in a family action seeks—

    (a) to oppose any crave in the initial writ;

    (b) to make a claim for—

        (i) aliment;

        (ii) an order for financial provision within the meaning of section 8(3) of the Act of 1985; or

        (iii) a section 11 order; or

    (c) an order—

        (i) under section 16(1)(b) or (3) of the Act of 1985 (setting aside or varying agreement as to financial provision);

        (ii) under section 18 of the Act of 1985 (which relates to avoidance transactions); or

        (iii) under the Act of 1981; or

    (d) to challenge the jurisdiction of the court.

(2) In an action to which this rule applies, the defender shall—

    (a) lodge a notice of intention to defend in Form F26 before the expiry of the period of notice; and

(b) make any claim or seek any order referred to in paragraph (1), as the case may be, in those defences by setting out in his defences—
    (i) craves;
    (ii) averments in the answers to the condescendence in support of those craves; and
    (iii) appropriate pleas-in-law.

(3) Where a defender intends to make an application for a section 11 order which, had it been made in an initial writ, would have required a warrant for intimation under rule 33.7, the defender shall include a crave in his notice of intention to defend for a warrant for intimation or to dispense with such intimation; and rule 33.7 shall, with the necessary modifications, apply to a crave for a warrant under this paragraph as it applies to a crave for a warrant under that rule.

NOTE
[1] As amended by SI 1996/2167 (effective November 1, 1996).

Abandonment by pursuer
33.35. Notwithstanding abandonment by a pursuer, the court may allow a defender to pursue an order or claim sought in his defences; and the proceedings in relation to that order or claim shall continue in dependence as if a separate cause.

Attendance of parties at Options Hearing
33.36. All parties shall, except on cause shown, attend personally the hearing under rule 9.12 (Options Hearing).

Decree by default
33.37.—[1] (1) In a family action in which the defender has lodged a notice of intention to defend, where a party fails—
    (a) to lodge, or intimate the lodging of, any production or part of process,
    (b) to implement an order of the sheriff within a specified period,
    (c) to appear or be represented at any diet, or
[2]   (d) otherwise to comply with any requirement imposed upon that party by these Rules;
that party shall be in default.
[3] (2) Where a party is in default under paragraph (1), the sheriff may—
    (a) where the family action is one mentioned in rule 33.1(1)(a) to (h), (n) or (o) allow the cause to proceed as undefended under Part II of this Chapter; or
    (b) where the family action is one mentioned in rule 33.1(1)(i) to (m), grant decree as craved; or
    (c) grant decree of absolvitor; or
    (d) dismiss the family action or any claim made or order sought; or
   (da) make such other order as he thinks fit to secure the expeditious progress of the cause; and
    (e) award expenses.
(3) Where no party appears at a diet in a family action, the sheriff may dismiss that action.
(4) In a family action, the sheriff may, on cause shown, prorogate the time for lodging any production or part of process, or for intimating or implementing any order.

NOTES
[1] As amended by SI 1996/2445 (effective November 1, 1996) (clerical error).
[2] As inserted by the Act of Sederunt (Ordinary Cause and Summary Application Rules) Amendment (Miscellaneous) 2006 (SSI 2006/410) (effective August 18, 2006).
[3] As amended by Act of Sederunt (Ordinary Cause Rules) Amendment (Family Law (Scotland) Act 2006 etc.) 2006, para.2 (SSI 2006/207) (effective May 4, 2006) and the Act of Sederunt (Ordinary Cause and Summary Application Rules) Amendment (Miscellaneous) 2006 (SSI 2006/410) (effective August 18, 2006).

PART IV

APPLICATIONS AND ORDERS RELATING TO CHILDREN IN CERTAIN ACTIONS

Application and interpretation of this Part
[1,2] **33.38.** This Part applies to an action of divorce, separation or declarator of nullity of marriage.

NOTES
[1] As amended by SI 1996/2167 (effective November 1, 1996).

[2] As amended by Act of Sederunt (Ordinary Cause Rules) Amendment (Family Law (Scotland) Act 2006 etc.) 2006, para.2 (SSI 2006/207) (effective May 4, 2006).

Applications in actions to which this Part applies
[1] **33.39.**—(1) An application for an order mentioned in paragraph (2) shall be made—
    (a) by a crave in the initial writ or defences, as the case may be, in an action to which this Part applies; or
    (b) where the application is made by a person other than the pursuer or defender, by minute in that action.
  (2) The orders referred to in paragraph (1) are—
    (a) an order for a section 11 order; and
    (b) an order for aliment for a child.

NOTE
[1] As amended by SI 1996/2167 (effective November 1, 1996).

33.40. [Repealed by SI 1996/2167 (effective November 1, 1996).]

33.41. [Repealed by SI 1996/2167 (effective November 1, 1996).]

33.42. [Repealed by SI 1996/2167 (effective November 1, 1996).]

Applications in depending actions by motion
[1] **33.43.** An application by a party in an action depending before the court to which this Part applies for, or for variation of, an order for—
    (a) interim aliment for a child under the age of 18, or
    (b) a residence order or a contact order,
shall be made by motion.

NOTE
[1] As amended by SI 1996/2167 (effective November 1, 1996).

Applications after decree relating to a section 11 order
[1] **33.44.**—[2] (1) An application after final decree for, or for the variation or recall of, a section 11 order or in relation to the enforcement of such an order shall be made by minute in the process of the action to which the application relates.
  (2) Where a minute has been lodged under paragraph (1), any party may apply by motion for any interim order which may be made pending the determination of the application.

NOTES
[1] As amended by SI 1996/2167 (effective November 1, 1996).
[2] As amended by SSI 2000/239 (effective October 2, 2000).

Applications after decree relating to aliment
33.45.—(1) An application after final decree for, or for the variation or recall of, an order for aliment for a child shall be made by minute in the process of the action to which the application relates.
  (2) Where a minute has been lodged under paragraph (1), any party may lodge a motion for any interim order which may be made pending the determination of the application.

Applications after decree by persons over 18 years for aliment
33.46.—(1) A person—
    (a) to whom an obligation of aliment is owed under section 1 of the Act of 1985,
    (b) in whose favour an order for aliment while under the age of 18 years was made in an action to which this Part applies, and
    (c) who seeks, after attaining that age, an order for aliment against the person in that action against whom the order for aliment in his favour was made,
shall apply by minute in the process of that action.
  (2) An application for interim aliment pending the determination of an application under paragraph (1) shall be made by motion.
  (3) Where a decree has been pronounced in an application under paragraph (1) or (2), any application for variation or recall of any such decree shall be made by minute in the process of the action to which the application relates.

Part V

Orders Relating to Financial Provision

Application and interpretation of this Part
33.47.—(1) This Part applies to an action of divorce.

(2) In this Part, "incidental order" has the meaning assigned in section 14(2) of the Act of 1985.

Applications in actions to which this Part applies
33.48.—(1) An application for an order mentioned in paragraph (2) shall be made—
- (a) by a crave in the initial writ or defences, as the case may be, in an action to which this Part applies; or
- (b) where the application is made by a person other than the pursuer or defender, by minute in that action.

(2) The orders referred to in paragraph (1) are—
- (a) an order for financial provision within the meaning of section 8(3) of the Act of 1985;
- (b) an order under section 16(1)(b) or (3) of the Act of 1985 (setting aside or varying agreement as to financial provision);
- (c) an order under section 18 of the Act of 1985 (which relates to avoidance transactions); and
- (d) an order under section 13 of the Act of 1981 (transfer or vesting of tenancy).

Applications in depending actions relating to incidental orders
33.49.—(1) In an action depending before the sheriff to which this Part applies—
- (a) the pursuer, notwithstanding rules 33.34(2) (application by defender for order for financial provision) and 33.48(1)(a) (application for order for financial provision in initial writ or defences), may apply by motion for an incidental order; and
- (b) the sheriff shall not be bound to determine such a motion if he considers that the application should properly be by a crave in the initial writ or defences, as the case may be.

(2) In an action depending before the sheriff to which this Part applies, an application under section 14(4) of the Act of 1985 for the variation or recall of an incidental order shall be made by minute in the process of the action to which the application relates.

Applications relating to interim aliment
33.50. An application for, or for the variation or recall of, an order for interim aliment for the pursuer or the defender shall be made by motion.

Applications relating to orders for financial provision
33.51.—(1) An application—
- (a) after final decree under any of the following provisions of the Act of 1985—
  - (i) section 8(1) for periodical allowance,
  - (ii) section 12(1)(b) (payment of capital sum or transfer of property),
  - (iii) section 12(4) (variation of date or method of payment of capital sum or date of transfer of property), or
  - (iv) section 13(4) (variation, recall, backdating or conversion of periodical allowance), or
- (b) after the grant or refusal of an application under—
  - (i) section 8(1) or 14(3) for an incidental order, or
  - (ii) section 14(4) (variation or recall of incidental order),

shall be made by minute in the process of the action to which the application relates.

(2) Where a minute is lodged under paragraph (1), any party may lodge a motion for any interim order which may be made pending the determination of the application.

[1] (3) An application under—
- (a) paragraph (5) of section 12A of the Act of 1985 (recall or variation of order in respect of a pension lump sum),
- (b) paragraph (7) of that section (variation of order in respect of pension lump sum to substitute trustees or managers), or
- (c) section 28(10) or 48(9) of the Welfare Reform and Pensions Act 1999,

shall be made by minute in the process of the action to which the application relates.

NOTE
[1] Inserted by SI 1996/2445 (effective November 1, 1996) and as amended by the Act of

Sederunt (Ordinary Cause, Summary Application, Summary Cause and Small Claim Rules) Amendment (Miscellaneous) 2003 (SSI 2003/26), para.2(9) (effective January 24, 2003).

Pension Protection Fund notification
[1] **33.51A.**—(1) In this rule—
"assessment period" shall be construed in accordance with section 132 of the Pensions Act 2004;
"pension arrangement" shall be construed in accordance with the definition in section 27 of the Act of 1985; and
"valuation summary" shall be construed in accordance with the definition in Schedule 2 to the Pension Protection Fund (Provision of Information) Regulations 2005.

(2) This rule applies where a party at any stage in the proceedings applies for an order under section 8 or section 16 of the Act of 1985.

(3) Where the party against whom an order referred to in paragraph (2) is sought has received notification in compliance with the Pension Protection Fund (Provision of Information) Regulations 2005 or does so after the order is sought—
(a) that there is an assessment period in relation to his pension arrangement; or
(b) that the Board of the Pension Protection Fund has assumed responsibility for all or part of his pension arrangement,
he shall comply with paragraph (4).

(4) The party shall—
(a) lodge the notification; and
(b) obtain and lodge as soon as reasonably practicable thereafter–
(i) a valuation summary; and
(ii) a forecast of his compensation entitlement.

(5) Subject to paragraph (6), the notification referred to in paragraph (4)(a) requires to be lodged—
(a) where the notification is received before the order is sought, within 7 days of the order being sought;
(b) where the notification is received after the order is sought, within 7 days of receiving the notification.

(6) Where an order is sought against the defender before the defences are lodged, and the notification is received before that step occurs, the notification shall be lodged with the defences.

(7) At the same time as lodging documents under paragraph (4), copies shall be sent to the other party to the proceedings.

NOTE
[1] As inserted by the Act of Sederunt (Sheriff Court Rules) (Miscellaneous Amendments) 2008 (SSI 2008/223) para.3(2) (effective July 1, 2008).

Applications after decree relating to agreements and avoidance transactions
33.52. An application for an order—
(a) under section 16(1)(a) or (3) of the Act of 1985 (setting aside or varying agreement as to financial provision), or
(b) under section 18 of the Act of 1985 (which relates to avoidance transactions),
made after final decree shall be made by minute in the process of the action to which the application relates.

PART VI

APPLICATIONS RELATING TO AVOIDANCE TRANSACTIONS

Form of applications
33.53.—(1) An application for an order under section 18 of the Act of 1985 (which relates to avoidance transactions) by a party to an action shall be made by including in the initial writ, defences or minute, as the case may be, appropriate craves, averments and pleas-in-law.

(2) An application for an order under section 18 of the Act of 1985 after final decree in an action, shall be made by minute in the process of the action to which the application relates.

Part VII

Financial Provision after Overseas Divorce or Annulment

Interpretation of this Part
33.54. In this Part—
"the Act of 1984" means the Matrimonial and Family Proceedings Act 1984;
"order for financial provision" has the meaning assigned in section 30(1) of the Act of 1984;
"overseas country" has the meaning assigned in section 30(1) of the Act of 1984.

[1] *Applications for financial provision after overseas divorce or annulment*
33.55.—(1) An application under section 28 of the Act of 1984 for an order for financial provision after a divorce or annulment in an overseas country shall be made by initial writ.
(2) An application for an order in an action to which paragraph (1) applies made before final decree under—
(a) section 13 of the Act of 1981 (transfer of tenancy of matrimonial home),
(b) section 29(4) of the Act of 1984 for interim periodical allowance, or
(c) section 14(4) of the Act of 1985 (variation or recall of incidental order),
shall be made by motion.
(3) An application for an order in an action to which paragraph (1) applies made after final decree under—
(a) section 12(4) of the Act of 1985 (variation of date or method of payment of capital sum or date of transfer of property),
(b) section 13(4) of the Act of 1985 (variation, recall, backdating or conversion of periodical allowance), or
(c) section 14(4) of the Act of 1985 (variation or recall of incidental order),
shall be made by minute in the process of the action to which the application relates.
[2] (4) An application under—
(a) paragraph (5) of section 12A of the Act of 1985 (recall or variation of order in respect of a pension lump sum), or
(b) paragraph (7) of that section (variation of order in respect of pension lump sum to substitute trustees or managers),
shall be made by minute in the process of the action to which the application relates.
(5) Where a minute has been lodged under paragraph (3), any party may apply by motion for an interim order pending the determination of the application.

NOTES
[1] Heading amended by SI 1996/2445 (effective November 1, 1996).
[2] Inserted by SI 1996/2445 (effective November 1, 1996).

Part VIII

Actions of Aliment

Interpretation of this Part
33.56. In this Part, "action of aliment" means a claim for aliment under section 2(1) of the Act of 1985.

Undefended actions of aliment
33.57.—(1) Where a motion for decree in absence under Chapter 7 (undefended causes) is lodged in an action of aliment, the pursuer shall, on lodging the motion, lodge all documentary evidence of the means of the parties available to him in support of the amount of aliment sought.
(2) Where the sheriff requires the appearance of parties, the sheriff clerk shall fix a hearing.

Applications relating to aliment
33.58.—(1) An application for, or for variation of, an order for interim aliment in a depending action of aliment shall be made by motion.
(2) An application after final decree for the variation or recall of an order for aliment in an action of aliment shall be made by minute in the process of the action to which the application relates.
(3) A person—
(a) to whom an obligation of aliment is owed under section 1 of the Act of 1985,

    (b) in whose favour an order for aliment while under the age of 18 years was made in an action of aliment, or

    (c) who seeks, after attaining that age, an order for aliment against the person in that action against whom the order for aliment in his favour was made,

shall apply by minute in the process of that action.

    (4) An application for interim aliment pending the determination of an application under paragraph (2) or (3) shall be made by motion.

    (5) Where a decree has been pronounced in an application under paragraph (2) or (3), any application for variation or recall of any such decree shall be made by minute in the process of the action to which the application relates.

Applications relating to agreements on aliment

    [1] **33.59.**—(1) Subject to paragraph (2) and rule 33A.53, an application under section 7(2) of the Act of 1985 (variation or termination of agreement on aliment) shall be made by summary application.

    (2) In a family action in which a crave for aliment may be made, an application under section 7(2) of the Act of 1985 shall be made by a crave in the initial writ or in defences, as the case may be.

NOTE

[1] As amended by Act of Sederunt (Ordinary Cause Rules) Amendment (Family Law (Scotland) Act 2006 etc.) 2006, para.2 (SSI 2006/207) (effective May 4, 2006).

PART IX

APPLICATIONS FOR ORDERS UNDER SECTION 11 OF THE CHILDREN (SCOTLAND) ACT 1995

Application of this Part

    [1,2] **33.60.** This Part applies to an application for a section 11 order in a family action other than in an action of divorce, separation or declarator of nullity of marriage.

NOTES

[1] Substituted by SI 1996/2167 (effective November 1, 1996).

[2] As amended by Act of Sederunt (Ordinary Cause Rules) Amendment (Family Law (Scotland) Act 2006 etc.) 2006, para.2 (SSI 2006/207) (effective May 4, 2006).

Form of applications

    [1] **33.61.** Subject to any other provision in this Chapter, an application for a section 11 order shall be made—

    (a) by an action for a section 11 order;

    (b) by a crave in the initial writ or defences, as the case may be, in any other family action to which this Part applies; or

    (c) where the application is made by a person other than a party to an action mentioned in paragraph (a) or (b), by minute in that action.

NOTE

[1] As amended by SI 1996/2167 (effective November 1, 1996).

Defenders in action for a section 11 order

    [1] **33.62.** In an action for a section 11 order, the pursuer shall call as a defender—

    (a) the parents or other parent of the child in respect of whom the order is sought;

    (b) any guardian of the child;

    (c) any person who has treated the child as a child of his family;

    (d) any person who in fact exercises care or control in respect of the child; and

    [2] (e) [*Repealed by SSI 2000/239 (effective October 2, 2000).*]

NOTE

[1] Substituted by SI 1996/2167 (effective November 1, 1996). Clerical error corrected by SI 1996/2445 (effective November 1, 1996).

Applications relating to interim orders in depending actions

    [1,2] **33.63.** An application, in an action depending before the sheriff to which this Part applies, for, or for the variation or recall of, an interim residence order or an interim contact order shall be made—

(a) by a party to the action, by motion; or

(b) by a person who is not a party to the action, by minute.

NOTES

[1] As amended by SI 1996/2167 (effective November 1, 1996).

[2] As amended by Act of Sederunt (Ordinary Cause Rules) Amendment (Family Law (Scotland) Act 2006 etc.) 2006, para.2 (SSI 2006/207) (effective May 4, 2006).

33.64. [Repealed by SI 1996/2167 (effective November 1, 1996).]

Applications after decree

[1] **33.65.**—(1) An application after final decree for variation or recall of a section 11 order shall be made by minute in the process of the action to which the application relates.

(2) Where a minute has been lodged under paragraph (1), any party may apply by motion for an interim order pending the determination of the application.

NOTE

[1] As amended by SI 1996/2167 (effective November 1, 1996).

Application for leave

[1] **33.65A.**—(1) Where leave of the court is required under section 11(3)(aa) of the Act of 1995 for the making of an application for a contact order under that section, the applicant must lodge along with the initial writ a written application in the form of a letter addressed to the sheriff clerk stating—

(a) the grounds on which leave is sought;

(b) whether or not the applicant has applied for legal aid.

(2) Where the applicant has applied for legal aid he must also lodge along with the initial writ written confirmation from the Scottish Legal Aid Board that it has determined, under regulation 7(2)(b) of the Civil Legal Aid (Scotland) Regulations 2002, that notification of the application should be dispensed with or postponed pending the making by the sheriff of an order for intimation under paragraph (4)(b).

(3) Subject to paragraph (4)(b), an application under paragraph (1) shall not be served or intimated to any party.

(4) The sheriff shall consider an application under paragraph (1) without hearing the applicant and may—

(a) refuse the application and pronounce an interlocutor accordingly; or

(b) if he is minded to grant the application order the applicant—

(i) to intimate the application to such persons as the sheriff considers appropriate; and

(ii) to lodge a certificate of intimation in, as near as may be, Form G8.

(5) If any person who receives intimation of an application under paragraph (4)(b) wishes to be heard he shall notify the sheriff clerk in writing within 14 days of receipt of intimation of the application.

(6) On receipt of any notification under paragraph (5) the sheriff clerk shall fix a hearing and intimate the date of the hearing to the parties.

(7) Where an application under paragraph (1) is granted, a copy of the sheriff's interlocutor must be served on the defender along with the warrant of citation.

NOTE

[1] As inserted by the Act of Sederunt (Sheriff Court Rules Amendment) (Adoption and Children (Scotland) Act 2007) 2009 (SSI 2009/284) (effective September 28, 2009).

PART X

ACTIONS UNDER THE MATRIMONIAL HOMES (FAMILY PROTECTION) (SCOTLAND) ACT 1981

Interpretation of this Part

33.66. Unless the context otherwise requires, words and expressions used in this Part which are also used in the Act of 1981 have the same meaning as in that Act.

Form of applications

33.67.—(1) Subject to any other provision in this Chapter, an application for an order under the Act of 1981 shall be made—

(a) by an action for such an order;

(b) by a crave in the initial writ or in defences, as the case may be, in any other family action; or

(c) where the application is made by a person other than a party to any action mentioned in paragraph (a) or (b), by minute in that action.

[1] (2) An application under section 7(1) (dispensing with consent of non-entitled spouse to a dealing) or section 11 (application in relation to attachment) shall, unless made in a depending family action, be made by summary application.

NOTE
[1] As amended by the Act of Sederunt (Debt Arrangement and Attachment (Scotland) Act 2002) 2002 (SSI 2002/560), art.4, Sch.3 (effective December 30, 2002).

Defenders
33.68. The applicant for an order under the Act of 1981 shall call as a defender—

(a) where he is seeking an order as a spouse, the other spouse;

[1] (b) where he is a third party making an application under section 7(1) dispensing with consent of non-entitled spouse to a dealing), or 8(1) (payment from non-entitled spouse in respect of loan), of the Act of 1981, both spouses;

(c) where the application is made under section 18 of the Act of 1981 (occupancy rights of cohabiting couples), or is one to which that section applies, the other partner; and

[2] (d) where the application is made under section 18A of the Act of 1981 (application for domestic interdict), the other partner.

NOTES
[1] As amended by Act of Sederunt (Ordinary Cause Rules) Amendment (Family Law (Scotland) Act 2006 etc.) 2006, para.2 (SSI 2006/207) (effective May 4, 2006).
[2] Inserted by Act of Sederunt (Ordinary Cause Rules) Amendment (Family Law (Scotland) Act 2006 etc.) 2006, para.2 (SSI 2006/207) (effective May 4, 2006).

Applications by motion
33.69.—(1) An application under any of the following provisions of the Act of 1981 shall be made by motion in the process of the depending action to which the application relates:—

(a) section 3(4) (interim order for regulation of rights of occupancy, etc.);

(b) section 4(6) (interim order suspending occupancy rights);

(c) section 7(1) (dispensing with consent of non-entitled spouse to a dealing);

(d) [*Omitted by Act of Sederunt (Ordinary Cause Rules) Amendment (Family Law (Scotland) Act 2006 etc.) 2006, para.2 (SSI 2006/207) (effective May 4, 2006).*]; and

(e) the proviso to section 18(1) (extension of period of occupancy rights).

(2) Intimation of a motion under paragraph (1) shall be given—

(a) to the other spouse or partner, as the case may be;

(b) where the motion is under paragraph (1)(a), (b) or (e) and the entitled spouse or partner is a tenant or occupies the matrimonial home by the permission of a third party, to the landlord or third party, as the case may be; and

(c) to any other person to whom intimation of the application was or is to be made by virtue of rule 33.7(1)(k) (warrant for intimation to certain persons in actions for orders under the Act of 1981) or 33.15 (order for intimation by sheriff).

Applications by minute
33.70.—(1) An application for an order under—

(a) section 5 of the Act of 1981 (variation and recall of orders regulating occupancy rights and of exclusion order), or

(b) [*Omitted by Act of Sederunt (Ordinary Cause Rules) Amendment (Family Law (Scotland) Act 2006 etc.) 2006, para.2 (SSI 2006/207) (effective May 4, 2006).*]

shall be made by minute.

(2) A minute under paragraph (1) shall be intimated—

(a) to the other spouse or partner, as the case may be;

(b) where the entitled spouse or partner is a tenant or occupies the matrimonial home by the permission of a third party, to the landlord or third party, as the case may be; and

(c) to any other person to whom intimation of the application was or is to be made by virtue of rule 33.7(1)(k) (warrant for intimation to certain persons in actions for orders under the Act of 1981) or 33.15 (order for intimation by sheriff).

Sist of actions to enforce occupancy rights
33.71. Unless the sheriff otherwise directs, the sist of an action by virtue of section 7(4) of the Act of 1981 (where action raised by non-entitled spouse to enforce occupancy rights) shall apply

only to such part of the action as relates to the enforcement of occupancy rights by a non-entitled spouse.

Certificates of delivery of documents to chief constable
33.72. [*Omitted by Act of Sederunt (Ordinary Cause Rules) Amendment (Family Law (Scotland) Act 2006 etc.) 2006, para.2 (SSI 2006/207) (effective May 4, 2006).*]

PART XI

SIMPLIFIED DIVORCE APPLICATIONS

Application and interpretation of this Part
33.73.—[1] (1) This Part applies to an application for divorce by a party to a marriage made in the manner prescribed in rule 33.74 (form of applications) if, but only if—
  (a) that party relies on the facts set out in section 1(2)(d) (no cohabitation for one year with consent of defender to decree), or section 1(2)(e) (no cohabitation for two years), or section 1(1)(b) (issue of interim gender recognition certificate) of the Act of 1976;
  (b) in an application under section 1(2)(d) of the Act of 1976, the other party consents to decree of divorce being granted;
  (c) no other proceedings are pending in any court which could have the effect of bringing the marriage to an end;
  (d) there are no children of the marriage under the age of 16 years;
  (e) neither party to the marriage applies for an order for financial provision on divorce;
  (f) neither party to the marriage suffers from mental disorder; and
  [2] (g) neither party to the marriage applies for postponement of decree under section 3A of the Act of 1976 (postponement of decree where impediment to religious marriage exists).

(2) If an application ceases to be one to which this Part applies at any time before final decree, it shall be deemed to be abandoned and shall be dismissed.

(3) In this Part "simplified divorce application" means an application mentioned in paragraph (1).

NOTES
[1] As amended by Act of Sederunt (Ordinary Cause Rules) Amendment (Family Law (Scotland) Act 2006 etc.) 2006, para.2 (SSI 2006/207) (effective May 4, 2006).
[2] Inserted by Act of Sederunt (Ordinary Cause Rules) Amendment (Family Law (Scotland) Act 2006 etc.) 2006, para.2 (SSI 2006/207) (effective May 4, 2006) and substituted by the Act of Sederunt (Ordinary Cause, Summary Application, Summary Cause and Small Claim Rules) Amendment (Miscellaneous) 2007 (SSI 2007/6), para.2(15) (effective February 26, 2007).

Form of applications
[2] **33.74.**—[1] (1) A simplified divorce application in which the facts set out in section 1(2)(d) of the Act of 1976 (no cohabitation for one year with consent of defender to decree) are relied on shall be made in Form F31 and shall only be of effect if—
  (a) it is signed by the applicant; and
  (b) the form of consent in Part 2 of Form F31 is signed by the party to the marriage giving consent.

(2) A simplified divorce application in which the facts set out in section 1(2)(e) of the Act of 1976 (no cohabitation for two years) are relied on shall be made in Form F33 and shall only be of effect if it is signed by the applicant.

[3] (3) A simplified divorce application in which the facts set out in section 1(1)(b) of the Act of 1976 (grounds of divorce: interim gender recognition certificate) are relied on shall be made in Form F33A and shall only be of effect if signed by the applicant.

NOTES
[1] As amended by SI 1996/2445 (effective November 1, 1996) (clerical error).
[2] As amended by Act of Sederunt (Ordinary Cause Rules) Amendment (Family Law (Scotland) Act 2006 etc.) 2006, para.2 (SSI 2006/207) (effective May 4, 2006).
[3] Inserted by Act of Sederunt (Ordinary Cause Rules) Amendment (Family Law (Scotland) Act 2006 etc.) 2006, para.2 (SSI 2006/207) (effective May 4, 2006).

Lodging of applications
[1] **33.75.** The applicant shall send a simplified divorce application to the sheriff clerk with—
  (a) an extract or certified copy of the marriage certificate;

(b) the appropriate fee; and

[2] (c) in an application under section 1(1)(b) of the Act of 1976 (grounds of divorce: interim gender recognition certificate), the interim gender recognition certificate or a certified copy within the meaning of rule 33.9A(3).

NOTES

[1] As amended by Act of Sederunt (Ordinary Cause Rules) Amendment (Family Law (Scotland) Act 2006 etc.) 2006, para.2 (SSI 2006/207) (effective May 4, 2006).

[2] Inserted by Act of Sederunt (Ordinary Cause Rules) Amendment (Family Law (Scotland) Act 2006 etc.) 2006, para.2 (SSI 2006/207) (effective May 4, 2006).

Citation and intimation

33.76.—(1) This rule is subject to rule 33.77 (citation where address not known).

(2) It shall be the duty of the sheriff clerk to cite any person or intimate any document in connection with a simplified divorce application.

(3) The form of citation—

[3] (a) in an application relying on the facts in section 1(2)(d) of the Act of 1976 shall be in Form F34;

(b) in an application relying on the facts in section 1(2)(e) of the Act of 1976 shall be in Form F35; and

[4] (c) in an application relying on the facts in section 1(1)(b) of the Act of 1976 shall be in Form F35A.

[1] (4) The citation or intimation required by paragraph (2) shall be made—

(a) by the sheriff clerk by registered post or the first class recorded delivery service in accordance with rule 5.3 (postal service or intimation);

[5] (b) on payment of an additional fee, by a sheriff officer in accordance with rule 5.4(1) to (4) (service within Scotland by sheriff officer); or

(c) where necessary, by the sheriff clerk in accordance with rule 5.5 (service on persons furth of Scotland).

[2] (5) Where citation or intimation is made in accordance with paragraph (4)(c), the translation into an official language of the country in which service is to be executed required by rule 5.5(6) shall be provided by the party lodging the simplified divorce application.

NOTES

[1] Substituted by SSI 2000/239 (effective October 2, 2000).

[2] Inserted by SSI 2000/239 (effective October 2, 2000).

[3] As amended by Act of Sederunt (Ordinary Cause Rules) Amendment (Family Law (Scotland) Act 2006 etc.) 2006, para.2 (SSI 2006/207) (effective May 4, 2006).

[4] Inserted by Act of Sederunt (Ordinary Cause Rules) Amendment (Family Law (Scotland) Act 2006 etc.) 2006, para.2 (SSI 2006/207) (effective May 4, 2006).

[5] As amended by the Act of Sederunt (Sheriff Court Rules) (Miscellaneous Amendments) 2010 (SSI 2010/279) para.2 (effective July 29, 2010).

Citation where address not known

[1] **33.77.**—(1) In a simplified divorce application in which the facts in section 1(2)(e) of the Act of 1976 (no cohabitation for two years) or section 1(1)(b) of the Act of 1976 (grounds of divorce: issue of interim gender recognition certificate) are relied on and the address of the other party to the marriage is not known and cannot reasonably be ascertained—

(a) citation shall be executed by displaying a copy of the application and a notice in Form F36 on the walls of court on a period of notice of 21 days; and

(b) intimation shall be made to—

(i) every child of the marriage between the parties who has reached the age of 16 years, and

(ii) one of the next of kin of the other party to the marriage who has reached that age, unless the address of such person is not known and cannot reasonably be ascertained.

(2) Intimation to a person referred to in paragraph (1)(b) shall be given by intimating a copy of the application and a notice of intimation in Form F37.

NOTE

[1] As amended by Act of Sederunt (Ordinary Cause Rules) Amendment (Family Law (Scotland) Act 2006 etc.) 2006, para.2 (SSI 2006/207) (effective May 4, 2006).

Opposition to applications

33.78.—(1) Any person on whom service or intimation of a simplified divorce application has been made may give notice by letter sent to the sheriff clerk that he challenges the jurisdiction of the court or opposes the grant of decree of divorce and giving the reasons for his opposition to the application.

(2) Where opposition to a simplified divorce application is made under paragraph (1), the sheriff shall dismiss the application unless he is satisfied that the reasons given for the opposition are frivolous.

(3) The sheriff clerk shall intimate the decision under paragraph (2) to the applicant and the respondent.

(4) The sending of a letter under paragraph (1) shall not imply acceptance of the jurisdiction of the court.

Evidence

33.79. Parole evidence shall not be given in a simplified divorce application.

Decree

33.80.—(1) The sheriff may grant decree in terms of the simplified divorce application on the expiry of the period of notice if such application has been properly served provided that, when the application has been served in a country to which the Hague Convention on the Service Abroad of Judicial and Extra-Judicial Documents in Civil and Commercial Matters dated November 15, 1965 applies, decree shall not be granted until it is established to the satisfaction of the sheriff that the requirements of Article 15 of that Convention have been complied with.

(2) The sheriff clerk shall, not sooner than 14 days after the granting of decree in terms of paragraph (1), issue to each party to the marriage an extract of the decree of divorce in Form F38.

Appeals

33.81. Any appeal against an interlocutor granting decree of divorce under rule 33.80 (decree) may be made, within 14 days after the date of decree, by sending a letter to the court giving reasons for the appeal.

Applications after decree

33.82. Any application to the court after decree of divorce has been granted in a simplified divorce application which could have been made if it had been made in an action of divorce shall be made by minute.

PART XII

VARIATION OF COURT OF SESSION DECREES

Application and interpretation of this Part

33.83.—(1) This Part applies to an application to the sheriff for variation or recall of any order to which section 8 of the Act of 1966 (variation of certain Court of Session orders) applies.

(2) In this Part, the "Act of 1966" means the Law Reform (Miscellaneous Provisions) (Scotland) Act 1966.

Form of application and intimation to Court of Session

33.84.—(1) An application to which this Part applies shall be made by initial writ.

(2) In such an application there shall be lodged with the initial writ a copy of the interlocutor, certified by a clerk of the Court of Session, which it is sought to vary.

(3) Before lodging the initial writ, a copy of the initial writ certified by the pursuer or his solicitor shall be lodged, or sent by first class recorded delivery post to the Deputy Principal Clerk of Session to be lodged in the process of the cause in the Court of Session in which the original order was made.

(4) The pursuer or his solicitor shall attach a certificate to the initial writ stating that paragraph (3) has been complied with.

[1] (5) The sheriff may, on cause shown, prorogate the time for lodging the certified copy of the interlocutor required under paragraph (2).

NOTE

[1] As amended by SI 1996/2445 (effective November 1, 1996) (clerical error).

Defended actions

33.85.—(1) Where a notice of intention to defend has been lodged and no request is made under rule 33.87 (remit of application to Court of Session), the pursuer shall within 14 days after the date of the lodging of a notice of intention to defend or within such other period as the sheriff may order, lodge in process the following documents (or copies) from the process in the cause in the Court of Session in which the original order was made:—

    (a) the pleadings;

    (b) the interlocutor sheets;

    (c) any opinion of the court; and

    (d) any productions on which he seeks to found.

(2) The sheriff may, on the joint motion of parties made at any time after the lodging of the documents mentioned in paragraph (1)—

    (a) dispense with proof;

    (b) whether defences have been lodged or not, hear the parties; and

    (c) thereafter, grant decree or otherwise dispose of the cause as he thinks fit.

Transmission of process to Court of Session

33.86.—(1) Where decree has been granted or the cause otherwise disposed of—

    (a) and the period for marking an appeal has elapsed without an appeal being marked, or

    (b) after the determination of the cause on any appeal,

the sheriff clerk shall transmit to the Court of Session the sheriff court process and the documents from the process of the cause in the Court of Session which have been lodged in the sheriff court process.

(2) A sheriff court process transmitted under paragraph (1) shall form part of the process of the cause in the Court of Session in which the original order was made.

Remit of application to Court of Session

33.87.—(1) A request for a remit to the Court of Session under section 8(3) of the Act of 1966 shall be made by motion.

(2) The sheriff shall, in respect of any such motion, order that the cause be remitted to the Court of Session; and, within 4 days after the date of such order, the sheriff clerk shall transmit the whole sheriff court process to the Court of Session.

(3) A cause remitted to the Court of Session under paragraph (2) shall form part of the process of the cause in the Court of Session in which the original order was made.

PART XIII

CHILD SUPPORT ACT 1991

Interpretation of this Part

[1] **33.88.** In this Part—

    "the Act of 1991" means the Child Support Act 1991;

    "child" has the meaning assigned in section 55 of the Act of 1991;

    "maintenance calculation" has the meaning assigned in section 54 of the Act of 1991.

NOTE

[1] As amended by SI 1996/2445 (effective November 1, 1996) and the Act of Sederunt (Ordinary Cause, Summary Application, Summary Cause and Small Claim Rules) Amendment (Miscellaneous) 2003 (SSI 2003/26), para.2(10) (effective January 24, 2003).

Restriction of expenses

33.89. Where the Secretary of State is named as a defender in an action for declarator of non-parentage or illegitimacy, and the Secretary of State does not defend the action, no expenses shall be awarded against the Secretary of State.

Effect of maintenance calculations

[1] **33.90.**—(1) The sheriff clerk shall, on receiving notification that a maintenance calculation has been made, cancelled or has ceased to have effect so as to affect an order of a kind prescribed for the purposes of section 10 of the Act of 1991, endorse on the interlocutor sheet relating to that order a certificate, in Form F39 or F40, as the case may be.

NOTE

[1] As amended by the Act of Sederunt (Ordinary Cause, Summary Application, Summary Cause and Small Claim Rules) Amendment (Miscellaneous) 2003 (SSI 2003/26), para.2(11) (effective January 24, 2003).

Effect of maintenance calculations on extracts relating to aliment
[1] **33.91.**—(1) Where an order relating to aliment is affected by a maintenance calculation, any extract of that order issued by the sheriff clerk shall be endorsed with the following certificate:—

> "A maintenance calculation having been made under the Child Support Act 1991 on (*insert date*), this order, in so far as it relates to the making or securing of periodical payments to or for the benefit of (*insert name(s) of child/children*), ceases to have effect from (*insert date 2 days after the date on which the maintenance calculation was made*)."

(2) Where an order relating to aliment has ceased to have effect on the making of a maintenance calculation, and that maintenance calculation is later cancelled or ceases to have effect, any extract of that order issued by the sheriff clerk shall be endorsed also with the following certificate:—

> "The jurisdiction of the child support officer under the Child Support Act 1991 having terminated on (*insert date*), this order, in so far as it relates to (*insert name(s) of child/children*), again shall have effect as from (*insert date of termination of child support officer's jurisdiction*).".

NOTE
[1] As amended by the Act of Sederunt (Ordinary Cause, Summary Application, Summary Cause and Small Claim Rules) Amendment (Miscellaneous) 2003 (SSI 2003/26), para.2(12) (effective January 24, 2003).

Applications to recall or vary an interdict
[1] **33.91A.** An application under section 32L(11)(b) of the Act of 1991 (orders preventing avoidance) for the variation or recall of an order for interdict is to be made by minute in the process of the action to which the application relates.

NOTE
[1] As inserted by the Act of Sederunt (Ordinary Cause Rules) Amendment (Child Maintenance and Other Payments Act 2008) 2010 (SSI 2010/120) r.2 (effective April 6, 2010).

[1] PART XIV

NOTE
[1] Inserted by SI 1996/2167 (effective November 1, 1996).

REFERRALS TO PRINCIPAL REPORTER

Application and interpretation of this Part
33.92.—(1) This Part applies where a sheriff, in a family action, refers a matter to the Principal Reporter under section 54 of the Act of 1995 (reference to the Principal Reporter by court).

(2) In this Part, "Principal Reporter" has the meaning assigned in section 93(1) of the Act of 1995.

Intimation to Principal Reporter
[1] **33.93.** Where a matter is referred by the sheriff to the Principal Reporter under section 54 of the Act of 1995, the interlocutor making the reference shall be intimated by the sheriff clerk forthwith to the Principal Reporter; and that intimation shall specify which of the conditions in paragraph (2)(a) to (h), (j), (k) or (l) of section 52 of that Act it appears to the sheriff has been satisfied.

NOTE
[1] As amended by Act of Sederunt (Ordinary Cause, Summary Application, Summary Cause and Small Claim Rules) Amendment (Miscellaneous) 2005 (SSI 2005/648), para.2 (effective January 2, 2006).

Intimation of decision by Principal Reporter
33.94.—(1) Where a matter has been referred by the sheriff to the Principal Reporter under section 54 of the Act of 1995 and the Principal Reporter, having made such investigation as he thinks appropriate and having reached the view that compulsory measures of supervision are necessary, arranges a children's hearing under section 69 of that Act (continuation or disposal of referral by children's hearing), the Principal Reporter shall intimate to the court which referred the matter to him—

    (a) the decision to arrange such children's hearing;

    (b) where there is no appeal made against the decision of that children's hearing once the period for appeal has expired, the outcome of the children's hearing; and

    (c) where such an appeal has been made, that an appeal has been made and, once determined, the outcome of that appeal.

(2) Where a matter has been referred by the sheriff to the Principal Reporter under section 54 of the Act of 1995 and the Principal Reporter, having made such investigation as he thinks appropriate and having considered whether compulsory measures of supervision are necessary, decides not to arrange a children's hearing under section 69 of that Act, the Principal Reporter shall intimate that decision to the court which referred the matter to him.

¹ PART XV

NOTE
  ¹ Inserted by SI 1996/2167 (effective November 1, 1996).

MANAGEMENT OF MONEY PAYABLE TO CHILDREN

33.95. Where the sheriff has made an order under section 13 of the Act of 1995 (awards of damages to children), an application by a person for an order by virtue of section 11(1)(d) of that Act (administration of child's property) may be made in the process of the cause in which the order under section 13 of that Act was made.

¹ CHAPTER 33A

CIVIL PARTNERSHIP ACTIONS

NOTE
  ¹ Inserted by Act of Sederunt (Ordinary Cause Rules) Amendment (Civil Partnership Act 2004) 2005 (SSI 2005/638), para.2 (effective December 8, 2005).

PART I

GENERAL PROVISIONS

Interpretation of this Chapter
  33A.1.—(1) In this Chapter, "civil partnership action" means—

    (a) an action of dissolution of civil partnership;

    (b) an action of separation of civil partners;

    (c) an action or application for an order under Chapter 3 or Chapter 4 of Part 3 of the Act of 2004;

    (d) an application for a declarator or other order under section 127 of the Act of 2004;

    (e) an action or application for financial provision after overseas proceedings as provided for in Schedule 11 to the Act of 2004;

  ¹ (f) an action for declarator of nullity of civil partnership.

  (2) In this Chapter, unless the context otherwise requires—

    "the Act of 1985" means the Family Law (Scotland) Act 1985;

    "the Act of 1995" means the Children (Scotland) Act 1995;

    "the Act of 2004" means the Civil Partnership Act 2004;

    "civil partnership" has the meaning assigned in section 1(1) of the Act of 2004;

    "contact order" has the meaning assigned in section 11(2)(d) of the Act of 1995;

    "Gender Recognition Panel" is to be construed in accordance with Schedule 1 to the Gender Recognition Act 2004;

    "interim gender recognition certificate" means the certificate issued under section 4 of the Gender Recognition Act 2004;

    "local authority" means a council constituted under section 2 of the Local Government etc. (Scotland) Act 1994;

    "mental disorder" has the meaning assigned in section 328 of the Mental Health (Care and Treatment) (Scotland) Act 2003;

    "order for financial provision" means, except in Part VII of this Chapter (financial provision after overseas proceedings as provided for in Schedule 11 to the Act of 2004), an order mentioned in section 8(1) of the Act of 1985;

    "parental responsibilities" has the meaning assigned in section 1(3) of the Act of 1995;

"parental rights" has the meaning assigned in section 2(4) of the Act of 1995;
"relevant interdict" has the meaning assigned in section 113(2) of the Act of 2004;
"residence order" has the meaning assigned in section 11(2)(c) of the Act of 1995;
"section 11 order" means an order under section 11 of the Act of 1995.

(3) For the purposes of rules 33A.2 (averments in actions of dissolution of civil partnership or separation of civil partners about other proceedings) and 33A.3 (averments where section 11 order sought) and, in relation to proceedings in another jurisdiction, Part XIII of this Chapter (sisting of civil partnership actions in Scotland), proceedings are continuing at any time after they have commenced and before they are finally disposed of.

NOTE
[1] Inserted by Act of Sederunt (Ordinary Cause Rules) Amendment (Family Law (Scotland) Act 2006 etc.) 2006, para.2 (SSI 2006/207) (effective May 4, 2006).

[1] *Averments in certain civil partnership actions about other proceedings*
33A.2.—[1] (1) This rule applies to an action of dissolution or declarator of nullity of civil partnership or separation of civil partners.

(2) In an action to which this rule applies, the pursuer shall state in the condescendence of the initial writ—
  (a) whether to his knowledge any proceedings are continuing in Scotland or in any other country in respect of the civil partnership to which the initial writ relates or are capable of affecting its validity or subsistence; and
  (b) where such proceedings are continuing—
      (i) the court, tribunal or authority before which the proceedings have been commenced;
      (ii) the date of commencement;
      (iii) the names of the parties;
      (iv) the date, or expected date of any proof (or its equivalent) in the proceedings; and
      (v) such other facts as may be relevant to the question of whether or not the action before the sheriff should be sisted under Part XIII of this Chapter.

(3) Where—
  (a) such proceedings are continuing;
  (b) the action before the sheriff is defended; and
  (c) either—
      (i) the initial writ does not contain the statement referred to in paragraph (2)(a); or
      (ii) the particulars mentioned in paragraph (2)(b) as set out in the initial writ are incomplete or incorrect,
any defences or minute, as the case may be, lodged by any person to the action shall include that statement and, where appropriate, the further or correct particulars mentioned in paragraph (2)(b).

NOTE
[1] As amended by Act of Sederunt (Ordinary Cause Rules) Amendment (Family Law (Scotland) Act 2006 etc.) 2006, para.2 (SSI 2006/207) (effective May 4, 2006).

Averments where section 11 order sought
33A.3.—(1) A party to a civil partnership action who makes an application in that action for a section 11 order in respect of a child shall include in his pleadings—
  [1] (a) where that action is an action of dissolution or declarator of nullity of civil partnership or separation of civil partners, averments giving particulars of any other proceedings known to him, whether in Scotland or elsewhere and whether concluded or not, which relate to the child in respect of whom the section 11 order is sought;
  (b) in any other civil partnership action—
      (i) the averments mentioned in paragraph (a); and
      (ii) averments giving particulars of any proceedings known to him which are continuing, whether in Scotland or elsewhere, and which relate to the civil partnership of either of the parents of that child.
  [2] (c) where the party seeks an order such as is mentioned in any of paragraphs (a) to (e) of subsection (2) of that section, an averment that no permanence order (as defined in section 80(2) of the Adoption and Children (Scotland) Act 2007) is in force in respect of the child.

(2) Where such other proceedings are continuing or have taken place and the averments of the applicant for such a section 11 order—
  (a) do not contain particulars of the other proceedings, or
  (b) contain particulars which are incomplete or incorrect,

any defences or minute, as the case may be, lodged by any party to the civil partnership action shall include such particulars or such further or correct particulars as are known to him.

(3) In paragraph 1(b)(ii), "child" includes a child of the family within the meaning assigned in section 101(7) of the Act of 2004.

NOTES

[1] As amended by Act of Sederunt (Ordinary Cause Rules) Amendment (Family Law (Scotland) Act 2006 etc.) 2006, para.2 (SSI 2006/207) (effective May 4, 2006).

[2] As inserted by the Act of Sederunt (Sheriff Court Rules Amendment) (Adoption and Children (Scotland) Act 2007) 2009 (SSI 2009/284) (effective September 28, 2009).

Averments where identity or address of person not known

33A.4. In a civil partnership action, where the identity or address of any person referred to in rule 33A.7 as a person in respect of whom a warrant for intimation requires to be applied for is not known and cannot reasonably be ascertained, the party required to apply for the warrant shall include in his pleadings an averment of that fact and averments setting out what steps have been taken to ascertain the identity or address, as the case may be, of that person.

Averments about maintenance orders

33A.5. In a civil partnership action in which an order for aliment or periodical allowance is sought, or is sought to be varied or recalled, by any party, the pleadings of that party shall contain an averment stating whether and, if so, when and by whom, a maintenance order (within the meaning of section 106 of the Debtors (Scotland) Act 1987) has been granted in favour of or against that party or of any other person in respect of whom the order is sought.

Averments where aliment or financial provision sought

33A.6.—(1) In this rule—

"the Act of 1991" means the Child Support Act 1991;

"child" has the meaning assigned in section 55 of the Act of 1991;

"crave relating to aliment" means—

(a) for the purposes of paragraph (2), a crave for decree of aliment in relation to a child or for recall or variation of such a decree; and

(b) for the purposes of paragraph (3), a crave for decree of aliment in relation to a child or for recall or variation of such a decree or for the variation or termination of an agreement on aliment in relation to a child;

"maintenance calculation" has the meaning assigned in section 54 of the Act of 1991.

(2) A civil partnership action containing a crave relating to aliment and to which section 8(6), (7), (8), or (10) of the Act of 1991 (top up maintenance orders) applies shall—

(a) include averments stating, where appropriate—

(i) that a maintenance calculation under section 11 of that Act (maintenance calculations) is in force;

(ii) the date of the maintenance calculation;

(iii) the amount and frequency of periodical payments of child support maintenance fixed by the maintenance calculation; and

(iv) the grounds on which the sheriff retains jurisdiction under section 8(6), (7), (8) or (10) of that Act; and

(b) unless the sheriff on cause shown otherwise directs, be accompanied by any document issued by the Secretary of State to the party intimating the making of the maintenance calculation referred to in sub paragraph (a).

(3) A civil partnership action containing a crave relating to aliment, and to which section 8(6), (7), (8) or (10) of the Act of 1991 does not apply, shall include averments stating—

(a) that the habitual residence of the absent parent, person with care or qualifying child, within the meaning of section 3 of that Act, is furth of the United Kingdom; or

(b) that the child is not a child within the meaning of section 55 of that Act.

(4) A civil partnership action involving parties in respect of whom a decision has been made in any application, review or appeal under the Act of 1991 relating to any child of those parties, shall—

(a) include averments stating that such a decision has been made and giving details of that decision; and

(b) unless the sheriff on cause shown otherwise directs, be accompanied by any document issued by the Secretary of State to the parties intimating that decision.

Warrants and forms for intimation

33A.7. —(1) Subject to paragraphs (5) and (7), in the initial writ in a civil partnership action, the pursuer shall include a crave for a warrant for intimation—

(a) in an action where the address of the defender is not known to the pursuer and cannot reasonably be ascertained, to—
    (i) every person who was a child of the family (within the meaning of section 101(7) of the Act of 2004) and who has reached the age of 16 years, and
    (ii) one of the next of kin of the defender who has reached that age,
unless the address of such a person is not known to the pursuer and cannot reasonably be ascertained, and a notice of intimation in Form CP1 shall be attached to the copy of the initial writ intimated to any such person;

(b) in an action where the defender is a person who is suffering from a mental disorder, to—
    (i) those persons mentioned in sub paragraph (a)(i) and (ii), unless the address of such person is not known to the pursuer and cannot reasonably be ascertained; and
    (ii) any person who holds the office of guardian, or continuing or welfare attorney to the defender under or by virtue of the Adults with Incapacity (Scotland) Act 2000,
and a notice of intimation in Form CP2 shall be attached to the copy of the initial writ intimated to any such person;

[1] (c) in an action of dissolution or declarator of nullity of civil partnership or separation of civil partners where the sheriff may make a section 11 order in respect of a child—
    (i) who is in the care of a local authority, to that authority and a notice of intimation in Form CP3 shall be attached to the initial writ intimated to that authority;
    (ii) who, being a child of one party to the civil partnership, has been accepted as a child of the family by the other party to the civil partnership and who is liable to be maintained by a third party, to that third party, and a notice of intimation in Form CP3 shall be attached to the initial writ intimated to that third party; or
    (iii) in respect of whom a third party in fact exercises care or control, to that third party, and a notice of intimation in Form CP4 shall be attached to the initial writ intimated to that third party;

(d) in an action where the pursuer craves a section 11 order, to any parent or guardian of the child who is not a party to the action, and a notice of intimation in Form CP5 shall be attached to the initial writ intimated to any such parent or guardian;

(e) in an action where the pursuer craves a residence order in respect of a child and he is—
    (i) not a parent of that child; and
    (ii) resident in Scotland when the initial writ is lodged,
to the local authority within which area the pursuer resides, and a notice of intimation in Form CP6 shall be attached to the initial writ intimated to that authority;

(f) in an action which includes a crave for a section 11 order, to the child to whom such an order would relate if not a party to the action, and a notice of intimation in Form CP7 shall be intimated to that child;

(g) in an action where the pursuer makes an application for an order under section 8(1)(aa) of the Act of 1985 (transfer of property) and—
    (i) the consent of a third party to such a transfer is necessary by virtue of an obligation, enactment or rule of law, or
    (ii) the property is subject to a security,
to the third party or creditor, as the case may be, and a notice of intimation in Form CP8 shall be attached to the initial writ intimated to any such person;

(h) in an action where the pursuer makes an application for an order under section 18 of the Act of 1985 (which relates to avoidance transactions), to—
    (i) any third party in whose favour the transfer of, or transaction involving, the property is to be or was made, and
    (ii) any other person having an interest in the transfer of, or transaction involving, the property,
and a notice of intimation in Form CP9 shall be attached to the initial writ intimated to any such person;

(i) in an action where the pursuer makes an application for an order under Chapter 3 of Part 3 of the Act of 2004, where the application is under section 102(1)(e), 102(4)(a), 103(1), 103(2), 104, 107 or 112 of that Act, and the entitled civil partner is a tenant or occupies the family home by permission of a third party, to the landlord or the third party, as the case may be and a notice of intimation in Form CP10 shall be attached to the initial writ intimated to any such person;

(j) in an action where the pursuer makes an application for an order under section 8(1)(ba) of the Act of 1985 (orders under section 12A of the Act of 1985 for pension lump sum), to the person responsible for the pension arrangement, and a notice of intimation in Form CP11 shall be attached to the initial writ intimated to any such person; and

   (k) in an action where a pursuer makes an application for an order under section 8(1)(baa) of the Act of 1985 (pension sharing orders), to the person responsible for the pension arrangement and a notice of intimation in Form CP12 shall be attached to the initial writ intimated to any such person.

(2) Expressions used in paragraph (1)(i) which are also used in Chapter 3 of Part 3 of the Act of 2004 have the same meaning as in that Chapter.

(3) A notice of intimation under paragraph (1) shall be on a period of notice of 21 days unless the sheriff otherwise orders; but the sheriff shall not order a period of notice of less than 2 days.

(4) In a civil partnership action, where the pursuer—

   (a) craves a residence order in respect of a child;

   (b) is not a parent of the child, and

   (c) is not resident in Scotland when the initial writ is lodged for warranting,

he shall include a crave for an order for intimation in Form CP6 to such local authority as the sheriff thinks fit.

(5) Where the address of a person mentioned in paragraph (1)(c), (d), (f), (g), (h), (i), (j) or (k) is not known and cannot reasonably be ascertained, the pursuer shall include a crave in the initial writ to dispense with intimation; and the sheriff may grant that crave or make such other order as he thinks fit.

(6) Where the identity or address of a person to whom intimation of a civil partnership action is required becomes known during the course of the action, the party who would have been required to insert a warrant for intimation to that person shall lodge a motion for a warrant for intimation to that person or to dispense with such intimation.

(7) Where a pursuer considers that to order intimation to a child under paragraph (1)(f) is inappropriate, he shall—

   (a) include a crave in the initial writ to dispense with intimation to that child; and

   (b) include in the initial writ averments setting out the reasons why such intimation is inappropriate;

and the sheriff may dispense with such intimation or make such other order as he thinks fit.

NOTE

[1] As amended by Act of Sederunt (Ordinary Cause Rules) Amendment (Family Law (Scotland) Act 2006 etc.) 2006, para.2 (SSI 2006/207) (effective May 4, 2006).

Intimation where alleged association

33A.8.—(1) In a civil partnership action where the pursuer founds upon an alleged association between the defender and another named person, the pursuer shall, immediately after the expiry of the period of notice, lodge a motion for an order for intimation to that person or to dispense with such intimation.

(2) In determining a motion under paragraph (1), the sheriff may—

   (a) make such order for intimation as he thinks fit; or

   (b) dispense with intimation; and

   (c) where he dispenses with intimation, order that the name of that person be deleted from the condescendence of the initial writ.

(3) Where intimation is ordered under paragraph (2), a copy of the initial writ and an intimation in Form CP13 shall be intimated to the named person.

(4) In paragraph (1), "association" means sodomy, incest, or any homosexual or heterosexual relationship.

Productions in action of dissolution of civil partnership or where section 11 order may be made

33A.9.—(1) This rule applies unless the sheriff directs otherwise.

[1] (2) In an action of dissolution or declarator of nullity of civil partnership, a warrant for citation shall not be granted without there being produced with the initial writ—

   (a) an extract of the relevant entry in the civil partnership register or an equivalent document; and

   (b) where the ground of action is that an interim gender recognition certificate has, after the date of registration of the civil partnership, been issued to either of the civil partners—

      (i) where the pursuer is the subject of the interim gender recognition certificate, the interim gender recognition certificate or, failing that, a certified copy of the interim gender recognition certificate; or

      (ii) where the defender is the subject of the interim gender recognition certificate, a certified copy of the interim gender recognition certificate.

(3) In a civil partnership action which includes a crave for a section 11 order, a warrant for

citation shall not be granted without there being produced with the initial writ an extract of the relevant entry in the register of births or an equivalent document.

(4) For the purposes of this rule, a certified copy of an interim gender recognition certificate shall be a copy of that certificate sealed with the seal of the Gender Recognition Panels and certified to be a true copy by an officer authorised by the President of Gender Recognition Panels.

NOTE
[1] As amended by Act of Sederunt (Ordinary Cause Rules) Amendment (Family Law (Scotland) Act 2006 etc.) 2006, para.2 (SSI 2006/207) (effective May 4, 2006).

Warrant of citation
33A.10. The warrant of citation in a civil partnership action shall be in Form CP14.

Form of citation and certificate
33A.11.—(1) Subject to rule 5.6 (service where address of person is not known), citation of a defender shall be in Form CP15, which shall be attached to a copy of the initial writ and warrant of citation and shall have appended to it a notice of intention to defend in Form CP16.

(2) The certificate of citation shall be in Form CP17 which shall be attached to the initial writ.

Execution of service on, or intimation to, local authority
33A.12.—(1) Where a local authority referred to in rule 33A.7(1)(e)(residence order sought by non parent resident in Scotland) or rule 33A.7(4) (residence order sought by pursuer not resident in Scotland) is named as a defender in an initial writ at the time it is lodged, service of the initial writ on that local authority shall be executed within 7 days after the date of granting of the warrant of citation.

(2) Where in a civil partnership action—
    (a) to which rule 33A.7(1)(e) applies, or
    (b) in which a crave under rule 33A.7(4) is required,
the local authority referred to in that provision is named as a defender in the initial writ at the time it is lodged, a notice in Form CP6 shall be attached to the copy of the initial writ served on that local authority.

(3) In any civil partnership action, the sheriff may, if he thinks fit, order intimation to a local authority; and such intimation shall be in Form CP6; and

(4) Where, by virtue of paragraph (3) of this rule, or rule 33A.7(1)(e), or rule 33A.7(4), intimation of an application for a residence order is to be made to a local authority, intimation to that local authority shall be given within 7 days after the date on which a warrant of citation, or an order for intimation, as the case may be, has been granted.

Service in cases of mental disorder of defender
33A.13.—(1) In a civil partnership action where the defender suffers or appears to suffer from mental disorder and is resident in a hospital or other similar institution, citation shall be executed by registered post or the first class recorded delivery service addressed to the medical officer in charge of that hospital or institution; and there shall be included with the copy of the initial writ—
    (a) a citation in Form CP15;
    (b) any notice required by rule 33A.14(1);
    (c) a request in Form CP18;
    (d) a form of certificate in Form CP19 requesting the medical officer to—
        (i) deliver and explain the initial writ, citation and any notice or form of notice of consent required under rule 33A.14(1) personally to the defender; or
        (ii) certify that such delivery or explanation would be dangerous to the health or mental condition of the defender; and
    (e) a stamped envelope addressed for return of that certificate to the pursuer or his solicitor, if he has one.

(2) The medical officer referred to in paragraph (1) shall send the certificate in Form CP19 duly completed to the pursuer or his solicitor, as the case may be.

(3) The certificate mentioned in paragraph (2) shall be attached to the certificate of citation.

(4) Where such a certificate bears that the initial writ has not been delivered to the defender, the sheriff may, at any time before decree—
    (a) order such further medical inquiry, and
    (b) make such order for further service or intimation,
as he thinks fit.

Notices in certain actions of dissolution of civil partnership or separation of civil partners

33A.14.—(1) In the following actions of dissolution of civil partnership or separation of civil partners there shall be attached to the copy of the initial writ served on the defender—

[1] (a) in an action relying on section 117(3)(c) of the Act of 2004 (no cohabitation for one year with consent of defender to decree)—

    (i) which is an action of dissolution of civil partnership, a notice in Form CP20 and a notice of consent in Form CP21;

    (ii) which is an action of separation of civil partners, a notice in Form CP22 and a form of notice of consent in Form CP23;

[1] (b) in an action relying on section 117(3)(d) of the Act of 2004 (no cohabitation for two years)—

    (i) which is an action of dissolution of civil partnership, a notice in Form CP24;

    (ii) which is an action of separation of civil partners, a notice in Form CP25.

[2] (c) in an action relying on section 117(2)(b) of the Act of 2004 (grounds of dissolution: interim gender recognition certificate), a notice in Form CP25A.

(2) The certificate of citation of an initial writ in an action mentioned in paragraph (1) shall state which notice or form mentioned in paragraph (1) has been attached to the initial writ.

NOTES

[1] As amended by Act of Sederunt (Ordinary Cause Rules) Amendment (Family Law (Scotland) Act 2006 etc.) 2006, para.2 (SSI 2006/207) (effective May 4, 2006).

[2] Inserted by Act of Sederunt (Ordinary Cause Rules) Amendment (Family Law (Scotland) Act 2006 etc.) 2006, para.2 (SSI 2006/207) (effective May 4, 2006).

Orders for intimation

33A.15.—(1) In any civil partnership action, the sheriff may, at any time—

    (a) subject to paragraph (2), order intimation to be made on such person as he thinks fit;

    (b) postpone intimation, where he considers that such postponement is appropriate and, in that case, the sheriff shall make such order in respect of postponement of intimation as he thinks fit; or

    (c) dispense with intimation, where he considers that such dispensation is appropriate.

(2) Where the sheriff is considering whether to make a section 11 order by virtue of section 12 of the Act of 1995 (restrictions on decrees for dissolution of civil partnership, separation or annulment affecting children), he shall, subject to paragraph (1)(c) and without prejudice to paragraph (1)(b) of this rule, order intimation in Form CP7 to the child to whom the section 11 order would relate unless—

    (a) intimation has been given to the child under rule 33A.7(1)(f); or

    (b) the sheriff considers that the child is not of sufficient age or maturity to express his views.

(3) Where a party makes a crave or averment in a civil partnership action which, had it been made in an initial writ, would have required a warrant for intimation under rule 33.7, that party shall include a crave in his writ for a warrant for intimation or to dispense with such intimation; and rule 33A.7 shall, with the necessary modifications, apply to a crave for a warrant under this paragraph as it applies to a crave for a warrant under that rule.

Appointment of curators ad litem to defenders

33A.16.—[1] (1) This rule applies to an action of dissolution or declarator of nullity of civil partnership or separation of civil partners where it appears to the court that the defender is suffering from a mental disorder.

(2) In an action to which this rule applies, the sheriff shall—

    (a) appoint a curator *ad litem* to the defender;

[1] (b) where the facts set out in section 117(3)(c) of the Act of 2004 (no cohabitation for one year with consent of defender to decree) are relied on—

    (i) make an order for intimation of the ground of the action to the Mental Welfare Commission for Scotland; and

    (ii) include in such an order a requirement that the Commission sends to the sheriff clerk a report indicating whether in its opinion the defender is capable of deciding whether or not to give consent to the granting of decree.

(3) Within 7 days after the appointment of a curator *ad litem* under paragraph (2)(a), the pursuer shall send to him—

    (a) a copy of the initial writ and any defences (including any adjustments and amendments) lodged; and

    (b) a copy of any notice in Form G5 sent to him by the sheriff clerk.

(4) On receipt of a report required under paragraph (2)(b)(ii), the sheriff clerk shall—

    (a) lodge the report in process; and

   (b) intimate that this has been done to—
       (i) the pursuer;
      (ii) the solicitor for the defender, if known; and
     (iii) the curator *ad litem*.

  (5) The curator *ad litem* shall lodge in process one of the writs mentioned in paragraph (6)—
   (a) within 14 days after the report required under paragraph (2)(b)(ii) has been lodged in process; or
   (b) where no such report is required, within 21 days after the date of his appointment under paragraph (2)(a).

  (6) The writs referred to in paragraph (5) are—
   (a) a notice of intention to defend;
   (b) defences to the action;
   (c) a minute adopting defences already lodged; and
   (d) a minute stating that the curator *ad litem* does not intend to lodge defences.

  (7) Notwithstanding that he has lodged a minute stating that he does not intend to lodge defences, a curator *ad litem* may appear at any stage of the action to protect the interests of the defender.

  (8) If, at any time, it appears to the curator *ad litem* that the defender is not suffering from mental disorder, he may report that fact to the court and seek his own discharge.

  (9) The pursuer shall be responsible, in the first instance, for payment of the fees and outlays of the curator *ad litem* incurred during the period from his appointment until—
   (a) he lodges a minute stating that he does not intend to lodge defences;
   (b) he decides to instruct the lodging of defences or a minute adopting defences already lodged; or
   (c) being satisfied after investigation that the defender is not suffering from mental disorder, he is discharged.

NOTE
[1] As amended by Act of Sederunt (Ordinary Cause Rules) Amendment (Family Law (Scotland) Act 2006 etc.) 2006, para.2 (SSI 2006/207) (effective May 4, 2006).

Applications for sist
  33A.17. An application for a sist, or the recall of a sist, under Part XIII of this Chapter shall be made by written motion.

Notices of consent to dissolution of civil partnership or separation of civil partners
  33A.18.—[1] (1) Where, in an action of dissolution of civil partnership or separation of civil partners in which the facts in section 117(3)(c) of the Act of 2004 (no cohabitation for one year with consent of defender to decree) are relied on, the defender wishes to consent to the grant of decree of dissolution of civil partnership or separation of civil partners he shall do so by giving notice in writing in Form CP21 (dissolution) or Form CP23 (separation), as the case may be, to the sheriff clerk.

  (2) The evidence of one witness shall be sufficient for the purpose of establishing that the signature on a notice of consent under paragraph (1) is that of the defender.

  (3) In an action of dissolution of civil partnership or separation of civil partners where the initial writ includes, for the purposes of section 117(3)(c) of the Act of 2004, an averment that the defender consents to the grant of decree, the defender may give notice by letter sent to the sheriff clerk stating that he has not so consented or that he withdraws any consent which he has already given.

  (4) On receipt of a letter under paragraph (3), the sheriff clerk shall intimate the terms of the letter to the pursuer.

  (5) On receipt of any intimation under paragraph (4), the pursuer may, within 14 days after the date of the intimation, if none of the other facts mentioned in section 117(3) of the Act of 2004 is averred in the initial writ, lodge a motion for the action to be sisted.

  (6) If no such motion is lodged, the pursuer shall be deemed to have abandoned the action and the action shall be dismissed.

  (7) If a motion under paragraph (5) is granted and the sist is not recalled or renewed within a period of 6 months from the date of the interlocutor granting the sist, the pursuer shall be deemed to have abandoned the action and the action shall be dismissed.

NOTE
[1] As amended by Act of Sederunt (Ordinary Cause Rules) Amendment (Family Law (Scotland) Act 2006 etc.) 2006, para.2 (SSI 2006/207) (effective May 4, 2006).

Procedure in respect of children

33A.19.—(1) In a civil partnership action, in relation to any matter affecting a child, where that child has—

    (a) returned to the sheriff clerk Form CP7, or

    (b) otherwise indicated to the court a wish to express views on a matter affecting him, the sheriff shall not grant any order unless an opportunity has been given for the views of that child to be obtained or heard.

(2) Where a child has indicated his wish to express his views, the sheriff shall order such steps to be taken as he considers appropriate to ascertain the views of that child.

(3) The sheriff shall not grant an order in a civil partnership action, in relation to any matter affecting a child who has indicated his wish to express his views, unless due weight has been given by the sheriff to the views expressed by that child, having due regard to his age and maturity.

Recording of views of the child

33A.20.—(1) This rule applies where a child expresses a view on a matter affecting him whether expressed personally to the sheriff or to a person appointed by the sheriff for that purpose or provided by the child in writing.

(2) The sheriff, or the person appointed by the sheriff, shall record the views of the child in writing; and the sheriff may direct that such views, and any written views, given by a child shall—

    (a) be sealed in an envelope marked "Views of the child confidential";

    (b) be kept in the court process without being recorded in the inventory of process;

    (c) be available to a sheriff only;

    (d) not be opened by any person other than a sheriff; and

    (e) not form a borrowable part of the process.

Appointment of local authority or reporter to report on a child

33A.21.—(1) This rule applies where, at any stage of a civil partnership action, the sheriff appoints—

    (a) a local authority, whether under section 11(1) of the Matrimonial Proceedings (Children) Act 1958 (reports as to arrangements for future care and upbringing of children) or otherwise, or

    (b) another person (referred to in this rule as a "reporter"), whether under a provision mentioned in sub paragraph (a) or otherwise,

to investigate and report to the court on the circumstances of a child and on proposed arrangements for the care and upbringing of the child.

(2) On making an appointment referred to in paragraph (1), the sheriff shall direct that the party who sought the appointment or, where the court makes the appointment of its own motion, the pursuer or minuter, as the case may be, shall—

    (a) instruct the local authority or reporter; and

    (b) be responsible, in the first instance, for the fees and outlays of the local authority or reporter appointed.

(3) Where a local authority or reporter is appointed—

    (a) the party who sought the appointment, or

    (b) where the sheriff makes the appointment of his own motion, the pursuer or minuter, as the case may be,

shall, within 7 days after the date of the appointment, intimate the name and address of the local authority or reporter to any local authority to which intimation of the family action has been made.

(4) On completion of a report referred to in paragraph (1), the local authority or reporter, as the case may be, shall send the report, with a copy of it for each party, to the sheriff clerk.

(5) On receipt of such a report, the sheriff clerk shall send a copy of the report to each party.

(6) Where a local authority or reporter has been appointed to investigate and report in respect of a child, an application for a section 11 order in respect of that child shall not be determined until the report of the local authority or reporter, as the case may be, has been lodged.

Referral to family mediation

33A.22. In any civil partnership action in which an order in relation to parental responsibilities or parental rights is in issue, the sheriff may, at any stage of the action, where he considers it appropriate to do so, refer that issue to a mediator accredited to a specified family mediation organisation.

Child Welfare Hearing

33A.23.—(1) Where—

(a) on the lodging of a notice of intention to defend in a civil partnership action in which the initial writ seeks or includes a crave for a section 11 order, a defender wishes to oppose any such crave or order, or seeks the same order as that craved by the pursuer,

(b) on the lodging of a notice of intention to defend in a civil partnership action, the defender seeks a section 11 order which is not craved by the pursuer, or

(c) in any other circumstances in a civil partnership action, the sheriff considers that a Child Welfare Hearing should be fixed and makes an order (whether at his own instance or on the motion of a party) that such a hearing shall be fixed,

the sheriff clerk shall fix a date and time for a Child Welfare Hearing on the first suitable court date occurring not sooner than 21 days after the lodging of such notice of intention to defend, unless the sheriff directs the hearing to be held on an earlier date.

(2) On fixing the date for the Child Welfare Hearing, the sheriff clerk shall intimate the date of the Child Welfare Hearing to the parties in Form CP26.

(3) The fixing of the date of the Child Welfare Hearing shall not affect the right of a party to make any other application to the court whether by motion or otherwise.

[1] (4) At the Child Welfare Hearing (which may be held in private), the sheriff shall seek to secure the expeditious resolution of disputes in relation to the child by ascertaining from the parties the matters in dispute and any information relevant to that dispute, and may—

(a) order such steps to be taken, make such order, if any, or order further procedure, as he thinks fit, and

(b) ascertain whether there is or is likely to be a vulnerable witness within the meaning of section 11(1) of the Act of 2004 who is to give evidence at any proof or hearing and whether any order under section 12(1) of the Act of 2004 requires to be made.

(5) All parties (including a child who has indicated his wish to attend) shall, except on cause shown, attend the Child Welfare Hearing personally.

(6) It shall be the duty of the parties to provide the sheriff with sufficient information to enable him to conduct the Child Welfare Hearing.

NOTE
[1]As substituted by the Act of Sederunt (Ordinary Cause, Summary Application, Summary Cause and Small Claim Rules) Amendment (Vulnerable Witnesses (Scotland) Act 2004) 2007, r.2(10) (effective November 1, 2007).

Applications for orders to disclose whereabouts of children
33A.24.—(1) An application in a civil partnership action for an order under section 33(1) of the Family Law Act 1986 (which relates to the disclosure of the whereabouts of a child) shall be made by motion.

(2) Where the sheriff makes an order under section 33(1) of the Family Law Act 1986, he may ordain the person against whom the order has been made to appear before him or to lodge an affidavit.

Applications in relation to removal of children
33A.25.—(1) An application in a civil partnership action for leave under section 51(1) of the Children Act 1975 (authority to remove a child from the care and possession of the applicant for a residence order) or for an order under section 35(3) of the Family Law Act 1986 (application for interdict or interim interdict prohibiting removal of child from jurisdiction) shall be made—

(a) by a party to the action, by motion; or

(b) by a person who is not a party to the action, by minute.

(2) An application under section 35(3) of the Family Law Act 1986 need not be served or intimated.

(3) An application in a civil partnership action under section 23(2) of the Child Abduction and Custody Act 1985 (declarator that removal of child from United Kingdom was unlawful) shall be made—

(a) in an action depending before the sheriff—

(i) by a party, in the initial writ, defences or minute, as the case may be, or by motion; or

(ii) by any other person, by minute; or

(b) after final decree, by minute in the process of the action to which the application relates.

Intimation to local authority before supervised contact order
33A.26. Where in a civil partnership action the sheriff, at his own instance or on the motion of a party, is considering making a contact order or an interim contact order subject to supervision by the social work department of a local authority, he shall ordain the party moving

for such an order to intimate to the chief executive of that local authority (where not already a party to the action and represented at the hearing at which the issue arises)—
    (a) the terms of any relevant motion;
    (b) the intention of the sheriff to order that the contact order be supervised by the social work department of that local authority; and
    (c) that the local authority shall, within such period as the sheriff has determined—
        (i) notify the sheriff clerk whether it intends to make representations to the sheriff; and
        (ii) where it intends to make representations in writing, do so within that period.

Joint minutes
    33A.27. Where any parties in a civil partnership action have reached agreement in relation to—
    (a) a section 11 order;
    (b) aliment for a child; or
    (c) an order for financial provision,
a joint minute may be entered into expressing that agreement; and, subject to rule 33A.19(3) (no order before views of child expressed), the sheriff may grant decree in respect of those parts of the joint minute in relation to which he could otherwise make an order, whether or not such a decree would include a matter for which there was no crave.

Affidavits
    33A.28. The sheriff in a civil partnership action may accept evidence by affidavit at any hearing for an order or interim order.

Part II

Undefended Civil Partnership Actions

Evidence in certain undefended civil partnership actions
    33A.29.—(1) This rule—
    (a) subject to sub paragraph (b), applies to all civil partnership actions in which no notice of intention to defend has been lodged, other than a civil partnership action—
        (i) for financial provision after overseas proceedings as provided for in Schedule 11 to the Act of 2004; or
        (ii) for an order under Chapter 3 or Chapter 4 of Part 3 or section 127 of the Act of 2004;
    (b) applies to a civil partnership action in which a curator *ad litem* has been appointed under rule 33A.16 where the curator *ad litem* to the defender has lodged a minute intimating that he does not intend to lodge defences;
    (c) applies to any civil partnership action which proceeds at any stage as undefended where the sheriff so directs;
    (d) applies to the merits of a civil partnership action which is undefended on the merits where the sheriff so directs, notwithstanding that the action is defended on an ancillary matter.
    (2) Unless the sheriff otherwise directs, evidence shall be given by affidavits.
    (3) Unless the sheriff otherwise directs, evidence relating to the welfare of a child shall be given by affidavit, at least one affidavit being emitted by a person other than a parent or party to the action.
    (4) Evidence in the form of a written statement bearing to be the professional opinion of a duly qualified medical practitioner, which has been signed by him and lodged in process, shall be admissible in place of parole evidence by him.

Procedure for decree in actions under rule 33A.29
    33A.30.—(1) In an action to which rule 33A.29 (evidence in certain undefended civil partnership actions) applies, the pursuer shall at any time after the expiry of the period for lodging a notice of intention to defend—
    (a) lodge in process the affidavit evidence; and
    (b) endorse a minute in Form CP27 on the initial writ.
    (2) The sheriff may, at any time after the pursuer has complied with paragraph (1), without requiring the appearance of parties—
    (a) grant decree in terms of the motion for decree; or
    (b) remit the cause for such further procedure, if any, including proof by parole evidence, as the sheriff thinks fit.

Extracts of undefended decree

33A.31. In an action to which rule 33A.29 (evidence in certain undefended civil partnership actions) applies, the sheriff clerk shall, after the expiry of 14 days after the grant of decree under rule 33A.30 (procedure for decree in actions under rule 33A.29), issue to the pursuer and the defender an extract decree.

No recording of evidence

33A.32. It shall not be necessary to record the evidence in any proof in a civil partnership action which is not defended.

Disapplication of Chapter 15

33A.33. Other than rule 15.1(1), Chapter 15 (motions) shall not apply to a civil partnership action in which no notice of intention to defend has been lodged, or to a civil partnership action in so far as it proceeds as undefended.

Late appearance and application for recall by defenders

[1] **33A.33A.**—(1) In a cause mentioned in rule 33A.1(a), (b) or (f), the sheriff may, at any stage of the action before the granting of final decree, make an order with such conditions, if any, as he thinks fit—

    (a) directing that a defender who has not lodged a notice of intention to defend be treated as if he had lodged such a notice and the period of notice had expired on the date on which the order was made; or

    (b) allowing a defender who has not lodged a notice of intention to defend to appear and be heard at a diet of proof although he has not lodged defences, but he shall not, in that event, be allowed to lead evidence without the pursuer's consent.

(2) Where the sheriff makes an order under paragraph (1), the pursuer may recall a witness already examined or lead other evidence whether or not he closed his proof before that order was made.

(3) Where no order under paragraph (1) has been sought by a defender who has not lodged a notice of intention to defend and decree is granted against him, the sheriff may, on an application made within 14 days of the date of the decree, and with such conditions, if any, as he thinks fit, make an order recalling the decree.

(4) Where the sheriff makes an order under paragraph (3), the cause shall thereafter proceed as if the defender had lodged a notice of intention to defend and the period of notice had expired on the date on which the decree was recalled.

(5) An application under paragraph (1) or (3) shall be made by note setting out the proposed defence and explaining the defender's failure to appear.

(6) An application under paragraph (1) or (3) shall not affect any right of appeal the defender may otherwise have.

(7) A note lodged in an application under paragraph (1) or (3) shall be served on the pursuer and any other party.

NOTE

[1] As inserted by the Act of Sederunt (Sheriff Court Rules) (Miscellaneous Amendments) 2008 (SSI 2008/223) para.2(3) (effective July 1, 2008).

PART III

DEFENDED CIVIL PARTNERSHIP ACTIONS

Notice of intention to defend and defences

33A.34.—(1) This rule applies where the defender in a civil partnership action seeks—

    (a) to oppose any crave in the initial writ;

    (b) to make a claim for—

        (i) aliment;

        (ii) an order for financial provision within the meaning of section 8(3) of the Act of 1985; or

        (iii) a section 11 order; or

    (c) an order—

        (i) under section 16(1)(b) or (3) of the Act of 1985 (setting aside or varying agreement as to financial provision);

        (ii) under section 18 of the Act of 1985 (which relates to avoidance transactions); or

        (iii) under Chapter 3 or Chapter 4 of Part 3 or section 127 of the Act of 2004; or

    (d) to challenge the jurisdiction of the court.

(2) In an action to which this rule applies, the defender shall—

(a) lodge a notice of intention to defend in Form CP16 before the expiry of the period of notice; and

(b) make any claim or seek any order referred to in paragraph (1), as the case may be, in those defences by setting out in his defences—

    (i) craves;

    (ii) averments in the answers to the condescendence in support of those craves; and

    (iii) appropriate pleas-in-law.

(3) Where a defender intends to make an application for a section 11 order which, had it been made in an initial writ, would have required a warrant for intimation under rule 33A.7, the defender shall include a crave in his notice of intention to defend for a warrant for intimation or to dispense with such intimation; and rule 33A.7 shall, with the necessary modifications, apply to a crave for a warrant under this paragraph as it applies to a crave for a warrant under that rule.

Abandonment by pursuer

33A.35. Notwithstanding abandonment by a pursuer of a civil partnership action, the court may allow a defender to pursue an order or claim sought in his defences; and the proceedings in relation to that order or claim shall continue in dependence as if a separate cause.

Attendance of parties at Options Hearing

33A.36. All parties to a civil partnership action shall, except on cause shown, attend personally the hearing under rule 9.12 (Options Hearing).

Decree by default

33A.37.—(1) In a civil partnership action in which the defender has lodged a notice of intention to defend, where a party fails—

(a) to lodge, or intimate the lodging of, any production or part of process;

(b) to implement an order of the sheriff within a specified period; or

(c) to appear or be represented at any diet,

that party shall be in default.

(2) Where a party is in default under paragraph (1), the sheriff may—

[1] (a) where the civil partnership action is one mentioned in rule 33A.1(1) (a), (b) or (f) allow that action to proceed as undefended under Part II of this Chapter; or

(b) where the civil partnership action is one mentioned in rule 33A.1(1)(c) to (e), grant decree as craved; or

(c) grant decree of absolvitor; or

(d) dismiss the civil partnership action or any claim made or order sought; and

(e) award expenses.

(3) Where no party appears at a diet in a civil partnership action, the sheriff may dismiss that action.

(4) In a civil partnership action, the sheriff may, on cause shown, prorogate the time for lodging any production or part of process, or for intimating or implementing any order.

NOTE

[1] As amended by Act of Sederunt (Ordinary Cause Rules) Amendment (Family Law (Scotland) Act 2006 etc.) 2006, para.2 (SSI 2006/207) (effective May 4, 2006).

PART IV

APPLICATIONS AND ORDERS RELATING TO CHILDREN IN CERTAIN ACTIONS

Application and interpretation of this Part

[1] **33A.38.** This Part applies to an action of dissolution or declarator of nullity of civil partnership or separation of civil partners.

NOTE

[1] As amended by Act of Sederunt (Ordinary Cause Rules) Amendment (Family Law (Scotland) Act 2006 etc.) 2006, para.2 (SSI 2006/207) (effective May 4, 2006).

Applications in actions to which this Part applies

33A.39.—(1) An application for an order mentioned in paragraph (2) shall be made—

(a) by a crave in the initial writ or defences, as the case may be, in an action to which this Part applies; or

(b) where the application is made by a person other than the pursuer or defender, by minute in that action.

(2) The orders referred to in paragraph (1) are:—

    (a) an order for a section 11 order; and

    (b) an order for aliment for a child.

Applications in depending actions by motion

33A.40. An application by a party in an action depending before the court to which this Part applies for, or for variation of, an order for—

    (a) interim aliment for a child under the age of 18; or

    (b) a residence order or a contact order,

shall be made by motion.

Applications after decree relating to a section 11 order

33A.41.—(1) An application after final decree for, or for the variation or recall of, a section 11 order or in relation to the enforcement of such an order shall be made by minute in the process of the action to which the application relates.

(2) Where a minute has been lodged under paragraph (1), any party may apply by motion for any interim order which may be made pending the determination of the application.

Applications after decree relating to aliment

33A.42.—(1) An application after final decree for, or for the variation or recall of, an order for aliment for a child shall be made by minute in the process of the action to which the application relates.

(2) Where a minute has been lodged under paragraph (1), any party may lodge a motion for any interim order which may be made pending the determination of the application.

Applications after decree by persons over 18 years for aliment

33A.43.—(1) A person—

    (a) to whom an obligation of aliment is owed under section 1 of the Act of 1985;

    (b) in whose favour an order for aliment while under the age of 18 years was made in an action to which this Part applies, and

    (c) who seeks, after attaining that age, an order for aliment against the person in that action against whom the order for aliment in his favour was made,

shall apply by minute in the process of that action.

(2) An application for interim aliment pending the determination of an application under paragraph (1) shall be made by motion.

(3) Where a decree has been pronounced in an application under paragraph (1) or (2), any application for variation or recall of any such decree shall be made by minute in the process of the action to which the application relates.

PART V

ORDERS RELATING TO FINANCIAL PROVISIONS

Application and interpretation of this Part

 33A.44.—(1) This Part applies to an action of dissolution or declarator of nullity of civil partnership.

(2) In this Part, "incidental order" has the meaning assigned in section 14(2) of the Act of 1985.

NOTE

[1] As amended by Act of Sederunt (Ordinary Cause Rules) Amendment (Family Law (Scotland) Act 2006 etc.) 2006, para.2 (SSI 2006/207) (effective May 4, 2006).

Applications in actions to which this Part applies

33A.45.—(1) An application for an order mentioned in paragraph (2) shall be made—

    (a) by a crave in the initial writ or defences, as the case may be, in an action to which this Part applies; or

    (b) where the application is made by a person other than the pursuer or defender, by minute in that action.

(2) The orders referred to in paragraph (1) are:—

    (a) an order for financial provision within the meaning of section 8(3) of the Act of 1985;

(b) an order under section 16(1)(b) or (3) of the Act of 1985 (setting aside or varying agreement as to financial provision);

(c) an order under section 18 of the Act of 1985 (which relates to avoidance transactions); and

(d) an order under section 112 of the Act of 2004 (transfer of tenancy).

Applications in depending actions relating to incidental orders

33A.46.—(1) In an action depending before the sheriff to which this Part applies—

(a) the pursuer or defender, notwithstanding rules 33A.34(2) (application by defender for order for financial provision) and 33A.45(1)(a) (application for order for financial provision in initial writ or defences), may apply by motion for an incidental order; and

(b) the sheriff shall not be bound to determine such a motion if he considers that the application should properly be by a crave in the initial writ or defences, as the case may be.

(2) In an action depending before the sheriff to which this Part applies, an application under section 14(4) of the Act of 1985 for the variation or recall of an incidental order shall be made by minute in the process of the action to which the application relates.

Applications relating to interim aliment

33A.47. An application for, or for the variation or recall of, an order for interim aliment for the pursuer or defender shall be made by motion.

Applications relating to orders for financial provision

33A.48.—(1) An application—

(a) after final decree under any of the following provisions of the Act of 1985—

(i) section 8(1) for periodical allowance;

(ii) section 12(1)(b) (payment of capital sum or transfer of property);

(iii) section 12(4) (variation of date or method of payment of capital sum or date of transfer of property); or

(iv) section 13(4) (variation, recall, backdating or conversion of periodical allowance); or

(b) after the grant or refusal of an application under—

(i) section 8(1) or 14(3) for an incidental order; or

(ii) section 14(4) (variation or recall of incidental order),

shall be made by minute in the process of the action to which the application relates.

(2) Where a minute is lodged under paragraph (1), any party may lodge a motion for any interim order which may be made pending the determination of the application.

(3) An application under—

(a) paragraph (5) of section 12A of the Act of 1985 (recall or variation of order in respect of a pension lump sum);

(b) paragraph (7) of that section (variation of order in respect of pension lump sum to substitute trustees or managers); or

(c) section 28(10) or 48(9) of the Welfare Reform and Pensions Act 1999,

shall be made by minute in the process of the action to which the application relates.

Applications after decree relating to agreements and avoidance transactions

33A.49. An application for an order—

(a) under section 16(1)(a) or (3) of the Act of 1985 (setting aside or varying agreements as to financial provision), or

(b) under section 18 of the Act of 1985 (which relates to avoidance transactions),

made after final decree shall be made by minute in the process of the action to which the application relates.

PART VI

APPLICATIONS RELATING TO AVOIDANCE TRANSACTIONS

Form of applications

33A.50. —(1) An application for an order under section 18 of the Act of 1985 (which relates to avoidance transactions) by a party to a civil partnership action shall be made by including in the initial writ, defences or minute, as the case may be, appropriate craves, averments and pleas in law.

(2) An application for an order under section 18 of the Act of 1985 after final decree in a civil

partnership action shall be made by minute in the process of the action to which the application relates.

PART VII

FINANCIAL PROVISION AFTER OVERSEAS PROCEEDINGS

Interpretation of this Part
33A.51. In this Part—
"order for financial provision" has the meaning assigned in paragraph 4 of Schedule 11 to the Act of 2004;
"overseas proceedings" has the meaning assigned in paragraph 1(1)(a) of Schedule 11 to the Act of 2004.

Applications for financial provision after overseas proceedings
33A.52.—(1) An application under paragraph 2(1) of Schedule 11 to the Act of 2004 for an order for financial provision after overseas proceedings shall be made by initial writ.

(2) An application for an order in an action to which paragraph (1) applies made before final decree under—
(a) section 112 of the Act of 2004 (transfer of tenancy of family home);
(b) paragraph 3(4) of Schedule 11 to the Act of 2004 for interim periodical allowance; or
(c) section 14(4) of the Act of 1985 (variation or recall of incidental order),
shall be made by motion.

(3) An application for an order in an action to which paragraph (1) applies made after final decree under—
(a) section 12(4) of the Act of 1985 (variation of date or method of payment of capital sum or date of transfer of property);
(b) section 13(4) of the Act of 1985 (variation, recall, backdating or conversion of periodical allowance); or
(c) section 14(4) of the Act of 1985 (variation or recall of incidental order),
shall be made by minute in the process of the action to which it relates.

(4) An application under—
(a) paragraph (5) of section 12A of the Act of 1985 (recall or variation of order in respect of a pension lump sum); or
(b) paragraph (7) of that section (variation of order in respect of pension lump sum to substitute trustees or managers),
shall be made by minute in the process of the action to which the application relates.

(5) Where a minute has been lodged under paragraph (3), any party may apply by motion for an interim order pending the determination of the application.

PART VIII

ACTIONS IN RESPECT OF ALIMENT

Applications relating to agreements on aliment
33A.53. In a civil partnership action in which a crave for aliment may be made, an application under section 7(2) of the Act of 1985 shall be made by a crave in the initial writ or in defences, as the case may be.

PART IX

APPLICATIONS FOR ORDERS UNDER SECTION 11 OF THE CHILDREN (SCOTLAND) ACT 1995

Application of this Part
[1] **33A.54.** This Part applies to an application for a section 11 order in a civil partnership action other than in an action of dissolution or declarator of nullity of civil partnership or separation of civil partners.

NOTE
[1] As amended by Act of Sederunt (Ordinary Cause Rules) Amendment (Family Law (Scotland) Act 2006 etc.) 2006, para.2 (SSI 2006/207) (effective May 4, 2006).

Form of applications

33A.55. Subject to any other provision in this Chapter, an application for a section 11 order shall be made—

(a) by a crave in the initial writ or defences, as the case may be, in a civil partnership action to which this Part applies; or

(b) where the application is made by a person other than a party to an action mentioned in paragraph (a), by minute in that action.

Applications relating to interim orders in depending actions

33A.56. An application, in an action depending before the sheriff to which this Part applies, for, or for the variation or recall of, an interim residence order or an interim contact order shall be made—

(a) by a party to the action, by motion; or

(b) by a person who is not a party to the action, by minute.

Applications after decree

33A.57.—(1) An application after final decree for variation or recall of a section 11 order shall be made by minute in the process of the action to which the application relates.

(2) Where a minute has been lodged under paragraph (1), any party may apply by motion for an interim order pending the determination of the application.

Application for leave

[1]**33A.57A.**—(1) Where leave of the court is required under section 11(3)(aa) of the Act of 1995 for the making of an application for a contact order under that section, the applicant must lodge along with the initial writ a written application in the form of a letter addressed to the sheriff clerk stating—

(a) the grounds of which leave is sought; and

(b) whether or not the applicant has applied for legal aid.

(2) Where the applicant has applied for legal aid he must also lodge along with the initial writ written confirmation from the Scottish Legal Aid Board that it has determined, under regulation 7(2)(b) of the Civil Legal Aid (Scotland) Regulations 2002, that notification of the application for legal aid should be dispensed with or postponed pending the making by the sheriff of an order for intimation under paragraph (4)(b).

(3) Subject to paragraph (4)(b) an application under paragraph (1) shall not be served or intimated to any party.

(4) The sheriff shall consider an application under paragraph (1) without hearing the applicant and may—

(a) refuse the application and pronounce an interlocutor accordingly; or

(b) if he is minded to grant the application order the applicant—

(i) to intimate the application to such persons as the sheriff considers appropriate; and

(ii) to lodge a certificate of intimation in, as near as may be, Form G8.

(5) If any person who receives intimation of an application under paragraph (4)(b) wishes to be heard he shall notify the sheriff clerk in writing within 14 days of receipt of intimation of the application.

(6) On receipt of any notification under paragraph (5) the sheriff clerk shall fix a hearing and intimate the date of the hearing to the parties.

(7) Where an application under paragraph (1) is granted, a copy of the sheriff's interlocutor must be served on the defender along with the warrant of citation.

NOTE

[1] As inserted by the Act of Sederunt (Sheriff Court Rules Amendment) (Adoption and Children (Scotland) Act 2007) 2009 (SSI 2009/284) (effective September 28, 2009).

PART X

ACTIONS RELATING TO OCCUPANCY RIGHTS AND TENANCIES

Application of this Part

33A.58. This Part applies to an action or application for an order under Chapter 3 or Chapter 4 of Part 3 or section 127 of the Act of 2004.

Interpretation of this Part

33A.59. Unless the context otherwise requires, words and expressions used in this Part which are also used in Chapter 3 or Chapter 4 of Part 3 of the Act of 2004 have the same meaning as in Chapter 3 or Chapter 4, as the case may be.

Form of application

33A.60.—(1) Subject to any other provision in this Chapter, an application for an order under this Part shall be made—

    (a) by an action for such an order;

    (b) by a crave in the initial writ or defences, as the case may be, in any other civil partnership action;

    (c) where the application is made by a person other than a party to any action mentioned in paragraph (a) or (b), by minute in that action.

(2) An application under section 107(1) (dispensation with civil partner's consent to dealing) or section 127 (application in relation to attachment) of the Act of 2004 shall, unless made in a depending civil partnership action, be made by summary application.

Defenders

33A.61. The applicant for an order under this Part shall call as a defender—

    (a) where he is seeking an order as a civil partner, the other civil partner; and

    (b) where he is a third party making an application under section 107(1) (dispensation with civil partner's consent to dealing), or 108(1) (payment from non-entitled civil partner in respect of loan) of the Act of 2004, both civil partners.

Applications by motion

33A.62.—(1) An application under any of the following provisions of the Act of 2004 shall be made by motion in the process of the depending action to which the application relates—

    (a) section 103(4) (interim order for regulation of rights of occupancy, etc.);

    (b) section 104(6) (interim order suspending occupancy rights);

    (c) section 107(1) (dispensation with civil partner's consent to dealing); and

    (d) [*Omitted by Act of Sederunt (Ordinary Cause Rules) Amendment (Family Law (Scotland) Act 2006 etc.) 2006, para.2 (SSI 2006/207) (effective May 4, 2006).*]

(2) Intimation of a motion under paragraph (1) shall be given—

    (a) to the other civil partner;

    (b) where the motion is under paragraph (1)(a) or (b) and the entitled civil partner is a tenant or occupies the family home by the permission of a third party, to the landlord or third party, as the case may be; and

    (c) to any other person to whom intimation of the application was or is to be made by virtue of rule 33A.7(1)(i) (warrant for intimation to certain persons in actions for orders under Chapter 3 of Part 3 of the Act of 2004) or rule 33A.15 (order for intimation by sheriff).

Applications by minute

33A.63. —(1) An application for an order under section 105 of the Act of 2004 (variation and recall of orders made under section 103 or section 104 of the Act of 2004) shall be made by minute.

(2) A minute under paragraph (1) shall be intimated—

    (a) to the other civil partner;

    (b) where the entitled civil partner is a tenant or occupies the family home by the permission of a third party, to the landlord or third party, as the case may be; and

    (c) to any other person to whom intimation of the application was or is to be made by virtue of rule 33A.7(1)(i) (warrant for intimation to certain persons in actions for orders under Chapter 3 of Part 3 of the Act of 2004) or rule 33A.15 (order for intimation by sheriff).

Sist of actions to enforce occupancy rights

33A.64. Unless the sheriff otherwise directs, the sist of an action by virtue of section 107(4) of the Act of 2004 (where action raised by non entitled civil partner to enforce occupancy rights) shall apply only to such part of the action as relates to the enforcement of occupancy rights by a non entitled civil partner.

Certificates of delivery of documents to chief constable

33A.65. [*Omitted by Act of Sederunt (Ordinary Cause Rules) Amendment (Family Law (Scotland) Act 2006 etc.) 2006, para.2 (SSI 2006/207) (effective May 4, 2006).*]

PART XI

SIMPLIFIED DISSOLUTION OF CIVIL PARTNERSHIP APPLICATIONS

Application and interpretation of this Part

33A.66.—(1) This Part applies to an application for dissolution of civil partnership by a party to a civil partnership made in the manner prescribed in rule 33A.67 (form of applications) if, but only if—

[1] (a) that party relies on the facts set out in section 117(3)(c) (no cohabitation for one year with consent of defender to decree), section 117(3)(d) (no cohabitation for two years), or section 117(2)(b) (issue of interim gender recognition certificate) of the Act of 2004;

   (b) in an application under section 117(3)(c) of the Act of 2004, the other party consents to decree of dissolution of civil partnership being granted;

   (c) no other proceedings are pending in any court which could have the effect of bringing the civil partnership to an end;

   (d) there is no child of the family (as defined in section 101(7) of the Act of 2004) under the age of 16 years;

   (e) neither party to the civil partnership applies for an order for financial provision on dissolution of civil partnership; and

   (f) neither party to the civil partnership suffers from mental disorder.

(2) If an application ceases to be one to which this Part applies at any time before final decree, it shall be deemed to be abandoned and shall be dismissed.

(3) In this Part "simplified dissolution of civil partnership application" means an application mentioned in paragraph (1).

NOTE

[1] As amended by Act of Sederunt (Ordinary Cause Rules) Amendment (Family Law (Scotland) Act 2006 etc.) 2006, para.2 (SSI 2006/207) (effective May 4, 2006).

Form of applications

33A.67.—(1) A simplified dissolution of civil partnership application in which the facts set out in section 117(3)(c) of the Act of 2004 (no cohabitation for two years with consent of defender to decree) are relied on shall be made in Form CP29 and shall only be of effect if—

   (a) it is signed by the applicant; and

   (b) the form of consent in Part 2 of Form CP29 is signed by the party to the civil partnership giving consent.

(2) A simplified dissolution of civil partnership application in which the facts set out in section 117(3)(d) of the Act of 2004 (no cohabitation for five years) are relied on shall be made in Form CP30 and shall only be of effect if it is signed by the applicant.

(3) A simplified dissolution of civil partnership application in which the facts set out in section 117(2)(b) of the Act of 2004 (issue of interim gender recognition certificate) are relied on shall be made in Form CP31 and shall only be of effect if it is signed by the applicant.

Lodging of applications

33A.68. The applicant shall send a simplified dissolution of civil partnership application to the sheriff clerk with—

   (a) an extract or certified copy of the civil partnership certificate;

   (b) the appropriate fee; and

   (c) in an application under section 117(2)(b) of the Act of 2004, the interim gender recognition certificate or a certified copy, within the meaning of rule 33A.9(4).

Citation and intimation

33A.69.—(1) This rule is subject to rule 33A.70 (citation where address not known).

(2) It shall be the duty of the sheriff clerk to cite any person or intimate any document in connection with a simplified dissolution of civil partnership application.

(3) The form of citation—

   (a) in an application relying on the facts in section 117(3)(c) of the Act of 2004 shall be in Form CP32;

   (b) in an application relying on the facts in section 117(3)(d) of the Act of 2004 shall be in Form CP33; and

   (c) in an application relying on the facts in section 117(2)(b) of the Act of 2004 shall be in Form CP34.

(4) The citation or intimation required by paragraph (2) shall be made—

   (a) by the sheriff clerk by registered post or the first class recorded delivery service in accordance with rule 5.3 (postal service or intimation);

¹ (b) on payment of an additional fee, by a sheriff officer in accordance with rule 5.4(1) to (4) (service within Scotland by sheriff officer); or

(c) where necessary, by the sheriff clerk in accordance with rule 5.5 (service on persons furth of Scotland).

(5) Where citation or intimation is made in accordance with paragraph (4)(c), the translation into an official language of the country in which service is to be executed required by rule 5.5(6) shall be provided by the party lodging the simplified dissolution of civil partnership application.

NOTE
¹ As amended by the Act of Sederunt (Sheriff Court Rules) (Miscellaneous Amendments) 2010 (SSI 2010/279) para.3 (effective July 29, 2010).

Citation where address not known
¹ **33A.70.**—(1) In a simplified dissolution of civil partnership application in which the facts in section 117(3)(d) (no cohabitation for two years) or section 117(2)(b) (issue of interim gender recognition certificate) of the Act of 2004 are relied on and the address of the other party to the civil partnership is not known and cannot reasonably be ascertained—

(a) citation shall be executed by displaying a copy of the application and a notice in Form CP35 on the walls of court on a period of notice of 21 days; and

(b) intimation shall be made to—

(i) every person who was a child of the family (within the meaning of section 101(7) of the Act of 2004) who has reached the age of 16 years, and

(ii) one of the next of kin of the other party to the civil partnership who has reached that age, unless the address of such person is not known and cannot reasonably be ascertained.

(2) Intimation to a person referred to in paragraph (1)(b) shall be given by intimating a copy of the application and a notice of intimation in Form CP36.

NOTE
¹ As amended by Act of Sederunt (Ordinary Cause Rules) Amendment (Family Law (Scotland) Act 2006 etc.) 2006, para.2 (SSI 2006/207) (effective May 4, 2006).

Opposition to applications
33A.71.—(1) Any person on whom service or intimation of a simplified dissolution of civil partnership application has been made may give notice by letter sent to the sheriff clerk that he challenges the jurisdiction of the court or opposes the grant of decree of dissolution of civil partnership and giving the reasons for his opposition to the application.

(2) Where opposition to a simplified dissolution of civil partnership application is made under paragraph (1), the sheriff shall dismiss the application unless he is satisfied that the reasons given for the opposition are frivolous.

(3) The sheriff clerk shall intimate the decision under paragraph (2) to the applicant and the respondent.

(4) The sending of a letter under paragraph (1) shall not imply acceptance of the jurisdiction of the court.

Evidence
33A.72. Parole evidence shall not be given in a simplified dissolution of civil partnership application.

Decree
33A.73.—(1) The sheriff may grant decree in terms of the simplified dissolution of civil partnership application on the expiry of the period of notice if such application has been properly served provided that, when the application has been served in a country to which the Hague Convention on the Service Abroad of Judicial and Extra Judicial Documents in Civil or Commercial Matters dated 15 November 1965 applies, decree shall not be granted until it is established to the satisfaction of the sheriff that the requirements of article 15 of that Convention have been complied with.

(2) The sheriff clerk shall, not sooner than 14 days after the granting of decree in terms of paragraph (1), issue to each party to the civil partnership an extract of the decree of dissolution of civil partnership in Form CP37.

Appeals
33A.74. Any appeal against an interlocutor granting decree of dissolution of civil partnership

under rule 33A.73 (decree) may be made, within 14 days after the date of decree, by sending a letter to the court giving reasons for the appeal.

Applications after decree
33A.75. Any application to the court after decree of dissolution of civil partnership has been granted in a simplified dissolution of civil partnership application which could have been made if it had been made in an action of dissolution of civil partnership shall be made by minute.

PART XII

REFERRALS TO PRINCIPAL REPORTER

Application and interpretation of this Part
33A.76.—(1) This Part applies where a sheriff, in a civil partnership action, refers a matter to the Principal Reporter under section 54 of the Act of 1995 (reference to the Principal Reporter by court).

(2) In this Part, "Principal Reporter" has the meaning assigned in section 93(1) of the Act of 1995.

Intimation to Principal Reporter
33A.77. Where a matter is referred by the sheriff to the Principal Reporter under section 54 of the Act of 1995, the interlocutor making the reference shall be intimated by the sheriff clerk forthwith to the Principal Reporter; and that intimation shall specify which of the conditions in paragraph (2)(a) to (h), (j), (k) or (l) of section 52 of the Act of 1995 it appears to the sheriff has been satisfied.

Intimation of decision by Principal Reporter
33A.78.—(1) Where a matter has been referred by the sheriff to the Principal Reporter under section 54 of the Act of 1995 and the Principal Reporter, having made such investigation as he thinks appropriate and having reached the view that compulsory measures of supervision are necessary, arranges a children's hearing under section 69 of that Act (continuation or disposal of referral by children's hearing), the Principal Reporter shall intimate to the court which referred the matter to him—
  (a) the decision to arrange such children's hearing;
  (b) where there is no appeal made against the decision of that children's hearing once the period for appeal has expired, the outcome of the children's hearing; and
  (c) where such an appeal has been made, that an appeal has been made and, once determined, the outcome of that appeal.

(2) Where a matter has been referred by the sheriff to the Principal Reporter under section 54 of the Act of 1995 and the Principal Reporter, having made such investigation as he thinks appropriate and having considered whether compulsory measures of supervision are necessary, decides not to arrange a children's hearing under section 69 of that Act, the Principal Reporter shall intimate that decision to the court which referred the matter to him.

PART XIII

SISTING OF CIVIL PARTNERSHIP ACTIONS

Application and interpretation of this Part
33A.79.—(1) This Part applies to any action for—
    dissolution of civil partnership;
    separation of civil partners.
(2) In this Part—
    "another jurisdiction" means any country outside Scotland.
    "related jurisdiction" means any of the following countries, namely, England and Wales, Northern Ireland, Jersey, Guernsey and the Isle of Man (the reference to Guernsey being treated as including Alderney and Sark).
(3) For the purposes of this Part—
  (a) neither the taking of evidence on commission nor a separate proof relating to any preliminary plea shall be regarded as part of the proof in the action; and
  (b) an action is continuing if it is pending and not sisted.
(4) Any reference in this Part to proceedings in another jurisdiction is to proceedings in a court or before an administrative authority of that jurisdiction.

Duty to furnish particulars of concurrent proceedings

33A.80. While any action to which this Part applies is pending in a sheriff court and proof in that action has not begun, it shall be the duty of the pursuer, and of any other person who has entered appearance in the action, to furnish, in such manner and to such persons and on such occasions as may be prescribed, such particulars as may be so prescribed of any proceedings which—

(a) he knows to be continuing in another jurisdiction; and

(b) are in respect of that civil partnership or capable of affecting its validity.

Mandatory sists

33A.81. Where before the beginning of the proof in any action for dissolution of civil partnership it appears to the sheriff on the application of a party to the civil partnership—

(a) that in respect of the same civil partnership proceedings for dissolution or nullity of civil partnership are continuing in a related jurisdiction; and

(b) that the parties to the civil partnership have resided together after the civil partnership was formed or treated as having been formed within the meaning of section 1(1) of the Act of 2004; and

(c) that the place where they resided together when the action was begun or, if they did not then reside together, where they last resided together before the date on which that action was begun is in that jurisdiction; and

(d) that either of the said parties was habitually resident in that jurisdiction throughout the year ending with the date on which they last resided together before the date on which that action was begun;

it shall be the duty of the sheriff, subject to rule 33A.83(2) below, to sist the action before him.

Discretionary sists

33A.82.—(1) Where before the beginning of the proof in any action to which this Part applies, it appears to the sheriff—

(a) that any other proceedings in respect of the civil partnership in question or capable of affecting its validity are continuing in another jurisdiction, and

(b) that the balance of fairness (including convenience) as between the parties to the civil partnership is such that it is appropriate for those other proceedings to be disposed of before further steps are taken in the action,

the sheriff may then if he thinks fit sist that action.

(2) In considering the balance of fairness and convenience for the purposes of paragraph (1)(b), the sheriff shall have regard to all factors appearing to be relevant, including the convenience of witnesses and any delay or expense which may result from the proceedings being sisted, or not being sisted.

(3) Paragraph (1) is without prejudice to the duty imposed by rule 33A.81 above.

(4) If, at any time after the beginning of the proof in any action to which this Part applies, the sheriff is satisfied that a person has failed to perform the duty imposed on him in respect of the action and any such other proceedings as aforesaid by rule 33A.80, paragraph (1) shall have effect in relation to that action and to the other proceedings as if the words "before the beginning of the proof" were omitted; but no action in respect of the failure of a person to perform such a duty shall be competent.

Recall of sists

33A.83.—(1) Where an action is sisted in pursuance of rule 33A.81 or 33A.82, the sheriff may if he thinks fit, on the application of a party to the action, recall the sist if it appears to him that the other proceedings by reference to which the action was sisted are sisted or concluded or that a party to those other proceedings has delayed unreasonably in prosecuting those other proceedings.

(2) Where an action has been sisted in pursuance of rule 33A.82 by reference to some other proceedings, and the sheriff recalls the sist in pursuance of the preceding paragraph, the sheriff shall not again sist the action in pursuance of the said rule 33A.82.

Orders in sisted actions

33A.84.—(1) The provisions of paragraphs (2) and (3) shall apply where an action to which this Part applies is sisted by reference to proceedings in a related jurisdiction for any of those remedies; and in this rule—

"the other proceedings", in relation to any sisted action, means the proceedings in another jurisdiction by reference to which the action was sisted;

"relevant order" means an interim order relating to aliment or children; and

"sisted" means sisted in pursuance of this Part.

(2) Where an action such as is mentioned in paragraph (1) is sisted, then, without prejudice to the effect of the sist apart from this paragraph—

    (a) the sheriff shall not have power to make a relevant order in connection with the sisted action except in pursuance of sub paragraph (c); and

    (b) subject to the said sub paragraph (c), any relevant order made in connection with the sisted action shall (unless the sist or the relevant order has been previously recalled) cease to have effect on the expiration of the period of three months beginning with the date on which the sist comes into operation; but

    (c) if the sheriff considers that as a matter of necessity and urgency it is necessary during or after that period to make a relevant order in connection with the sisted action or to extend or further extend the duration of a relevant order made in connection with the sisted action, the sheriff may do so, and the order shall not cease to have effect by virtue of sub paragraph (b).

(3) Where any action such as is mentioned in paragraph (1) is sisted and at the time when the sist comes into operation, an order is in force, or at a subsequent time an order comes into force, being an order made in connection with the other proceedings and providing for any of the following matters, namely periodical payments for a party to the civil partnership in question, periodical payments for a child, the arrangements to be made as to with whom a child is to live, contact with a child, and any other matter relating to parental responsibilities or parental rights, then, as from the time when the sist comes into operation (in a case where the order is in force at that time) or (in any other case) on the coming into force of the order—

    (a) any relevant order made in connection with the sisted action shall cease to have effect in so far as it makes for a civil partner or child any provision for any of the said matters as respects which the same or different provision for that civil partner or child is made by the other order; and

    (b) the sheriff shall not have power in connection with the sisted action to make a relevant order containing for a civil partner or child provision for any of the matters aforesaid as respects which any provision for that civil partner or child is made by the other order.

(4) Nothing in this paragraph affects any power of a sheriff—

    (a) to vary or recall a relevant order in so far as the order is for the time being in force; or

    (b) to enforce a relevant order as respects any period when it is or was in force; or

    (c) to make a relevant order in connection with an action which was, but is no longer, sisted.

[1] CHAPTER 33B

FINANCIAL PROVISION FOR FORMER COHABITANTS

Interpretation of this Chapter

    33B. In this Chapter—

    "the Act" means the Family Law (Scotland) Act 2006;

    "cohabitant" has the meaning given in section 25 of the Act;

    "the deceased" means the cohabitant referred to in section 29(1)(a) of the Act;

    "net intestate estate" has the meaning given in section 29(10) of the Act;

    "the survivor" means the cohabitant referred to in section 29(1)(b) of the Act.

    33B.—(1) An application under—

    (a) section 28(2) of the Act for an order for financial provision where cohabitation ends otherwise than by death; or

    (b) section 29(2) of the Act for an order for financial provision by the survivor on intestacy,

shall be made by initial writ.

(2) In an initial writ under paragraph (1)(b) the pursuer shall—

    (a) name the deceased's executor as the defender; and

    (b) include a crave for a warrant for intimation to any person having an interest in the deceased's net intestate estate, and a notice of intimation in Form CO1 shall be attached to the initial writ intimated to any such person.

(3) Where the identity or address of any person referred to in paragraph (2)(b) is not known and cannot be ascertained, the pursuer shall include in his pleadings an averment of that fact and averments setting out what steps have been taken to identify the identity or address, as the case may be, of that person.

(4) An application under section 29(9) of the Act for variation of the date or method of payment of a capital sum shall be made by minute in the process of the action to which the application relates.

NOTE
¹ Inserted by Act of Sederunt (Ordinary Cause Rules) Amendment (Family Law (Scotland) Act 2006 etc.) 2006, para.2 (SSI 2006/207) (effective May 4, 2006).

CHAPTER 34

ACTIONS RELATING TO HERITABLE PROPERTY

PART I

SEQUESTRATION FOR RENT

[*Revoked by the Act of Sederunt (Sheriff Court Rules Amendment) (Diligence) 2008 (SSI 2008/ 121) r.2(1)(a) (effective April 1, 2008).*]

PART II

REMOVING

Action of removing where fixed term of removal
34.5.—(1) Subject to section 21 of the Agricultural Holdings (Scotland) Act 1991 (notice to quit and notice of intention to quit)—
  (a) where the tenant has bound himself to remove by writing, dated and signed—
     (i) within 12 months after the term of removal; or
    (ii) where there is more than one ish, after the ish first in date to remove;
    an action of removing may be raised at any time; and
  (b) where the tenant has not bound himself, an action of removing may be raised at any time, but—
     (i) in the case of a lease of lands exceeding two acres in extent for three years and upwards, an interval of not less than one year nor more than two years shall elapse between the date of notice of removal and the term of removal first in date;
    (ii) in the case of a lease of lands exceeding two acres in extent, whether written or verbal, held from year to year or under tacit relocation, or for any other period less than three years, an interval of not less than six months shall elapse between the date of notice of removal and the term of removal first in date; and
    (iii) in the case of a house let with or without land attached not exceeding two acres in extent, as also of land not exceeding two acres in extent without houses, as also of mills, fishings, shootings, and all other heritable subjects excepting land exceeding two acres in extent, and let for a year or more, 40 days at least shall elapse between the date of notice of removal and the term of removal first in date.
  (2) In any defended action of removing the sheriff may order the defender to find caution for violent profits.
  (3) In an action for declarator of irritancy and removing by a superior against a vassal, the pursuer shall call as parties the last entered vassal and such heritable creditors and holders of postponed ground burdens as are disclosed by a search for 20 years before the raising of the action, and the expense of the search shall form part of the pursuer's expenses of process.

Form of notice of removal
34.6.—¹ (1) A notice under the following sections of the Sheriff Courts (Scotland) Act 1907 shall be in Form H2:—
  (a) section 34 (notice in writing to remove where lands exceeding two acres held on probative lease),
  (b) section 35 (letter of removal where tenant in possession of lands exceeding two acres), and
  (c) section 36 (notice of removal where lands exceeding two acres occupied by tenant without written lease).
  (2) A letter of removal shall be in Form H3.

NOTE
¹ As amended by SI 1996/2445 (effective November 1, 1996).

Form of notice under section 37 of the Act of 1907
[1] **34.7.** A notice under section 37 of the Sheriff Courts (Scotland) Act 1907 (notice of termination of tenancy) shall be in Form H4.

NOTE
[1] As amended by SI 1996/2445 (effective November 1, 1996).

Giving notice of removal
[1] **34.8.**—(1) A notice under section 34, 35, 36, 37 or 38 of the Sheriff Courts (Scotland) Act 1907 (which relate to notices of removal) may be given by—
    (a) a sheriff officer
    (b) the person entitled to give such notice, or
    (c) the solicitor or factor of such person,
posting the notice by registered post or the first class recorded delivery service at any post office within the United Kingdom in time for it to be delivered at the address on the notice before the last date on which by law such notice must be given, addressed to the person entitled to receive such notice, and bearing the address of that person at the time, if known, or, if not known, to the last known address of that person.

(2) A sheriff officer may also give notice under a section of the Sheriff Courts (Scotland) Act 1907 mentioned in paragraph (1) in any manner in which he may serve an initial writ; and, accordingly, rule 5.4 (service within Scotland by sheriff officer) shall, with the necessary modifications, apply to the giving of notice under this paragraph as it applies to service of an initial writ.

NOTE
[1] As amended by SI 1996/2445 (effective November 1, 1996).

Evidence of notice to remove
34.9.—(1) A certificate of the sending of notice under rule 34.8 dated and endorsed on the lease or an extract of it, or on the letter of removal, signed by the sheriff officer or the person sending the notice, his solicitor or factor, or an acknowledgement of the notice endorsed on the lease or an extract of it, or on the letter of removal, by the party in possession or his agent, shall be sufficient evidence that notice has been given.

(2) Where there is no lease, a certificate of the sending of such notice shall be endorsed on a copy of the notice or letter of removal.

Applications under Part II of the Conveyancing and Feudal Reform (Scotland) Act 1970
34.10.—(1) An application or counter-application to the sheriff under any of the following provisions of Part II of the Conveyancing and Feudal Reform (Scotland) Act 1970 (which relates to the standard security) shall be made by initial writ where any other remedy is craved:—
    (a) section 18(2) (declarator that obligations under contract performed);
    (b) section 20(3) (application by creditor for warrant to let security subjects);
    (c) section 22(1) (objections to notice of default);
    (d) section 22(3) (counter-application for remedies under the Act);
    (e) section 24(1) (application by a creditor for warrant to exercise remedies on default); and
    (f) section 28(1) (decree of foreclosure).

(2) An interlocutor of the sheriff disposing of an application or counter-application under paragraph (1) shall be final and not subject to appeal except as to a question of title or any other remedy granted.

Service on unnamed occupiers
[1] **34.11.**—(1) Subject to paragraph (2), this rule applies only to a crave for removing in an action of removing against a person or persons in possession of heritable property without right or title to possess the property.

(2) This rule shall not apply with respect to a person who has or had a title or other right to occupy the heritable property and who has been in continuous occupation since that title or right is alleged to have come to an end.

(3) Where this rule applies, the pursuer may apply by motion to shorten or dispense with the period of notice or other period of time in these Rules relating to the conduct of the action or the extracting of any decree.

(4) Where the name of a person in occupation of the heritable property is not known and cannot reasonably be ascertained, the pursuer shall call that person as a defender by naming him as an "occupier".

(5) Where the name of a person in occupation of the heritable property is not known and cannot reasonably be ascertained, the initial writ shall be served (whether or not it is also served on a named person), unless the court otherwise directs, by a sheriff officer—

    (a) affixing a copy of the initial writ and a citation in Form H5 addressed to "the occupiers" to the main door or other conspicuous part of the premises, and if practicable, depositing a copy of each of those documents in the premises; or

    (b) in the case of land only, inserting stakes in the ground at conspicuous parts of the occupied land to each of which is attached a sealed transparent envelope containing a copy of the initial writ and a citation in Form H5 addressed to "the occupiers".

NOTE

[1] Inserted by the Act of Sederunt (Sheriff Court Ordinary Cause Rules Amendment) (Miscellaneous) 2000 (S.S.I. 2000 No. 239) (effective October 2, 2000).

[1] *Applications under the Mortgage Rights (Scotland) Act 2001*

34.12.—(1) In an action to which rule 3.2(3) applies, an application under either of the following provisions of the Mortgage Rights (Scotland) Act 2001 shall be made by minute in the action—

    (a) section 1(2) (application to the court for an order under section 2);

    (b) section 2(5) (application to vary or revoke an order or to further continue proceedings).

(2) Any such minute may be lodged by a person who is entitled to make an application even although that person has not been called as a defender and such a person may appear or be represented at any hearing to determine the application.

NOTE

[1] Inserted by the Act of Sederunt (Amendment of Ordinary Cause Rules and Summary Applications, Statutory Applications and Appeals etc. Rules) (Applications under the Mortgage Rights (Scotland) Act 2001) 2002 (SSI 2002 No.7), para.2(5).

CHAPTER 35

ACTIONS OF MULTIPLEPOINDING

Application of this Chapter

35.1.—(1) This Chapter applies to an action of multiplepoinding.

Application of Chapters 9 and 10

35.2. Chapter 10 (additional procedure) and the following rules in Chapter 9 (standard procedure in defended causes) shall not apply to an action of multiplepoinding:—

    rule 9.1   (notice of intention to defend),

    rule 9.2   (fixing date for Options Hearing),

    rule 9.4   (lodging of pleadings before Options Hearing),

    rule 9.8   (adjustment of pleadings),

    rule 9.9   (effect of sist on adjustment),

    rule 9.10 (open record),

    rule 9.11 (record for Options Hearing),

    rule 9.12 (Options Hearing),

    rule 9.15 (applications for time to pay directions).

Parties

35.3.—(1) An action of multiplepoinding may be brought by any person holding, or having an interest in, or claim on, the fund *in medio*, in his own name.

(2) The pursuer shall call as defenders to such an action—

    (a) all persons so far as known to him as having an interest in the fund *in medio*; and

    (b) where he is not the holder of the fund, the holder of that fund.

Condescendence of fund in medio

35.4.—(1) Where the pursuer is the holder of the fund *in medio*, he shall include a detailed statement of the fund in the condescendence in the initial writ.

(2) Where the pursuer is not the holder of the fund *in medio*, the holder shall, before the expiry of the period of notice—

    (a) lodge in process—

     (i) a condescendence of the fund *in medio*, stating any claim or lien which he may profess to have on that fund;

    (ii) a list of all persons known to him as having an interest in the fund; and

  (b) intimate a copy of the condescendence and list to any other party.

Warrant of citation in multiplepoindings

35.5. The warrant of citation of the initial writ in an action of multiplepoinding shall be in Form M1.

Citation

35.6.—(1) Subject to rule 5.6 (service where address of person is not known), citation of any person in an action of multiplepoinding shall be in Form M2 which shall be attached to a copy of the initial writ and warrant of citation and shall have appended to it a notice of appearance in Form M4.

(2) The certificate of citation shall be in Form M3 and shall be attached to the initial writ.

Advertisement

35.7. The sheriff may make an order for advertisement of the action in such newspapers as he thinks fit.

Lodging of notice of appearance

35.8. Where a party intends to lodge—

  (a) defences to challenge the jurisdiction of the court or the competency of the action,

  (b) objections to the condescendence of the fund *in medio*, or

  (c) a claim on the fund,

he shall, before the expiry of the period of notice, lodge a notice of appearance in Form M4.

Fixing date for first hearing

35.9. Where a notice of appearance, or a condescendence on the fund *in medio* and list under rule 35.4(2)(a) has been lodged, the sheriff clerk shall—

  (a) fix a date and time for the first hearing, which date shall be the first suitable court day occurring not sooner than 4 weeks after the expiry of the period of notice;

  (b) on fixing the date for the first hearing forthwith intimate that date in Form M5 to each party; and

  (c) prepare and sign an interlocutor recording the date of the first hearing.

Hearings

35.10.—(1) The sheriff shall conduct the first, and any subsequent hearing, with a view to securing the expeditious progress of the cause by ascertaining from parties the matters in dispute.

(2) The parties shall provide the sheriff with sufficient information to enable him to—

  (a) conduct the hearing as provided for in this Chapter,

  (b) consider any child witness notice or vulnerable witness application that has been lodged where no order has been made, or

  (c) ascertain whether there is or is likely to be a vulnerable witness within the meaning of section 11(1) of the Act of 2004 who is to give evidence at any proof or hearing and whether any order under section 12(1) of the Act of 2004 requires to be made.

(3) At the first, or any subsequent hearing, the sheriff shall fix a period within which defences, objections or claims shall be lodged, and appoint a date for a second hearing.

(4) Where the list lodged under rule 35.4(2)(a) contains any person who is not a party to the action, the sheriff shall order—

  (a) the initial writ to be amended to add that person as a defender;

  (b) service of the pleadings so amended to be made on that person, with a citation in Form M6; and

  (c) intimation to that person of any condescendence of the fund *in medio* lodged by a holder of the fund who is not the pursuer.

(5) Where a person to whom service has been made under paragraph (4) lodges a notice of appearance under rule 35.8, the sheriff clerk shall intimate to him in Form M5 the date of the next hearing fixed in the action.

Rule 35.10 focuses on the need for efficiency throughout the course of an action of multiplepoinding, so that the case may be disposed of as quickly and satisfactorily as possible. These provisions are similar to the rules for the conduct of options hearings and procedural hearings in other ordinary causes. (See for example OCR rules 9.12(1), (2) and 10.6(1).)

NOTE
[1]As inserted by the Act of Sederunt (Ordinary Cause, Summary Application, Summary Cause and Small Claim Rules) Amendment (Vulnerable Witnesses (Scotland) Act 2004) 2007, r.2(11) (effective November 1, 2007).

Lodging defences, objections and claims
35.11.—(1) Defences, objections and claims by a party shall be lodged with the sheriff clerk in a single document under separate headings.

(2) Each claimant shall lodge with his claim any documents founded on in his claim, so far as they are within his custody or power.

Disposal of defences
35.12.—(1) Where defences have been lodged, the sheriff may order the initial writ and defences to be adjusted and thereafter close the record and regulate further procedure.

(2) Unless the sheriff otherwise directs, defences shall be disposed of before any further procedure in the action.

The rules set out consecutive procedural stages by which defences, objections and claims are successively disposed of. Unless the sheriff otherwise directs, defences challenging the jurisdiction or competency of an action are dealt with first, before any further procedure. After defences have been lodged, the sheriff may order the initial writ and defences to be adjusted. He then closes the record and regulates further procedure, usually by appointing parties to debate. If the sheriff sustains the objections to jurisdiction or to the competency of the action, the case comes to an end here. If he rejects them, the case will continue to a new hearing at which further procedure will be determined.

Objections to fund in medio
35.13.—(1) Where objections to the fund *in medio* have been lodged, the sheriff may, after disposal of any defences, order the condescendence of the fund and objections to be adjusted, and thereafter close the record and regulate further procedure.

(2) If no objections to the fund *in medio* have been lodged, or if objections have been lodged and disposed of, the sheriff may, on the motion of the holder of the fund, and without ordering intimation to any party approve the condescendence of the fund and find the holder liable only in one single payment.

Preliminary pleas in multiplepoindings
35.14.—(1) A party intending to insist on a preliminary plea shall, not later than 3 days before any hearing to determine further procedure following the lodging of defences, objections or claims, lodge with the sheriff clerk a note of the basis of the plea.

(2) Where a party fails to comply with the provisions of paragraph (1), he shall be deemed to be no longer insisting on the plea and the plea shall be repelled by the sheriff at the hearing referred to in paragraph (1).

(3) If satisfied that there is a preliminary matter of law which justifies a debate, the sheriff shall, after having heard parties and considered the note lodged under this rule, appoint the action to debate.

Consignation of the fund and discharge of holder
35.15.—(1) At any time after the condescendence of the fund *in medio* has been approved, the sheriff may order the whole or any part of the fund to be sold and the proceeds of the sale consigned into court.

(2) After such consignation the holder of the fund *in medio* may apply for his exoneration and discharge.

(3) The sheriff may allow the holder of the fund *in medio*, on his exoneration and discharge, his expenses out of the fund as a first charge on the fund.

Further service or advertisement
35.16. The sheriff may at any time, of his own motion or on the motion of any party, order further service on any person or advertisement.

Ranking of claims
35.17.—(1) After disposal of any defences, and approval of the condescendence of the fund *in medio*, the sheriff may, where there is no competition on the fund, rank and prefer the claimants and grant decree in terms of that ranking.

(2) Where there is competition on the fund, the sheriff may order claims to be adjusted and thereafter close the record and regulate further procedure.

Remit to reporter
35.18.—(1) Where several claims have been lodged, the sheriff may remit to a reporter to prepare a scheme of division and report.

(2) The expenses of such remit, when approved by the sheriff, shall be made a charge on the fund, to be deducted before division.

CHAPTER 36

ACTIONS OF DAMAGES

[1] PART AI

SPECIAL PROCEDURE FOR ACTIONS FOR, OR ARISING FROM PERSONAL INJURIES

NOTE
[1] As inserted by the Act of Sederunt (Ordinary Cause Rules Amendment) (Personal Injuries Actions) 2009 (SSI 2009/285) r.2 (effective November 2, 2009).

Application and interpretation

Application and interpretation of this Part
36.A1.—(1) This Part applies to a personal injuries action.

(2) In this Part—
　　"personal injuries action" means an action of damages for, or arising from, personal
　　　　injuries or death of a person from personal injuries; and
　　"personal injuries procedure" means the procedure established by rules 36.G1 to 36.L1.

(3) In the definition of "personal injuries action", "personal injuries" includes any disease or impairment, whether physical or mental.

Raising a personal injuries action

Form of initial writ
36.B1.—(1) Subject to rule 36.C1, the initial writ in a personal injuries action shall be in Form PI1 and there shall be annexed to it a brief statement containing—
　　(a) averments in numbered paragraphs relating only to those facts necessary to establish
　　　　the claim;
　　(b) the names of every medical practitioner from whom, and every hospital or other
　　　　institution in which, the pursuer or, in an action in respect of the death of a person,
the deceased received treatment for the personal injuries.

(2) An initial writ may include—
　　(a) warrants for intimation so far as permitted under these Rules, and
　　(b) a specification of documents in Form PI2.

Actions based on clinical negligence
36.C1.—(1) An initial writ in a personal injuries action may include a draft interlocutor in Form PI4.

(2) At the same time as an initial writ which includes a draft interlocutor in Form PI4 is presented for warranting, the pursuer may lodge a written application in the form of a letter addressed to the sheriff clerk for authority to raise the action, where it is based on alleged clinical negligence, as an ordinary cause.

(3) On the making of an application under paragraph (2), the initial writ shall be placed before a sheriff in chambers and in the absence of the parties.

(4) On consideration of the initial writ in accordance with paragraph (3), the sheriff may—
　　(a) if he considers that there are exceptional reasons for not following personal injuries
　　　　procedure such as would justify the granting of a motion under rule 36.F1, grant
　　　　authority for the cause to proceed as an ordinary cause by signing the draft
　　　　interlocutor in the initial writ; or
　　(b) fix a hearing.

(5) The sheriff clerk shall notify the parties of the date and time of any hearing under paragraph (4)(b).

(6) At a hearing under paragraph (4)(b), the sheriff may refuse the application or, if he considers that there are exceptional reasons for not following personal injuries procedure such as would justify the granting of a motion under rule 36.F1, grant authority for the cause to proceed as an ordinary cause by signing the draft interlocutor in the initial writ.

(7) Where the sheriff grants authority for the cause to proceed as an ordinary cause under paragraph (4)(a) or (6)—

(a) the sheriff or, as the case may be, the sheriff clerk shall sign a warrant in accordance with rule 5.1 (signature of warrants);

(b) the cause shall thereafter proceed in accordance with Chapter 9 (standard procedure in defended causes) rather than in accordance with personal injuries procedure.

(8) In this rule—

"clinical negligence" means a breach of a duty of care by a health care professional in connection with that person's diagnosis or the care and treatment of any person, by act or omission, whilst the health care professional was acting in his professional capacity; and

"health care professional" includes a doctor, dentist, nurse, midwife, health visitor, pharmacy practitioner, registered ophthalmic practitioner, registered dispensing optician, member of Professions Allied to Medicine, member of the Allied Health Professions, a person who is a member of ambulance personnel, a member of laboratory staff or a relevant technician.

Inspection and recovery of documents

36.D1.—(1) This rule applies where the initial writ in a personal injuries action contains a specification of documents by virtue of rule 36.B1(2)(b).

(2) On the granting of a warrant for citation, an order granting commission and diligence for the production and recovery of the documents mentioned in the specification shall be deemed to have been granted and the sheriff clerk shall certify Form PI2 to that effect by attaching thereto a docquet in Form PI3.

(3) An order which is deemed to have been made under paragraph (2) shall be treated for all purposes as an interlocutor granting commission and diligence signed by the sheriff.

(4) The pursuer may serve an order under paragraph (2) and the provisions of Chapter 28 (recovery of evidence) shall thereafter apply, subject to any necessary modifications, as if the order were an order obtained on an application under rule 28.2 (applications for commission and diligence for recovery of documents etc.).

(5) Nothing in this rule shall affect the right of a party to apply under rule 28.2 for a commission and diligence for recovery of documents or for an order under section 1 of the Administration of Justice (Scotland) Act 1972 in respect of any document or other property whether or not mentioned in the specification annexed to the initial writ.

Personal injuries action: application of other rules and withdrawal from personal injuries procedure

Application of other rules

36.E1.—(1) Subject to rule 36.F1, a defended personal injuries action shall, instead of proceeding in accordance with Chapter 9 (standard procedure in defended causes), proceed in accordance with personal injuries procedure.

(2) Paragraph (1) does not apply to a personal injuries action in respect of which the sheriff has granted an application under rule 36.C1(2).

(3) Paragraphs (4) to (14) apply to a personal injuries action proceeding in accordance with personal injuries procedure.

(4) Despite paragraph (1), the following rules of Chapter 9 apply—

(a) rule 9.1 (notice of intention to defend);

(b) rule 9.3 (return of initial writ);

(c) rule 9.5 (process folder);

(d) rule 9.6 (defences); and

(e) rule 9.7 (implied admissions).

(5) But the defences shall not include a note of pleas-in-law.

(6) In the application of rule 18.3(1) (applications to amend), a minute of amendment lodged in process shall include, where appropriate, confirmation as to whether any warrants are sought under rule 36.B1(2)(a) or whether a specification of documents is sought under rule 36.B1(2)(b).

(7) In the application of rule 18.5(1)(a) (service of amended pleadings), the sheriff shall order any timetable issued in terms of rule 36.G1 to be served together with a copy of the initial writ or record.

(8) Rule 18.5(3) (fixing of hearing following service of amended pleadings and lodging of notice of intention to defend) shall not apply.

(9) In the application of rule 19.1 (counterclaims) a counterclaim may also include—

(a) warrants for intimation so far as permitted under these Rules; and

(b) a specification of documents in Form PI2.

(10) In rule 19.4 (disposal of counterclaims), paragraph (b) shall not apply.

(11) In the application of rule 20.4(3) (service on third party), any timetable already issued in terms of rule 36.G1 shall also be served with a third party notice.

(12) In the application of rule 20.6 (procedure following answers)—

    (a) paragraphs (1) and (2) shall not apply; and

    (b) where a third party lodges answers, any timetable already issued under rule 36.G1 shall apply to the third party.

(13) Chapters 22 (preliminary pleas) and 28A (pre-proof hearing) shall not apply.

(14) In relation to an action proceeding in accordance with personal injuries procedure—

    (a) references elsewhere in these Rules to the condescendence of an initial writ or to the articles of the condescendence shall be construed as references to the statement required under rule 36.B1(1) and the numbered paragraphs of that statement;

    (b) references elsewhere in these Rules to pleas-in-law, an open record, a closed record or a record for an Options Hearing shall be ignored;

[1]   (c) references elsewhere in these Rules to any action carried out before or after the closing of the record shall be construed as references to that action being carried out before, or as the case may be, after, the date fixed for completion of adjustment under rule 36.G1(1A)(c).

NOTE

[1] As amended by the Act of Sederunt (Sheriff Court Rules) (Miscellaneous Amendments) 2010 (SSI 2010/279) para.4 (effective July 29, 2010).

Disapplication of personal injuries procedure

36.F1.—(1) Any party to a personal injuries action proceeding in accordance with personal injuries procedure may, within 28 days of the lodging of defences (or, where there is more than one defender the first lodging of defences), by motion apply to have the action withdrawn from personal injuries procedure and to be appointed to proceed as an ordinary cause.

(2) No motion under paragraph (1) shall be granted unless the sheriff is satisfied that there are exceptional reasons for not following personal injuries procedure.

(3) In determining whether there are exceptional reasons justifying the granting of a motion made under paragraph (1), the sheriff shall have regard to—

    (a) the likely need for detailed pleadings;

    (b) the length of time required for preparation of the action; and

    (c) any other relevant circumstances.

(4) Where the sheriff appoints the cause to proceed as an ordinary cause under paragraph (1)—

    (a) the sheriff clerk shall fix a date and time for an Options Hearing;

    (b) the cause shall thereafter proceed in accordance with Chapter 9 rather than in accordance with personal injuries procedure;

    (c) the pursuer shall within 14 days thereof lodge a revised initial writ as nearly as may be in Form G1; and

    (d) the defender shall thereafter adjust his defences so as to comply with rule 9.6(2).

Personal injuries procedure

Allocation of diets and timetables

36.G1.—[1] (1) The sheriff clerk shall, on the lodging of defences in the action or, where there is more than one defender, the first lodging of defences—

    (a) allocate a diet of proof of the action, which shall be no earlier than 4 months (unless the sheriff on cause shown directs an earlier diet to be fixed) and no later than 9 months from the date of the first lodging of defences; and

    (b) issue a timetable stating—

        (i) the date of the diet mentioned in subparagraph (a); and

        (ii) the dates no later than which the procedural steps mentioned in paragraph (1A) are to take place.

[1] (1A) Those procedural steps are—

    (a) application for a third party notice under rule 20.1;

    (b) the pursuer executing a commission for recovery of documents under rule 36.D1;

    (c) the parties adjusting their pleadings;

    (d) the pursuer lodging a statement of valuation of claim in process;

    (e) the pursuer lodging a record;

    (f) the defender (and any third party to the action) lodging a statement of valuation of claim in process;

    (g) the parties each lodging in process a list of witnesses together with any productions upon which they wish to rely; and

(h) the pursuer lodging in process the minute of the pre-proof conference.

[1] (1B) The dates mentioned in paragraph (1)(b)(ii) are to be calculated by reference to periods specified in Appendix 3, which, with the exception of the period specified in rule 36.K1(2), the sheriff principal may vary for his sheriffdom or for any court within his sheriffdom.

(2) A timetable issued under paragraph (1)(b) shall be in Form PI5 and shall be treated for all purposes as an interlocutor signed by the sheriff; and so far as the timetable is inconsistent with any provision in these Rules which relates to a matter to which the timetable relates, the timetable shall prevail.

(3) Where a party fails to comply with any requirement of a timetable other than that referred to in paragraph (8) or rule 36.K1(3), the sheriff clerk may fix a date and time for the parties to be heard by the sheriff.

(4) The pursuer shall lodge a certified copy of the record, which shall consist of the pleadings of the parties, in process by the date specified in the timetable and shall at the same time send one copy to the defender and any other parties.

(5) The pursuer shall, on lodging the certified copy of the record as required by paragraph (4), apply by motion to the sheriff, craving the court—

    (a) to allow to parties a preliminary proof on specified matters;

    (b) to allow a proof; or

    (c) to make some other specified order.

(6) The motion lodged under paragraph (5) shall specify the anticipated length of the preliminary proof, or proof, as the case may be.

(7) In the event that any party proposes to crave the court to make any order other than an order allowing a proof under paragraph (5)(b), that party shall, on making or opposing (as the case may be) the pursuer's motion, specify the order to be sought and give full notice in the motion or the notice of opposition thereto of the grounds thereof.

(8) Where the pursuer fails to lodge a record by the date specified in the timetable issued under paragraph (1), the sheriff clerk shall fix a date and time for the parties to be heard by the sheriff.

[2] (8A) A party who seeks to rely on the evidence of a person not on his or her list lodged in accordance with paragraph (1A)(g) must, if any other party objects to such evidence being admitted, seek leave of the sheriff to admit that evidence whether it is to be given orally or not; and such leave may be granted on such conditions, if any, as the sheriff thinks fit.

[2] (8B) The list of witnesses intimated in accordance with paragraph (1A)(g) must include the name, occupation (where known) and address of each intended witness and indicate whether the witness is considered to be a vulnerable witness within the meaning of section 11(1) of the Act of 2004 and whether any child witness notice or vulnerable witness application has been lodged in respect of that witness.

[3] (9) A production which is not lodged in accordance with paragraph (1A)(g) shall not be used or put in evidence at proof unless—

    (a) by consent of parties; or

    (b) with the leave of the sheriff on cause shown and on such conditions, if any, as to expenses or otherwise as the court thinks fit.

(10) In a cause which is one of a number of causes arising out of the same cause of action, the sheriff may—

    (a) on the motion of a party to that cause; and

    (b) after hearing parties to all those causes, appoint that cause or any part of those causes to be the leading cause and to sist the other causes pending the determination of the leading cause.

(11) In this rule, "pursuer" includes additional pursuer or minuter as the case may be.

NOTES

[1] As substituted and inserted by the Act of Sederunt (Sheriff Court Rules) (Miscellaneous Amendments) 2010 (SSI 2010/279) para.4 (effective July 29, 2010).

[2] As inserted by the Act of Sederunt (Sheriff Court Rules) (Miscellaneous Amendments) 2010 (SSI 2010/279) para.4 (effective July 29, 2010).

[3] As amended by the Act of Sederunt (Sheriff Court Rules) (Miscellaneous Amendments) 2010 (SSI 2010/279) para.4 (effective July 29, 2010).

Applications for sist or for variation of timetable

36.H1.—[1] (1) The action may be sisted or the timetable varied by the sheriff on an application by any party to the action by motion.

(2) An application under paragraph (1)—

    (a) shall be placed before the sheriff; and

    (b) shall be granted only on special cause shown.

(3) Any sist of an action in terms of this rule shall be for a specific period.

(4) Where the timetable issued under rule 36.G1 is varied under this rule, the sheriff clerk shall issue a revised timetable in Form PI5.

(5) A revised timetable issued under paragraph (4) shall have effect as if it were a timetable issued under rule 36.G1 and any reference in this Part to any action being taken in accordance with the timetable shall be construed as a reference to its being taken in accordance with the timetable as varied under this rule.

NOTE
[1] As amended by the Act of Sederunt (Sheriff Court Rules) (Miscellaneous Amendments) 2010 (SSI 2010/279) para.4 (effective July 29, 2010).

Statements of valuation of claim
36.J1.—(1) Each party to the action shall make a statement of valuation of claim in Form PI6.

(2) A statement of valuation of claim (which shall include a list of supporting documents) shall be lodged in process.

(3) Each party shall, on lodging a statement of valuation of claim—
    (a) intimate the list of documents included in the statement of valuation of claim to every other party; and
    (b) lodge each of those documents.

(4) Nothing in paragraph (3) shall affect—
    (a) the law relating to, or the right of a party to object to, the recovery of a document on the ground of privilege or confidentiality; or
    (b) the right of a party to apply under rule 28.2 for a commission and diligence for recovery of documents or an order under section 1 of the Administration of Justice (Scotland) Act 1972.

(5) Without prejudice to paragraph (2) of rule 36.L1, where a party has failed to lodge a statement of valuation of claim in accordance with a timetable issued under rule 36.G1, the sheriff may, at any hearing under paragraph (3) of that rule—
    (a) where the party in default is the pursuer, dismiss the action; or
    (b) where the party in default is the defender, grant decree against the defender for an amount not exceeding the pursuer's valuation.

Pre-proof conferences
36.K1.—(1) For the purposes of this rule, a pre-proof conference is a conference of the parties, which shall be held not later than four weeks before the date assigned for the proof—
    (a) to discuss settlement of the action; and
    (b) to agree, so far as is possible, the matters which are not in dispute between them.

(2) Subject to any variation of the timetable in terms of rule 36.H1, a joint minute of a pre-proof conference, made in Form PI7, shall be lodged in process by the pursuer not later than three weeks before the date assigned for proof.

(3) Where a joint minute in Form PI7 has not been lodged in accordance with paragraph (2) and by the date specified in the timetable the sheriff clerk shall fix a date and time for the parties to be heard by the sheriff.

[1] (4) If a party is not present during the pre-proof conference, the representative of such party shall have access to the party or another person who has authority to commit the party in settlement of the action.

NOTE
[1] As substituted by the Act of Sederunt (Sheriff Court Rules) (Miscellaneous Amendments) 2010 (SSI 2010/279) para.4 (effective July 29, 2010).

Incidental hearings
36.L1.—(1) Where the sheriff clerk fixes a date and time for a hearing under paragraph (3) or (8) of rule 36.G1 or paragraph (3) of rule 36.K1 he shall—
    (a) fix a date not less than seven days after the date of the notice referred to in subparagraph (b);
    (b) give notice to the parties to the action—
        (i) of the date and time of the hearing; and
        (ii) requiring the party in default to lodge in process a written explanation as to why the timetable has not been complied with and to intimate a copy to all other parties, not less than two clear working days before the date of the hearing.

(2) At the hearing, the sheriff—
    (a) shall consider any explanation provided by the party in default;

(b) may award expenses against that party; and

(c) may make any other appropriate order, including decree of dismissal.

PART I

INTIMATION TO CONNECTED PERSONS IN CERTAIN ACTIONS OF DAMAGES

Application and interpretation of this Part

36.1.—(1) This Part applies to an action of damages in which, following the death of any person from personal injuries, damages are claimed—

(a) by the executor of the deceased, in respect of the injuries from which the deceased died; or

(b) by any relative of the deceased, in respect of the death of the deceased.

(2) In this Part—

"connected person" means a person, not being a party to the action, who has title to sue the defender in respect of the personal injuries from which the deceased died or in respect of his death;

"relative" has the meaning assigned to it in Schedule 1 to the Damages (Scotland) Act 1976.

Averments

36.2. In an action to which this Part applies, the pursuer shall aver in the condescendence, as the case may be—

(a) that there are no connected persons;

(b) that there are connected persons, being the persons specified in the crave for intimation;

(c) that there are connected persons in respect of whom intimation should be dispensed with on the ground that—

(i) the names or whereabouts of such persons are not known to, and cannot reasonably be ascertained by, the pursuer; or

(ii) such persons are unlikely to be awarded more than £200 each.

Warrants for intimation

36.3.—(1) Where the pursuer makes averments under rule 36.2(b) (existence of connected persons), he shall include a crave in the initial writ for intimation to any person who is believed to have title to sue the defender in an action in respect of the death of the deceased or the personal injuries from which the deceased died.

(2) A notice of intimation in Form D1 shall be attached to the copy of the initial writ where intimation is given on a warrant under paragraph (1).

Applications to dispense with intimation

36.4.—(1) Where the pursuer makes averments under rule 36.2(c) (dispensing with intimation to connected persons), he shall apply by crave in the initial writ for an order to dispense with intimation.

(2) In determining an application under paragraph (1), the sheriff shall have regard to—

(a) the desirability of avoiding a multiplicity of actions; and

(b) the expense, inconvenience or difficulty likely to be involved in taking steps to ascertain the name or whereabouts of the connected person.

(3) Where the sheriff is not satisfied that intimation to a connected person should be dispensed with, he may—

(a) order intimation to a connected person whose name and whereabouts are known;

(b) order the pursuer to take such further steps as he may specify in the interlocutor to ascertain the name or whereabouts of any connected person; and

(c) order advertisement in such manner, place and at such times as he may specify in the interlocutor.

Subsequent disclosure of connected persons

36.5. Where the name or whereabouts of a person, in respect of whom the sheriff has dispensed with intimation on a ground specified in rule 36.2(c) (dispensing with intimation to connected persons), subsequently becomes known to the pursuer, the pursuer shall apply to the sheriff by motion for a warrant for intimation to such a person; and such intimation shall be made in accordance with rule 36.3(2).

Connected persons entering process

36.6.—(1) A connected person may apply by minute craving leave to be sisted as an additional pursuer to the action.

(2) Such a minute shall also crave leave of the sheriff to adopt the existing grounds of action, and to amend the craves, condescendence and pleas-in-law.

(3) The period within which answers to a minute under this rule may be lodged shall be 14 days from the date of intimation of the minute.

[1] (4) Rule 14.13 (procedure following grant of minute) shall not apply to a minute to which this rule applies.

NOTE

[1] As amended by S.I. 1996 No. 2445 (effective November 1, 1996).

Failure to enter process

36.7. Where a connected person to whom intimation is made in accordance with this Part—
  (a) does not apply to be sisted as an additional pursuer to the action,
  (b) subsequently raises a separate action against the same defender in respect of the same personal injuries or death, and
  (c) would, apart from this rule, be awarded the expenses or part of the expenses of that action,

he shall not be awarded those expenses except on cause shown.

PART II

INTERIM PAYMENTS OF DAMAGES

Application and interpretation of this Part

36.8.—(1) This Part applies to an action of damages for personal injuries or the death of a person in consequence of personal injuries.

(2) In this Part—
  "defender" includes a third party against whom the pursuer has a crave for damages;
  "personal injuries" includes any disease or impairment of a physical or mental condition.

Applications for interim payment of damages

36.9.—(1) In an action to which this Part applies, a pursuer may, at any time after defences have been lodged, apply by motion for an order for interim payment of damages to him by the defender or, where there are two or more of them, by any one or more of them.

(2) The pursuer shall intimate a motion under paragraph (1) to every other party on a period of notice of 14 days.

(3) On a motion under paragraph (1), the sheriff may, if satisfied that—
  (a) the defender has admitted liability to the pursuer in the action, or
  (b) if the action proceeded to proof, the pursuer would succeed in the action on the question of liability without any substantial finding of contributory negligence on his part, or on the part of any person in respect of whose injury or death the claim of the pursuer arises, and would obtain decree for damages against any defender,

ordain that defender to make an interim payment to the pursuer of such amount as the sheriff thinks fit, not exceeding a reasonable proportion of the damages which, in the opinion of the sheriff, are likely to be recovered by the pursuer.

(4) Any such payment may be ordered to be made in one lump sum or otherwise as the sheriff thinks fit.

[1] (5) No order shall be made against a defender under this rule unless it appears to the sheriff that the defender is—
  (a) a person who is insured in respect of the claim of the pursuer;
  (b) a public authority;
  (c) a person whose means and resources are such as to enable him to make the interim payment; or
  (d) the person's liability will be met by—
    (i) an insurer under section 151 of the Road Traffic Act 1988; or
    (ii) an insurer acting under the Motor Insurers Bureau Agreement, or the Motor Insurers Bureau where it is acting itself.

(6) Notwithstanding the grant or refusal of a motion for an interim payment, a subsequent motion may be made where there has been a change of circumstances.

(7) Subject to Part IV (management of damages payable to persons under legal disability) an interim payment shall be paid to the pursuer unless the sheriff otherwise directs.

(8) This rule shall, with the necessary modifications, apply to a counterclaim for damages for personal injuries made by a defender as it applies to an action in which the pursuer may apply for an order for interim payment of damages.

NOTE
[1] Amended by the Act of Sederunt (Ordinary Cause, Summary Application and Small Claim Rules) Amendment (Miscellaneous) 2004 (SSI 2004/197) (effective May 21, 2004), para.2(13).

Adjustment on final decree
36.10. Where a defender has made an interim payment under rule 36.9, the sheriff may, when final decree is pronounced, make such order with respect to the interim payment as he thinks fit to give effect to the final liability of that defender to the pursuer; and in particular may order—
    (a) repayment by the pursuer of any sum by which the interim payment exceeds the amount which that defender is liable to pay to the pursuer; or
    (b) payment by any other defender or a third party, of any part of the interim payment which the defender who made it is entitled to recover from him by way of contribution or indemnity or in respect of any remedy or relief relating to, or connected with, the claim of the pursuer.

PART III

PROVISIONAL DAMAGES FOR PERSONAL INJURIES

Application and interpretation of this Part
36.11.—(1) This Part applies to an action of damages for personal injuries.
    (2) In this Part—
        "the Act of 1982" means the Administration of Justice Act 1982;
        "further damages" means the damages referred to in section 12(4)(b) of the Act of 1982;
        "provisional damages" means the damages referred to in section 12(4)(a) of the Act of 1982.

Applications for provisional damages
36.12. An application under section 12(2)(a) of the Act of 1982 for provisional damages for personal injuries shall be made by including in the initial writ—
    (a) a crave for provisional damages;
    (b) averments in the condescendence supporting the crave, including averments—
        (i) that there is a risk that, at some definite or indefinite time in the future, the pursuer will, as a result of the act or omission which gave rise to the cause of action, develop some serious disease or suffer some serious deterioration of his physical or mental condition; and
        (ii) that the defender was, at the time of the act or omission which gave rise to the cause of action, a public authority, public corporation or insured or otherwise indemnified in respect of the claim; and
    (c) an appropriate plea-in-law.

Applications for further damages
36.13.—(1) An application for further damages by a pursuer in respect of whom an order under section 12(2)(b) of the Act of 1982 has been made shall be made by minute in the process of the action to which it relates and shall include—
    (a) a crave for further damages;
    (b) averments in the statement of facts supporting that crave; and
    (c) appropriate pleas-in-law.
    (2) On lodging such a minute in process, the pursuer shall apply by motion for warrant to serve the minute on—
    (a) every other party; and
    (b) where such other party is insured or otherwise indemnified, his insurer or indemnifier, if known to the pursuer.
    (3) Any such party, insurer or indemnifier may lodge answers to such a minute in process within 28 days after the date of service on him.
    (4) Where answers have been lodged under paragraph (3), the sheriff may, on the motion of any party, make such further order as to procedure as he thinks fit.

PART IV

MANAGEMENT OF DAMAGES PAYABLE TO PERSONS UNDER LEGAL DISABILITY

Orders for payment and management of money
  [1] **36.14.**—(1) In an action of damages in which a sum of money becomes payable, by virtue of a decree or an extra-judicial settlement, to or for the benefit of a person under legal disability (other than a person under the age of 18 years), the sheriff shall make such order regarding the payment and management of that sum for the benefit of that person as he thinks fit.
  (2) An order under paragraph (1) shall be made on the granting of decree for payment or of absolvitor.

NOTE
  [1] As amended by SI 1996/2167 (effective November 1, 1996).

Methods of management
  36.15. In making an order under rule 36.14(1), the sheriff may—
    (a) appoint a judicial factor to apply, invest or otherwise deal with the money for the benefit of the person under legal disability;
    (b) order the money to be paid to—
      (i) the Accountant of Court, or
      (ii) the guardian of the person under legal disability,
      as trustee, to be applied, invested or otherwise dealt with and administered under the directions of the sheriff for the benefit of the person under legal disability;
    (c) order the money to be paid to the sheriff clerk of the sheriff court district in which the person under legal disability resides, to be applied, invested or otherwise dealt with and administered, under the directions of the sheriff of that district, for the benefit of the person under legal disability; or
    (d) order the money to be paid directly to the person under legal disability.

Subsequent orders
  36.16.—(1) Where the sheriff has made an order under rule 36.14(1), any person having an interest may apply for an appointment or order under rule 36.15, or any other order for the payment or management of the money, by minute in the process of the cause to which the application relates.
  (2) An application for directions under rule 36.15(b) or (c) may be made by any person having an interest by minute in the process of the cause to which the application relates.

Management of money paid to sheriff clerk
  36.17.—(1) A receipt in Form D2 by the sheriff clerk shall be a sufficient discharge in respect of the amount paid to him under this Part.
  (2) The sheriff clerk shall, at the request of any competent court, accept custody of any sum of money in an action of damages ordered to be paid to, applied, invested or otherwise dealt with by him, for the benefit of a person under legal disability.
  (3) Any money paid to the sheriff clerk under this Part shall be paid out, applied, invested or otherwise dealt with by the sheriff clerk only after such intimation, service and enquiry as the sheriff may order.
  (4) Any sum of money invested by the sheriff clerk under this Part shall be invested in a manner in which trustees are authorised to invest by virtue of the Trustee Investments Act 1961.

[1] PART IV A

PRODUCTIONS IN CERTAIN ACTIONS OF DAMAGES

NOTE
  [1] As inserted by the Act of Sederunt (Sheriff Court Ordinary Cause Rules Amendment) (Miscellaneous) 2000 (SSI 2000/239) (effective October 2, 2000).

Application of this Part
  [1] **36.17A.** This Part applies to an action of damages for personal injuries or the death of a person in consequence of personal injuries, which, by virtue of rule 36.C1 or rule 36.F1, is to proceed as an ordinary cause.

NOTE
[1] As amended by the Act of Sederunt (Ordinary Cause Rules Amendment) (Personal Injuries Actions) 2009 (SSI 2009/285) r.2 (effective November 2, 2009).

Averments of medical treatment
36.17B. The condescendence of the initial writ in an action to which this Part applies shall include averments naming—
   (a) every general medical practitioner or general medical practice from whom; and
   (b) every hospital or other institution in which,
the pursuer or, in an action in respect of the death of a person, the deceased received treatment for the injuries sustained, or disease suffered, by him.

Lodging of medical reports
36.17C.—(1) In an action to which this Part applies, the pursuer shall lodge as productions, with the initial writ when it is presented for warranting in accordance with rule 5.1, all medical reports on which he intends, or intends to reserve the right, to rely in the action.
   (2) Where no medical report is lodged as required by paragraph (1), the defender may apply by motion for an order specifying a period within which such a report shall be lodged in process.

PART V

SEX DISCRIMINATION ACT 1975

Causes under section 66 of the Act of 1975
36.18. [*Omitted by the Act of Sederunt (Ordinary Cause, Summary Application, Summary Cause and Small Claim Rules) Amendment (Equality Act 2006 etc.) 2006 (SSI 2006/509) (effective November 3, 2006).*]

[1] PART VI

MESOTHELIOMA ACTIONS: SPECIAL PROVISIONS

NOTE
[1] As inserted by the Act of Sederunt (Ordinary Cause Rules Amendment) (Personal Injuries Actions) 2009 (SSI 2009/285) r.2 (effective November 2, 2009).

Mesothelioma actions: special provisions
36.19.—(1) This Part applies where liability to a relative of the pursuer may arise under section 1(2A) and (2B) of the Damages (Scotland) Act 1976 (liability where the personal injury in consequence of which the deceased died is mesothelioma).
   (2) On settlement of the pursuer's claim, the pursuer may apply by motion for all or any of the following—
   (a) a sist for a specified period;
   (b) discharge of any diet;
   (c) where the action is one to which the personal injuries procedure in Part A1 of this Chapter applies, variation of the timetable issued under rule 36.G1.
   (3) Paragraphs (4) to (7) apply where a motion under paragraph (2) has been granted.
   (4) As soon as reasonably practicable after the death of the pursuer, any agent who immediately prior to the death was instructed in a cause by the deceased pursuer shall notify the court of the death.
   (5) The notification under paragraph (4) shall be by letter to the sheriff clerk and shall be accompanied by a certified copy of the death certificate relative to the deceased pursuer.
   (6) A relative of the deceased may apply by motion for the recall of the sist and for an order for further procedure.
   (7) On expiration of the period of any sist pronounced on a motion under paragraph (2), the sheriff clerk may fix a date and time for the parties to be heard by the sheriff.

CHAPTER 37

CAUSES UNDER THE PRESUMPTION OF DEATH (SCOTLAND) ACT 1977

Interpretation of this Chapter
37.1. In this Chapter—

"the Act of 1977" means the Presumption of Death (Scotland) Act 1977;

"action of declarator" means an action under section 1(1) of the Act of 1977;

"missing person" has the meaning assigned in section 1(1) of the Act of 1977.

Parties to, and service and intimation of, actions of declarator

37.2.—[1,2] (1) In an action of declarator—

(a) the missing person shall be named as the defender;

(b) subject to paragraph (2), service on that person shall be executed by advertisement in such newspaper or other publication as the sheriff thinks fit of such facts relating to the missing person and set out in the initial writ as the sheriff may specify; and

(c) the period of notice shall be 21 days from the date of publication of the advertisement unless the sheriff otherwise directs.

[2] (2) The advertisement mentioned in paragraph (1) shall be in Form P1.

(3) Subject to paragraph (5), in an action of declarator, the pursuer shall include a crave for a warrant for intimation to—

(a) the missing person's—

(i) spouse, and

(ii) children, or, if he has no children, his nearest relative known to the pursuer,

(b) any person, including any insurance company, who so far as known to the pursuer has an interest in the action, and

(c) the Lord Advocate,

in the following terms:— "For intimation to (*name and address*) as [husband *or* wife, child *or* nearest relative] [a person having an interest in the presumed death] of (*name and last known address of the missing person*) and to the Lord Advocate.".

[3] (4) A notice of intimation in Form P2 shall be attached to the copy of the initial writ where intimation is given on a warrant under paragraph (3).

(5) The sheriff may, on the motion of the pursuer, dispense with intimation on a person mentioned in paragraph (3)(a) or (b).

(6) An application by minute under section 1(5) of the Act of 1977 (person interested in seeking determination or appointment not sought by pursuer) shall contain a crave for the determination or appointment sought, averments in the answers to the condescendence in support of that crave and an appropriate plea-in-law.

(7) On lodging a minute under paragraph (6), the minuter shall—

(a) send a copy of the minute by registered post or the first class recorded delivery service to each person to whom intimation of the action has been made under paragraph (2); and

(b) lodge in process the Post Office receipt or certificate of posting of that minute.

NOTES

[1] As amended by the Act of Sederunt (Sheriff Court Ordinary Cause Rules Amendment) (Miscellaneous) 1996 (SI 1996/2445) (effective November 1, 1996) (clerical error).

[2] Substituted by the Act of Sederunt (Sheriff Court Ordinary Cause Rules Amendment) (Miscellaneous) 2000 (SSI 2000/239) (effective October 2, 2000).

[3] As amended by the Act of Sederunt (Sheriff Court Ordinary Cause Rules Amendment) (Miscellaneous) 2000 (SSI 2000/239) (effective October 2, 2000).

Further advertisement

37.3. Where no minute has been lodged indicating knowledge of the present whereabouts of the missing person, at any time before the determination of the action, the sheriff may, of his own motion or on the motion of a party, make such order for further advertisement as he thinks fit.

Applications for proof

37.4.—(1) In an action of declarator where no minute has been lodged, the pursuer shall, after such further advertisement as may be ordered under rule 37.3, apply to the sheriff by motion for an order for proof.

(2) A proof ordered under paragraph (1) shall be by affidavit evidence unless the sheriff otherwise directs.

Applications for variation or recall of decree

37.5.—(1) An application under section 4(1) of the Act of 1977 (variation or recall of decree) shall be made by minute in the process of the action to which it relates.

(2) On the lodging of such a minute, the sheriff shall make an order—

(a) for service on the missing person, where his whereabouts have become known;

    (b) for intimation to those persons mentioned in rule 37.2(3) or to dispense with intimation to a person mentioned in rule 37.2(3)(a) or (b); and

    (c) for any answers to the minute to be lodged in process within such period as the sheriff thinks fit.

(3) An application under section 4(3) of the Act of 1977 (person interested seeking determination or appointment not sought by applicant for variation order) shall be made by lodging answers containing a crave for the determination or appointment sought.

(4) A person lodging answers containing a crave under paragraph (3) shall, as well as sending a copy of the answers to the minuter—

    (a) send a copy of the answers by registered post or the first class recorded delivery service to each person on whom service or intimation of the minute was ordered; and

    (b) lodge in process the Post Office receipt or certificate of posting of those answers.

Appointment of judicial factors

37.6.—(1) The Act of Sederunt (Judicial Factors Rules) 1992 shall apply to an application for the appointment of a judicial factor under section 2(2)(c) or section 4(2) of the Act of 1977 as it applies to a petition for the appointment of a judicial factor.

(2) In the application of rule 37.5 (applications for variation or recall of decree) to an application under section 4(1) of the Act of 1977 in a cause in which variation or recall of the appointment of a judicial factor is sought, for reference to a minute there shall be substituted references to a note.

CHAPTER 38

EUROPEAN COURT

Interpretation of this Chapter

38.1.—(1) In this Chapter—

"appeal" includes an application for leave to appeal;

"the European Court" means the Court of Justice of the European Communities;

"reference" means a reference to the European Court for

[1] (a) a preliminary ruling under Article 234 of the E.E.C. Treaty, Article 150 of the Euratom Treaty or Article 41 of the E.C.S.C. Treaty; or

    (b) a ruling on the interpretation of the Conventions, as defined in section 1(1) of the Civil Jurisdiction and Judgments Act 1982, under Article 3 of Schedule 2 to that Act.

(2) The expressions "E.E.C. Treaty", "Euratom Treaty" and "E.C.S.C. Treaty" have the meanings assigned respectively in Schedule 1 to the European Communities Act 1972.

NOTE

[1] As amended by the Act of Sederunt (Sheriff Court Ordinary Cause Rules Amendment) (Miscellaneous) 2000 (S.S.I. 2000 No. 239) (effective October 2, 2000).

Applications for reference

38.2.—(1) A reference may be made by the sheriff of his own motion or on the motion of a party.

(2) [*Repealed by S.S.I. 2000 No.239 (effective October 2, 2000).*]

Preparation of case for reference

38.3.—(1) Where the sheriff decides that a reference shall be made, he shall continue the cause for that purpose and, within 4 weeks after the date of that continuation, draft a reference.

[1] (1A) Except in so far as the sheriff may otherwise direct, a reference shall be prepared in accordance with Form E1, having regard to the guidance set out in the Notes for Guidance issued by the Court of Justice of the European Communities.

(2) On the reference being drafted, the sheriff clerk shall send a copy to each party.

(3) Within 4 weeks after the date on which copies of the draft have been sent to parties, each party may—

    (a) lodge with the sheriff clerk, and

    (b) send to every other party,

a note of any adjustments he seeks to have made in the draft reference.

(4) Within 14 days after the date on which any such note of adjustments may be lodged, the sheriff, after considering any such adjustments, shall make and sign the reference.

(5) The sheriff clerk shall forthwith intimate the making of the reference to each party.

Sist of cause
38.4.—(1) Subject to paragraph (2), on a reference being made, the cause shall, unless the sheriff when making such a reference otherwise orders, be sisted until the European Court has given a preliminary ruling on the question referred to it.

(2) The sheriff may recall a sist made under paragraph (1) for the purpose of making an interim order which a due regard to the interests of the parties may require.

Transmission of reference
38.5.—(1) Subject to paragraph (2), a copy of the reference, certified by the sheriff clerk, shall be transmitted by the sheriff clerk to the Registrar of the European Court.

(2) Unless the sheriff otherwise directs, a copy of the reference shall not be sent to the Registrar of the European Court where an appeal against the making of the reference is pending.

(3) For the purpose of paragraph (2), an appeal shall be treated as pending—
    (a) until the expiry of the time for making that appeal; or
    (b) where an appeal has been made, until that appeal has been determined.

CHAPTER 39

PROVISIONS IN RELATION TO CURATORS AD LITEM

Fees and outlays of curators ad litem in respect of children
¹ **39.1.**—(1) This rule applies to any civil proceedings whether or not the child is a party to the action.

(2) In an action where the sheriff appoints a curator ad litem to a child, the pursuer shall in the first instance, unless the court otherwise directs, be responsible for the fees and outlays of the curator ad litem incurred during the period from his appointment until the occurrence of any of the following events:
    (a) he lodges a minute stating that he does not intend to lodge defences or to enter the process;
    (b) he decides to instruct the lodging of defences or a minute adopting defences already lodged; or(c) the discharge, before the occurrence of the events mentioned in sub paragraphs (a) and (b), of the curator.

¹ CHAPTER 40

COMMERCIAL ACTIONS

Application and interpretation of this Chapter
40.1.—(1) This Chapter applies to a commercial action.

(2) In this Chapter—
    (a) "commercial action" means—an action arising out of, or concerned with, any transaction or dispute of a commercial or business nature including, but not limited to, actions relating to—
        (i) the construction of a commercial document;
        (ii) the sale or hire purchase of goods;
        (iii) the export or import of merchandise;
        (iv) the carriage of goods by land, air or sea;
        (v) insurance;
        (vi) banking;
        (vii) the provision of services;
        (viii) a building, engineering or construction contract; or

(ix) a commercial lease; and
(b) "commercial action" does not include an action in relation to consumer credit transactions.

(3) A commercial action may be raised only in a sheriff court where the Sheriff Principal for the sheriffdom has directed that the procedure should be available.

Proceedings before a nominated sheriff
40.2. All proceedings in a commercial action shall be brought before—
(a) a sheriff of the sheriffdom nominated by the Sheriff Principal; or
(b) where a nominated sheriff is not available, any other sheriff of the sheriffdom.

Procedure in commercial actions
40.3.—(1) In a commercial action the sheriff may make such order as he thinks fit for the progress of the case in so far as not inconsistent with the provisions in this Chapter.

(2) Where any hearing is continued, the reason for such continuation shall be recorded in the interlocutor.

Election of procedure for commercial actions
40.4. The pursuer may elect to adopt the procedure in this Chapter by bringing an action in Form G1A.

Transfer of action to be a commercial action
40.5.—(1) In an action within the meaning of rule 40.1(2) in which the pursuer has not made an election under rule 40.4, any party may apply by motion at any time to have the action appointed to be a commercial action.

(2) An interlocutor granted under paragraph (1) shall include a direction as to further procedure.

Appointment of a commercial action as an ordinary cause
40.6.—(1) At any time before, or at the Case Management Conference, the sheriff shall appoint a commercial action to proceed as an ordinary cause—
(a) on the motion of a party where—
(i) detailed pleadings are required to enable justice to be done between the parties; or
(ii) any other circumstances warrant such an order being made; or
(b) on the joint motion of parties.

(2) If a motion to appoint a commercial action to proceed as an ordinary action is refused, no subsequent motion to appoint the action to proceed as an ordinary cause shall be considered except on a material change of circumstances.

(3) Where the sheriff orders that a commercial action shall proceed as an ordinary cause the interlocutor granting such shall prescribe—
(a) a period of adjustment, if appropriate; and
(b) the date, time and place for any options hearing fixed.

(4) In determining what order to make in deciding that a commercial action proceed as an ordinary cause the sheriff shall have regard to the periods prescribed in rule 9.2.

Special requirements for initial writ in a commercial action
40.7.—(1) Where the construction of a document is the only matter in dispute no pleadings or pleas-in-law require to be included in the initial writ.

(2) There shall be appended to an initial writ in Form G1A a list of the documents founded on or adopted as incorporated in the initial writ.

Notice of Intention to Defend
40.8.—(1) Where the defender intends to—
(a) challenge the jurisdiction of the court;
(b) state a defence; or
(c) make a counterclaim,
he shall, before the expiry of the period of notice lodge with the sheriff clerk a notice of intention to defend in Form O7 and shall, at the same time, send a copy to the pursuer.

(2) The lodging of a notice of intention to defend shall not imply acceptance of the jurisdiction of the court.

Defences
40.9.—(1) Where a notice of intention to defend has been lodged, the defender shall lodge defences within 7 days after the expiry of the period of notice.

(2) There shall be appended to the defences a list of the documents founded on or adopted as incorporated in the defences.

(3) Subject to the requirement that each article of condescendence in the initial writ need not be admitted or denied, defences shall be in the form of answers that allow the extent of the dispute to be identified and shall have appended a note of the pleas in law of the defender.

Fixing date for Case Management Conference

40.10.—(1) On the lodging of defences, the sheriff clerk shall fix a date and time for a Case Management Conference, which date shall be on the first suitable court day occurring not sooner than 14 days, nor later than 28 days after the date of expiry of the period of notice.

(2) On fixing the date for the Case Management Conference, the sheriff clerk shall—
    (a) forthwith intimate to the parties the date and time of the Case Management Conference; and
    (b) prepare and sign an interlocutor recording that information.

(3) The fixing of the date of the Case Management Conference shall not affect the right of a party to make application by motion, to the court.

Applications for summary decree in a commercial action

40.11. Where a pursuer, in terms of rule 17.2(1) (applications for summary decree), or a defender in terms of rule 17.3(1) (application of summary decree to counterclaims), applies for summary decree in a commercial action, the period of notice mentioned in rule 17.2(3) shall be 48 hours.

Case Management Conference

40.12.—(1) At the Case Management Conference in a commercial action the sheriff shall seek to secure the expeditious resolution of the action.

(2) Parties shall be prepared to provide such information as the sheriff may require to determine—
    (a) whether, and to what extent, further specification of the claim and defences is required; and
    (b) the orders to make to ensure the expeditious resolution of the action; and
[1] (c) whether there is or is likely to be a vulnerable witness within the meaning of section 11(1) of the Act of 2004 who is to give evidence at any proof or hearing, consider any child witness notice or vulnerable witness application that has been lodged where no order has been made and consider whether any order under section 12(1) of the Act of 2004 requires to be made.

(3) The orders the sheriff may make in terms of paragraph 2(b) may include but shall not be limited to—
    (a) the lodging of written pleadings by any party to the action which may be restricted to particular issues;
    (b) the lodging of a statement of facts by any party which may be restricted to particular issues;
    (c) allowing an amendment by a party to his pleadings;
    (d) disclosure of the identity of witnesses and the existence and nature of documents relating to the action or authority to recover documents either generally or specifically;
    (e) the lodging of documents constituting, evidencing or relating to the subject matter of the action or any invoices, correspondence or similar documents;
    (f) the exchanging of lists of witnesses;
    (g) the lodging of reports of skilled persons or witness statements;
    (h) the lodging of affidavits concerned with any of the issues in the action;
    (i) the lodging of notes of arguments setting out the basis of any preliminary plea;
    (j) fixing a debate or proof, with or without any further preliminary procedure, to determine the action or any particular aspect thereof;
    (k) the lodging of joint minutes of admission or agreement;
    (l) recording admissions made on the basis of information produced; or
    (m) any order which the sheriff thinks will result in the speedy resolution of the action (including the use of alternative dispute resolution), or requiring the attendance of parties in person at any subsequent hearing.

(4) In making any order in terms of paragraph (3) the sheriff may fix a period within which such order shall be complied with.

(5) The sheriff may continue the Case Management Conference to a specified date where he considers it necessary to do so—
    (a) to allow any order made in terms of paragraph (3) to be complied with; or
    (b) to advance the possibility of resolution of the action.

(6) Where the sheriff makes an order in terms of paragraph (3) he may ordain the pursuer to—
  (a) make up a record; and
  (b) lodge that record in process,
within such period as he thinks fit.

NOTE
[1]As inserted by the Act of Sederunt (Ordinary Cause, Summary Application, Summary Cause and Small Claim Rules) Amendment (Vulnerable Witnesses (Scotland) Act 2004) 2007, r.2(12) (effective November 1, 2007).

Lodging of productions
  40.13. Prior to any proof or other hearing at which the documents listed in terms of rules 40.7(2) and 40.9(2) are to be referred to parties shall, in addition to lodging the productions in terms of rule 21.1, prepare, for the use of the sheriff, a working bundle in which the documents are arranged chronologically or in another appropriate order.

Hearing for further procedure
  40.14. At any time before final judgement, the sheriff may—
  (a) of his own motion or on the motion of any party, fix a hearing for further procedure; and
  (b) make such other order as he thinks fit.

Failure to comply with rule or order of sheriff
  40.15. Any failure by a party to comply timeously with a provision in this Chapter or any order made by the sheriff in a commercial action shall entitle the sheriff, of his own motion—
  (a) to refuse to extend any period for compliance with a provision in these Rules or an order of the court;
  (b) to dismiss the action or counterclaim, as the case may be, in whole or in part;
  (c) to grant decree in respect of all or any of the craves of the initial writ or counterclaim, as the case may be; or
  (d) to make an award of expenses,
as he thinks fit.

Determination of action
  40.16. It shall be open to the sheriff, at the end of any hearing, to restrict any interlocutor to a finding.

Parts of Process
  40.17. All parts of process lodged in a commercial action shall be clearly marked "Commercial Action".

[1] CHAPTER 41

PROTECTION FROM ABUSE (SCOTLAND) ACT 2001

NOTE
  [1] Inserted by the Act of Sederunt (Ordinary Cause Rules) Amendment (Applications under the Protection from Abuse (Scotland) Act 2001) 2002 (SSI 2002/128), para.2.

Interpretation
  41.1.—(1) In this Chapter a section referred to by number means the section so numbered in the Protection from Abuse (Scotland) Act 2001.
  (2) Words and expressions used in this Chapter which are also used in the Protection from Abuse (Scotland) Act 2001 have the same meaning as in that Act.

Attachment of power of arrest to interdict
  [1] **41.2.**—(1) An application under section 1(1) (application for attachment of power of arrest to interdict)—
  (a) shall be made in the crave in the initial writ, defences or counterclaim in which the interdict to which it relates is applied for, or, if made after the application for interdict, by motion in the process of the action in which the interdict was sought, or by minute, with answers if appropriate, should the sheriff so order; and
  (b) shall be intimated to the person against whom the interdict is sought or was obtained.

[2] (2) Where the sheriff attaches a power of arrest under section 1(2) or (1A) (order attaching power of arrest) the following documents shall be served along with the power of arrest in accordance with section 2(1) (documents to be served along with power of arrest)—

(a) a copy of the application for interdict;

(b) a copy of the interlocutor granting interdict; and

(c) where the application to attach the power of arrest was made after the interdict was granted, a copy of the certificate of service of the interdict.

(3) After the power of arrest has been served, the following documents shall be delivered by the person who obtained the power to the chief constable in accordance with section 3(1) (notification to police)—

(a) a copy of the application for interdict;

(b) a copy of the interlocutor granting interdict;

(c) a copy of the certificate of service of the interdict; and

(d) where the application to attach the power of arrest was made after the interdict was granted—

   (i) a copy of the application for the power of arrest;

   (ii) a copy of the interlocutor granting it; and

   (iii) a copy of the certificate of service of the power of arrest and the documents that required to be served along with it in accordance with section 2(1).

NOTES

[1] As amended by the Act of Sederunt (Ordinary Cause, Summary Application, Summary Cause and Small Claim Rules) Amendment (Miscellaneous) 2003 (SSI 2003/26), para.2(13) (effective January 24, 2003).

[2] As amended by Act of Sederunt (Ordinary Cause Rules) Amendment (Family Law (Scotland) Act 2006 etc.) 2006, para.2 (SSI 2006/207) (effective May 4, 2006).

Extension or recall of power of arrest

41.3.—(1) An application under either of the following provisions shall be made by minute in the process of the action in which the power of arrest was attached—

(a) section 2(3) (extension of duration of power of arrest);

(b) section 2(7) (recall of power of arrest).

(2) Where the sheriff extends the duration of, or recalls, a power of arrest, the person who obtained the extension or recall must deliver a copy of the interlocutor granting the extension or recall in accordance with section 3(1).

Documents to be delivered to chief constable in relation to recall or variation of interdict

41.4. Where an interdict to which a power of arrest has been attached under section 1(2) is varied or recalled, the person who obtained the variation or recall must deliver a copy of the interlocutor varying or recalling the interdict in accordance with section 3(1).

Certificate of delivery of documents to chief constable

41.5.—Where a person is in any circumstances required to comply with section 3(1) he shall, after such compliance, lodge in process a certificate of delivery in Form PA1.".

[1] CHAPTER 42

NOTE

[1] Inserted by the Act of Sederunt (Ordinary Cause Rules) Amendment (Competition Appeal Tribunal) 2004 (SSI 2004/350), para.2 (effective August 20, 2004).

COMPETITION APPEAL TRIBUNAL

Interpretation

42.1. In this Chapter—

"the 1998 Act" means the Competition Act 1998; and

"the Tribunal" means the Competition Appeal Tribunal established by section 12 of the Enterprise Act 2002.

Transfer of proceedings to the Tribunal

42.2.—(1) A party in proceedings for a monetary claim to which section 47A of the 1998 Act applies may apply by motion to the sheriff for an order transferring the proceedings, or any part of them, to the Tribunal.

(2) Where the sheriff orders that such proceedings (or any part of them) are transferred to the Tribunal, the sheriff clerk shall, within 7 days from the date of such order—

    (a) transmit the process (or the appropriate part) to the clerk of the Tribunal;

    (b) notify each party to the proceedings in writing of the transmission under sub paragraph (a); and

    (c) certify, by making an appropriate entry on the interlocutor sheet, that he has made all notifications required under sub paragraph (b).

(3) Transmission of the process under paragraph (2)(a) shall be valid notwithstanding any failure by the sheriff clerk to comply with paragraph (2)(b) and (c).

[1] Chapter 43

Causes Relating to Articles 81 and 82 of the Treaty Establishing the European Community

NOTE

[1] Inserted by Act of Sederunt (Ordinary Cause Rules) Amendment (Causes Relating to Articles 81 and 82 of the Treaty Establishing the European Community) 2006 (SSI 2006/293) (effective June 16, 2006).

Intimation of actions to the Office of Fair Trading

    43.1—(1) In this rule—

      "the Treaty" means the Treaty establishing the European Community; and

      "the OFT" means the Office of Fair Trading.

    (2) In an action where an issue under Article 81 or 82 of the Treaty is raised—

    (a) by the pursuer in the initial writ;

    (b) by the defender in the defences;

    (c) by any party in the pleadings;

intimation of the action shall be given to the OFT by the party raising the issue by a notice of intimation in Form OFT1.

    (3) The initial writ, defences or pleadings in which the issue under Article 81 or 82 of the Treaty is raised shall include a crave for warrant for intimation to the OFT.

    (4) A certified copy of an interlocutor granting a warrant under paragraph (3) shall be sufficient authority for the party to intimate by notice in Form OFT1.

    (5) A notice of intimation under paragraph (2) shall be on a period of notice of 21 days unless the sheriff otherwise orders; but the sheriff shall not order a period of notice of less than 2 days.

    (6) There shall be attached to the notice of intimation—

    (a) a copy of the initial writ, defences or pleadings (including any adjustments and amendments), as the case may be;

    (b) a copy of the interlocutor allowing intimation of the notice; and

    (c) where the pleadings have not been amended in accordance with any minute of amendment, a copy of that minute.

[1] Chapter 44

Equality Enactments

NOTE

[1] As inserted by the Act of Sederunt (Ordinary Cause, Summary Application, Summary Cause and Small Claim Rules) Amendment (Equality Act 2006 etc.) 2006 (SSI 2006/509), (effective November 3, 2006).

Application and interpretation

    44.1.—(1) This Chapter applies to claims under the equality enactments.

    (2) In this Chapter, "claims under the equality enactments" means proceedings in reparation for breach of statutory duty under any of the following enactments:—

    (a) Sex Discrimination Act 1975;

    (b) Race Relations Act 1976;

    (c) Disability Discrimination Act 1995;

    (d) Equality Act 2006.

Intimation to Commission

    [1] **44.2.** The pursuer shall send a copy of the initial writ to the Commission by registered or recorded delivery post.

[1] As inserted by the Act of Sederunt (Sheriff Court Rules) (Miscellaneous Amendments) 2008 (SSI 2008/223) para.4(3)(b) (effective July 1, 2008).

Assessor

44.3.—(1) The sheriff may, of his own motion or on the motion of any party, appoint an assessor.

(2) The assessor shall be a person who the sheriff considers has special qualifications to be of assistance in determining the cause.

Taxation of Commission expenses

44.4. [*Omitted by the Act of Sederunt (Sheriff Court Rules) (Miscellaneous Amendments) 2008 (SSI 2008/223) para.4(3)(c) (effective July 1, 2008).*]

National security

44.5.—(1) Where, on a motion under paragraph (3) or of his own motion, the sheriff considers it expedient in the interests of national security, he may—

(a) exclude from all or part of the proceedings—
  (i) the pursuer;
  (ii) the pursuer's representatives;
  (iii) any assessors;
(b) permit a pursuer or representative who has been excluded to make a statement to the court before the commencement of the proceedings or the part of the proceedings, from which he is excluded;
(c) take steps to keep secret all or part of the reasons for his decision in the proceedings.

(2) The sheriff clerk shall, on the making of an order under paragraph (1) excluding the pursuer or his representatives, notify the Advocate General for Scotland of that order.

(3) A party may apply by motion for an order under paragraph (1).

(4) The steps referred to in paragraph (1)(c) may include the following—

(a) directions to the sheriff clerk; and
(b) orders requiring any person appointed to represent the interests of the pursuer in proceedings from which the pursuer or his representatives are excluded not to communicate (directly or indirectly) with any persons (including the excluded pursuer)—
  (i) on any matter discussed or referred to;
  (ii) with regard to any material disclosed,

during or with reference to any part of the proceedings from which the pursuer or his representatives are excluded.

(5) Where the sheriff has made an order under paragraph (4)(b), the person appointed to represent the interests of the pursuer may apply by motion for authority to seek instructions from or otherwise communicate with an excluded person.

[1] CHAPTER 45

VULNERABLE WITNESSES (SCOTLAND) ACT 2004

NOTE

[1]As inserted by the Act of Sederunt (Ordinary Cause, Summary Application, Summary Cause and Small Claim Rules) Amendment (Vulnerable Witnesses (Scotland) Act 2004) 2007, r.2(13) (effective November 1, 2007).

Interpretation

45.1. In this Chapter—

"child witness notice" has the meaning given in section 12(2) of the Act of 2004;
"review application" means an application for review of arrangements for vulnerable witnesses pursuant to section 13 of the Act of 2004;
"vulnerable witness application" has the meaning given in section 12(6) of the Act of 2004.

Child Witness Notice

45.2. A child witness notice lodged in accordance with section 12(2) of the Act of 2004 shall be in Form G19.

Vulnerable Witness Application

45.3. A vulnerable witness application lodged in accordance with section 12(6) of the Act of 2004 shall be in Form G20.

Intimation

45.4.—(1) The party lodging a child witness notice or vulnerable witness application shall intimate a copy of the child witness notice or vulnerable witness application to all the other parties to the proceedings and complete a certificate of intimation.

(2) A certificate of intimation referred to in paragraph (1) shall be in Form G21 and shall be lodged with the child witness notice or vulnerable witness application.

Procedure on lodging child witness notice or vulnerable witness application

45.5.—(1) On receipt of a child witness notice or vulnerable witness application, the sheriff may—

    (a) make an order under section 12(1) or (6) of the Act of 2004 without holding a hearing;

    (b) require further information from any of the parties before making any further order;

    (c) fix a date for a hearing of the child witness notice or vulnerable witness application.

(2) The sheriff may, subject to any statutory time limits, make an order altering the date of the proof or other hearing at which the child or vulnerable witness is to give evidence and make such provision for intimation of such alteration to all parties concerned as he deems appropriate.

(3) An order fixing a hearing for a child witness notice or vulnerable witness application shall be intimated by the sheriff clerk–

    (a) on the day the order is made; and

    (b) in such manner as may be prescribed by the sheriff,

to all parties to the proceedings and such other persons as are named in the order where such parties or persons are not present at the time the order is made.

Review of arrangements for vulnerable witnesses

45.6.—(1) A review application shall be in Form G22.

(2) Where the review application is made orally, the sheriff may dispense with the requirements of paragraph (1).

Intimation of review application

45.7.—(1) Where a review application is lodged, the applicant shall intimate a copy of the review application to all other parties to the proceedings and complete a certificate of intimation.

(2) A certificate of intimation referred to in paragraph (1) shall be in Form G23 and shall be lodged together with the review application.

Procedure on lodging a review application

45.8.—(1) On receipt of a review application, the sheriff may—

    (a) if he is satisfied that he may properly do so, make an order under section 13(2) of the Act of 2004 without holding a hearing or, if he is not so satisfied, make such an order after giving the parties an opportunity to be heard;

    (b) require of any of the parties further information before making any further order;

    (c) fix a date for a hearing of the review application.

(2) The sheriff may, subject to any statutory time limits, make an order altering the date of the proof or other hearing at which the child or vulnerable witness is to give evidence and make such provision for intimation of such alteration to all parties concerned as he deems appropriate.

(3) An order fixing a hearing for a review application shall be intimated by the sheriff clerk—

    (a) on the day the order is made; and

    (b) in such manner as may be prescribed by the sheriff,

to all parties to the proceedings and such other persons as are named in the order where such parties or persons are not present at the time the order is made.

Determination of special measures

45.9. When making an order under section 12(1) or (6) or 13(2) of the Act of 2004 the sheriff may, in light thereof, make such further orders as he deems appropriate in all the circumstances.

Intimation of an order under section 12(1) or (6) or 13(2)

45.10. An order under section 12(1) or (6) or 13(2) of the Act of 2004 shall be intimated by the sheriff clerk—

    (a) on the day the order is made; and

    (b) in such manner as may be prescribed by the sheriff,

to all parties to the proceedings and such other persons as are named in the order where such parties or persons are not present at the time the order is made.

Taking of evidence by commissioner
45.11.—(1) An interlocutor authorising the special measure of taking evidence by a commissioner shall be sufficient authority for the citing the witness to appear before the commissioner.

(2) At the commission the commissioner shall—
    (a) administer the oath *de fideli administratione* to any clerk appointed for the commission; and
    (b) administer to the witness the oath in Form G14, or where the witness elects to affirm, the affirmation in Form G15.

(3) The commission shall proceed without interrogatories unless, on cause shown, the sheriff otherwise directs.

Commission on interrogatories
45.12.—(1) Where interrogatories have not been dispensed with, the party citing or intending to cite the vulnerable witness shall lodge draft interrogatories in process.

(2) Any other party may lodge cross-interrogatories.

(3) The interrogatories and cross-interrogatories, when adjusted, shall be extended and returned to the sheriff clerk for approval and the settlement of any dispute as to their contents by the sheriff.

(4) The party who cited the vulnerable witness shall—
    (a) provide the commissioner with a copy of the pleadings (including any adjustments and amendments), the approved interrogatories and any cross-interrogatories and a certified copy of the interlocutor of his appointment;
    (b) instruct the clerk; and
    (c) be responsible in the first instance for the fee of the commissioner and his clerk.

(5) The commissioner shall, in consultation with the parties, fix a diet for the execution of the commission to examine the witness.

Commission without interrogatories
45.13. Where interrogatories have been dispensed with, the party citing or intending to cite the vulnerable witness shall—
    (a) provide the commissioner with a copy of the pleadings (including any adjustments and amendments) and a certified copy of the interlocutor of his appointment;
    (b) fix a diet for the execution of the commission in consultation with the commissioner and every other party;
    (c) instruct the clerk; and
    (d) be responsible in the first instance for the fees of the commissioner and his clerk.

Lodging of video record and documents
45.14.—(1) Where evidence is taken on commission pursuant to an order made under section 12(1) or (6) or 13(2) of the Act of 2004 the commissioner shall lodge the video record of the commission and relevant documents with the sheriff clerk.

(2) On the video record and any documents being lodged the sheriff clerk shall—
    (a) note—
        (i) the documents lodged;
        (ii) by whom they were lodged; and
        (iii) the date on which they were lodged, and
    (b) intimate what he has noted to all parties concerned.

Custody of video record and documents
45.15.—(1) The video record and documents referred to in rule 45.14 shall, subject to paragraph (2), be kept in the custody of the sheriff clerk.

(2) Where the video record of the evidence of a witness is in the custody of the sheriff clerk under this rule and where intimation has been given to that effect under rule 45.14(2), the name and address of that witness and the record of his evidence shall be treated as being in the knowledge of the parties; and no party shall be required, notwithstanding any enactment to the contrary—
    (a) to include the name of that witness in any list of witnesses; or
    (b) to include the record of his evidence in any list of productions.

Application for leave for party to be present at the commission
45.16. An application for leave for a party to be present in the room where the commission proceedings are taking place shall be by motion.

¹ Chapter 46

Companies Act 2006

NOTE
¹ As inserted by the Act of Sederunt (Sheriff Court Rules) (Miscellaneous Amendments) 2010 (SSI 2010/279) para.5 (effective July 29, 2010).

Leave to raise derivative proceedings
46.1.—(1) Where leave of the court is required under section 266(1) (derivative proceedings: requirement for leave and notice) of the Companies Act 2006 (the "2006 Act"), the applicant must lodge, along with the initial writ, a written application in the form of a letter addressed to the sheriff clerk stating the grounds on which leave is sought.

(2) Subject to paragraph (4), an application under paragraph (1) is not to be served on, or intimated to, any party.

(3) The application is to be placed before the sheriff, who shall consider it for the purposes of section 266(3) of the 2006 Act without hearing the applicant.

(4) Service under section 266(4)(a) of the 2006 Act may be given by any of the methods provided for in Chapter 5 (citation, service and intimation) and a certificate of service must be lodged.

(5) If the company wishes to be heard it must, within 21 days after the date of service of the application, lodge written submissions setting out its position in relation to the application.

(6) Subject to section 266(4)(b) of the 2006 Act, the next stage in the proceedings is a hearing at which the applicant and the company may be heard.

(7) The sheriff clerk is to fix the hearing and intimate its date to the applicant and the company.

(8) Where an application under paragraph (1) is granted, a copy of the sheriff's interlocutor must be served on the defender along with the warrant of citation.

Application to continue proceedings as derivative proceedings
46.2. An application under section 267(2) (application to continue proceedings as derivative proceedings) of the 2006 Act is to be in the form of a minute and Chapter 14 (applications by minute) applies with the necessary modifications.

Rule 1.4   APPENDIX 1

Forms

Rule 3.1(1)(a)   FORM G1

Form of initial writ

INITIAL WRIT

SHERIFFDOM OF (*insert name of sheriffdom*)
AT (*insert place of sheriff court*)

[A.B.] (*design and state any special capacity in which the pursuer is suing*). Pursuer.
Against
[C.D.] (*design and state any special capacity in which the defender is being sued*). Defender.

The Pursuer craves the court (*here state the specific decree, warrant or order sought*).

CONDESCENDENCE
(*State in numbered paragraphs the facts which form the ground of action*)

PLEAS-IN-LAW
(*State in numbered sentences*)

Signed
[A.B.], Pursuer.
or [X.Y.], Solicitor for the pursuer (*state designation and business address*)

Rule 3.1(1)(b) and 40.4 [1] FORM G1A

Form of initial writ in a commercial action

SHERIFFDOM OF *(insert name of sheriffdom)*
AT *(insert place of sheriff court)*

COMMERCIAL ACTION

[A.B.] *(design and state any special capacity in which the pursuer is being sued)*. Pursuer.
Against
[C.D.] *(design and state any special capacity in which the defender is being sued)*. Defender.

[A.B.] for the Pursuer craves the court *(specify the orders sought)*

CONDESCENDENCE
(provide the following, in numbered paragraphs—

information sufficient to identify the transaction or dispute from which the action arises;

a summary of the circumstances which have resulted in the action being raised; and

details setting out the grounds on which the action proceeds.)

Note: Where damages are sought, the claim may be summarised in the pleadings—

in the form of a statement of damages; or

by lodging with the initial writ a schedule detailing the claim.

PLEAS-IN-LAW
(state in numbered sentences)

Signed
[A.B.], Pursuer
or [X.Y.], Solicitor for the Pursuer *(state designation and business address)*

NOTE
[1] Inserted by the Act of Sederunt (Ordinary Cause Rules) Amendment (Commercial Actions) 2001 (SSI 2001/8) (effective March 1, 2001).

Rule 4.2(1) FORM G2

[Omitted by Act of Sederunt (Sheriff Court Caveat Rules) 2006 (SI 2006/198), effective April 28, 2006]

Rule 5.6(1)(a) FORM G3

Form of advertisement

NOTICE TO [C.D.] Court ref. no.
An action has been raised in Sheriff Court by [A.B.], Pursuer, calling as a Defender [C.D.] whose last known address was *(insert last known address of defender)*. If [C.D.] wishes to defend the action [*where notice is given in a family action add*: or make any claim or seek any order] he [*or she*] should immediately contact the sheriff clerk at *(insert address)* from whom the service copy initial writ may be obtained. If he [*or she*] fails to do so decree may be granted against him [*or her*].

Signed
[X.Y.], *(add designation and business address)*
Solicitor for the pursuer
or [P.Q.], *(add business address)*
Sheriff officer

Rule 5.6(1)(b)   FORM G4

Form of notice for walls of court

NOTICE TO [C.D.]   Court ref. no.
An action has been raised in   Sheriff Court by [A.B.], Pursuer, calling as a Defender
[C.D.] whose last known address was (*insert last known address of defender*). If [C.D.] wishes to
defend the action [*where notice is to be given in a family action add*: or make any claim or seek
any order] he [*or* she] should immediately contact the sheriff clerk at (*insert address*) from whom
the service copy initial writ may be obtained. If he [*or* she] fails to do so decree may be granted
against him [*or* her].

Date (*insert date*)   (*Signed*)
                                   Sheriff clerk (depute)
                                   Telephone no. (*insert telephone number of sheriff clerk's
                                   office*)

Rule 6.A2(2)   [1] FORM G4A

Statement to accompany application for interim diligence

DEBTORS (SCOTLAND) ACT 1987 Section 15D [or DEBT ARRANGEMENT AND
ATTACHMENT (SCOTLAND) ACT 2002 Section 9C]
Sheriff Court...................
In the Cause (Cause Reference No.)
[A.B.] *(designation and address)*
                                                              Pursuer

against

[C.D.] *(designation and address)*
                                                              Defender

STATEMENT

1. The applicant is the pursuer [*or* defender] in the action by [A.B] *(design)* against [C.D.]
(design).

2. [The following persons have an interest *(specify names and addresses)*].

3. The applicant is [*or* is not] seeking the grant under section 15E(1) of the 1987 Act of warrant
for diligence [*or* section 9D(1) of the 2002 Act of interim attachment] in advance of a hearing on
the application.

4. [*Here provide such other information as may be prescribed by regulations made by the Scottish
Ministers under section 15D(2)(d) of the 1987 Act or 9C(2)(d) of the 2002 Act*]

                                   (Signed)

                                   Solicitor [*or* Agent] for A.B. [*or* C.D.]
                                   (*include full designation*)

NOTE
[1] As inserted by the Act of Sederunt (Sheriff Court Rules Amendment) (Diligence) (SSI 2008/
121) r.5(7) (effective April 1, 2008).

Rule 6.A8   [1] FORM G4B

Form of schedule of arrestment on the dependence

SCHEDULE OF ARRESTMENT ON THE DEPENDENCE

Date: (*date of execution*)

Time: (*time arrestment executed*)

To: (*name and address of arrestee*)

IN HER MAJESTY'S NAME AND AUTHORITY AND IN NAME AND AUTHORITY OF THE SHERIFF, I, *(name)*, Sheriff Officer, by virtue of:

- an initial writ containing warrant which has been granted for arrestment on the dependence of the action at the instance of *(name and address of pursuer)* against *(name and address of defender)* and dated *(date)*;

- a counterclaim containing a warrant which has been granted for arrestment on the dependence of the claim by *(name and address of creditor)* against *(name and address of debtor)* and dated *(date of warrant)*;

- an order of the Sheriff at *(place)* dated *(date of order)* granting warrant [for arrestment on the dependence of the action raised at the instance of *(name and address of pursuer)* against *(name and address of defender)*] [*or* for arrestment on the dependence of the claim in the counterclaim [*or* third party notice] by *(name and address of creditor)* against *(name and address or debtor)*],

arrest in your hands (i) the sum of *(amount)*, in excess of the Protected Minimum Balance, where applicable *(see Note 1)*, more or less, due by you to *(defender's name)* [*or name and address of common debtor if common debtor is not the defender*] or to any other person on his [*or* her] [*or* its] [*or* their] behalf; and (ii) all moveable things in your hands belonging or pertaining to the said *(name of common debtor)*, to remain in your hands under arrestment until they are made forthcoming to *(name of pursuer)* [*or name and address of creditor if he is not the pursuer*] or until further order of the court.

This I do in the presence of *(name, occupation and address of witness)*.

(Signed)

Sheriff Officer

(Address)

NOTE

1.   This Schedule arrests in your hands (i) funds due by you to *(name of common debtor)* and (ii) goods or other moveables held by you for him. **You should not pay any funds to him or hand over any goods or other moveables to him without taking legal advice.**

2.   This Schedule may be used to arrest a ship or cargo. If it is, you should consult your legal adviser about the effect of it.

3.   The Protected Minimum Balance is the sum referred to in section 73F(4) of the Debtors (Scotland) Act 1987. This sum is currently set at *[insert current sum]*. The Protected Minimum Balance applies where the arrestment attaches funds standing to the credit of a debtor in an account held by a bank or other financial institution and the debtor is an individual. The Protected Minimum Balance does not apply where the account is held in the name of a company, a limited liability partnership, a partnership or an unincorporated association or where the account is operated by the debtor as a trading account.

4.   Under section 73G of the Debtors (Scotland) Act 1987 you must also, within the period of 3 weeks beginning with the day on which the arrestment is executed, disclose to the creditor the nature and value of the funds and/or moveable property which have been attached. This disclosure must be in the form set out in Schedule 8 to the Diligence (Scotland) Regulations 2009. Failure to comply may lead to a financial penalty under section 73G of the Debtors (Scotland) Act 1987 and may also be dealt with as a contempt of court. You must, at the same time, send a copy of the disclosure to the debtor and to any person known to you who owns (or claims to own) attached property and to any person to whom attached funds are (or are claimed to be due), solely or in common with the debtor.

IF YOU WISH FURTHER ADVICE CONTACT ANY CITIZENS ADVICE BUREAU/ LOCAL ADVICE CENTRE/SHERIFF CLERK OR SOLICITOR

NOTE
[1] As inserted by the Act of Sederunt (Sheriff Court Rules Amendment) (Diligence) 2008 (SSI 2008/121) r.5(7) (effective April 1, 2008) and substituted by the Act of Sederunt (Sheriff Court Rules Amendment) (Diligence) 2009 (SSI 2009/107) (effective April 22, 2009).

Rule 6.A8   [1] FORM G4C

Form of certificate of execution of arrestment on the dependence

CERTIFICATE OF EXECUTION

I, (*name*), Sheriff Officer, certify that I executed an arrestment on the dependence, by virtue of an interlocutor of the Sheriff at (*place*) on (*date*) obtained at the instance of (*name and address of party arresting*) against (*name and address of defender*) on (*name of arrestee*)–

* by delivering the schedule of arrestment to (*name of arrestee or other person*) at (*place*) personally on (*date*).

* by leaving the schedule of arrestment with (*name and occupation of person with whom left*) at (*place*) on (*date*) [and by posting a copy of the schedule to the arrestee by registered post or first class recorded delivery to the address specified on the receipt annexed to this certificate].

* by depositing the schedule of arrestment in (*place*) on (*date*). (*Specify that enquiry made and reasonable grounds exist for believing that the person on whom service is to be made resides at the place but is not available*) [and by posting a copy of the schedule to the arrestee by registered post or first class recorded delivery to the address specified on the receipt annexed to this certificate].

* by affixing the schedule of arrestment to the door at (*place*) on (*date*). (*Specify that enquiry made and that reasonable grounds exist for believing that the person on whom service is to be made resides at the place but is not available*) [and by posting a copy of the schedule to the arrestee by registered post or first class recorded delivery to the address specified on the receipt annexed to this certificate].

* by leaving the schedule of arrestment with (*name and occupation of person with whom left*) at (*place of business*) on (*date*) [and by posting a copy of the schedule to the arrestee by registered post or first class recorded delivery to the address specified on the receipt annexed to this certificate].

* by depositing the schedule of arrestment at (*place of business*) on (*date*). (*Specify that enquiry made and that reasonable grounds exist for believing that the person on whom service is to be made carries on business at that place*) [and by posting a copy of the schedule to the arrestee by registered post or first class recorded delivery to the address specified on the receipt annexed to this certificate].

* by affixing the schedule of arrestment to the door at (*place of business*) on (*date*). (*Specify that enquiry made and that reasonable grounds exist for believing that the person on whom service is to be made carries on business at that place.*) [and by posting a copy of the schedule to the arrestee by registered post or first class recorded delivery to the address specified on the receipt annexed to this certificate].

* by leaving the schedule of arrestment at (*registered office*) on (*date*), in the hands of (*name of person*) [and by posting a copy of the schedule to the arrestee by registered post or first class recorded delivery to the address specified on the receipt annexed to this certificate].

* by depositing the schedule of arrestment at (*registered office*) on (*date*) [and by posting a copy of the schedule to the arrestee by registered post or first class recorded delivery to the address specified on the receipt annexed to this certificate].

* by affixing the schedule of arrestment to the door at (*registered office*) on (*date*) [and by posting a copy of the schedule to the arrestee by registered post or first class recorded delivery to the address specified on the receipt annexed to this certificate].

I did this in the presence of (*name, occupation and address of witness*).

(*Signed*)

Sheriff Officer

(*Address*)

(*Signed*)

(Witness)

*Delete where not applicable

NOTE

A copy of the Schedule of arrestment on the dependence is to be attached to this certificate.

NOTE
[1] As inserted by the Act of Sederunt (Sheriff Court Rules Amendment) (Diligence) 2008 (SSI 2008/121) r.5(7) (effective April 1, 2008) and substituted by the Act of Sederunt (Sheriff Court Rules Amendment) (Diligence) 2009 (SSI 2009/107) (effective April 22, 2009).

Rules 9.2(2)(a) and 33.16(3)(b)   [1] FORM G5

Form of intimation of Options Hearing

Sheriff Court (*insert address and telephone number*)   Court ref. no.

[A.B.] (*design*) Pursuer against [C.D.] (*design*) Defender

You are given notice that in this action:—

| (*insert date*) | is the last day for lodging defences; |

| (*insert date*) | is the last day for making adjustments to the writ or defences; |

| (*insert date, time and place*) | is the date, time and place for the Options Hearing. |

Date (*insert date*)   (*Signed*)
Sheriff clerk (depute)

NOTE:
    If you fail to comply with the terms of this notice or with any of the rules 9.3, 9.4, 9.6, 9.10 and 9.11 of the Standard Procedure of the Ordinary Cause Rules of the Sheriff Court or, where applicable, rule 33.37 (decree by default in a family action), decree by default may be granted in terms of rule 16.2(2) of those Rules.

NOTE TO BE ADDED WHERE PARTY UNREPRESENTED

> **NOTE**
> **IF YOU ARE UNCERTAIN WHAT ACTION TO TAKE** you should consult a solicitor. You may be eligible for legal aid depending on your income, and you can get information from any Citizens Advice Bureau or other advice agency.

NOTE
[1] As amended by S.I. 1996 No. 2445 (effective November 1, 1996).

Rule 15.1(1)(b)   FORM G6

Form of motion

SHERIFFDOM OF (*insert name of sheriffdom*)   Court ref. no.
AT (*insert place of sheriff court*)

MOTION FOR THE PURSUER [*or* DEFENDER]
in the cause
[A.B.] (*insert designation and address*)
Pursuer
against
[C.D.] (*insert designation and address*)
Defender

The (*insert description of party*) moves the court to (*insert details of motion and, where appropriate, the reason(s) for seeking the order*).

List the documents or parts of process lodged with the motion:—

(*Insert description of document or name part of process*)

Date (*insert date*)   (*Signed*)
                                                  Party (*insert name and
                                                  description of party*)
                                                  or Solicitor for party
                                                  (*insert designation and business
                                                  address*)

Rule 15.2(1)   [1] FORM G7

Form of intimation of motion

SHERIFFDOM OF (*insert name of sheriffdom*)   Court ref. no.
AT (*insert place of sheriff court*)

in the cause

[A.B.] (*insert name and address*)
                                                  Pursuer
against
[C.D.] (*insert name and address*)
                                                  Defender

LAST DATE FOR LODGING NOTICE OF OPPOSITION:

APPLICATION IS MADE BY MOTION FOR THE ORDER(S) SOUGHT IN THE ATTACHED FORM (*attach a copy of the motion in Form G6*)

* A copy of the document(s) or part(s) of process referred to in Form G6 is/are attached.

OPPOSITION TO THE MOTION MAY BE MADE by completing Form G9 (notice of opposition to motion) and lodging it with the sheriff clerk at (*insert address*) on or before the last date for lodging notice of opposition. A copy of the notice of opposition must be sent immediately to any other party in the action.

IN THE EVENT OF A NOTICE OF OPPOSITION BEING LODGED the sheriff clerk will assign a date, time and place for hearing parties on the motion. Intimation of this hearing will be sent to parties by the sheriff clerk.

IF NO NOTICE OF OPPOSITION IS LODGED, the motion may be considered by the sheriff without the attendance of parties.

Date (*insert date*)   (*Signed*)
                                                  Pursuer (*or as the case may be*)
                                                  [*or* Solicitor for pursuer [*or as the case may be*]
                                                  (*insert name and business address*)]

EXPLANATORY NOTE TO BE ADDED WHERE PARTY TO WHOM INTIMATION IS MADE IS NOT LEGALLY REPRESENTED

IF YOU ARE UNCERTAIN WHAT ACTION TO TAKE you should consult a solicitor. You may also obtain advice from a Citizens Advice Bureau or other advice agency.

NOTE: If YOU intend to oppose the motion you must appear or be represented on the date of the hearing. If you return Form G9 (notice of opposition to motion) and then fail to attend or be represented at the court hearing, the court may consider the motion in your absence and may grant the order(s) sought.

* Delete if not applicable

NOTE
[1] Substituted by S.I. 1996 No. 2445 (effective November 1, 1996).

Rule 14.4(1)(a)   [1] FORM G7A

Form of intimation of minute (answers lodged)

SHERIFFDOM OF (*insert name of sheriffdom*)   Court ref. no.
AT (*insert place of sheriff court*)

in the cause

[A.B.] (*insert name and address*)
                    Pursuer
against

[C.D.] (*insert name and address*)
                    Defender

LAST DATE FOR LODGING ANSWERS:

APPLICATION IS MADE BY MOTION FOR THE ORDER(S) SOUGHT IN THE MINUTE ATTACHED (*attach a copy of minute and interlocutor*)

* A copy of the document(s) or part(s) of process referred to in the minute is/are attached.

IN THE EVENT OF ANSWERS BEING LODGED the sheriff clerk will assign a date, time and place for hearing parties on the minute and answers. Intimation of this hearing will be sent to parties by the sheriff clerk.

IF NO ANSWERS ARE LODGED, the motion may be considered by the sheriff without the attendance of parties.

Date (*insert date*)   (*Signed*)
                    Pursuer (*or as the case may be*)
                    [*or* Solicitor for pursuer [*or as the case may be*]
                    (*Add name and business address*)]

EXPLANATORY NOTE TO BE ADDED WHERE PARTY TO WHOM INTIMATION IS MADE IS NOT LEGALLY REPRESENTED

IF YOU ARE UNCERTAIN WHAT ACTION TO TAKE you should consult a solicitor. You may also obtain advice from a Citizens Advice Bureau or other advice agency.

NOTE: If you intend to oppose the minute you must appear or be represented on the date of the hearing. If you return Form G9 (notice of opposition to minute) and then fail to attend or be represented at the court hearing, the court may consider the minute in your absence and may grant the order(s) sought.

* Delete if not applicable

NOTE
[1] Inserted by S.I. 1996 No. 2445 (effective November 1, 1996).

Rule 14.4(1)(a)   [1] FORM G7B

Form of intimation of minute (no order for answers or no hearing fixed)

SHERIFFDOM OF (*insert name of sheriffdom*)   Court ref. no.
AT (*insert place of sheriff court*)

in the cause

[A.B.] (*insert name and address*)
                    Pursuer
against
[C.D.] (*insert name and address*)
                    Defender

LAST DATE FOR LODGING NOTICE OF OPPOSITION:

APPLICATION IS MADE BY MINUTE FOR THE ORDER(S) SOUGHT IN THE MINUTE ATTACHED (*attach a copy of minute and interlocutor*)

* A copy of the document(s) or part(s) of process referred to in the minute is/are attached.

OPPOSITION TO THE MOTION MAY BE MADE by completing Form G9 (notice of opposition to motion) and lodging it with the sheriff clerk at (*insert address*) on or before the last date for lodging notice of opposition. A copy of the notice of opposition must be sent immediately to any other party in the action.

IN THE EVENT OF A NOTICE OF OPPOSITION BEING LODGED the sheriff clerk will assign a date, time and place for hearing parties on the minute. Intimation of this hearing will be sent to parties by the sheriff clerk.

IF NO NOTICE OF OPPOSITION IS LODGED, the minute may be considered by the sheriff without the attendance of parties.

Date (*insert date*)

(*Signed*)

Pursuer (*or as the case may be*)
[*or* Solicitor for pursuer [*or as the case may be*]
(*Add name and business address*)]

EXPLANATORY NOTE TO BE ADDED WHERE PARTY TO WHOM INTIMATION IS MADE IS NOT LEGALLY REPRESENTED

IF YOU ARE UNCERTAIN WHAT ACTION TO TAKE you should consult a solicitor. You may also obtain advice from a Citizens Advice Bureau or other advice agency.

NOTE: If YOU intend to oppose the minute you must appear or be represented on the date of the hearing. If you return Form G9 (notice of opposition to minute) and then fail to attend or be represented at the court hearing, the court may consider the motion in your absence and may grant the order(s) sought.

* Delete if not applicable

NOTE
[1] Inserted by S.I. 1996 No. 2445 (effective November 1, 1996).

Rule 14.4(1)(a) [1] FORM G7C

Form of intimation of minute (hearing fixed)

SHERIFFDOM OF (*insert name of sheriffdom*)   Court ref. no.
AT (*insert place of sheriff court*)

in the cause

[A.B.] (*insert name and address*)
Pursuer

against
[C.D.] (*insert name and address*)
Defender

DATE AND TIME FOR HEARING MINUTE:

*DATE FOR LODGING ANSWERS OR AFFIDAVIT EVIDENCE:

APPLICATION IS MADE FOR THE ORDER(S) SOUGHT IN THE MINUTE ATTACHED (*attach a copy of minute and interlocutor*)

* A copy of the document(s) or part(s) of process referred to in the minute is/are attached.

IF YOU WISH TO OPPOSE THE MINUTE OR MAKE ANY REPRESENTATIONS you must attend or be represented at (*insert name and address of court*) on the date and time referred to above.

* If an order has been made for you to lodge answers or affidavit evidence these must be lodged with the sheriff clerk (*insert address*) on or before the above date.

IF YOU FAIL TO ATTEND OR BE REPRESENTED the minute may be determined in your absence.

Date (*insert date*)   (*Signed*)
                                                     Pursuer (*or as the case may be*)
                                                     [*or* Solicitor for pursuer [*or as the case may be*]
                                                     (*Add name and business address*)]

EXPLANATORY NOTE TO BE ADDED WHERE PARTY TO WHOM INTIMATION IS MADE IS NOT LEGALLY REPRESENTED

> **IF YOU ARE UNCERTAIN WHAT ACTION TO TAKE** you should consult a solicitor. You may also obtain advice from a Citizens Advice Bureau or other advice agency.

> NOTE: If you intend to oppose the minute you must appear or be represented on the date of the hearing. If you return Form G9 (notice of opposition to minute) and then fail to attend or be represented at the court hearing, the court may consider the minute in your absence and may grant the order(s) sought.

* Delete if not applicable

NOTE
   [1] Inserted by SI 1996/2445 (effective November 1, 1996).

Rules 14.6 and 15.1(2)   [1] FORM G8

Form of certificate of intimation of motion or minute

CERTIFICATE OF INTIMATION OF MOTION [*or* MINUTE]

I certify that intimation of the motion [*or* minute] was made to (*insert names of parties or solicitors for the parties, as appropriate*) by (*insert method of intimation; where intimation is by facsimile transmission, insert fax number to which intimation sent*) on (*insert date of intimation*).

Date (*insert date*)   (*Signed*)
                                                     Solicitor [*or* Sheriff Officer]
                                                     (*Add name and business address*)

NOTE
   [1] Substituted by SI 1996/2445 (effective November 1, 1996).

Rules 14.7(1)(a) and 15.3(1)(a)   [1] FORM G9

Form of notice of opposition to motion or minute

NOTICE OF OPPOSITION TO MOTION [*or* MINUTE]

SHERIFFDOM OF (*insert name of sheriffdom*)   Court ref. no.:
AT (*insert place of sheriff court*)

in the cause

[A.B.] (*insert name and address*)
                                                     Pursuer
against
[C.D.] (*insert name and address*)
                                                     Defender

Notice of opposition to motion [*or* minute] given by (*insert name of party opposing motion*) to (*insert names of all other parties, or solicitors for the parties, to the action*) by (*insert method of intimation; where intimation is made by facsimile transmission, insert fax number to which notice of opposition sent*) on (*insert date of intimation*).

Date (*insert date*)   (*Signed*)
                                                        Pursuer (*or as the case may be*)
                                                        (*insert name and address of party*)
                                                        [*or* Solicitor for Pursuer [*or as the case may be*]
                                                        (*Add name and business address*)]

NOTE
   [1] Substituted by SI 1996/2445 (effective November 1, 1996).

Rule 24.2(3)   [1] FORM G10

Form of intimation to a party whose solicitor has withdrawn

SHERIFFDOM OF (*insert name of sheriffdom*)
AT (*insert place of sheriff court*)

in the cause

[A.B.] (*insert designation*)
                                        Pursuer
                    against
[C.D.] (*insert designation*)
                                        Defender

Court ref. no.

The court has been informed that your solicitors have ceased to act for you.

As a result the sheriff has ordered that you appear or be represented on (*insert date and time*) within the Sheriff Court at the above address. A copy of the order is attached.

When you appear you will be asked by the sheriff to state whether you intend to proceed with your action [*or* defences *or* answers].

> **NOTE:**
> **IF YOU ARE UNCERTAIN WHAT ACTION TO TAKE** you should consult a solicitor.
> You may also obtain advice from a Citizens Advice Bureau or other advice agency.

NOTE
   [1] As amended by SI 1996/2445 (effective November 1, 1996).

Rule 28.3(1)   [1] FORM G11

Form of notice in optional procedure for commission and diligence

Court ref. no.

Order by the Sheriff Court at (*insert address*)

In the cause

[A.B.] (*design*) Pursuer
                    against
[C.D.] (*design*) Defender

To (*insert name and designation of party or parties or haver, from whom documents are sought to be recovered*)

You are given notice that you are required to produce to the sheriff clerk at the above address within seven days of (*insert date on which service was executed. N.B. Rule 5.3(2) relating to postal service or intimation*):

   (1) this order; which must be produced intact;
   (2) a certificate signed and completed in terms of the form appended to this notice; and
   (3) all documents in your possession falling within the enclosed specification, with an inventory of such documents signed by you relating to this order and your certificate.

Production may be made by lodging the documents with the sheriff clerk at the above address, by posting them by registered post or the first class recorded delivery service addressed to the sheriff clerk at the above address.

Date (*insert date*)   Signed
   Solicitor for party (*add designation and
   business address of the solicitor for the
   party in whose favour commission and
   diligence granted*)

NOTE
   If you claim confidentiality for any of the documents produced by you, such documents must nevertheless be produced, but may be placed in a special sealed packet by themselves, marked "confidential".
   Claims for necessary outlays within certain specified limits may be paid. Claims should be made in writing to the person who has obtained the order that you produce the documents.

CERTIFICATE

I hereby certify with reference to the order of the Sheriff Court at *(insert place of sheriff court)* in the cause (*insert court ref. no.*) and the relative specification of documents, served upon me and marked respectively X and Y:

(1) that the documents which are produced and which are numbered in the inventory signed by me and marked Z, are the whole documents in my possession falling under the specification [*or* that I have no documents in my possession falling within the specification];

(2) that, to the best of my knowledge and belief, there are in existence other documents falling within the specification, but not in my possession, namely (*describe them by reference to one or more of the descriptions of documents in the specification*), which were last seen by me on or about (*insert date*), at (*insert place*), in the hands of (*insert name and address of the person*) [*or that I know of the existence of no documents in the possession of any person, other than myself, which fall within the specification*].

Signed

NOTE
   [1] Substituted by Act of Sederunt (Ordinary Cause, Summary Application, Summary Cause and Small Claim Rules) Amendment (Miscellaneous) 2005 (SSI 2005/648), para.2 (effective January 2, 2006).

Rules 28.4(4) and 29.7(4)   FORM G12

Form of certificate of citation of witness or haver

I certify that on (*insert date of citation*)   I duly cited [K.L.], (*design*) to attend at (*insert name of sheriff court*) Sheriff Court on (*insert date*) at (*insert time*) as a witness for the pursuer [*or* defender] in the action at the instance of [A.B.] (*design*), Pursuer, against [C.D.] (*design*), Defender, [and I required him [*or* her] to bring with him [*or* her] (*specify documents*)]. This I did by (*state mode of citation*).

Date (*insert date*)   (*Signed*)
                                         [P.Q.], Sheriff officer;
                                         or [X.Y.], (*add designation and business address*)
                                         Solicitor for the pursuer [*or* defender]

Rule 28.4(4) and 29.7(4)   [1] FORM G13

Form of citation of witness or haver

                                                        (*date*)

CITATION

SHERIFFDOM OF (*insert name of sheriffdom*)

AT (*insert place of sheriff court*)

To [A.B.] (*design*)

(*Name*) who is pursuing/defending a case against (*name*) [*or* is a (*specify*) in the case of (*name*) against (*name*) has asked you to be a witness. You must attend the above sheriff court on (*insert date*) at (*insert time*) for that purpose, [and to bring with you (*specify documents*)].

- If you would like to know more about being a witness
- are a child under the age of 16
- think you may be a vulnerable witness within the meaning of section 11(1) of the Vulnerable Witnesses (Scotland) Act 2004 (that is someone the court considers may be less able to give their evidence due to mental disorder or fear or distress connected to giving your evidence at the court hearings)

you should contact (*specify the solicitor acting for the party or the litigant citing the witness*) for further information.

If you are a vulnerable witness (including a child under the age of 16), then you should be able to use a special measure (such measures include the use of a screen, a live TV link or a supporter, or a commissioner) to help you give evidence.

Expenses

You may claim back money which you have to spend and any earnings you have lost within certain specified limits, because you have to come to court on the above date. These may be paid to you if you claim within specified time limits. Claims should be made to the person who has asked you to attend court. Proof of any loss of earnings should be given to that person.

If you wish your travelling expenses to be paid before you go to court, you should apply for payment to the person who has asked you to attend court.

Failure to attend

It is very important that you attend court and you should note that failure to do so may result in a warrant being granted for your arrest. In addition, if you fail to attend without any good reason, having requested and been paid your travelling expenses, you may be ordered to pay a penalty not exceeding £250.

If you have any questions about anything in this citation, please contact (*specify the solicitor acting for the party or the party litigant citing the witness*) for further information.

Signed

[P.Q.], Sheriff Officer,

or [X.Y.], (*add designation and business address*)

Solicitor for the pursuer [*or defender*] [*or specify*]

NOTE
[1] As substituted by SSI 2007/463 (effective November 1, 2007).

Rules 28.4(6)(b), 28.10(4)(b) and 29.16   FORM G14

Form of oath for witness

The witness to raise his right hand and repeat after the sheriff [*or* commissioner]: "I swear by Almighty God that I will tell the truth, the whole truth and nothing but the truth".

Rules 28.4(6)(b), 28.10(4)(b) and 29.16   FORM G15

Form of affirmation for witness

The witness to repeat after the sheriff [*or* commissioner]: "I solemnly, sincerely and truly declare and affirm that I will tell the truth, the whole truth and nothing but the truth".

¹ FORM G16   **Rules 28.14(3) and 28.14A(2)**

Form of minute for [letter of request] [taking of evidence in the European Community]*

SHERIFFDOM OF (*insert name of sheriffdom*)
AT (*insert place of sheriff court*)

MINUTE FOR PURSUER [DEFENDER]*

in the cause

[A.B.] (*insert designation and address*)

Pursuer

against

[C.D.] (*insert designation and address*)

Defender

Court ref. no.

The Minuter states that the evidence specified in the attached [letter of request] [Form A] [Form I]* is required for the purpose of these proceedings and craves the court to issue [a letter of request] [that Form]* to (*specify in the case of a letter of request the central or other appropriate authority of the country or territory in which the evidence is to be obtained, and in the case of Form A or I the applicable court, tribunal, central body or competent authority*) to obtain the evidence specified.

Date (*insert date*)   Signed

            (*insert designation and address*)

* *delete as applicable*

NOTE
¹ As substituted by the Act of Sederunt (Taking of Evidence in the European Community) 2003 (SSI 2003/601).

FORM G17   **Rule 28.14(3)**

Form of letter of request

LETTER OF REQUEST

1. Sender   (*insert name and address*)

2. Central authority of the requested state (*insert name and address*)

3. Person to whom the executed request is to (*insert name and address*)
be returned

4. The undersigned applicant has the honour to submit the following request:

5. a. Requesting judicial authority   (*insert name and address*)

  b. To the competent authority   (*insert name of requested state*)

6. Names and addresses of the parties and
their representatives

 a. Pursuer

 b. Defender

 c. Other parties

7. Nature and purpose of the proceedings
and summary of facts

8. Evidence to be obtained or other judicial
act to be performed

(*Items to be completed where applicable*)

9. Identity and address of any person to be
examined

10. Questions to be put to the persons to be examined or statement of the subject-matter about which they are to be examined	(*or see attached list*)
11. Documents or other property to be inspected	(*specify whether it is to be produced, copied, valued, etc.*)
12. Any requirement that the evidence be given on oath or affirmation and any special form to be used	(*in the event that the evidence cannot be taken in the manner requested, specify whether it is to be taken in such manner as provided by local law for the formal taking of evidence*)
13. Special methods or procedure to be followed	
14. Request for notification of the time and place for the execution of the request and identity and address of any person to be notified	
15. Request for attendance or participation of judicial personnel of the requesting authority at the execution of the letter of request	
16. Specification of privilege or duty to refuse to give evidence under the law of the state of origin	
17. The fees and expenses (costs) incurred will be borne by	(*insert name and address*)

(*Items to be included in all letters of request*)

18. Date of request

19. Signature and seal of the requesting authority

FORM G18   Rule 30.3(2)

Form of certificate of rate of exchange

CERTIFICATE OF RATE OF EXCHANGE

I (*insert designation and address*) certify that the rates current in London for the purchase of (*state the unit of currency in which the decree is expressed*) on (*insert date*) was (*state rate of exchange*) to the £ sterling and at this rate the sum of (*state the amount of the sum in the decree*) amounts to (*insert sterling equivalent*).

Date (*insert date*)

Signed
> For and on behalf of the bank manager or other official

Rule 45.2   [1] FORM G19

Form of child witness notice

VULNERABLE WITNESSES (SCOTLAND) ACT 2004 Section 12

Received the   *day of*   *20*

(*Date of receipt of this notice*)

.... (*signed*)

Sheriff Clerk

CHILD WITNESS NOTICE

Sheriff Court.........

..........20.........

Court Ref. No.

1. The applicant is the pursuer [*or* defender] in the action by [A.B.] (*design*) against [C.D.] (*design*).

2. The applicant has cited [*or* intends to cite] [E.F.] (*date of birth*) as a witness.

3. [E.F.] is a child witnesses under section 11 of the Vulnerable Witnesses (Scotland) Act 2004 [and was under the age of sixteen on the date of the commencement of proceedings].

4. The applicant considers that the following special measure[s] is [are] the most appropriate for the purpose of taking the evidence of [E.F.][*or* that [E.F.] should give evidence without the benefit of any special measure]:-

(delete as appropriate and specify any special measure(s) sought).

5. [(a) The reason[s] this [these] special measure[s] is [are] considered the most appropriate is [are] as follows:-

(here specify the reason(s) for the special measure(s) sought)].

OR

[(b) The reason[s] it is considered that [E.F.] should give evidence without the benefit of any special measure is [are]:-

(here explain why it is felt that no special measures are required)].

6. [E.F.] and the parent[s] of [*or* person[s] with parental responsibility for] [E.F.] has [have] expressed the following view[s] on the special measure[s] that is [are] considered most appropriate [*or* [the appropriateness of [E.F.] giving evidence without the benefit of any special measure]:-

(delete as appropriate and set out the views(s) expressed and how they were obtained)

7. Other information considered relevant to this application is as follows:-

(here set out any other information relevant to the child witness notice).

8. The applicant asks the court to –

(a) consider this child witness notice;

(b) make an order authorising the special measure[s] sought; *or*

(c) make an order authorising the giving of evidence by [E.F.] without the benefit of special measures.

(delete as appropriate)

(*Signed*)

[A.B. *or* C.D.]

[or Legal representative of A.B. [*or* C.D.]] (*include full designation*)

NOTE: This form should be suitably adapted where section 16 of the Act of 2004 applies.

NOTE

[1] As inserted by the Act of Sederunt (Ordinary Cause, Summary Application, Summary Cause and Small Claim Rules) Amendment (Vulnerable Witnesses (Scotland) Act 2004) 2007 (SSI 2007/463) (effective November 1, 2007).

¹ FORM G20

Form of vulnerable witness application

Rule 45.3

VULNERABLE WITNESSES (SCOTLAND) ACT 2004 Section 12

Received the ....day of ....20............

(Date of receipt of this notice)

.................*(signed)*

Sheriff Clerk

VULNERABLE WITNESS APPLICATION

Sheriff Court ....20 ....

Court Ref. No.

1. The applicant is the pursuer [*or* defender] in the action by [A.B] (*design*) against [C.D.] (*design*).

2. The applicant has cited [*or* intends to cite] [E.F.] (*date of birth*) as a witness.

3. The applicant considers that [E.F.] is a vulnerable witness under section 11(1)(b) of the Vulnerable Witnesses (Scotland) Act 2004 for the following reasons:–

(*here specify reasons witness is considered to be a vulnerable witness*).

4. The applicant considers that the following special measure[s] is [are] the most appropriate for the purpose of taking the evidence of [E.F.]:–

(*specify any special measure(s) sought*).

5. The reason[s] this [these] special measure[s] is [are] considered the most appropriate is [are] as follows:–

(*here specify the reason(s) for the special measures(s) sought*).

6. [E.F.] has expressed the following view[s] on the special measure[s] that is [are] considered most appropriate:–

(*set out the views expressed and how they were obtained*).

7. Other information considered relevant to this application is as follows:–

(*here set out any other information relevant to the vulnerable witness application*).

8. The applicant asks the court to–

(a) consider this vulnerable witness application;

(b) make an order authorising the special measure[s] sought.

....(*Signed*)

[A.B. *or* C.D.]

[*or* Legal representative of A.B. [*or* C.D.]] (*include full designation*)

NOTE: This form should be suitably adapted where section 16 of the Act of 2004 applies.

NOTE
[1] As inserted by the Act of Sederunt (Ordinary Cause, Summary Application, Summary Cause and Small Claim Rules) Amendment (Vulnerable Witnesses (Scotland) Act 2004) 2007 (SSI 2007/463) (effective November 1, 2007).

[1] FORM G21

Form of certificate of intimation

Rule 45.4(1)

VULNERABLE WITNESSES (SCOTLAND) ACT 2004 Section 12

CERTIFICATE OF INTIMATION

Sheriff Court ....20......

Court Ref. No.

I certify that intimation of the child witness notice [*or* vulnerable witness application] relating to (*insert name of witness*) was made to (*insert names of parties or solicitors for parties, as appropriate*) by (*insert method of intimation; where intimation is by facsimile transmission, insert fax number to which intimation sent*) on (*insert date of intimation*).

Date: ....

....................(*Signed*)

Solicitor [*or* Sheriff Officer]

(*include full business designation*)

NOTE
[1] As inserted by the Act of Sederunt (Ordinary Cause, Summary Application, Summary Cause and Small Claim Rules) Amendment (Vulnerable Witnesses (Scotland) Act 2004) 2007 (SSI 2007/463) (effective November 1, 2007).

¹ FORM G22

Form of application for review

Rule 45.6

VULNERABLE WITNESSES (SCOTLAND) ACT 2004 Section 13

Received the ....day of...................20....

(date of receipt of this notice)

....*(signed)*

Sheriff Clerk

APPLICATION FOR REVIEW OF ARRANGEMENTS FOR VULNERABLE WITNESS

Sheriff Court... ....20...

Court Ref. No.

1. The applicant is the pursuer [*or* defender] in the action by [A.B.] (*design*) against [C.D.] (*design*).

2. A proof [*or* hearing] is fixed for (*date*) at (*time*).

3. [E.F.] is a witness who is to give evidence at, or for the purposes of, the proof [*or* hearing]. [E.F.] is a child witness [*or* vulnerable witness] under section 11 of the Vulnerable Witnesses (Scotland) Act 2004.

4. The current arrangements for taking the evidence of [E.F.] are (*here specify current arrangements*).

5. The current arrangements should be reviewed as (*here specify reasons for review*).

6. [E.F.] [and the parent[s] of [*or* person[s] with parental responsibility for] [E.F.]] has [have] expressed the following view[s] on [the special measure[s] that is [are] considered most appropriate] [*or* the appropriateness of [E.F.] giving evidence without the benefit of any special measure]:–

(*delete as appropriate and set out the view(s) expressed and how they were obtained*).

7. The applicant seeks (here specify the order sought).

(*Signed*)

[A.B. *or* C.D.]

[*or* Legal representative of A.B. [*or* C.D.]] (*include full designation*)

NOTE: This form should be suitably adapted where section 16 of the Act of 2004 applies.

NOTE
¹ As inserted by the Act of Sederunt (Ordinary Cause, Summary Application, Summary Cause and Small Claim Rules) Amendment (Vulnerable Witnesses (Scotland) Act 2004) 2007 (SSI 2007/463) (effective November 1, 2007).

[1] FORM G23

Form of certificate of intimation

Rule 45.7(2)

VULNERABLE WITNESSES (SCOTLAND) ACT 2004 Section 13

CERTIFICATE OF INTIMATION

Sheriff Court ....20......

Court Ref. No.

I certify that intimation of the review application relating to (*insert name of witness*) was made to (*insert names of parties or solicitors for parties, as appropriate*) by (*insert method of intimation; where intimation is by facsimile transmission, insert fax number to which intimation sent*) on (*insert date of intimation*).

Date: ....

(*Signed*)

Solicitor [*or* Sheriff Officer]

(*include full business designation*)

NOTE
[1] As inserted by the Act of Sederunt (Ordinary Cause, Summary Application, Summary Cause and Small Claim Rules) Amendment (Vulnerable Witnesses (Scotland) Act 2004) 2007 (SSI 2007/463) (effective November 1, 2007).

FORM O1   **Rule 3.3(1)**

Form of warrant of citation

(*Insert place and date*) Grants warrant to cite the defender (*insert name and address*) by serving upon him [*or* her] a copy of the writ and warrant on a period of notice of (*insert period of notice*) days, and ordains him [*or* her], if he [*or* she] intends to defend the action or make any claim, to lodge a notice of intention to defend with the sheriff clerk at (*insert place of sheriff court*) within the said period of notice after such service [and grants warrant to arrest on the dependence].

[Meantime grants interim interdict; *or* grants warrant to arrest to found jurisdiction; *or* sequestrates and grants warrant to inventory; *or otherwise, as the case may be.*]

Signed
Sheriff [*or* sheriff clerk]

Rule 3.3(2)   [1] FORM O2

Form of warrant of citation where time to pay direction or time order may be applied for

(*Insert place and date*) Grants warrant to cite the defender (*insert name and address*) by serving a copy of the writ and warrant, with Form O3, on a period of notice of (*insert period of notice*) days and ordains him [*or* her] if he [*or* she]—

    (a) intends to defend the action or make any claim, to lodge a notice of intention to defend; *or*

    (b) admits the claim and intends to apply for a time to pay direction [*or* time order] [and apply for recall or restriction of an arrestment] to lodge the appropriate part of Form O3 duly completed;

with the sheriff clerk at (*insert place of sheriff court*) within the said period of notice after such service [and grants warrant to arrest on the dependence].

[Meantime grants interim interdict, *or* grants warrant to arrest to found jurisdiction; *or* sequestrates and grants warrant to inventory; *or otherwise, as the case may be.*]

Signed

Sheriff [*or* sheriff clerk]

NOTE
[1] As amended by the Act of Sederunt (Ordinary Cause, Summary Application, Summary Cause and Small Claim Rules) Amendment (Miscellaneous) 2007 (SSI 2007/6), para.2(16) (effective January 29, 2007).

Rule 3.3(4) [1] FORM O2A

Form of warrant in an action to which rule 3.2(3) applies

(*Insert place and date*) Grants warrant to cite the defender (*insert name and address*) by serving a copy of the writ and warrant and Form O7 on a period of notice of (*insert period of notice*) days and ordains him [*or* her] if he [*or* she]—

  (a) intends to defend the action or make any claim, to lodge a notice of intention to defend with the sheriff clerk at (*insert place of sheriff court*) within the said period of notice after such service [and grants warrant to arrest on the dependence]; or
  (b) intends to apply for an order under section 2 of the Mortgage Rights (Scotland) Act 2001, to lodge a minute applying for an order under that section before the conclusion of the proceedings.

[Meantime grants interim interdict *or otherwise as the case may be.*]

NOTE
[1] Inserted by the Act of Sederunt (Amendment of Ordinary Cause Rules and Summary Applications, Statutory Applications and Appeals etc. Rules) (Applications under the Mortgage Rights (Scotland) Act 2001) 2002 (SSI 2002/7), para.5.

[1] FORM O3

Form of notice to be served on defender in ordinary action where time to pay direction or time order may be applied for

Rule 3.3(3), ACTION RAISED BY
7.3(2) and
18.5(1)(a)

PURSUER   DEFENDER

AT   SHERIFF COURT

(Including address)

COURT REF. NO.

DATE OF EXPIRY OF
PERIOD OF NOTICE

**THIS SECTION MUST BE COMPLETED BY THE
PURSUER BEFORE SERVICE**

(1) Time to pay directions

The Debtors (Scotland) Act 1987 gives you the right to apply to the court
for a "time to pay direction" which is an order permitting you to pay any
sum of money you are ordered to pay to the pursuer (which may include
interest and court expenses) either by way of instalments or deferred lump
sum. A deferred lump sum means that you must pay all the amount at one
time within a period specified by the court.

When making a time to pay direction the court may recall or restrict an
arrestment made on your property by the pursuer in connection with the
action or debt (for example, your bank account may have been frozen).

(2) Time Orders

The Consumer Credit Act 1974 allows you to apply to the court for a
"time order" during a court action, to ask the court to give you more time
to pay a loan agreement. **A time order is similar to a time to pay direction,
but can only be applied for where the court action is about a credit
agreement regulated by the Consumer Credit Act.** The court has power to
grant a time order in respect of a regulated agreement to reschedule
payment of the sum owed. This means that a time order can change:

- the amount you have to pay each month
- how long the loan will last
- in some cases, the interest rate payable

A time order can also stop the creditor taking away any item bought by
you on hire purchase or conditional sale under the regulated agreement,
so long as you continue to pay the instalments agreed.

**HOW TO APPLY FOR A TIME TO PAY DIRECTION OR TIME
ORDER WHERE YOU ADMIT THE CLAIM AND YOU DO NOT
WANT TO DEFEND THE ACTION**

1. The appropriate application forms are attached to this notice. If
   you want to make an application you should lodge the
   completed application with the sheriff clerk at the above address
   before the expiry of the period of notice, the date of which is
   given above. No court fee is payable when lodging the
   application.

2. Before completing the application please read carefully the notes
   on how to complete the application. In the event of difficulty you
   may contact the court's civil department at the address above or
   any sheriff clerk's office, solicitor, Citizens Advice Bureau or
   other advice agency. Written guidance can also be obtained from
   the Scottish Court Service website (www.scotcourts.gov.uk).

NOTE

Where this form is being served on a defender along with Form O9 (notice
to additional defender) the reference to "date of expiry of period of
notice" should be amended to "date for lodging of defences or an
application for a time to pay direction or time order" and the reference to
"before the expiry of the period of notice" should be amended to "on or
before the date for lodging of defences or an application for a time to pay
direction or time order".

WHAT WILL HAPPEN NEXT

If the pursuer objects to your application, a hearing will be fixed and the court will advise you in writing of the date and time.

If the pursuer does not object to your application, a copy of the court order for payment (called an extract decree) will be served on you by the pursuer's solicitor advising when instalment payments should commence or deferred payment be made.

Court ref. no.

APPLICATION FOR A TIME TO PAY DIRECTION UNDER THE DEBTORS (SCOTLAND) ACT 1987

*PART A

By

*(This section must be completed by pursuer before service)

DEFENDER

In an action raised by

PURSUER

HOW TO COMPLETE THE APPLICATION

PLEASE WRITE IN INK USING BLOCK CAPITALS

PART A of the application will have been completed in advance by the pursuer and gives details of the pursuer and you as the defender.

PART B If you wish to apply to pay by instalments enter the amount and tick the appropriate box at B3(1). If you wish to apply to pay the full sum due in one deferred payment enter the period of deferment you propose at B3(2).

PART C Give full details of your financial position in the space provided.

PART D If you wish the court, when making the time to pay direction, to recall or restrict an arrestment made in connection with the action, enter the appropriate details about what has been arrested and the place and date of the arrestment at D5, and attach the schedule of arrestment or copy.

Sign the application where indicated. Retain the copy initial writ and the form of notice which accompanied this application form as you may need them at a later stage. You should ensure that your application arrives at the court before the expiry of the period of notice.

PART B

1. The applicant is a defender in the action brought by the above named pursuer.

2. The defender admits the claim and applies to the court for a time to pay direction.

3. The defender applies

(1) To pay by instalments of £

(Tick one box only)

EACH WEEK   FORTNIGHT   MONTH

OR

(2) To pay the sum ordered in one payment within

WEEKS/MONTHS

Please state in this box why you say a time to pay direction should be made. In doing so, please consider the Note below.

NOTE

Under the 1987 Act, the court is required to make a time to pay direction if satisfied that it is reasonable in the circumstances to do so, and having regard in particular to the following matters—

> **The nature of and reasons for the debt in relation to which decree is granted or the order is sought**
>
> **Any action taken by the creditor to assist the debtor in paying the debt**
>
> **The debtor's financial position**
>
> **The reasonableness of any proposal by the debtor to pay that debt**
>
> **The reasonableness of any refusal or objection by the creditor to any proposal or offer by the debtor to pay the debt.**

PART C

4. **Defender's financial position**

I am employed /self employed / unemployed

My net income is:	weekly, fortnightly or monthly	My outgoings are:	weekly, fortnightly or monthly
Wages	£	Mortgage/rent	£
State benefits	£	Council tax	£
Tax credits	£	Gas/electricity etc	£
Other	£	Food	£
		Credit and loans	£
		Phone	£
		Other	£
Total	£	Total	£

People who rely on your income
(e.g. spouse/civil partner/partner/
children) – how many

Here list all assets (if any) e.g. value of house; amounts in bank or building society accounts; shares or other investments:

Here list any outstanding debts:

PART D

5. The defender seeks to recall or restrict an arrestment of which the details are as follows (*please state, and attach the schedule of arrestment or copy*).

6. This application is made under sections 1(1) and 2(3) of the Debtors (Scotland) Act 1987.

Therefore the defender asks the court

*to make a time to pay direction

*to recall the above arrestment

*to restrict the above arrestment (*in which case state restriction wanted*)

Date (*insert date*)

Signed

Defender

Court ref. no.

APPLICATION FOR A TIME ORDER UNDER THE CONSUMER CREDIT ACT 1974

*PART A

By

*(This section must be completed by pursuer before service)

DEFENDER

In an action raised by

PURSUER

HOW TO COMPLETE THE APPLICATION

PLEASE WRITE IN INK USING BLOCK CAPITALS

PART A of the application will have been completed in advance by the pursuer and gives details of the pursuer and you as the defender.

PART B If you wish to apply to pay by instalments enter the amount and tick the appropriate box at B3. If you wish the court to make any additional orders, please give details at B4. Please give details of the regulated agreement at B5.

PART C Give full details of your financial position in the space provided.

Sign the application where indicated. Retain the copy initial writ and the form of notice which accompanied this application form as you may need them at a later stage. You should ensure that your application arrives at the court before the expiry of the period of notice.

PART B

1. The Applicant is a defender in the action brought by the above named pursuer.

I/WE WISH TO APPLY FOR A TIME ORDER under the Consumer Credit Act 1974

2. **Details of order(s) sought**

The defender wishes to apply for a time order under section 129 of the Consumer Credit Act 1974

The defender wishes to apply for an order in terms of section ..... of the Consumer Credit Act 1974

3. **Proposals for payment**

I admit the claim and apply to pay the arrears and future instalments as follows:

By instalments of £ .... per *week/fortnight/month

No time to pay direction or time to pay order has been made in relation to this debt.

4. **Additional orders sought**

The following additional order(s) is (are) sought: (*specify*)

The order(s) sought in addition to the time order is (are) sought for the following reasons:

5. **Details of regulated agreement**

    (a) Date of agreement

    (b) Reference number of agreement

(*Please attach a copy of the agreement*)

    (c) Names and addresses of other parties to agreement

    (d) Name and address of person (if any) who acted as surety (guarantor) to the agreement

    (e) Place where agreement signed (e.g. the shop where agreement signed, including name and address)

    (f) Details of payment arrangements

        i. The agreement is to pay instalments of £ ..... per week/ month

        ii. The unpaid balance is £ ..... / I do not know the amount of arrears

        iii. I am £ ..... in arrears / I do not know the amount of arrears

PART C

4. Defender's financial position

I am employed /self employed / unemployed

My net income is:	weekly, fortnightly or monthly	My outgoings are:	weekly, fortnightly or monthly
Wages	£	Mortgage/rent	£
State benefits	£	Council tax	£
Tax credits	£	Gas/electricity etc	£
Other	£	Food	£
Credit and loans	£	Phone	£
		Other	£
Total	£	Total	£

People who rely on your income (e.g. spouse/civil partner/partner/ children) – how many

Here list all assets (if any) e.g. value of house; amounts in bank or building society accounts; shares or other investments:

Here list any outstanding debts:

Therefore the defender asks the court to make a time order

Date   Signed

                                           Defender

NOTE
[1] As amended by SSI 2007/6 (effective January 29, 2007) and substituted by the Act of Sederunt (Sheriff Court Rules) (Miscellaneous Amendments) 2009 (SSI 2009/294) r.2 (effective December 1, 2009).

Rule 7.3(4)   [1] FORM O3A

Form of pursuer's response objecting to application for time to pay direction or time order

Court ref no:

SHERIFFDOM OF (*insert name of sheriffdom*)

AT (*insert place of sheriff court*)

PURSUER'S RESPONSE OBJECTING TO APPLICATION FOR TIME TO PAY DIRECTION OR TIME ORDER

in the cause

[A.B.], (*insert designation and address*), Pursuer
against
[C.D.], (*insert designation and address*), Defender

1.   The pursuer received a copy application for a time to pay direction or time order lodged by the defender on (*date*).

2.   The pursuer does not accept the offer.

3.   The debt is (*please specify the nature of the debt*).

4.   The debt was incurred on (*specify date*) and the pursuer has contacted the defender in relation to the debt on (*specify date(s)*).

*5.   The contractual payments were (*specify amount*).

*6.   (*Specify any action taken by the pursuer to assist the defender to pay the debt*).

*7.   The defender has made payment(s) towards the debt of (*specify amount(s)*) on (*specify date(s)*).

*8.   The debtor has made offers to pay (*specify amount(s)*) on (*specify date(s)*) which offer(s) was [were] accepted [*or* rejected] and (*specify amount*) was paid on (*specify date(s)*).

9.   (*Here set out any information you consider relevant to the court's determination of the application*).

*delete as appropriate

Minute for decree

(*Signed*)
Pursuer *or* Solicitor for pursuer

(*Date*)

NOTE
[1] As inserted by Act of Sederunt (Sheriff Court Rules) (Miscellaneous Amendments) 2009 (SSI 2009/294) r.2 (effective December 1, 2009).

Rule 5.2(1)   [1] FORM O4

Form of Citation

CITATION

SHERIFFDOM OF (*insert name of Sheriffdom*)
AT (*insert place of sheriff court*)

[A.B.], (*insert designation and address*), Pursuer, against [C.D.], (*insert designation and address*), Defender

Court Ref No:

(*Insert place and date*). You [C.D.], are hereby served with this copy writ and warrant, with Form 07 (notice of intention to defend).

Form 07 is served on you for use should you wish to intimate an intention to defend this action.

IF YOU WISH TO DEFEND THIS ACTION you should consult a solicitor with a view to lodging a notice of intention to defend (Form 07). The notice of intention to defend, together with the court fee of £ (*insert amount*) must be lodged with the Sheriff Clerk at the above address within 21 days (*or insert the appropriate period of notice*) of (*insert the date on which service was executed NB. Rule 5.3(2) relating to postal service*).

A copy of any notice of intention to defend should be sent to the Solicitor for the pursuer at the same time as your notice of intention to defend is lodged with the Sheriff Clerk.

IF YOU ARE UNCERTAIN WHAT ACTION TO TAKE you should consult a solicitor. You may be eligible for legal aid depending on your income, and you can get information about legal aid from a solicitor. You may also obtain advice from any Citizens' Advice Bureau or other advice agency.

PLEASE NOTE THAT IF YOU DO NOTHING IN ANSWER TO THIS DOCUMENT the court may regard you as admitting the claim made against you and the pursuer may obtain decree against you in your absence.

Signed
[P.Q.], Sheriff Officer
or [X.Y.] (*add designation and business address*)
Solicitor for the Pursuer

NOTE
[1] Substituted by the Act of Sederunt (Sheriff Court Ordinary Cause Rules Amendment) (Miscellaneous) 2000 (SSI 2000/239) (effective October 2, 2000).

Rule 5.2(2) [1] FORM 05

Form of citation where time to pay direction or time order may be applied for

CITATION

SHERIFFDOM OF (*insert name of Sheriffdom*)
AT (*insert place of Sheriff Court*)

[A.B.], (*insert designation and address*) Pursuer against [C.D.], (*insert designation and address*) Defender

Court Ref No:

(*insert place and date*). You [C.D.], are hereby served with this copy writ and warrant, together with the following forms—

Form 03 (application for time to pay direction or time order); and
Form 07 (notice of intention to defend).

Form 03 is served on you because it is considered that you may be entitled to apply for a time to pay direction or time order [and for the recall or restriction of an arrestment used on the dependence of the action or in security of the debt referred to in the copy writ]. See Form 03 for further details.

IF YOU ADMIT THE CLAIM AND WISH TO APPLY FOR A TIME TO PAY DIRECTION OR TIME ORDER, you must complete Form 03 and return it to the Sheriff Clerk at (*insert address*) within 21 days (*or insert the appropriate period of notice*) of (*insert the date on which service was executed. NB Rule 5.3 (2) relating to postal service*).

IF YOU ADMIT THE CLAIM AND WISH TO AVOID A COURT ORDER BEING MADE AGAINST YOU, the whole sum claimed including interest and any expense due should be paid to the pursuer or his solicitor in good time before the expiry of the period of notice.

Form 07 is served on you for use should you wish to intimate an intention to defend the action.

IF YOU WISH TO DEFEND THIS ACTION you should consult a solicitor with a view to lodging a notice of intention to defend (Form 07). The notice of intention to defend, together with the court fee of £ (*insert amount*) must be lodged with the Sheriff Clerk at the above address within 21 days (*or insert the appropriate period of notice*) of (*insert the date on which service was executed. NB Rule 5.3(2) relating to postal service*).

A copy of any notice of intention to defend should be sent to the Solicitor for the pursuer at the same time as your notice of intention to defend is lodged with the Sheriff Clerk.

IF YOU ARE UNCERTAIN WHAT ACTION TO TAKE you should consult a solicitor. You may be eligible for legal aid depending on your income, and you can get information about legal aid from a solicitor. You may also obtain advice from any Citizens' Advice Bureau or other advice agency.

PLEASE NOTE THAT IF YOU DO NOTHING IN ANSWER TO THIS DOCUMENT the court may regard you as admitting the claim made against you and the pursuer may obtain decree against you in your absence.

Signed
[P.Q.], Sheriff Officer
or [X.Y.] (*add designation and business address*)
Solicitor for the Pursuer

NOTE
[1] As substituted by the Act of Sederunt (Sheriff Court Ordinary Cause Rules Amendment) (Miscellaneous) 2000 (SSI 2000/239) (effective October 2, 2000) and amended by the Act of Sederunt (Ordinary Cause, Summary Application, Summary Cause and Small Claim Rules) Amendment (Miscellaneous) 2007 (SSI 2007/6), para.2(16) (effective January 29, 2007).

Rule 5.2(2A)   [1] **FORM O5A**

Form of citation in an action to which rule 3.2(3) applies

CITATION

SHERIFFDOM OF (*insert name of Sheriffdom*)
AT (*insert place of Sheriff Court*)

[A.B.], (*insert designation and address*) Pursuer against [C.D.], (*insert designation and address*), Defender

Court Ref No:
(*Insert place and date*). You [C.D.], are hereby served with this copy writ and warrant, with Form O7 (notice of intention to defend).

Form O7 is served on you for your use should you wish to intimate an intention to defend this action.

IF YOU WISH TO DEFEND THIS ACTION you should consult a solicitor with a view to lodging a notice of intention to defend (Form O7). The notice of intention to defend, together with the court fee of £ (*insert amount*), must be lodged with the Sheriff Clerk at the above address within 21 days (*or insert the appropriate period of notice*) of (*insert the date on which service was executed NB Rule 5.3(2) relating to postal service*).

A copy of any notice of intention to defend should be sent to the Solicitor for the pursuer at the same time as your notice of intention to defend is lodged with the Sheriff Clerk.

IF YOU WISH TO MAKE AN APPLICATION FOR AN ORDER UNDER SECTION 2 OF THE MORTGAGE RIGHTS (SCOTLAND) ACT 2001 you should consult a solicitor with a view to lodging a minute applying for an order under that section. The minute, together with the court fee of £ (*insert amount*), must be lodged with the Sheriff Clerk at the above address before the conclusion of the proceedings.

IF YOU ARE UNCERTAIN AS TO WHAT ACTION TO TAKE you should consult a solicitor. You may be eligible for legal aid depending on your income, and you can get information about legal aid from a solicitor. You may also obtain advice from any Citizens' Advice Bureau, or other advice agency.

PLEASE NOTE THAT IF YOU DO NOTHING IN ANSWER TO THIS DOCUMENT the court may regard you as admitting the claim made against you and the pursuer may obtain decree against you in your absence.

> Signed
> [P.Q.], Sheriff Officer,
> or [X.Y.] (*add designation and business address*)
> Solicitor for the Applicant

NOTE
[1] As inserted by the Act of Sederunt (Amendment of Ordinary Cause Rules and Summary Applications, Statutory Applications and Appeals etc. Rules) (Applications under the Mortgage Rights (Scotland) Act 2001) 2002 (SSI 2002 No.7), para.2(6).

Rule 5.2(3) [1] FORM O6

Form of certificate of citation

CERTIFICATE OF CITATION

(*Insert place and date*) I, hereby certify that upon the day of I duly cited [C.D.], Defender, to answer to the foregoing writ. This I did by (*state method of service; if by officer and not by post, add*: in presence of [L.M.], (*insert designation*), witness hereto with me subscribing; *and where service executed by post state whether by registered post or the first class recorded delivery service*).

(*In actions in which a time to pay direction may be applied for, state whether Form O2 and Form O3 were sent in accordance with rule 3.3*).

(*In actions to which rule 3.2(3) applies, state whether Form O2A was sent in accordance with rule 3.3*).

> Signed
> [P.Q.], Sheriff officer
> [L.M.], witness
> or [X.Y.]. (*add designation and business address*)
> Solicitor for the pursuer

NOTE
[1] As substituted by the Act of Sederunt (Amendment of Ordinary Cause Rules and Summary Applications, Statutory Applications and Appeals etc. Rules) (Applications under the Mortgage Rights (Scotland) Act 2001) 2002 (SSI 2002 No.7), para.2(6).

Rules 5.2(1) and 9.1(1) [1] FORM 07

Form of notice of intention to defend

NOTICE OF INTENTION TO DEFEND

*PART A   in an action raised at   Sheriff Court
Court Ref No

(*Insert name and business address of solicitor for the Pursuer*)

Pursuer

Solicitor for the pursuer

Defender

*(This section to be completed by the Pursuer
before service)
DATE OF SERVICE: DATE OF EXPIRY OF PERIOD OF NOTICE:

PART B

(This section to be completed by the defender or defender¿s solicitors, and both parts of this form to
be returned to the Sheriff Clerk (*insert address of Sheriff Clerk*) on or before the date of expiry of
the period of notice referred to in PART A above. At the same time a copy of the form should be
sent to the Solicitor for the Pursuer).

(*Insert place and date*)

[C.D.], (*insert designation and address*), Defender, intends to defend the action raised by [A.B.],
(*insert designation and address*), Pursuer, against him (and others).

                    Signed
                    [C.D.], Defender
                    or [X.Y.], (*add designation and business address*)
                    Solicitor for the defender

NOTE
[1] As substituted by the Act of Sederunt (Sheriff Court Ordinary Cause Rules Amendment)
(Miscellaneous) 2000 (SSI 2000/239) (effective October 2, 2000).

Paragraph 4(4)

Rule 13A.3(1)   [1] FORM O7A

Form of minute of intervention by the Commission for Equality and Human Rights

SHERIFFDOM OF (*insert name of sheriffdom*)... Court ref. no.

AT *(insert place of sheriff court)*

APPLICATION FOR LEAVE TO INTERVENE BY THE COMMISSION FOR
EQUALITY AND HUMAN RIGHTS

in the cause

[A.B.] (*designation and address*), Pursuer
against
[C.D.] (*designation and address*), Defender

[*Here set out briefly:*
    (a) the Commission's reasons for believing that the proceedings are relevant to a matter in
       connection with which the Commission has a function;
    (b) the issue in the proceedings which the Commission wishes to address; and
    (c) the propositions to be advanced by the Commission and the Commission's reasons for
       believing that they are relevant to the proceedings and that they will assist the court.]

NOTE
[1] As inserted by the Act of Sederunt (Sheriff Court Rules) (Miscellaneous Amendments) 2008
(SSI 2008/223) para.4(4) (effective July 1, 2008).

Rule 13B.2(1) [1] FORM O7B

Form of minute of intervention by the Scottish Commission for Human Rights

SHERIFFDOM OF *(insert name of sheriffdom)*...Court ref. no.

AT *(insert place of sheriff court)*

APPLICATION FOR LEAVE TO INTERVENE BY THE SCOTTISH COMMISSION FOR HUMAN RIGHTS

in the cause

[A.B.] *(designation and address)*, Pursuer
against
[C.D.] *(designation and address)*, Defender

[*Here set out briefly:*
 (a) the issue in the proceedings which the Commission intends to address;
 (b) a summary of the submission the Commission intends to make.]

NOTE
[1] As inserted by the Act of Sederunt (Sheriff Court Rules) (Miscellaneous Amendments) 2008 (SSI 2008/223) para.4(4) (effective July 1, 2008).

Rule 13B.3(1) [1] FORM O7C

Invitation to the Scottish Commission for Human Rights to intervene

SHERIFFDOM OF *(insert name of sheriffdom)*...Court ref. no.

AT *(insert place of sheriff court)*

INVITATION TO THE SCOTTISH COMMISSION FOR HUMAN RIGHTS TO INTERVENE

in the cause

[A.B.] *(designation and address)*, Pursuer
against
[C.D.] *(designation and address)*, Defender

[*Here set out briefly:*
 (a) the facts, procedural history and issues in the proceedings;
 (b) the issue in the proceedings on which the court seeks a submission.]

NOTE
[1] As inserted by the Act of Sederunt (Sheriff Court Rules) (Miscellaneous Amendments) 2008 (SSI 2008/223) para.4(4) (effective July 1, 2008).

Rule 18.5(1)(a)(i) [1] FORM O8

Form of notice to additional or substitute defender where time to pay direction or time order may be applied for

SHERIFFDOM OF *(insert name of sheriffdom)*

AT *(insert place of sheriff court)*

To [E.F.] *(insert designation and address of additional* [or *substitute*] defender)   Court ref. no.

You [E.F.] are given notice that in this action in which [A.B.] is the pursuer and [C.D.] is the defender, your name has, by order of the court dated *(insert date of court order)* been added [*or* substituted] as a defender to the said action; and the action, originally against [C.D.] is now [*or* also] directed against you.

Enclosed with this notice are the following documents—
  Copies of the [*insert as appropriate*, pleadings as adjusted *or* closed record];
  Form O3 (application for a time to pay direction or time order); and
  Form O7 (notice of intention to defend).

Form O3 is served on you because it is considered that you may be entitled to apply for a time to pay direction or time order [and for the recall or restriction of an arrestment used on the dependence of the action or in security of the debt referred to in the copy writ]. See Form O3 for further details.

IF YOU ADMIT THE CLAIM AND WISH TO APPLY FOR A TIME TO PAY DIRECTION OR TIME ORDER, you must complete Form O3 and return it to the sheriff clerk at (*insert address*) within 21 days (*or insert the appropriate period of notice*) of (*insert the date on which service was executed. N.B. Rule 5.3(2) relating to postal citation*).

IF YOU ADMIT THE CLAIM AND WISH TO AVOID A COURT ORDER BEING MADE AGAINST YOU, the whole sum claimed including interest and any expenses due should be paid to the pursuer or his solicitor in good time before the expiry of the period of notice.

Form O7 is served on you for use should you wish to intimate an intention to defend the action.

IF YOU WISH TO DEFEND THIS ACTION you should consult a solicitor with a view to lodging a notice of intention to defend (Form O7). The notice of intention to defend, together with the court fee of £ (*insert amount*) must be lodged with the sheriff clerk at the above address within 21 days (*or insert the appropriate period of notice*) of (*insert the date on which service was executed. N.B. See Rule 5.3(2) relating to postal service*).

IF YOU ARE UNCERTAIN WHAT ACTION TO TAKE you should consult a solicitor. You may be eligible for legal aid depending on your income, and you can get information about legal aid from a solicitor. You may also obtain advice from any Citizens Advice Bureau or other advice agency.

PLEASE NOTE THAT IF YOU DO NOTHING IN ANSWER TO THIS DOCUMENT the court may regard you as admitting the claim made against you and the pursuer may obtain decree against you in your absence.

Signed
[P.Q.], Sheriff officer
or [X.Y.] (*add designation and business address*)
Solicitor for the pursuer [*or* defender]

NOTE
[1] As amended by the Act of Sederunt (Ordinary Cause, Summary Application, Summary Cause and Small Claim Rules) Amendment (Miscellaneous) 2007 (SSI 2007/6), para.2(16) (effective January 29, 2007).

Rule 18.5(1)(a)(ii)   FORM O9

Form of notice to additional or substitute defender

SHERIFFDOM OF (*insert name of sheriffdom*)

AT (*insert place of sheriff court*)

To [E.F.] (*insert designation and address of additional* [or *substitute*] defender)   Court ref. no.

You [E.F.] are given notice that in this action in which [A.B.] is the pursuer and [C.D.] is the defender, your name has, by order of the court dated (*insert date of court order*) been added [*or* substituted] as a defender to the said action; and the action, originally against the said [C.D.] is now [*or* also] directed against you.

Enclosed with this notice are the following documents—
   Copies of the [*insert as appropriate* pleadings as adjusted *or* closed record]; and
   Form O7 (notice of intention to defend).

Form O7 is served on you for use should you wish to intimate an intention to defend the action.

IF YOU WISH TO DEFEND THIS ACTION you should consult a solicitor with a view to lodging a notice of intention to defend (Form O7). The notice of intention to defend, together with the court fee of £ (*insert amount*) must be lodged with the sheriff clerk at the above address with 28 days (*or insert the appropriate period of notice*) of (*insert the date on which service was executed. N.B. Rule 5.3(2) relating to postal service*).

IF YOU ARE UNDERTAIN WHAT ACTION TO TAKE you should consult a solicitor. You may be eligible for legal aid depending on your income, and you can get information about legal aid from a solicitor. You may also obtain advice from any Citizens Advice Bureau or other advice agency.

PLEASE NOTE THAT IF YOU DO NOTHING IN ANSWER TO THIS DOCUMENT the court may regard you as admitting the claim made against you and the pursuer may obtain decree against you in your absence.

Signed
[P.Q.], Sheriff officer
or [X.Y.] (*add designation and business* address)
Solicitor for the pursuer [*or* defender]

Rule 20.1 [1] FORM O10

Form of third party notice

SHERIFFDOM OF (*insert name of sheriffdom*) Court ref. no.
AT (*insert place of sheriff court*)

THIRD PARTY NOTICE
in the cause

[A.B.], (*insert designation and address*), Pursuer
against
[C.D.], (*insert designation and address*), Defender

To [E.F.]

You are given notice by [C.D.] of an order granted by Sheriff (*insert name of sheriff*) in this action in which [A.B.] is the pursuer and [C.D.] the defender. In the action the pursuer claims against the defender the sum of £ as damages in respect of (*insert brief account of the circumstances of the claim*) as more fully appears in the [*insert as appropriate*, pleadings as adjusted *or* amended *or* closed record] enclosed.

> *The defender admits [*or* denies] liability to the pursuer but claims that, if he [*or* she] is liable to the pursuer, you are liable to relieve him [*or* her] wholly [*or* partially] of his [*or* her] liability because (*set forth contract or other right of contribution, relief, or indemnity*) as more fully appears from the defences lodged by him [*or* her] in the action.
>
> or

*Delete as appropriate.

> *The defender denies liability for the injury claimed to have been suffered by the pursuer and maintains that liability, if any, to the pursuer rests solely on you [along with (*insert names of any other person whom defender maintains is liable to him [or her] by way of contribution, relief or indemnity*)] as more fully appears from the defences lodged by him [*or* her] in the action.
>
> or
>
> *The defender denies liability for the injury said to have been suffered by the pursuer but maintains that if there is any liability he [*or* she] shares that with you, as more fully appears from the defences lodged by him [*or* her] in the action.
>
> or
>
> *The defender admits liability in part for the injury suffered by the pursuer but disputes the amount of damages and maintains that liability falls to be shared by you, as more fully appears from the defences lodged by him [*or* her] in the action.
>
> or
>
> *The defender admits liability in part for the injury suffered by the pursuer and for the damages claimed but maintains that liability falls to be shared by you, as more fully appears from the defences lodged by him [*or* her] in the action.

or
(Otherwise as the case may be)

IF YOU WISH TO resist either the claim of the pursuer against the defender, or the claim of the defender against you, you must lodge answers with the sheriff clerk at the above address within 28 days of (*insert the date on which service was executed. N.B. Rule 5.3(2) relating to postal service*). You must also pay the court fee of £ (*insert amount*).

Date (*insert date*)   (*Signed*)

Solicitor for the defender.

NOTE
[1] As amended by S.I. 1996 No. 2445 (effective November 1, 1996) (clerical error).

Rule 31.4(1)   [1] FORM A1

Form of note of appeal to the sheriff principal

SHERIFFDOM OF (*insert name of sheriffdom*)

AT (*insert name of sheriff court*)

Court ref. no.

in the cause

[A.B.] (*insert name and address*)

Pursuer [*or as the case may be*]

against

[C.D.] (*insert name and address*)

Defender [*or as the case may be*]

The pursuer (*or defender or as the case may be*) appeals to the sheriff principal on the following grounds:—

(*state grounds on which appeal is to proceed*)

[and requests the sheriff to write a note].

Date (*insert date*)   (*Signed*)

[*or* Solicitor for pursuer [*or
as the case may be*]
(*add name and business address*)]

NOTE
[1] Inserted by S.I. 1996 No. 2445 (effective November 1, 1996).

Rule 33.7(1)(a)   FORM F1

Form of intimation to children and next-of-kin in an action of divorce or separation
where the defender's address is not known

Court ref. no.

To (*insert name and address as in warrant*)

You are given NOTICE that an action of divorce [*or* separation] has been raised against (*insert name*) your (*insert relationship, e.g. father, mother, brother or other relative as the case may be*). If you know of his [*or* her] present address, you are requested to inform the sheriff clerk (*insert address of sheriff clerk*) in writing immediately. If you wish to appear as a party you must lodge a minute with the sheriff clerk for leave to do so. Your minute must be lodged within 21 days of (*insert date on which intimation was given. N.B. Rule 5.3(2) relating to postal service or intimation*).

Date (*insert date*)   (*Signed*)

Solicitor for the pursuer (*add designation
and business address*)

> **NOTE**
> If you decide to lodge a minute it may be in your best interest to consult a solicitor. The minute should be lodged with the sheriff clerk together with the appropriate fee of (*insert amount*) and a copy of this intimation.

> **IF YOU ARE UNCERTAIN WHAT ACTION TO TAKE** you should consult a solicitor. You may be entitled to legal aid depending on your financial circumstances, and you can get information about legal aid from a solicitor. You may also obtain advice from any Citizens Advice Bureau or other advice agency.

Rule 33.7(1)(b)   FORM F2

Form of intimation to alleged adulterer in action of divorce or separation

To (*insert name and address as in warrant*)   Court ref. no.

You are given NOTICE that in this action, you are alleged to have committed adultery. A copy of the initial writ is attached. If you wish to dispute the truth of the allegation made against you, you must lodge a minute with the sheriff clerk (*insert address of sheriff clerk*) for leave to appear as a party. Your minute must be lodged within 21 days of (*insert date on which intimation was given. N.B. Rule 5.3(2) relating to postal service or intimation*).

Date (*insert date*)   (*Signed*)
                       Solicitor for the pursuer

> **NOTE**
> If you decide to lodge a minute it may be in your best interest to consult a solicitor. The minute should be lodged with the sheriff clerk together with the appropriate fee of (*insert amount*) and a copy of this intimation.

> **IF YOU ARE UNCERTAIN WHAT ACTION TO TAKE** you should consult a solicitor. You may be entitled to legal aid depending on your financial circumstances, and you can get information about legal aid from a solicitor. You may also obtain advice from any Citizens Advice Bureau or other advice agency.

Rule 33.7(1)(c)   FORM F3

Form of intimation to children, next-of-kin and *curator bonis* in an action of divorce or separation where the defender suffers from a mental disorder

To (*insert name and address as in warrant*)   Court ref. no.

You are given NOTICE that an action of divorce [*or separation*] has been raised against (*insert name and designation*) your (*insert relationship, e.g. father, mother, brother or other relative, or ward, as the case may be*). A copy of the initial writ is enclosed. If you wish to appear as a party, you must lodge a minute with the sheriff clerk (*insert address of sheriff clerk*), for leave to do so. Your minute must be lodged within 21 days of (*insert date on which intimation was given. N.B. Rule 5.3(2) relating to postal service or intimation*).

Date (*insert date*)   (*Signed*)
                       Solicitor for the pursuer (*insert designation and business address*)

> **NOTE**
> If you decide to lodge a minute it may be in your best interest to consult a solicitor. The minute should be lodged with the sheriff clerk together with the appropriate fee of (*insert amount*) and a copy of this intimation.

> **IF YOU ARE UNCERTAIN WHAT ACTION TO TAKE** you should consult a solicitor. You may be entitled to legal aid depending on your financial circumstances, and you can get information about legal aid from a solicitor. You may also obtain advice from any Citizens Advice Bureau or other advice agency.

Rule 33.7(1)(d)   FORM F4

Form of intimation to additional spouse of either party in proceedings relating to a
polygamous marriage

To (*name and address as in warrant*)   Court ref. no.

You are given NOTICE that this action for divorce [*or* separation], involves (*insert name and
designation*) your spouse. A copy of the initial writ is attached. If you wish to appear as a party,
you must lodge a minute with the sheriff clerk (*insert address of sheriff clerk*) for leave to do so.
Your minute must be lodged within 21 days of (*insert date on which intimation was given. N.B.
Rule 5.3(2) relating to postal service or intimation*).

Date (*insert date*)   (*Signed*)
                                              Solicitor for the pursuer

---
NOTE
If you decide to lodge a minute it may be in your best interest to consult a solicitor. The
minute should be lodged with the sheriff clerk together with the appropriate fee of (*insert
amount*) and a copy of this intimation.

IF YOU ARE UNCERTAIN WHAT ACTION TO TAKE you should consult a solicitor.
You may be entitled to legal aid depending on your financial circumstances, and you can get
information about legal aid from a solicitor. You may also obtain advice from any Citizens
Advice Bureau or other advice agency.

Rule 33.7(1)(e)(i) and (ii)   [1] FORM F5

Form of intimation to a local authority or third party who may be liable to maintain a child

To (*insert name and address as in warrant*)   Court ref. no.

YOU ARE GIVEN NOTICE that in this action, the court may make an order under section 11
of the Children (Scotland) Act 1995 in respect of (*insert name and address*), a child in your care
[*or* liable to be maintained by you]. A copy of the initial writ is attached. If you wish to appear
as a party, you must lodge a minute with the sheriff clerk (*insert address of sheriff clerk*) for
leave to do so. Your minute must be lodged within 21 days of (*insert date on which intimation
was given. N.B. Rule 5.3(2) relating to postal service or intimation*).

Date (*insert date*)   (*Signed*)
                                              Solicitor for the pursuer

---
NOTE
If you decide to lodge a minute it may be in your best interests to consult a solicitor. The
minute should be lodged with the sheriff clerk together with the appropriate fee of (*insert
amount*) and a copy of this intimation.

IF YOU ARE UNCERTAIN WHAT ACTION TO TAKE you should consult a solicitor.
You may be entitled to legal aid depending on your financial circumstances, and you can get
information about legal aid from a solicitor. You may also obtain advice from any Citizens
Advice Bureau or other advice agency.

NOTE
[1] Substituted by S.I. 1996 No. 2167 (effective November 1, 1996).

Rule 33.7(1)(e)(iii)   [1] FORM F6

Form of intimation to person who in fact exercises care or control of a child

To (*insert name and address as in warrant*)   Court ref. no.

YOU ARE GIVEN NOTICE that in this action, the court may make an order under section 11
of the Children (Scotland) Act 1995 in respect of (*insert name and address*) a child at present in
your care or control. A copy of the initial writ is attached. If you wish to appear as a party, you
must lodge a minute with the sheriff clerk (*insert address of sheriff clerk*) for leave to do so. Your

minute must be lodged within 21 days of (*insert date on which intimation was given. N.B. Rule 5.3(2) relating to postal service or intimation*).

Date (*insert date*)   (*Signed*)
                                              Solicitor for the pursuer

---

NOTE
If you decide to lodge a minute it may be in your best interests to consult a solicitor. The minute should be lodged with the sheriff clerk together with the appropriate fee of (*insert amount*) and a copy of this intimation.

IF YOU ARE UNCERTAIN WHAT ACTION TO TAKE you should consult a solicitor. You may be entitled to legal aid depending on your financial circumstances, and you can get information about legal aid from a solicitor. You may also obtain advice from any Citizens Advice Bureau or other advice agency.

NOTE
[1] Substituted by S.I. 1996 No. 2167 (effective November 1, 1996).

Rule 33.7(1)(f)   [1] FORM F7

Form of notice to parent or guardian in action for a section 11 order in respect of a child

1. YOU ARE GIVEN NOTICE that in this action, the pursuer is applying for an order under section 11 of the Children (Scotland) Act 1995 in respect of the child (*insert name of child*). A copy of the initial writ is served on you and is attached to this notice.

2. If you wish to oppose this action, or oppose the granting of any order applied for by the pursuer in respect of the child, you must lodge a notice of intention to defend (Form F26). See Form F26 attached for further details.

Date (*insert date*)   (*Signed*)
                                              Pursuer
                                              or Solicitor for the pursuer (*add designation and business address*)

NOTE: IF YOU ARE UNCERTAIN WHAT ACTION TO TAKE you should consult a solicitor. You may be entitled to legal aid depending on your financial circumstances, and you can get information about legal aid from a solicitor. You may also obtain advice from any Citizens Advice Bureau or other advice agency.

NOTE
[1] Substituted by S.I. 1996 No. 2167 (effective November 1, 1996).

Rules 33.7(1)(g), 33.7(4)   [1] FORM F8
and 33.12(2) and (3)

Form of notice to local authority requesting a report in respect of a child

To (*insert name and address*)   Court ref. no.

1. YOU ARE GIVEN NOTICE that in an action in the Sheriff Court at (*insert address*) the pursuer has applied for a residence order in respect of the child (*insert name of child*). A copy of the initial writ is enclosed.

2. You are required to submit to the court a report on all the circumstances of the child and on the proposed arrangements for the care and upbringing of the child.

Date (*insert date*)   (*Signed*)
                                              Solicitor for the pursuer (*add designation and business address*)

NOTE
[1] Substituted by S.I. 1996 No. 2167 (effective November 1, 1996).

Rule 33.7(1)(h)   ¹ FORM F9

Form of intimation in an action which includes a crave for a section 11 order

PART A   Court ref. No.

> This part must be completed by the
> Pursuer's solicitor in language a child is
> capable of understanding.

To (1)

The Sheriff (the person who has to decide about your future) has been asked by (2)   to
decide:—

(a) (3) and (4)

(b) (5)

(c) (6)

If you want to tell the Sheriff what you think about the things your (2)   has asked the
Sheriff to decide about your future you should complete Part B of this form and send it to the
Sheriff Clerk at (7) by (8)   . An envelope which does not need a postage stamp is enclosed
for you to use to return the form.

> **IF YOU DO NOT UNDERSTAND THIS FORM OR IF YOU WANT HELP TO
> COMPLETE IT you may get help from a SOLICITOR or contact the SCOTTISH CHILD
> LAW CENTRE ON the FREE ADVICE TELEPHONE LINE ON 0800 328 8970.**

If you return the form it will be given to the Sheriff. The Sheriff may wish to speak with you and
may ask you to come and see him or her.

NOTES FOR COMPLETION

(1) Insert name and address of child.	(2) Insert relationship to the child of party making the application to court.
(3) Insert appropriate wording for residence order sought.	(4) Insert address.
(5) Insert appropriate wording for contact order sought.	(6) Insert appropriate wording for any other order sought.
(7) Insert address of sheriff clerk.	(8) Insert the date occurring 21 days after the date on which intimation is given. N.B. Rule 5.3(2) relating to intimation and service.
(9) Insert court reference number.	(10) Insert name and address of parties to the action.

PART B

IF YOU WISH THE SHERIFF TO KNOW YOUR VIEWS ABOUT YOUR FUTURE YOU
SHOULD COMPLETE THIS PART OF THE FORM

To the Sheriff Clerk, (7)

Court Ref. No. (9)

(10) ....

QUESTION (1): DO YOU WISH THE SHERIFF TO KNOW WHAT YOUR VIEWS ARE
ABOUT YOUR FUTURE?

(PLEASE TICK BOX)

Yes	
No	

If you have ticked YES please also answer Question (2) *or* (3)

QUESTION (2): WOULD YOU LIKE A FRIEND, RELATIVE OR OTHER PERSON TO TELL THE SHERIFF YOUR VIEWS ABOUT YOUR FUTURE?

(PLEASE TICK BOX)

Yes	
No	

If you have ticked YES please write the name and address of the person you wish to tell the Sheriff your views in Box (A) below. You should also tell that person what your views are about your future.

BOX A:	(NAME)	
	(ADDRESS)	
	....	
	Is this person:— A friend? ☐ A relative?	
	☐	
	A teacher? ☐ Other?	
	☐	

OR

QUESTION (3): WOULD YOU LIKE TO WRITE TO THE SHERIFF AND TELL HIM WHAT YOUR VIEWS ARE ABOUT YOUR FUTURE?

(PLEASE TICK BOX)

Yes	
No	

If you decide that you wish to write to the Sheriff you can write what your views are about your future in Box (B) below or on a separate piece of paper. If you decide to write your views on a separate piece of paper you should send it along with this form to the Sheriff Clerk in the envelope provided.

BOX B: WHAT I HAVE TO SAY ABOUT MY FUTURE:—

NAME: ....
ADDRESS: ....
DATE: ....

NOTE
[1] Substituted by SI 1996/2167 (effective November 1, 1996) and amended by SSI 2003/26 (effective January 24, 2003).

Rule 33.7(1)(a)   FORM F10

Form of intimation to creditor in application for order for the transfer of property under section 8 of the Family Law (Scotland) Act 1985

To (*insert name and address as in warrant*)   Court ref. no.

You are given NOTICE that in this action an order is sought for the transfer of property (*specify the order*), over which you hold a security. A copy of the initial writ is attached. If you wish to appear as a party, you must lodge a minute with the sheriff clerk (*insert address of sheriff clerk*) for leave to do so. Your minute must be lodged within 21 days of (*insert date on which intimation was given. N.B. Rule 5.3(2) relating to postal service or intimation*).

Date (*insert date*)   (*Signed*)
                                        Solicitor for the pursuer

NOTE

If you decide to lodge a minute it may be in your best interests to consult a solicitor. The minute should be lodged with the sheriff clerk together with the appropriate fee of (*insert amount*) and a copy of this intimation.

IF YOU ARE UNCERTAIN WHAT ACTION TO TAKE you should consult a solicitor. You may be entitled to legal aid depending on your financial circumstances, and you can get information about legal aid from a solicitor. You may also obtain advice from any Citizens Advice Bureau or other advice agency.

Rule 33.7(1)(j)   FORM F11

Form of intimation in an action where the pursuer makes an application for an order under section 18 of the Family Law (Scotland) Act 1985

To (*insert name and address as in warrant*)   Court ref. no.

You are given NOTICE that in this action, the pursuer craves the court to make an order under section 18 of the Family Law (Scotland) Act 1985. A copy of the initial writ is attached. If you wish to appear as a party, you must lodge a minute with the sheriff clerk (*insert address of sheriff clerk*) for leave to do so. Your minute must be lodged within 21 days of (*insert date on which intimation was given. N.B. Rule 5.3(2) relating to postal service or intimation*).

Date (*insert date*)   (*Signed*)
                                        Solicitor for the pursuer

NOTE

If you decide to lodge a minute it may be in your best interests to consult a solicitor. The minute should be lodged with the sheriff clerk together with the appropriate fee of (*insert amount*) and a copy of this intimation.

IF YOU ARE UNCERTAIN WHAT ACTION TO TAKE you should consult a solicitor. You may be entitled to legal aid depending on your financial circumstances, and you can get information about legal aid from a solicitor. You may also obtain advice from any Citizens Advice Bureau or other advice agency.

Rule 33.7(1)(k)   FORM F12

Form of intimation in an action where a non-entitled pursuer makes an application for an order under the Matrimonial Homes (Family Protection) (Scotland) Act 1981

To (*insert name and address as in warrant*)   Court ref. no.

You are given NOTICE that in this action, the pursuer craves the court to make an order under section   (*insert the section under which the order(s) is sought*) of the Matrimonial Homes (Family Protection) (Scotland) Act 1981. A copy of the initial writ is attached. If you wish to appear as a party, you must may lodge a minute with the sheriff clerk (*insert address of sheriff clerk*) for leave to do so. Your minute must be lodged within 21 days of (*insert date on which intimation was given. N.B. Rule 5.3(2) relating to postal service or intimation*).

Date (*insert date*)   (*Signed*)
                                        Solicitor for the pursuer

NOTE

If you decide to lodge a minute it may be in your best interests to consult a solicitor. The minute should be lodged with the sheriff clerk together with the appropriate fee of (*insert amount*) and a copy of this intimation.

IF YOU ARE UNCERTAIN WHAT ACTION TO TAKE you should consult a solicitor. You may be entitled to legal aid depending on your financial circumstances, and you can get information about legal aid from a solicitor. You may also obtain advice from any Citizens Advice Bureau or other advice agency.

Rule 33.7(1)(l) [1] FORM F12A

Form of intimation to person responsible for pension arrangement in relation to order for payment in respect of pension lump sum under section 12A of the Family Law (Scotland) Act 1985

To (*insert name and address as in warrant*)   Court ref. no.

You are given NOTICE that in this action the pursuer has applied for an order under section 8 of the Family Law (Scotland) Act 1985 for a capital sum in circumstances where the matrimonial property includes rights in a pension scheme under which a lump sum is payable. The relevant pension scheme is (*give brief details, including number, if known*). If you wish to apply to appear as a party, you must lodge a minute with the sheriff clerk (*insert address of sheriff clerk*) for leave to do so. Your minute must be lodged within 21 days of (*insert date on which intimation was given. N.B. rule 5.3(2) relating to postal service or intimation.*)

Date (*insert date*)   (*Signed*)
                                        Solicitor for the pursuer
                                        (*add designation and business address*)

NOTE
If you decide to lodge a minute it may be in your best interests to consult a solicitor. The minute should be lodged with the sheriff clerk together with the appropriate fee of (*insert amount*) and a copy of this intimation.

IF YOU ARE UNCERTAIN WHAT ACTION TO TAKE you should consult a solicitor. You may be entitled to legal aid depending on your financial circumstances, and you can get information about legal aid from a solicitor. You may also obtain advice from any Citizens Advice Bureau or other advice agency.

NOTE
[1] Inserted by S.I. 1996 No. 2445 (effective November 1, 1996) and amended by the Act of Sederunt (Ordinary Cause Rules) Amendment (No.2)(Pension Sharing on Divorce etc.) 2000 (S.S.I. 2000 No. 408) para. 2(3)(a).

Rule 33.7(1)(m) [1] FORM F12B

Form of intimation to person responsible for the pension arrangement in relation to pension sharing order under section 8(1)(baa) of the Family Law (Scotland) Act 1985.

Court ref. no.

To (*insert name and address as in warrant*)

You are given NOTICE that in this action the pursuer has applied under section 8 of the Family Law (Scotland) Act 1985 for a pension sharing order in circumstances where the matrimonial property includes rights in a pension scheme. The relevant pension scheme is (*give brief details, including number, if known*). If you wish to apply to appear as a party, you must lodge a minute with the sheriff clerk (*insert address of sheriff clerk*) for leave to do so. Your minute must be lodged within 21 days of (*insert date on which intimation was given, N.B. rule 5.3(2) relating to postal service or intimation.*)

Date (*insert date*)   (*Signed*)
                                        Solicitor for the pursuer
                                        (*add designation and business address*)

NOTE
If you decide to lodge a minute it may be in your best interests to consult a solicitor. The minute should be lodged with the sheriff clerk together with the appropriate fee of (insert amount) and a copy of this intimation.

IF YOU ARE UNCERTAIN WHAT ACTION TO TAKE you should consult a solicitor. You may be entitled to legal aid depending on your financial circumstances, and you can get information about legal aid from a solicitor. You may also obtain advice from any Citizens Advice Bureau or other advice agency.

NOTE
[1] Inserted by the Act of Sederunt (Ordinary Cause Rules) Amendment (No.2)(Pension Sharing on Divorce etc.) 2000 (S.S.I. 2000 No. 408) para. 2(3)(b).

Rule 33.8(3)   FORM F13

Form of intimation to person with whom an improper association is alleged to have occurred

To (*insert name and address as in warrant*)   Court ref. no.

You are given NOTICE that in this action, the defender is alleged to have had an improper association with you. A copy of the initial writ is attached. If you wish to dispute the truth of the allegation made against you, you must lodge a minute with the sheriff clerk (*insert address of sheriff clerk*) for leave to appear as a party. Your minute must be lodged within 21 days of (*insert date on which intimation was given. N.B. Rule 5.3(2) relating to postal service or intimation*).

Date (*insert date*)   (*Signed*)
                                                  Solicitor for the pursuer

> **NOTE**
> If you decide to lodge a minute it may be in your best interests to consult a solicitor. The minute should be lodged with the sheriff clerk together with the appropriate fee of (*insert amount*) and a copy of this intimation.

> **IF YOU ARE UNCERTAIN WHAT ACTION TO TAKE** you should consult a solicitor. You may be entitled to legal aid depending on your financial circumstances, and you can get information about legal aid from a solicitor. You may also obtain advice from any Citizens Advice Bureau or other advice agency.

Rule 33.10   FORM F14

Form of warrant of citation in family action

(*Insert place and date*)

Grants warrant to cite the defender (*insert name and address of defender*) by serving upon him [*or* her] a copy of the writ and warrant upon a period of notice of (*insert period of notice*) days, and ordains the defender to lodge a notice of intention to defend with the sheriff clerk at (*insert address of sheriff court*) if he [*or* she] wishes to:
  (a) challenge the jurisdiction of the court;
  (b) oppose any claim made or order sought;
  (c) make any claim or seek any order.

[Meantime grants interim interdict, *or* warrant to arrest on the dependence].

Rules 33.11(1) and 33.13(1)(a)   FORM F15

Form of citation in family action

CITATION

SHERIFFDOM OF (*insert name of sheriffdom*)
AT (*insert place of sheriff court*)

[A.B.], (*insert designation and address*), Pursuer, against [C.D.], (*insert designation and address*), Defender.

(*Insert place and date*)   Court ref. no.

You [C.D.], are hereby served with this copy writ and warrant, with Form F26 (notice of intention to defend) [and (*insert details of any other form of notice served, e.g. any of the forms served in accordance with rule 33.14*.)].

> **Form F26** is served on you for use should you wish to intimate an intention to defend the action.
>
> **IF YOU WISH TO—**
>   (a) challenge the jurisdiction of the court;

(b) oppose any claim made or order sought;

(c) make any claim or seek any order; or

(d) seek any order;

you should consult a solicitor with a view to lodging a notice of intention to defend (Form F26). The notice of intention to defend, together with the court fee of £ (*insert amount*) must be lodged with the sheriff clerk at the above address within 21 days (*or insert appropriate period of notice*) of (*insert the date on which service was executed. N.B. Rule 5.3(2) relating to postal service or intimation*).

IF YOU ARE UNCERTAIN WHAT ACTION TO TAKE you should consult a solicitor. You may be entitled to legal aid depending on your financial circumstances, and you can get information about legal aid from a solicitor. You may also obtain advice from any Citizens Advice Bureau or other advice agency.

PLEASE NOTE THAT IF YOU DO NOTHING IN ANSWER TO THIS DOCUMENT the court may regard you as admitting the claim made against you and the pursuer may obtain decree against you in your absence.

Signed

[P.Q.], Sheriff officer

or

[X.Y.], (*add designation and business address*)

Solicitor for the pursuer

Rule 33.11(2)   FORM F16

Form of certificate of citation in family action

CERTIFICATE OF CITATION

(*Insert place and date*) I,   hereby certify that upon the   day of   I duly cited [C.D.], Defender, to answer to the foregoing writ. This I did by (*state method of service; if by officer and not by post, add*: in presence of [L.M.], (*insert designation*), witness hereto with me subscribing; *and* (*insert details of any forms of intimation or notice sent including details of the person to whom intimation sent and the method of service*).

Signed

[P.Q.], Sheriff officer

[L.M.], witness

or

[X.Y.] (*add designation and business address*)

Solicitor for the pursuer

Rule 33.13(1)(c)   FORM F17

Form of request to medical officer of hospital or similar institution

To (*insert name and address of medical officer*)

In terms of rule 33.13(1)(c) of the Ordinary Cause Rules of the Sheriff Court a copy of the initial writ at the instance of (*insert name and address of pursuer*), Pursuer, against (*insert name and address of defender*), Defender, is enclosed and you are requested to

(a) deliver it personally to (*insert name of defender*), and

(b) explain the contents to him or her,

unless you are satisfied that such delivery or explanation would be dangerous to his or her health or mental condition. You are further requested to complete and return to me in the enclosed stamped addressed envelope the certificate appended hereto, making necessary deletions.

Date (*insert date*)   (*Signed*)

Solicitor for the pursuer (*add designation and business address*)

Rules 33.13(1)(d) and 33.13(2)   FORM F18

Form of certificate by medical officer of hospital or similar institution

Court ref. no.

I (*insert name and designation*) certify that I have received a copy initial writ in an action of (*type of family action to be inserted by the party requesting service*) at the instance of (*insert name and designation*), Pursuer, against (*insert name and designation*), Defender, and that

* I have on the   day of   personally delivered a copy thereof to the said defender who is under my care at (*insert address*) and I have explained the contents or purport thereof to him or her, *or*
* I have not delivered a copy thereof to the said defender who is under my care at (*insert address*) and I have not explained the contents or purport thereof to him or her because (*state reasons*).

Date (*insert date*)   (*Signed*)
                                             Medical officer (*add designation and
                                             address*)

     * Delete as appropriate.

Rule 33.14(1)(a)(i)   ¹ FORM F19

Form of notice to defender where it is stated that defender consents to the granting of decree of divorce

YOU ARE GIVEN NOTICE that the copy initial writ served on you with this notice states that you consent to the grant of decree of divorce.

1. If you do so consent the consequences for you are that:—

² (a) provided the pursuer establishes the fact that he [*or* she] has not cohabited with you at any time during a continuous period of one year after the date of your marriage and immediately preceding the bringing of this action and that you consent, a decree of divorce will be granted;
   (b) on the grant of a decree of divorce you may lose your rights of succession to the pursuer's estate; and
   (c) decree of divorce will end the marriage thereby affecting any right to such pension as may depend on the marriage continuing, or, on your being left a widow the state widow's pension will not be payable to you when the pursuer dies.

Apart from these, there may be other consequences for you depending upon your particular circumstances.

2. You are entitled, whether or not you consent to the grant of decree of divorce in this action, to apply to the sheriff in this action—

   (a) to make financial or other provision for you under the Family Law (Scotland) Act 1985;
   (b) for an order under section 11 of the Children (Scotland) Act 1995 in respect of any child of the marriage, or any child accepted as such, who is under 16 years of age; or
   (c) for any other competent order.

3. IF YOU WISH TO APPLY FOR ANY OF THE ABOVE ORDERS you should consult a solicitor with a view to lodging a notice of intention to defend (Form F26).

4. If, after consideration, you wish to consent to the grant of decree of divorce in this action, you should complete and sign the attached notice of consent (Form F20) and send it to the sheriff clerk at the sheriff court referred to in the initial writ within 21 days of (*insert the date on which service was executed. N.B. Rule 5.3(2) relating to postal service*).

5. If at a later stage, you wish to withdraw your consent to decree being granted against you in this action, you must inform the sheriff clerk immediately in writing.

Date (*insert date*)   (*Signed*)
                                             Solicitor for the pursuer (*add designation
                                             and business address*)

NOTES
[1] Substituted by SI 1996/2167 (effective November 1, 1996).
[2] As amended by Act of Sederunt (Ordinary Cause Rules) Amendment (Family Law (Scotland) Act 2006 etc.) 2006, para.2 (SSI 2006/207) (effective May 4, 2006).

Rules 33.14(1)(a)(i) and 33.18(1) FORM F20

Form of notice of consent in actions of divorce under section 1(2)(d) of the Divorce (Scotland) Act 1976

Court ref. no.

[A.B.], (*insert designation and address*), Pursuer, against [C.D.], (*insert designation and address*), Defender.

I (*full name and address of the defender to be inserted by pursuer or pursuer's solicitor before sending notice*) have received a copy of the initial writ in the action against me at the instance of (*full name and address of pursuer to be inserted by pursuer or pursuer's solicitor before sending notice*). I understand that it states that I consent to the grant of decree of divorce in this action. I have considered the consequences for me mentioned in the notice (Form F19) sent to me with this notice. I consent to the grant of decree of divorce in this action.

Date (*insert date*) (*Signed*)
Defender

Rule 33.14(1)(a)(ii) [1] FORM F21

Form of notice to defender where it is stated that defender consents to the granting of decree of separation

YOU ARE GIVEN NOTICE that the copy initial writ served on you with this notice states that you consent to the grant of decree of separation.

1. If you do so consent the consequences for you are that—

[2] (a) provided the pursuer establishes the fact that he [*or she*] has not cohabited with you at any time during a continuous period of one year after the date of your marriage and immediately preceding the bringing of this action and that you consent, a decree of separation will be granted;
   (b) on the grant of a decree of separation you will be obliged to live apart from the pursuer but the marriage will continue to subsist; you will continue to have a legal obligation to support your wife [*or husband*] and children;

Apart from these, there may be other consequences for you depending upon your particular circumstances.

2. You are entitled, whether or not you consent to the grant of decree of separation in this action, to apply to the sheriff in this action—

   (a) to make financial or other provision for you under the Family Law (Scotland) Act 1985;
   (b) for an order under Section 11 of the Children (Scotland) Act 1995 in respect of any child of the marriage, or any child accepted as such, who is under 16 years of age; or
   (c) for any other competent order.

3. IF YOU WISH TO APPLY FOR ANY OF THE ABOVE ORDERS you should consult a solicitor with a view to lodging a notice of intention to defend (Form F26).

4. If, after consideration, you wish to consent to the grant of decree of separation in this action, you should complete and sign the attached notice of consent (Form F22) and send it to the sheriff clerk at the sheriff court referred to in the initial writ and other papers within 21 days of (*insert the date on which service was executed. N.B. Rule 5.3(2) relating to postal service or intimation*).

5. If at a later stage you wish to withdraw your consent to decree being granted against you in this action, you must inform the sheriff clerk immediately in writing.

Date (*insert date*)   (*Signed*)
                                                                         Solicitor for the pursuer (*add designation
                                                                         and business address*)

NOTES
[1] Substituted by SI 1996/2167 (effective November 1, 1996).
[2] As amended by Act of Sederunt (Ordinary Cause Rules) Amendment (Family Law (Scotland) Act 2006 etc.) 2006, para.2 (SSI 2006/207) (effective May 4, 2006).

Rules 33.14(1)(a)(ii) and 33.18(1)   FORM F22

Form of notice of consent in actions of separation under section 1(2)(d) of the Divorce (Scotland) Act 1976

                                                                                   Court ref. no.

[A.B.], (*insert designation and address*), Pursuer against [C.D.], (*insert designation and address*), Defender.

I (*full name and address of the defender to be inserted by pursuer or pursuer's solicitor before sending notice*) confirm that I have received a copy of the initial writ in the action against me at the instance of (*full name and address of pursuer to be inserted by pursuer or pursuer's solicitor before sending notice*). I understand that it states that I consent to the grant of decree of separation in this action. I have considered the consequences for me mentioned in the notice (Form F21) sent together with this notice. I consent to the grant of decree of separation in this action.

Date (*insert date*)   (*Signed*)
                                                                         Defender

Rule 33.14(1)(b)(i)   [1] FORM F23

[2] Form of notice to defender in an action of divorce where it is stated there has been two years' non-cohabitation

YOU ARE GIVEN NOTICE that—

[2] 1. The copy initial writ served on you with this notice states that there has been no cohabitation between you and the pursuer at any time during a continuous period of two years after the date of the marriage and immediately preceding the commencement of this action. If the pursuer establishes this as a fact and the sheriff is satisfied that the marriage has broken down irretrievably, a decree will be granted.

2. Decree of divorce will end the marriage thereby affecting any right to such pension as may depend on the marriage continuing, or, on your being left a widow the state widow's pension will not be payable to you when the pursuer dies. You may also lose your rights of succession to the pursuer's estate.

[2] 3. You are entitled, whether or not you dispute that there has been no such cohabitation during that two year period, to apply to the sheriff in this action—

   (a) to make financial or other provision for you under the Family Law (Scotland) Act 1985;
   (b) for an order under section 11 of the Children (Scotland) Act 1995 in respect of any child of the marriage, or any child accepted as such, who is under 16 years of age; or
   (c) for any other competent order.

4. IF YOU WISH TO APPLY FOR ANY OF THE ABOVE ORDERS you should consult a solicitor with a view to lodging a notice of intention to defend (Form F26).

Date (*insert date*)   (*Signed*)
                                                                         Solicitor for the pursuer (*add designation
                                                                         and business address*)

NOTES
[1] Substituted by SI 1996/2167 (effective November 1, 1996).
[2] As amended by Act of Sederunt (Ordinary Cause Rules) Amendment (Family Law (Scotland) Act 2006 etc.) 2006, para.2 (SSI 2006/207) (effective May 4, 2006).

Rule 33.14(1)(b)(ii)   [1] FORM F24

[2] Form of notice to defender in an action of separation where it is stated there has been two years' non-cohabitation

YOU ARE GIVEN NOTICE that—

[2] 1. The copy initial writ served on you together with this notice states that there has been no cohabitation between you and the pursuer at any time during a continuous period of two years after the date of the marriage and immediately preceding the commencement of this action and that if the pursuer establishes this as a fact, and the sheriff is satisfied that there are grounds justifying decree of separation, a decree will be granted.

2. On the granting of decree of separation you will be obliged to live apart from the pursuer but the marriage will continue to subsist. You will continue to have a legal obligation to support your wife [*or* husband] and children.

[2] 3. You are entitled, whether or not you dispute that there has been no such cohabitation during that two year period, to apply to the sheriff in this action—

    (a) to make provision under the Family Law (Scotland) Act 1985;
    (b) for an order under section 11 of the Children (Scotland) Act 1995 in respect of any child of the marriage, or any child accepted as such, who is under 16 years of age; or
    (c) for any other competent order.

4. IF YOU WISH TO APPLY FOR ANY OF THE ABOVE ORDERS you should consult a solicitor with a view to lodging a notice of intention to defend (Form F26).

Date (*insert date*)   (*Signed*)
                                     Solicitor for the pursuer (*add designation and business address*)

NOTES
[1] Substituted by SI 1996/2167 (effective November 1, 1996).
[2] As amended by Act of Sederunt (Ordinary Cause Rules) Amendment (Family Law (Scotland) Act 2006 etc.) 2006, para.2 (SSI 2006/207) (effective May 4, 2006).

Rule 33.14(1)(c)   [1] FORM F24A

Form of notice to defender in action of divorce where an interim gender recognition certificate has been issued

YOU ARE GIVEN NOTICE that—

1. The copy initial writ served on you together with this notice states that an interim gender recognition certificate has been issued to you [*or* the pursuer]. If the pursuer establishes this as a fact, decree will be granted.

2. Decree of divorce will end the marriage thereby affecting any right to such pension as may depend on the marriage continuing, or, on your being left a widow the state widow's pension will not be payable to you when the pursuer dies. You may also lose your rights of succession to the pursuer's estate.

3. If the pursuer is entitled to a decree of divorce, you are nevertheless entitled to apply to the sheriff in this action—

    (a) to make financial or other provision for you under the Family Law (Scotland) Act 1985;
    (b) for an order under section 11 of the Children (Scotland) Act 1995 in respect of any child of the marriage, or any child accepted as such, who is under 16 years of age; or
    (c) for any competent order.

4. IF YOU WISH TO APPLY FOR ANY OF THE ABOVE ORDERS you should consult a solicitor with a view to lodging a notice of intention to defend (Form F26).

Date (*insert date*)

(*Signed*)
Solicitor for the pursuer (*add designation and business address*)

NOTE
[1] Inserted by Act of Sederunt (Ordinary Cause Rules) Amendment (Family Law (Scotland) Act 2006 etc.) 2006, para.2 (SSI 2006/207) (effective May 4, 2006).

FORM F25

[Removed by SI 1996/2167 (effective November 1, 1996).]

Rules 33.11(1) and 33.34(2)(a)   [1] FORM F26

Form of notice of intention to defend in family action

NOTICE OF INTENTION TO DEFEND

PART A

PART A (This section to be completed by the pursuer's solicitor before service.) [*Insert name and business address of solicitor for the pursuer*]	Court ref. No. In an action brought in Sheriff Court	Date of expiry of period of notice
	Pursuer	
	Defender Date of service:	

PART B

(This section to be completed by the defender or defender's solicitor, and both parts of the form to be returned to the Sheriff Clerk at the above Sheriff Court on or before the date of expiry of the period of notice referred to in Part A above.)

(*Insert place and date*)

[C.D.] (*Insert designation and address*), Defender, intends to
    (a) challenge the jurisdiction of the court;
    (b) oppose a crave in the initial writ;
    (c) make a claim;
    (d) seek an order;

in the action against him [*or* her] raised by [A.B.], (*insert designation and address*), Pursuer.

PART C

(This section to be completed by the defender or the defender's solicitor where an order under section 11 of the Children (Scotland) Act 1995 in respect of a child is opposed by the defender).

DO YOU WISH TO OPPOSE THE MAKING OF ANY ORDER CRAVED BY THE PURSUER IN RESPECT OF A CHILD?

YES/NO*

*delete as appropriate

If you answered YES to the above question, please state here the order(s) which you wish to oppose and the reasons why the court should not make such order(s).

PART D

(This section to be completed by the defender or the defender's solicitor where an order under section 11 of the Children (Scotland) Act 1995 in respect of a child is sought by the defender).

DO YOU WISH THE COURT TO MAKE ANY ORDER UNDER SECTION 11 OF THE CHILDREN (SCOTLAND) ACT 1995 IN RESPECT OF A CHILD?

YES/NO*

*delete as appropriate

If you answered YES to the above question, please state here the order(s) which you wish the court to make and the reasons why the court should make such order(s).

PART E

IF YOU HAVE COMPLETED PART D OF THIS FORM YOU MUST INCLUDE EITHER CRAVE (1) OR (2) BELOW (*delete as appropriate)

(1)* Warrant for intimation of notice in terms of Form F9 on the child(ren) (*insert full name(s) and date(s) of birth*) is sought.

(2)* I seek to dispense with intimation on the child(ren) (*insert full name(s) and date(s) of birth*) for the following reasons:—

Signed
[C.D.] Defender [*or* [X.Y.] *(add designation and business address)*
Solicitor for Defender]

NOTE
¹ Substituted by Act of Sederunt (Ordinary Cause, Summary Application, Summary Cause and Small Claim Rules) Amendment (Miscellaneous) 2005 (SSI 2005/648), para.2 (effective January 2, 2006).

Rule 33.29(1)(b)   FORM F27

Form of minute for decree in family action to which rule 33.28 applies

(*Insert name of solicitor for the pursuer*) having considered the evidence contained in the affidavits and the other documents all as specified in the schedule hereto, and being satisfied that upon the evidence a motion for decree (in terms of the crave of the initial writ) [*or in such restricted terms as may be appropriate*] may properly be made, moves the court accordingly.

In respect whereof
Signed
Solicitor for the Pursuer (*add designation and business address*)

SCHEDULE
(*Number and specify documents considered*)

Rules 33.40(c) and 33.64(1)(c)   FORM F28

Form of notice of intimation to local authority or third party to whom care of a child is to be given

To (*name and address as in warrant*)   Court ref. no.

You are given NOTICE that in this action, the sheriff proposes to commit to your care the child (*insert name and address*). A copy of the initial writ is attached. If you wish to appear as a party, you must lodge a minute with the sheriff clerk (*insert address of sheriff clerk*) for leave to do so. Your minute must be lodged within 21 days of (*insert date on which intimation was given. N.B. Rule 5.3(2) relating to postal service or intimation*).

Date (*insert date*)   (*Signed*)
                                                         Solicitor for the pursuer

---

NOTE
If you decide to lodge a minute it may be in your best interest to consult a solicitor. The minute should be lodged with the sheriff clerk together with the appropriate fee of (*insert amount*) and a copy of this intimation.

IF YOU ARE UNCERTAIN WHAT ACTION TO TAKE you should consult a solicitor. You may be entitled to legal aid depending on your financial circumstances, and you can get information about legal aid from a solicitor. You may also obtain advice from any Citizens Advice Bureau or other advice agency.

Rules 33.41 and 33.64(2)   FORM F29

Form of notice of intimation to local authority of supervision order

[A.B.], (*insert designation and address*), Pursuer, against [C.D.], (*insert designation and address*), Defender.

To (*insert name and address of local authority*)   Court ref. no.

You are given NOTICE that on (*insert date*) in the Sheriff Court at (*insert place*) the sheriff made a supervision order under section 12 of the Matrimonial Proceedings (Children) Act 1958 [*or* section 11(1)(b) of the Guardianship Act 1973] placing the child (*insert name and address of child*) under your supervision. A certified copy of the sheriff's interlocutor is attached.

Date (*insert date*)   (*Signed*)
                                                         Sheriff clerk (depute)

Rules 33.72(1) and 33.72(2)   FORM F30

[*Omitted by Act of Sederunt (Ordinary Cause Rules) Amendment (Family Law (Scotland) Act 2006 etc.) 2006, para.2 (SSI 2006/207) (effective May 4, 2006).*]

Rule 33.74(1)   [1,2,3] FORM F31

Form of simplified divorce application under section 1(2)(d) of the Divorce (Scotland) Act 1976

Sheriff Clerk
Sheriff Court House
....
....
(Telephone) ....

APPLICATION FOR DIVORCE WITH CONSENT OF OTHER PARTY TO THE MARRIAGE (HUSBAND AND WIFE HAVING LIVED APART FOR AT LEAST ONE YEAR)

Before completing this form, you should have read the leaflet entitled "Do it yourself Divorce", which explains the circumstances in which a divorce may be sought by this method. If simplified procedure appears to suit your circumstances, you may use this form to apply for divorce. Below you will find directions designed to assist you with your application. Please follow them carefully. In the event of difficulty, you may contact any sheriff clerk's office or Citizens Advice Bureau.

Directions for making application

WRITE IN INK, USING BLOCK CAPITALS

Application   1. Complete and sign Part 1 of the form (pages 3–7), paying particular
(Part 1)   attention to the notes opposite each section.

Consent of
husband/wife
(Part 2)

2. When you have completed Part 1 of the form, attach the (blue) instruction sheet SP3 to it and send both documents to your spouse for completion of the consent at Part 2 (page 9).

NOTE: If your spouse does NOT complete and sign the form of consent, your application cannot proceed further under the simplified procedure. In that event, if you still wish to obtain a divorce, you should consult a solicitor.

Affidavit
(Part 3)

3. When the application has been returned to you with the consent (Part 2) duly completed and signed, you should take the form to a Justice of the Peace, Notary Public, Commissioner for Oaths or other duly authorised person so that your affidavit at Part 3 (page 10) may be completed and sworn.

Returning
completed
application
form to court

4. When directions 1–3 above have been complied with, your application is now ready to be sent to the sheriff clerk at the above address. With it you must enclose:

(i) your marriage certificate (the document headed "Extract of an entry in a Register of Marriages", which will be returned to you in due course), and

(ii) either a cheque or postal order in respect of the court fee, crossed and made payable to "the Scottish Court Service" or a completed fee exemption form,

    or   a completed form SP15, claiming exemption from the court fee.

5. Receipt of your application will be promptly acknowledged. Should you wish to withdraw the application for any reason, please contact the sheriff clerk immediately.

PART 1

WRITE IN INK, USING BLOCK CAPITALS

1. NAME AND ADDRESS OF APPLICANT

Surname ....

Other name(s) in full ....

....

Present address ....

....

Daytime telephone number (if any)

....

2. NAME AND ADDRESS OF SPOUSE

Surname ....

Other name(s) in full ....

....

Present address ....

....

Daytime telephone number (if any) ....

3. JURISDICTION

Please indicate with a tick (✔) in the appropriate box or boxes which of the following apply:

PART A

(i)   My spouse and I are habitually resident in Scotland   ☐

(ii)   My spouse and I were last habitually resident in Scotland, and one of us still resides there   ☐

(iii) My spouse is habitually resident in Scotland   ☐

(iv) I am habitually resident in Scotland having resided there for at least a year immediately before this application was made   ☐

(v) I am habitually resident in Scotland having resided there for at least six months immediately before this application was made and am domiciled in Scotland ☐

(vi) My spouse and I are domiciled in Scotland ☐

If you have ticked one or more of the boxes in Part A, you should go direct to Part C. You should only complete Part B if you have not ticked any boxes in Part A

PART B

(i) I am domiciled in Scotland ☐

(ii) My spouse is domiciled in Scotland ☐

AND

(iii) No court of a Contracting State has jurisdiction under the Council Regulation (E.C.) No. 2201/2003 of 27th November 2003 concerning jurisdiction and the recognition and enforcement of judgments in matrimonial matters and in matters of Parental Responsibility (O.J. No L.338, 23.12.2003, p.1) ☐

PART C

(i) I have lived at the address shown above for at least 40 days immediately before the date I signed this application ☐

(ii) My spouse has lived at the address shown above for at least 40 days immediately before the date I signed this application ☐

(iii) I lived at the address shown above for a period of at least 40 days ending not more than 40 days before the date I signed this application and have no known residence in Scotland at that date ☐

(iv) My spouse lived at the address shown above for a period of at least 40 days ending not more than 40 days before the date I signed this application and has no known residence in Scotland at that date ☐

4. DETAILS OF PRESENT MARRIAGE

Place of Marriage .... (Registration District)

Date of Marriage: Day .... month .... year ....

5. PERIOD OF SEPARATION

(i) Please the date on which you ceased to live with your spouse. (If more than 1 year, just give the month and year)
Day ...... Month ...... Year ......

(ii) Have you lived with your spouse since that date?   *[YES/NO]

(iii) If yes, for how long in total did you live together before finally separating again?
.... months

6. RECONCILIATION

Is there any reasonable prospect of reconciliation with your spouse?   *[YES/NO]

Do you consider that the marriage has broken down irretrievably?   *[YES/NO]

7. CONSENT

Does your spouse consent to a divorce being granted?   *[YES/NO]

8. MENTAL DISORDER

Does your spouse have any mental disorder (whether mental illness,   *[YES/NO]
personality disorder or learning disability)?   (if yes, give details)

9. CHILDREN

Are there any children of the marriage under the age of 16?   *[YES/NO]

10. OTHER COURT ACTIONS

Are you aware of any court actions currently proceeding in any   *[YES/NO]
country (including Scotland) which may affect your
marriage?   (If yes, give details)   *Delete as appropriate

11. DECLARATION AND REQUEST FOR DIVORCE

I confirm that the facts stated in paragraphs 1–10 above apply to my marriage.

I do NOT ask the sheriff to make any financial provision in connection with this application.

I do NOT ask the court to postpone the grant of decree under section 3A of the Divorce (Scotland) Act 1976.

I request the sheriff to grant decree of divorce from my spouse.

Date   Signature of applicant's spouse ....

IMPORTANT
Part 1 MUST be completed, signed and dated before sending the application form to your spouse.

PART 2

NOTICE TO CONSENTING SPOUSE

(Insert name and address of consenting spouse)

CONSENT TO APPLICATION FOR DIVORCE (HUSBAND AND WIFE HAVING LIVED APART FOR AT LEAST ONE YEAR)

In Part 1 of the enclosed application form your spouse is applying for divorce on the ground that the marriage has broken down irretrievably because you and he [*or* she] have lived apart for at least one year and you consent to the divorce being granted.

Such consent must be given formally in writing at Part 2 of the application form. BEFORE completing that part, you are requested to read it over carefully so that you understand the effect of consenting to divorce. Thereafter if you wish to consent—

(a) check the details given by the Applicant at Part 1 of the form to ensure that they are correct to the best of your knowledge;

(b) complete Part 2 (Consent by Applicant's spouse to divorce) by entering your name and address at the appropriate place and adding your signature and the date; and

(c) return the whole application form to your spouse at the address given in Part 1.

Once your husband or wife has completed the remainder of the form and has submitted it to the court, a copy of the whole application (including your consent) will later be served upon you formally by the sheriff clerk.

In the event of the divorce being granted, you will automatically be sent a copy of the extract decree. (Should you change your address before receiving the copy extract decree, please notify the sheriff clerk immediately.)

If you do NOT wish to consent please return the application form, with Part 2 uncompleted, to your spouse and advise him or her of your decision.

The sheriff will NOT grant a divorce on this application if Part 2 of the form is not completed by you.

Sheriff clerk (depute)
Sheriff Court (*insert address*)

CONSENT BY APPLICANT'S SPOUSE TO DIVORCE

NOTE: Before completing this part of the form, please read the notes opposite (page 8)

I, ...
(Insert full name, in BLOCK letters, of Applicant's spouse)

residing at

....
(Insert address, also in BLOCK letters)

....
....

HEREBY STATE THAT

    (a) I have read Part 1 of this application;

    (b) the Applicant has lived apart from me for a continuous period of one year immediately preceding the date of the application (paragraph 11 of Part 1);

    (c) I do not ask the sheriff to make any financial provision for me including—
        (i) the payment by the Applicant of a periodical allowance (i.e. a regular payment of money weekly or monthly, etc. for maintenance);
        (ii) the payment by the Applicant of a capital sum (i.e. a lump sum payment);

    (d) I understand that divorce may result in the loss to me of property rights;

    (e) I do not ask the court to postpone the grant of decree under section 3A of the Divorce (Scotland) Act 1976; and

    (f) I CONSENT TO DECREE OF DIVORCE BEING GRANTED IN RESPECT OF THIS APPLICATION.

Date   Signature ....

NOTE: You may withdraw your consent, even after giving it, at any time before divorce is granted by the sheriff. Should you wish to do so, please contact the sheriff clerk immediately.

PART 3

APPLICANT'S AFFIDAVIT

To be completed by the Applicant only after Parts 1 and 2 have been signed and dated.

I, *(insert Applicant's full name)* ....
   residing at *(insert Applicant's present home address)* ....
....
....

SWEAR that to the best of my knowledge and belief:

    (1) the facts stated in Part 1 of this Application are true; and

    (2) the signature in Part 2 of this Application is that of my *husband/wife.

Signature of Applicant ....

To be completed by Justice of the Peace, Notary Public or Commissioner for Oaths	SWORN at *(insert place)* ....
	this .... day of ....19........
	before me *(insert full name)* ....
	(insert full address) ....
	....
	....
	Signature ....
	*Justice of the Peace/Notary Public/Commissioner for Oaths
	*Delete as appropriate

NOTES
[1] As amended by SI 1996/2445 (effective November 1, 1996) and the Act of Sederunt (Ordinary Cause Rules) Amendment (Form of Simplified Divorce Application) 2003 (SSI 2003/25), para.2(2)(a) (effective January 31, 2003).

[2] As amended by Act of Sederunt (Ordinary Cause Rules) Amendment (Family Law (Scotland) Act 2006 etc.) 2006, para.2 (SSI 2006/207) (effective May 4, 2006).

[3] As amended by the Act of Sederunt (Ordinary Cause, Summary Application, Summary

Cause and Small Claim Rules) Amendment (Miscellaneous) 2007 (SSI 2007/6), para.2(16)(f) (effective February 26, 2007).

FORM F32

[Repealed by SI 1996/2445 (effective November 1, 1996).]

Rule 33.74(2)   [1,2,3] FORM F33

Form of simplified divorce application under section 1(2)(e) of the Divorce (Scotland) Act 1976

Sheriff Clerk
Sheriff Court House

....

....

(Telephone) ....

APPLICATION FOR DIVORCE (HUSBAND AND WIFE HAVING LIVED APART FOR AT LEAST TWO YEARS)

Before completing this form, you should have read the leaflet entitled "Do it yourself Divorce", which explains the circumstances in which a divorce may be sought by this method. If the simplified procedure appears to suit your circumstances, you may use this form to apply for divorce.

Below you will find directions to assist you with your application. Please follow them carefully. In the event of difficulty, you may contact any sheriff clerk's office or Citizens Advice Bureau.

Directions for making application

WRITE IN INK, USING BLOCK CAPITALS

Application (Part 1)	1. Complete and sign Part 1 of the form (pages 3–7), paying particular attention to the notes opposite each section.
Affidavits (Part 2)	2. When you have completed Part 1, you should take the form to a Justice of the Peace, Notary Public, Commissioner for Oaths or other duly authorised person in order that your affidavit in Part 2 (page 8) may be completed and sworn.
Returning completed application form to court	3. When directions 1 and 2 above have been complied with, your application is now ready to be sent to the sheriff clerk at the above address. With it you must enclose:

(i) your marriage certificate (the document headed "Extract of an entry in a Register of Marriages", which will be returned to you in due course). Check the notes on page 2 to see if you need to obtain a letter from the General Register Office stating that there is no record of your spouse having divorced you, and
(ii) either a cheque or postal order in respect of the court fee, crossed and made out to "the Scottish Court Service" or a completed fee exemption form.

4. Receipt of your application will be promptly acknowledged. Should you wish to withdraw the application for any reason, please contact the sheriff clerk immediately.

PART 1

WRITE IN INK, USING BLOCK CAPITALS

1. NAME AND ADDRESS OF APPLICANT

Surname ....

Other name(s) in full ....
Present address ....
....
....
Daytime telephone number (if any) ....

2. NAME OF SPOUSE

Surname ....

Other name(s) in full ....

3. ADDRESS OF SPOUSE (if the address of your spouse is not known, please enter "not known" in this paragraph and proceed to paragraph 4)

Present address ....

....

....

Daytime telephone (if any) ....

4. Only complete this paragraph if you do not know the present address of your spouse

NEXT-OF-KIN

Name ....

Address ....

....

....

Relationship
to your spouse ....

CHILDREN OF THE MARRIAGE

Names and dates of birth	Addresses
....	....
....	....
....	....
....	....

If insufficient space is available to list all the children of the marriage, please continue on a separate sheet and attach to this form.

5. JURISDICTION   Please indicate with a tick (✔) in the appropriate box or boxes which of the following apply:

PART A

(i)   My spouse and I are habitually resident in Scotland

(ii) My spouse and I were last habitually resident in Scotland, and one of us still resides there

(iii) My spouse is habitually resident in Scotland

(iv) I am habitually resident in Scotland having resided there for at least a year immediately before this application was made

(v)   I am habitually resident in Scotland having resided there for at least six months immediately before this application was made and am domiciled in Scotland

(vi) My spouse and I are domiciled in Scotland

If you have ticked one or more of the boxes in Part A, you should go direct to Part C. You should only complete Part B if you have not ticked any boxes in Part A

PART B

(i)   I am domiciled in Scotland

(ii) My spouse is domiciled in Scotland

☐

AND

(iii) No court of a Contracting State has jurisdiction under the Council Regulation (E.C.) No. 2201/2003 of 27th November 2003 concerning jurisdiction and the recognition and enforcement of judgments in matrimonial matters and in matters of Parental Responsibility (O.J. No L.338, 23.12.2003, p.1)

☐

PART C

(i) I have lived at the address shown above for at least 40 days immediately before the date I signed this application

☐

(ii) My spouse has lived at the address shown above for at least 40 days immediately before the date I signed this application

☐

(iii) I lived at the address shown above for a period of at least 40 days ending not more than 40 days before the date I signed this application and have no known residence in Scotland at that date

☐

(iv) My spouse lived at the address shown above for a period of at least 40 days ending not more than 40 days before the date I signed this application and has no known residence in Scotland at that date

☐

6. DETAILS OF PRESENT MARRIAGE

Place of Marriage .... (Registration District)

Date of Marriage: Day .... month .... year ....

7. PERIOD OF SEPARATION

(i) Please state the date on which you ceased to live with your spouse. (If more than 2 years, just give the month and year) Day .... Month .... Year ....

(ii) Have you lived with your spouse since that date? *[YES/NO]

(iii) If yes, for how long in total did you live together before finally separating again?

.... months

8. RECONCILIATION

Is there any reasonable prospect of reconciliation with your spouse? *[YES/NO]

Do you consider that the marriage has broken down irretrievably? *[YES/NO]

9. MENTAL DISORDER

Does your spouse have any mental disorder (whether mental illness, personality disorder or learning disability)? (If yes, give details) *[YES/NO]

10. CHILDREN

Are there any children of the marriage under the age of 16? *[YES/NO]

11. OTHER COURT ACTIONS

Are you aware of any court actions currently proceeding in any country (including Scotland) which may affect your marriage? *[YES/NO]
(If yes, give details)

*Delete as appropriate

12. DECLARATION AND REQUEST FOR DIVORCE

I confirm that the facts stated in paragraphs 1–12 above apply to my marriage.

I do NOT ask the sheriff to make any financial provision in connection with this application.

I do NOT ask the court to postpone the grant of decree under section 3A of the Divorce (Scotland) Act 1976.

I request the sheriff to grant decree of divorce from my husband or wife.

Date ....
Signature of Applicant ....

PART 2

APPLICANT'S AFFIDAVIT

(To be completed by the Applicant only after Part 1 has been signed and dated.)

I, (*insert full name*) ....

residing at (*insert present home address*) ....

....

SWEAR that to the best of my knowledge and belief the facts stated in Part 1 of this Application are true.

Signature of Applicant ....

To be completed by Justice of the Peace, Notary Public or Commissioner for Oaths	SWORN at (*insert place*) this .... day of .... 19......... before me (*insert full name*) .... of (*insert full address*) ....

Signature ....

*Justice of the Peace/Notary Public/Commissioner for Oaths

*Delete as appropriate

NOTES

[1] As amended by SI 1996/2445 (effective November 1, 1996) and the Act of Sederunt (Ordinary Cause Rules) Amendment (Form of Simplified Divorce Application) 2003 (SSI 2003/25), para.2(2)(b) (effective January 31, 2003).
[2] As amended by Act of Sederunt (Ordinary Cause Rules) Amendment (Family Law (Scotland) Act 2006 etc.) 2006, para.2 (SSI 2006/207) (effective May 4, 2006).
[3] As amended by the Act of Sederunt (Ordinary Cause, Summary Application, Summary Cause and Small Claim Rules) Amendment (Miscellaneous) 2007 (SSI 2007/6), para.2(16)(g) (effective February 26, 2007).

Rule 33.74(1)(3)   [1,2] FORM F33A

Form of simplified divorce application under section 1(1)(b) of the Divorce (Scotland) Act 1976

Sheriff Clerk
Sheriff Court House

....
....

(Telephone) ....

APPLICATION FOR DIVORCE (INTERIM GENDER RECOGNITION CERTIFICATE ISSUED TO ONE OF THE PARTIES AFTER THE MARRIAGE

Before completing this form, you should have read the leaflet entitled "Do it yourself Divorce", which explains the circumstances in which a divorce may be sought by this method. If the simplified procedure appears to suit your circumstances, you may use this form to apply for divorce. Below you will find directions designed to assist you with your application. Please follow them carefully. In the event of difficulty, you may contact any sheriff clerk's office or Citizen's Advice Bureau.

Directions for making application

WRITE IN INK, USING BLOCK CAPITALS

Application
(Part 1)

1. Complete and sign Part 1 of the form (pages 3–7), paying particular attention to the notes opposite each section.

Affidavits
(Part 2)

2. When you have completed Part 1, you should take the form to a Justice of the Peace, Notary Public, Commissioner for Oaths or other duly authorised person so that your affidavit at Part 2 (page 8) may be completed and sworn.

Returning
completed
application
form to court

3. When directions 1–2 above have been complied with, your application is now ready to be sent to the sheriff clerk at the above address. With it you must enclose:

   (i) your marriage certificate (the document headed "Extract of an entry in a Register of Marriages, which will be returned to you in due course). Check the notes on page 2 to see if you also need to obtain a letter from the General Register Office stating that there is no record that your spouse has divorced you, and,

   (ii) either a cheque or postal order in respect of the court fee, crossed and made payable to "Scottish Court Service or a completed fee exemption form, and

   (iii) the interim gender recognition certificate or a copy sealed with the seal of the Gender Recognition Panels and certified to be a true copy by an officer authorised by the President of Gender Recognition Panels.

4. Receipt of your application will be promptly acknowledged. Should you wish to withdraw the application for any reason, please contact the sheriff clerk immediately.

PART 1

WRITE IN INK, USING BLOCK CAPITALS

1. NAME AND ADDRESS OF APPLICANT

Surname ....

Other name(s) in full ....

....

Present address ....

....

Daytime telephone number (if any) ....

2. NAME OF SPOUSE

Surname ....

Other name(s) in full ....

3. ADDRESS OF SPOUSE (if the address of your spouse is not known, please enter "not known" in this paragraph and proceed to paragraph 4)

Present address ....

....

Daytime telephone (if any) ....

4. Only complete this paragraph if you do not know the present address of your spouse

NEXT-OF-KIN

Name ....

Address ....

....

....

Relationship to your spouse ....

CHILDREN OF THE MARRIAGE

Names and dates of birth	Addresses
....	....
	....
....	....
	....
....	....
	....

If insufficient space is available to list all the children of the marriage, please continue on a separate sheet and attach to this form.

5. JURISDICTION

Please indicate with a tick (✔) in the appropriate box or boxes which of the following apply:

PART A

(i) My spouse and I are habitually resident in Scotland

(ii) My spouse and I were last habitually resident in Scotland, and one of us still resides there

(iii) My spouse is habitually resident in Scotland

(iv) I am habitually resident in Scotland having resided there for at least a year immediately before this application was made

(v) I am habitually resident in Scotland having resided there for at least six months immediately before this application was made and am domiciled in Scotland

(vi) My spouse and I are domiciled in Scotland

If you have ticked one or more of the boxes in Part A, you should go direct to Part C. You should only complete Part B if you have not ticked any boxes in Part A

PART B

(i) I am domiciled in Scotland

(ii) My spouse is domiciled in Scotland

AND

(iii) No court of a Contracting State has jurisdiction under Council Regulation (E.C.) No. 2201/2003 of 27th November 2003 concerning jurisdiction and the recognition and enforcement of judgments in matrimonial matters and matters of parental responsibility (O.J. No. L. 338, 23.12.2003, p.1.)

PART C

(i) I have lived at the address shown above for at least 40 days immediately before the date I signed this application

(ii) My spouse has lived at the address shown above for at least 40 days immediately before the date I signed this application

(iii) I lived at the address shown above for a period of at least 40 days ending not more than 40 days before the date I signed this application and have no known residence in Scotland at that date

(iv) My spouse lived at the address shown above for a period of at least 40 days ending not more than 40 days before the date I signed this application and has no known residence in Scotland at that date

6. DETAILS OF PRESENT MARRIAGE

Place of Marriage .... (Registration District)

Date of Marriage: Day .... month .... year ....

7. DETAILS OF ISSUE OF INTERIM GENDER RECOGNITION CERTIFICATE

(i) Please state whether the interim gender recognition certificate has been issued to you or your spouse

(ii) Please state the date the interim gender recognition certificate was issued

Day .... Month .... Year ....

8. MENTAL DISORDER

Does your spouse have any mental disorder (whether mental illness, personality disorder or learning disability)?　　(If yes, give details)　　*[YES/NO]

9. CHILDREN

Are there any children of the marriage under the age of 16?　　*[YES/NO]

10. OTHER COURT ACTIONS

Are you aware of any court actions currently proceeding in any country (including Scotland) which may affect your marriage?　　(If yes, give details)　　*[YES/NO]

* Delete as appropriate

11. DECLARATION AND REQUEST FOR DIVORCE

I confirm that the facts stated in paragraphs 1-10 above apply to my marriage.

I do NOT ask the sheriff to make any financial provision in connection with this application.

I do NOT ask the court to postpone the grant of decree under section 3A of the Divorce (Scotland) Act 1976.

I request the sheriff to grant decree of divorce from my husband or wife.

Date　　　　　Signature of Applicant ....

PART 2

APPLICANT'S AFFIDAVIT

To be completed by the Applicant only after Part 1 has been signed and dated.

I, (*Insert Applicant's full name*) ....

residing at (*insert Applicant's present home address*) ....

....

....

SWEAR that to the best of my knowledge and belief the facts stated in Part 1 of this Application are true.

Signature of Applicant ....

SWORN at (*insert place*) ....

To be completed by Justice of the Peace, Notary Public or Commissioner for Oaths	this .... day of .... 20.................
	before me (*insert full name*) ....
	of (*insert full address*) ....
	....
	....
	Signature ....

*Justice of the Peace/Notary Public/Commissioner for Oaths

*Delete as appropriate

NOTES

[1] Inserted by Act of Sederunt (Ordinary Cause Rules) Amendment (Family Law (Scotland) Act 2006 etc.) 2006, para.2 (SSI 2006/207) (effective May 4, 2006).

[2] As amended by the Act of Sederunt (Ordinary Cause, Summary Application, Summary Cause and Small Claim Rules) Amendment (Miscellaneous) 2007 (SSI 2007/6), para.2(16)(h) (effective February 26, 2007).

Rule 33.76(3)(a)   [1,2] FORM F34

Form of citation in application relying on the facts in section 1(2)(d) of the Divorce (Scotland) Act 1976

(*Insert name and address of non-applicant spouse*)

APPLICATION FOR DIVORCE (HUSBAND AND WIFE HAVING LIVED APART FOR AT LEAST ONE YEAR WITH CONSENT OF OTHER PARTY)

Your spouse has applied to the sheriff for divorce on the ground that the marriage has broken down irretrievably because you and he or she have lived apart for a period of at least one year and you consent to divorce being granted.

A copy of the application is hereby served upon you.

1. Please note:
    (a) that the sheriff may not make financial provision under this procedure and that your spouse is making no claim for—
        (i) the payment by you of a periodical allowance (i.e. a regular payment of money weekly or monthly, etc. for maintenance);
        (ii) the payment by you of a capital sum (i.e. a lump sum payment);
    (b) that no application may be made under this procedure for postponement of decree under section 3A of the Divorce (Scotland) Act 1976 (postponement of decree where impediment to religious marriage exists).

2. Divorce may result in the loss to you of property rights (e.g. the right to succeed to the Applicant's estate on his or her death) or the right, where appropriate, to a widow's pension.

3. If you wish to oppose the granting of a divorce, you should put your reasons in writing and send your letter to the address shown below. Your letter must reach the sheriff clerk before (*insert date*).

4. In the event of the divorce being granted, you will be sent a copy of the extract decree. Should you change your address before receiving the copy extract decree, please notify the sheriff clerk immediately.

> Signed
> Sheriff clerk (depute)
> (*insert address and telephone number of the sheriff clerk*)
> *or* Sheriff officer

NOTE: If you wish to exercise your right to make a claim for financial provision, or if you wish to apply for postponement of decree under section 3A of the Divorce (Scotland) Act 1976 (postponement of decree where impediment to religious marriage exists), you should immediately advise the sheriff clerk that you oppose the application for that reason, and thereafter consult a solicitor.

NOTES

[1] As amended by Act of Sederunt (Ordinary Cause Rules) Amendment (Family Law (Scotland) Act 2006 etc.) 2006, para.2 (SSI 2006/207) (effective May 4, 2006).

[2] As amended by the Act of Sederunt (Ordinary Cause, Summary Application, Summary Cause and Small Claim Rules) Amendment (Miscellaneous) 2007 (SSI 2007/6), para.2(16)(i) (effective February 26, 2007).

Rule 33.76(3)(b) [1,2] **FORM F35**

Form of citation in application relying on the facts in section 1(2)(e) of the Divorce (Scotland) Act 1976

(Insert name and address of non-applicant spouse)

APPLICATION FOR DIVORCE (HUSBAND AND WIFE HAVING LIVED APART FOR AT LEAST TWO YEARS)

Your spouse has applied to the sheriff for divorce on the ground that the marriage has broken down irretrievably because you and he or she have lived apart for a period of at least two years.

A copy of the application is hereby served upon you.

1. Please note:
    (a) that the sheriff may not make financial provision under this procedure and that your spouse is making no claim for—
        (i) the payment by you of a periodical allowance (i.e. a regular payment of money weekly or monthly, etc., for maintenance);
        (ii) the payment by you of a capital sum (i.e. a lump sum payment);
    (b) that no application may be made under this procedure for postponement of decree under section 3A of the Divorce (Scotland) Act 1976 (postponement of decree where impediment to religious marriage exists).
2. Divorce may result in the loss to you of property rights (e.g. the right to succeed to the Applicant's estate on his or her death) or the right, where appropriate, to a widow's pension.

3. If you wish to oppose the granting of a divorce, you should put your reasons in writing and send your letter to the address shown below. Your letter must reach the sheriff clerk before *(insert date)*.

4. In the event of the divorce being granted, you will be sent a copy of the extract decree. Should you change your address before receiving the copy extract decree, please notify the sheriff clerk immediately.

> Signed
> Sheriff clerk (depute)
> *(insert the address and telephone*
> number of the sheriff court)
> *or* Sheriff officer

NOTE: If you wish to exercise your right to make a claim for financial provision, or if you wish to apply for postponement of decree under section 3A of the Divorce (Scotland) Act 1976 (postponement of decree where impediment to religious marriage exists), you should immediately advise the sheriff clerk that you oppose the application for that reason, and thereafter consult a solicitor.

NOTES

[1] As amended by Act of Sederunt (Ordinary Cause Rules) Amendment (Family Law (Scotland) Act 2006 etc.) 2006, para.2 (SSI 2006/207) (effective May 4, 2006).

[2] As amended by the Act of Sederunt (Ordinary Cause, Summary Application, Summary Cause and Small Claim Rules) Amendment (Miscellaneous) 2007 (SSI 2007/6), para.2(16)(j) (effective February 26, 2007).

Rule 33.76(3)(c)   [1,2] FORM 35A

Form of citation in application on grounds under section 1(1)(b) of the Divorce (Scotland)
Act 1976

(*Insert name and address of non-applicant spouse*)

APPLICATION FOR DIVORCE (INTERIM GENDER RECOGNITION CERTIFICATE
ISSUED TO ONE OF THE PARTIES AFTER THE MARRIAGE)

> Your spouse has applied to the sheriff for divorce on the ground that an interim gender
> recognition certificate has been issued to you or your spouse after your marriage.

A copy of the application is hereby served upon you.

1. Please note that the sheriff may not make financial provision under this procedure and that
your spouse is making no claim for—
> (a) the payment by you of a periodical allowance (i.e. a regular payment of money weekly
>   or monthly, etc. for maintenance);
> (b) the payment by you of a capital sum (i.e. a lump sum payment).

2. Divorce may result in the loss to you of property rights (e.g. the right to succeed to the
Applicant's estate on his or her death) or the right, where appropriate, to a pension.

2A. Please note that no application may be made under this procedure for postponement of
decree under section 3A of the Divorce (Scotland) Act 1976 (postponement of decree where
impediment to religious marriage exists).

3. If you wish to oppose the granting of a decree of divorce, you should put your reasons in
writing and send your letter to the address shown below. Your letter must reach the sheriff clerk
before (*insert date*).

4. In the event of the decree of divorce being granted, you will be sent a copy of the extract
decree. Should you change your address before receiving the copy extract decree, please notify
the sheriff clerk immediately.

> (*Signed*)
> Sheriff clerk (depute)
> (*insert address and telephone number of
> the sheriff clerk*)
> [*or* Sheriff officer]

NOTE: If you wish to exercise your right to make a claim for financial provision, or if you wish
to apply for postponement of decree under section 3A of the Divorce (Scotland) Act 1976
(postponement of decree where impediment to religious marriage exists), you should
immediately advise the sheriff clerk that you oppose the application for that reason, and
thereafter consult a solicitor.

NOTES
[1] Inserted by Act of Sederunt (Ordinary Cause Rules) Amendment (Family Law (Scotland)
Act 2006 etc.) 2006, para.2 (SSI 2006/207) (effective May 4, 2006).
[2] As amended by the Act of Sederunt (Ordinary Cause, Summary Application, Summary
Cause and Small Claim Rules) Amendment (Miscellaneous) 2007 (SSI 2007/6), para.2(16)(k)
(effective February 26, 2007).

Rule 33.77(1)(a)   FORM F36

Form of intimation of simplified divorce application for display on the walls of court

                                        Court ref. no.

An application for divorce has been made in this sheriff court by [A.B.], (*insert designation and
address*), Applicant, naming [C.D.], (*insert designation and address*) as Respondent.

If [C.D.] wishes to oppose the granting of decree of divorce he [*or* she] should immediately
contact the sheriff clerk from whom he [*or* she] may obtain a copy of the application.

Date (*insert date*)

> Signed
> Sheriff clerk (depute)

Rule 33.77(2) FORM F37

Form of intimation to children and next-of-kin in simplified divorce application

To (*insert name and address*) Court ref. no.

You are hereby given NOTICE that an application for divorce has been made against (*insert name of respondent*) your (*insert relationship e.g. father, mother, brother or other relative as the case may be*). A copy of this application is attached.

If you know of his or her present address, you are requested to inform the sheriff clerk (*insert address of sheriff clerk*) in writing immediately. You may also, if you wish, oppose the granting of decree of divorce by sending a letter to the court giving your reasons for your opposition to the application. Your letter must be sent to the sheriff clerk within 21 days of (*insert date on which intimation was given. N.B. Rule 5.3(2) relating to postal service or intimation*).

Date (*insert date*)

Signed
Sheriff clerk (depute)

NOTE
IF YOU ARE UNCERTAIN WHAT ACTION TO TAKE you should consult a solicitor. You may be entitled to legal aid depending on your financial circumstances, and you can get information about legal aid from a solicitor. You may also obtain advice from any Citizens Advice Bureau or other advice agency.

Rule 33.80(2) FORM F38

Form of extract decree of divorce in simplified divorce application

At (*insert place and date*)
in an action in the Sheriff Court of the Sheriffdom of (*insert name of sheriffdom*) at (*insert place of sheriff court*)

at the instance of [A.B.], (*insert full name of applicant*), Applicant,

against (*insert full name of respondent*), Respondent,

who were married at (*insert place*) on (*insert date*),

the sheriff pronounced decree divorcing the Respondent from the Applicant.

Extracted at (*insert place and date*)

by me, sheriff clerk of the Sheriffdom of (*insert name of sheriffdom*).

Signed
Sheriff clerk (depute)

Rule 33.90 FORM F39

Form of certificate relating to the making of a maintenance assessment under the Child Support Act 1991

Sheriff Court (*insert address*)
Date (*insert date*)

I certify that notification has been received from the Secretary of State under section 10 of the Child Support Act 1991 of the making of a maintenance assessment under that Act which supersedes the decree or order granted on (*insert date*) in relation to aliment for (*insert the name(s) of child(ren)*) with effect from (*insert date*).

Signed
Sheriff clerk (depute)

Rule 33.90   FORM F40

Form of certificate relating to the cancellation or ceasing to have effect of a maintenance
assessment under the Child Support Act 1991

Sheriff Court (*insert address*)
Date (*insert date*)

I certify that notification has been received from the Secretary of State under section 10 of the
Child Support Act 1991 that the maintenance assessment made on (*insert date*) has been
cancelled [*or* ceased to have effect] on (*insert date*).

                                        Signed
                                        Sheriff clerk (depute)

Rule 33.22A(2)   [1] FORM F41

Form of intimation to parties of a Child Welfare Hearing

Sheriff Court (*insert address and telephone number*)   Court Ref No:

In the action [A.B.], (*design*), Pursuer against [C.D.], (*design*), Defender

YOU ARE GIVEN NOTICE that a Child Welfare Hearing has been fixed for (*insert time*) on
(*insert date*) at (*insert place*).

Date (*insert date*)   Signed
                                        Sheriff Clerk (Depute)

NOTE
Please note that in terms of Rule 33.22A(5) parties to the action must attend personally

---
*IF YOU ARE UNCERTAIN WHAT ACTION TO TAKE you should consult a solicitor.
You may be eligible for legal aid depending on your financial circumstances, and you can get
information about legal aid from a solicitor. You may also obtain information from any
Citizens' Advice Bureau or other advice agency.
---

*This section to be deleted where service is to be made on a solicitor.

NOTE
[1] Substituted by SSI 2000/239 (effective October 2, 2000).

Rule 33.27A(1)   [1] FORM F42

Form of Certificate under Article 32 of Council Regulation (EC) No. 1347/2000 of 29th May
2000 on jurisdiction and the recognition and enforcement of judgments in matrimonial matters
and in matters of parental responsibility for children of both spouses

Matrimonial matters

Sheriffdom of *(insert name of sheriffdom)*

at *(insert place of Sheriff Court)*

I hereby certify, pursuant to Article 32 of Council Regulation (EC) No. 1347/2000 of 29th May
2000 on jurisdiction and the recognition and enforcement of judgments in matrimonial matters
and in matters of parental responsibility for children of both spouses, concerning judgments in
matrimonial matters, the following:

1. Member State of origin: *(insert country)*

2. Court or authority issuing the certificate:

2.1 Name: Sheriff Court of *(insert name)*

2.2 Address: *(insert address of sheriff court)*

2.3 Tel/Fax/E-mail: *(insert Tel/Fax/E-mail)*

3. Marriage:

3.1 Wife:

    3.1.1 Full Name: *(insert name)*

    3.1.2 Country and place of birth: *(insert country and place)*

    3.1.3 Date of birth: *(insert date)*

3.2 Husband:

    3.2.1 Full Name: *(insert name)*

    3.2.2 Country and place of birth: *(insert country and place)*

    3.2.3 Date of birth: *(insert date)*

3.3 Country, place (where available) and date of marriage

    3.3.1 Country of marriage : *(insert country)*

    3.3.2 Place of marriage (where available): *(insert place)*

    3.3.3 Date of marriage: *(insert date)*

4. Court which delivered the judgment:

4.1 Name of Court: *(insert name)*

4.2 Place of Court: *(insert place)*

5. Judgment:

5.1 Date: *(insert date)*

5.2 Case reference number: *(insert reference number)*

5.3 Type of judgment:

5.3.1	Divorce	☐
5.3.3	Legal separation	☐

5.4 Was the Judgment given in default of appearance ?

5.4.1	No	☐
5.4.2	Yes	☐

6. Name of parties to whom legal aid has been granted: *(insert names)*

7. Is the judgment subject to further appeal under the law of the Member State of origin?

7.1	No	☐
7.2	Yes	☐

8. Date of legal effect in the Member State where the judgment was given:

8.1 of divorce: *(insert date)*

8.2 of separation: *(insert date)*

(Signed)

Sheriff Clerk

(Place and date)

NOTE

[1] Inserted by Act of Sederunt (Ordinary Cause Rules) Amendment (European Matrimonial and Parental Responsibility Jurisdiction and Judgments) 2001 (SSI 2001/144), para.4 (effective April 2, 2001).

Rule 33.27A(1) ¹ FORM F43

Form of Certificate under Article 32 of Council Regulation (EC) No. 1347/2000 of 29th May 2000 on jurisdiction and the recognition and enforcement of judgments in matrimonial matters and in matters of parental responsibility for children of both spouses

Parental Responsibility

Sheriffdom of *(insert name of sheriffdom)*

at *(insert place of Sheriff Court)*

I hereby certify, pursuant to Article 32 of Council Regulation (EC) No. 1347/2000 of 29th May 2000 on jurisdiction and the recognition and enforcement of judgments in Matrimonial matters and in matters of parental responsibility for children of both spouses, concerning judgments in matters of parental responsibility, the following:

1. Member State of origin: *(insert country)*

2. Court or authority issuing the certificate:

2.1 Name: Sheriff Court of *(insert name)*

2.2 Address: *(insert address of sheriff court)*

2.3 Tel/Fax/E-mail: *(insert tel/fax/e-mail)*

3. Parents:

3.1 Mother:

    3.1.1 Full Name: *(insert name)*

    3.1.2 Date and place of birth: *(insert date and place)*

3.2 Father:

    3.2.1 Full Name: *(insert name)*

    3.2.2 Date and place of birth: *(insert date and place)*

4. Court which delivered Judgment:

4.1 Name of Court: *(insert name)*

4.2 Place of Court; *(insert place)*

5. Judgment:

5.1 Date: *(insert date)*

5.2 Case Reference number: *(insert reference number)*

5.3 Was the Judgment given in default of appearance?

| 5.3.1 | No | ☐ |
| 5.3.2 | Yes | ☐ |

6. Children who are covered by the judgment:

6.1 Full Name and date of birth: *(insert name and date of birth)*

6.2 Full Name and date of birth: *(insert name and date of birth)*

6.3 Full Name and date of birth: *(insert name and date of birth)*

6.4 Full Name and date of birth: *(insert name and date of birth)*

7. Names of parties to whom legal aid has been granted: *(insert names)*

8. Attestation of enforceability and service

8.1 Is the judgment enforceable according to the law of the Member State of origin?

8.1.1	No	☐
8.1.2	Yes	☐

8.2 Has the judgment been served on the party against whom enforcement is sought?

8.2.1	Yes	☐

8.2.1.1 Full name of party: *(insert name)*

8.2.1.2 Date of service: *(insert date)*

8.2.2	No	☐

(Place and date)   (*Signed*)
                                                          Sheriff Clerk

NOTE
[1] Inserted by Act of Sederunt (Ordinary Cause Rules) Amendment (European Matrimonial and Parental Responsibility Jurisdiction and Judgments) 2001 (SSI 2001/144), para.4 (effective April 2, 2001).

Rule 33A.7(1)(a)   [1] FORM CP1

Form of intimation to children and next-of-kin in an action of dissolution of civil partnership or separation of civil partners where defender's address is not known

Court ref. no.

To *(insert name and address as in warrant)*

You are given NOTICE that an action of dissolution of a civil partnership [*or* separation of civil partners] has been raised against *(insert name)* your *(insert relationship, e.g. father, mother, brother or other relative as the case may be)*. If you know of his [*or* her] present address, you are requested to inform the sheriff clerk *(insert address of sheriff clerk)* in writing immediately. If you wish to appear as a party you must lodge a minute with the sheriff clerk for leave to do so. Your minute must be lodged within 21 days of *(insert date on which intimation was given. N.B. Rule 5.3(2) relating to postal service or intimation)*.

Date *(insert date)*

                                        (*Signed*)

                                        Solicitor for the pursuer

                                        (*insert designation and business address*)

NOTE
If you decide to lodge a minute it may be in your best interests to consult a solicitor. The minute should be lodged with the sheriff clerk together with the appropriate fee of (*insert amount*) and a copy of this intimation.

IF YOU ARE UNCERTAIN WHAT ACTION TO TAKE you should consult a solicitor. You may be entitled to legal aid depending on your financial circumstances, and you can get information about legal aid from a solicitor. You may also obtain advice from any Citizens Advice Bureau or other advice agency.

NOTE
[1] Inserted by Act of Sederunt (Ordinary Cause Rules) Amendment (Civil Partnership Act 2004) 2005 (SSI 2005/638), para.3 (effective December 8, 2005).

Rule 33A.7(1)(b)   [1] FORM CP2

Form of intimation to children, next-of-kin, guardian and attorney in action of dissolution of civil partnership or separation of civil partners where defender suffers from a mental disorder

Court ref. no.

To (*insert name and address as in warrant*)

You are given NOTICE that an action of dissolution of a civil partnership [*or* separation of civil partners] has been raised against (*insert name*) your (*insert relationship, e.g. father, mother, brother or other relative, ward or granter of a power of attorney as the case may be*). A copy of the initial writ is enclosed. If you wish to appear as a party, you must lodge a minute with the sheriff clerk (*insert address of sheriff clerk*), for leave to do so. Your minute must be lodged within 21 days of (*insert date on which intimation was given. N.B. Rule 5.3(2) relating to postal service or intimation*).

Date (*insert date*)

(*Signed*)

Solicitor for the pursuer

(*insert designation and business address*)

> **NOTE**
> If you decide to lodge a minute it may be in your best interests to consult a solicitor. The minute should be lodged with the sheriff clerk together with the appropriate fee of (*insert amount*) and a copy of this intimation.

> **IF YOU ARE UNCERTAIN WHAT ACTION TO TAKE** you should consult a solicitor. You may be entitled to legal aid depending on your financial circumstances, and you can get information about legal aid from a solicitor. You may also obtain advice from any Citizens Advice Bureau or other advice agency.

NOTE
   [1] Inserted by Act of Sederunt (Ordinary Cause Rules) Amendment (Civil Partnership Act 2004) 2005 (SSI 2005/638), para.3 (effective December 8, 2005).

Rule 33A.7(1)(c)(i) and (ii)   [1] FORM CP3

Form of intimation to a local authority or third party who may be liable to maintain a child in a civil partnership action

Court ref. no.

To (*insert name and address as in warrant*)

YOU ARE GIVEN NOTICE that in this action, the court may make an order under section 11 of the Children (Scotland) Act 1995 in respect of (*insert name and address*), a child in your care [*or liable to be maintained by you*]. A copy of the initial writ is attached. If you wish to appear as a party, you must lodge a minute with the sheriff clerk (*insert address of sheriff clerk*), for leave to do so. Your minute must be lodged within 21 days of (*insert date on which intimation was given. N.B. Rule 5.3(2) relating to postal service or intimation*).

Date (*insert date*)

(*Signed*)

Solicitor for the pursuer

(*insert designation and business address*)

> **NOTE**
> If you decide to lodge a minute it may be in your best interests to consult a solicitor. The minute should be lodged with the sheriff clerk together with the appropriate fee of (*insert amount*) and a copy of this intimation.

> **IF YOU ARE UNCERTAIN WHAT ACTION TO TAKE** you should consult a solicitor. You may be entitled to legal aid depending on your financial circumstances, and you can get information about legal aid from a solicitor. You may also obtain advice from any Citizens

NOTE
[1] Inserted by Act of Sederunt (Ordinary Cause Rules) Amendment (Civil Partnership Act 2004) 2005 (SSI 2005/638), para.3 (effective December 8, 2005).

Rule 33A.7(1)(c)(iii) [1] FORM CP4

Form of intimation to person who in fact exercises care or control of a child in a civil partnership action

Court ref. no.

To (*insert name and address as in warrant*)

YOU ARE GIVEN NOTICE that in this action, the court may make an order under section 11 of the Children (Scotland) Act 1995 in respect of (*insert name and address*), a child at present in your care or control. A copy of the initial writ is attached. If you wish to appear as a party, you must lodge a minute with the sheriff clerk (*insert address of sheriff clerk*), for leave to do so. Your minute must be lodged within 21 days of (*insert date on which intimation was given. N.B. Rule 5.3(2) relating to postal service or intimation*).

Date (*insert date*)

(*Signed*)

Solicitor for the pursuer

(*insert designation and business address*)

NOTE
If you decide to lodge a minute it may be in your best interests to consult a solicitor. The minute should be lodged with the sheriff clerk together with the appropriate fee of (*insert amount*) and a copy of this intimation.

IF YOU ARE UNCERTAIN WHAT ACTION TO TAKE you should consult a solicitor. You may be entitled to legal aid depending on your financial circumstances, and you can get information about legal aid from a solicitor. You may also obtain advice from any Citizens Advice Bureau or other advice agency.

NOTE
[1] Inserted by Act of Sederunt (Ordinary Cause Rules) Amendment (Civil Partnership Act 2004) 2005 (SSI 2005/638), para.3 (effective December 8, 2005).

Rule 33A.7(1)(d) [1] FORM CP5

Form of notice to parent or guardian in a civil partnership action which includes a crave for a section 11 order in respect of a child

Court ref. no.

1. YOU ARE GIVEN NOTICE that in this action, the pursuer is applying for an order under section 11 of the Children (Scotland) Act 1995 in respect of the child (*insert name of child*). A copy of the initial writ is served on you and is attached to this notice.

2. If you wish to oppose this action, or oppose the granting of any order applied for by the pursuer in respect of the child, you must lodge a notice of intention to defend (Form CP16). See Form CP16 attached for further details.

Date (*insert date*)

(*Signed*)

Pursuer

[*or* Solicitor for the pursuer]

(*insert designation and business address*)

NOTE: IF YOU ARE UNCERTAIN WHAT ACTION TO TAKE you should consult a solicitor. You may be entitled to legal aid depending on your financial circumstances, and you can get information about legal aid from a solicitor. You may also obtain advice from any Citizens Advice Bureau or other advice agency.

NOTE

[1] Inserted by Act of Sederunt (Ordinary Cause Rules) Amendment (Civil Partnership Act 2004) 2005 (SSI 2005/638), para.3 (effective December 8, 2005).

Rule 33A.7(1)(e), 33A.7(4)   [1] FORM CP6
and 33A.12(2) and (3)

Form of notice to local authority requesting a report in respect of a child in a civil partnership action

Court ref. no.

To (*insert name and address*)

1. YOU ARE GIVEN NOTICE that in an action in the Sheriff Court at (*insert address*) the pursuer has applied for a residence order in respect of the child (*insert name of child*). A copy of the initial writ is enclosed.

2. You are required to submit to the court a report on all the circumstances of the child and on the proposed arrangements for the care and upbringing of the child.

Date (*insert date*)

(*Signed*)

Solicitor for the pursuer

(*insert designation and business address*)

NOTE

[1] Inserted by Act of Sederunt (Ordinary Cause Rules) Amendment (Civil Partnership Act 2004) 2005 (SSI 2005/638), para.3 (effective December 8, 2005).

Rule 33A.7(1)(f), 33A.15(2)   [1] FORM CP7
and 33A.19(1)(a)

Form of intimation in a civil partnership action which includes a crave for a section 11 order

Court ref. no.

PART A

This part must be completed by the Pursuer's solicitor in language a child is capable of understanding.

To (1)

The Sheriff (the person who has to decide about your future) has been asked by (2)   to decide:–

(a) (3) and (4)

(b) (5)

(c) (6)

If you want to tell the Sheriff what you think about the things your (2)   has asked the Sheriff to decide about your future you should complete Part B of this form and send it to the Sheriff Clerk at (7) by (8)   . An envelope which does not need a postage stamp is enclosed for you to use to return the form.

IF YOU DO NOT UNDERSTAND THIS FORM OR IF YOU WANT HELP TO COMPLETE IT you may get help from a SOLICITOR or contact the SCOTTISH CHILD LAW CENTRE on the FREE ADVICE TELEPHONE LINE ON 0800 328 8970.

If you return the form it will be given to the Sheriff. The Sheriff may wish to speak with you and ask you to come and see him or her.

NOTES FOR COMPLETION

(1) Insert name and address of child	(2) Insert relationship to the child of party making the application to court.
(3) Insert appropriate wording for residence	(4) Insert address
(5) Insert appropriate wording for contact order sought.	(6) Insert appropriate wording for any other order sought.
(7) Insert address of sheriff clerk.	(8) Insert the date occurring 21 days after the date on which intimation is given. N.B. Rule 5.3(2) relating to intimation and service.
(9) Insert court reference number.	(10) Insert name and address of parties to the action.

PART B

IF YOU WISH THE SHERIFF TO KNOW YOUR VIEWS ABOUT YOUR FUTURE YOU SHOULD COMPLETE THIS PART OF THE FORM

To the Sheriff Clerk, (7)

Court Ref. No. (9)

(10)...

QUESTION (1): DO YOU WISH THE SHERIFF TO KNOW WHAT YOUR VIEWS ARE ABOUT YOUR FUTURE?

(PLEASE TICK BOX)

Yes	
No	

If you have ticked YES please also answer Question (2) *or* (3)

QUESTION (2): WOULD YOU LIKE A FRIEND, RELATIVE OR OTHER PERSON TO TELL THE SHERIFF YOUR VIEWS ABOUT YOUR FUTURE?

(PLEASE TICK BOX)

Yes	
No	

If you have ticked YES please write the name and address of the person you wish to tell the Sheriff your views in Box (A) below. You should also tell that person what your views are about your future.

BOX A:	(NAME)		
	(ADDRESS)		
	....		
	Is this person:	A friend? ☐	A relative? ☐
		A teacher? ☐	Other? ☐

OR

QUESTION (3): WOULD YOU LIKE TO WRITE TO THE SHERIFF AND TELL HIM WHAT YOUR VIEWS ARE ABOUT YOUR FUTURE?

(PLEASE TICK BOX)

Yes	
No	

If you decide that you wish to write to the Sheriff you can write what your views are about your future in Box (B) below or on a separate piece of paper. If you decide to write your views on a separate piece of paper you should send it along with this form to the Sheriff Clerk in the envelope provided.

BOX B: WHAT I HAVE TO SAY ABOUT MY FUTURE:–

NAME: ....

ADDRESS: ....

DATE: ....

NOTE
[1] Inserted by Act of Sederunt (Ordinary Cause Rules) Amendment (Civil Partnership Act 2004) 2005 (SSI 2005/638), para.3 (effective December 8, 2005).

Rule 33A.7(1)(g)   [1]FORM CP8

Form of intimation to creditor in application for order for the transfer of property under section 8 of the Family Law (Scotland) Act 1985 in a civil partnership action

Court ref. no.

To (*insert name and address as in warrant*)

You are given NOTICE that in this action, an order is sought for the transfer of property (*specify the order*), over which you hold a security. A copy of the initial writ is attached. If you wish to appear as a party, you must lodge a minute with the sheriff clerk (*insert address of sheriff clerk*), for leave to do so. Your minute must be lodged within 21 days of (*insert date on which intimation was given. N.B. Rule 5.3(2) relating to postal service or intimation*).

Date (*insert date*)

(*Signed*)

Solicitor for the pursuer

(*insert designation and business address*)

> **NOTE**
> If you decide to lodge a minute it may be in your best interests to consult a solicitor. The minute should be lodged with the sheriff clerk together with the appropriate fee of (*insert amount*) and a copy of this intimation.

> **IF YOU ARE UNCERTAIN WHAT ACTION TO TAKE** you should consult a solicitor. You may be entitled to legal aid depending on your financial circumstances, and you can get information about legal aid from a solicitor. You may also obtain advice from any Citizens Advice Bureau or other advice agency.

NOTE
[1] Inserted by Act of Sederunt (Ordinary Cause Rules) Amendment (Civil Partnership Act 2004) 2005 (SSI 2005/638), para.3 (effective December 8, 2005).

Rule 33A.7(1)(h) [1] FORM CP9

Form of intimation in a civil partnership action where the pursuer makes an application for an order under section 18 of the Family Law (Scotland) Act 1985

Court ref. no.

To (*insert name and address as in warrant*)

You are given NOTICE that in this action, the pursuer craves the court to make an order under section 18 of the Family Law (Scotland) Act 1985. A copy of the initial writ is attached. If you wish to appear as a party, you must lodge a minute with the sheriff clerk (*insert address of sheriff clerk*), for leave to do so. Your minute must be lodged within 21 days of (*insert date on which intimation was given. N.B. Rule 5.3(2) relating to postal service or intimation*).

Date (*insert date*)

(*Signed*)

Solicitor for the pursuer

(*insert designation and business address*)

> **NOTE**
> If you decide to lodge a minute it may be in your best interests to consult a solicitor. The minute should be lodged with the sheriff clerk together with the appropriate fee of (*insert amount*) and a copy of this intimation.

> **IF YOU ARE UNCERTAIN WHAT ACTION TO TAKE** you should consult a solicitor. You may be entitled to legal aid depending on your financial circumstances, and you can get information about legal aid from a solicitor. You may also obtain advice from any Citizens Advice Bureau or other advice agency.

NOTE
[1] Inserted by Act of Sederunt (Ordinary Cause Rules) Amendment (Civil Partnership Act 2004) 2005 (SSI 2005/638), para.3 (effective December 8, 2005).

Rule 33A.7(1)(i) [1] FORM CP10

Form of intimation in an action where an application is made under Chapter 3 of Part 3 of the Civil Partnership Act 2004

Court ref. no

To (*insert name and address as in warrant*)

You are given NOTICE that in this action the pursuer craves the court to make an order under Section (*insert the section under which the order(s) is sought*) of Chapter 3 of Part 3 of the Civil Partnership Act 2004. A copy of the initial writ is attached. If you wish to appear as a party, you must lodge a minute with the sheriff clerk (*insert address of sheriff clerk*), for leave to do so. Your minute must be lodged within 21 days of (*insert date on which intimation was given. N.B. Rule 5.3(2) relating to postal service or intimation*).

Date (*insert date*)

(*Signed*)

Solicitor for the pursuer

(*insert designation and business address*)

NOTE

If you decide to lodge a minute it may be in your best interests to consult a solicitor. The minute should be lodged with the sheriff clerk together with the appropriate fee of (*insert amount*) and a copy of this intimation.

IF YOU ARE UNCERTAIN WHAT ACTION TO TAKE you should consult a solicitor. You may be entitled to legal aid depending on your financial circumstances, and you can get information about legal aid from a solicitor. You may also obtain advice from any Citizens Advice Bureau or other advice agency.

NOTE

[1] Inserted by Act of Sederunt (Ordinary Cause Rules) Amendment (Civil Partnership Act 2004) 2005 (SSI 2005/638), para.3 (effective December 8, 2005).

Rule 33A.7(1)(j) [1] FORM CP11

Form of intimation to person responsible for pension arrangement in relation to an order for payment in respect of pension lump sum under section 12A of the Family Law (Scotland) Act 1985 in a civil partnership action

Court ref. no.

To (*insert name and address as in warrant*)

Rule 33A.7(1)(j)You are given NOTICE that in this action, the pursuer has applied for an order under section 8 of the Family Law (Scotland) Act 1985 for a capital sum in circumstances where the family property includes rights in a pension arrangement under which a lump sum is payable. The relevant pension arrangement is (*give brief details, including number, if known*). If you wish to appear as a party, you must lodge a minute with the sheriff clerk (*insert address of sheriff clerk*), for leave to do so. Your minute must be lodged within 21 days of (*insert date on which intimation was given. N.B. Rule 5.3(2) relating to postal service or intimation*).

Date (*insert date*)

(*Signed*)

Solicitor for the pursuer

(*insert designation and business address*)

NOTE

If you decide to lodge a minute it may be in your best interests to consult a solicitor. The minute should be lodged with the sheriff clerk together with the appropriate fee of (*insert amount*) and a copy of this intimation.

IF YOU ARE UNCERTAIN WHAT ACTION TO TAKE you should consult a solicitor. You may be entitled to legal aid depending on your financial circumstances, and you can get information about legal aid from a solicitor. You may also obtain advice from any Citizens Advice Bureau or other advice agency.

NOTE

[1] Inserted by Act of Sederunt (Ordinary Cause Rules) Amendment (Civil Partnership Act 2004) 2005 (SSI 2005/638), para.3 (effective December 8, 2005).

Rule 33A.7(1)(k) [1] FORM CP12

Form of intimation to person responsible for pension arrangement in relation to pension sharing order under section 8(1)(baa) of the Family Law (Scotland) Act 1985 in a civil partnership action

Court ref. no.

To (*insert name and address as in warrant*)

You are given NOTICE that in this action, the pursuer has applied under section 8 of the Family Law (Scotland) Act 1985 for a pension sharing order in circumstances where the family property includes rights in a pension arrangement. The relevant pension arrangement is (*give brief details, including number, if known*). If you wish to appear as a party, you must lodge a minute with the sheriff clerk (*insert address of sheriff clerk*), for leave to do so. Your minute must be lodged within 21 days of (*insert date on which intimation was given. N.B. Rule 5.3(2) relating to postal service or intimation*).

Date (*insert date*)

(*Signed*)

Solicitor for the pursuer

(*insert designation and business address*)

> **NOTE**
> If you decide to lodge a minute it may be in your best interests to consult a solicitor. The minute should be lodged with the sheriff clerk together with the appropriate fee of (*insert amount*) and a copy of this intimation.

> **IF YOU ARE UNCERTAIN WHAT ACTION TO TAKE** you should consult a solicitor. You may be entitled to legal aid depending on your financial circumstances, and you can get information about legal aid from a solicitor. You may also obtain advice from any Citizens Advice Bureau or other advice agency.

NOTE
[1] Inserted by Act of Sederunt (Ordinary Cause Rules) Amendment (Civil Partnership Act 2004) 2005 (SSI 2005/638), para.3 (effective December 8, 2005).

Rule 33A.8(3) [1] FORM CP13

Form of intimation to person with whom an association is alleged to have occurred in a civil partnership action

Court ref. no.

To (*insert name and address as in warrant*)

You are given NOTICE that in this action, the defender is alleged to have had an association with you. A copy of the initial writ is attached. If you wish to dispute the truth of the allegation made against you, you must lodge a minute with the sheriff clerk (*insert address of sheriff clerk*), for leave to appear as a party. Your minute must be lodged within 21 days of (*insert date on which intimation was given. N.B. Rule 5.3(2) relating to postal service or intimation*).

Date (*insert date*)

(*Signed*)

Solicitor for the pursuer

(*insert designation and business address*)

> **NOTE**
> If you decide to lodge a minute it may be in your best interests to consult a solicitor. The minute should be lodged with the sheriff clerk together with the appropriate fee of (*insert amount*) and a copy of this intimation.

> **IF YOU ARE UNCERTAIN WHAT ACTION TO TAKE** you should consult a solicitor. You may be entitled to legal aid depending on your financial circumstances, and you can get information about legal aid from a solicitor. You may also obtain advice from any Citizens Advice Bureau or other advice agency.

NOTE
[1] Inserted by Act of Sederunt (Ordinary Cause Rules) Amendment (Civil Partnership Act 2004) 2005 (SSI 2005/638), para.3 (effective December 8, 2005).

Rule 33A.10   [1] FORM CP14

Form of warrant of citation in a civil partnership action

Court ref. no.

(*Insert place and date*)

Grants warrant to cite the defender (*insert name and address of defender*) by serving upon him [*or* her] a copy of the writ and warrant upon a period of notice of (*insert period of notice*) days, and ordains the defender to lodge a notice of intention to defend with the sheriff clerk at (*insert address of sheriff court*), if he [*or* she] wishes to:

    (a) challenge the jurisdiction of the court;

    (b) oppose any claim made or order sought;

    (c) make any claim or seek any order.

[Meantime grants interim interdict, *or* warrant to arrest on the dependence].

NOTE
[1] Inserted by Act of Sederunt (Ordinary Cause Rules) Amendment (Civil Partnership Act 2004) 2005 (SSI 2005/638), para.3 (effective December 8, 2005).

Rule 33A.11(1) and 33A.13(1)(a)   [1] FORM CP15

Form of citation in a civil partnership action

CITATION

SHERIFFDOM OF (*insert name of sheriffdom*)

AT (*insert place of sheriff court*)

[A.B.], (*insert designation and address*), Pursuer, against [C.D.], (*insert designation and address*), Defender.

(*Insert place and date*)   Court ref. no.

You [C.D.], are hereby served with this copy writ and warrant, with Form CP16 (notice of intention to defend) [and (*insert details of any other form of notice served, e.g. any of the forms served in accordance with rule 33A.14.*)].

> Form CP16 is served on you for use should you wish to intimate an intention to defend the action.
>
> **IF YOU WISH TO—**
>
> (a) challenge the jurisdiction of the court;
> (b) oppose any claim made or order sought;
> (c) make any claim; or
> (d) seek any order;
>
> you should consult a solicitor with a view to lodging a notice of intention to defend (Form CP16). The notice of intention to defend, together with the court fee of £ (*insert amount*) must be lodged with the sheriff clerk at the above address within 21 days (*or insert appropriate period of notice*) of (*insert the date on which service was executed. N.B. Rule 5.3(2) relating to postal service or intimation*).

IF YOU ARE UNCERTAIN WHAT ACTION TO TAKE you should consult a solicitor. You may be entitled to legal aid depending on your financial circumstances, and you can get information about legal aid from a solicitor. You may also obtain advice from any Citizens Advice Bureau or other advice agency.

PLEASE NOTE THAT IF YOU DO NOTHING IN ANSWER TO THIS DOCUMENT the court may regard you as admitting the claim made against you and the pursuer may obtain decree against you in your absence.

(*Signed*)

[P.Q.], Sheriff officer

[*or*

[X.Y.], (*insert designation and business address*)

Solicitor for the pursuer]

NOTE
[1] Inserted by Act of Sederunt (Ordinary Cause Rules) Amendment (Civil Partnership Act 2004) 2005 (SSI 2005/638), para.3 (effective December 8, 2005).

Rules 33A.11(1) and 33A.34(2)(a)   [1] **FORM CP16**

Form of notice of intention to defend in a civil partnership action

NOTICE OF INTENTION TO DEFEND

PART A

PART A (This section to be completed by the pursuer's solicitor before service.) [*Insert name and business address of solicitor for the pursuer*]	Court ref. No. In an action brought in Sheriff Court Pursuer Defender Date of service	Date of expiry of period of notice

PART B

(This section to be completed by the defender or defender's solicitor, and both parts of the form to be returned to the Sheriff Clerk at the above Sheriff Court on or before the date of expiry of the period of notice referred to in Part A above.)

(*Insert place and date*)

[C.D.] (*Insert designation and address*), Defender, intends to
    (a) challenge the jurisdiction of the court;
    (b) oppose a crave in the initial writ;
    (c) make a claim;
    (d) seek an order;
in the action against him [*or* her] raised by [A.B.], (*insert designation and address*), Pursuer.

PART C

(This section to be completed by the defender or the defender's solicitor where an order under section 11 of the Children (Scotland) Act 1995 in respect of a child is opposed by the defender).

DO YOU WISH TO OPPOSE THE MAKING OF ANY ORDER CRAVED BY THE PURSUER IN RESPECT OF A CHILD?

YES/NO*

*delete as appropriate

If you answered YES to the above question, please state here the order(s) which you wish to oppose and the reasons why the court should not make such order(s).

PART D

(This section to be completed by the defender or the defender's solicitor where an order under section 11 of the Children (Scotland) Act 1995 in respect of a child is sought by the defender).

DO YOU WISH THE COURT TO MAKE ANY ORDER UNDER SECTION 11 OF THE CHILDREN (SCOTLAND) ACT 1995 IN RESPECT OF A CHILD?

YES/NO*

*delete as appropriate

If you answered YES to the above question, please state here the order(s) which you wish the court to make and the reasons why the court should make such order(s).

PART E

IF YOU HAVE COMPLETED PART D OF THIS FORM YOU MUST INCLUDE EITHER CRAVE (1) OR (2) BELOW (*delete as appropriate)

(1)* Warrant for intimation of notice in terms of Form CP7 on the child(ren) (*insert full name(s) and date(s) of birth*) is sought.

(2)* I seek to dispense with intimation on the child(ren) (*insert full name(s) and date(s) of birth*) for the following reasons:–

> Signed
> [C.D.] Defender [*or* [X.Y.]
> (*add designation and business address*)
> Solicitor for Defender]

NOTE
[1] Inserted by Act of Sederunt (Ordinary Cause Rules) Amendment (Civil Partnership Act 2004) 2005 (SSI 2005/638), para.3 (effective December 8, 2005).

Rule 33A.11(2) [1] FORM CP17

Form of certificate of citation in a civil partnership action

CERTIFICATE OF CITATION

(*Insert place and date*) I,   hereby certify that upon the   day of   I duly cited [C.D.], Defender, to answer to the foregoing writ. This I did by (*state method of service; if by officer and not by post, add:* in the presence of [L.M.], (*insert designation*), witness hereto with me subscribing; *and insert details of any forms of intimation or notice sent including details of the person to whom intimation sent and the method of service*).

> (*Signed*)
> [P.Q.], Sheriff officer
> [L.M.], witness
> [*or*
> [X.Y.] (*add designation and business address*)
> Solicitor for the pursuer]

NOTE
[1] Inserted by Act of Sederunt (Ordinary Cause Rules) Amendment (Civil Partnership Act 2004) 2005 (SSI 2005/638), para.3 (effective December 8, 2005).

Rule 33A.13(1)(c) [1] FORM CP18

Form of request to medical officer of hospital or similar institution in a civil partnership action

To (*insert name and address of medical officer*)

In terms of rule 33A.13(1)(c) of the Ordinary Cause Rules of the Sheriff Court a copy of the initial writ at the instance of (*insert name and address of pursuer*), Pursuer, against (*insert name and address of defender*), Defender, is enclosed and you are requested to

(a) deliver it personally to (*insert name of defender*), and

(b) explain the contents to him or her,

unless you are satisfied that such delivery or explanation would be dangerous to his or her health or mental condition. You are further requested to complete and return to me in the enclosed stamped addressed envelope the certificate appended hereto, making necessary deletions.

Date (*insert date*)   (*Signed*)

                                             Solicitor for the pursuer

                                             (*insert designation and business address*)

NOTE
[1] Inserted by Act of Sederunt (Ordinary Cause Rules) Amendment (Civil Partnership Act 2004) 2005 (SSI 2005/638), para.3 (effective December 8, 2005).

Rule 33A.13(1)(d) and 33A.13(2) [1] FORM CP19

Form of certificate by medical officer of hospital or similar institution in a civil partnership action

Court ref. no.

I (*insert name and designation*) certify that I have received a copy initial writ in an action of (*type of civil partnership action to be inserted by the party requesting service*) at the instance of (*insert name and designation*), Pursuer, against (*insert name and designation*), Defender, and that

* I have on the   day of   personally delivered a copy thereof to the said defender who is under my care at (*insert address*) and I have explained the contents or purport thereof to him or her, *or*
* I have not delivered a copy thereof to the said defender who is under my care at (*insert address*) and I have not explained the contents thereof to him or her because (*state reasons*).

Date (*insert date*)

(*Signed*)

                                             Medical officer (*add designation and address*)

* Delete as appropriate.

NOTE
[1] Inserted by Act of Sederunt (Ordinary Cause Rules) Amendment (Civil Partnership Act 2004) 2005 (SSI 2005/638), para.3 (effective December 8, 2005).

Rule 33A.14(1)(a)(i) [1] FORM CP20

Form of notice to defender where it is stated that defender consents to granting decree of dissolution of a civil partnership

YOU ARE GIVEN NOTICE that the copy initial writ served on you with this notice states that you consent to the grant of decree of dissolution of your civil partnership.

1. If you do so consent the consequences for you are that—

[2] (a) provided the pursuer establishes the fact that he [*or* she] has not cohabited with you at any

time during a continuous period of one year after the date of registration of your civil partnership and immediately preceding the bringing of this action and that you consent, a decree of dissolution of your civil partnership will be granted;

(b) on the grant of a decree of dissolution of your civil partnership you may lose your rights of succession to the pursuer's estate; and

(c) decree of dissolution will end your civil partnership thereby affecting any right to such pension as may depend on the civil partnership continuing, or, your right to any state pension that may have been payable to you on the death of your civil partner.

Apart from these, there may be other consequences for you depending upon your particular circumstances.

2. You are entitled, whether or not you consent to the grant of decree of dissolution of your civil partnership, to apply to the sheriff in this action—

(a) to make financial or other provision for you under the Family Law (Scotland) Act 1985;

(b) for an order under section 11 of the Children (Scotland) Act 1995 in respect of any child of the family within the meaning of section 101(7) of the Civil Partnership Act 2004; or

(c) for any other competent order.

3. IF YOU WISH TO APPLY FOR ANY OF THE ABOVE ORDERS you should consult a solicitor with a view to lodging a notice of intention to defend (Form CP16).

4. If, after consideration, you wish to consent to the grant of decree of dissolution of your civil partnership in this action, you should complete and sign the attached notice of consent (Form CP21) and send it to the sheriff clerk at the sheriff court referred to in the initial writ within 21 days of (*insert the date on which service was executed N.B. Rule 5.3(2) relating to postal service*).

5. If, at a later stage, you wish to withdraw your consent to decree being granted against you in this action, you must inform the sheriff clerk immediately in writing.

Date (*insert date*)

(*Signed*)

Solicitor for the pursuer

(*insert designation and business address*)

NOTES
[1] Inserted by Act of Sederunt (Ordinary Cause Rules) Amendment (Civil Partnership Act 2004) 2005 (SSI 2005/638), para.3 (effective December 8, 2005).
[2] As amended by Act of Sederunt (Ordinary Cause Rules) Amendment (Family Law (Scotland) Act 2006 etc.) 2006, para.2 (SSI 2006/207) (effective May 4, 2006).

Rules 33A.14(1)(a)(i) and 33A.18(1)   [1] FORM CP21

Form of notice of consent in actions of dissolution of a civil partnership under section 117(3)(c) of the Civil Partnership Act 2004

Court ref. no.

[A.B.], (*insert designation and address*), Pursuer, against [C.D.], (*insert designation and address*), Defender.

I, (*full name and address of the defender to be inserted by pursuer or pursuer's solicitor before sending notice*) have received a copy of the initial writ in the action against me at the instance of (*full name and address of pursuer to be inserted by pursuer or pursuer's solicitor before sending notice*). I understand that it states that I consent to the grant of decree of dissolution of the civil partnership in this action. I have considered the consequences for me mentioned in the notice (Form CP20) sent to me with this notice. I consent to the grant of decree of dissolution of the civil partnership in this action.

Date (*insert date*)   (*Signed*)

Defender

NOTE
  [1] Inserted by Act of Sederunt (Ordinary Cause Rules) Amendment (Civil Partnership Act 2004) 2005 (SSI 2005/638), para.3 (effective December 8, 2005).

Rule 33A.14(1)(a)(ii)   [1] FORM CP22

Form of notice to defender where it is stated that defender consents to the granting of decree of separation of civil partners

YOU ARE GIVEN NOTICE that the copy initial writ served on you with this notice states that you consent to the grant of decree of separation of you and your civil partner.

1. If you do so consent the consequences for you are that—

[2] (a) provided the pursuer establishes the fact that he [*or she*] has not cohabited with you at any time during a continuous period of one year after the date of registration of your civil partnership and immediately preceding the bringing of this action and that you consent, a decree of separation of civil partners will be granted;

(b) on the grant of a decree of separation of civil partners you will be obliged to live apart from the pursuer but the civil partnership will continue to subsist; you will continue to have a legal obligation to support your civil partner and any child of the family within the meaning of section 101(7) of the Civil Partnership Act 2004; and

Apart from these, there may be other consequences for you depending upon your particular circumstances.

2. You are entitled, whether or not you consent to the grant of decree of separation of civil partners, to apply to the sheriff in this action—

(a) to make financial or other provision for you under the Family Law (Scotland) Act 1985;

(b) for an order under section 11 of the Children (Scotland) Act 1995 in respect of any child of the family within the meaning of section 101(7) of the Civil Partnership Act 2004; or

(c) for any other competent order.

3. IF YOU WISH TO APPLY FOR ANY OF THE ABOVE ORDERS you should consult a solicitor with a view to lodging a notice of intention to defend (Form CP16).

4. If, after consideration, you wish to consent to the grant of decree of separation of civil partners in this action, you should complete and sign the attached notice of consent (Form CP23) and send it to the sheriff clerk at the sheriff court referred to in the initial writ and other papers within 21 days of (*insert the date on which service was executed. N.B. Rule 5.3(2) relating to postal service or intimation*).

5. If, at a later stage, you wish to withdraw your consent to decree being granted against you in this action, you must inform the sheriff clerk immediately in writing.

Date (*insert date*)

(*Signed*)

Solicitor for the pursuer (*add*

designation and business address)

NOTES
  [1] Inserted by Act of Sederunt (Ordinary Cause Rules) Amendment (Civil Partnership Act 2004) 2005 (SSI 2005/638), para.3 (effective December 8, 2005).
  [2] As amended by Act of Sederunt (Ordinary Cause Rules) Amendment (Family Law (Scotland) Act 2006 etc.) 2006, para.2 (SSI 2006/207) (effective May 4, 2006).

Rules 33A.14(1)(a)(ii) and 33A.18(1)   [1] FORM CP23

Form of notice of consent in actions of separation of civil partners under section 120 of the Civil Partnership Act 2004

Court ref. no

[A.B.], (*insert designation and address*), Pursuer against [C.D.], (*insert designation and address*), Defender.

I, (*full name and address of the defender to be inserted by pursuer or pursuer's solicitor before sending notice*) confirm that I have received a copy of the initial writ in the action against me at the instance of (*full name and address of pursuer to be inserted by pursuer or pursuer's solicitor before sending notice*). I understand that it states that I consent to the grant of decree of separation of civil partners in this action. I have considered the consequences for me mentioned in the notice (Form CP22) sent together with this notice. I consent to the grant of decree of separation of civil partners in this action.

Date (*insert date*)

(*Signed*)

Defender

NOTE

[1] Inserted by Act of Sederunt (Ordinary Cause Rules) Amendment (Civil Partnership Act 2004) 2005 (SSI 2005/638), para.3 (effective December 8, 2005).

Rule 33A.14(1)(b)(i) [1,2] FORM CP24

Form of notice to defender in an action for dissolution of a civil partnership where it is stated there has been two years' non-cohabitation

YOU ARE GIVEN NOTICE that—

1. The copy initial writ served on you with this notice states that there has been no cohabitation between you and the pursuer at any time during a continuous period of two years after the date of registration of the civil partnership and immediately preceding the commencement of this action. If the pursuer establishes this as a fact and the sheriff is satisfied that the civil partnership has broken down irretrievably, a decree will be granted.

2. Decree of dissolution will end the civil partnership thereby affecting any right to such pension as may depend on the civil partnership continuing or your right to any state pension that may have been payable to you on the death of your civil partner. You may also lose your rights of succession to the pursuer's estate.

3. You are entitled, whether or not you dispute that there has been no such cohabitation during that five year period, to apply to the sheriff in this action—

    (a) to make financial or other provision for you under the Family Law (Scotland) Act

    (b) for an order under section 11 of the Children (Scotland) Act 1995 in respect of any child of the family within the meaning of section 101(7) of the Civil Partnership Act 2004; or

    (c) for any other competent order.

4. IF YOU WISH TO APPLY FOR ANY OF THE ABOVE ORDERS you should consult a solicitor with a view to lodging a notice of intention to defend (Form CP16).

Date (*insert date*)

(*Signed*)

Solicitor for the pursuer (*add*

designation and business address)

NOTES

[1] Inserted by Act of Sederunt (Ordinary Cause Rules) Amendment (Civil Partnership Act 2004) 2005 (SSI 2005/638), para.3 (effective December 8, 2005).

[2] As amended by Act of Sederunt (Ordinary Cause Rules) Amendment (Family Law (Scotland) Act 2006 etc.) 2006, para.2 (SSI 2006/207) (effective May 4, 2006).

Rule 33A.14(1)(b)(ii) [1,2] FORM CP25

Form of notice to defender in an action for separation of civil partners where it is stated there has been two years' non-cohabitation

YOU ARE GIVEN NOTICE that—

1. The copy initial writ served on you with this notice states that there has been no cohabitation between you and the pursuer at any time during a continuous period of five years after the date of registration of the civil partnership and immediately preceding the commencement of this action. If the pursuer establishes this as a fact and the sheriff is satisfied that there are grounds justifying a decree of separation of civil partners, a decree will be granted.

2. On the granting of decree of separation you will be obliged to live apart from the pursuer but the civil partnership will continue to subsist. You will continue to have a legal obligation to support your civil partner and any child of the family within the meaning of section 101(7) of the Civil Partnership Act 2004.

3. You are entitled, whether or not you dispute that there has been no such cohabitation during that two year period, to apply to the sheriff in this action—

    (a) to make provision under the Family Law (Scotland) Act 1985;

    (b) for an order under section 11 of the Children (Scotland) Act 1995 in respect of any child of the family within the meaning of section 101(7) of the Civil Partnership Act 2004; or

    (c) for any other competent order.

4. IF YOU WISH TO APPLY FOR ANY OF THE ABOVE ORDERS you should consult a solicitor with a view to lodging a notice of intention to defend (Form CP16).

Date (*insert date*)

                                     (*Signed*)

                                     Solicitor for the pursuer (*add*

                                     designation and business address)

NOTES
[1] Inserted by Act of Sederunt (Ordinary Cause Rules) Amendment (Civil Partnership Act 2004) 2005 (SSI 2005/638), para.3 (effective December 8, 2005).
[2] As amended by Act of Sederunt (Ordinary Cause Rules) Amendment (Family Law (Scotland) Act 2006 etc.) 2006, para.2 (SSI 2006/207) (effective May 4, 2006).

Rule 33A.14(1)(c)   [1] FORM CP25A

Form of notice to defender in action of dissolution of civil partnership where an interim gender recognition certificate has been issued

YOU ARE GIVEN NOTICE that—

1. The copy initial writ served on you together with this notice states that an interim gender recognition certificate has been issued to you [*or* the pursuer]. If the pursuer establishes this as a fact, decree will be granted.

2. Decree of dissolution will end the civil partnership thereby affecting any right to such pension as may depend on the civil partnership continuing or your right to any state pension that may have been payable to you on the death of your civil partner. You may also lose your rights of succession to the pursuer's estate.

3. If the pursuer is entitled to decree of dissolution you are nevertheless entitled to apply to the sheriff in this action—
    (a) to make financial or other provision for you under the Family Law (Scotland) Act 1985;
    (b) for an order under section 11 of the Children (Scotland) Act 1995 in respect of any child of the family within the meaning of section 101(7) of the Civil Partnership Act 2004; or
    (c) for any other competent order.

4. IF YOU WISH TO APPLY FOR ANY OF THE ABOVE ORDERS you should consult a solicitor with a view to lodging a notice of intention to defend (Form CP16).

Date *(insert date)*   (*Signed*)

                                     Solicitor for the pursuer (*add designation and business address*)

NOTE
[1] Inserted by Act of Sederunt (Ordinary Cause Rules) Amendment (Family Law (Scotland) Act 2006 etc.) 2006, para.2 (SSI 2006/207) (effective May 4, 2006).

Rule 33A.23(2) [1] FORM CP26

Form of intimation to parties of a Child Welfare Hearing in a civil partnership action

Sheriff court (*insert address and telephone number*) Court ref. no.

In this action [A.B.], (*design*), Pursuer, against [C.D.] (*design*), Defender

YOU ARE GIVEN NOTICE that a Child Welfare Hearing has been fixed for (*insert time*) on (*insert date*) at (*insert place*).

Date (*insert date*) Signed...
Sheriff Clerk (Depute)

NOTE
[1] Inserted by Act of Sederunt (Ordinary Cause Rules) Amendment (Civil Partnership Act 2004) 2005 (SSI 2005/638), para.3 (effective December 8, 2005).

Rule 33A.30(1)(b) [1] FORM CP27

Form of minute for decree in a civil partnership action to which rule 33A.29 applies

(*Insert name of solicitor for the pursuer*) having considered the evidence contained in the affidavits and the other documents all as specified in the schedule hereto, and being satisfied that upon the evidence a motion for decree (in terms of the crave of initial writ) [*or in such restricted terms as may be appropriate*] may be properly be made, moves the court accordingly.

In respect whereof

Signed

Solicitor for the Pursuer (*add designation and business address*)

SCHEDULE

(*Number and specify documents considered*)

NOTE
[1] Inserted by Act of Sederunt (Ordinary Cause Rules) Amendment (Civil Partnership Act 2004) 2005 (SSI 2005/638), para.3 (effective December 8, 2005).

Rules 33A.65(1) and 33A.65(2) [1] FORM CP28

Form of certificate of delivery of documents to chief constable in a civil partnership action

[*Omitted by Act of Sederunt (Ordinary Cause Rules) Amendment (Family Law (Scotland) Act 2006 etc.) 2006, para.2 (SSI 2006/207) (effective May 4, 2006).*]

Rule 33A.67(1) [1,2] FORM CP29

Form of simplified dissolution of civil partnership application under section 117(3)(c) of the Civil Partnership Act 2004

Sheriff Clerk

Sheriff Court House

....
....

(Telephone)..

APPLICATION FOR DISSOLUTION OF A CIVIL PARTNERSHIP WITH CONSENT OF

OTHER PARTY TO THE CIVIL PARTNERSHIP (CIVIL PARTNERS HAVING LIVED APART FOR AT LEAST ONE YEAR)

Before completing this form, you should have read the leaflet entitled "Do it yourself Dissolution", which explains the circumstances in which a dissolution of a civil partnership may be sought by this method. If the simplified procedure appears to suit your circumstances, you may use this form to apply for dissolution of your civil partnership. Below you will find directions designed to assist you with your application. Please follow them carefully. In the event of difficulty, you may contact any sheriff clerk's office or Citizen Advice Bureau.

Directions for making application

WRITE IN INK, USING BLOCK CAPITALS

Application (Part 1)	1. Complete and sign Part 1 of the form (pages 3-7), paying particular attention to the notes opposite each section.
Consent of civil partner (Part 2)	2. When you have completed Part 1 of the form, attach the (blue) instruction sheet SP3 to it and send both documents to your civil partner for completion of the consent at Part 2 (page 9).

NOTE: If your civil partner does NOT complete and sign the form of consent, your application cannot proceed further under the simplified procedure. In that event, if you still wish to obtain a dissolution of your civil partnership, you should consult a solicitor.

Affidavit (Part 3)	3. When the application has been returned to you with the consent (Part 2) duly completed and signed, you should take the form to a Justice of the Peace, Notary Public, Commissioner for Oaths or other duly authorised person so that your affidavit at Part 3 (page 10) may be completed and sworn.
Returning completed application form to court	4. When directions 1-3 above have been complied with, your application is now ready to be sent to the sheriff clerk at the above address. With it you must enclose:

(i) an extract of the registration of your civil partnership in the civil partnership register (the document headed "Extract of an entry in the Register of Civil Partnerships", which will be returned to you in due course), or an equivalent document, and

(ii) either a cheque or postal order in respect of the court fee, crossed and made payable to "the Scottish Court Service",

or a completed form SP15, claiming exemption from the court fee.

5. Receipt of your application will be promptly acknowledged. Should you wish to withdraw the application for any reason, please contact the sheriff clerk immediately.

PART 1

WRITE IN INK, USING BLOCK CAPITALS

1. NAME AND ADDRESS OF APPLICANT

Surname ....

Other name(s) in full ....

....

Present address ....

....

Daytime telephone number (if any) ....

2. NAME AND ADDRESS OF CIVIL PARTNER

Surname ....

Other name(s) in full ....

....

Present address ....

....

Daytime telephone number (if any) ....

3. JURISDICTION Please indicate with a tick ( ) in the appropriate box or boxes which of the following apply:

PART A

    (i) My civil partner and I are habitually resident in Scotland   ☐

   (ii) My civil partner and I were last habitually resident in Scotland,   ☐
       and one of us still resides there

  (iii) My civil partner is habitually resident in Scotland   ☐

  (iv) I am habitually resident in Scotland having resided there for at   ☐
       least a year immediately before this application was made

   (v) I am habitually resident in Scotland having resided there for at   ☐
       least six months immediately before this application was made
       and am domiciled in Scotland

If you have ticked one or more of the boxes in Part A, you should go direct to Part C. You should only complete Part B if you have not ticked any of the boxes in Part A

PART B

    (i) I am domiciled in Scotland   ☐

   (ii) My civil partner is domiciled in Scotland   ☐

  (iii) No court has, or is recognised as having, jurisdiction under   ☐
       regulations made under section 219 of the Civil Partnership Act 2004

PART C

    (i) I have lived at the address shown above for at least 40 days   ☐
       immediately before the date I signed this application

   (ii) My civil partner has lived at the address shown above for at least   ☐
       40 days immediately before the date I signed this application

  (iii) I lived at the address shown above for a period of at least 40 days   ☐
       ending not more than 40 days before the date I signed this
       application and have no known residence in Scotland at that date

  (iv) My civil partner lived at the address shown above for a period of   ☐
       at least 40 days ending not more than 40 days before the date I
       signed this application and has no known residence in Scotland at
       that date

4. DETAILS OF PRESENT CIVIL PARTNERSHIP

Place of Registration of Civil Partnership...(Registration District)

Date of Registration of Civil Partnership: Day...................month.................year....................

5. PERIOD OF SEPARATION

    (i) Please state the date on which you ceased to live with your civil partner. (If more than 1
       year, just give the month and year)

       Day...........Month.........Year............

   (ii) Have you lived with your civil partner since that date?   *[YES/NO]

  (iii) If yes, for how long in total did you live together before finally separating again?

                       ....months

6. RECONCILIATION

Is there any reasonable prospect of reconciliation with your civil partner? *[YES/NO]

Do you consider that the civil partnership has broken down irretrievably? *[YES/NO]

7. CONSENT

Does your civil partner consent to a dissolution of the civil partnership *[YES/NO] being granted?

8. MENTAL DISORDER

Does your civil partner have any mental disorder (whether mental illness, personality disorder or learning disability)? *[YES/NO]

Is your civil partner suffering from any mental disorder *[YES/NO]

(whether illness or handicap)?(If yes, give details)

9. CHILDREN

Are there any children of the family under the age of 16? *[YES/NO]

10. OTHER COURT ACTIONS

Are you aware of any court actions currently proceeding in any country (including Scotland) which may affect your civil partnership? *[YES/NO]

(If yes, give details)

* Delete as appropriate

11. REQUEST FOR DISSOLUTION OF THE CIVIL PARTNERSHIP AND DISCLAIMER OF FINANCIAL PROVISION

I confirm that the facts stated in paragraphs 1-10 above apply to my civil partnership.

I do NOT ask the sheriff to make any financial provision in connection with this application.

I request the sheriff to grant decree of dissolution of my civil partnership.

Date   Signature of Applicant ....

IMPORTANT

Part 1 MUST be completed, signed and dated before sending the application form to your civil partner.

PART 2

NOTICE TO CONSENTING CIVIL PARTNER

(Insert name and address of consenting civil partner)

CONSENT TO APPLICATION FOR DISSOLUTION OF A CIVIL PARTNERSHIP (CIVIL PARTNERS HAVING LIVED APART FOR AT LEAST ONE YEAR)

In Part 1 of the enclosed application form your civil partner is applying for dissolution of your civil partnership on the ground the civil partnership has broken down irretrievably because you and he [*or* she] have lived apart for at least one year and you consent to the dissolution being granted.

Such consent must be given formally in writing at Part 2 of the application form. BEFORE completing that part, you are requested to read it over carefully so that you understand the effect of consenting to the dissolution of the civil partnership. Thereafter if you wish to consent—

(a) check the details given by the Applicant at Part 1 of the form to ensure that they are correct to the best of your knowledge;

(b) complete Part 2 (Consent by Applicant's civil partner to dissolution) by entering your name and address at the appropriate place and adding your signature and the date; and

(c) return the whole application form to your civil partner at the address given in Part 1.

Once your civil partner has completed the remainder of the form and has submitted it to the court, a copy of the whole application (including your consent) will later be served upon you formally by the sheriff clerk.

In the event of the dissolution of the civil partnership being granted, you will automatically be sent a copy of the extract decree. (Should you change your address before receiving the copy extract decree, please notify the sheriff clerk immediately.)

If you do NOT wish to consent please return the application form, with Part 2 uncompleted, to your civil partner and advise him or her of your decision.

The sheriff will NOT grant a dissolution of your civil partnership on this application if Part 2 of the form is not completed by you.

CONSENT BY APPLICANT'S CIVIL PARTNER TO DISSOLUTION OF CIVIL PARTNERSHIP

NOTE: Before completing this part of the form, please read the notes opposite (page 8)

I, ...

(Insert full name, in BLOCK letters, of Applicant's civil partner)

residing at ....

....

....

(Insert address, also in BLOCK letters)

HEREBY STATE THAT

    (a) I have read Part 1 of this application;

    (b) the Applicant has lived apart from me for a continuous period of one year immediately preceding the date of the application (paragraph 11 of Part 1);

    (c) I do not ask the sheriff to make any financial provision for me including—

        (i) the payment by the Applicant of a periodical allowance (i.e. a regular payment of money weekly or monthly, etc. for maintenance);

        (ii) the payment by the Applicant of a capital sum (i.e. a lump sum payment);

    (d) I understand that dissolution of my civil partnership may result in the loss to me of property rights; and

    (e) I CONSENT TO DECREE OF DISSOLUTION BEING GRANTED IN RESPECT OF THIS APPLICATION

Date   Signature ....

NOTE: You may withdraw your consent, even after giving it, at any time before the dissolution of the civil partnership is granted by the sheriff. Should you wish to do so, please contact the sheriff clerk immediately.

PART 3

APPLICANT'S AFFIDAVIT

To be completed by the Applicant only after Parts 1 and 2 have been signed and dated.

I, *(Insert Applicant's full name)* ....

residing at *(insert Applicant's present home address)* ....

....

....

SWEAR that to the best of my knowledge and belief:

        (1) the facts stated in Part 1 of this Application are true; and

        (2) the signature in Part 2 of this Application is that of my civil partner.

Signature of Applicant ....

SWORN at *(insert place)* ....

To be completed by
Justice of the Peace, this..................day of..........................20..............
Notary Public or
Commissioner for before me (*insert full name*) ....

Oaths (*insert full address*) ....

....

....

Signature ....

*Justice of the Peace/ Notary Public/Commissioner for Oaths

* Delete as appropriate

NOTES
[1] Inserted by Act of Sederunt (Ordinary Cause Rules) Amendment (Civil Partnership Act 2004) 2005 (SSI 2005/638), para.3 (effective December 8, 2005).
[2] As amended by Act of Sederunt (Ordinary Cause Rules) Amendment (Family Law (Scotland) Act 2006 etc.) 2006, para.2 (SSI 2006/207) (effective May 4, 2006).

Rule 33A.67(2) [1] FORM CP30

Form of simplified dissolution of civil partnership application under section 117(3)(d) of the Civil Partnership Act 2004

Sheriff Clerk

Sheriff Court House

....

....

(Telephone)..

APPLICATION FOR DISSOLUTION OF A CIVIL PARTNERSHIP (CIVIL PARTNERS HAVING LIVED APART FOR AT LEAST TWO YEARS)

Before completing this form, you should have read the leaflet entitled "Do it yourself Dissolution", which explains the circumstances in which a dissolution of a civil partnership may be sought by this method. If the simplified procedure appears to suit your circumstances, you may use this form to apply for dissolution of your civil partnership. Below you will find directions designed to assist you with your application. Please follow them carefully. In the event of difficulty, you may contact any sheriff clerk's office or Citizen Advice Bureau.

Directions for making application

WRITE IN INK, USING BLOCK CAPITALS

Application   1. Complete and sign Part 1 of the form (pages 3-7), paying particular
(Part 1)   attention to the notes opposite each section.

Affidavits   2. When you have completed Part 1, you should take the form to a Justice of
(Part 2)   the Peace, Notary Public, Commissioner for Oaths or other duly authorised
                  person so that your affidavit at Part 2 (page 8) may be completed and sworn.

Returning   3. When directions 1-2 above have been complied with, your application now
completed   ready to be sent to the sheriff clerk at the above address. With it you must
application   enclose:
form to court
                  (i) an extract of the registration of your civil partnership in the civil
                  partnership register (the document headed "Extract of an entry in the Register
                  of Civil Partnerships", which will be returned to you in due course), or an
                  equivalent document. Check the notes on page 2 to see if you need to obtain a
                  letter from the General Register Office stating that there is no record of your
                  civil partner having dissolved the civil partnership, and

(ii) either a cheque or postal order in respect of the court fee, crossed and made payable to "the Scottish Court Service",

or a completed fee exemption form.

4. Receipt of your application will be promptly acknowledged. Should you wish to withdraw the application for any reason, please contact the sheriff clerk immediately.

PART 1

WRITE IN INK, USING BLOCK CAPITALS

1. NAME AND ADDRESS OF APPLICANT

Surname ....

Other name(s) in full. ....

....

Present address. ....

....

Daytime telephone number (if any) ....

2. NAME OF CIVIL PARTNER

Surname ....

Other name(s) in full ....

3. ADDRESS OF CIVIL PARTNER (If the address of your civil partner is not known, please enter "not known" in this paragraph and proceed to paragraph 4)

Present address ....

....

....

Daytime telephone number (if any) ....

4. Only complete this paragraph if you do not know the present address of your civil partner

NEXT-OF-KIN Name. ....

Address ....

....

....

Relationship to your civil partner ....

CHILDREN OF THE FAMILY

Names and dates of birth   Addresses

....

                                                        ....

....

                                                        ....

If insufficient space is available to list all the children of the family, please continue on a separate sheet and attach to this form.

5. JURISDICTION

Please indicate with a tick (✔) in the appropriate box or boxes which of the following apply:

PART A

   (i) My civil partner and I are habitually resident in Scotland □

  (ii) My civil partner and I were last habitually resident in Scotland, □
and one of us still resides there

 (iii) My civil partner is habitually resident in Scotland □

 (iv) I am habitually resident in Scotland having resided there for at □
least a year immediately before this application was made

  (v) I am habitually resident in Scotland having resided there for at □
least six months immediately before this application was made
and am domiciled in Scotland

If you have ticked one or more of the boxes in Part A, you should go direct to Part C. You should only complete Part B if you have not ticked any of the boxes in Part A.

PART B

   (i) I am domiciled in Scotland □

  (ii) My civil partner is domiciled in Scotland □

 (iii) No court has, or is recognised as having, jurisdiction under □
regulations made under section 219 of the Civil Partnership Act 2004

PART C

   (i) I have lived at the address shown above for at least 40 days □
immediately before the date I signed this application

  (ii) My civil partner has lived at the address shown above for at least □
40 days immediately before the date I signed this application

 (iii) I lived at the address shown above for a period of at least 40 days □
ending not more than 40 days before the date I signed this
application and have no known residence in Scotland at that date

 (iv) My civil partner lived at the address shown above for a period of □
at least 40 days ending not more than 40 days before the date I
signed this application and has no known residence in Scotland at that date

6. DETAILS OF PRESENT CIVIL PARTNERSHIP

Place of Registration of Civil Partnership...(Registration District)

Date of Registration of Civil Partnership: Day....................month......................year ....

7. PERIOD OF SEPARATION

   (i) Please state the date on which you ceased to live with your civil partner. (If more than 2 years, just give the month and year)

      Day...........Month.........Year............

  (ii) Have you lived with your civil partner since that date?   *[YES/NO]

 (iii) If yes, for how long in total did you live together before finally separating again?

                                             ....months

8. RECONCILIATION

Is there any reasonable prospect of reconciliation with your civil partner?   *[YES/NO]

Do you consider that the civil partnership has broken down irretrievably?   *[YES/NO]

9. MENTAL DISORDER

Does your civil partner have any mental disorder (whether mental illness,
personality disorder or learning disability)?   *[YES/NO]

(If yes, give details)

10. CHILDREN

Are there any children of the family under the age of 16?   *[YES/NO]

11. OTHER COURT ACTIONS

Are you aware of any court actions currently proceeding in any country

(including Scotland) which may affect your civil partnership?   *[YES/NO]

(If yes, give details)   * Delete as appropriate

12. DECLARATION AND REQUEST FOR DISSOLUTION OF THE CIVIL PARTNER-SHIP

I confirm that the facts stated in paragraphs 1-11 above apply to my civil partnership.

I do NOT ask the sheriff to make any financial provision in connection with this application.

I request the sheriff to grant decree of dissolution of my civil partnership.

Date   Signature of Applicant...

PART 2

APPLICANT'S AFFIDAVIT

To be completed by the Applicant only after Part 1 has been signed and dated.

I, (*Insert Applicant's full name*) ....

residing at (*insert Applicant's present home address*) ....

....

....

SWEAR that to the best of my knowledge and belief the facts stated in Part 1 of this Application are true.

Signature of Applicant...

                    SWORN at (*insert place*) ....

To be completed by   this...day of.............................20 ....
Justice of the Peace,
Notary Public or   before me (*insert full name*) ....
Commissioner for
Oaths   (*insert full address*) ....

                           ....

                           ....

                    Signature ....

                    *Justice of the Peace/ Notary Public/Commissioner for Oaths

                    * Delete as appropriate

NOTES

[1] Inserted by Act of Sederunt (Ordinary Cause Rules) Amendment (Civil Partnership Act 2004) 2005 (SSI 2005/638), para.3 (effective December 8, 2005).

[2] As amended by Act of Sederunt (Ordinary Cause Rules) Amendment (Family Law (Scotland) Act 2006 etc.) 2006, para.2 (SSI 2006/207) (effective May 4, 2006).

Rule 33A.67(3) [1,2] FORM CP31

Form of simplified dissolution of a civil partnership application on grounds under section 117(2)(b) of the Civil Partnership Act 2004

Sheriff Clerk

Sheriff Court House

....

....

(Telephone) ....

APPLICATION FOR DISSOLUTION OF A CIVIL PARTNERSHIP (INTERIM GENDER RECOGNITION CERTIFICATE ISSUED TO ONE OF THE CIVIL PARTNERS AFTER REGISTRATION OF THE CIVIL PARTNERSHIP)

Before completing this form, you should have read the leaflet entitled "Do it yourself Dissolution", which explains the circumstances in which a dissolution of a civil partnership may be sought by this method. If the simplified procedure appears to suit your circumstances, you may use this form to apply for dissolution of your civil partnership. Below you will find directions designed to assist you with your application. Please follow them carefully. In the event of difficulty, you may contact any sheriff clerk's office or Citizen Advice Bureau.

Directions for making application

WRITE IN INK, USING BLOCK CAPITALS

Application (Part 1)	1. Complete and sign Part 1 of the form (pages 3-7), paying particular attention to the notes opposite each section
Affidavits (Part 2)	2. When you have completed Part 1, you should take the form to a Justice of the Peace, Notary Public, Commissioner for Oaths or other duly authorised person so that your affidavit at Part 2 (page 8) may be completed and sworn.
Returning Completed Application form to court	3. When directions 1-2 above have been complied with, your application is now ready to be sent to the sheriff clerk at the above address. With it you must enclose: form to court

(i) an extract of the registration of your civil partnership in the civil partnership register (the document headed "Extract of an entry in the Register of Civil Partnerships", which will be returned to you in due course), or an equivalent document. Check the notes on page 2 to see if you need to obtain a letter from the General Register Office stating that there is no record of your civil partner having dissolved the civil partnership,

(ii) either a cheque or postal order in respect of the court fee, crossed and made payable to "the Scottish Court Service" or a completed fee exemption form, and

(iii) the interim gender recognition certificate or a copy sealed with the seal of the Gender Recognition Panels and certified to be a true copy by an officer authorised by the President of Gender Recognition Panels.

4. Receipt of your application will be promptly acknowledged. Should you wish to withdraw the application for any reason, please contact the sheriff clerk immediately.

PART 1

WRITE IN INK, USING BLOCK CAPITALS

1. NAME AND ADDRESS OF APPLICANT

Surname ....

Other name(s) in full ....

....

Present address ....

....

Daytime telephone number (if any) ....

2. NAME OF CIVIL PARTNER

Surname ....

Other name(s) in full ....

3. ADDRESS OF CIVIL PARTNER (If the address of your civil partner is not known, please enter "not known" in this paragraph and proceed to paragraph 4)

Present address ....

....

....

Daytime telephone number (if any) ....

4. Only complete this paragraph if you do not know the present address of your civil partner

NEXT-OF-KIN

Name ....

Address ....

....

....

Relationship to your civil partner ....

CHILDREN OF THE FAMILY

Names and dates of birth   Addresses

....

                                                        ....

....

                                                        ....

If insufficient space is available to list all the children of the family, please continue on a separate sheet and attach to this form.

5. JURISDICTION

Please indicate with a tick (✔) in the appropriate box or boxes which of the following apply:

PART A

(i) My civil partner and I are habitually resident in Scotland ☐

(ii) My civil partner and I were last habitually resident in Scotland, and one of us still resides there ☐

(iii) My civil partner is habitually resident in Scotland ☐

(iv) I am habitually resident in Scotland having resided there for at least a year immediately before this application was made ☐

(v) I am habitually resident in Scotland having resided there for at least six months immediately before this application was made and am domiciled in Scotland ☐

If you have ticked one or more of the boxes in Part A, you should go direct to Part C. You should only complete Part B if you have not ticked any of the boxes in Part A

PART B

(i) I am domiciled in Scotland ☐

   (ii) My civil partner is domiciled in Scotland ☐

   (iii) No court has, or is recognised as having, jurisdiction under ☐
regulations made under section 219 of the Civil Partnership Act 2004

PART C

   (i) I have lived at the address shown above for at least 40 days ☐
immediately before the date I signed this application

   (ii) My civil partner has lived at the address shown above for at least ☐
40 days immediately before the date I signed this application

   (iii) I lived at the address shown above for a period of at least 40 days ☐
ending not more than 40 days before the date I signed this
application and have no known residence in Scotland at that date

   (iv) My civil partner lived at the address shown above for a period of ☐
at least 40 days ending not more than 40 days before the date I
signed this application and has no known residence in Scotland at
that date

6. DETAILS OF PRESENT CIVIL PARTNERSHIP

Place of Registration of Civil Partnership .... (Registration District)

Date of Registration of Civil Partnership: Day....................month....................year..................

7. DETAILS OF ISSUE OF INTERIM GENDER RECOGNITION CERTIFICATE

   (i) Please state whether the interim gender recognition certificate has been issued to you or
your civil partner

   (ii) Please state the date the interim gender recognition certificate was issued
Day....................Month...................Year............

8. MENTAL DISORDER

Does your civil partner have any mental disorder (whether mental illness,
personality disorder or learning disability)?   *[YES/NO]

(If yes, give details)

9. CHILDREN Are there any children of the family under the age of 16?   *[YES/NO]

10. OTHER COURT ACTIONS

Are you aware of any court actions currently proceeding in any
country (including Scotland) which may affect your civil partnership?   *[YES/NO]

(If yes, give details)   * Delete as appropriate

11. DECLARATION AND REQUEST FOR DISSOLUTION OF THE CIVIL PARTNERSHIP

I confirm that the facts stated in paragraphs 1-10 above apply to my civil partnership.

I do NOT ask the sheriff to make any financial provision in connection with this application.

I request the sheriff to grant decree of dissolution of my civil partnership.

Date   Signature of Applicant...

PART 2

APPLICANT'S AFFIDAVIT

To be completed by the Applicant only after Part 1 has been signed and dated.

I, (*Insert Applicant's full name*) ....

residing at (*insert Applicant's present home address*) ....

....

....

SWEAR that to the best of my knowledge and belief the facts stated in Part 1 of this Application are true.

Signature of Applicant ....

<table>
<tr><td></td><td>SWORN at (insert place) ....</td></tr>
<tr><td>To be completed by
Justice of the Peace,</td><td>this....................................day of..........................20 ....</td></tr>
<tr><td>Notary Public or
Commissioner for
Oaths</td><td>before me (insert full name) ....</td></tr>
<tr><td></td><td>(insert full address) ....</td></tr>
</table>

....

....

Signature ....

*Justice of the Peace/ Notary Public/Commissioner for Oaths

* Delete as appropriate

NOTES
[1] Inserted by Act of Sederunt (Ordinary Cause Rules) Amendment (Civil Partnership Act 2004) 2005 (SSI 2005/638), para.3 (effective December 8, 2005).
[2] As amended by Act of Sederunt (Ordinary Cause Rules) Amendment (Family Law (Scotland) Act 2006 etc.) 2006, para.2 (SSI 2006/207) (effective May 4, 2006).

Rule 33A.69(3)(a)   [1,2] FORM CP32

Form of citation in application relying on facts in section 117(3)(c) of the Civil Partnership Act 2004

(*Insert name and address of non-applicant civil partner*)

APPLICATION FOR DISSOLUTION OF A CIVIL PARTNERSHIP (CIVIL PARTNERS HAVING LIVED APART FOR AT LEAST ONE YEAR WITH THE CONSENT OF THE OTHER CIVIL PARTNER)

Your civil partner has applied to the sheriff for dissolution of your civil partnership on the ground that the civil partnership has broken down irretrievably because you and he or she have lived apart for a period of at least one year and you consent to decree of dissolution being granted.

A copy of the application is hereby served upon you.

1. Please note that the sheriff may not make financial provision under this procedure and that your civil partner is making no claim for—

(a) the payment by you of a periodical allowance (i.e. a regular payment of money weekly or monthly, etc. for maintenance);

(b) the payment by you of a capital sum (i.e. a lump sum payment).

2. Dissolution of your civil partnership may result in the loss to you of property rights (e.g. the right to succeed to the Applicant's estate on his or her death) or the right, where appropriate, to a pension.

3. If you wish to oppose the granting of a decree of dissolution of your civil partnership, you should put your reasons in writing and send your letter to the address shown below. Your letter must reach the sheriff clerk before (*insert date*).

4. In the event of the decree of dissolution of your civil partnership being granted, you will be sent a copy of the extract decree. Should you change your address before receiving the copy extract decree, please notify the sheriff clerk immediately.

Signed

Sheriff clerk (depute)

(*insert address and telephone number of the sheriff clerk*)

[*or* Sheriff officer]

NOTE: If you wish to exercise your right to make a claim for financial provision you should immediately advise the sheriff clerk that you oppose the application for that reason, and thereafter consult a solicitor.

NOTES
[1] Inserted by Act of Sederunt (Ordinary Cause Rules) Amendment (Civil Partnership Act 2004) 2005 (SSI 2005/638), para.3 (effective December 8, 2005).
[2] As amended by Act of Sederunt (Ordinary Cause Rules) Amendment (Family Law (Scotland) Act 2006 etc.) 2006, para.2 (SSI 2006/207) (effective May 4, 2006).

Rule 33A.69(3)(b)   [1,2] FORM CP33

Form of citation in application relying on facts in section 117(3)(d) of the Civil Partnership Act 2004

(*Insert name and address of non-applicant civil partner*)

APPLICATION FOR DISSOLUTION OF A CIVIL PARTNERSHIP (CIVIL PARTNERS HAVING LIVED APART FOR AT LEAST TWO YEARS)

Your civil partner has applied to the sheriff for dissolution of your civil partnership on the ground that the civil partnership has broken down irretrievably because you and he or she have lived apart for a period of at least two years.

A copy of the application is hereby served upon you.

1. Please note:

   (a) that the sheriff may not make financial provision under this procedure and that your civil partner is making no claim for—

      (i) the payment by you of a periodical allowance (i.e. a regular payment of money weekly or monthly, etc. for maintenance);

      (ii) the payment by you of a capital sum (i.e. a lump sum payment);

   (b) [*Omitted by Act of Sederunt (Ordinary Cause Rules) Amendment (Family Law (Scotland) Act 2006 etc.) 2006, para.2 (SSI 2006/207) (effective May 4, 2006).*]

2. Dissolution of your civil partnership may result in the loss to you of property rights (e.g. the right to succeed to the Applicant's estate on his or her death) or the right, where appropriate, to a pension.

3. If you wish to oppose the granting of a decree of dissolution of your civil partnership, you should put your reasons in writing and send your letter to the address shown below. Your letter must reach the sheriff clerk before (*insert date*).

4. In the event of the decree of dissolution of your civil partnership being granted, you will be sent a copy of the extract decree. Should you change your address before receiving the copy extract decree, please notify the sheriff clerk immediately.

Signed

Sheriff clerk (depute)

(*insert address and telephone number of the sheriff clerk*)

[*or* Sheriff officer]

NOTE: If you wish to exercise your right to make a claim for financial provision you should immediately advise the sheriff clerk that you oppose the application for that reason, and thereafter consult a solicitor.

NOTES

[1] Inserted by Act of Sederunt (Ordinary Cause Rules) Amendment (Civil Partnership Act 2004) 2005 (SSI 2005/638), para.3 (effective December 8, 2005).

[2] As amended by Act of Sederunt (Ordinary Cause Rules) Amendment (Family Law (Scotland) Act 2006 etc.) 2006, para.2 (SSI 2006/207) (effective May 4, 2006).

Rule 33A.69(3)(c)   [1] FORM CP34

Form of citation in application on grounds under section 117(2)(b) of the Civil Partnership Act 2004

(*Insert name and address of non-applicant civil partner*)

APPLICATION FOR DISSOLUTION OF A CIVIL PARTNERSHIP (INTERIM GENDER RECOGNITION CERTIFICATE ISSUED TO ONE OF THE CIVIL PARTNERS AFTER THE REGISTRATION OF THE CIVIL PARTNERSHIP)

Your civil partner has applied to the sheriff for dissolution of your civil partnership on the ground that an interim gender recognition certificate has been issued to you or your civil partner after your civil partnership was registered.

A copy of the application is hereby served upon you.

1. Please note that the sheriff may not make financial provision under this procedure and that your civil partner is making no claim for—

  (a) the payment by you of a periodical allowance (i.e. a regular payment of money weekly or monthly, etc. for maintenance);

  (b) the payment by you of a capital sum (i.e. a lump sum payment).

2. Dissolution of your civil partnership may result in the loss to you of property rights (e.g. the right to succeed to the Applicant's estate on his or her death) or the right, where appropriate, to a pension.

3. If you wish to oppose the granting of a decree of dissolution of your civil partnership, you should put your reasons in writing and send your letter to the address shown below. Your letter must reach the sheriff clerk before (*insert date*).

4. In the event of the decree of dissolution of your civil partnership being granted, you will be sent a copy of the extract decree. Should you change your address before receiving the copy extract decree, please notify the sheriff clerk immediately.

> Signed
>
> Sheriff clerk (depute)
>
> (*insert address and telephone number of the sheriff clerk*)
>
> [*or* Sheriff officer]

NOTE: If you wish to exercise your right to make a claim for financial provision you should immediately advise the sheriff clerk that you oppose the application for that reason, and thereafter consult a solicitor.

NOTE

[1] Inserted by Act of Sederunt (Ordinary Cause Rules) Amendment (Civil Partnership Act 2004) 2005 (SSI 2005/638), para.3 (effective December 8, 2005).

Rule 33A.70(1)(a)   [1] FORM CP35

Form of intimation of simplified dissolution of a civil partnership application for display on the walls of court

Court ref. no.

An application for dissolution of a civil partnership has been made in this sheriff court by [A.B.], (*insert designation and address*), Applicant, naming [C.D.], (*insert designation and address*) as Respondent.

If [C.D.] wishes to oppose the granting of decree of dissolution of the civil partnership he [*or* she] should immediately contact the sheriff clerk from whom he [*or* she] may obtain a copy of the application.

Date (*insert date*)

Signed

Sheriff clerk (depute)

NOTE
[1] Inserted by Act of Sederunt (Ordinary Cause Rules) Amendment (Civil Partnership Act 2004) 2005 (SSI 2005/638), para.3 (effective December 8, 2005).

Rule 33A.70(2) [1] FORM CP36

Form of intimation to children of the family and next-of-kin in a simplified dissolution of a civil partnership application

Court ref. no.

To (*insert name and address*)

You are hereby given NOTICE that an application for dissolution of a civil partnership has been made against (*insert name of respondent*) your (*insert relationship e.g. father, mother, brother or other relative as the case may be*). A copy of this application is attached.

If you know of his or her present address, you are requested to inform the sheriff clerk (*insert address of sheriff clerk*) in writing immediately. You may also, if you wish, oppose the granting of the decree of dissolution by sending a letter to the court giving your reasons for your opposition to the application. Your letter must be sent to the sheriff clerk within 21 days of (*insert date on which intimation was given. N.B. Rule 5.3(2) relating to postal service or intimation*).

Date (*insert date*)

Signed

Sheriff clerk (depute)

IF YOU ARE UNCERTAIN WHAT ACTION TO TAKE you should consult a solicitor. You may be entitled to legal aid depending on your financial circumstances, and you can get information about legal aid from a solicitor. You may also obtain advice from any Citizens Advice Bureau or other advice agency.

NOTE
[1] Inserted by Act of Sederunt (Ordinary Cause Rules) Amendment (Civil Partnership Act 2004) 2005 (SSI 2005/638), para.3 (effective December 8, 2005).

Rule 33A.73(2) [1] FORM CP37

Form of extract decree of dissolution of a civil partnership in an application for a simplified dissolution of a civil partnership

At (*insert place and date*)

in an action in the Sheriff Court of the Sheriffdom of (*insert name of sheriffdom*) at (*insert place of sheriff court*)

at the instance of (*insert full name of applicant*), Applicant,

against (*insert full name of respondent*), Respondent,

whose civil partnership was registered at (*insert place*) on (*insert date*),

the sheriff pronounced decree dissolving the civil partnership of the Applicant and the Respondent.

Extracted at (*insert place and date*)

by me, sheriff clerk of the Sheriffdom of (*insert name of sheriffdom*).

Signed

Sheriff clerk (depute)

NOTE
[1] Inserted by Act of Sederunt (Ordinary Cause Rules) Amendment (Civil Partnership Act 2004) 2005 (SSI 2005/638), para.3 (effective December 8, 2005).

Rule 33B.2(2)(b)   [1] FORM CO1

Form of intimation of application for financial provision on intestacy under section 29(2) of the Family Law (Scotland) Act 2006

To: (insert name and address as in warrant)   Court ref no.

You are given NOTICE that the pursuer has applied for an order for financial provision on intestacy under section 29(2) of the Family Law (Scotland) Act 2006. A copy of the initial writ is attached. If you wish to appear as a party, you must lodge a minute with the sheriff clerk (*insert address of sheriff clerk*) for leave to do so. Your minute must be lodged within 21 days of (*insert date on which intimation is given. N.B. rule 5.3(2) relating to postal service or intimation*).

Date (insert date)   (signed)

                                        Solicitor for the pursuer

---

NOTE
If you decide to lodge a minute it may be in your best interests to consult a solicitor. The minute should be lodged with the sheriff clerk together with the appropriate fee of (*insert amount*) and a copy of this intimation.

IF YOU ARE UNCERTAIN WHAT ACTION TO TAKE you should consult a solicitor. You may be entitled to legal aid depending on your financial circumstances, and you can get information about legal aid from a solicitor. You may also obtain advice from any Citizens Advice Bureau or other advice agency.

NOTE
[1] Inserted by Act of Sederunt (Ordinary Cause Rules) Amendment (Family Law (Scotland) Act 2006 etc.) 2006, para.2 (SSI 2006/207) (effective May 4, 2006).

Rule 34.1(2)   [1] FORM H1

Form of notice informing defender of right to apply for certain orders under the Debtors (Scotland) Act 1987 on sequestration for rent

[*Revoked by the Act of Sederunt (Sheriff Court Rules Amendment) (Diligence) 2008 (SSI 2008/121) r.2(1)(a) (effective April 1, 2008).*]

Rule 34.6(1)   FORM H2

Form of notice of removal

To (*insert name, designation, and address of party in possession*). You are required to remove from (*describe subjects*) at the term of (*or if different terms, state them and the subjects to which they apply*), in terms of lease (*describe it*) [*or in terms of your letter of removal dated (insert date)*] [*or otherwise as the case may be*].

Date (*insert date*)   Signed
                                        (*add designation and address*)

Rule 34.6(2)   FORM H3

Form of letter of removal

To (*insert name and designation of addressee*)
(*Insert place and date*) I am to remove from (*state subjects by usual name or short description sufficient for identification*) at the term of (*insert term and date*)

                                        [K.L.] (*add designation and address*).

(If not holograph, to be attested thus— [M.N.] (*add designation and address*), witness.)

Rule 34.7 FORM H4

Form of notice of removal under section 37 of the 1907 Act

NOTICE OF REMOVAL UNDER SECTION 37 OF THE SHERIFF COURTS (SCOT-LAND) ACT 1907

To (*insert designation and address*).
You are required to remove from (*insert description of heritable subjects, land, ground, etc.*) at the term of [Whitsunday *or* Martinmas], (*insert date*)

Date (*insert date*)   Signed
                          (*add designation and address*)

Rule 34.11(4) [1] FORM H5

Form of citation of unnamed occupiers

CITATION

SHERIFFDOM OF (*insert name of sheriffdom*)

AT (insert place of sheriff court)

[A.B.] (*insert designation and address*)

Pursuer

against

The Occupier[s] of (*address*)

Defender

An action has been brought in the above Sheriff Court by [A.B.]. [A.B.] calls as a defender the occupier[s] of the property at (*insert address*). If the occupier[s] [or any of them] wish[es] to challenge the jurisdiction of the court or to defend the action, he [or she [or it] [or they]] should contact the sheriff clerk at (*insert address of sheriff court*) immediately and in any event by (*date on which period of notice expires*).

                          Signed
                          Sheriff [or Sheriff Clerk]

NOTE
[1] Inserted by SSI 2000/239 (effective October 2, 2000).

Rule 35.5 FORM M1

Form of warrant of citation in an action of multiplepoinding

(*Insert place and date*) Grants warrant to cite the defender (*insert name and address*) by serving a copy of the writ and warrant upon a period of notice of (*insert period of notice*) days, and ordains him [*or* her], if he [*or* she] intends to lodge:—
(a) defences challenging the jurisdiction of the court or the competence of the action; or
(b) objections to the condescendence on the fund *in medio*; or
(c) a claim on the fund;
to lodge a notice of appearance with the sheriff clerk at (*insert name and address of sheriff court*) within the said period of notice after such service [and grants warrant to arrest on the dependence].

[*Where the holder of the fund in medio is a defender, insert:* Appoints the holder of the fund *in medio* to
(a) lodge with the sheriff clerk at (*insert place of sheriff court*) within the said period of notice after such service
   (i) a detailed condescendence on the fund *in medio*; and
   (ii) a list of parties having an interest in the fund; and
(b) intimate to all parties to the action a copy of the condescendence and list.]

FORM M2

Form of citation in an action of multiplepoinding

Rule 35.6(1)   CITATION

Court ref. no.

SHERIFFDOM OF (*insert name of sheriffdom*)

AT (*insert place of sheriff court*)

[A.B.], (*insert designation and address*), Pursuer, against [C.D.], (*insert designation and address*), Defender.

(*Insert place and date*) You [C.D.] are hereby served with this copy writ and warrant, together with Form M4 (notice of appearance).

[*Where the defender is the holder of the fund in medio, insert the following paragraph:–*
As holder of the fund *in medio* you must lodge with the sheriff clerk at the above address within (*insert period of notice*)days of (*insert date on which service was executed. N.B. Rule 5.3(2) relating to postal service*)-
    (a) a detailed condescendence on the fund *in medio*; and
    (b) a list of parties having an interest in the fund.
You must at the same time intimate to all other parties to the action a copy of
    (a) the detailed condescendence on the fund; and
    (b) the list of parties having an interest in the fund.]

Form M4 is served on you for use should you wish to intimate that you intend to lodge:-
    (a) defences challenging the jurisdiction of the court or the competence of the action; or
    (b) objections to the condescendence on the fund *in medio*; or
    (c) a claim on the fund.

IF YOU WISH TO APPEAR IN THIS ACTION you should consult a solicitor with a view to lodgng a notice of appearnce (Form M4). The notice of appearance, together with the court fee of #(*insert amount*) must be lodged with the sheriff clerk at the above address within (*insert the appropriat period of notice*) days of (*insert the date on which service was executed. N.B. Rule 5.3(2) relating to postal service*).

IF YOU ARE UNCERTAIN WHAT ACTION TO TAKE you should consult a solicitor. You may be eligible for legal aid depending on your income. You can get information about legal aid from a solicitor. You may also obtain advice from any Citizens Advice Bureau or other advice agency.

PLEASE NOTE THAT IF YOU DO NOTHING IN ANSWER TO THIS DOCUMENT the court may regard you as having no interest in the fund *in medio* and will proceed accordingly.

Signed
[P.Q.], Sheriff officer,
or [X.Y.] (*add designation and business address*)
Solicitor for the pursuer

FORM M3

Form of certificate of citation in an action of multiplepoinding

Rule 35.6(2)   CERTIFICATE OF CITATION

(*Insert place and date*)

I,hereby certify that upon theday of
I duly cited [C.D.], Defender, to answer to the foregoing writ. This I
did by (*state method of service; if by officer and not by post, add:* in
presence of [L.M.], (*insert designation*), witness hereto with me
subscribing *and where service is executed by post state whether made
by registered post of the first class recorded delivery service*):

Signed
[P.Q.], Sheriff officer
[L.M.], witness
or [X.Y.] (*add designation and business address*)
Solicitor for the pursuer

FORM M4   **Rules 35.6(1) and 35.8**

Form of notice of appearance in an action of multiplepoinding

NOTICE OF APPEARANCE (MULTIPLEPOINDING)

*PART A
Court Ref. No.

(*insert name and business address of solicitor for the pursuer*)	in an action raised at Sheriff Court
	Pursuer
Solicitor for the pursuer	**Defender**

*(This section to be completed by the pursuer
before service)

DATE OF SERVICE: DATE OF EXPIRY OF PERIOD OF NOTICE:

*PART B
*This section to be completed by the defender or the defender's solicitor and both parts of this form
returned to the sheriff clerk at (*insert address of sheriff clerk*) on or before the expiry of the period
of notice referred to in PART A above)

(*Insert place and date*)
[C.D.] (*design*), Defender, intends to lodge:

**Tick the
appropriate
boxes**

☐   defences challenging the jurisdiction of the court or the competence of the action.

☐   objections to the condescendence on the fund in medio

☐   a claim on the fund in medio.

Signed
[C.D.] Defender,
or [X.Y.] (*add designation and business address*)
Solicitor for the defender

FORM M5   **Rules 35.9(b) and 35.10(5)**

Form of intimation of first hearing in an action of multiplepoinding

SHERIFFDOM OF (*insert name of sheriffdom*)   Court ref. no.
AT (*insert place of sheriff court*)

[A.B.] (*insert designation and address*), Pursuer, against [C.D.] (*insert designation and address*), Defender.

You are given notice that in this action of multiplepoinding

| *Insert date, time and place*) |

is the date, time and place for the first hearing.

Date (*insert date*)   Signed
                                         Sheriff clerk (dispute)

NOTE
If the pursuer fails to return the writ in terms of rule 9.3 of the Ordinary Cause Rules of the Sheriff Court or any party fails to comply with the terms of this notice or to provide the sheriff at the hearing with sufficient information to enable it to be conducted it in terms of rule 35.10 of these rules, the sheriff may make such order or finding against that party so failing as he thinks fit.

NOTE TO BE ADDED WHERE PARTY UNREPRESENTED

NOTE
IF YOU ARE UNCERTAIN WHAT ACTION TO TAKE you should consult a solicitor. You may be eligible for legal aid depending on your income. You can get information about legal aid from a solicitor. You may also obtain advice from any Citizens Advice Bureau or other advice agency.

FORM M6   **Rule 35.10(4)(b)**

Form of citation of person having an interest in the fund in an action of multiplepoinding

CITATION

SHERIFFDOM OF (*insert name of sheriffdom*)   Court ref. no.
AT (*insert place of sheriff court*)

[A.B.], (*insert designation and address*), Pursuer, against [C.D.], (*insert designation and address*), Defender.

(*Insert place and date*) In the above action the court has been advised that you (*insert name and address*) have an interest in (*insert details of the fund in medio*). You are hereby served with a copy of the pleadings in this action, together with Form M4 (notice of appearance).

Form M4 is served on you for use should you wish to intimate that you intend to lodge:

(a) defences challenging the jurisdiction of the court or the competence of the action; or
(b) objections to the condescendence on the fund *in medio*; or
(c) a claim on the fund.

IF YOU WISH TO APPEAR IN THIS ACTION you should consult a solicitor with a view to lodging a notice of appearance (Form M4). The notice of appearance, together with the court fee of £ (*insert amount*) must be lodged with the sheriff clerk at the above address within   days of (*insert date on which service was executed N.B. Rule 5.3(2) relating to postal service*).

NOTE:
IF YOU ARE UNCERTAIN WHAT ACTION TO TAKE you should consult a solicitor. You may be eligible for legal aid depending on your income. You can get information about legal aid from a solicitor. You may also obtain advice from any Citizens Advice Bureau or other advice agency.

PLEASE NOTE THAT IF YOU DO NOTHING IN ANSWER TO THIS DOCUMENT the court may regard you as having no interest in the fund *in medio* and will proceed accordingly.

Signed
[P.Q.], Sheriff officer,
or [X.Y.] (*add designation and business address*)
Solicitor for the pursuer

Rule 36.B1   [1] FORM PI1

Form of initial writ in a personal injuries action

Court ref. no.

INITIAL WRIT

(Personal Injuries Action)

SHERIFFDOM OF (*insert name of sheriffdom*)

AT (*insert place of sheriff court*)

[A.B.] (*design and state any special capacity in which pursuer is suing*), Pursuer

against

[C.D.] (*design and state any special capacity in which defender is being sued*), Defender

The pursuer craves the court to grant decree—

(a) for payment by the defender to the pursuer of the sum of (*amount of sum in words and figures*);

(b) (*enter only if a claim for provisional damages is sought in terms of rule 36.12*) for payment by the defender to the pursuer of (*enter amount in words and figures*) of provisional damages; and

(c) for the expenses of the action.

STATEMENT OF CLAIM

1. The pursuer is (*state designation, address, National Insurance Number (where applicable), occupation and date of birth of pursuer*). (In an action arising out of the death of a relative state designation of the deceased and relation to the pursuer).

2. The defender is (*state designation, address and occupation of the defender*).

3. The court has jurisdiction to hear this claim against the defender because (*state briefly ground of jurisdiction*).

4. (*State briefly the facts necessary to establish the claim*).

5. (*State briefly the personal injuries suffered and the heads of claim. Give names and addresses of medical practitioners and hospitals or other institutions in which the person injured received treatment*).

6. (*State whether claim based on fault at common law or breach of statutory duty; if breach of statutory duty, state provision of enactment*).

(*Signed*)

[A.B.], Pursuer

or [X.Y.], Solicitor for the pursuer (*insert designation and business address*)

NOTE
[1] As inserted by the Act of Sederunt (Ordinary Cause Rules Amendment) (Personal Injuries Actions) 2009 (SSI 2009/285) r.2 (effective November 2, 2009) and amended by the Act of Sederunt (Sheriff Court Rules) (Miscellaneous Amendments) 2010 (SSI 2010/279) para.4 (effective July 29, 2010).

Rule 36.B1   [1] FORM PI2

Form of order of court for recovery of documents in personal injuries action

Court ref. no.

SHERIFFDOM OF (*insert name of sheriffdom*)

AT (*insert place of sheriff court*)

SPECIFICATION OF DOCUMENTS

in the cause

[A.B.] (*designation and address*), Pursuer

against

[C.D.] (*designation and address*), Defender

Date: (*date of posting or other method of service*)

To: (*name and address of party or parties from whom the following documents are sought to be recovered*)

You are hereby required to produce to the agent for the pursuer within seven days of the service on you of this Order:

[*Insert such of the following calls as are required*].

1.   All books, medical records, reports, charts, X-rays, notes and other documents of (*specify the name of each medical practitioner or general practitioner practice named in initial writ in accordance with rule 36.B1(1)(b)*), and relating to the pursuer [*or, as the case may be, the deceased*] from (*insert date*), in order that excerpts may be taken therefrom at the sight of the Commissioner of all entries showing or tending to show the nature, extent and cause of the pursuer's [*or, as the case may be, the deceased's*] injuries when he attended his doctor on or after (*specify date*) and the treatment received by him since that date.

2.   All books, medical records, reports, charts, X-rays, notes and other documents of (*specify, in separate calls, the name of each hospital or other institution named in initial writ in accordance with rule 36.B1(1)(b)*), and relating to the pursuer [*or, as the case may be, the deceased*] from (*insert date*), in order that excerpts may be taken therefrom at the sight of the Commissioner of all entries showing or tending to show the nature, extent and cause of the pursuer's [*or, as the case may be, the deceased's*] injuries when he was admitted to that institution on or about (*specify date*), the treatment received by him since that date and his certificate of discharge, if any.

3.   The medical records and capability assessments held by the defender's occupational health department relating to the pursuer [*or, as the case may be, the deceased*], except insofar as prepared for or in contemplation of litigation, in order that excerpts may be taken therefrom at the sight of the Commissioner of all entries showing or tending to show the nature and extent of any injuries, symptoms and conditions from which the pursuer [*or, as the case may be, the deceased*] was suffering and the nature of any assessment and diagnosis made thereof on or subsequent to (*specify date*).

4.   All wage books, cash books, wage sheets, computer records and other earnings information relating to the pursuer [*or, as the case may be, the deceased*] (N.I. number (*specify*

number)) held by or on behalf of (*specify employer*), for the period (*specify dates commencing not earlier than 26 weeks prior to the date of the accident or the first date of relevant absence, as the case may be*) in order that excerpts may be taken therefrom at the sight of the Commissioner of all entries showing or tending to show—

(a) the pursuer's [*or, as the case may be, the deceased's*] earnings, both gross and net of income tax and employee National Insurance Contributions, over the said period;

(b) the period or periods of the pursuer's [*or, as the case may be, the deceased's*] absence from employment over the said period and the reason for absence;

(c) details of any increases in the rate paid over the period (*specify dates*) and the dates on which any such increases took effect;

(d) the effective date of, the reasons for and the terms (including any terms relative to any pension entitlement) of the termination of the pursuer's [*or, as the case may be, the deceased's*] employment;

(e) the nature and extent of contributions (if any) to any occupational pension scheme made by the pursuer [*or, as the case may be, the deceased*] and his employer;

(f) the pursuer's present entitlement (if any) to any occupational pension and the manner in which said entitlement is calculated.

5.   All accident reports, memoranda or other written communications made to the defender or anyone on his behalf by an employee of the defender who was present at or about the time at which the pursuer [*or, as the case may be, the deceased*] sustained the injuries in respect of which the initial writ in this cause was issued and relevant to the matters contained in the statement of claim.

6.   Any assessment current at the time of the accident referred to in the initial writ or at the time of the circumstances referred to in the initial writ giving rise to the cause of action (as the case may be) undertaken by or on behalf of the defender for the purpose of regulation 3 of the Management of Health and Safety at Work Regulations 1992 and subsequently regulation 3 of the Management of Health and Safety at Work Regulations 1999 [*or (specify the regulations or other legislative provision under which the risk assessment is required)*] in order that excerpts may be taken therefrom at the sight of the Commissioner of all entries relating to the risks posed to workers [*or (specify the matters set out in the statement of claim to which the risk assessment relates)*].

7.   Failing principals, drafts, copies or duplicates of the above or any of them.

(Signature, name and business address of the agent for the pursuer)

NOTES:

1.   The documents recovered will be considered by the parties to the action and they may or may not be lodged in the court process. A written receipt will be given or sent to you by the pursuer, who may thereafter allow them to be inspected by the other parties. The party in whose possession the documents are will be responsible for their safekeeping.

2.   Payment may be made, within certain limits, in respect of claims for outlays incurred in relation to the production of documents. Claims should be made in writing to the person who has obtained an order that you produce the documents.

3.   If you claim that any of the documents produced by you is **confidential** you must still produce such documents but may place them in a separate sealed packet by themselves, marked "CONFIDENTIAL". In that event they must be delivered or sent by post to the sheriff clerk. Any party who wishes to open the sealed packet must apply to the sheriff by motion. A party who makes such an application must intimate the motion to you.

4.   Subject to paragraph 3 above, you may produce these documents by sending them by registered post or by the first class recorded delivery service or registered postal packet, or by hand to (*name and address of the agent for the pursuer*).

CERTIFICATE

(*Date*)

I hereby certify with reference to the above order in the cause (*cause reference number*) and the enclosed specification of documents, served on me and marked respectively X and Y—

    1.   That the documents which are produced and which are listed in the enclosed inventory signed by me and marked Z, are all the documents in my possession falling within the specification. *OR* That I have no documents in my possession falling within the specification.

    2.   That, to the best of my knowledge and belief, there are in existence other documents falling within the specification, but not in my possession. These documents are as follows: (*describe them by reference to the descriptions of documents in the specification*). They were last seen by me on or about (*date*), at (*place*), in the hands of (*name and address of the person*). *OR* That I know of the existence of no documents in the possession of any person, other than me, which fall within the specification.

(*Signed*)

(*Name and address*)

NOTE
   [1] As inserted by the Act of Sederunt (Ordinary Cause Rules Amendment) (Personal Injuries Actions) 2009 (SSI 2009/285) r.2 (effective November 2, 2009).

Rule 36.D1   [1] FORM PI3

Form of docquet for deemed grant of recovery of documents in a personal injuries action

Court ref. no.

Court (*insert court*)

Date (*insert date*)

Commission and diligence for the production and recovery of the documents called for in this specification of documents is deemed to have been granted.

(*Signed*)

Sheriff Clerk (depute)

NOTE
   [1] As inserted by the Act of Sederunt (Ordinary Cause Rules Amendment) (Personal Injuries Actions) 2009 (SSI 2009/285) r.2 (effective November 2, 2009) and amended by the Act of Sederunt (Sheriff Court Rules) (Miscellaneous Amendments) 2010 (SSI 2010/279) para.4 (effective July 29, 2010).

Rule 36.C1   [1] FORM PI4

Form of interlocutor granting authority to raise action based on clinical negligence as an ordinary cause

(*To be inserted on the first page of the initial writ, above the crave(s)*)

Authority

The sheriff, having considered the application of the pursuer [and having heard agents thereon], being satisfied that, although this is a personal injuries action, there are exceptional reasons for not following the personal injuries procedure in Part A1 of Chapter 36 of the Ordinary Cause Rules 1993 such as would justify the granting of a motion under rule 36.F1, grants authority for the cause to proceed as an ordinary cause.

(*Signed*)

Sheriff

Date (*date*)

NOTE
[1] As inserted by the Act of Sederunt (Ordinary Cause Rules Amendment) (Personal Injuries Actions) 2009 (SSI 2009/285) r.2 (effective November 2, 2009).

Rule 36.G1 [1] FORM PI5

Form of timetable

TIMETABLE

Court ref. no.

In the cause

[A.B.], Pursuer

against

[C.D.], Defender

This timetable has effect as if it were an interlocutor of the sheriff

1.   The diet allocated for the proof in this action will begin on (*date*). Subject to any variation under rule 36.H1, this order requires the parties to undertake the conduct of this action within the periods specified in paragraphs 2 to 9 below.

2.   Any motion under rule 20.1 (third party notice) shall be made by (*date*).

3.   Where the pursuer has obtained a commission and diligence for the recovery of documents by virtue of rule 36.D1, the pursuer shall serve an order under rule 28.3 not later than (*date*).

4.   The pursuer shall lodge a statement of valuation of claim under rule 36.J1 not later than (*date*).

5.   For the purposes of rule 36.G1, the adjustment period shall end on (*date*).

6.   The pursuer shall lodge a record not later than (*date*).

7.   The defender and any third party convened in the action shall lodge a statement of valuation of claim under rule 36.J1 not later than (*date*).

8.   Not later than (*date*) parties shall lodge lists of witnesses and productions.

9.   Not later than (*date*) the pursuer shall lodge a pre-proof minute under rule 36.K1.

NOTE
[1] As inserted by the Act of Sederunt (Ordinary Cause Rules Amendment) (Personal Injuries Actions) 2009 (SSI 2009/285) r.2 (effective November 2, 2009).

Rule 36.J1 [1] FORM PI6

Form of statement of valuation of claim

Court ref. no.

Head of claim	Components	Valuation
Solatium	Past	£x
	Future	£x
Interest on past solatium	Percentage applied to past solatium (*state percentage rate*)	£x

Past wage loss	Date from which wage loss claimed: (*date*)	£x
	Date to which wage loss claimed: (*date*)	
	Rate of net wage loss (per week, per month or per annum)	
Interest on past wage loss	Percentage applied to past wage loss: (*state percentage rate*)	£x
Future wage loss	Multiplier: (*state multiplier*)	£x
	Multiplicand: (*state multiplicand and show how calculated*)	
	Discount factor applied (if appropriate): (*state factor*)	
	Or specify any other method of calculation	
Past services	Date from which services claimed: (*date*)	£x
	Date to which services claimed: (*date*)	
	Nature of services: (............)	
	Person by whom services provided: (............)	
	Hours per week services provided: (............)	
	Net hourly rate claimed: (..........)	
	Total amount claimed: (..........)	
	Interest	
Future loss of capacity to provide personal services	Multiplier: (*insert multiplier*)	£x
	Multiplicand: (*insert multiplicand, showing how calculated*)	

Needs and other expenses	One off	£x
	Multiplier: (*insert multiplier*)	
	Multiplicand: (*insert multiplicand*)	
	Interest	
Any other heads as appropriate (*specify*)		
Total		£x (*insert total valuation of claim*)
List of Supporting Documents—		

NOTE

[1] As inserted by the Act of Sederunt (Ordinary Cause Rules Amendment) (Personal Injuries Actions) 2009 (SSI 2009/285) r.2 (effective November 2, 2009) and amended by the Act of Sederunt (Sheriff Court Rules) (Miscellaneous Amendments) 2010 (SSI 2010/279) para.4 (effective July 29, 2010).

Rule 36.K1 [1] FORM PI7

Minute of pre-proof conference

Court ref. no.

SHERIFFDOM OF (*insert sheriffdom*) AT (*insert place*)

Joint minute of pre-proof conference

in the cause

[*A.B.*], Pursuer

against

[*C.D.*], Defender

[E.F.] for the pursuer and

[G.H.] for the defender hereby state to the court:

1.   That the pre-proof conference was held in this case [*at (place)* or *by (telephone conference or video conference or other remote means)*] on [*date*].

2.   That the following persons were present—
      (*State names and designations of persons attending conference*)

3.   That the following persons were available to provide instructions by telephone or video conference—
      (*State names and designations or persons available to provide instructions by telephone or video conference*)

4.   That the persons participating in the conference discussed settlement of the action.

5.   That the following questions were addressed—

Section 1

		Yes	No
1.	Is the diet of proof still required?		
2.	If the answer to question 1 is "yes", does the defender admit liability? (If "no", complete section 2) If yes, does the defender plead contributory negligence? If yes, is the degree of contributory negligence agreed? If yes, state % degree of fault attributed to the pursuer.		
3.	If the answer to question 1 is "yes", is the quantum of damages agreed? (If "no", complete section 3)		

Section 2

[To be inserted only if the proof is still required]

It is estimated that the hearing will last   days

NB. If the estimate is more than 2 days then this should be brought to the attention of the sheriff clerk. This may affect prioritisation of the case.

During the course of the pre-proof conference, the pursuer called on the defender to agree certain facts, questions of law and matters of evidence.

Those calls, and the defender's responses, are as follows—

Call	Response	
	Admitted	*Denied*
1.		
2.		
3.		
4.		

During the course of the pre-proof conference, the defender called on the pursuer to agree certain facts, questions of law and matters of evidence.

Those calls, and the pursuer's responses, are as follows—

Call	Response	
	Admitted	*Denied*
1.		
2.		
3.		
4.		

Section 3

Quantum of damages

Please indicate where agreement has been reached on an element of damages.

Head of claim	*Components*	*Not agreed*	*Agreed at*
Solatium	Past		
	Future		
Interest on past solatium	Percentage applied to past solatium (*state percentage*)		

Past wage loss	Date from which wage lost claimed		
	Date to which wage loss claimed		
	Rate of net wage loss (per week, per month or per annum)		
Interest on past wage loss			
Future wage loss	Multiplier		
	Multiplicand (showing how calculated)		
Past necessary services	Date from which services claimed		
	Date to which services claimed		
	Hours per week services provided		
	Net hourly rate claimed		
Past personal services	Date from which services claimed		
	Date to which services claimed		
	Hours per week services provided		
	Net hourly rate claimed		
Interest on past services			
Future necessary services	Multiplier		
	Multiplicand (showing how calculated)		
Future personal services	Multiplier		
	Multiplicand (showing how calculated)		
Needs and other expenses	One off		
	Multiplier		
	Multiplicand (showing how calculated)		
Any other heads as appropriate (specify)			

Signed by each party/his or her solicitor

NOTE
[1] As inserted by the Act of Sederunt (Ordinary Cause Rules Amendment) (Personal Injuries Actions) 2009 (SSI 2009/285) r.2 (effective November 2, 2009) and amended by the Act of Sederunt (Sheriff Court Rules) (Miscellaneous Amendments) 2010 (SSI 2010/279) para.4 (effective July 29, 2010).

Rule 36.3(2)   FORM D1

Form of intimation to connected person in damages action

SHERIFFDOM OF (*insert name of sheriffdom*)   Court ref.no.

AT (*insert place of sheriff court*)

You are given NOTICE that an action has been raised in the above sheriff court by (*insert name and designation of pursuer*) against (*insert name and designation of defender*).
A copy of the initial writ is attached.

It is believed that you may have a title or interest to sue the said (*insert name of defender*) in an action based upon [the injuries from which the late (*insert name and designation*) died] [or the death of the late (*insert name and designation*)]. You may therefore be entitled to enter this action as an additional pursuer. If you wish to do so, you may apply by lodging a minute with the sheriff clerk at the above address to be sisted as an additional pursuer within (*insert the appropriate period of notice*) days of (*insert the date on which service was executed N.B. Rule 5.3(2) relating to postal service*).

Signed
Solicitor for the pursuer

NOTE
The minute must be lodged with the sheriff clerk with the court fee of (*insert amount*) and a motion seeking leave for the minute to be received and for answers to be lodged. When lodging the minute you must present to the sheriff clerk a copy of the initial writ and this intimation.

IF YOU ARE UNCERTAIN WHAT ACTION TO TAKE you should consult a solicitor. You may be eligible for legal aid depending on your income, and you can obtain information about legal aid from any solicitor. You may also obtain advice from any Citizens Advice Bureau or other advice agency.

Rule 36.17(1)   FORM D2

Form of receipt for payment into court

RECEIPT

In the Sheriff Court of (*insert name of sheriffdom*) at (*insert place of sheriff court*) in the cause, (*state names of parties or other appropriate description*) [A.B.] (*insert designation*) has this day paid into court the sum of (*insert sum concerned*) being a payment into court in terms of rule 36.14 of the Ordinary Cause Rules of the Sheriff Court of money which in an action of damages, has become payable to a person under legal disability.

[*If the payment is made under rule 36.15(c) add:* [the custody of which money has been accepted at the request of (*insert name of court making request*).]

Date (*insert date*)   Signed
Sheriff clerk (depute)

Rule 37.2(2)   [1] FORM P1

Form of advertisement in an action of declarator under section 1(1) of the Presumption of Death (Scotland) Act 1977

(insert such facts relating to the missing person as set out in the initial writ as the sheriff may specify).

Sheriff Court (*insert address*)   Court ref. no.

An action has been raised in (*insert name of sheriff court*) by [A.B.], Pursuer, to declare that [C.D.], Defender, whose last known address was (*insert last known address of [C.D.]*) is dead.

Any person wishing to defend the action must apply to do so by (*insert date, being [21] days after the date of the advertisement*) by lodging a minute seeking to be sisted a a party to the action with the sheriff clerk at the above address.

A copy of the initial writ may be obtained from the sheriff clerk at the above address.

Date (*insert date*)   Signed

                       [X.Y.] (*add designation and business address*) Solicitor for the pursuer *or* [P.Q.] Sheriff officer

NOTE

[1] As amended by the Act of Sederunt (Sheriff Court Ordinary Cause Rules Amendment) (Miscellaneous) 2000 (SSI 2000/239) (effective October 2, 2000).

Rule 37.2(4)   FORM P2

Form of intimation to missing person's spouse and children or nearest known relative

To (*insert name and address as in warrant*)   Court ref. no.

You are given notice that in this action the pursuer craves the court to declare that (*insert the name and last known address of missing person*) is dead. A copy of the initial writ is enclosed.

If you wish to appear as a party, and make an application under section 1 (5) of the Presumption of Death (Scotland) Act 1977 craving the court to make any determination or appointment not sought by the pursuer, you must lodge a minute with the sheriff clerk at (*insert address of sheriff clerk*).

Your minute must be lodged within [   ] days of (*insert the date on which intimation was given N.B. Rule 5.3(2) relating to postal service or intimation*).

Date (*insert date*)   Signed

                       Solicitor for the pursuer

                       (*add designation and business address*)

NOTE

If you decide to lodge a minute it may be in your best interest to consult a solicitor. The minute should be lodged with the sheriff clerk with the appropriate fee of £ (*insert amount*) and a copy of this intimation.

IF YOU ARE UNCERTAIN WHAT ACTION TO TAKE you should consult a solicitor. You may be entitled to legal aid depending on your financial circumstances. You can get information about legal aid from a solicitor. You may also obtain advice from any Citizen's Advice Bureau or other advice agency.

Rule 38.3(1A)   [1] FORM E1

Form of reference to the European Court

REQUEST
for
PRELIMINARY RULING
of
THE COURT OF JUSTICE OF THE EUROPEAN COMMUNITIES
from
THE SHERIFFDOM OF *insert name of sheriffdom*) at (*insert place of court*)
in the cause
[A.B.] (*insert designation and address*), Pursuer
against
[C.D.] (*insert designation and address*), Defender

[Here set out a clear and succinct statement of the case giving rise to the request for the ruling of the European Court in order to enable the European Court to consider and understand the issues of Community law raised and to enable governments of Member States and other interested parties to submit observations. The statement of the case should include:

    (a) particulars of the parties;
    (b) the history of the dispute between the parties;
    (c) the history of the proceedings;
    (d) the relevant facts as agreed by the parties or found by the court or, failing such agreement or finding, the contentions of the parties on such facts;

    (e) the nature of the issues of law and fact between the parties;

    (f) the Scots law, so far as relevant;

    (g) the Treaty provisions or other acts, instruments or rules of Community law concerned; and

    (h) an explanation of why the reference is being made.]

The preliminary ruling of the Court of Justice of the European Communities is accordingly requested on the following questions:

    1, 2, etc. [Here set out the question on which the ruling is sought, identifying the Treaty provisions or other acts, instruments or rules of Community law concerned.]
    Dated the day of 20 .

NOTE
[1] As substituted by the Act of Sederunt (Sheriff Court Ordinary Cause Rules Amendment) (Miscellaneous) 2000 (SSI 2000/239) (effective October 2, 2000).

Rule 41.5   [1] FORM PA1

Form of certificate of delivery of documents to chief constable

(*Insert place and date*) I, hereby certify that upon the day of I duly delivered to (insert name and address) chief constable of (*insert name of constabulary*) (*insert details of the documents delivered*). This I did by (*state method of delivery*).

Signed

Solicitor/sheriff officer

(*add designation and business address*)

NOTE
[1] As inserted by the Act of Sederunt (Ordinary Cause Rules) (Applications under the Protection from Abuse (Scotland) Act 2001) 2002 (SSI 2002/128), para. 2(3) and Sched.

Rule 43.1(2)   [1]FORM OFT1

Form of notice of intimation to the Office of Fair Trading

Date: (*date of posting or other method of intimation*)

To: The Office of Fair Trading

TAKE NOTICE

(*Name and address of pursuer or defender*) has brought an action against [*or* has defended an action brought by] (*name and address of defender or pursuer*). The action raises an issue under Article 81 or 82 of the Treaty establishing the European Community. A copy of the initial writ is [*or* pleadings and interlocutor allowing intimation are] attached.

If you wish to submit written observations to the court, these should be addressed to the sheriff clerk (*insert address of sheriff clerk*) and must be lodged within 21 days of (*insert date on which intimation was given. N.B. rule 5.3(2) relating to postal service or intimation*).

If you wish to submit oral observations to the court, you must lodge a minute with the sheriff clerk (*insert address of sheriff clerk*) for leave to do so. Your minute must be lodged within 21 days of (*insert date on which intimation was given. N.B. rule 5.3(2) relating to postal service or intimation*).

Date (*insert date*)   (*Signed*)
                                  Solicitor for pursuer/defender

NOTE
[1] As inserted by Act of Sederunt (Ordinary Cause Rules) Amendment (Causes Relating to Articles 81 and 82 of the Treaty Establishing the European Community) 2006 (SSI 2006/293) (effective June 16, 2006).

Rule 30.6(1) APPENDIX 2

FORMS FOR EXTRACT DECREES

FORM 1

Form of extract decree for payment

EXTRACT DECREE FOR PAYMENT

Sheriff Court   Court ref. no.

Date of decree   * In absence

Pursuer(s)   Defender(s)

The sheriff granted decree against the   for payment to the   of the undernoted sums.

Sum decerned for £   with interest at   per cent a year from   until payment and expenses against the   of £   .

* A time to pay direction was made under section 1(1) of the Debtors (Scotland) Act 1987.

* The amount is payable by instalments of £   per   commencing within   of intimation of this extract decree.

* The amount is payable by lump sum within   of intimation of this extract decree.

This extract is warrant for all lawful execution hereon.

Date   Sheriff clerk (depute)

* Delete as appropriate.

FORM 2

Form of extract decree ad factum praestandum

EXTRACT DECREE *AD FACTUM PRAESTANDUM*

Sheriff Court   Court ref. no.

Date of decree   * In absence

Pursuer(s)   Defender(s)

The sheriff ordained the defender(s)

and granted decree against the   for payment of expenses of £   .

This extract is warrant for all lawful execution hereon.

Date   Sheriff clerk (depute)

* Delete as appropriate.

FORM 3

Form of extract decree of removing

EXTRACT DECREE OF REMOVING

Sheriff Court   Court ref. no.

Date of decree   * In absence

Pursuer(s)   Defender(s)

The sheriff ordained the defender(s) to remove* himself/herself/themselves and his/her/their sub-tenants, dependents and others, and all effects from the premises at the undernoted address and to leave those premises vacant** [and that after a charge of   days].

In the event that the defender(s) fail(s) to remove the sheriff granted warrant to sheriff officers to eject the defender(s), sub-tenants, dependents and others, with all effects, from those premises so as to leave them vacant.

The Sheriff granted decree against the   for payment of expenses of £   .

Full address of premises:—

This extract is warrant for all lawful execution hereon.

Date   Sheriff clerk (depute)

** Delete as appropriate.
** Delete if period of charge is not specified in the decree.

FORM 4

Form of extract decree of declarator

EXTRACT DECREE OF DECLARATOR

Sheriff Court   Court ref. no.

Date of decree   * In absence

Pursuer(s)   Defender(s)

The sheriff found and declared that

and granted decree against the   for payment of expenses of £   .

This extract is warrant for all lawful execution hereon.

Date   Sheriff clerk (depute)

* Delete as appropriate.

FORM 5

Form of extract decree of furthcoming

EXTRACT DECREE OF FURTHCOMING

Sheriff Court   Court ref. no.

Date of decree   * In absence

Date of original decree

Pursuer(s)   Defender(s)/Arrestee(s)

Common Debtor(s)

The sheriff granted against the arrestee(s) for payment of the undernoted sums.

Sum decerned for £   or such other sum(s) as may be owing by the arrestee(s) to the common debtor(s) by virtue of the original decree dated above in favour of the pursuer(s) against the common debtor(s).

Expenses of £   * payable out of the arrested fund / payable by the common debtor(s).

This extract is warrant for all lawful execution hereon.

Date   Sheriff clerk (depute)

* Delete as appropriate.

FORM 6

Form of extract decree of absolvitor

EXTRACT DECREE OF ABSOLVITOR

Sheriff Court   Court ref. no.

Date of first warrant   Date of decree

Pursuer(s)   Defender(s)

(Insert the nature of crave(s) in the above action)

The sheriff absolved the   defender(s)

and granted decree against the   for payment of expenses of £   .

This extract is warrant for all lawful execution hereon.

Date   Sheriff clerk (depute)

FORM 7

Form of extract decree of dismissal

EXTRACT DECREE OF DISMISSAL

Sheriff Court   Court ref. no.

Date of first warrant   Date of decree

Pursuer(s)   Defender(s)

The sheriff dismissed the action against the   defender(s)

and granted decree against the   for payment of expenses of £   .

    * This extract is warrant for all lawful execution hereon.

Date   Sheriff clerk (depute)

     * Delete as appropriate.

FORM 8

[Repealed by the Act of Sederunt (Sheriff Court Ordinary Cause Rules Amendment) (Miscellaneous) 1996 (S.I. 1996 No. 2445) (effective November 1, 1996).]

FORM 9

Form of extract decree

EXTRACT DECREE

Sheriff Court   Court ref. no.

Date of decree   * In absence

Pursuer(s)   Defender(s)

The sheriff

and granted decree against the   for payment of expenses of £   .

    This extract is warrant for all lawful execution hereon.

Date   Sheriff clerk (depute)

     * Delete as appropriate.

¹ FORM 10

Form of extract decree of divorce

EXTRACT DECREE OF DIVORCE

Sheriff Court   Court Ref No

Date of Decree   *In absence

Pursuer   Defender

Date of parties marriage   Place of parties marriage

The sheriff granted decree

(1) divorcing the defender from the Pursuer;

*(2) ordering that the following child(ren):

        Full name(s)   Date(s) of birth

Reside with the *pursuer/defender and finding the *pursuer/defender entitled to be in contact with the following child(ren): as follows:

All in terms of the Children (Scotland) Act 1995.

*(3) ordaining payment
    *(a)   by the   to the   of a periodical allowance of £ per
    *(b)   by the   to the   of a capital sum of £
    *(c)   by the   to the   of £   per   as aliment for each child until that
           child attains years of age, said sum payable in advance and beginning at the date of this
           decree with interest thereon at the rate of per cent a year until payment;
    *(d)   by the   to the   of £ of expenses;

*(4) finding the   liable to the   in expenses as the same may be subsequently taxed.

                 This extract is warrant for all lawful execution hereon.

Date: (*insert date*)   Sheriff Clerk (depute)
       *Delete as appropriate.

¹ FORM 11

Form of extract decree of separation and aliment

EXTRACT DECREE OF SEPARATION AND ALIMENT

Sheriff Court   Court Ref No

Date of Decree   *In absence

Pursuer   Defender

The sheriff found and declared that the pursuer is entitled to live separately from the defender from the date of decree and for all time thereafter.

The Sheriff ordered that the following child(ren):

        Full name(s)   Date(s) of birth

Reside with the *pursuer/defender

And found the *pursuer/defender entitled to be in contact with the following child(ren):

as follows:

All in terms of the Children (Scotland) Act 1995.

*The sheriff ordained payment by the   to the   of £   per   as aliment for the   , said sum payable in advance and beginning at the date of this decree with interest thereon at   per cent a year until payment.

*The sheriff ordained payment by the   to the   of £   per   as aliment for each child, until that child attains   years of age, said sum payable in advance and beginning at the date of this decree with interest thereon at   per cent a year until payment;

and granted decree against the   for payment of £   .

This extract is warrant for all lawful execution hereon.

Date: (*insert date*)   Sheriff Clerk (Depute)*Delete as appropriate.

[1] FORM 12

Form of extract decree: Residence Order/Contact Order and aliment

EXTRACT DECREE OF RESIDENCE ORDER/CONTACT ORDER AND ALIMENT

Sheriff Court   Court Ref No

Date of Decree   *In absence

Pursuer   Defender

The Sheriff granted decree against the *pursuer/defender.

The Sheriff ordered that the following child(ren):

Full name(s)   Date(s) of birth

reside with the *pursuer/defender and found the *pursuer/defender entitled to be in contact with the following child(ren):

as follows:

All in terms of the Children (Scotland) Act 1995.

*The sheriff ordained payment by the   to the of £   per   as aliment for each child, until that child attains   years of age, said sum payable in advance and beginning at the date of this decree with interest thereon at   per cent a year until payment;

and granted decree with interest thereon at per cent a year until payment;and granted decree against the for payment of expenses of £   .

This extract is warrant for all lawful execution hereon.

Date: (*insert date*)   Sheriff Clerk (Depute)
        *Delete as appropriate.

NOTE

[1] As substituted by the Act of Sederunt (Sheriff Court Ordinary Cause Rules Amendment) (Miscellaneous) 2000 (S.S.I. 2000 No. 239) (effective October 2, 2000).

SCHEDULE OF TIMETABLE UNDER PERSONAL INJURIES PROCEDURE

Steps referred to under rule 36.G1(1A)	Period of time within which action must be carried out*
Application for a third party notice under rule 20.1(rule 36.G1(1A)(a))	Not later than 28 days after defences have been lodged
Pursuer executing a commission for recovery of documents under rule 36.D1 (rule 36.G1(1A)(b))	Not later than 28 days after defences have been lodged
Parties adjusting their pleadings (rule 36.G1(1A)(c))	Not later than 8 weeks after defences have been lodged
Pursuer lodging a statement of valuation of claim in process (rule 36.G1(1A)(d))	Not later than 8 weeks after defences have been lodged
Pursuer lodging a record (rule 36.G1(1A)(e))	Not later than 10 weeks after defences have been lodged
Defender (and any third party to the action) lodging a statement of valuation of claim in process (rule 36.G1(1A)(f))	Not later than 12 weeks after defences have been lodged
Parties lodging in process a list of witnesses together with any productions upon which they wish to rely (rule 36.G1(1A)(g))	Not later than 8 weeks before the date assigned for the proof
Pursuer lodging in process the minute of the pre-proof conference (rule 36.G1(1A)(h))	Not later than 21 days before the date assigned for the proof

*NOTE: Where there is more than one defender in an action, references in the above table to defences having been lodged should be read as references to the first lodging of defences.

NOTE
[1] As inserted by the Act of Sederunt (Ordinary Cause Rules Amendment) (Personal Injuries Actions) 2009 (SSI 2009/285) r.2 (effective November 2, 2009) and substituted by the Act of Sederunt (Sheriff Court Rules) (Miscellaneous Amendments) 2010 (SSI 2010/279) para.4 (effective July 29, 2010).

Sheriff Courts (Civil Jurisdiction and Procedure) (Scotland) Act 1963

(1963 c. 22)

An Act to increase the amount by reference to which actions are classified as summary causes in the sheriff court in Scotland; to increase the amount by reference to which the small debt jurisdiction of the sheriff is limited; to amend the law with regard to the bringing of actions between spouses for interim aliment of small amounts in the sheriff's small debt court and with regard to the jurisdiction of the sheriff in such actions brought as aforesaid; and for purposes connected with the matters aforesaid.
[10th July 1963]

1, 2. [*Repealed by the Sheriff Courts (Scotland) Act 1971, Sch.2.*]

Actions for aliment of small amounts

[1] **3.**—(1) An action under section 2 of the Family Law (Scotland) Act 1985 for aliment only (whether or not expenses are also sought) may be brought before the sheriff as a summary cause if the aliment claimed in the action does not exceed—

    (a) in respect of a child under the age of 18 years, the sum of £35 per week; and

    (b) in any other case, the sum of £70 per week;

and any provision in any enactment limiting the jurisdiction of the sheriff in a summary cause by reference to any amount, or limiting the period for which a decree granted by him shall have effect, shall not apply in relation to such an action.

    (2) *[Repealed by the Civil Jurisdiction and Judgments Act 1982, Sch.14.]*

    [2] (3) The Secretary of State may by order vary the amounts prescribed in paragraphs (a) and (b) of subsection (1) above.

    (4) The power to make an order under subsection (3) above shall be exercisable by statutory instrument subject to annulment in pursuance of a resolution of either House of Parliament and shall include power to vary or revoke any order made thereunder.

NOTES

[1] Substituted by the Family Law (Scotland) Act 1985, s.23.

[2] As amended by SI 1999/678, Art. 2, Sch.(effective May 19, 1999).

Citation, construction and commencement

4.—(1) This Act may be cited as the Sheriff Courts (Civil Jurisdiction and Procedure) (Scotland) Act 1963.

    (2) In this Act the expression "the principal Act" means the Sheriff Courts (Scotland) Act 1907, as amended by any other enactment, and the principal Act and this Act shall be construed together as one.

    (3) This Act shall come into operation on 1st October 1963.

Sheriff Courts (Scotland) Act 1971

(1971 c. 58)

An Act to amend the law with respect to sheriff courts in Scotland, and for purposes connected therewith.   [27th July 1971]

PART I

CONSTITUTION, ORGANISATION AND ADMINISTRATION

General duty of the Secretary of State

Secretary of State to be responsible for organisation and administration of sheriff courts

1. Subject to the provisions of this Act, the Secretary of State shall be under a duty to secure the efficient organisation and administration of the sheriff courts, and for the purpose of carrying out that duty shall have, in addition to any functions conferred on him by or under any other enactment, the functions conferred on him by the following provisions of this Act.

Sheriffdoms

Power of Secretary of State to alter sheriffdoms

2.—(1) The Secretary of State may by order alter the boundaries of sheriffdoms, form new sheriffdoms, or provide for the abolition of sheriffdoms existing at the time of the making of the order.

(2) An order under subsection (1) above may contain all such provisions as appear to the Secretary of State to be necessary or expedient for rendering the order of full effect and any incidental, supplemental or consequential provisions which appear to him to be necessary or expedient for the purposes of the order, including, but without prejudice to the generality of the foregoing words—

    (a) provision for the abolition of any office,

    (b) provisions amending, repealing or revoking any enactment (whether passed or made before or after the commencement of this Act, and including any enactment contained in or made under this Act).

(3) Where an order under subsection (1) above includes, by virtue of subsection (2)(a) above, provision for the abolition of any office, then—

    (a) that provision shall have effect notwithstanding the provisions of any enactment (including any enactment contained in this Act), or of any instrument in terms of which any person holds that office;

[1] (b) the Secretary of State may, with the concurrence of the Minister for the Civil Service, pay to or in respect of any person who suffers loss of employment, or loss or diminution of emoluments, which is attributable to the said provision such amount by way of compensation as may appear to the Secretary of State to be reasonable in all the circumstances but no payment shall be made under this provision to or in respect of any person who is mentioned in section 51(2) of the Scotland Act 1998.

(4) The power to make orders under subsection (1) above shall be exercisable by statutory instrument, but no order shall be made under that subsection unless a draft of the order has been laid before Parliament and approved by a resolution of each House of Parliament.

NOTE
[1] As amended by SI 1999/1820, art.4, Sch.2, para.50 (effective July 1, 1999).

Sheriff court districts and places where sheriff courts are to be held

Sheriff court districts and places where sheriff courts are to be held

    3.—(1) Subject to any alterations made by an order under section 2(1) of this Act or under subsection (2) below—

    (a) the sheriff court districts existing immediately before the commencement of this Act shall continue to exist after such commencement, and

    (b) sheriff courts shall, after such commencement, continue to be held at the places at which they were in use to be held immediately before such commencement.

(2) The Secretary of State may by order—

    (a) alter the boundaries of sheriff court districts, form new districts, or provide for the abolition of districts existing at the time of the making of the order;

    (b) provide that sheriff courts shall be held, or shall cease to be held, at any place.

(3) An order under subsection (2) above may contain all such provisions as appear to the Secretary of State to be necessary or expedient for rendering the order of full effect and any incidental, supplemental or consequential provisions which appear to him to be necessary or expedient for the purposes of the order, including, but without prejudice to the generality of the foregoing words, provisions amending, repealing or revoking any enactment (whether passed or made before or after the commencement of this Act, and including any enactment contained in or made under this Act).

[1] (4) The Secretary of State may, with the concurrence of the Minister for the Civil Service, pay to or in respect of any person who suffers loss of

employment, or loss or diminution of emoluments, which is attributable to an order under subsection (2) above such amount by way of compensation as may appear to the Secretary of State to be reasonable in all the circumstances but no payment shall be made under this provision to or in respect of any person who is mentioned in section 51(2) of the Scotland Act 1998.

(5) The power to make orders under subsection (2) above shall be exercisable by statutory instrument.

(6) Without prejudice to subsection (1) above, any enactment or other instrument in force immediately before the commencement of this Act shall, to the extent that it fixes sheriff court districts or the places at which sheriff courts are to be held, cease to have effect.

NOTE
[1] As amended by SI 1999/1820, art.4, Sch.2, para.50 (effective July 1, 1999).

Sheriffs principal and sheriffs

Offices of sheriff principal and sheriff

4.—(1) The office of sheriff (that is to say, the office known formerly as the office of sheriff depute, but known immediately before the commencement of this Act as the office of sheriff) shall be known as the office of sheriff principal, the office of sheriff substitute shall be known as the office of sheriff, and the office of honorary sheriff substitute shall be known as the office of honorary sheriff.

(2) Accordingly, any enactment or other document in force or having effect at the commencement of this Act which refers whether expressly or by implication, or which falls to be construed as referring, or as including a reference, to the office of sheriff (as defined in subsection (1) above), or to the office of sheriff substitute, or to the holder of any of the said offices, shall be construed in accordance with subsection (1) above.

[1] (3) Section 28 of the Interpretation Act 1889, shall not apply for the interpretation of this Act.

NOTE
[1] As amended by the Interpretation Act 1978 (c.30), Sch.3.

Qualification for offices of sheriff principal and sheriff

5.—(1) A person shall not be appointed to the office of sheriff principal or sheriff unless he is, and has been for at least ten years, legally qualified.

For the purposes of this subsection, a person shall be legally qualified if he is an advocate or a solicitor.

[1] (2) Without prejudice to sections 11(3) and 11A of this Act, in this section "sheriff principal" does not include a temporary sheriff principal and "sheriff" does not include a part-time sheriff or an honorary sheriff.

NOTE
[1] As amended by the Bail, Judicial Appointments etc. (Scotland) Act 2000 (asp.9), s.12 and Sch., para.1.

[1] Retiring age for sheriff principal and sheriff]

5A.—(1) A sheriff principal or sheriff shall vacate his office on the day on which he attains the age of 70.

(2) Subsection (1) above is subject to section 26(4) to (6) of the Judicial Pensions and Retirement Act 1993 (power to authorise continuance in office up to the age of 75).

[2] (3) Without prejudice to sections 11(4A) and (4B) and 11B(3) of this Act, in this section, "sheriff principal" does not include a temporary sheriff principal and "sheriff" does not include a part-time sheriff.

NOTES
[1] As inserted by the Judicial Pensions and Retirement Act 1993 (c.8), Sch.6, para.10.
[2] As inserted by the Bail, Judicial Appointments etc. (Scotland) Act 2000 (asp 9) s.12 and Sch., para.1.

Disqualification of sheriffs principal and sheriffs
6.—(1) A sheriff principal to whom this subsection applies, or a sheriff, shall not, so long as he holds office as such—
    (a) engage, whether directly or indirectly, in any private practice or business, or be in partnership with or employed by, or act as agent for, any person so engaged;
    (b) [*Repealed by the Law Reform (Miscellaneous Provisions) (Scotland) Act 1985 (c.73), s.20 and Sch.4.*]
(2) Subsection (1) above shall apply to any person holding the office of sheriff principal who is appointed to that office after the commencement of this Act and on whose appointment the Secretary of State directs that that subsection shall apply to him.
(3) The sheriff principal of any sheriffdom, not being either a sheriff principal who is restricted by the terms of his appointment from engaging in private practice or a sheriff principal to whom subsection (1) above applies, shall not, so long as he holds office as such, advise, or act as an advocate in any court, in any cause civil or criminal arising within or coming from that sheriffdom.
(4) Any reference in any enactment passed before the commencement of this Act to a sheriff principal who is restricted by the terms of his appointment from engaging in private practice shall be construed as including a reference to a sheriff principal to whom subsection (1) above applies.
[1] (5) Without prejudice to the giving of any direction under section 11 (5) of this Act, in this section "sheriff principal" does not include a temporary sheriff principal and "sheriff" does not include a part-time sheriff or an honorary sheriff.

NOTE
[1] As amended by the Bail, Judicial Appointments etc. (Scotland) Act 2000 (asp 9) s.12 and Sch., para.1.

Jurisdiction of sheriff
[1] 7.—(1) For removal of doubt it is hereby declared that a sheriff by virtue of his appointment as such, has and is entitled to exercise the jurisdiction and powers attaching to the office of sheriff in all parts of the sheriffdom for which he is appointed.
(2) Without prejudice to section 11A(4) of this Act, in this section, "sheriff" does not include a part-time sheriff.

NOTE
[1] Existing text renumbered as s.7(1) and s.7(2) inserted by the Bail, Judicial Appointments etc. (Scotland) Act 2000 (asp 9) s.12 and Sch., para.1.

Sheriff may be appointed to assist Secretary of State
8. Notwithstanding anything in section 6 of this Act, a person holding the office of sheriff principal or sheriff may, without relinquishing that office, be appointed by the Secretary of State to assist him to discharge the functions vested in him in relation to the organisation and administration of the sheriff courts, but a person so appointed shall not perform his duties as the holder of the office of sheriff principal or sheriff, as the case may be, while he retails that appointment.

Functions of Secretary of State in relation to sheriffs principal, sheriffs, etc.

Power of Secretary of State to give administrative directions

[1] **9.**—(1) For the purpose of securing the efficient organisation and administration of the sheriff courts and, in particular, the speedy and efficient disposal of business in those courts, the Secretary of State may give such directions of an administrative nature as appear to him to be necessary or expedient, and any sheriff principal or sheriff, and any officer or servant engaged in the administration of the sheriff courts, to whom a direction is given under this section shall, subject to the provisions of this Act, give effect to that direction.

(2) In this section, "sheriff" does not include a part-time sheriff.

NOTE

[1] Existing text renumbered as s.9(1) and s.9(2) inserted by the Bail, Judicial Appointments etc. (Scotland) Act 2000 (asp 9) s.12 and Sch., para.1.

Scottish Ministers may authorise sheriff principal or direct sheriff to act in another sheriffdom

10.—[1,2] (1) Where a vacancy occurs in the office of sheriff principal of any sheriffdom the Scottish Ministers may, if it appears to them expedient so to do in order to avoid delay in the administration of justice in that sheriffdom, authorise the sheriff principal of any other sheriffdom to perform the duties of sheriff principal in the first-mentioned sheriffdom (in addition to his own duties) until the Scottish Ministers otherwise decide.

[1,2] (1A) Where the sheriff principal of any sheriffdom is unable to perform, or rules that he is precluded from performing, all of, or some part of, his duties as sheriff principal the Scottish Ministers may authorise the sheriff principal of any other sheriffdom to perform the duties of sheriff principal, or as the case may be that part of those duties, in the first-mentioned sheriffdom (in addition to his own duties) until the Scottish Ministers otherwise decides.

[2] (2) Where as regards any sheriffdom—

    (a) a sheriff is by reason of illness or otherwise unable to perform his duties as sheriff, or

    (b) a vacancy occurs in the office of sheriff, or

    (c) any other reason it appears to the Scottish Ministers expedient so to do in order to avoid delay in the administration of justice in that sheriffdom,

the Scottish Ministers may direct a sheriff appointed for any other sheriffdom to perform, in accordance with the terms of the direction, the duties of sheriff in the first-mentioned sheriffdom (in addition to or in place of his own duties) until otherwise directed by the Scottish Ministers, and any sheriff to whom a direction is given under this subsection shall give effect to that direction.

(3) A sheriff principal authorised, or a sheriff directed, under this section to perform duties in any sheriffdom shall for that purpose, without the necessity of his receiving a commission in that behalf, have and be entitled to exercise the jurisdiction and powers attaching to the office of sheriff principal or, as the case may be, sheriff in that sheriffdom.

[2] (4) The Scottish Ministers may, pay to a sheriff principal or a sheriff, in respect of any duties performed by that sheriff principal or sheriff (in addition to his own duties) in pursuance of an authority or direction under this section, such remuneration and allowances as may appear to the Secretary of State, with the consent of the Treasury to be reasonable in all the circumstances.

[3] (5) In this section "sheriff" does not include an honorary or a part-time sheriff.

NOTES
[1] Subss (1) and (1A) substituted for subs. (1) by the Law Reform (Miscellaneous Provisions) (Scotland) Act 1980, s.10(a).
[2] As amended by SI 1999/1820, Art.4, Sch. para.50 (effective July 1, 1999).
[3] As amended by the Bail, Judicial Appointments etc. (Scotland) Act 2000 (asp.9), s.12 and Sch., para.1.

Secretary of State may appoint temporary sheriffs principal and sheriffs

11.—[1] (1) Where a vacancy occurs in the office of sheriff principal of any sheriffdom the Secretary of State may, if it appears to him expedient so to do in order to avoid delay in the administration of justice in that sheriffdom, appoint a person to act as sheriff principal of the sheriffdom.

[1] (1A) Where the sheriff principal of any sheriffdom is unable to perform, or rules that he is precluded from performing, all of, or some part of, his duties as sheriff principal the Secretary of State may appoint a person to act as sheriff principal of the sheriffdom, or as the case may be to perform that part of the duties of the sheriff principal.

[1] (1B) A person appointed under subsection (1) or (1A) above shall be known as a temporary sheriff principal.

(2) [*Repealed by the Bail, Judicial Appointments etc. (Scotland) Act 2000 (asp 9) (Scottish Act), Pt 2 (c.2) s.6(1). Notwithstanding the coming into force of that repeal—*

    (a) a temporary sheriff may continue to exercise the jurisdiction and powers of a sheriff for the purposes of any proceedings commenced or other matter which began before such coming into force; and

    (b) a temporary sheriff shall, for those purposes and for the purposes of any further proceedings arising out of the proceedings or other matter referred to in paragraph (a) above, be treated as continuing to be a temporary sheriff.]

[2] (3) A person shall not be appointed to be a temporary sheriff principal unless he is legally qualified and has been so qualified—

    (a) for at least ten years;

For the purposes of this subsection, a person shall be legally qualified if he is an advocate or a solicitor.

[2] (4) The appointment of a temporary sheriff principal shall subsist until recalled by the Secretary of State.

[2,3] (4A) No appointment under this section of a person to be a temporary sheriff principal shall extend beyond the day on which the person reaches the age of 70.

[3] (4B) Subsection (4A) above is subject to section 26(4) to (6) of the Judicial Pensions and Retirement Act 1993 (power to authorise continuance in office up to the age of 75).

[2] (5) If the Secretary of State, on appointing any person to be a temporary sheriff principal, so directs, the provisions of section 6(1) of this Act shall apply in relation to that person as they apply in relation to a person holding the office of sheriff.

[2] (6) A person appointed to be temporary sheriff principal of any sheriffdom shall for the purposes of his appointment, without the necessity of his receiving a commission in that behalf, have and be entitled to exercise the jurisdiction and powers attaching to the office of sheriff principal or sheriff in that sheriffdom.

(7) The appointment of any person holding the office of sheriff to be a temporary sheriff principal shall not affect the commission held by that person as sheriff, but he shall not, while his appointment as a temporary sheriff principal subsists, perform any duties by virtue of the said commission.

[2] (8) The Secretary of State may pay to any person appointed to be a temporary sheriff principal such remuneration and allowances as the Treasury, on the recommendation of the Secretary of State, may determine.

NOTES

[1] Subsections (1), (1A) and (1B) substituted for subs. (1) by the Law Reform (Miscellaneous Provisions) (Scotland) Act 1980 (c.55), s.10(b). As amended by the Bail, Judicial Appointments etc. (Scotland) Act 2000 (asp.9), s.6, s.12 and Sch., para.1.

[2] As amended by the Bail, Judicial Appointments etc. (Scotland) Act 2000 (asp.9), Sch., para.1.

[3] Inserted by the Judicial Pensions and Retirement Act 1993 (c.8), Sch.6, para.11.

Appointment of part-time sheriffs

[1] **11A**—(1) The Scottish Ministers may, under this section, appoint persons to act as sheriffs, and persons so appointed shall be known as "part-time sheriffs".

(2) In making those appointments, the Scottish Ministers shall comply with such requirements as to procedure and consultation as may be prescribed by regulations made by them.

(3) A person shall not be appointed a part-time sheriff unless qualified under section 5(1) of this Act to be appointed to the office of sheriff.

(4) A part-time sheriff shall, without the necessity of receiving a commission in that behalf, be entitled to exercise in every sheriffdom the jurisdiction and powers attaching to the office of sheriff.

[2] (5) The number of persons holding appointments as part-time sheriffs shall not, at any one time, exceed 80 or such other number as may be fixed in substitution by order made by the Scottish Ministers.

(6) A part-time sheriff shall be subject to such instructions, arrangements and other provisions as fall to be made under this Act by the sheriff principal of the sheriffdom in which the part-time sheriff is sitting.

(7) In the performance of their functions under this Act, sheriffs principal shall together have regard to the desirability of securing that every part-time sheriff—

> (a) is given the opportunity of sitting on not fewer than 20 days; and
> (b) does not sit for more than 100 days,

in each successive period of 12 months beginning with the day of the part-time sheriff's appointment as such.

(8) The Scottish Ministers shall pay to part-time sheriffs such remuneration and allowances as they determine.

NOTES

[1] As inserted by the Bail, Judicial Appointments etc. (Scotland) Act 2000 (asp 9) s.7 (effective August 9, 2000).

[2] As amended by the Maximum Number of Part-Time Sheriffs (Scotland) Order 2006 (SSI 2006/257) (effective May 10, 2006).

Limitation, termination etc. of appointment of part-time sheriffs

[1] **11B.**—(1) An appointment as a part-time sheriff shall, subject to subsections (2) to (4) below, last for 5 years.

(2) A part-time sheriff may resign at any time by giving notice to that effect to the Scottish Ministers.

(3) An appointment of a person as a part-time sheriff shall not extend beyond the day when the person reaches the age of 70.

[2] (4) A part-time sheriff's appointment shall come to an end upon the part-time sheriff's being removed from office under section 12E of this Act.

(5) A part-time sheriff whose appointment comes to an end by operation of subsection (1) above may be reappointed and, except in the circumstances set out in subsection (6) below, shall be reappointed.

(6) The circumstances mentioned in subsection (5) above are that—

> (a) the part-time sheriff has declined that reappointment;
> (b) the part-time sheriff is aged 69 or over;
> (c) a sheriff principal has made a recommendation to the Scottish Ministers against the reappointment;

    (d) the part-time sheriff has not sat for a total of 50 or more days in the preceding five year period; or

    (e) the Scottish Ministers have, since the part-time sheriff was last appointed, made an order under section 11A(5) of this Act reducing the number of persons who may hold appointment as part-time sheriffs.

(7) A part-time sheriff whose appointment comes to an end by resignation under subsection (2) above may be reappointed.

(8) The provisions of section 11A and this section of this Act apply to a reappointment under subsections (5) and (7) above as they apply to an appointment.

(9) A part-time sheriff who is a solicitor in practice shall not carry out any function as a part-time sheriff in a sheriff court district in which his or her main place of business as such solicitor is situated.

NOTES

[1] As inserted by the Bail, Judicial Appointments etc. (Scotland) Act 2000 (asp 9) s.7 (effective August 9, 2000).

[2] As amended by the Judiciary and Courts (Scotland) Act 2008 (Consequential Modifications) Order 2009 (SSI 2009/334) art.3(1) (effective April 1, 2010).

Removal of part-time sheriffs from office

[1] **11C**—(1) A part-time sheriff may be removed from office by and only by order of the tribunal constituted by and under subsection (3) below ("the tribunal").

(2) The tribunal may order the removal from office of a part-time sheriff only if, after investigation carried out at the request of the Scottish Ministers, it finds that the part-time sheriff is unfit for office by reason of inability, neglect of duty or misbehaviour.

(3) The tribunal shall consist of the following three members, who shall be appointed by the Lord President of the Court of Session—

    (a) either a Senator of the College of Justice or a sheriff principal (who shall preside);

    (b) a person who is, and has been for at least ten years, legally qualified within the meaning of section 5(1) of this Act; and

    (c) one other person.

(4) Regulations, made by the Scottish Ministers—

    (a) may make provision enabling the tribunal, at any time during an investigation, to suspend a part-time sheriff from office and providing as to the effect and duration of such suspension; and

    (b) shall make such further provision as respects the tribunal as the Scottish Ministers consider necessary or expedient, including provision for the procedure to be followed by and before it.

NOTE

[1] As inserted by the Bail, Judicial Appointments etc. (Scotland) Act 2000 (asp 9) s.7 (effective August 9, 2000).

Regulations and orders under sections 11A and 11C

[1] **11D**—(1) Regulations under section 11A or section 11C and orders under section 11A of this Act shall be made by statutory instrument.

(2) No such regulations or order shall be made unless laid in draft before, and approved by a resolution of, the Scottish Parliament.".

NOTE

[1] As inserted by the Bail, Judicial Appointments etc. (Scotland) Act 2000 (asp 9) s.7 (effective August 9, 2000).

Removal from office, and suspension, of sheriff principal or sheriff

[1] **12.**—(1) The Lord President of the Court of Session and the Lord

Justice Clerk may of their own accord and shall, if they are requested so to do by the Secretary of State, undertake jointly an investigation into the fitness for office of any sheriff principal or sheriff and, as soon as practicable after completing that investigation, shall report in writing to the Secretary of State either—

(a) that the sheriff principal or sheriff is fit for office, or

(b) that the sheriff principal or sheriff is unfit for office by reason of inability, neglect of duty or misbehaviour,

and shall in either case include in their report a statement of their reasons for so reporting.

(2) The Secretary of State may, if a report is made to him under subsection (1) above to the effect that any sheriff principal or sheriff is unfit for office by reason of inability, neglect of duty or misbehaviour, make an order removing that sheriff principal or sheriff from office.

(3) An order under subsection (2) above—

(a) shall be made by statutory instrument, which shall be subject to annulment in pursuance of a resolution of either House of Parliament,

(b) shall not be made so as to come into operation before the expiry, in relation to the order, of the period of forty days mentioned in section 5(1) of the Statutory Instruments Act 1946.

(4) The Lord President of the Court of Session and the Lord Justice Clerk may, on undertaking an investigation under subsection (1) above or at any time during the course of such an investigation, if they think it proper so to do, recommend in writing to the Secretary of State that the sheriff principal or sheriff who is the subject of the investigation be suspended from office, and the Secretary of State may, on receiving such a recommendation as aforesaid, suspend that sheriff principal or sheriff from office.

(5) A sheriff principal or a sheriff suspended from office under subsection (4) above shall remain so suspended until the Secretary of State otherwise directs.

(6) The suspension from office of a sheriff principal or a sheriff under subsection (4) above shall not affect the payment to him of his salary in respect of the period of his suspension.

[2] (7) In this section "sheriff principal" does not include a temporary sheriff principal and "sheriff" does not include a part-time sheriff or an honorary sheriff.

NOTES

[1] Extended by the District Courts (Scotland) Act 1975 (c.20), s.5(8).

[2] As amended by the Bail, Judicial Appointments etc. (Scotland) Act 2000 (asp.9), s.12 and Sch., para.1.

Functions of Secretary of State with respect to residence and leave of absence of sheriffs principal

13.—(1) The Secretary of State may require any sheriff principal (being a sheriff principal who is restricted by the terms of his appointment from engaging in private practice or to whom section 6(1) of this Act applies) to reside ordinarily at such place as the Secretary of State may specify.

(2) The Secretary of State may approve such leave of absence for any sheriff principal (being a sheriff principal who is restricted by the terms of his appointment from engaging in private practice or to whom section 6(1) of this Act applies) as appears to the Secretary of State to be proper, but the amount of leave so approved (other than leave granted on account of ill-health) shall not, unless the Secretary of State for special reasons otherwise permits, exceed seven weeks in any year.

Functions of Secretary of State with respect to number, residence and place of duties of sheriffs

14.—(1) The Secretary of State may, with the approval of the Treasury, by order prescribe the number of sheriffs to be appointed for each sheriffdom.

(2) The Secretary of State may require any sheriff to reside ordinarily at such place as the Secretary of State may specify.

(3) The Secretary of State—

(a) shall, on the appointment of a person to hold the office of sheriff for any sheriffdom,

(b) may, at any subsequent time while the said person holds that office,

give to that person a direction designating the sheriff court district or districts in which he is to perform his duties as sheriff:

Provided that a direction given to a sheriff under this subsection shall be subject to any instruction given to that sheriff under section 15 of this Act by the sheriff principal of the sheriffdom, being an instruction given for the purpose of giving effect to any special provision made by the sheriff principal under section 16(1)(b) of this Act.

(4) If for the purpose of securing the efficient organisation and administration of the sheriff courts, and after consultation with the Lord President of the Court of Session the Secretary of State by order so directs, a person holding the office of sheriff for any sheriffdom shall, on such date as may be specified in the order, cease to hold that office and shall, on and after that date, without the necessity of his receiving a commission in that behalf, hold instead the office of sheriff for such other sheriffdom as may be so specified; and on making an order under this subsection with respect to any person the Secretary of State shall give to that person a direction under subsection (3) above designating the sheriff court district or districts in which he is to perform his duties as sheriff.

[1] (5) In this section "sheriff" does not include an honorary or a part-time sheriff.

NOTE

[1] As amended by the Bail, Judicial Appointments etc. (Scotland) Act 2000 (asp 9), s. 12 and Sched., para. 1.

Functions of the sheriff principal in relation to sheriffs, etc.

General functions of sheriff principal

15.—(1) Subject generally to the provisions of this Act, and in particular to the provisions of this or any other Act conferring functions on the Secretary of State or anything done under any such provision, the sheriff principal of each sheriffdom shall be under a duty to secure the speedy and efficient disposal of business in the sheriff courts of that sheriffdom, and for the purpose of carrying out that duty shall have, in addition to any functions conferred on him by or under any other enactment, the functions conferred on him by the following provisions of this Act.

[1] (2) For the purpose of securing the effective discharge of any of the said functions the sheriff principal of any sheriffdom may give such instructions of an administrative nature as appear to him to be necessary or expedient, and any sheriff appointed for that sheriffdom any part-time sheriff, and any officer or servant engaged in the administration of the sheriff courts in the sheriffdom, to whom an instruction is given under this section shall, subject to the provisions of this Act, give effect to that instruction.

NOTE

[1] As amended by the Bail, Judicial Appointments etc. (Scotland) Act 2000 (asp.9), s.12 and Sch., para.1.

Functions of sheriff principal with respect to duties and leave of absence of sheriffs

16.—[1] (1) The sheriff principal of each sheriffdom shall make such arrangements as appear to him necessary or expedient for the purpose of securing the speedy and efficient disposal of business in the sheriff courts of that sheriffdom and in particular, but without prejudice to the generality of the foregoing words, may—

    (a) subject to any direction given by the Secretary of State under section 9 of this Act, provide for the division of such business as aforesaid between the sheriff principal, the sheriffs appointed for the sheriffdom and any part-time sheriffs, and for the distribution of the business (so far as allocated to the sheriffs) amongst those sheriffs;

    (b) where any of those sheriffs is by reason of illness or otherwise unable to perform his duties as sheriff, or a vacancy occurs in the office of sheriff in the sheriffdom, or for any other reason it appears to the sheriff principal expedient so to do in order to avoid delay in the administration of justice in the sheriffdom, make special provision of a temporary nature for the disposal of any part of the said business either by the sheriff principal or by any of the sheriffs appointed for the sheriffdom or by any part-time sheriffs, in addition to or in place of the sheriff principal's or, as the case may be, that sheriff's own duties;

so, however, that nothing done under this subsection shall enable a sheriff or part-time sheriff to dispose of business which he does not otherwise have power to dispose of.

(2) The sheriff principal of any sheriffdom may approve such leave of absence for any sheriff appointed for that sheriffdom as appears to the sheriff principal to be proper, but the amount of leave so approved (other than leave granted on account of ill-health) shall not, unless the Secretary of State for special reasons otherwise permits, exceed seven weeks in any year.

[1] (3) In subsection (2) above "sheriff" shall not include a part-time or an honorary sheriff.

NOTE
[1] As amended by the Bail, Judicial Appointments etc. (Scotland) Act 2000 (asp.9), s.12 and Sch., para.1.

Sheriff principal may fix sittings and business of sheriff courts in sheriffdom, and sessions for civil business

17.—(1) The sheriff principal of each sheriffdom may by order prescribe—

    (a) the number of sheriff courts to be held at each of the places within that sheriffdom at which a court is required under or by virtue of this Act to be held,

[1] (b) subject to section 25(2) of this Act, the days on which and the times at which those courts are to be held,

    (c) the descriptions of business to be disposed of at those courts.

(2) The sheriff principal of each sheriffdom shall by order prescribe the dates of the sessions to be held in the sheriff courts of that sheriffdom for the disposal of civil business, and may prescribe different dates in relation to different courts, so however that—

    (a) there shall be held in the courts of each sheriffdom three sessions in each year for the disposal of civil business, that is to say, a winter session, a spring session and a summer session;

    (b) the dates of the sessions prescribed under this subsection shall not be such as to allow, in any court, a vacation of longer than two weeks at Christmas time, four weeks in the spring and eight weeks in the summer.

(3) The sheriff principal of each sheriffdom shall, before the end of the spring session in each year, fix in respect of each sheriff court in that sheriffdom at least one day during the vacation immediately following that session for the disposal of civil business in that court, and shall, before the end of the summer session in each year, fix in respect of each court at least two days during the vacation immediately following that session for the said purpose; but civil proceedings in the sheriff courts may proceed during

vacation as during session, and interlocutors may competently be pronounced during vacation in any such proceedings.

(4) A sheriff principal shall give notice of any matter prescribed or fixed by him under the foregoing provisions of this section in such manner as he may think sufficient for bringing that matter to the attention of all persons having an interest therein.

(5) Subject to anything done under subsection (1) above, or by an order under section 2(1) or section 3(2) of this Act, after the commencement of this Act—

(a) there shall be held at each of the places at which a sheriff court was in use to be held immediately before such commencement the same number of courts as was in use to be held there immediately before such commencement;

(b) the court days and times in use to be observed in any sheriff court immediately before such commencement (whether in pursuance of any enactment or other instrument or otherwise) shall continue to be observed in that court;

(c) the descriptions of business in use to be dealt with on court days in any sheriff court immediately before such commencement shall continue to be dealt with on those days.

(6) Without prejudice to subsection (5) above, any enactment or other instrument in force immediately before the commencement of this Act shall, to the extent that it contains provisions with respect to any matter which the sheriff principal has power to prescribe under subsection (1) above, cease to have effect.

NOTE
[1] See the Bail etc. (Scotland) Act 1980 (c.44), s.10(2).

Secretary of State may exercise certain functions of sheriff principal in certain circumstances
    18. If in any case the Secretary of State considers—

(a) that the exercise by the sheriff principal of any sheriffdom of any of the functions conferred on him by sections 15 to 17 of this Act, or

(b) that the failure of the sheriff principal of any sheriffdom to exercise any of the said functions,

is prejudicial to the speedy and efficient disposal of business in the sheriff courts of that sheriffdom or to the efficient organisation or administration of the sheriff courts generally, or is otherwise against the interests of the public, the Secretary of State may—

(i) (in the circumstances mentioned in paragraph (a) above) rescind that exercise of that function by the sheriff principal and, if he thinks fit, himself exercise that function in that case;

(ii) (in the circumstances mentioned in paragraph (b) above) himself exercise that function in that case,

and the exercise of any function of a sheriff principal by the Secretary of State under this section shall have effect as if it were an exercise of that function by the sheriff principal.

Miscellaneous

Travelling allowances for sheriffs principal
    [1] **19.** The Scottish Court Service may pay to any sheriff principal such allowances as it may determine in respect of the travelling expenses incurred by the sheriff principal in the performance of the duties of his office.

NOTE
[1] As amended by the Judiciary and Courts (Scotland) Act 2008 (Consequential Modifications) Order 2009 (SSI 2009/334) art.3(2) (effective April 1, 2010).

Extension of purposes for which Lord Advocate may give instructions to procurators fiscal

20. The purposes for which the Lord Advocate may issue instructions to procurators fiscal under section 8(1) of the Sheriff Courts and Legal Officers (Scotland) Act 1927 shall include, in addition to the purpose mentioned in the said section 8(1), the speedy and efficient disposal of business in the sheriff courts.

21. [*Repealed by the House of Commons Disqualification Act 1975 (c.24), Sch.3.*]

Saving for existing functions

22. Nothing in the foregoing provisions of this Act shall affect the discharge by any person of any function lawfully held by him immediately before the commencement of this Act, except in so far as the discharge of that function is or would be inconsistent with any of those provisions or anything done thereunder.

PART II

COURT HOUSES, BUILDINGS AND OFFICES

23–30. [Not reproduced.]

PART III

CIVIL JURISDICTION, PROCEDURE AND APPEALS

Civil Jurisdiction

Upper limit to privative jurisdiction of sheriff court to be £5,000

[1] **31.** Section 7 of the Sheriff Courts (Scotland) Act 1907 (which provides that all causes not exceeding £50 in value which are competent in the sheriff court are to be brought in that court only, and are not to be subject to review by the Court of Session) shall have effect as if for the words "£50" there were substituted the words "£5,000".

NOTE

[1] As substituted subject to savings specified in SSI 2007/507 art.4 by the Sheriff Courts (Scotland) Act 1971 (Privative Jurisdiction and Summary Cause) Order (SSI 2007/507), art.2 (effective January 14, 2008).

Regulation of procedure in civil proceedings

Power of Court of Session to regulate civil procedure in sheriff court

[1] **32.**—[2] (1) Subject to the provisions of this section, the Court of Session may by act of sederunt regulate and prescribe the procedure and practice to be followed in any civil proceedings in the sheriff court (including any matters incidental or relating to any such procedure or practice), and, without prejudice to the generality of the foregoing words, the power conferred on the Court of Session by this section shall extend to—

    (a) regulating the procedure to be followed in connection with execution or diligence following on any civil proceedings;

    (b) prescribing the manner in which, the time within which, and the conditions on which, an appeal may be taken to the sheriff principal from an interlocutor of a sheriff, or to the Court of Session from an interlocutor of a sheriff principal or a sheriff (including an interlocutor applying the verdict of a jury), or any application may be made to the sheriff court, or anything required or authorised to be done in relation to any civil proceedings shall or may be done;

    (c) prescribing the form of any document to be used in, or for the purposes of, any civil proceedings or any execution or diligence following thereon, and the person by whom, and the manner in which, any such document as aforesaid is to be authenticated;

(d) regulating the procedure to be followed in connection with the production and recovery of documents;

[3] (e) providing in respect of any category of civil proceedings for written statements (including affidavits) and reports, admissible under section 2(1)(b) of the Civil Evidence (Scotland) Act 1988, to be received in evidence, on such conditions as may be prescribed, without being spoken to by a witness;

[6](ea) regulating the procedure to be followed in connection with the making of orders under sections 12(1) and (6) and 13(2) of theVulnerable Witnesses (Scotland) Act 2004 (asp 3) ("the 2004 Act");

(eb) regulating, so far as not regulated by the 2004 Act, the use of special measures authorised by virtue of that Act to be used;

(f) making such provision as may appear to the Court of Session to be necessary or expedient with respect to the payment, investment or application of any sum of money awarded to or in respect of a person under legal disability in any action in the sheriff court;

(g) regulating the summoning, remuneration and duties of assessors;

(h) making such provision as may appear to the Court of Session to be necessary or expedient for carrying out the provisions of this Act or of any enactment conferring powers or imposing duties on sheriffs principal or sheriffs or relating to proceedings in the sheriff courts;

(i) regulating the expenses which may be awarded by the sheriff to parties in proceedings before him;

[4] (j) permitting a person who is not an advocate or solicitor and is not represented by an advocate or solicitor to transmit, whether orally or in writing, the views of a child to the sheriff for the purposes of any enactment which makes provision (however expressed) for the sheriff to have regard to those views;

[5] (k) prescribing the procedure to be followed in appointing a person under section 3(4) of the Adults with Incapacity (Scotland) Act 2000 (asp 4) and the functions of such a person.

[7] (l) permitting a party to proceedings which relate to [an interim attachment, an attachment, a money attachment, a land attachment or a residual attachment][7] to be represented, in such circumstances as may be specified in the act of sederunt, by a person who is neither an advocate nor a solicitor.

[8] (m) permitting a debtor appearing before a sheriff under section 12 of the Bankruptcy (Scotland) Act 1985 (c.66) (award of sequestration) to be represented, in such circumstances as may be specified in the act of sederunt, by a person who is neither an advocate nor a solicitor.

Provided that nothing contained in an act of sederunt made under this section shall derogate from—

(i) the provisions of sections 35 to 38 of this Act (as amended by the Law Reform (Miscellaneous Provisions) (Scotland) Act 1985) with respect to summary causes, or

(ii) the provisions of subsection (8) of section 20 of the Race Relations Act 1968 with respect to the remuneration to be paid to assessors appointed under subsection (7) of that section.

(2) An act of sederunt under this section may contain such incidental, supplemental or consequential provisions as appear to the Court of Session to be necessary or expedient for the purposes of that act, including, but without prejudice to the generality of the foregoing words, provisions amending, repealing or revoking any enactment (whether passed or made before or after the commencement of this Act) relating to matters with respect to which an act of sederunt may be made under this section.

(3) Before making an act of sederunt under this section with respect to any

matter the Court of Session shall (unless that act embodies, with or without modifications, draft rules submitted to them by the Sheriff Court Rules Council under section 34 of this Act) consult the said Council, and shall take into consideration any views expressed by the Council with respect to that matter.

(4) Section 34 of the Administration of Justice (Scotland) Act 1933 (power of Court of Session to regulate civil procedure in sheriff court) shall cease to have effect, but any act of sederunt made under or having effect by virtue of that section shall, if and so far as it is in force immediately before the commencement of this Act, continue in force and shall have effect, and be treated, as if it had been made under this section.

NOTES

[1] See also the Maintenance Orders (Reciprocal Enforcement) Act 1972 (c.18), ss.19 and 31(3). Extended: see the Children Act 1975 (c.72), s.66, the Banking Act 1979 (c.37), s.31(7)(b), the Debtors (Scotland) Act 1987 (c.18), s.97 and the Child Support Act 1991 (c.48), ss.39(2) and 49 and the Children (Scotland) Act 1995 (c.36), s.91, (effective October 1, 1996: SI 1996/2203). Applied: see the Children Act 1975 (c.72), s.78. See also the Presumption of Death (Scotland) Act 1977 (c.27), s.15(1).

[2] As amended by the Law Reform (Miscellaneous Provisions) (Scotland) Act 1985 (c.73), Sch.2, para.12.

[3] Substituted by the Civil Evidence (Scotland) Act 1988 (c.32), s.2(4).

[4] Inserted by the Children (Scotland) Act 1995 (c.36), Sch.4, para.18(2) (effective November 1, 1995: SI 1995/2787).

[5] As inserted by the Adults with Incapacity (Scotland) Act 2000 (asp 4), s. 88 and Sch.5, para.13.

[6] As amended by the Vulnerable Witnesses (Scotland) Act 2004 (asp 3), s.14, and brought into force by the Vulnerable Witnesses (Scotland) Act 2004 Commencement Order 2005 (SSI 2005/168) (effective April 1, 2005) but only in respect of proceedings in the sheriff court under Part II of the Children (Scotland) Act 1995 in respect of appeals under section 51(1) and applications under sections 68 and 85 of that Act and only in respect of child witnesses.

[7] As inserted by the Debt Arrangement and Attachment (Scotland) Act 2002 (asp 17) Pt 2 s.43 (effective December 17, 2002) and substituted by the Bankruptcy and Diligence etc. (Scotland) Act 2007 (asp 3) Sch.5 para.10 (effective April 1, 2008 for the purpose specified in SSI 2008/115 art.3(2)–(3) and Sch.1; not yet in force otherwise).

[8] As inserted by the Bankruptcy and Diligence etc. (Scotland) Act 2007 (asp 3) Pt 1 s.33 (effective April 1, 2008).

Sheriff Court Rules Council

33.—[0] (1) There shall be established a body (to be known as the Sheriff Court Rules Council, and hereafter in this section and section 34 called "the Council") which shall have the functions conferred on it by section 34, and which shall consist of—

    (a) two sheriffs principal, three sheriffs, one advocate, five solicitors and two whole-time sheriff clerks, all appointed by the Lord President of the Court of Session, after consultation with such persons as appear to him to be appropriate;

    (b) two persons appointed by the Lord President after consultation with the Secretary of State, being persons appearing to the Lord President to have—

        (i) a knowledge of the working procedures and practices of the civil courts;

        (ii) a knowledge of consumer affairs; and

        (iii) an awareness of the interests of litigants in the civil courts; and

    (c) one person appointed by the Secretary of State, being a person appearing to the Secretary of State to be qualified for such appointment.

(2) The members of the Council shall, so long as they retain the respective qualifications mentioned in subsection (1) above, hold office for three years and be eligible for re-appointment.

(3) Any vacancy in the membership of the Council occurring by reason of

death, resignation or other cause before the expiry of the period for which the member whose place is so vacated was appointed shall be filled—

[0](a) if the member was appointed by the Lord President of the Court of Session, by the appointment by the Lord President, after such consultation as is mentioned in paragraph (a) or, as the case may be, (b) of subsection (1) above, of a person having the same qualifications as that member,

 (b) if the member was appointed by the Secretary of State, by the appointment by the Secretary of State of another person appearing to the Secretary of State to have qualifications suitable for such appointment,

and a person so appointed to fill a vacancy shall hold office only until the expiry of the said period.

[1] (4) The Lord President of the Court of Session shall appoint one of the two sheriffs principal who are members of the Council as chairman thereof, and the Secretary of State shall appoint a secretary to the Council.

(5) The Council shall have power to regulate the summoning of meetings of the Council and the procedure at such meetings, so however that—

 (a) the Council shall meet within one month of its being established and thereafter at intervals of not more than six months, and shall meet at any time on a requisition in that behalf made by the chairman of the Council or any three members thereof, and

 (b) at any meeting of the Council six members shall be a quorum.

(6) The Rules Council for the sheriff court established under section 35 of the Administration of Justice (Scotland) Act 1933 is hereby dissolved, and the said section 35 shall cease to have effect.

NOTES

[0] As amended by the Law Reform (Miscellaneous Provisions) (Scotland) Act 1990 (c.40), Sch.8, para.26.

[1] As amended by the Law Reform (Miscellaneous Provisions) (Scotland) Act 1985 (c.73), Sch.2, para.13 and Sch.4.

Functions of Sheriff Court Rules Council

34.—(1) As soon as practicable after it has been established the Council shall review generally the procedure and practice followed in civil proceedings in the sheriff court (including any matters incidental or relating to that procedure or practice) and, in the light of that review and of the provisions of this Act, shall prepare and submit to the Court of Session draft rules, being rules which—

 (a) are designed to regulate and prescribe that procedure and practice (including any such matters as aforesaid), and

 (b) are such as the Court of Session have power to make by act of sederunt under section 32 of this Act,

and the Court of Session shall make an act of sederunt under the said section 32 embodying those rules with such modifications, if any, as they think expedient.

(2) After submitting draft rules to the Court of Session under subsection (1) above the Council shall keep under review the procedure and practice followed in civil proceedings in the sheriff court (including any matters incidental or relating to that procedure or practice), and the Council may prepare and submit to the Court of Session draft rules designed to deal with any of the matters relating to the sheriff court which the Court of Session have power under section 32 of this Act to regulate or prescribe by act of sederunt, and the Court of Session shall consider any draft rules so submitted and shall, if they approve the rules, make an act of sederunt under the said section 32 embodying those rules with such modifications if any, as they think expedient.

(3) For the purpose of assisting it in the discharge of its functions under

the foregoing provisions of this section the Council may invite representations on any aspect of the procedure or practice in civil proceedings in the sheriff court (including any matters incidental or relating to that procedure or practice), and shall consider any such representations received by it, whether in response to such an invitation as aforesaid or otherwise.

Summary causes

Summary causes

35.—(1) The definition of "summary cause" contained in paragraph (i) of section 3 of the Sheriff Courts (Scotland) Act 1907 shall cease to have effect, and for the purposes of the procedure and practice in civil proceedings in the sheriff court there shall be a form of process, to be known as a "summary cause", which shall be used for the purposes of all civil proceedings brought in that court, being proceedings of one or other of the following descriptions, namely—

[1] (a) actions for payment of money not exceeding £5,000[1a] in amount (exclusive of interest and expenses);

[1,6] (b) actions of multiplepoinding, actions of furthcoming, where the value of the fund *in medio*, or the value of the arrested fund or subject, as the case may be, does not exceed £5,000[1a] (exclusive of interest and expenses);

[2] (c) actions *ad factum praestandum* and actions for the recovery of possession of heritable or moveable property, other than actions in which there is claimed in addition, or as an alternative, to a decree *ad factum praestandum* or for such recovery, as the case may be, a decree for payment of money exceeding £5,000[1a] in amount (exclusive of interest and expenses);

(d) proceedings which, according to the law and practice existing immediately before the commencement of this Act, might competently be brought in the sheriff's small debt court or where required to be conducted and disposed of in the summary manner in which proceedings were conducted and disposed of under the Small Debt Acts;

and any reference in the following provisions of this Act, or in any other enactment (whether passed or made before or after the commencement of this Act) relating to civil procedure in the sheriff court, to a summary cause shall be construed as a reference to a summary cause within the meaning of this subsection.

[3] (1A) For the avoidance of doubt it is hereby declared that nothing in subsection (1) above shall prevent the Court of Session from making different rules of procedure and practice in relation to different descriptions of summary cause proceedings.

[4,5] (2) There shall be a form of summary cause process, to be known as a "small claim", which shall be used for the purposes of such descriptions of summary cause proceedings as are prescribed by the Secretary of State by order.

[4] (3) No enactment or rule of law relating to admissibility or corroboration of evidence before a court of law shall be binding in a small claim.

[4] (4) An order under subsection (2) above shall be by statutory instrument but shall not be made unless a draft of it has been approved by a resolution of each House of Parliament.

NOTES

[1] As amended by SI 1976/900 and SI 1981/842.

[1a] As substituted subject to savings specified in SSI 2007/507 art.4 by the Sheriff Courts (Scotland) Act 1971 (Privative Jurisdiction and Summary Cause) Order (SSI 2007/507), art.3 (effective January 14, 2008).

[2] As amended by SI 1976/900 and SI 1981/842. Excluded by the Land Tenure Reform (Scotland) Act 1974 (c.38), s.9(6).

[3] As inserted by the Law Reform (Miscellaneous Provisions) (Scotland) Act 1985 (c.73), Sch.2, para.14, with effect from December 30, 1985.

[4] New subss (2)–(4) substituted for subs. (2) by the Law Reform (Miscellaneous Provisions) (Scotland) Act 1985 (c.73), s.18(1).

[5] As amended by SI 1999/678, art.2, Sch.(effective May 19, 1999).

[6] As amended by Bankruptcy and Diligence etc. (Scotland) Act 2007 (asp 3) Sch.6(1) para.1 (effective April 1, 2008: as SSI 2008/115).

Procedure in summary causes

36.—(1) In relation to summary causes the power conferred on the Court of Session by section 32 of this Act shall extend to the making of rules permitting a party to such a cause, in such circumstances as may be specified in the rules, to be represented by a person who is neither an advocate nor a solicitor.

(2) A summary cause shall be commenced by a summons in, or as nearly as is practicable in, such form as may be prescribed by rules under the said section 32.

[1] (3) The evidence, if any, given in a summary cause shall not be recorded.

(4) [*Repealed by the Debtors (Scotland) Act 1987 (c.18), Sch.8.*]

NOTE

[1] Excluded by the Maintenance Orders (Reciprocal Enforcement) Act 1972 (c.18), s.4(4)(b).

Further provisions as to small claims

[1] **36A.** Where the pursuer in a small claim is not—

(a) a partnership or a body corporate; or

(b) acting in a representative capacity,

he may require the sheriff clerk to effect service of the summons on his behalf.

NOTE

[1] As inserted by the Law Reform (Miscellaneous Provisions) (Scotland) Act 1985 (c.73), s.18(2).

Expenses in small claims

[1] **36B.**—[2] (1) No award of expenses shall be made in a small claim in which the value of the claim does not exceed such sum as the Secretary of State shall prescribe by order.

[2] (2) Any expenses which the sheriff may award in any other small claim shall not exceed such sum as the Secretary of State shall prescribe by order.

(3) Subsections (1) and (2) above do not apply to a party to a small claim—

(a) who being a defender—

   (i) has not stated a defence; or

   (ii) having stated a defence, has not proceeded with it; or

   (iii) having stated and proceeded with a defence, has not acted in good faith as to its merits; or

(b) on whose part there has been unreasonable conduct in relation to the proceedings or the claim;

nor do they apply in relation to an appeal to the sheriff principal.

(4) An order under this section shall be by statutory instrument but shall not be made unless a draft of it has been approved by a resolution of each House of Parliament.

NOTES

[1] As inserted by the Law Reform (Miscellaneous Provisions) (Scotland) Act 1985 (c.73), s.18(2).

[2] As amended by SI 1999/678, art.2, Sch. (effective May 19, 1999).

Remits

[5] **37.**—[1] (1) In the case of any ordinary cause brought in the sheriff court the sheriff—

(a) shall at any stage, on the joint motion of the parties to the cause, direct that the cause be treated as a summary cause, and in that case the cause shall be treated for all purposes (including appeal) as a summary cause and shall proceed accordingly;

(b) may, subject to section 7 of the Sheriff Courts (Scotland) Act 1907, on the motion of any of the parties to the cause, if he is of the opinion that the importance or difficulty of the cause make it appropriate to do so, remit the cause to the Court of Session.

(2) In the case of any summary cause, the sheriff at any stage—

(a) shall, on the joint motion of the parties to the cause, and

(b) may, on the motion of any of the parties to the cause, if he is of the opinion that the importance or difficulty of the cause makes it appropriate to do so,

direct that the cause be treated as an ordinary cause, and in that case the cause shall be treated for all purposes (including appeal) as an ordinary cause and shall proceed accordingly:

Provided that a direction under this subsection may, in the case of an action for the recovery of possession of heritable or moveable property, be given by the sheriff of his own accord.

[2] (2A) In the case of any action in the sheriff court, being an action for divorce or an action in relation to the custody, guardianship or adoption of a child the sheriff may, of his own accord, at any stage remit the action to the Court of Session.

[4] (2B) In the case of any small claim the sheriff at any stage—

(a) may, if he is of the opinion that a difficult question of law or a question of fact of exceptional complexity is involved, of his own accord or on the motion of any party to the small claim;

(b) shall, on the joint motion of the parties to the small claim,

direct that the small claim be treated as a summary cause (not being a small claim) or ordinary cause, and in that case the small claim shall be treated for all purposes (including appeal) as a summary cause (not being a small claim) or ordinary cause as the case may be.

[4] (2C) In the case of any cause which is not a small claim by reason only of any monetary limit applicable to a small claim or to summary causes, the sheriff at any stage shall, on the joint motion of the parties to the cause, direct that the cause be treated as a small claim and in that case the cause shall be treated for all purposes (including appeal) as a small claim and shall proceed accordingly.

[5] (2D) In the case of any action in the sheriff court where the matter to which the action relates could competently be determined by the Land Court by virtue of the Agricultural Holdings (Scotland) Act 1991 (c.55) or the Agricultural Holdings (Scotland) Act 2003 (asp 11), the sheriff may (of his own accord or on the motion of any of the parties) at any stage remit the case to the Land Court if he is of the opinion that it is appropriate to do so.

[3] (3) A decision—

(a) to remit, or not to remit, under subsection (2A), (2B) or (2C) above; or

(b) to make, or not to make, a direction by virtue of paragraph (b) of, or the proviso to, subsection (2) above,

shall not be subject to review; but from a decision to remit, or not to remit, under subsection (1)(b) above an appeal shall lie to the Court of Session.

(4) In this section "sheriff" includes a sheriff principal.

NOTES

[1] As amended by the Law Reform (Miscellaneous Provisions) (Scotland) Act 1980 (c.55), s.16(a). See the Land Tenure Reform (Scotland) Act 1974 (c.38), s.9(6).

[2] Added by the Law Reform (Miscellaneous Provisions) (Scotland) Act 1980 (c.55), s.16(b). As amended by the Divorce Jurisdiction, Court Fees and Legal Aid (Scotland) Act 1983 (c.12), Sch.1, para.12, the Law Reform (Parent and Child) (Scotland) Act 1986 (c.9), Sch.1, para.11,

the Age of Legal Capacity (Scotland) Act 1991 (c.50), Sch.1, para.35, and the Children (Scotland) Act 1995 (c.36), Sch.4, para.18(3) (effective April 1, 1997: SI 1996/3201).

[3] As substituted by the Law Reform (Miscellaneous Provisions) (Scotland) Act 1980 (c.55), s.16(c). As amended by the Law Reform (Miscellaneous Provisions) (Scotland) Act 1985 (c.73), s.18(3)(b).

[4] Added by the Law Reform (Miscellaneous Provisions) (Scotland) Act 1988, s.18(3).

[5] As inserted by the Agricultural Holdings (Scotland) Act 2003 (asp 11), Pt 7, s.86(1).

Appeal in summary causes

[1] **38.** In the case of—

(a) any summary cause an appeal shall lie to the sheriff principal on any point of law from the final judgment of the sheriff; and

(b) any summary cause other than a small claim an appeal shall lie to the Court of Session on any point of law from the final judgment of the sheriff principal, if the sheriff principal certifies the cause as suitable for such an appeal,

but save as aforesaid an interlocutor of the sheriff or the sheriff principal in any such cause shall not be subject to review.

NOTE

[1] As amended by the Law Reform (Miscellaneous Provisions) (Scotland) Act 1985 (c.73), s.18(4). Excluded by the Debtors (Scotland) Act 1987 (c.18), s.103(1).

Miscellaneous and supplemental

39, 40. [*Repealed by the Law Reform (Miscellaneous Provisions) (Scotland) Act 1980 (c.55), Sch.3.*]

Power of Her Majesty to vary limit to privative jurisdiction of sheriff court, etc.

[1] **41.**—(1) If it appears to Her Majesty in Council that the sum of £250 specified in any provisions of this Act mentioned in subsection (2) below (or such other sum as may be specified in that provision by virtue of an Order in Council under this section) should be varied, Her Majesty may by Order in Council, specifying the provision and the sum in question, direct that the provision shall be amended so as to substitute for that sum such other sum as may be specified in the Order.

(2) The provisions referred to in subsection (1) above are—
section 31,
paragraphs (a), (b) and (c) of section 35.

(3) An Order in Council under this section may contain such incidental, supplemental or consequential provisions as appear to Her Majesty in Council to be necessary or expedient for the purposes of the Order.

(4) Any Order in Council made under this section may be revoked by a subsequent Order in Council under this section which substitutes another sum for the sum specified in the Order which is thereby revoked.

(5) No recommendation shall be made to Her Majesty in Council to make an Order under this section unless a draft of the Order has been laid before Parliament and approved by resolution of each House of Parliament.

NOTE

[1] As amended by the Law Reform (Miscellaneous Provisions) (Scotland) Act 1980 (c.55), Sch.3.

Application of provisions regarding jurisdiction and summary causes

42. The following provisions of this Act, namely—
section 31,
sections 35 to 40,
section 46(2) so far as relating to the enactments mentioned in Part II of Schedule 2,

Schedule 1 (except paragraph 1),
shall not apply in relation to any proceedings commenced before the
commencement of this Act.

PART IV

MISCELLANEOUS AND GENERAL

Orders, etc.

43.—(1) Any power conferred by this Act to make an order shall include a
power exercisable in the like manner and subject to the like conditions (if
any) to vary or revoke the order by a subsequent order.

(2) It is hereby declared that any power conferred by this Act to include
incidental, consequential or supplemental provisions in any instrument
made under this Act includes a power to include transitional provisions in
that instrument.

Expenses

44.—(1) There shall be paid out of moneys provided by Parliament any
sums payable by the Secretary of State in consequence of the provisions of
this Act.

(2) Any sums payable under or by virtue of this Act to the Secretary of
State shall be paid into the Consolidated Fund.

(3) In the application of section 4(1) of the Local Government (Scotland)
Act 1966 (variation of rate support grant orders) to a rate support grant
order made before the transfer date appointed under section 30 of this Act
for a grant period ending after that date, the Secretary of State shall take
into account any relief obtained, or likely to be obtained, by local
authorities—

(a) which is attributable to the coming into operation of Part II of this
   Act, and

(b) which was not taken into account in making the rate support grant
   order the variation of which is in question.

The provisions of this subsection are without prejudice to section 4(4) of
the said Act of 1966 (under which an order under that section may vary the
matters prescribed by a rate support grant order).

Interpretation

45.—[1] (1) In this Act, unless the contrary intention appears—

(a) references to a sheriff principal include reference to a temporary
   sheriff principal, and references to the office of sheriff principal
   include references to an appointment as a temporary sheriff
   principal;

(b) references to a sheriff include references to a part-time sheriff
   and an honorary sheriff, and references to the office of sheriff
   include references to an appointment as a part-time sheriff and
   to the office of honorary sheriff;

(c) references to an honorary sheriff are references to a person
   holding the office of honorary sheriff in his capacity as such.

(2) In this Act—

(a) "enactment" includes an order, regulation, rule or other
   instrument having effect by virtue of an Act;

(b) any references to any enactment shall, unless the contrary
   intention appears, be construed as a reference to that enactment
   as amended or extended, and as including a reference thereto as
   applied, by or under any other enactment (including this Act).

(3) Subject to the foregoing provisions of this section and to any other
express provision of this Act, expressions used in this Act and in the Sheriff

Courts (Scotland) Act 1907 shall have the same meanings in this Act as in that Act.

NOTE
[1] As amended by the Bail, Judicial Appointments etc. (Scotland) Act 2000 (asp 9), s. 12 and Sched., para.1.

Amendment and repeal of enactments

46.—(1) Schedule 1 to this Act (which contains certain minor and consequential amendments of enactments) shall have effect.

(2) The enactments mentioned in Schedule 2 to this Act are hereby repealed to the extent specified in relation thereto in column 3 of that Schedule.

Short title, commencement and extent

47.—(1) This Act may be cited as the Sheriff Courts (Scotland) Act 1971.

[1] (2) This Act shall come into operation on such date as the Secretary of State may appoint by order made by statutory instrument, and different dates may be appointed for different provisions of this Act, or for different purposes.

Any reference in any provision of this Act to the commencement of this Act shall, unless otherwise provided by any such order, be construed as a reference to the date on which that provision comes into operation.

[2] (3) This Act, except section 4 (offices of sheriff principal and sheriff), shall extend to Scotland only.

NOTES
[1] See SI 1971/1582; SI 1973/276 and SI 1976/236. Power fully exercised.
[2] As amended by the House of Commons Disqualification Act 1975 (c.24), Sch.3.

SCHEDULES

SCHEDULE 1

Minor and Consequential Amendment of Enactments

General

1. In any enactment passed or made before the commencement of this Act, for any reference to a county, where it appears in relation to a sheriff or a sheriff substitute or in any similar context, there shall, unless the contrary intention appears, be substituted a reference to a sheriffdom.

. . . . . .

SCHEDULE 2

Repeal of Enactments

. . . . . .

District Courts (Scotland) Act 1975

(1975 c. 20)

[Repealed by the Justice of the Peace Courts (Sheriffdom of South Strathclyde, Dumfries and Galloway) etc. Order 2009 (SSI 2009/332) art.7 (effective February 22, 2010).]

[1] Fatal Accidents and Sudden Deaths Inquiry (Scotland) Act 1976

(1976 c.14)

An Act to make provision for Scotland for the holding of public inquiries in respect of fatal accidents, deaths of persons in legal custody, sudden, suspicious and unexplained deaths and deaths occurring in circumstances giving rise to serious public concern.
[April 13, 1976.]

NOTE
[1] See the Anatomy Act 1984 (c.14), s.4(6).

Investigation of death and application for public inquiry

1.—(1) Subject to the provisions of any enactment specified in Schedule 1 to this Act and subsection (2) below, where—
  (a) in the case of a death to which this paragraph applies—
    (i) it appears that the death has resulted from an accident occurring in Scotland while the person who has died, being an employee, was in the course of his employment or, being an employer or self-employed person, was engaged in his occupation as such; or
    (ii) the person who has died was, at the time of his death, in legal custody; or
  (b) it appears to the Lord Advocate to be expedient in the public interest in the case of a death to which this paragraph applies that an inquiry under this Act should be held into the circumstances of the death on the ground that it was sudden, suspicious or unexplained, or has occurred in circumstances such as to give rise to serious public concern,
the procurator fiscal for the district with which the circumstances of the death appear to be most closely connected shall investigate those circumstances and apply to the sheriff for the holding of an inquiry under this Act into those circumstances.

(2) Paragraph (a) of subsection (1) above applies to a death occurring in Scotland after the commencement of this Act (other than such a death in a case where criminal proceedings have been concluded against any person in respect of the death or any accident from which the death resulted, and the Lord Advocate is satisfied that the circumstances of the death have been sufficiently established in the course of such proceedings), and paragraph (b) of that subsection applies to a death occurring there at any time after the date three years before such commencement.

(3) An application under subsection (1) above—
  (a) shall be made to the sheriff with whose sheriffdom the circumstances of the death appear to be most closely connected;
  (b) shall narrate briefly the circumstances of the death so far as known to the procurator fiscal;
  (c) may, if it appears that more deaths than one have occurred as a

result of the same accident or in the same or similar circumstances, relate to both or all such deaths.

(4) For the purposes of subsection (1)(a)(ii) above, a person is in legal custody if—

(a) he is detained in, or is subject to detention in, a prison, remand centre, detention centre, borstal institution, or young offenders institution, all within the meaning of the Prisons (Scotland) Act 1952; or

(b) he is detained in a police station, police cell, or other similar place; or

[1](ba) he is detained in, or is subject to detention in, service custody premises (within the meaning of section 300 of the Armed Forces Act 2006);

(c) he is being taken—

[2] (i) to any of the places specified in paragraphs (a) and (b) and (ba) of this subsection to be detained therein; or

(ii) from any such place in which immediately before such taking he was detained.

NOTES

[1] As inserted by the Armed Forces Act 2006 (c.52) Sch.16 para.72 (effective October 31, 2009).

[2] As substituted by the Armed Forces Act 2006 (c.52) Sch.16 para.72 (effective October 31, 2009).

Citation of witnesses for precognition

2.—(1) The procurator fiscal may, for the purpose of carrying out his investigation under section 1(1) of this Act, cite witnesses for precognition by him, and this section shall be sufficient warrant for such citation.

(2) If any witness cited under subsection (1) above—

(a) fails without reasonable excuse and after receiving reasonable notice to attend for precognition by the procurator fiscal at the time and place mentioned in the citation served on him; or

(b) refuses when so cited to give information within his knowledge regarding any matter relevant to the investigation in relation to which such precognition is taken,

the procurator fiscal may apply to the sheriff for an order requiring the witness to attend for such precognition or to give such information at a time and place specified in the order; and the sheriff shall, if he considers it expedient to do so, make such an order.

[1] (3) If the witness fails to comply with the order of the sheriff under subsection (2) above, he shall be liable to be summarily punished forthwith by a fine not exceeding level 3 on the standard scale or by imprisonment for any period not exceeding 20 days.

NOTE

[1] As amended by the Criminal Procedure (Consequential Provisions) (Scotland) Act 1995 (c.40), Sch.4, para.10.

Holding of public inquiry

3.—(1) On an application under section 1 of this Act being made to him, the sheriff shall make an order—

(a) fixing a time and place for the holding by him of an inquiry under this Act (hereafter in this Act referred to as "the inquiry"), which shall be as soon thereafter as is reasonably practicable in such court-house or other premises as appear to him to be appropriate, having regard to the apparent circumstances of the death; and

(b) granting warrant to cite witnesses and havers to attend at the inquiry at the instance of the procurator fiscal or of any person who may be entitled by virtue of this Act to appear at the inquiry.

(2) On the making of an order under subsection (1) above, the procurator fiscal shall—

   (a) intimate the holding of the inquiry and the time and place fixed for it to the wife or husband or the nearest known relative and, in a case where the inquiry is being held in respect of such a death as is referred to in section 1(1)(a)(i) of this Act, to the employer, if any, of the person whose death is the subject of the inquiry, and to such other person or class of persons as may be prescribed in rules made under section 7(1)(g) of this Act; and

   (b) give public notice of the holding of the inquiry and of the time and place fixed for it.

(3) Where an application under section 1 of this Act relates to more than one death, the order made under subsection (1) above shall so relate; and in this Act references to a death shall include references to both or all deaths or to each death as the case may require, and in subsection (2)(a) above the reference to the person whose death is the subject of the inquiry shall include a reference to each person whose death is the subject of the inquiry.

Conduct of public inquiry

4.—(1) At the inquiry, it shall be the duty of the procurator fiscal to adduce evidence with regard to the circumstances of the death which is the subject of the inquiry.

(2) The wife or husband, or the nearest known relative, and, in a case where the inquiry is being held in respect of such a death as is referred to in section 1(1)(a)(i) of this Act, the employer, if any, of the person whose death is the subject of the inquiry, an inspector appointed under section 19 of the Health and Safety at Work etc. Act 1974 and any other person who the sheriff is satisfied has an interest in the inquiry may appear and adduce evidence at the inquiry.

(3) Subject to subsection (4) below, the inquiry shall be open to the public.

(4) Where a person under the age of 17 is in any way involved in the inquiry, the sheriff may, at his own instance or on an application made to him by any party to the inquiry, make an order providing that—

   (a) no report of the inquiry which is made in a newspaper or other publication or a sound or television broadcast shall reveal the name, address or school, or include any particulars calculated to lead to the identification of that person;

   (b) no picture relating to the inquiry which is or includes a picture of that person shall be published in any newspaper or other publication or televised broadcast.

[1] (5) Any person who contravenes an order made under subsection (4) above shall be guilty of an offence and shall be liable on summary conviction to a fine not exceeding level 4 on the standard scale in respect of each offence.

(6) The sheriff may, either at his own instance or at the request of the procurator fiscal or of any party who may be entitled by virtue of this Act to appear at the inquiry, summon any person having special knowledge and being willing to do so, to act as an assessor at the inquiry.

(7) Subject to the provisions of this Act and any rules made under section 7 of this Act, the rules of evidence, the procedure and the powers of the sheriff to deal with contempt of court and to enforce the attendance of witnesses at the inquiry shall be as nearly as possible those applicable in an ordinary civil cause brought before the sheriff sitting alone.

NOTE

[1] As amended by virtue of the Criminal Procedure (Scotland) Act 1975 (c.21), ss.289F and 289G.

Criminal proceedings and compellability of witnesses

5.—(1) The examination of a witness or haver at the inquiry shall not be a bar to criminal proceedings being taken against him.

(2) No witness at the inquiry shall be compellable to answer any question tending to show that he is guilty of any crime or offence.

Sheriff's determination, etc.
6.—(1) At the conclusion of the evidence and any submissions thereon, or as soon as possible thereafter, the sheriff shall make a determination setting out the following circumstances of the death so far as they have been established to his satisfaction—

(a) where and when the death and any accident resulting in the death took place;

(b) the cause or causes of such death and any accident resulting in the death;

(c) the reasonable precautions, if any, whereby the death and any accident resulting in the death might have been avoided;

(d) the defects, if any, in any system of working which contributed to the death or any accident resulting in the death; and

(e) any other facts which are relevant to the circumstances of the death.

(2) The sheriff shall be entitled to be satisfied that any circumstances referred to in subsection (1) above have been established by evidence, notwithstanding that that evidence is not corroborated.

(3) The determination of the sheriff shall not be admissible in evidence or be founded on in any judicial proceedings, of whatever nature, arising out of the death or out of any accident from which the death resulted.

(4) On the conclusion of the inquiry

(a) the sheriff clerk shall send to the Lord Advocate a copy of the determination of the sheriff and, on a request being made to him, send to any Minister or Government Department or to the Health and Safety Commission, a copy of

(i) the application made under section 1 of this Act;

(ii) the transcript of the evidence;

(iii) any report or documentary production used in the inquiry;

(iv) the determination of the sheriff, and

(b) the procurator fiscal shall send to the Registrar General of Births, Deaths and Marriages for Scotland the name and last known address of the person who has died and the date, place and cause of his death.

(5) Upon payment of such fee as may be prescribed in rules made under paragraph (i) of section 7(1) of this Act, any person—

(a) may obtain a copy of the determination of the sheriff;

(b) who has an interest in the inquiry may, within such period as may be prescribed in rules made under paragraph (j) of the said section 7(1), obtain a copy of the transcript of the evidence,

from the sheriff clerk.

Rules
¹ **7.**—(1) The Secretary of State may, by rules, provide in relation to inquiries under this Act—

(a) as to the form of any document to be used in or for the purposes of such inquiries;

(b) for the representation, on such conditions as may be specified in the rules, of any person who is entitled by virtue of this Act to appear at the inquiry;

(c) for the authorisation by the sheriff of the taking and holding in safe custody of anything which it may be considered necessary to produce;

(d) for the inspection by the sheriff or any person authorised by him of any land, premises, article, or other thing;

(e) that written statements and reports may, on such conditions as may be specified in the rules, be admissible in lieu of parole evidence;

(f) as to the duties, remuneration and other conditions of appointment of any assessor summoned under section 4 of this Act, and for keeping of lists of persons willing to act as such;

(g) as to intimation of the holding of the inquiry;

(h) as to the payment of fees to solicitors and expenses to witnesses and havers;

(i) as to the payment of a fee by a person obtaining a copy of the determination of the sheriff or a copy of the transcript of the evidence;

(j) as to the period within which a person entitled may obtain a copy of the transcript of the evidence at the inquiry;

(k) as to such other matters relating to procedure as the Lord Advocate thinks appropriate.

(2) The power to make rules conferred by any provision of this Act shall be exercisable by statutory instrument.

(3) Rules made by the Lord Advocate under this Act may contain such incidental, consequential and supplemental provisions as appear to him to be necessary or proper for bringing the rules into operation and giving full effect thereto.

NOTE

[1] As amended by SI 1999/678, Art.2, Sch. (effective May 19, 1999).

Minor and consequential amendments and repeals
8. [Not reprinted.]

Application to continental shelf
[1] **9.** For the purposes of this Act a death or any accident from which death has resulted which has occurred—

(a) in connection with any activity falling within subsection (2) of section 23 of the Oil and Gas (Enterprise) Act 1982; and

(b) in that area, or any part of that area, in respect of which it is provided by Order in Council under subsection (1) of that section that questions arising out of acts or omissions taking place therein shall be determined in accordance with the law in force in Scotland,

shall be taken to have occurred in Scotland.

NOTE

[1] As amended by the Oil and Gas (Enterprise) Act 1982 (c.23), Sch.3, para.34 and substituted by the Petroleum Act 1998 (c.17), Sch.4 para.9 (effective February 15, 1999).

Interpretation, transitional, citation, commencement and extent
10.—(1) Any reference in this Act to any other enactment shall be construed as a reference to that enactment as amended by or under any other enactment including this Act.

(2)–(3) [*Repealed by the Statute Law (Repeals) Act 1989 (c.43), Sch.1, Pt I.*]

(4) This Act may be cited as the Fatal Accidents and Sudden Deaths Inquiry (Scotland) Act 1976.

(5) [*Repealed by the Statute Law (Repeals) Act 1989 (c.43), Sch.1, Pt I.*]

(6) This Act, other than subsections (4) and (5) of section 4 and section 9 of this Act, extends to Scotland only.

. . . . . .

Vulnerable Witnesses (Scotland) Act 2004

(asp 3)

[April 14, 2004]

. . . .

PART 2

CIVIL PROCEEDINGS

Evidence of children and other vulnerable witnesses: special measures

Establishment of grounds of referral to children's hearings: restrictions on evidence

PART 3

MISCELLANEOUS AND GENERAL

Abolition of the competence test

. . . . . .

PART 2

CIVIL PROCEEDINGS

Evidence of children and other vulnerable witnesses: special measures

Interpretation of this Part
11.—(1) For the purposes of this Part of this Act, a person who is giving

or is to give evidence in or for the purposes of any civil proceedings is a vulnerable witness if—

    (a) the person is under the age of 16 on the date of commencement of the proceedings (such a vulnerable witness being referred to in this Part as a "child witness"), or

    (b) where the person is not a child witness, there is a significant risk that the quality of the evidence to be given by the person will be diminished by reason of—

        (i) mental disorder (within the meaning of section 328 of the Mental Health (Care and Treatment) (Scotland) Act 2003 (asp 13)), or

        (ii) fear or distress in connection with giving evidence in the proceedings.

(2) In considering whether a person is a vulnerable witness by virtue of subsection (1)(b) above, the court must take into account—

    (a) the nature and circumstances of the alleged matter to which the proceedings relate,

    (b) the nature of the evidence which the person is likely to give,

    (c) the relationship (if any) between the person and any party to the proceedings,

    (d) the person's age and maturity,

    (e) any behaviour towards the person on the part of—

        (i) any party to the proceedings,

        (ii) members of the family or associates of any such party,

        (iii) any other person who is likely to be a party to the proceedings or a witness in the proceedings, and

    (f) such other matters, including—

        (i) the social and cultural background and ethnic origins of the person,

        (ii) the person's sexual orientation,

        (iii) the domestic and employment circumstances of the person,

        (iv) any religious beliefs or political opinions of the person, and

        (v) any physical disability or other physical impairment which the person has,

    as appear to the court to be relevant.

(3) For the purposes of subsection (1)(a) above, proceedings are taken to have commenced when the petition, summons, initial writ or other document initiating the proceedings is served, and, where the document is served on more than one person, the proceedings shall be taken to have commenced when the document is served on the first person on whom it is served.

(4) In subsection (1)(b), the reference to the quality of evidence is to its quality in terms of completeness, coherence and accuracy.

(5) In this Part—

    "child witness notice" has the meaning given in section 12(2),

    "civil proceedings" includes, in addition to such proceedings in any of the ordinary courts of law, any proceedings to which section 91 (procedural rules in relation to certain applications etc.) of the Children (Scotland) Act 1995 (c. 36) applies,

    "court" is to be construed in accordance with the meaning of "civil proceedings",

    "special measure" means any of the special measures set out in, or prescribed under, section 18,

    "vulnerable witness application" has the meaning given in section 12(6)(a).

Orders authorising the use of special measures for vulnerable witnesses

    12.—(1) Where a child witness is to give evidence in or for the purposes of any civil proceedings, the court must, before the proof or other hearing at which the child is to give evidence, make an order—

    (a) authorising the use of such special measure or measures as the court considers to be the most appropriate for the purpose of taking the child witness's evidence, or

    (b) that the child witness is to give evidence without the benefit of any special measure.

(2) The party citing or intending to cite a child witness must lodge with the court a notice (referred to in this Part as a "child witness notice")—

    (a) specifying the special measure or measures which the party considers to be the most appropriate for the purpose of taking the child witness's evidence, or

    (b) if the party considers that the child witness should give evidence without the benefit of any special measure, stating that fact,

and the court must have regard to the child witness notice in making an order under subsection (1) above.

(3) If a child witness notice specifies any of the following special measures, namely—

    (a) the use of a live television link in accordance with section 20 where the place from which the child witness is to give evidence by means of the link is another part of the court building in which the court-room is located,

    (b) the use of a screen in accordance with section 21, or

    (c) the use of a supporter in accordance with section 22 in conjunction with either of the special measures referred to in paragraphs (a) and (b) above,

that special measure is, for the purposes of subsection (1)(a) above, to be taken to be the most appropriate for the purposes of taking the child witness's evidence.

(4) The court may make an order under subsection (1)(b) above only if satisfied—

    (a) that the child witness has expressed a wish to give evidence without the benefit of any special measure and that it is appropriate for the child witness so to give evidence, or

    (b) that—

        (i) the use of any special measure for the purpose of taking the evidence of the child witness would give rise to a significant risk of prejudice to the fairness of the proceedings or otherwise to the interests of justice, and

        (ii) that risk significantly outweighs any risk of prejudice to the interests of the child witness if the order is made.

(5) Subsection (6) below applies in relation to a person other than a child witness who is to give evidence in or for the purpose of any civil proceedings (referred to in this section as "the witness").

(6) The court may—

    (a) on an application (referred to in this Part as a "vulnerable witness application") made to it by the party citing or intending to cite the witness, and

    (b) if satisfied that the witness is a vulnerable witness,

make an order authorising the use of such special measure or measures as the court considers most appropriate for the purpose of taking the witness's evidence.

(7) In deciding whether to make an order under subsection (6) above, the court must—

    (a) have regard to—

        (i) the possible effect on the witness if required to give evidence without the benefit of any special measure, and

        (ii) whether it is likely that the witness would be better able to give evidence with the benefit of a special measure, and

    (b) take into account the matters specified in section 11(2)(a) to (f).

Review of arrangements for vulnerable witnesses

13.—(1) In any civil proceedings in which a person who is giving or is to give evidence (referred to in this section as "the witness") appears to the court to be a vulnerable witness, the court may at any stage in the proceedings (whether before or after the commencement of the proof or other hearing at which the witness is giving or is to give evidence or before or after the witness has begun to give evidence)—

    (a) on the application of the party citing or intending to cite the witness, or

    (b) of its own motion,

review the current arrangements for taking the witness's evidence and make an order under subsection (2) below.

(2) The order which may be made under this subsection is—

    (a) where the current arrangements for taking the witness's evidence include the use of a special measure or combination of special measures authorised by an order under section 12 or under this subsection (referred to as the "earlier order"), an order varying or revoking the earlier order, or

    (b) where the current arrangements for taking the witness's evidence do not include any special measure, an order authorising the use of such special measure or measures as the court considers most appropriate for the purpose of taking the witness's evidence.

(3) An order under subsection (2)(a) above varying an earlier order may—

    (a) add to or substitute for any special measure authorised by the earlier order such other special measure as the court considers most appropriate for the purpose of taking the witness's evidence, or

    (b) where the earlier order authorises the use of a combination of special measures for that purpose, delete any of the special measures so authorised.

(4) The court may make an order under subsection (2)(a) above revoking an earlier order only if satisfied that—

    (a) the witness has expressed a wish to give or, as the case may be, continue to give evidence without the benefit of any special measure and that it is appropriate for the witness so to give evidence, or

    (b) that—

        (i) the use, or continued use, of the special measure for the purpose of taking the witness's evidence would give rise to a significant risk of prejudice to the fairness of the proceedings or otherwise to the interests of justice, and

        (ii) that risk significantly outweighs any risk of prejudice to the interests of the witness if the order is made.

(5) Subsection (7) of section 12 applies to the making of an order under subsection (2)(b) of this section as it applies to the making of an order under subsection (6) of that section but as if the references to the witness were to the witness within the meaning of this section.

(6) In this section, "current arrangements" means the arrangements in place at the time the review under this section is begun.

Procedure in connection with orders under sections 12 and 13

14.—(1) In section 5 (power to regulate procedure etc. in the Court of Session by act of sederunt) of the Court of Session Act 1988 (c. 36), after paragraph (d) there is inserted—

    "(da) to regulate the procedure to be followed in proceedings in the Court in connection with the making of orders under sections 12(1) and (6) and 13(2) of the Vulnerable Witnesses (Scotland) Act 2004 (asp 3) ("the 2004 Act");

    (db) to regulate, so far as not regulated by the 2004 Act, the use in any proceedings in the Court of any special measures authorised by virtue of that Act to be used;".

(2) In section 32(1) (power of Court of Session to regulate civil procedure in the sheriff court) of the Sheriff Courts (Scotland) Act 1971 (c. 58), after paragraph (e) there is inserted—

> "(ea) regulating the procedure to be followed in connection with the making of orders under sections 12(1) and (6) and 13(2) of the Vulnerable Witnesses (Scotland) Act 2004 (asp 3) ("the 2004 Act");
>
> (eb) regulating, so far as not regulated by the 2004 Act, the use of special measures authorised by virtue of that Act to be used;".

Vulnerable witnesses: supplementary provision

15.—(1) Subsection (2) below applies where—

(a) a party is considering for the purposes of a child witness notice or a vulnerable witness application which of the special measures is or are the most appropriate for the purpose of taking the evidence of the person to whom the notice or application relates, or

(b) the court is making an order under section 12(1) or (6) or 13(2).

(2) The party or, as the case may be, the court must—

(a) have regard to the best interests of the witness, and

(b) take account of any views expressed by—

    (i) the witness (having regard, where the witness is a child witness, to the witness's age and maturity), and

    (ii) where the witness is a child witness, the witness's parent.

(3) For the purposes of subsection (2)(b) above, where the witness is a child witness—

(a) the witness is to be presumed to be of sufficient age and maturity to form a view if aged 12 or older, and

(b) in the event that any views expressed by the witness are inconsistent with any views expressed by the witness's parent, the views of the witness are to be given greater weight.

(4) In this section—

"parent", in relation to a child witness, means any person having parental responsibilities within the meaning of section 1(3) of the Children (Scotland) Act 1995 (c. 36) in relation to the child witness,

"the witness" means—

(a) in the case referred to in subsection (1)(a) above, the person to whom the child witness notice or vulnerable witness application relates,

(b) in the case referred to in subsection (1)(b) above, the person to whom the order would relate.

Party to proceedings as a vulnerable witness

16.—Where a child witness or other person who is giving or is to give evidence in or for the purposes of any civil proceedings (referred to in this section as "the witness") is a party to the proceedings—

(a) sections 12 and 13 have effect in relation to the witness as if references in those sections to the party citing or intending to cite the witness were references to the witness, and

(b) section 15 has effect in relation to the witness as if—

    (i) in subsection (1), paragraph (a) were omitted, and

    (ii) in subsection (2), the words "The party or, as the case may be," were omitted.

Crown application and saving provision

17.—(1) Sections 11 to 15 of this Act apply to the Crown.

(2) Nothing in section 12 or 13 of this Act affects any power or duty which a court has otherwise than by virtue of those sections to make or authorise

any special arrangements for taking the evidence of any person in any civil proceedings.

The special measures
   18.—(1) The special measures which may be authorised to be used by virtue of section 12 or 13 of this Act for the purpose of taking the evidence of a vulnerable witness are—
   (a) taking of evidence by a commissioner in accordance with section 19,
   (b) use of a live television link in accordance with section 20,
   (c) use of screen in accordance with section 21,
   (d) use of a supporter in accordance with section 22, and
   (e) such other measures as the Scottish Ministers may, by order made by statutory instrument, prescribe.
   (2) An order under subsection (1)(e) above is not to be made unless a draft of the statutory instrument containing the order has been laid before and approved by a resolution of the Scottish Parliament.

Taking of evidence by a commissioner
   19.—(1) Where the special measure to be used is taking of evidence by a commissioner, the court must appoint a commissioner to take the evidence of the vulnerable witness in respect of whom the special measure is to be used.
   (2) Proceedings before a commissioner appointed under subsection (1) above must be recorded by video recorder.
   (3) A party to the proceedings—
   (a) must not, except by leave of the court, be present in the room where such proceedings are taking place, but
   (b) is entitled by such means as seem suitable to the court to watch and hear the proceedings.
   (4) The recording of the proceedings made in pursuance of subsection (2) above is to be received in evidence without being sworn to by witnesses.

Live television link
   20.—(1) Where the special measure to be used is a live television link, the court must make such arrangements as seem to it appropriate for the vulnerable witness in respect of whom the special measure is to be used to give evidence by means of such a link.
   (2) Where—
   (a) the live television link is to be used in proceedings in a sheriff court, but
   (b) that court lacks accommodation or equipment necessary for the purpose of receiving such a link,
the sheriff may by order transfer the proceedings to any sheriff court in the same sheriffdom which has such accommodation or equipment available.
   (3) An order may be made under subsection (2) above—
   (a) at any stage in the proceedings (whether before or after the commencement of the proof or other hearing at which the vulnerable witness is to give evidence), or
   (b) in relation to a part of the proceedings.

Screens
   21.—(1) Where the special measure to be used is a screen, the screen must be used to conceal the parties to the proceedings from the sight of the vulnerable witness in respect of whom the special measure is to be used.
   (2) However, the court must make arrangements to ensure that the parties are able to watch and hear the vulnerable witness giving evidence.
   (3) Subsections (2) and (3) of section 20 apply for the purposes of use of a screen under this section as they apply for the purposes of use of a live television link under that section but as if—

(a) references to the live television link were references to the screen, and

(b) the reference to receiving such a link were a reference to the use of a screen.

Supporters

22.—(1) Where the special measure to be used is a supporter, another person ("the supporter") nominated by or on behalf of the vulnerable witness in respect of whom the special measure is to be used may be present alongside the witness for the purpose of providing support whilst the witness is giving evidence.

(2) Where the person nominated as the supporter is to give evidence in the proceedings, that person may not act as the supporter at any time before giving evidence.

(3) The supporter must not prompt or otherwise seek to influence the vulnerable witness in the course of giving evidence.

Establishment of grounds of referral to children's hearings: restrictions on evidence

23. Establishment of grounds of referral to children's hearings: restrictions on evidence

After section 68 (application to sheriff to establish grounds of referral) of the Children (Scotland) Act 1995 (c. 36) there is inserted—

"**68A** Restrictions on evidence in certain cases involving sexual abuse

(1) This section applies in relation to—

(a) an application under section 65(7) or (9) of this Act in which the ground of referral to be established is a condition mentioned in—

(i) paragraph (b) of subsection (2) of section 52 of this Act where that condition is alleged to be satisfied by reference to sexual behaviour engaged in by any person,

(ii) paragraph (d), (e) or (f) of that subsection where that condition is alleged to be satisfied by reference to a relevant offence, or

(iii) paragraph (g) of that subsection, or

(b) an application under section 85 of this Act for a review of a finding that any such ground of referral is established.

(2) In hearing the application, the sheriff shall not admit, or allow questioning designed to elicit, evidence which shows or tends to show that the child who is the subject of the application or any other witness giving evidence at the hearing (such child or other witness being referred to in this section and section 68B of this Act as "the witness")—

(a) is not of good character (whether in relation to sexual matters or otherwise),

(b) has, at any time, engaged in sexual behaviour not forming part of the subject matter of the ground of referral,

(c) has, at any time (other than shortly before, at the same time as or shortly after the acts which form part of the subject matter of the ground of referral), engaged in such behaviour, not being sexual behaviour, as might found the inference that the witness is not a credible or reliable witness, or

(d) has, at any time, been subject to any such condition or predisposition as might found the inference referred to in paragraph (c) above.

(3) In subsection (1)(a)(ii) above, "relevant offence" means—

(a) an offence mentioned in paragraph 1 or 4 of Schedule 1 (offences against children under the age of 17 to which special provisions apply) to the Criminal Procedure (Scotland) Act 1995 (c. 46), or

(b) any other offence mentioned in that Schedule where there is a substantial sexual element in the alleged commission of the offence.

(4) In subsection (2)(b) and (c) above—

  (a) "the subject matter of the ground of referral" means—

    (i) in the case of an application in which the ground of referral to be established is the condition referred to in paragraph (a)(i) of subsection (1) above, the sexual behaviour referred to in that paragraph,

    (ii) in the case of any other application, the acts or behaviour constituting the offence by reference to which the ground of referral is alleged to be established,

    and

  (b) the reference to engaging in sexual behaviour includes a reference to undergoing or being made subject to any experience of a sexual nature.

68B Exceptions to restrictions under section 68A

(1) The sheriff hearing an application referred to in subsection (1) of section 68A of this Act may, on an application by any party to the proceedings, admit such evidence or allow such questioning as is referred to in subsection (2) of that section if satisfied that—

  (a) the evidence or questioning will relate only to a specific occurrence or occurrences of sexual or other behaviour or to specific facts demonstrating—

    (i) the character of the witness, or

    (ii) any condition or predisposition to which the witness is or has been subject,

  (b) that occurrence or those occurrences of behaviour or facts are relevant to establishing the ground of referral, and

  (c) the probative value of the evidence sought to be admitted or elicited is significant and is likely to outweigh any risk of prejudice to the proper administration of justice arising from its being admitted or elicited.

(2) In subsection (1) above—

  (a) the reference to an occurrence or occurrences of sexual behaviour includes a reference to undergoing or being made subject to any experience of a sexual nature,

  (b) "the proper administration of justice" includes—

    (i) appropriate protection of the witness's dignity and privacy, and

    (ii) ensuring the facts and circumstances of which the sheriff is made aware are relevant to an issue to be put before the sheriff and commensurate with the importance of that issue to the sheriff's decision on the question whether the ground of referral is established.

(3) In this section, "the witness" means the child who is the subject of the application referred to in section 68A(1) or other witness in respect of whom the evidence is sought to be admitted or elicited.".

PART 3

MISCELLANEOUS AND GENERAL

Abolition of the competence test

Abolition of the competence test for witnesses in criminal and civil proceedings
   24.—(1) The evidence of any person called as a witness (referred to in this section as "the witness") in criminal or civil proceedings is not inadmissible solely because the witness does not understand—

(a) the nature of the duty of a witness to give truthful evidence, or
(b) the difference between truth and lies.

(2) Accordingly, the court must not, at any time before the witness gives evidence, take any step intended to establish whether the witness understands those matters.

. . . . . .

Enforcement Abroad of Sheriff Court Judgments 1962

(S.I. 1962 No. 1517)

[17th July 1962]

The Lords of Council and Session, under and by virtue of the powers conferred upon them by section 34(1) of the Administration of Justice (Scotland) Act 1933 and of all other powers competent to them in that behalf, do hereby enact as follows:—

Interpretation
1. In this Act of Sederunt—
    "sheriff" includes sheriff-substitute;
    "sheriff clerk" includes sheriff clerk depute;
    "initial writ" means the statement of claim, petition, note of appeal, or
        other document by which the action is initiated.

[1] **2.** An application for a certified copy of a judgment obtained in a sheriff court, made for the purpose of the enforcement of the judgment in a country other than a country to which Parts I and II of the Civil Jurisdiction and Judgments Act 1982 applies, shall be made in that sheriff court by minute lodged in the process in which the judgment was obtained. There shall be lodged with the minute either an extract decree setting forth the judgment or a copy of the judgment. The sheriff, on being satisfied, by affidavit or by other proper evidence, as to the purpose for which the application is being made, shall pronounce an order ordaining the sheriff clerk to issue a certified copy of the judgment. The certificate shall be in the following terms:—

> "I certify that the foregoing is a true copy of a judgment obtained in the   Sheriff Court and that this certificate is issued for the purpose of the enforcement of the judgment in a country other than a country to which Parts I and II of the Civil Jurisdiction and Judgments Act 1982 applies and in obedience to an order by the Sheriff of   dated
>
> (Signed)
> Sheriff Clerk."

NOTE
[1] As amended by S.I. 1986 No. 1947.

3. There shall be issued along with the foregoing certificate the following further certificate also certified by the sheriff clerk—

> A certificate, enumerating and identifying and having annexed to it; (1) a copy of the initial writ by which the proceedings were initiated, showing the manner in which the initial writ was served on the defender or respondent and whether the defender or respondent appeared thereto, and the objections made to the jurisdiction if any; (2) a copy of the pleadings, if any, in the proceedings; (3) a copy of the opinion or note, if any, of the sheriff, and (4) a statement of such other particulars as it may be necessary to give to the foreign tribunal

in which it is sought to obtain execution of the judgment. Copies of the foregoing documents shall be supplied where necessary by the person making the application.

4. This Act of Sederunt may be cited as the Act of Sederunt (Enforcement Abroad of Sheriff Court Judgments) 1962, and shall come into operation on 17th July 1962.

Computer Evidence in the Sheriff Court 1969

(S.I. 1969 No. 1643)

[18th November 1969]

The Lords of Council and Session, by virtue of the powers conferred upon them by section 34 of the Administration of Justice (Scotland) Act 1933 and section 15(6) of the Law Reform (Miscellaneous Provisions)(Scotland) Act 1968, do hereby enact and declare as follows:—

1. A party to any civil proceedings who wishes to rely on a statement contained in a document produced by a computer shall, not later than the date of closing the record, send to every other party to the proceedings a copy of the statement together with a notice in writing—
  (a) intimating that the party intends to rely on the statement;
  (b) stating that the statement is contained in a document produced by a computer; and
¹ (c) informing the party to whom it is addressed that he may give a counter-notice in terms of paragraph 3 hereof;
and the party so giving notice may within fourteen days thereafter lodge in process a certificate in terms of section 13(4) of the Law Reform (Miscella neous Provisions) (Scotland) Act 1968 relating to the document.

NOTE
¹ Substituted by S.I. 1970 No. 456.

2. When a certificate in terms of section 13(4) of the Law Reform (Miscellaneous Provisions) (Scotland) Act 1968 shall have been lodged in process, a copy thereof shall be sent to every other party to the proceedings within fourteen days after the date of the notice referred to in paragraph 1 hereof.

3. Any party who receives such a notice as is mentioned in paragraph 1 hereof may, within twenty-one days thereafter, by counter-notice in writing addressed to the party who served the notice, require him, within twenty-one days, to furnish him in writing with all or any of the following information—
  (a) any such information as might have been the subject of a certificate under section 13(4) of the Law Reform (Miscellaneous Provisions) (Scotland) Act 1968, except in so far as such information is the subject of a certificate lodged in process as aforesaid;
  (b) the name, occupation, business address and place of residence of a person occupying at the material time a responsible position in relation to each of (i) the operation of the device involved in the production of the document, (ii) the management of the activities for the purposes of which the computer was used to store or process information, (iii) the supply of information to the computer, (iv) the operation of the computer, and (v) the operation of any equipment

by means of which the document containing the statement was produced by the computer; and

(c) the name, occupation, business address and place of residence of the person who signed any certificate lodged in process in terms of section 13(4) of the Law Reform (Miscellaneous Provisions) (Scot land) Act 1968.

4. Subject to the provisions of section 15(8) of the Law Reform (Miscella neous Provisions) (Scotland) Act 1968, a party upon whom a counter-notice has been served in terms of paragraph 3 hereof shall not be entitled to rely upon the statement in the document to which the notice under paragraph 1 hereof related, unless the counter-notice shall have been withdrawn by the party who gave it or unless the court shall be satisfied that the counter-notice was complied with so far as was reasonably possible.

5. Any party to whom information is furnished under a counter-notice by virtue of paragraph 3 hereof may, not later than twenty-eight days before the date of the proof or trial, by notice in writing require that the party wishing to rely on the statement in the document produced by a computer should call as a witness any person of whom particulars were furnished under sub-paragraph (b) or (c) of paragraph 3 hereof.

6. (i) Subject to the provisions of section 15(8) of the Law Reform (Miscellaneous Provisions) (Scotland) Act 1968 a party who has been required to call any person as a witness in terms of paragraph 5 hereof shall not be entitled to rely upon the statement in the document to which the notice under paragraph 1 hereof related unless the notice requiring that person to be called as a witness shall have been withdrawn by the party who gave it, or unless that person shall be adduced as a witness, or unless the court shall be satisfied that such person is dead, or beyond the seas, or unfit by reason of his bodily or mental condition to attend as a witness, or cannot with reasonable diligence be identified or found, or cannot reasonably be expected (having regard to the passage of time and to all the circumstances) to have any recollection of matters relevant to the accuracy or otherwise of the statement in the document.

(ii) In the event that such person is not to be adduced as a witness for any reason aforesaid, the party wishing to rely on the statement in the document produced by a computer shall give notice in writing to every other party to the proceedings that such witness is not to be adduced and the reason therefor.

(iii) The notice referred to in sub-paragraph (ii) hereof shall be given not later than fourteen days after the date of the notice under paragraph 5 hereof or, if such reason could not reasonably have become known to him within that period, immediately such reason shall become known.

7. This Act of Sederunt shall apply to all civil proceedings in the Sheriff Court.

8. This Act of Sederunt may be cited as the Act of Sederunt (Computer Evidence in the Sheriff Court) 1969, and shall come into operation on 1st December 1969.

Interest in Sheriff Court Decrees or Extracts 1975

(SI 1975/948)

[4th June 1975]

The Lords of Council and Session, under and by virtue of the powers conferred upon them by section 4 of the Administration of Justice (Scotland) Act 1972 and of all other powers competent to them in that behalf, do hereby enact and declare as follows:—

¹ **1.** In the case of any decree or extract in an action commenced on or after 1st July 1975 the provisions of section 9 of the Sheriff Courts (Scotland) Extracts Act 1892 as amended by the Act of Sederunt (Interest in Sheriff Court Decrees or Extracts) 1972 shall not apply. Instead there shall be substituted a new section 9 as follows:—

"where interest is included in a decree or extract, it shall be deemed to be at the rate of eight *per centum per annum*, unless otherwise stated".

NOTE

¹ Twelve per cent substituted for eleven per cent, with effect from 5th April 1983, by SI 1983/409.

Fifteen per cent substituted for twelve per cent, with effect from 16th August 1985, by SI 1985/1179.

Eight per cent substituted for fifteen per cent, with effect from 1st April 1993, by SI 1993/769.

2. This Act of Sederunt may be cited as the Act of Sederunt (Interest in Sheriff Court Decrees or Extracts) 1975, and shall come into operation on 2nd July 1975.

Fatal Accidents and Sudden Deaths Inquiry Procedure (Scotland) Rules 1977

(SI 1977/191)

[7th February 1977]

In exercise of the powers conferred on me by section 7(1) of the Fatal Accidents and Sudden Deaths Inquiry (Scotland) Act 1976 and of all other powers enabling me in that behalf I hereby make the following rules:—

Citation and commencement
1. These rules may be cited as the Fatal Accidents and Sudden Deaths Inquiry Procedure (Scotland) Rules 1977 and shall come into operation on 1st March 1977.

Interpretation
2.—(1) In these rules, unless the context otherwise requires,—
"the Act" means the Fatal Accidents and Sudden Deaths Inquiry (Scotland) Act 1976;
"inquiry" means an inquiry under the Act;
"officer of law" has the meaning assigned to it by section 462 of the Criminal Procedure (Scotland) Act 1975;
¹ "the Ordinary Cause Rules" means Schedule 1 to the Sheriff Courts (Scotland) Act 1907;

"procurator fiscal" has the meaning assigned to it by section 462 of the Criminal Procedure (Scotland) Act 1975;

"sheriff clerk" includes sheriff clerk depute and any person duly authorised to execute the duties of sheriff clerk.

(2) In these rules, unless the context otherwise requires, a reference to any enactment shall be construed as a reference to that enactment as amended or re-enacted by any subsequent enactment.

(3) The Interpretation Act 1889 shall apply for the interpretation of these rules as it applies for the interpretation of an Act of Parliament.

NOTE
[1] As inserted by the Fatal Accidents and Sudden Deaths Inquiry Procedure (Scotland) Amendment Rules (SSI 2007/478), r.2(2)(c) (effective November 1, 2007).

Application for holding of inquiry
3. The application for the holding of an inquiry in accordance with section 1(1) of the Act and the sheriff's first warrant thereon shall be in the case of such a death as is referred to in section 1(1)(a) of the Act in the form as nearly as may be of Form 1 of the Schedule to these rules, and in the case of such a death as is referred to in section 1(1)(b) of the Act in the form as nearly as may be of Form 2 of the said Schedule.

Notice of holding of inquiry
4.—(1) Intimation of the holding of an inquiry in accordance with section 3(2)(a) of the Act shall be made by notice in writing in the form as nearly as may be of Form 3 of the Schedule to these rules, given not less than 21 days before the date of the inquiry.

(2) Such notice shall be given to the following persons, besides those specified in the said section 3(2)(a),—

[1] (za) any civil partner of the person who has died;
  (a) in the case of such a death as is referred to in section 1(1)(a)(i) of the Act, to the Health and Safety Commission;
  (b) in the case of such a death as is referred to in section 1(1)(a)(ii) of the Act, to any minister, government department or other authority in whose legal custody the person who has died was at the time of his death;
[2] (c) in the case of a death occurring in the circumstances specified in section 9 of the Act, or a death resulting from an accident occurring in those circumstances, to the Secretary of State for Employment;
  (d) in any case where it is competent for a minister or government department under any statute other than the Act to cause public inquiry to be made into the circumstances of the death, to such minister or government department.

(3) Public notice of the holding of an inquiry in accordance with section 3(2)(b) of the Act shall be given by publishing in at least two newspapers circulating in the sheriff court district where the inquiry is to be held, not less than 21 days before the date of the inquiry, an advertisement in the form as nearly as may be of Form 4 of the Schedule to these rules.

NOTES
[1] As inserted by the Fatal Accidents and Sudden Deaths Inquiry Procedure (Scotland) Amendment Rules (SSI 2007/478), r.2(3) (effective November 1, 2007).
[2] As amended by SI 1992/1568 (effective July 3, 1992).

Custody of productions
5. The sheriff may at the time of making an order for the holding of an inquiry or at any time thereafter, upon the application of the procurator fiscal, or of any other person entitled to appear at the inquiry or at his own instance, grant warrant to officers of law to take possession of anything connected with the death which is the subject of inquiry and which it may be

considered necessary to produce at the inquiry and to hold any such thing in safe custody, subject to inspection by any persons interested.

Inspection of land, premises, etc.
6. The sheriff may at the time of making an order for the holding of an inquiry or at any time thereafter, upon the application of the procurator fiscal or of any other person entitled to appear at the inquiry or at his own instance, inspect or grant warrant for any person to inspect any land, premises, article or other thing the inspection of which the sheriff considers desirable for the purposes of the inquiry.

Representation
7.—(1) The procurator fiscal may appear on his own behalf at an inquiry or be represented by an assistant or depute procurator fiscal or by Crown counsel.

(2) Any person entitled to appear at an inquiry in terms of section 4(2) of the Act may appear on his own behalf or be represented by an advocate or a solicitor or, with the leave of the sheriff, by any other person.

Citation of witnesses or havers
8. The citation of a witness or haver to appear at an inquiry shall be in the form as nearly as may be of Form 5 of the Schedule to these rules, and an execution of citation in the form as nearly as may be of Form 6 of the said Schedule shall be sufficient evidence of such citation.

Vulnerable witness procedure—forms
[1] **8A.**—(1) This rule applies where a vulnerable witness (within the meaning of section 11(1) of the 2004 Act) is to give evidence at an inquiry and the application of the Ordinary Cause Rules in relation to the vulnerable witness would otherwise require any of the forms in column 1 of the Table below to be used.

(2) The form used instead shall be as nearly as may be the corresponding form of the Schedule to these Rules that is specified in column 2 of the Table.

TABLE 1

Column 1—*Ordinary Cause Rules form*	Column 2—*Inquiry form*
child witness notice (Form G19)	Form 7
vulnerable witness application (Form G20)	Form 8
certificate of intimation (Form G21)	Form 9
review application (Form G22)	Form 10
certificate of intimation (Form G23)	Form 11

NOTE
[1] As inserted by the Fatal Accidents and Sudden Deaths Inquiry Procedure (Scotland) Amendment Rules (SSI 2007/478), r.2(4) (effective November 1, 2007).

Vulnerable witness procedure—preliminary hearing
[1] **8B.** If any preliminary hearing is held before the inquiry, the sheriff shall ascertain whether there is or is likely to be a vulnerable witness (within the meaning of section 11(1) of the 2004 Act) who is to give evidence at the inquiry, consider any child witness notice or vulnerable witness application that has been lodged where no order has been made under section 12 of the 2004 Act and consider whether any order under section 12 of that Act requires to be made.

NOTE
[1] As inserted by the Fatal Accidents and Sudden Deaths Inquiry Procedure (Scotland) Amendment Rules (SSI 2007/478), r.2(4) (effective November 1, 2007).

Adjournment of inquiry
9. The sheriff may at any time adjourn the inquiry to a time and place specified by him at the time of adjournment.

Written statements
10.—(1) The sheriff may admit in place of oral evidence by any person in an inquiry, to the like extent as such oral evidence, a written statement by that person signed by that person and sworn or affirmed to be true by that person before a notary public, commissioner for oaths or justice of the peace, or before a commissioner appointed by the sheriff for that purpose:
Provided that such a statement may only be admitted if—
(a) all persons who appear or are represented at the inquiry agree to its admission; or
(b) the sheriff considers that its admission will not result in unfairness in the conduct of the inquiry to any person who appears or is represented at the inquiry.
(2) A certificate that the statement has been so sworn and affirmed, annexed to the statement and signed by the person making the statement and by the person before whom it is sworn or affirmed, shall be sufficient evidence that it has been so sworn or affirmed.
(3) Any statement which is admitted in evidence by virtue of this rule shall, unless the sheriff otherwise directs, be read aloud at the inquiry; and where the sheriff directs that a statement or any part of it shall not be read aloud he shall state his reason for so directing and, where appropriate, an account shall be given orally of what the sheriff has directed not to be read aloud.
(4) Any document or object referred to as a production and identified in a written statement tendered in evidence under this rule shall be treated as if it had been produced and had been identified in court by the maker of the statement.

Sheriff's determination
11.—(1) The sheriff's determination shall be in writing and shall be signed by him.
(2) The sheriff's determination shall, except in the circumstances specified in paragraph (3) of this rule, be read out by him in public.
(3) Where the sheriff requires time to prepare his determination and considers that in the circumstances it is not reasonable to fix an adjourned sitting of the inquiry for the sole purpose of reading out the determination, the sheriff shall not be required to read out the determination, but the sheriff clerk shall send free of charge a copy of the determination, to the procurator fiscal and to any person who appeared or was represented at the inquiry and shall allow any person to inspect a copy of the determination at the sheriff clerk's office free of charge during the period of three months after the date when the determination was made.

Assessors
12.—(1) A request to the sheriff to summon a person to act as an assessor in terms of section 4(6) of the Act shall be made by written motion lodged with the sheriff clerk not less than seven days before the date of the inquiry.
(2) The appointment of an assessor shall not affect the admissibility of expert evidence in the inquiry.

Recording of evidence

13. Evidence given in an inquiry shall be recorded in the same manner as evidence given in an ordinary civil cause in the sheriff court:

Provided that where the evidence shall have been taken down in shorthand it shall not be necessary to extend such evidence unless the sheriff shall so direct or unless a copy of the transcript of evidence shall be duly requested by any person entitled thereto in terms of the Act and these rules.

Time-limit for obtaining copy of transcript of evidence

14. A person shall be entitled to obtain a copy of the transcript of the evidence in accordance with section 6(5)(*b*) of the Act only if he makes application therefor to the sheriff clerk within a period of three months after the date when the sheriff's determination was made.

Fee on obtaining copy of determination, or of transcript of evidence

15.—(1) The fee payable upon obtaining a copy of the sheriff's determination in accordance with section 6(5)(*a*) of the Act shall be such fee as is payable to sheriff clerks for copying documents relating to civil proceedings in the sheriff court.

(2) The fee payable upon obtaining a copy of the transcript of the evidence in accordance with section 6(5)(*b*) of the Act shall be—

(*a*) where the copy is made by a shorthand writer, such copying fee as is payable by the sheriff clerk to the shorthand writer;

(*b*) where the copy is made by the sheriff clerk, such fee as is payable to sheriff clerks for copying documents relating to civil proceedings in the sheriff court.

Service of documents

16.—(1) The notice intimating the holding of an inquiry in accordance with section 3(2)(*a*) of the Act, the citation of a witness for precognition by the procurator fiscal, the citation of a witness or haver to attend at an inquiry, and any interlocutor, warrant or other order of the sheriff or writ following thereon issued in connection with an inquiry may be served on a person in any of the following manners:–

(*a*) the procurator fiscal or the solicitor for any person entitled to appear at the inquiry, as appropriate, may post the document in a registered or recorded delivery letter addressed to the person on whom the document requires to be served at his residence or place of business or at any address specified by him for the purpose of receiving documents;

(*b*) a police officer (where the document is issued by the procurator fiscal) or a sheriff officer may—

   (i) serve the document personally on the person on whom it requires to be served; or

   (ii) leave the document in the hands of an inmate or employee at that person's residence or place of business or any address specified by him for the purpose of receiving documents;

   (iii) introduce the document into that person's residence or place of business or any address so specified by means of a letterbox or other lawful means; or

   (iv) affix the document to the door of that person's residence or place of business or any place so specified;

Provided that when it proves difficult for any reason to serve any document on any person the sheriff, on being satisfied that all reasonable steps have been taken to serve it, may dispense with service of such document or order such other steps as he may think fit.

Dispensing power of sheriff

17. The sheriff may in his discretion relieve any person from the consequences of any failure to comply with the provisions of these rules if the failure resulted from mistake, oversight or any cause other than wilful non-observance of these rules and in granting such relief may impose such terms and conditions as appear to him to be just; and in any such case the sheriff may make such order as appears to him to be just regarding extension of time, lodging or amendment of papers or otherwise, so as to enable the inquiry to proceed as if such failure had not happened.

SCHEDULE

Rule 3   FORM 1

UNDER THE FATAL ACCIDENTS AND SUDDEN DEATHS INQUIRY (SCOTLAND) ACT 1976

To the Sheriff of   at (*place of court*)

The APPLICATION of the Procurator Fiscal for the District of

From information received by the applicant it appears that (*narrate briefly the apparent facts of the death*);

In terms of the said Act an inquiry requires to be held into the circumstances of said death.

May it therefore please your Lordship to fix a time and place for the holding by your Lordship of such in inquiry; to grant warrant to cite witnesses and havers to attend at such inquiry, at the instance of the applicant, and of any other person who may be entitled by virtue of said Act to appear thereat; to grant warrant to officers of law to take possession of, and hold in safe custody, subject to inspection by any person interested, anything which it may be considered necessary to produce at the inquiry.

According to Justice, &c.

(*Signature*)
Procurator Fiscal

(*Place and date*). The Sheriff having considered the foregoing application orders that inquiry into the circumstances of the death of   within designed, be held on the   day of   19 , at (*time*), within the Sheriff Court House at   ; grants warrant to cite witnesses and havers as craved; also grants warrant to officers of law to take possession of, and to hold in safe custody, subject to the inspection by any person interested, anything which it may be considered necessary to produce at the inquiry.
(*Signature*)

Rule 3   FORM 2

UNDER THE FATAL ACCIDENTS AND SUDDEN DEATHS INQUIRY (SCOTLAND) ACT 1976

To the Sheriff of   at (*place of court*)

The APPLICATION of the Procurator Fiscal for the District of

From information received by the applicant is appears that (*narrate briefly the apparent facts of the death*);

and it appears to the Lord Advocate to be expedient in the public interest that an inquiry under the said Act should be held into the circumstances of said death.

May it therefore please your Lordship to fix a time and place for the holding by your Lordship of such an inquiry; to grant warrant to cite witnesses and havers to attend at such inquiry, at the instance of the applicant and of any other person who may be entitled by virtue of said Act to appear thereat; to grant warrant to officers of law to take possession of, and hold in safe custody, subject to inspection by any person interested, anything which it may be considered necessary to produce at the inquiry.

According to Justice, &c.

(*Signature*)
Procurator Fiscal

(*Place and date*). The Sheriff having considered the foregoing application orders that inquiry into the circumstances of the death of   within designed, be held on the   day of   19 , at (*time*) within the Sheriff Court House at   ; grants warrant to cite witnesses and havers as craved; also grants warrant to officers of law to take possession of, and to hold in safe custody, subject to the inspection by any person interested, anything which it may be considered necessary to produce at the inquiry.

(*Signature*)

Rule 4(1)   FORM 3

(*Address of procurator fiscal*)

(*Date*)

(*Name and address of
person to whom notice
is given*)

Dear Sir

DEATH OF (*insert name of deceased*)

I have to intimate that an inquiry under the Fatal Accidents and Sudden Deaths Inquiry (Scotland) Act 1976 into the circumstances of the death of (*insert name and address of deceased*) will be held on the   day of   at (*time*) within the Sheriff Court House at (*address*).

* [You have the right to appear, call witnesses and lead evidence at the inquiry. You may attend in person or be represented by an advocate or a solicitor instructed by you or, with the leave of the sheriff, by some other person.]

Yours faithfully,

(*Signature*)
Procurator Fiscal

  * To be inserted only when the person to whom notice is given is the wife, husband or nearest known relative, or the employer, of the deceased.

Rule 4(3)   FORM 4

ADVERTISEMENT

Under the Fatal Accidents and Sudden Deaths Inquiry (Scotland) Act 1976

The Sheriff of

will hold an inquiry on the   day of (*month*) 19   at (*time*) within the Sheriff Court House at (*address*) into the circumstances of the death of (*name, occupation, address*).

(*Signature*)
Procurator Fiscal for the District of

Rule 8   FORM 5

To (*name and designation*).

  YOU are cited to attend at the Sheriff Court House at (*address*) on (*date*) at (*time*) as a witness at the instance of (*insert* "the Procurator Fiscal for the District of   " *or name and address of person calling witness*) at the INQUIRY then to be held into the circumstances of the DEATH of (*name and address of deceased*) [and are required to bring with

you   ] and if you fail to attend you may be ordered to pay a penalty not
exceeding*

*(Signature and designation of procurator fiscal,
police officer, sheriff officer or solicitor)*

* (Insert penalty specified in rule [74(2)] of the First Schedule to the Sheriff Courts (Scotland)
Act 1907 [as amended]).

Rule 8   FORM 6

I certify that on (*date*) I lawfully cited (*name and designation*) to attend at the Sheriff Court
House at (*address*) on (*date*) at (*time*) as a witness at the instance of (*insert* "the Procurator
Fiscal for the District of   " *or name and address of person calling witness*) at the
INQUIRY then to be held into the circumstances of the DEATH of (*name and address of
deceased*) [and I required him to bring with him   ].

This I did by (*specify exactly how served*).

*(Signature and designation of procurator fiscal,
police officer, sheriff officer or solicitor)*

Enforcement of Judgments under the Civil Jurisdiction and Judgments Act 1982, 1986

(SI 1986/1947)

[13th November 1986]

The Lords of Council and Session, under and by virtue of the powers
conferred on them by section 32 of the Sheriff Courts (Scotland) Act 1971,
section 48 of the Civil Jurisdiction and Judgments Act 1982 and of all other
powers enabling them in that behalf, do hereby enact and declare:—

Citation and commencement
   1.—(1) This Act of Sederunt may be cited as the Act of Sederunt
(Enforcement of Judgments under the Civil Jurisdiction and Judgments Act
1982) 1986 and shall come into operation on 1st January 1987.
   (2) This Act of Sederunt shall be inserted in the Books of Sederunt.

Interpretation
   2.—[1] (1) In this Act of Sederunt—
      "the 1982 Act" means the Civil Jurisdiction and Judgments Act 1982;
      "the 1968 Convention" and "the Lugano Convention" have the
         meanings respectively assigned in section 1 of the 1982 Act;
      "authentic instrument" means an instrument referred to in Articles 50
         or 51 of the 1968 Convention and the Lugano Convention;
      "court settlement" means a settlement referred to in Article 51 of the
         1968 Convention and the Lugano Convention; and
      "Ordinary Cause Rules" means the First Schedule to the Sheriff Courts
         (Scotland) Act 1907.
   (2) A form referred to by number means the form so numbered in the
Schedule to this Act of Sederunt or a form substantially to the same effect,
with such variation as circumstances may require.

NOTE
[1] As amended by SI 1993/2346 (effective October 25, 1993).

Enforcement of sheriff court judgments in other parts of the United Kingdom (Money provisions)

3.—(1) An application for a certificate under paragraph 2 of Schedule 6 to the 1982 Act shall be made in writing to the sheriff clerk and shall be accompanied by an affidavit—

(a) stating the sum or aggregate of the sums, including expenses, payable and unsatisfied;

(b) verifying that the time for bringing an appeal against the judgment has expired and no appeal has been brought within that time, or that any appeal has been finally disposed of; and that enforcement of the judgment has not been suspended and the time available for the enforcement has not expired; and

(c) stating the address of the party entitled to enforce, and the usual or last known address of the party liable to execution on, the judgment.

(2) A certificate under paragraph 4 of Schedule 6 to the 1982 Act shall be in Form 1 and be signed by the sheriff clerk.

Enforcement of sheriff court judgments in other parts of the United Kingdom (Non-money provisions)

4.—(1) An application for a certified copy of an interlocutor or extract decree and, where appropriate, a copy of the note or opinion of the sheriff under paragraph 2 of Schedule 7 to the 1982 Act shall be made in writing to the sheriff clerk and shall be accompanied by an affidavit—

(a) verifying that the time for bringing an appeal against the judgment has expired and no appeal has been brought within that time, or any appeal has been finally disposed of; and that enforcement of the judgment has not been suspended and the time available for the enforcement has not expired; and

(b) stating the address of the party entitled to enforce, and the usual or last known address of the party liable to execution on, the judgment.

(2) A copy of an interlocutor, decree, note or opinion issued under paragraph 4 of Schedule 7 to the 1982 Act shall have appended to it a certificate in Form 2 signed by the sheriff clerk.

Enforcement of sheriff court interlocutors and decrees in another Contracting State

5.—[1] (1) Before an application is made under section 12 of the 1982 Act for a copy of a judgment or a certificate giving particulars relating to the judgment and the proceedings in which it was given, the party wishing to enforce the judgment shall serve the judgment on all parties against whom the judgment has been given in accordance with rule 5.4 or 5.5 of the Ordinary Cause Rules, as the case may be, accompanied by a notice in Form 4; and the execution of such service shall be in Form 5 unless a form of execution of service is provided by the person effecting service in the other Contracting State where service was effected.

(2) An application under section 12 of the 1982 Act shall be made in writing to the sheriff clerk for—

(*a*) a certificate in Form 3;

(*b*) a certified copy interlocutor; and

(*c*) if required, a certified copy of the opinion of the sheriff.

(3) A certificate shall not be issued under sub-paragraph (2)(*a*) unless there is produced and lodged in the process of the cause an execution of service required under sub-paragraph (1).

NOTE
[1] As amended by SI 1993/2346 (effective October 25, 1993).

Recognition and enforcement in Scotland of foreign maintenance orders

6.—[*Repealed by SI 1997/291, r.1.4, Sch.2 (effective April 1, 1997).*]

¹ **6A.**—(1) Paragraphs 5 and 6 shall apply to the recognition and enforcement of an authentic instrument or court settlement as they apply to the recognition and enforcement of a judgment under the 1982 Act, but with such modifications as circumstances may require.

(2) Where paragraph 5 applies in relation to an authentic instrument, an application under section 12 of the 1982 Act shall be made, in writing, to the sheriff clerk for—

(*a*) a certificate in Form 3A; and

(*b*) a certified copy of the authentic instrument.

NOTE

¹ Inserted by SI 1993/2346 (effective October 25, 1993).

Consequential amendments

7.—(1) In paragraph 2 of the Act of Sederunt (Enforcement Abroad of Sheriff Court Judgments) 1962, for the word "abroad" wherever it occurs, substitute the words "in a country other than a country to which Parts I and II of the Civil Jurisdiction and Judgments Act 1982 applies".

(2) In rule 13(1) of the Act of Sederunt (Maintenance Orders (Reciprocal Enforcement) Act 1972 Rules) 1974, after the word "Act", where it second and third appears in that rule, insert the words "or any other enactment".

SCHEDULE

Paragraph 3(2)   FORM 1

CERTIFICATE BY SHERIFF CLERK UNDER SECTION 18 OF, AND PARAGRAPH 4(1) OF SCHEDULE 6 TO, THE CIVIL JURISDICTION AND JUDGMENTS ACT 1982

Sheriff Court (*address*)

.... (Pursuer) v. ....(Defender)

I,   Sheriff Clerk at   Sheriff Court,
hereby certify:—

1. That [AB] obtained judgment against [CD] in the above sheriff court on (*date*) for payment of   with   of expenses of which   is unsatisfied.

2. That the money provision in the judgment carries interest at the rate of   *per centum per annum* from the   day of   19   until payment.

3. That the time for appealing against the judgment has expired [and no appeal has been brought within that time] [*or* and an appeal having been brought within that time has been finally disposed of].

4. That enforcement of the judgment has not for the time being been suspended and that the time available for its enforcement has not expired.

5. That this certificate is issued under section 18 of, and paragraph 4(1) of Schedule 6 to, the Civil Jurisdiction and Judgments Act 1982 and paragraph 3(2) of the Act of Sederunt (Enforcement of Judgments under the Civil Jurisdiction and Judgments Act 1982) 1986.

Dated at (*place*) this   day of   19 .

(*Signed*)
Sheriff Clerk

Paragraph 4(2)   FORM 2

CERTIFICATE BY SHERIFF CLERK UNDER SECTION 18 OF, AND PARAGRAPH 4(1)(*b*) OF SCHEDULE 7 TO, THE CIVIL JURISDICTION AND JUDGMENTS ACT 1982

Sheriff Court (*address*)

I,   Sheriff Clerk at   Sheriff Court,
hereby certify:—

1. That [AB] obtained judgment against [CD] in the above sheriff court on (*date*).

2. That the copy of the interlocutor attached is a true copy of the decree [*or other order*] [and that the copy of the note or opinion of the sheriff attached is a true copy thereof].

3. That the time for appealing against the interlocutor has expired [and no appeal has been brought within that time] [*or* and an appeal having been brought within that time has been finally disposed of].

4. That enforcement of the decree [*or other order*] has not for the time being been suspended and that the time available for its enforcement has not expired.

5. That this certificate is issued under section 18 of, and paragraph 4(1)(*b*) of Schedule 7 to, the Civil Jurisdiction and Judgments Act 1982 and paragraph 4(2) of the Act of Sederunt (Enforcement of Judgments under the Civil Jurisdiction and Judgments Act 1982) 1986.

Dated at (*place*) this   day of   19 .

(*Signed*)
Sheriff Clerk

Paragraph 5(2)   FORM 3

CERTIFICATE BY SHERIFF CLERK UNDER SECTION 12 OF THE CIVIL JURISDICTION AND JUDGMENTS ACT 1982

Sheriff Court (*address*)

.... (Pursuer) v. ....(Defender)

I,   Sheriff Clerk at   Sheriff Court,
hereby certify:—

1. That the initial writ raised by the pursuer, [AB] (*address*), was executed by citation of the defender, [CD] (*address*), served on him on the   day of   19 by (*state mode of service*).

2. That in the initial writ the pursuer sought [payment of the sum of £   in respect of (*state briefly the nature of the claim*) [and (*state other craves of the writ*)].

3. That [no] notice of intention to defend the action was lodged by the defender [on the   day of   19] [and lodged defences on the   day of   19].

4. That decree [*or other order*] was granted against the defender by the Sheriff of   at   for payment of the sum of £   [*or state briefly the terms of the interlocutor or opinion of the sheriff*] [and (*state briefly any other craves of the initial writ*)] together with expenses of the action in the sum of £   , all in terms of the certified copy interlocutor attached hereto.

5. That [no] objection to the jurisdiction of the court has been made [on the grounds that   ].

6. That the decree includes interest at the rate of   *per centum per annum* on the total of the sum of £   and expenses of £   from the   day of   19 until payment.

7. That the interlocutor containing the decree has been served on the defender.

8. That the time within which an appeal may be brought against the interlocutor [expires on   [*or* has expired]].

9. That an [*or* no] appeal against the interlocutor has been brought [and has been finally disposed of].

10. That enforcement of the decree has not for the time being been suspended and the time available for its enforcement has not expired.

11. That the whole pleadings of the parties are contained in the closed record [*or* initial writ] a copy of which is attached.

12. That the pursuer [*or* defender] benefited from legal aid.

13. That this certificate is issued under section 12 of the Civil Jurisdiction and Judgments Act 1982 and paragraph 5(2) of the Act of Sederunt (Enforcement of Judgments under the Civil Jurisdiction and Judgments Act 1982) 1986.

Dated at (*place*) this   day of   19

(*Signed*)
Sheriff Clerk

Paragraph 6A(2)   [1] FORM 3A

CERTIFICATE BY SHERIFF CLERK UNDER SECTION 12 OF THE CIVIL JURISDICTION AND JUDGMENTS ACT 1982 (AUTHENTIC INSTRUMENTS)

Sheriff Court (*address*)

Authentic Instrument between (*names of parties*)

I, (*name*) sheriff clerk at (*name of court*) Sheriff Court, (*address*) hereby certify:—

1. That the attached copy instrument is a true copy of an authentic instrument registered in the Sheriff Court Books on (*date*).

2. That a copy of the authentic instrument so registered was served on the said (*name of debtor*) on (*date*).

3. That (*state briefly the obligation contained in the authentic instrument*).

4. That enforcement of the authentic instrument has not for the time being been suspended and the time available for enforcement has not expired.

5. That this certificate is issued under section 12 of the Civil Jurisdiction and Judgments Act 1982 as modified by the Civil Jurisdiction and Judgments (Authentic Instruments and Court Settlements) Order 1993.

Dated at (*insert place*) this   day of   19 .

(*Signed*)
Sheriff Clerk

NOTE
[1] Inserted by SI 1993/2346 (effective 25th October 1993).

Paragraph 5(1)   FORM 4

NOTICE TO ACCOMPANY SERVICE COPY OF JUDGMENT

To [AB] (*address*)

You are hereby served with a copy of the interlocutor of the Sheriff of   at   given
on the   day of   19 . [In terms of this interlocutor you are required to (*state
requirements of interlocutor*). Your failure to do so may result in further steps being taken to
enforce the interlocutor.]

(*Signed*)
(*Address*)
Solicitor [*or* Sheriff Officer]

(*Place and date*)

Paragraph 5(1)   FORM 5

EXECUTION OF SERVICE OF JUDGMENT AND NOTICE WHERE SERVICE EFFECTED BY OFFICER OF COURT
OR SOLICITOR IN SCOTLAND

(*place and date*)

I, [AB] (*address*), hereby certify that upon the   day of   19 , I duly served a
copy of this judgment together with notice in terms of paragraph 5(1) of the Act of Sederunt
(Enforcement of Judgments under the Civil Jurisdiction and Judgments Act 1982) 1986 upon
[CD], defender. This I did by posting (*set forth mode of service; if by officer and not by post,
add* in presence of EF (*address*) witness, hereto with me subscribing).

(*Signed*)
(*Address*)
Solicitor for Pursuer
[*or* Defender]

[or

(*Signed*)
Sheriff Officer

(*Signed*)
Witness]

Paragraph 6(8)   FORM 6

[*Revoked by SI 1997/291, r.1.4, Sched. 2 (effective April 1, 1997).*]

Summary Suspension 1993

(SI 1993/3128)

[December 10, 1993]

The Lords of Council and Session, under and by virtue of the powers
conferred on them by section 32 of the Sheriff Courts (Scotland) Act 1971
and of all other powers enabling them in that behalf, having approved, with
modifications, draft rules submitted to them by the Sheriff Court Rules
Council in accordance with section 34 of that Act, do hereby enact and
declare:

Citation and commencement
1.—(1) This Act of Sederunt may be cited as the Act of Sederunt (Summary Suspension) 1993 and shall come into force on 1st January 1994.
(2) This Act of Sederunt shall be inserted in the Books of Sederunt.

Summary application for suspension of charge
2. Where a charge for payment has been executed on any decree to which section 5(5) of the Sheriff Courts (Scotland) Act 1907 applies the person so charged may apply to the sheriff in the sheriff court having jurisdiction over him for suspension of such charge and diligence.

Sist of diligence
3.—(1) On sufficient caution being found or other security given for—
(a) the sum charged for with interest and expenses, and
(b) a further sum to be fixed by the sheriff in respect of expenses to be incurred in the suspension process.
the sheriff may sist diligence, order intimation and answers, and proceed to dispose of the cause in a summary manner.
(2) The following rules of the Ordinary Cause Rules 1993 shall, with the necessary modifications, apply to an applicant under paragraph 2—
rule 27.4 (methods of finding caution or giving security)
rule 27.5 (cautioners and guarantors)
rule 27.6 (forms of bonds of caution and other securities)
rule 27.7 (sufficiency of caution or security and objections)
rule 27.8 (insolvency or death of cautioner or guarantor).

Objections
4. Where objections are taken to the competency or regularity of suspension proceedings, the decision of the sheriff on such objections may be appealed to the sheriff principal whose decision shall be final and not subject to appeal.

Savings for proceedings arising out of causes already commenced
5. Nothing in this Act of Sederunt shall affect suspension proceedings arising out of causes commenced before the date of coming into force of this Act of Sederunt, which shall proceed according to the law and practice in force immediately before that date.

Act of Sederunt (Summary Applications, Statutory Applications and Appeals etc. Rules) 1999

(SI 1999/929)

[19th March 1999]

ARRANGEMENT OF RULES

CHAPTER 1: GENERAL

CHAPTER 2: SUMMARY APPLICATION RULES

CHAPTER 3: RULES ON APPLICATIONS UNDER SPECIFIC STATUTES

Part II

Betting and Gaming Appeals

[Omitted by the Act of Sederunt (Sheriff Court Rules) (Miscellaneous Amendments) 2008 (SSI 2008/223) para.14(3)(effective July 1, 2008).]

Part III

Coal Mining Subsidence Act 1991

Part IV

Conveyancing and Feudal Reform (Scotland) Act 1970

Part V

Copyright, Designs and Trade Marks

Part VI

Drug Trafficking Act 1994

Part VII

Licensing (Scotland) Act 1976

Part VIII

Mental Health (Scotland) Act 1984

PART IX

PROCEEDS OF CRIME (SCOTLAND) ACT 1995

PART X

RATING (DISABLED PERSONS) ACT 1978

PART XI

REPRESENTATION OF THE PEOPLE ACT 1983

PART XII

REQUESTS OR APPLICATIONS UNDER THE MODEL LAW ON INTERNATIONAL COMMERCIAL ARBITRATION

PART XIII

SEX DISCRIMINATION ACT 1975

[*Omitted by the Act of Sederunt (Ordinary Cause, Summary Application, Summary Cause and Small Claim Rules) Amendment (Equality Act 2006 etc.) 2006 (SSI 2006/509) (effective November 3, 2006).*]

PART XIV

ACCESS TO HEALTH RECORDS ACT 1990

PART XV

RACE RELATIONS ACT 1976

[*Omitted by the Act of Sederunt (Ordinary Cause, Summary Application, Summary Cause and Small Claim Rules) Amendment (Equality Act 2006 etc.) 2006 (SSI 2006/509) (effective November 3, 2006).*]

PART XVI

ADULTS WITH INCAPACITY (SCOTLAND) ACT 2000

PART XVII

ANTI-TERRORISM, CRIME AND SECURITY ACT 2001

PART XVIII

LOCAL GOVERNMENT (SCOTLAND) ACT 1973

Part IX

Proceeds of Crime Act 2002

Part XX

International Criminal Court (Scotland) Act 2001

Part XXI

Immigration and Asylum Act 1999

Part XXII

Crime and Disorder Act 1998

Part XXIII

Ethical Standards in Public Life etc. (Scotland) Act 2000

Part XXIV

International Protection of Adults

Part XXX

Mental Health (Care and Treatment) (Scotland) Act 2003

Part XXXI

Football Banning Orders

Part XXXII

Animal Health and Welfare

Part XXXIII

Equality Enactments

Part XXXIV

Licensing (Scotland) Act 2005

Part XXXV

Adult Support and Protection (Scotland) Act 2007

Part XXXVI

UK Borders Act 2007

The Lords of Council and Session, under and by virtue of the powers conferred on them by Schedule 1, paragraphs 24(1), 28D and 28(2), Schedule 2, paragraph 7 and Schedule 3, paragraph 13(3) to the Betting Gaming and Lotteries Act 1963, Schedule 2, paragraphs 33(1), 34(1), 45 and 47, and Schedule 9, paragraph 15 to the Gaming Act 1968, section 32 of the Sheriff Courts (Scotland) Act 1971, sections 66(5A) and 75 of the Sex Discrimination Act 1975, section 39(9) of the Licensing (Scotland) Act 1976, Schedule 3, paragraph 12 to the Lotteries and Amusements Act 1976, sections 136, 139, 146, 147, 152, 153, 182(3) and 185 of the Representation of the People Act 1983, sections 114(3), 204(3) and 231(3) of the Copyright, Designs and Patents Act 1988, section 19(3) of the Trade Marks Act 1994, section 46 of the Drug Trafficking Act 1994, Regulation 5(3) of the Olympics Association Right (Infringement Proceedings) Regulations 1995, and sections 31(5) and 48 of, and Schedule 1, paragraph 11 to, the Proceeds of Crime (Scotland) Act 1995 and of all other powers enabling them in that behalf, having approved draft rules submitted to them by the Sheriff Court Rules Council in accordance with section 34 of the Sheriff Courts (Scotland) Act 1971, do hereby enact and declare:

Chapter 1

General

Citation and commencement

1.1—(1) This Act of Sederunt may be cited as the Act of Sederunt (Summary Applications, Statutory Applications and Appeals etc. Rules) 1999 and shall come into force on 1st July 1999.

(2) This Act of Sederunt shall be inserted in the Books of Sederunt.

Interpretation

1.2—[1] (1) In this Act of Sederunt, unless the context otherwise requires—
[2] "the 2004 Act" means the Vulnerable Witnesses (Scotland) Act 2004;

"enactment" includes an enactment comprised in, or in an instrument made under, an Act of the Scottish Parliament;

"Ordinary Cause Rules" means the First Schedule to the Sheriff Courts (Scotland) Act 1907;

"sheriff clerk" includes sheriff clerk depute; and

"summary application" has the meaning given by section 3(p) of the Sheriff Courts (Scotland) Act 1907.

(2) Unless the context otherwise requires, any reference in this Act of Sederunt to a specified Chapter, Part or rule shall be construed as a reference to the Chapter, Part or rule bearing that number in this Act of Sederunt, and a reference to a specified paragraph, sub-paragraph or head shall be construed as a reference to the paragraph, sub-paragraph or head so numbered or lettered in the provision in which that reference occurs.

(3) Any reference in this Act of Sederunt to a numbered Form shall, unless the context otherwise requires, be construed as a reference to the Form so numbered in Schedule 1 to this Act of Sederunt and includes a form substantially to the same effect with such variation as circumstances may require.

[3] (4) In this Act of Sederunt, references to a solicitor include a reference to a member of a body which has made a successful application under section 25 of the Law Reform (Miscellaneous Provisions) (Scotland) Act 1990 but only to the extent that the member is exercising rights acquired by virtue of section 27 of that Act.

NOTES
[1] As amended by the Act of Sederunt (Ordinary Cause, Summary Application, Summary Cause and Small Claim Rules) Amendment (Miscellaneous) 2007 (SSI 2007/6), para.3(2) (effective January 29, 2007).
[2] As inserted by the Act of Sederunt (Ordinary Cause, Summary Application, Summary Cause and Small Claim Rules) Amendment (Vulnerable Witnesses (Scotland) Act 2004) (SSI 2007/463), r.3(2) (effective November 1, 2007).
[3] As inserted by the Act of Sederunt (Sheriff Court Rules Amendment) (Sections 25 to 29 of the Law Reform (Miscellaneous Provisions) (Scotland) Act 1990) 2009 (SSI 2009/164) r.3 (effective May 20, 2009).

Revocation

1.3 The Acts of Sederunt mentioned in column (1) of Schedule 2 to this Act of Sederunt are revoked to the extent specified in column (3) of that Schedule.

Application

1.4 Unless otherwise provided in this Act of Sederunt or in any other enactment, any application or appeal to the sheriff shall be by way of summary application and the provisions of Chapter 2 of this Act of Sederunt shall apply accordingly.

CHAPTER 2

SUMMARY APPLICATION RULES

PART I

INTERPRETATION

Interpretation

2.1 In this Chapter, unless the context otherwise requires—
"decree" includes any judgment, deliverance, interlocutor, act, order, finding or authority which may be extracted;

"defender" means any person other than the pursuer who is a party to a summary application; and

"pursuer" means any person making a summary application.

PART II

GENERAL RULES

Application

2.2 This Part applies to summary applications.

Relief from failure to comply with rules

2.3—(1) The sheriff may relieve a party from the consequences of failure to comply with a provision in this Part which is shown to be due to mistake, oversight or other excusable cause, on such conditions as he thinks fit.

(2) Where the sheriff relieves a party from the consequences of a failure to comply with a provision in this Part of these Rules under paragraph (1), he may make such order as he thinks fit to enable the summary application to proceed as if the failure to comply with the provision had not occurred.

The initial writ

2.4—(1) Unless otherwise prescribed by any other enactment, a summary application shall be commenced by initial writ in Form 1.

(2) The initial writ shall be written, typed or printed on A4 size paper of durable quality and shall not be backed or folded.

(3) Where the pursuer has reason to believe that an agreement exists prorogating jurisdiction over the subject-matter of the summary application to another court, the initial writ shall contain details of that agreement.

(4) Where the pursuer has reason to believe that proceedings are pending before another court involving the same cause of action and between the same parties as those named in the instance of the initial writ, the initial writ shall contain details of those proceedings.

[2] (4A) In an action which relates to a regulated agreement within the meaning given by section 189(1) of the Consumer Credit Act 1974 the initial writ shall include an averment that such an agreement exists and details of the agreement.

(5) An article of condescendence shall be included in the initial writ averring—

(a) the ground of jurisdiction; and

(b) the facts upon which the ground of jurisdiction is based.

(6) Where the residence, registered office or place of business, as the case may be, of the defender is not known and cannot reasonably be ascertained, the pursuer shall set out in the instance of the initial writ that the whereabouts of the defender are not known and aver in the condescendence what steps have been taken to ascertain his present whereabouts.

(7) The initial writ shall be signed by the pursuer or his solicitor (if any) and the name and address of that solicitor shall be stated on the back of every service copy of that writ.

(8) The initial writ shall include averments about those persons who appear to the pursuer to have an interest in the application and in respect of whom a warrant for citation is sought.

[1] (9) Where warrant to arrest on the dependence is sought, the initial writ shall include averments to justify the grant of such a warrant.

NOTES

[1] As inserted by the Act of Sederunt (Ordinary Cause, Summary Application and Small Claim Rules) Amendment (Miscellaneous) 2004 (SSI 2004/197) para.3(2) (effective May 21, 2004).

[2] As inserted by the Act of Sederunt (Sheriff Court Rules) (Miscellaneous Amendments) 2009 (SSI 2009/294) r.3 (effective December 1, 2009) as substituted by the Act of Sederunt

(Amendment of the Act of Sederunt (Sheriff Court Rules) (Miscellaneous Amendments) 2009) 2009 (SSI 2009/402) (effective November 30, 2009).

Order for intimation to interested persons by sheriff
2.5 The sheriff may make an order for intimation to any person who appears to him to have an interest in the summary application.

Time limits
2.6—[1](1) This rule applies to a summary application where the time within which the application being an appeal under statute or an application in the nature of an appeal may be made is not otherwise prescribed.

(2) An application to which this rule applies shall be lodged with the sheriff clerk within 21 days after the date on which the decision, order, scheme, determination, refusal or other act complained of was intimated to the pursuer.

(3) On special cause shown, the sheriff may hear an application to which this rule applies notwithstanding that it was not lodged within the period prescribed in paragraph (2).

NOTE
[1] As amended by the Act of Sederunt (Ordinary Cause, Summary Application and Small Claim Rules) Amendment (Miscellaneous) 2004 (SSI 2004/197) para.3(3) (effective May 21, 2004).

Warrants, forms and certificate of citation
[4] **2.7**—(1) Subject to paragraph (2), a warrant for citation or intimation may be signed by the sheriff or sheriff clerk.

[3](1A) A warrant for arrestment on the dependence may be signed by the sheriff, if the sheriff considers it appropriate.

(2) A warrant containing a period of notice shorter than the period of notice to be given to a defender under rule 3.6(1)(a) or (b), as the case may be, of the Ordinary Cause Rules or any other warrant which the sheriff clerk may not sign, shall be signed by the sheriff.

(3) Where the sheriff clerk refuses to sign a warrant which he may sign, the party presenting the summary application may apply to the sheriff for the warrant.

(4) Where citation is necessary—
[1] (a) the warrant of citation shall, subject to paragraphs (5) and (7A)(a) and rule 3.18.3(1) (appeals under section 103J of the Local Government (Scotland) Act 1973), be in Form 2; and
[1] (b) citation shall, subject to paragraphs (7) and (7A)(b) and rules 2.13 (service where address of person is not known) and 3.18.3(2) (appeals under section 103J of the Local Government (Scotland) Act 1973), be in Form 3.

(5) Where a time to pay direction under the Debtors (Scotland) Act 1987 or a time order under the Consumer Credit Act 1974 may be applied for by the defender, the warrant of citation shall be in Form 4.

(6) Where a warrant of citation in accordance with Form 4 is appropriate, there shall be served on the defender (with the initial writ and warrant) a notice in Form 5.

(7) Where a time to pay direction under the Debtors (Scotland) Act 1987 or a time order under the Consumer Credit Act 1974 may be applied for by the defender, citation shall be in Form 6 which shall be attached to a copy of the initial writ and warrant of citation.

[2] (7A) In a summary application falling within section 1(1)(b) or (c) of the Mortgage Rights (Scotland) Act 2001—
(a) the warrant of citation shall be in Form 6A; and
(b) citation shall be in Form 6B which shall be attached to a copy of the initial writ and warrant of citation.

(8) Where citation is necessary, the certificate of citation shall be in Form 7 which shall be attached to the initial writ.

(9) Where citation is by a sheriff officer, one witness shall be sufficient for the execution of citation.

(10) Where citation is by a sheriff officer, the certificate of citation shall be signed by the sheriff officer and the witness and shall state—

(a) the method of citation; and

(b) where the method of citation was other than personal or postal citation, the full name and designation of any person to whom the citation was delivered.

(11) Where citation is executed under paragraph (3) of rule 2.11 (depositing or affixing by sheriff officer), the certificate shall include a statement—

(a) of the method of service previously attempted;

(b) of the circumstances which prevented such service being executed; and

(c) that a copy of the document was sent in accordance with the provisions of paragraph (4) of that rule.

NOTES

[1] As amended by the Act of Sederunt (Summary Applications, Statutory Applications and Appeals etc. Rules) Amendment (No.2) (Local Government (Scotland) Act 1973) 2002 (SSI 2002/130), para.2(2) (effective March 8, 2002).

[2] As inserted by the Act of Sederunt (Amendment of Ordinary Cause Rules and Summary Applications, Statutory Applications and Appeals etc. Rules) (Applications under the Mortgage Rights (Scotland) Act 2001) 2002 (SSI 2002/7) para.3(2)(c) (effective January 17, 2002).

[3] As inserted by the Act of Sederunt (Ordinary Cause, Summary Application and Small Claim Rules) Amendment (Miscellaneous) 2004 (SSI 2004/197) para.3(4) (effective May 21, 2004).

[4] As amended by the Act of Sederunt (Ordinary Cause, Summary Application, Summary Cause and Small Claim Rules) Amendment (Miscellaneous) 2007 (SSI 2007/6), para.3(3) (effective January 29, 2007).

Orders against which caveats may be lodged
2.8 [*Omitted by Act of Sederunt (Sheriff Court Caveat Rules) 2006 (SI 2006/198), effective April 28, 2006*]

Form, lodging and renewal of caveats
2.9 [*Omitted by Act of Sederunt (Sheriff Court Caveat Rules) 2006 (SI 2006/198), effective April 28, 2006*]

Postal service or intimation
2.10—(1) In any summary application in which service or intimation of any document or citation of any person may be by recorded delivery, such service, intimation or citation shall be by the first class recorded delivery service.

(2) Notwithstanding the terms of section 4(2) of the Citation Amendment (Scotland) Act 1882 (time from which period of notice reckoned), where service or intimation is by post, any period of notice contained in the warrant of citation shall run from the beginning of the day after the date of posting.

(3) On the face of the envelope used for postal service or intimation under this rule there shall be written or printed the following notice:—

"This envelope contains a citation to or intimation from (*specify the court*). If delivery cannot be made at the address shown it is to be returned immediately to:— The Sheriff Clerk (*insert address of sheriff clerk's office*).".

(4) The certificate of citation or intimation in the case of postal service shall have attached to it any relevant postal receipts.

Service within Scotland by sheriff officer

2.11—(1) An initial writ, decree, charge, warrant or any other order or writ following upon such initial writ or decree served by a sheriff officer on any person shall be served—

(a) personally; or

(b) by being left in the hands of a resident at the person's dwelling place or an employee at his place of business.

(2) Where service is executed under paragraph (1)(b), the certificate of citation or service shall contain the full name and designation of any person in whose hands the initial writ, decree, charge, warrant or other order or writ, as the case may be, was left.

(3) Where a sheriff officer has been unsuccessful in executing service in accordance with paragraph (1), he may, after making diligent enquiries, serve the document question by—

(a) depositing it in that person's dwelling place or place of business; or

(b) affixing it to the door of that person's dwelling place or place of business.

(4) Subject to rule 2.18 (service of schedule of arrestment), where service is executed under paragraph (3), the sheriff officer shall, as soon as possible after such service, send a letter containing a copy of the document by ordinary first class post to the address at which he thinks it most likely that the person on whom service has been executed may be found.

[1] (5) Where the firm which employs the sheriff officer has in its possession—

(a) the document or a copy of it certified as correct by the pursuer's solicitor, the sheriff officer may serve the writ upon the defender without having the document or certified copy in his possession, in which case he shall if required to do so by the person on whom service is executed and within a reasonable time of being so required, show the document or certified copy to the person; or

(b) a certified copy of the interlocutor pronounced allowing service of the document, the sheriff officer may serve the document without having in his possession the certified copy interlocutor if he has in his possession a facsimile copy of the certified copy interlocutor (which he shall show, if required, to the person on whom service is executed).

NOTE

[1] As inserted by the Act of Sederunt (Ordinary Cause, Summary Application, Summary Cause and Small Claim Rules) Amendment (Miscellaneous) 2003 (SSI 2003/26), para.3(3) (effective January 24, 2003).

Service on persons furth of Scotland

[1,2] **2.12**—(1) Subject to the following provisions of this rule, an initial writ, decree, charge, warrant or any other order or writ following upon such initial writ or decree served on a person furth of Scotland shall be served—

(a) at a known residence or place of business in England, Wales, Northern Ireland, the Isle of Man, the Channel Islands or any country with which the United Kingdom does not have a convention providing for service of writs in that country—

  (i) in accordance with the rules for personal service under the domestic law of the place in which service is to be executed; or

  (ii) by posting in Scotland a copy of the document in question in a registered letter addressed to the person at his residence or place of business;

(b) in a country which is a party to the Hague Convention on the Service Abroad of Judicial and Extra-Judicial Documents in Civil or Commercial Matters dated 15th November 1965 or the Convention in Schedule 1 or 3C to the Civil Jurisdiction and Judgments Act 1982—

  (i) by a method prescribed by the internal law of the country where service is to be executed for the service of documents in domestic actions upon persons who are within its territory;

  (ii) by or through the central, or other appropriate, authority in the country where service is to be executed at the request of the Secretary of State for Foreign and Commonwealth Affairs;

  (iii) by or through a British Consular Office in the country where service is to be executed at the request of the Secretary of State for Foreign and Commonwealth Affairs;

  (iv) where the law of the country in which the person resides permits, by posting in Scotland a copy of the document in a registered letter addressed to the person at his residence; or

  (v) where the law of the country in which service is to be executed permits, service by an *huissier*, other judicial officer or competent official of the country where service is to be executed; or

 (c) in a country with which the United Kingdom has a convention on the service of writs in that country other than the conventions mentioned in sub-paragraph (b), by one of the methods approved in the relevant convention.

[2,3] (1A) In a country to which the EC Service Regulation applies, service—

 (a) may be effected by the methods prescribed in paragraph (1)(b)(ii) or (iii) only in exceptional circumstances; and

 (b) is effected only if the receiving agency has informed the person that acceptance of service may be refused on the ground that the document has not been translated in accordance with paragraph (6).

(2) Any document which requires to be posted in Scotland for the purposes of this rule shall be posted by a solicitor or a sheriff officer, and on the face of the envelope there shall be written or printed the notice set out in rule 2.10(3).

(3) In the case of service by a method referred to in paragraph (1)(b)(ii) and (iii), the pursuer shall—

 (a) send a copy of the writ and warrant of service with citation attached, or other document, as the case may be, with a request for service by the method indicated in the request to the Secretary of State for Foreign and Commonwealth Affairs; and

 (b) lodge in process a certificate signed by the authority which executed service stating that it has been, and the manner in which it was, served.

(4) In the case of service by a method referred to in paragraph (1)(b)(v), the pursuer or the sheriff officer shall—

 (a) send a copy of the writ and warrant for service with citation attached, or other document, as the case may be, with a request for service by the method indicated in the request to the official in the country in which service is to be executed; and

 (b) lodge in process a certificate of the official who executed service stating that it has been, and the manner in which it was, served.

(5) Where service is executed, in accordance with paragraph (1)(a)(i) or (1)(b)(i) other than on another party in the United Kingdom, the Isle of Man or the Channel Islands, the party executing service shall lodge a certificate by a person who is conversant with the law of the country concerned and who practises or has practised law in that country or is a duly accredited representative of the Government of that country, stating that the method of service employed is in accordance with the law of the place where service was executed.

(6) Every writ, document, citation or notice on the face of the envelope mentioned in rule 2.10(3) shall be accompanied by a translation in—

[2] (a) an official language of the country in which service is to be executed; or

   (b) in a country to which the EC Service Regulation applies, a language of the member state of transmission that is understood by the person on whom service is being executed.

(7) A translation referred to in paragraph (6) shall be certified as correct by the person making it and the certificate shall—

   (a) include his full name, address and qualifications; and

   (b) be lodged with the execution of citation or service.

[4] (8) In this rule "the EC Service Regulation" means Regulation (EC) No. 1393/2007 of the European Parliament and of the Council of 13th November 2007 on the service in the Member States of judicial and extrajudicial documents in civil or commercial matters (service of documents), and repealing Council Regulation (EC) No. 1348/2000, as amended from time to time.

NOTES

[1] As amended by the Act of Sederunt (Ordinary Cause, Summary Application, Summary Cause and Small Claim Rules) Amendment (Miscellaneous) 2003 (SSI 2003/26), para.3(4) (effective January 24, 2003).

[2] As amended and inserted by the Act of Sederunt (Ordinary Cause, Summary Application and Small Claim Rules) Amendment (Miscellaneous) 2004 (SSI 2004/197) (effective May 21, 2004), para.3(5) and substituted by the Act of Sederunt (Sheriff Court Ordinary Cause, Summary Application, Summary Cause and Small Claims Rules) Amendment (Council Regulation (EC) No. 1348 of 2000 Extension to Denmark) 2007 (SSI 2007/440) r.3(2) (effective October 9, 2007).

[3] As amended by the Act of Sederunt (Sheriff Court Rules) (Miscellaneous Amendments) (No.2) 2008 (SSI 2008/365) r.8(a) (effective November 13, 2008).

[4] As substituted by the Act of Sederunt (Sheriff Court Rules) (Miscellaneous Amendments) (No.2) 2008 (SSI 2008/365) r.8(b) (effective November 13, 2008).

Service where address of person is not known

2.13—(1) Where the address of a person to be cited or served with a document is not known and cannot reasonably be ascertained, the sheriff shall grant warrant for citation or service upon that person by—

   (a) the publication of an advertisement in Form 9 in a specified newspaper circulating in the area of the last known address of that person; or

   (b) displaying on the walls of court a copy of the instance and crave of the initial writ, the warrant of citation and a notice in Form 10;

and any period of notice contained in the warrant of citation shall run from the date of publication of the advertisement or display on the walls of court, as the case may be.

(2) Where service requires to be executed under paragraph (1), the pursuer shall lodge a service copy of the initial writ and a copy of any warrant of citation with the sheriff clerk from whom they may be uplifted by the person for whom they are intended.

(3) Where a person has been cited or served in accordance with paragraph (1) and, after the summary application has commenced, his address becomes known, the sheriff may allow the initial writ to be amended subject to such conditions as to re-service, intimation, expenses or transfer of the summary application as he thinks fit.

(4) Where advertisement in a newspaper is required for the purpose of citation or service under this rule, a copy of the newspaper containing the advertisement shall be lodged with the sheriff clerk by the pursuer.

(5) Where display on the walls of court is required under paragraph (1)(b), the pursuer shall supply to the sheriff clerk for that purpose a certified copy of the instance and crave of the initial writ and any warrant of citation.

Persons carrying on business under trading or descriptive name

2.14—(1) A person carrying on a business under a trading or descriptive name may be designed in the instance of the initial writ by such trading or descriptive name alone, and an extract of a—

(a) decree pronounced in the sheriff court; or

(b) decree proceeding upon any deed, decree arbitral, bond, protest of a bill, promissory note or banker's note or upon any other obligation or document on which execution may proceed, recorded in the sheriff court books,

against such person under such trading or descriptive name, shall be a valid warrant for diligence against such person.

(2) An initial writ, decree, charge, warrant or any other order or writ following upon such initial writ or decree in a summary application in which a person carrying on business under a trading or descriptive name is designed in the instance of the initial writ by that name shall be served—

(a) at any place of business or office at which such business is carried on within the sheriffdom of the sheriff court in which the cause is brought; or

(b) where there is no place of business within that sheriffdom, at any place where such business is carried on (including the place of business or office of the clerk or secretary of any company, corporation or association or firm).

Endorsation unnecessary

2.15 An initial writ, decree, charge, warrant or any other order or writ following upon such initial writ or decree may be served, enforced or otherwise lawfully executed anywhere in Scotland without endorsation by a sheriff clerk and, if executed by a sheriff officer, may be so executed by a sheriff officer of the court which granted it or by a sheriff officer of the sheriff court district in which it is to be executed.

Re-service

2.16 Where it appears to the sheriff that there has been any failure or irregularity in citation or service on a person, he may order the pursuer to re-serve the initial writ on such conditions as the sheriff thinks fit.

No objection to regularity of citation, service or intimation

2.17—(1) A person who appears in a summary application shall not be entitled to state any objection to the regularity of the execution of citation, service or intimation on him, and his appearance shall remedy any defect in such citation, service or intimation.

(2) Nothing in paragraph (1) shall preclude a party from pleading that the court has no jurisdiction.

Service of schedule of arrestment

2.18 If a schedule of arrestment has not been personally served on an arrestee, the arrestment shall have effect only if a copy of the schedule is also sent by registered post or the first class recorded delivery service to—

(a) the last known place of residence of the arrestee; or

(b) if such a place of residence is not known, or if the arrestee is a firm or corporation, to the arrestee's principal place of business if known, or, if not known, to any known place of business of the arrestee,

and the sheriff officer shall, on the certificate of execution, certify that this has been done and specify the address to which the copy of the schedule was sent.

Form of schedule of arrestment on the dependence

[1] **2.18A.**—(1) An arrestment on the dependence shall be served by serving the schedule of arrestment on the arrestee in Form 10A.

(2) A certificate of execution shall be lodged with the sheriff clerk in Form 10B.

NOTE

[1] As inserted by the Act of Sederunt (Sheriff Court Rules Amendment) (Diligence) 2009 (SSI 2009/107) r.4 (effective April 22, 2009).

Arrestment on dependence before service

2.19—(1) An arrestment on the dependence of a summary application used before service shall cease to have effect if the initial writ is not served within 20 days from the date of arrestment and either—

   (a) in the case where the pursuer is entitled to minute for decree in absence on the expiry of a period of notice contained in the warrant of citation, decree in absence has not been pronounced within 20 days after the expiry of the period of notice; or
   (b) in the case where the pursuer is not entitled to minute for decree in absence prior to the first hearing of the summary application, there is no appearance by the pursuer at the first hearing and the summary application drops from the roll.

(2) After such an arrestment has been executed, the party who executed it shall forthwith report the execution to the sheriff clerk.

Movement of arrested property

2.20—(1) Any person having an interest may apply by motion for a warrant authorising the movement of a vessel or cargo which is the subject of an arrestment to found jurisdiction or on the dependence of a summary application.

(2) Where the court grants a warrant sought under paragraph (1), it may make such further order as it thinks fit to give effect to that warrant.

Transfer to another sheriff court

2.21—(1) The sheriff may, on cause shown, remit a summary application to another sheriff court.

(2) Subject to paragraph (4), where a summary application in which there are two or more defenders has been brought in the sheriff court of the residence or place of business of one of them, the sheriff may transfer the summary application to any other sheriff court which has jurisdiction over any of the defenders.

(3) Subject to paragraph (4), where a plea of no jurisdiction is sustained, the sheriff may transfer the summary application to the sheriff court before which it appears to him the summary application ought to have been brought.

(4) The sheriff shall not transfer a summary application to another sheriff court under paragraph (2) or (3) except—

   (a) on the motion of a party; and
   (b) where he considers it expedient to do so having regard to the convenience of the parties and their witnesses.

(5) On making an or er under paragraph (1), (2) or (3), the sheriff—

   (a) shall state his reasons for doing so in the interlocutor; and
   (b) may make the order on such conditions as to expenses or otherwise as he thinks fit.

(6) The court to which a summary application is transferred under paragraph (1), (2) or (3) shall accept the summary application.

(7) A transferred summary application shall proceed in all respects as if it had been originally brought in the court to which it is transferred.

(8) An interlocutor transferring a summary application may, with leave of the sheriff, be appealed to the sheriff principal but shall not be subject to appeal to the Court of Session.

Applications for time to pay directions or time orders
[1] **2.22**—(1) This rule applies to a summary application in which—
   (a) a time to pay direction may be applied for under the Debtors (Scotland) Act 1987; or
   (b) a time order may be applied for under the Consumer Credit Act 1987.
(2) A defender may apply for a time to pay direction or time order and, where appropriate, for recall or restriction of an arrestment—
   (a) by appearing and making the appropriate motion at a diet fixed for hearing of the summary application;
[2] (b) except where the warrant of citation contains a shorter period of notice than the period of notice to be given to a defender under rule 3.6(1)(a) or (b), as the case may be, of the Ordinary Cause Rules, by completing and returning the appropriate portion of Form 5 to the sheriff clerk at least 14 days before the first diet fixed for hearing of the summary application or the expiry of the period of notice or otherwise, as the case may be in the warrant of citation; or
   (c) by application to the court at any stage before final decree.
[3] (3) On lodging an application under paragraph (2)(b), the defender shall send a copy of it to the pursuer by first class ordinary post.
[3] (4) Where the pursuer objects to the application of the defender lodged under paragraph (2)(b) he shall—
   (a) complete and lodge with the sheriff clerk Form 5A prior to the date fixed for the hearing of the summary application; and
   (b) send a copy of that form to the defender.
[3] (5) The sheriff clerk shall then fix a hearing in relation to the application under paragraph (2)(b) and intimate the hearing to the pursuer and the defender.
[3] (6) The sheriff may determine an application under paragraph (2)(c) without the defender having to appear.

NOTES
[1] As amended by the Act of Sederunt (Ordinary Cause, Summary Application, Summary Cause and Small Claim Rules) Amendment (Miscellaneous) 2007 (SSI 2007/6), para.3(4) (effective January 29, 2007).
[2] As amended by the Act of Sederunt (Sheriff Court Rules) (Miscellaneous Amendments) 2009 (SSI 2009/294) r.3 (effective December 1, 2009).
[3] Para.(3) substituted for paras (3)–(6) by the Act of Sederunt (Sheriff Court Rules) (Miscellaneous Amendments) 2009 (SSI 2009/294) r.3 (effective December 1, 2009).

[1] *Applications under the Mortgage Rights (Scotland) Act 2001*
2.22A—(1) This rule applies to a summary application to which rule 2.7(7A) applies.
(2) Subject to paragraph (3), an application under either of the following provisions of the Mortgage Rights (Scotland) Act 2001 shall be made by minute in the summary application—
   (a) section 1(2) (application to the court for an order under section 2);
   (b) section 2(5) (application to vary or revoke an order or to further continue proceedings).
(3) A defender may apply orally for an order under section 2 when the summary application first calls in court or as the sheriff otherwise directs.
(4) A minute under paragraph (2) may be lodged by a person who is entitled to make an application even although that person has not been called as a defender and such a person may appear or be represented at any hearing to determine the application made in the minute.
(5) Except where the sheriff otherwise directs, any such minute shall be lodged in accordance with, and regulated by, Chapter 14 of the Ordinary Cause Rules.

NOTE
[1] As inserted by the Act of Sederunt (Amendment of Ordinary Cause Rules and Summary

Applications, Statutory Applications and Appeals etc. Rules) (Applications under the Mortgage Rights (Scotland) Act 2001) 2002 (SSI 2002/7), para.3(3) (effective January 17, 2002).

Remuneration of assessors
2.23 Where an assessor is appointed by the sheriff to assist him in determining the summary application, the remuneration to be paid to such assessor shall be part of the expenses of the application.

Deposits for expenses
2.24 Where, under any enactment, the sheriff requires the pursuer to deposit a sum of money to cover the expenses of an appeal under the enactment, such sum shall, subject to the provisions of that enactment, not exceed an amount which is twenty-five times the amount of the fee payable at that time in respect of lodging the initial writ.

When decrees extractable
2.25—(1) Subject to the following paragraphs—
   (a) subject to sub-paragraph (c), a decree in absence may be extracted after the expiry of 14 days from the date of decree;
   (b) subject to sub-paragraph (c), any decree pronounced in a defended summary application may be extracted at any time after whichever is the later of the following—
      (i) the expiry of the period within which an application for leave to appeal may be made and no such application has been made;
      (ii) the date on which leave to appeal has been refused and there is no right of appeal from such refusal;
      (iii) the expiry of the period within which an appeal may be marked and no appeal has been marked; or
      (iv) the date on which an appeal has been finally disposed of; and
   (c) where the sheriff has, in pronouncing decree, reserved any question of expenses, extract of that decree may be issued only after the expiry of 14 days from the date of the interlocutor disposing of the question of expenses unless the sheriff otherwise directs.
(2) The sheriff may, on cause shown, grant a motion to allow extract to be applied for and issued earlier than a date referred to in paragraph (1).
(3) In relation to a decree referred to in paragraph (1)(b) or (c), paragraph (2) shall not apply unless—
   (a) the motion under that paragraph is made in the presence of the parties; or
   (b) the sheriff is satisfied of proper intimation of the motion has been made in writing to every party not present at the hearing of the motion.
(4) Nothing in this rule shall affect the power of the sheriff to supersede extract.

Form of extract decree
2.26 The extract of a decree shall be in Form 11.

Form of warrant for execution
2.27 An extract of a decree on which execution may proceed shall include a warrant for execution in the following terms:— "This extract is warrant for all lawful execution hereon.".

Date of decree in extract
2.28—(1) Where the sheriff principal has adhered to the decision of the sheriff following an appeal, the date to be inserted in the extract decree as the date of decree shall be the date of the decision of the sheriff principal.

(2) Where a decree has more than one date it shall not be necessary to specify in an extract what was done on each date.

Decrees in absence where defender furth of Scotland

2.29—(1) Where a defender is domiciled in another part of the United Kingdom or in another Contracting State, the sheriff shall not grant decree in absence until it has been shown that the defender has been able to receive the initial writ in sufficient time to arrange for his defence or that all necessary steps have been taken to that end, and for the purposes of this paragraph—

(a) the question whether a person is domiciled in another part of the United Kingdom shall be determined in accordance with sections 41 and 42 of the Civil Jurisdiction and Judgments Act 1982;

(b) the question whether a person is domiciled in another Contracting State shall be determined in accordance with Article 52 of the Convention in Schedule 1 or 3C to that Act, as the case may be; and

(c) the term "Contracting State" has the meaning assigned in section 1 of that Act.

(2) Where an initial writ has keen served in a country to which the Hague Convention on the Service Abroad of Judicial and Extra-Judicial Documents in Civil or Commercial Matters dated 15th November 1965 applies, decree shall not be granted until it is established to the satisfaction of the sheriff that the requirements of Article 15 of the Convention have been complied with.

Motion procedure

2.30 Except where the sheriff otherwise directs, any motion relating to a summary application shall be made in accordance with, and regulated by, Chapter 15 of the Ordinary Cause Rules.

Power of sheriff to make orders

2.31 The sheriff may make such order as he thinks fit for the progress of a summary application in so far as it is not inconsistent with section 50 of the Sheriff Courts (Scotland) Act 1907.

Live links

[1] **2.32**—(1) On cause shown, a party may apply by motion for authority for the whole or part of—

(a) the evidence of a witness or the party to be given; or

(b) a submission to be made,

through a live link.

(2) In paragraph (1)—

[2] "witness" means a person who has been or may be cited to appear before the court as a witness, except a vulnerable witness within the meaning of section 11(1) of the 2004 Act;

"submission" means any oral submission which would otherwise be made to the court by the party or his representative in person including an oral submission in support of a motion; and

"live link" means a live television link or such other arrangement as may be specified in the motion by which the witness, party or representative, as the case may be, is able to be seen and heard in the proceedings or heard in the proceedings and is able to see and hear or hear the proceedings while at a place which is outside the courtroom.

NOTES

[1] As inserted by the Act of Sederunt (Ordinary Cause, Summary Application, Summary Cause and Small Claim Rules) Amendment (Miscellaneous) 2007 (SSI 2007/6), para.3(5) (effective January 29, 2007).

[2] As amended by the Act of Sederunt (Ordinary Cause, Summary Application, Summary

Cause and Small Claim Rules) Amendment (Vulnerable Witnesses (Scotland) Act 2004) 2007 (SSI 2007/463), r.3(3) (effective November 1, 2007).

Enquiry when fixing hearing

[1] **2.33.** Where the sheriff fixes a hearing he shall make enquiry whether there is or is likely to be a vulnerable witness within the meaning of section 11(1) of the 2004 Act who is to give evidence at any proof or hearing, consider any child witness notice or vulnerable witness application that has been lodged where no order has been made and consider whether any order under section 12(1) of the 2004 Act requires to be made.

NOTE

[1] As inserted by the Act of Sederunt (Ordinary Cause, Summary Application, Summary Cause and Small Claim Rules) Amendment (Vulnerable Witnesses (Scotland) Act 2004) 2007 (SSI 2007/463) r.3(4) (effective November 1, 2007).

Vulnerable witness procedure

[1] **2.34.** Except where the sheriff otherwise directs, where a vulnerable witness is to give evidence in a hearing of a summary application any child witness notice or vulnerable application relating to the vulnerable witness shall be made in accordance with and regulated by Chapter 45 of the Ordinary Cause Rules.

NOTE

[1] As inserted by the Act of Sederunt (Ordinary Cause, Summary Application, Summary Cause and Small Claim Rules) Amendment (Vulnerable Witnesses (Scotland) Act 2004) 2007 (SSI 2007/463), r.3(4) (effective November 1, 2007).

Representation

[1,2] **2.35.**—(1) A party may be represented by any person authorised under any enactment to conduct proceedings in the sheriff court in accordance with the terms of that enactment.

(2) The person referred to in paragraph (1) may do everything for the preparation and conduct of an action as may have been done by an individual conducting his own action.

NOTES

[1] As inserted by the Act of Sederunt (Ordinary Cause, Summary Application, Summary Cause and Small Claim Rules) Amendment (Miscellaneous) 2007 (SSI 2007/6), para.3(5) (effective January 29, 2007).

[2] As renumbered by the Act of Sederunt (Sheriff Court Rules) (Miscellaneous Amendments) 2008 (SSI 2008/223) r.14(2) (effective July 1, 2008).

Expenses

[1,2] **2.36.**—(1) A party who—

    (a) is or has been represented by a person authorised under any enactment to conduct proceedings in the sheriff court; and

    (b) would have been found entitled to expenses if he had been represented by a solicitor or an advocate,

May be awarded expenses or outlays to which a party litigant may be found entitled under the Litigants in Person (Costs and Expenses) Act 1975 or any enactment under that Act.

NOTES

[1] As inserted by the Act of Sederunt (Ordinary Cause, Summary Application, Summary Cause and Small Claim Rules) Amendment (Miscellaneous) (SSI 2007/6), para.3(5) (effective January 29, 2007).

[2] As renumbered by the Act of Sederunt (Sheriff Court Rules) (Miscellaneous Amendments) 2008 (SSI 2008/223) r.14(2) (effective July 1, 2008).

Interventions by the CEHR
[1] **2.37.**—(1) In this rule and in rule 2.38, "the CEHR" means the Commission for Equality and Human Rights.

(2) The CEHR may apply to the sheriff for leave to intervene in any summary application in accordance with this Rule.

(3) An application for leave to intervene shall be by way of minute of intervention in Form 11AA and the CEHR shall—

   (a) send a copy of it to all the parties; and
   (b) lodge it in process, certifying that sub-paragraph (a) has been complied with.

(4) A minute of intervention shall set out briefly–

   (a) the CEHR's reasons for believing that the proceedings are relevant to a matter in connection with which the CEHR has a function;
   (b) the issue in the proceedings which the CEHR wishes to address; and
   (c) the propositions to be advanced by the CEHR and the CEHR's reasons for believing that they are relevant to the proceedings and that they will assist the sheriff.

(5) The sheriff may—

   (a) refuse leave without a hearing;
   (b) grant leave without a hearing unless a hearing is requested under paragraph (6);
   (c) refuse or grant leave after such a hearing.

(6) A hearing, at which the applicant and the parties may address the court on the matters referred to in paragraph (8)(c) may be held if, within 14 days of the minute of intervention being lodged, any of the parties lodges a request for a hearing.

(7) Any diet in pursuance of paragraph (6) shall be fixed by the sheriff clerk who shall give written intimation of the diet to the CEHR and all the parties.

(8) The sheriff may grant leave only if satisfied that–

   (a) the proceedings are relevant to a matter in connection with which the CEHR has a function;
   (b) the propositions to be advanced by the CEHR are relevant to the proceedings and are likely to assist him; and
   (c) the intervention will not unduly delay or otherwise prejudice the rights of the parties, including their potential liability for expenses.

(9) In granting leave the sheriff may impose such terms and conditions as he considers desirable in the interests of justice, including making provision in respect of any additional expenses incurred by the parties as a result of the intervention.

(10) The sheriff clerk shall give written intimation of a grant or refusal of leave to the CEHR and all the parties.

(11) This rule is without prejudice to any other entitlement of the CEHR by virtue of having title and interest in relation to the subject matter of any proceedings by virtue of section 30(2) of the Equality Act 2006 or any other enactment to seek to be sisted as a party in those proceedings.

(12) Nothing in this rule shall affect the power of the sheriff to make such other direction as he considers appropriate in the interests of justice.

(13) Any decision of the sheriff in proceedings under this rule and rule 2.38 shall be final and not subject to appeal.

NOTE
[1] As inserted by the Act of Sederunt (Sheriff Court Rules) (Miscellaneous Amendments) 2008 (SSI 2008/223) r.5(2) (effective July 1, 2008).

Form of intervention
[1] **2.38.**—(1) An intervention by the CEHR shall be by way of a written

submission which (including any appendices) shall not exceed 5000 words.

(2) The CEHR shall lodge the submission and send a copy of it to all the parties by such time as the sheriff may direct.

(3) The sheriff may in exceptional circumstances—

    (a) allow a longer written submission to be made;

    (b) direct that an oral submission is to be made.

(4) Any diet in pursuance of paragraph (3)(b) shall be fixed by the sheriff clerk who shall give written intimation of the diet to the CEHR and all the parties.

NOTE

[1] As inserted by the Act of Sederunt (Sheriff Court Rules) (Miscellaneous Amendments) 2008 (SSI 2008/223) r.5(2) (effective July 1, 2008).

Interventions by the SCHR

[1] **2.39.**—(1) In this rule and in rules 2.40 and 2.41—

    "the Act of 2006" means the Scottish Commission for Human Rights Act 2006;

    "the SCHR" means the Scottish Commission for Human Rights.

(2) An application for leave to intervene shall be by way of minute of intervention in Form 11AB and the SCHR shall—

    (a) send a copy of it to all the parties; and

    (b) lodge it in process, certifying that subparagraph (a) has been complied with.

(3) In granting leave the sheriff may impose such terms and conditions as he considers desirable in the interests of justice, including making provision in respect of any additional expenses incurred by the parties as a result of the intervention.

(4) The sheriff clerk shall give written intimation of a grant or refusal of leave to the SCHR and all the parties.

(5) Any decision of the sheriff in proceedings under this rule and rules 2.40 and 2.41 shall be final and not subject to appeal.

NOTE

[1] As inserted by the Act of Sederunt (Sheriff Court Rules) (Miscellaneous Amendments) 2008 (SSI 2008/223) r.5(2) (effective July 1, 2008).

Invitations to intervene

[1] **2.40.**—(1) An invitation to intervene under section 14(2)(b) of the Act of 2006 shall be in Form 11AC and the sheriff clerk shall send a copy of it to the SCHR and all the parties.

(2) An invitation under paragraph (1) shall be accompanied by—

    (a) a copy of the pleadings in the proceedings; and

    (b) such other documents relating to those proceedings as the sheriff thinks relevant.

(3) In issuing an invitation under section 14(2)(b) of the Act of 2006, the sheriff may impose such terms and conditions as he considers desirable in the interests of justice, including making provision in respect of any additional expenses incurred by the parties as a result of the intervention.

NOTE

[1] As inserted by the Act of Sederunt (Sheriff Court Rules) (Miscellaneous Amendments) 2008 (SSI 2008/223) r.5(2) (effective July 1, 2008).

Form of intervention

[1]**2.41.**—(1) An intervention by the SCHR shall be by way of a written submission which (including any appendices) shall not exceed 5000 words.

(2) The SCHR shall lodge the submission and send a copy of it to all the parties by such time as the sheriff may direct.

(3) The sheriff may in exceptional circumstances—
(a) allow a longer written submission to be made;
(b) direct that an oral submission is to be made.
(4) Any diet in pursuance of paragraph (3)(b) shall be fixed by the sheriff clerk who shall give written intimation of the diet to the SCHR and all the parties.

NOTE
[1] As inserted by the Act of Sederunt (Sheriff Court Rules) (Miscellaneous Amendments) 2008 (SSI 2008/223) r.5(2) (effective July 1, 2008).

CHAPTER 3

RULES ON APPLICATIONS UNDER SPECIFIC STATUTES

PART I

ADMINISTRATION OF JUSTICE (SCOTLAND) ACT 1972

Interpretation and application
[1] **3.1.1**—(1) In this Part,
(a) "the Act" means the Administration of Justice (Scotland) Act 1972; and
(b) "listed items" means a list of the documents and other property which the applicant in terms of rule 3.1.2 wishes to be made the subject of the order.
(2) This Part applies to applications under section 1(1) of the Act.

NOTE
[1] As amended by the Act of Sederunt (Summary Applications, Statutory Applications and Appeals etc. Rules) Amendment (No.2) (Administration of Justice (Scotland) Act 1972) 2000 (SSI 2000/387) (effective November 20, 2000).

Applications under section 1(1) of the Act
3.1.2—(1) An application for an order under section 1(1) of the Act (orders for inspection of documents and other property, etc.) shall be made by summary application where the proceedings in respect of which the application is made have not been commenced.
[1] (2) The summary application shall contain—
(a) the listed items;
(b) the address of the premises within which the applicant believes the listed items are to be found; and
(c) the facts which give rise to the applicant's belief that, were the order not to be granted, the listed items, or any of them, would cease to be available for the purposes of section 1 of the Act.

NOTE
[1] As inserted by the Act of Sederunt (Summary Applications, Statutory Applications and Appeals etc. Rules) Amendment (No.2) (Administration of Justice (Scotland) Act 1972) 2000 (SSI 2000/387) r.2(4) (effective November 20, 2000).

Accompanying documents
[1] **3.1.3** The applicant shall lodge with the summary application—
(a) an affidavit supporting the averments in the summary application; and
(b) an undertaking by the applicant that he—
(i) will comply with any order of the sheriff as to payment of compensation if it is subsequently discovered that the order, or the implementation of the order, has caused loss to the respondent or, where the haver is not the respondent, to the haver;

(ii) will bring within a reasonable time of the execution of the order any proceedings which he decides to bring; and

(iii) will not, without leave of the sheriff, use any information, documents or other property obtained as a result of the order, except for the purpose of any proceedings which he decides to bring and to which the order relates.

NOTE
[1] As inserted by the Act of Sederunt (Summary Applications, Statutory Applications and Appeals etc. Rules) Amendment (No.2) (Administration of Justice (Scotland) Act 1972) 2000 (SSI 2000/387) r.2(4) (effective November 20, 2000).

Modification of undertakings
[1] **3.1.4** The sheriff may, on cause shown, modify, by addition, deletion or substitution, the undertaking mentioned in rule 3.1.3.

NOTE
[1] As inserted by the Act of Sederunt (Summary Applications, Statutory Applications and Appeals etc. Rules) Amendment (No.2) (Administration of Justice (Scotland) Act 1972) 2000 (SSI 2000/387) r.2(4) (effective November 20, 2000).

Intimation and service of application
[1] **3.1.5**—(1) Before granting the summary application, the sheriff may order such intimation or service of the summary application to be given or executed, as the case may be, as he thinks fit.

(2) Any person receiving intimation or service of the summary application by virtue of an order under paragraph (1) may appear and oppose the summary application.

NOTE
[1] As inserted by the Act of Sederunt (Summary Applications, Statutory Applications and Appeals etc. Rules) Amendment (No.2) (Administration of Justice (Scotland) Act 1972) 2000 (SSI 2000/387) r.2(4) (effective November 20, 2000).

Form of order
[1] **3.1.6** An order made under this Part shall—
(a) be in Form 11A; and
(b) include in addition a warrant of citation in Form 2.

NOTE
[1] As inserted by the Act of Sederunt (Summary Applications, Statutory Applications and Appeals etc. Rules) Amendment (No.2) (Administration of Justice (Scotland) Act 1972) 2000 (SSI 2000/387) r.2(4) (effective November 20, 2000).

Caution and other security
[1] **3.1.7** On granting, in whole or in part, the summary application the sheriff may order the applicant to find such caution or other security as he thinks fit.

NOTE
[1] As inserted by the Act of Sederunt (Summary Applications, Statutory Applications and Appeals etc. Rules) Amendment (No.2) (Administration of Justice (Scotland) Act 1972) 2000 (SSI 2000/387) r.2(4) (effective November 20, 2000).

Execution of an order
[1] **3.1.8** The order made in terms of rule 3.1.6 shall be served by the Commissioner in person and it shall be accompanied by a copy of the affidavit referred to in rule 3.1.3(a).

NOTE
[1] As inserted by the Act of Sederunt (Summary Applications, Statutory Applications and Appeals etc. Rules) Amendment (No.2) (Administration of Justice (Scotland) Act 1972) 2000 (SSI 2000/387) r.2(4) (effective November 20, 2000).

Duties of a Commissioner

[1] **3.1.9** The Commissioner appointed by the sheriff shall, on executing the order—

(a) give to the haver a copy of the notice in Form 11B;

(b) explain to the haver—

  (i) the meaning and effect of the order; and

  (ii) that he may be entitled to claim that some or all of the listed items are confidential or privileged;

(c) inform the haver of his right to seek legal advice;

(d) enter the premises and take all reasonable steps to fulfil the terms of the order;

(e) where the order has authorised the recovery of any of the listed items, prepare an inventory of all the listed items to be recovered before recovering them; and

(f) send any recovered listed items to the sheriff clerk to await the further order of the sheriff.

NOTE
[1] As inserted by the Act of Sederunt (Summary Applications, Statutory Applications and Appeals etc. Rules) Amendment (No.2) (Administration of Justice (Scotland) Act 1972) 2000 (SSI 2000/387) r.2(4) (effective November 20, 2000).

Confidentiality

[1] **3.1.10**—(1) Where confidentiality is claimed for any listed item, that listed item shall, where practicable, be enclosed in a sealed envelope.

(2) A motion to have such a sealed envelope opened may be made by the party who obtained the order and he shall intimate the terms of the motion, by registered post or first class recorded delivery, to the person claiming confidentiality.

(3) A person claiming confidentiality may oppose a motion made under paragraph (2).

NOTE
[1] As inserted by the Act of Sederunt (Summary Applications, Statutory Applications and Appeals etc. Rules) Amendment (No.2) (Administration of Justice (Scotland) Act 1972) 2000 (SSI 2000/387) r.2(4) (effective November 20, 2000).

Restrictions on service

[1] **3.1.11**—(1) Except on cause shown, the order may be served on Monday to Friday only, between the hours of 9am and 5pm only.

(2) The order shall not be served at the same time as a search warrant granted in the course of a criminal investigation.

(3) The Commissioner may be accompanied only by—

(a) any person whom he considers necessary to assist him to execute the order;

(b) such representatives of the applicant as are named in the order,

and if it is likely that the premises will be occupied by an unaccompanied female and the Commissioner is not female, one of the people accompanying the Commissioner shall be female.

(4) If it appears to the Commissioner when he comes to serve the order that the premises are occupied by an unaccompanied female and the Commissioner is neither female nor accompanied by a female, the Commissioner shall not enter the premises.

NOTE

[1] As inserted by the Act of Sederunt (Summary Applications, Statutory Applications and Appeals etc. Rules) Amendment (No.2) (Administration of Justice (Scotland) Act 1972) 2000 (SSI 2000/387) r.2(4) (effective November 20, 2000).

Right of haver to consult

[1] **3.1.12** The haver may seek legal or other professional advice of his choice and where the purpose of seeking this advice is to help him to decide whether to ask the sheriff to vary the order the Commissioner shall not commence to search for or to take any other steps to take possession of or preserve the listed items.

NOTE

[1] As inserted by the Act of Sederunt (Summary Applications, Statutory Applications and Appeals etc. Rules) Amendment (No. 2) (Administration of Justice (Scotland) Act 1972) 2000 (SSI 2000/387) (effective November 20, 2000).

PART II

BETTING AND GAMING APPEALS

[*Revoked by the Act of Sederunt (Sheriff Court Rules) (Miscellaneous Amendments) 2008 (SSI 2008/223) para.14(3)(effective July 1, 2008).*]

PART III

COAL MINING SUBSIDENCE ACT 1991

Interpretation and application

3.3.1—(1) In this Part—

"the Act" means the Coal Mining Subsidence Act 1991;

"agreement or consent" means the agreement or consent referred to in section 41 of the Act);

"person" means a person referred to in section 41 of the Act;

"any person with responsibility for subsidence affecting any land" has the meaning given in section 43 of the Coal Industry Act 1994.

(2) This Part applies to proceedings under section 41 of the Act.

Applications under section 41 of the Act

3.3.2—(1) An application under section 41 of the Act (disputes about withholding of agreement or consent) shall specify—

(a) the person with whom any person with responsibility for subsidence affecting any land has reached agreement and from whom any person with responsibility for subsidence affecting any land obtained consent; and

(b) the steps which have been taken to obtain the agreement or consent of the person who is withholding such agreement or consent.

(2) An application under section 41 of the Act made in relation to the exercise of a power under section 5(3) or (5) of the Act, shall, when lodged with the sheriff clerk, be accompanied by the notice of proposed remedial action under section 4(2) of the Act.

PART IV

CONVEYANCING AND FEUDAL REFORM (SCOTLAND) ACT 1970

Application

3.4.1—(1) In this Part, "the Act" means the Conveyancing and Feudal Reform (Scotland) Act 1970.

(2) This Part applies to applications and counter applications under Part II of the Act.

Disposal of applications under Part II of the Act
3.4.2 An interlocutor of the sheriff disposing of an application or counter application under Part II of the Act shall be final and not subject to appeal except as to a question of title or as to any other remedy granted.

PART V

COPYRIGHT, DESIGNS AND TRADE MARKS

Interpretation
3.5.1 In this Part—
"the 1988 Act" means the Copyright, Designs and Patents Act 1988;
"the 1994 Act" means the Trade Marks Act 1994; and
"the 1995 Regulations" means the Olympics Association Right (Infringement Proceedings) Regulations 1995.

Orders for delivery up, forfeiture, destruction or other disposal
3.5.2 An application to the sheriff made under sections 99, 114, 195, 204, 230, 231 or 298 of the 1988 Act, under sections 16 or 19 of the 1994 Act or under Regulation 3 or 5 of the 1995 Regulations, shall be made—
(a) by motion or incidental application, as the case may be, where proceedings have been commenced; or
(b) by summary application where no proceedings have been commenced.

Service of notice on interested persons
3.5.3. Where an application has been made under section 114, 204, 231 or 298 of the 1988 Act, section 19 of the 1994 Act or Regulation 5 of the 1995 Regulations—
(a) the application shall—
  (i) specify the name and address of any person known or believed by the applicant to have an interest in the subject matter of the application; or
  (ii) state that to the best of the applicant's knowledge and belief no other person has such an interest; and
(b) the sheriff shall order that there be intimated to any person who has such an interest, a copy of the pleadings and any motion, incidental application or summary application, as the case maybe.

Procedure where leave of court required
3.5.4—(1) Where leave of the court is required under the 1988 Act before the action may proceed, the pursuer shall lodge along with the initial writ or summons a motion or incidental application, as the case may be, stating the grounds upon which leave is sought.
(2) The sheriff may hear the pursuer on the motion or incidental application and may grant or refuse it or make such other order in relation to it as he considers appropriate prior to determination.
(3) Where such motion or incidental application is granted, a copy of the sheriff's interlocutor shall be served upon the defender along with the warrant of citation.

PART VI

DRUG TRAFFICKING ACT 1994

[Revoked by the Act of Sederunt (Summary Applications, Statutory Applications and Appeals etc. Rules) Amendment (No.5) (Proceeds of Crime Act 2002) 2002 (SSI 2002/563), para.2(3) (effective December 30, 2002), subject to savings outlined in para.2(3).]

PART VII

LICENSING (SCOTLAND) ACT 1976

Interpretation and application
3.7.1—(1) In this Part, "the Act" means the Licensing (Scotland) Act 1976.
(2) This Part applies to appeals under section 39 of the Act.

Service
3.7.2 The appellant shall serve a copy of the initial writ on—
 (a) the clerk to the licensing board and the chief constable;
 (b) if he was the applicant at the hearing before the licensing board, upon all parties who appeared at the hearing; and
 (c) if he was an objector at the hearing, upon the applicant.

Statement of reasons of licensing board
3.7.3—(1) Where the appellant has received from the licensing board a statement of reasons for its decision, he shall lodge a copy thereof with the sheriff clerk along with the initial writ.
(2) The sheriff may, at any time prior to pronouncing a final interlocutor, require the licensing board to state the ground of refusal of an application and to give their reasons for finding such ground to be established.

PART VIII

MENTAL HEALTH (SCOTLAND) ACT 1984

Interpretation and application
3.8.1.—(1) In this Part, "the Act" means the Mental Health (Scotland) Act 1984.
(2) This Part applies to—
 (a) applications for admission submitted to a sheriff under section 21 of the Act;
 (b) guardianship applications submitted to a sheriff under section 40 of the Act; and
 (c) community care applications submitted under section 35A of the Act.

Appointment of hearing
3.8.2—(1) On an application being submitted, the sheriff shall appoint a hearing subject, in the case of an application for admission, to section 21(3A) of the Act.
(2) The sheriff may, where he considers it appropriate in all the circumstances, appoint that the hearing of an application shall take place in a hospital or other place.

Service of application
3.8.3—(1) The sheriff clerk shall serve or cause to be served on the patient a copy of the application, with the exception of any medical recommendation, together with a notice in Form 12.

(2) Where the patient is not a resident patient in a hospital, the notice and copy application shall be served on him personally by sheriff officer.

(3) Where the patient is a resident patient in a hospital, the notice and copy application shall be served together with a notice in Form 13 on his responsible medical officer—

(a) by first class recorded delivery service; or

(b) personally by sheriff officer.

(4) Where the patient is already the subject of a guardianship order, the notice and copy application (including any medical recommendations) shall, in addition to any other service required by this rule, be served on the guardian—

(a) by first class recorded delivery service; or

(b) personally a sheriff officer.

Duties of responsible medical officer

3.8.4—(1) On receipt of a notice in Form 13 the responsible medical officer shall, subject to rule 3.8.5(1)—

(a) deliver the notice in Form 12 to the patient; and

(b) as soon as practicable thereafter, complete and return to the court a certificate of such delivery in Form 14.

[1] (2) Where, in the opinion of the responsible medical officer, it would be prejudicial to the patient's health or treatment if the patient were to be present during the proceedings—

(a) in an application to which rule 3.8.3(3) applies, the responsible medical officer shall set forth his reasons for his opinion in the certificate in Form 14; and

(b) in any other case, the responsible medical officer or the special medical officer, as the case may be, shall set forth his reasons for his opinion in writing and send them to the sheriff clerk.

NOTE

[1] As amended by SSI 2003/26, para.3(5) (clerical error).

Appointment of curator ad litem

3.8.5—(1) Where two medical certificates are produced stating that it would be prejudicial to the health or treatment of the patient if personal service were effected in terms of rule 3.8.3(2) or 3.8.4(1) the sheriff—

(a) may dispense with such service; and

(b) if he does so, shall appoint a curator *ad litem* to receive the application and represent the interest of that patient.

(2) The sheriff may appoint a curator *ad litem* to represent the interests of the patient where he is satisfied that—

(a) the patient should be excluded from the whole or any part of the proceedings under section 113(2) of the Act; or

(b) in any other case, it is in all the circumstances appropriate to do so.

(3) The sheriff clerk shall serve the application on the curator *ad litem* by handing, or sending by first class recorded delivery service, to him a copy of the application and of the order appointing him as the curator.

Appointment of solicitor by court

3.8.6 Where the patient has indicated that he wishes to be represented at the hearing but has not nominated a representative, the sheriff may appoint a solicitor to take instructions from the patient.

Intimation to representatives

3.8.7 Where in any proceedings under the Act, the sheriff clerk is aware that the patient is represented by any person and that representative would not otherwise receive intimation of any diet, a copy of the notice served on the patient shall be intimated to the representative by the sheriff clerk by first class recorded delivery service.

Service by sheriff officer
   3.8.8—(1) Where a copy of an application and any notice has been served personally by sheriff officer, he shall prepare and return to the court an execution of such service setting forth in detail the manner and circumstances of such service.
   (2) Where a sheriff officer has been unable to effect personal service under this Part, he shall report to the court the reason why service was not effected.

Variation of conditions of community care order
   3.8.9—(1) Where, after consulting the persons referred to in subsections (1) and (2) of section 35D of the Act (variation of conditions of community care order), an application is made by the special medical officer for the variation of a community care order under that section, the special medical officer shall—
   (a) complete Form 22 in Schedule 2 to the Mental Health (Prescribed Forms) (Scotland) Regulations 1996; and
   (b) lodge that form with the sheriff clerk, together with a certified copy of the community care order to which the application for variation relates.

Hearing
   3.8.10—(1) Any hearing to determine an application under rule 3.8.9 shall take place within 28 days after receipt by the sheriff clerk of Form 22 and the community care order referred to in that rule.
   (2) Intimation of the date of the hearing referred to in paragraph (1) shall be given by the Stationery sheriff clerk by first class recorded delivery service to such persons as the sheriff may direct; and any intimation of such date to the patient shall be made personally by sheriff officer.

Appeal against community care order
   3.8.11 An application by way of appeal for the revocation of a community care order under section 35F of the Act shall be in Form 15.

Part IX

Proceeds of Crime (Scotland) Act 1995

Interpretation and application
   3.9.1—(1) In this Part—
   "the Act" means the Proceeds of Crime (Scotland) Act 1995; and
   "administrator" means the person appointed under paragraph 1(1) of Schedule 1 to Act.
   (2) This Part applies to proceedings under sections 28, 29, 30, 31 and 33 of, and paragraphs 1, 2, 4, 6 and 12 of Schedule 1 to, the Act.

Service of restraint orders
   3.9.2 Where the sheriff pronounces an interlocutor making a restraint order under section 28(1) of the Act (application for restraint order), the prosecutor shall serve a copy of that interlocutor on every person named in the interlocutor as restrained by the order.

Recall or variation of restraint orders
   3.9.3—(1) An application to the sheriff under any of the following provisions of the Act shall be made by note in the process containing the interlocutor malting the restraint order to which the application relates—

(a) section 29(4) or (5) (recall of restraint orders in relation to realisable property);
(b) section 30(3) or (4) (recall of restraint orders in relation to forfeitable property);
(c) section 31(1) (variation or recall of restraint order).

(2) In respect of an application by note under paragraph (1)(c) by a person having an interest for an order for variation or recall under section 31(1)(b) of the Act—

(a) [*Revoked by the Act of Sederunt (Ordinary Cause, Summary Application, Summary Cause and Small Claim Rules) Amendment (Miscellaneous) 2005 (SSI 2005/648) r.3(2) (effective January 2, 2006).*]
(b) the period of notice for lodging answers to the note shall be 14 days or such other period as the sheriff thinks fit.

Applications for interdict
3.9.4—(1) An application to the sheriff under section 28(8) of the Act (interdict) may be made—

(a) in the application made under section 28(1) of the Act; or
(b) if made after a restraint order has been made, by note in the process of the application for that order.

(2) An application under section 28(8) of the Act by note under paragraph (1)(b) shall not be intimated, served or advertised before that application is granted.

Applications in relation to arrestment
3.9.5—(1) An application to the sheriff under section 33(1) of the Act (arrestment of property affected by restraint order by the prosecutor for warrant for arrestment may be made—

(a) in the application made under section 28(1) of the Act; or
(b) if made after a restraint order has been applied for, by note in the process of the application for that order.

(2) An application to the sheriff under section 33(2) of the Act, to loose, restrict or recall an arrestment shall be made by note in the process of the application for the restraint order.

(3) An application to the sheriff under section 33(4) of the Act (recall or restriction of arrestment) shall be made by note in the process containing the interlocutor making the restraint order to which the application relates.

Appeals to the Court of Session
3.9.6—(1) This rule applies to appeals against an interlocutor of the sheriff refusing, varying or recalling or refusing to vary or recall a restraint order.

(2) An appeal to which this rule applies shall be marked within 14 days after the date of the interlocutor concerned.

(3) An appeal to which this rule applies shall be marked by writing a note of appeal on the interlocutor sheet, or other written record containing the interlocutor appealed against, or on a separate sheet lodged with the sheriff clerk, in the following terms:— "The applicant appeals to the Court of Session.".

(4) A note of appeal to which this rule applies shall—

(a) be signed by the appellant;
(b) bear the date on which it is signed; and
(c) where the appellant is represented, specify the name and address of the solicitor or other agent who will be acting for him in the appeal.

(5) The sheriff clerk shall transmit the process within 4 days after the appeal is marked to the Deputy Principal Clerk of Session.

(6) Within the period specified in paragraph (5), the sheriff clerk shall—

(a) send written notice of the appeal to every other party; and
(b) certify on the interlocutor sheet that he has done so.

(7) Failure of the sheriff clerk to comply with paragraph (6) shall not invalidate the appeal.

Applications for appointment of administrators

3.9.7—(1) An application to the sheriff under paragraph 1 of Schedule 1 to the Act (appointment of administrators) shall be made—

  (a) where made after a restraint order has been made, by note in the process of the application for that order; or
  (b) in any other case, by summary application.

(2) The notification to be made by the sheriff clerk under paragraph 1 (3)(a) of Schedule 1 to the Act shall be made by intimation of a copy of the interlocutor to the person required to give possession of property to an administrator.

Incidental applications in an administration

3.9.8—(1) An application to the sheriff under any of the following provisions of Schedule to the Act shall be made by note in the process of the application for appointment of the administrator—

  (a) paragraph 1(1) with respect to an application after appointment of an administrator to require a person to give property to him;
  (b) paragraph 1(4) (making or altering a requirement or removal of administrator);
  (c) paragraph 1(5) (appointment of new administrator on death, resignation or removal of administrator);
  (d) paragraph 2(1)(n) (directions as to functions of administrator);
  (e) paragraph 4 (directions for application of proceeds).

(2) An application to the sheriff under any of the following provisions of Schedule 1 to the Act shall be made in the application for appointment of an administrator under paragraph 1(1) of that Schedule or, if made after the application has been made, by note in the process—

  (a) paragraph 2(1)(o) (special powers of administrator);
  (b) paragraph 2(3) (vesting of property in administrator);
  (c) paragraph 12 (order to facilitate the realisation of property).

Requirements where order to facilitate realisation of property considered

3.9.9 Where the sheriff considers making an order under paragraph 12 of Schedule 1 to the Act (order to facilitate the realisation of property)—

  (a) the sheriff shall fix a date for a hearing in the first instance; and
  (b) the applicant or noter, as the case may be, shall serve a notice in Form 16 on any person who has an interest in the property.

Documents for Accountant of Court

3.9.10—(1) A person who has lodged any document in the process of an application for the appointment of an administrator shall forthwith send a copy of that document to the Accountant of Court.

(2) The sheriff clerk shall transmit to the Accountant of Court any part of the process as the Accountant of Court may request in relation to an administration which is in dependence before the sheriff unless such part of the process is, at the time of request, required by the sheriff.

Procedure for fixing and finding caution

3.9.11 Rules 9 to 12 of the Act of Sederunt (Judicial Factors Rules) 1992 (fixing and finding caution in judicial factories) shall, with the necessary modifications, apply to the fixing and finding of caution by an administrator under this Part as they apply to the fixing and finding of caution by a judicial factor.

Administrator's title to act

3.9.12 An administrator appointed under this Part shall not be entitled to act until he has obtained a copy of the interlocutor appointing him.

Duties of administrator

3.9.13—(1) The administrator shall, as soon as possible, but within three months after the date of his appointment, lodge with the Accountant of Court—

    (a) an inventory of the property in respect of which he has been appointed;

    (b) all vouchers, securities, and other documents which are in his possession; and

    (c) a statement of that property which he has in his possession or intends to realise.

(2) An administrator shall maintain accounts of his intromissions with the property in his charge and shall, subject to paragraph (3)—

    (a) within six months after the date of his appointment; and

    (b) at six monthly intervals after the first account during the subsistence of his appointment,

lodge with the Accountant of Court an account of his intromissions in such form, with such supporting vouchers and other documents, as the Accountant of Court may require.

(3) The Accountant of Court may waive the lodging of an account where the administrator certifies that there have been no intromissions during a particular accounting period.

State of funds and scheme of division

3.9.14—(1) The administrator shall—

    (a) where there are funds available for division, prepare a state of funds after application of sums in accordance with paragraph 4(2) of Schedule 1 to the Act, and a scheme of division amongst those who held property which has been realised under the Act and lodge them and all relevant documents with the Accountant of Court; or

    (b) where there are no funds available for division, prepare a state of funds only and lodge it with the Accountant of Court, and give to the Accountant of Court such explanations as he shall require.

(2) The Accountant of Court shall—

    (a) make a written report on the state of funds and any scheme of division including such observations as he considers appropriate for consideration by the sheriff; and

    (b) return the state of funds and any scheme of division to the administrator with his report.

(3) The administrator shall, on receiving the report of the Accountant of Court—

    (a) lodge in process the report, the state of funds and any scheme of division;

    (b) intimate a copy of it to the prosecutor; and

    (c) intimate to each person who held property which has been realised under the Act a notice stating—

        (i) that the state of funds and scheme of division or the state of funds only, as the case may be, and the report of the Accountant of Court, have been lodged in process; and

        (ii) the amount for which that person has been ranked, and whether he is to be paid in full, or by a dividend, and the amount of it, or that no funds are available for payment.

Objections to scheme of division

3.9.15—(1) A person wishing to be heard by the sheriff in relation to the distribution of property under paragraph 4(3) of Schedule 1 to the Act shall lodge a note of objection in the process to which the scheme of division relates within 21 days of the date of the notice intimated under rule 3.9.14(3)(c).

(2) After the period for lodging a note of objection has expired and no

note of objection has been lodged, the administrator may apply by motion for approval of the scheme of division and state of funds, or the state of funds only, as the case may be.

(3) After the period for lodging a note of objection has expired and a note of objection has been lodged, the sheriff shall dispose of such objection after hearing any objector and the administrator and making such inquiry as he thinks fit.

(4) If any objection is sustained to any extent, the necessary alterations shall be made to the state of funds and any scheme of division and shall be approved by the sheriff.

Application for discharge of administrator
3.9.16—(1) Where the scheme of division is approved by the sheriff and the administrator delivered or conveyed to the persons entitled the sums or receipts allocated to them in the scheme, the administrator may apply for his discharge.

(2) An application to the sheriff for discharge of the administrator shall be made by note in the process of the application under paragraph 1(1) of Schedule 1 to the Act.

Appeals against determination of outlays and remuneration
3.9.17 An appeal to the sheriff under paragraph 6(2) of Schedule 1 to the Act (appeal against a determination by the Accountant of Court) shall be made by note in the process of the application in which the administrator was appointed.

PART X

RATING (DISABLED PERSONS) ACT 1978

Interpretation and application
3.10.1—(1) In this Part, "the Act" means the Rating (Disabled Persons) Act 1978.

(2) This Part applies to appeals under section 6(5) or 6(5A) of the Act.

Appeals under section 6(5) or 6(5A) of the Act
3.10.2 Any appeal under this Part shall be lodged within 42 days of the date on which the application to the rating authority is refused by the authority.

PART XI

REPRESENTATION OF THE PEOPLE ACT 1983

Interpretation and application
[1] **3.11.1**—(1) In this Part—
"sheriff clerk" means, except in rules 3.11.2, 3.11.22 and 3.11.23 the sheriff clerk of the sheriff court district where the trial of the election petition is to take place;
"the Act" means the Representation of the People Act 1983.
(2) In this Part—
(a) rules 3.11.2 to 3.11.21 apply to election petitions under the Act; and
(b) rules 3.11.22 to 3.11.24 apply to registration appeals under section 56 of the Act where the appellant is a person—
(i) whose entry in the register is an anonymous entry; or
(ii) who has applied for such an entry.

NOTE
[1] As substituted by the Act of Sederunt (Summary Applications, Statutory Applications and

Appeals etc. Rules) Amendment (Registration Appeals) 2008 (SSI 2008/41), r.2(2) (effective March 17, 2008).

Initiation of proceedings

3.11.2—(1) The election petition shall be lodged with the sheriff clerk of a sheriff court district within which the election questioned has taken place.

(2) The sheriff clerk shall without delay transmit it to the sheriff principal who shall forthwith appoint—

(a) the time and place for trial of the petition;

(b) the amount of the security to be given by the petitioner; and

(c) if he thinks fit, answers to be lodged within a specified time after service.

(3) Service in terms of section 136(3) of the Act (security for costs) shall be effected—

(a) personally within—
  (i) 5 days; or
  (ii) such other period as the sheriff principal may appoint,
  of the giving of security; or

(b) by first class recorded delivery post within—
  (i) 5 days; or
  (ii) such other period as the sheriff principal may appoint,
  of the giving of security.

Security for expenses by bond of caution

3.11.3—(1) If the security proposed is in whole or in part by bond of caution, it shall be given by lodging with the sheriff clerk a bond for the amount specified by the sheriff principal.

(2) Such bond shall—

(a) recite the nature of the petition; and

(b) bind and oblige the cautioner and the petitioner jointly and severally, and their respective heirs, executors and successors whomsoever, that the petitioner shall make payment of all costs, charges and expenses that may be payable by him to any person by virtue of any order or decree pronounced in the petition.

(3) The sufficiency of the cautioner must be attested to the satisfaction of the sheriff clerk, as in the case of judicial bonds of caution.

Objections to bond of caution

3.11.4—(1) Objections to a bond of caution shall be lodged with the sheriff clerk within 14 days of service in terms of section 136(3) of the Act.

(2) Objections shall be heard and disposed of by the sheriff clerk.

(3) If any objection is allowed, it may be removed by a deposit of such sum of money as the sheriff clerk shall determine, made in the manner provided in rule 3.11.5 and within 5 days after the date of the sheriff clerk's determination.

Security by deposit

3.11.5—(1) Security tendered in whole or in part by deposit of money shall be made in such bank the sheriff clerk may select.

(2) The deposit receipt shall be—

(a) taken in joint name of the petitioner and the sheriff clerk;

(b) handed to the sheriff clerk; and

(c) held by the sheriff clerk subject to the orders of the court in the petition.

Amendment of pleadings

3.11.6—(1) Subject to paragraph (2), the sheriff principal shall have power at any stage to allow petition and any answers to be amended upon such condition as to expenses or otherwise as he shall think fit.

(2) No amendment altering the ground upon which the election was questioned in the petition as presented shall be competent, except to the extent sanctioned by section 129(6) of the Act (time for presentation or amendment of petition questioning local election).

Notice of date and place of trial

3.11.7—(1) The sheriff clerk shall, as soon as he receives intimation of the time and place fixed for trial—

(a) display a notice thereof on the walls of his principal office; and

(b) send by first class post one copy of such notice to—

(i) the petitioner;

(ii) the respondent;

(iii) the Lord Advocate; and

(iv) the returning officer.

(2) The returning officer on receipt of notice from the sheriff clerk shall forthwith publish the time and place fixed for trial in the area for which the election questioned was held.

(3) Subject to paragraph (4), display of a notice in accordance with paragraph (1)(a) shall be deemed to be notice in the prescribed manner within the meaning of section 139(1) of the Act (trial of petition) and such notice shall not be vitiated by any miscarriage of or relating to all or any copies sent by post.

(4) At any time before the trial it shall be competent for any party interested to bring any miscarriage of notice sent by post before the sheriff principal, who shall deal therewith as he may consider fit.

Clerk of court

3.11.8 The sheriff clerk shall attend and act as clerk of court at the trial of the petition.

Shorthand writer's charges

3.11.9 The shorthand writer's charges, as approved by the sheriff principal, shall be paid in the first instance by the petitioner.

Appeals

3.11.10 The application to state a special case referred to in section 146(1) of the (special case for determination of the Court of Session) shall be made by minute in the petition proceedings.

List of votes objected to and of objections

3.11.11—(1) When a petitioner claims the seat for an unsuccessful candidate, alleging that such candidate had a majority of lawful votes, he and the respondent shall, 5 days before the day fixed for the trial, respectively deliver to the sheriff clerk, and send by first class post to the other party and the Lord Advocate, a list of the votes intended to be objected to, and of the objections to each such vote.

(2) The sheriff clerk shall allow inspection of such list to all parties concerned.

(3) No evidence shall be allowed to be given against any vote or in support of any objection not specified in such list, except by leave of the sheriff principal granted upon such terms as to the amendment of the list, postponement of the trial, and payment of expenses as to him may seem fit.

Petition against undue return

3.11.12—(1) When on the trial of a petition complaining of an undue return and claiming the office for some person, the respondent intends to give evidence to prove that that person was not duly elected, such respondent shall, 5 days before the day appointed for the trial, deliver to the sheriff clerk, and send by first class post to the petitioner and the Lord

Advocate, a list of the objections to the election upon which he intends to rely.

(2) No evidence shall be allowed to be given by a respondent in support of any objection to the election not specified in such list except by leave of the sheriff principal granted upon such terms as to the amendment of the list, postponement of the trial, and payment of expenses as to him may seem fit.

Prescribed officer
3.11.13 The sheriff clerk shall be the prescribed officer for the purposes of sections 143(1) (expense of witnesses) and 155(2) (neglect or refusal to pay costs) of the Act.

Leave to abandon
3.11.14—(1) Application for leave to withdraw a petition in terms of section 147(1) of the Act (withdrawal of petition), shall be made by minute in Form 17 and shall be preceded by written notice of the intention to make it, sent by first class post to—
    (a) the respondent;
    (b) the Lord Advocate; and
    (c) the returning officer.

(2) The returning officer shall forthwith publish the fact of his having received such notice in the area for which the election questioned was held.

(3) The sheriff principal, upon the application being laid before him, shall by interlocutor, fix the time, not being earlier than 8 days after the date of the interlocutor, and place for hearing it.

(4) The petitioner shall, at least 6 days before the day fixed for the hearing, publish in a newspaper circulating in the district named in the interlocutor a notice in Form 18.

Death of petitioner
3.11.15—(1) In the event of the death of the sole petitioner, or of the last survivor of several petitioners, the sheriff clerk shall forthwith, upon the fact being brought to his knowledge, insert in a newspaper circulating in the district a notice in Form 19.

(2) The time within which any person who might have been a petitioner in respect of the election may apply to the court by minute in the petition proceedings to be substituted as a petitioner shall be 21 days from the date of publication of such notice.

Notice by respondent that he does not oppose petition
3.11.16—(1) Notice that a respondent does not intend to oppose a petition shall be given by leaving a written notice to that effect at the office of the sheriff clerk at least 6 days (exclusive of the day of leaving such notice) before the day fixed for the trial.

(2) On such notice being left with the sheriff clerk, or on its being brought to his knowledge that a respondent other than a returning officer has died, resigned, or otherwise ceased to hold the office to which the petition relates, the sheriff clerk shall forthwith—
    (a) advertise the fact once in a newspaper circulating in the district; and
    (b) send intimation thereof by first class post to—
        (i) the petitioner;
        (ii) the Lord Advocate; and
        (iii) the returning officer, who shall publish the fact in the district.

(3) The advertisement to be made by the sheriff clerk shall state the last day on which, under this Part, application to be admitted as a respondent to oppose the petition can be made.

Application to be admitted as respondent
3.11.17 Application to be admitted as a respondent to oppose a petition

on the occurrence of any of the events mentioned in section 153(1) of the Act (withdrawal and substitution of respondents before trial) must be made by minute in the petition proceedings within 10 days after the date of publication of the advertisement mentioned in rule 3.11.16, unless the sheriff principal on cause shown sees fit to extend the time.

Public notice of trial not proceeding
3.11.18—(1) This rule applies where after the notice of trial has been published the sheriff clerk receives notice
  (a) the petitioner's intention to apply for leave to withdraw;
  (b) the respondent's intention not to oppose;
  (c) the abatement of the petition by death; or
  (d) the occurrence of any of the events mentioned in section 153(1) of the Act.
(2) Where this rule applies the sheriff clerk shall forthwith give notice by advertisement inserted once in a newspaper circulating in the district, that the trial will not proceed on the day fixed.

Notice to a party's agent sufficient
3.11.19 Where a party to proceedings under this Part is represented by a solicitor any reference to such party shall, where appropriate, be construed as a reference to the solicitor representing that party and a notice sent to his solicitor shall be held to be notice to the party.

Cost of publication
3.11.20 Where under this Part the returning officer or the sheriff clerk requires to have published a notice or advertisement, the cost shall be paid in the first instance by the petitioner or in the case of a notice under rule 3.11.15 from the estate of the sole or last surviving petitioner and shall form part of the general expenses of the petition.

Expenses
3.11.21 The expenses of petitions and other proceedings under the Act shall be taxed by the auditor of the sheriff court.

Application for serial number
[1] **3.11.22**—(1) Where a person desiring to appeal wishes to prevent his identity being disclosed he may, before lodging the appeal, apply to the sheriff clerk for a serial number to be assigned to him for all purposes connected with the appeal.
(2) On receipt of an application for a serial number, the sheriff clerk shall assign such a number to the applicant and shall enter a note of it opposite the name of the applicant in the register of such serial numbers.
(3) The contents of the register of serial numbers and the names of the persons to whom each number relates shall be treated as confidential by the sheriff clerk and shall not be disclosed to any person other than–
  (a) the sheriff;
  (b) the registration officer whose decision or determination is the subject of the appeal.
(4) In this rule and in rule 3.11.23 "sheriff clerk" means the sheriff clerk of the sheriff court district in which the appeal is or is to be raised.

NOTE
[1] As inserted by the Act of Sederunt (Summary Applications, Statutory Applications and Appeals etc. Rules) Amendment (Registration Appeals) (SSI 2008/41), r.2(3) (effective March 17, 2008).

Confidentiality
[1] **3.11.23** Unless the sheriff otherwise directs, all documents lodged in

process of an appeal to which this rule applies are to be available only to the sheriff and the parties; and such documents are to be treated as confidential by all persons involved in, or party to, the proceedings and by the sheriff clerk.

NOTE
[1] As inserted by the Act of Sederunt (Summary Applications, Statutory Applications and Appeals etc. Rules) Amendment (Registration Appeals) (SSI 2008/41), r.2(3) (effective March 17, 2008).

Hearing
[1] **3.11.24** The hearing of an appeal to which this rule applies is to be in private.

NOTE
[1] As inserted by the Act of Sederunt (Summary Applications, Statutory Applications and Appeals etc. Rules) Amendment (Registration Appeals) (SSI 2008/41), r.2(3) (effective March 17, 2008).

PART XII

REQUESTS OR APPLICATIONS UNDER THE MODEL LAW ON INTERNATIONAL COMMERCIAL ARBITRATION

Interpretation
3.12.1 In this Part, "the Model Law" means the United Nations Commission on International Trade Law Model Law on International Commercial Arbitration as set out in Schedule 7 to the Law Reform (Miscellaneous Provisions) (Scotland) Act 1990.

Application
3.12.2—(1) Subject to sub-paragraph (2), any request or application which may be made to the sheriff under the Model Law shall be made by summary application.

(2) Where proceedings involving the same arbitration and the same parties are already pending before the sheriff under this Part, a further application or request may be made by note in the same process.

(3) The sheriff shall order service of such summary application or note to be made on such persons as he considers appropriate.

Recognition and enforcement of awards
3.12.3—(1) There shall be lodged along with an application under Article 35 of the Model Law—
  (a) the original arbitration agreement or certified copy thereof;
  (b) the duly authenticated original award or certified copy thereof and
  (c) where appropriate, a duly certified translation in English of the agreement and award.

(2) An application under this paragraph shall specify whether to the knowledge of the applicant—
  (a) the arbitral award has been recognised, or is being enforced, in any other jurisdiction; and
  (b) an application for setting aside or suspension of the arbitral award has been made to a court of the country in which or under whose law the award was made.

(3) Where the sheriff is satisfied that an arbitral award should be recognised and enforced, he shall so order and shall instruct the sheriff clerk to register the award in the Books of the Sheriff Court for execution.

PART XIII

SEX DISCRIMINATION ACT 1975

[Omitted by the Act of Sederunt (Ordinary Cause, Summary Application, Summary Cause and Small Claim Rules) Amendment (Equality Act 2006 etc.) 2006 (SSI 2006/509) (effective November 3, 2006).]

[1] PART XIV

ACCESS TO HEALTH RECORDS ACT 1990

NOTE
[1] As inserted by the Act of Sederunt (Summary Applications, Statutory Applications and Appeals etc. Rules) Amendment 2000 (SSI 2000/148), para.2(2) (effective July 3, 2000).

Interpretation and application
3.14.1—(1) In this Part—
"the Act" means the Access to Health Records Act 1990; and
"the Reg" means the Access to Health Records (Steps to Secure Compliance and Complaints Procedures) (Scotland) Regulations 1991.
(2) This Part applies to applications under section 8(1) of the Act (applications to the court for order to comply with requirement of the Act).

Accompanying documents
3.14.2 An application shall specify those steps prescribed in the Regulations which have been taken by the person concerned to securecompliance with any requirement of the Act, and when lodged in process shall be accompanied by—
(a) a copy of the application under section 3 of the Act (applications for access to a health record);
(b) a copy of the complaint under regulation 3 or 4 of the Regulations (complaint about non-compliance with the Act); and
(c) if applicable, a copy of the report under regulation 6 of the Regulations (report in response to complaint).

Time of making application
3.14.3 The application shall be made where the applicant—
(a) has received a report in accordance with regulation 6 of the Regulations, within one year of the date of the report;
(b) has not received such a report, within 18 months of the date of the complaint.

PART XV

RACE RELATIONS ACT 1976

[Omitted by the Act of Sederunt (Ordinary Cause, Summary Application, Summary Cause and Small Claim Rules) Amendment (Equality Act 2006 etc.) 2006 (SSI 2006/509) (effective November 3, 2006).]

[1] Part XVI

ADULTS WITH INCAPACITY (SCOTLAND) ACT 2000

NOTE
[1] As inserted by the Act of Sederunt (Summary Applications, Statutory Applications and Appeals etc. Rules) Amendment (Adults with Incapacity) 2001 (SSI 2001/142), r.3(2).

Interpretation
[2] **3.16.1** In this Part—
"the 2000 Act" means the Adults with Incapacity (Scotland) Act 2000;
[3] "the 2003 Act" means the Mental Health (Care and Treatment) (Scotland) Act 2003;
[4] "adult" means a person who is the subject of an application under the 2000 Act and—

    (a) has attained the age of 16 years; or
    (b) in relation to an application for a guardianship order, will attain the age of 16 years within 3 months of the date of the application;

"authorised establishment" has the meaning ascribed to it in section 35(2) of the 2000 Act;

"continuing attorney" means a person on whom there has been conferred a power of attorney granted under section 15(1) of the 2000 Act;

[1] "guardianship order" means an order made under section 58(4) of the 2000 Act;

"incapable" has the meaning ascribed to it at section 1(6) of the 2000 Act, and "incapacity" shall be construed accordingly;

[1] "intervention order" means an order made under section 53(1) of the 2000 Act;

[1] "local authority" has the meaning ascribed to it by section 87(1) of the 2000 Act;

"managers" has the meaning ascribed to it in paragraph 1 of Schedule 1 to the 2000 Act;

[1] "Mental Welfare Commission" has the meaning ascribed to it by section 87(1) of the 2000 Act;

[5] "named person" has the meaning ascribed to it by section 329 of the Mental Health (Care and Treatment) (Scotland) Act 2003;

"nearest relative" means, subject to section 87(2) of the 2000 Act, the person who would be, or would be exercising the functions of, the adult's nearest relative under sections 53 to 57 of the 1984 Act if the adult were a patient within the meaning of that Act and notwithstanding that the person neither is or was caring for the adult for the purposes of section 53(3) of that Act;

"power of attorney" includes a factory and commission;

"primary carer" means the person or organisation primarily engaged in caring for an adult;

"Public Guardian" shall be construed in accordance with section 6 of the 2000 Act; and

"welfare attorney" means a person on whom there has been conferred a power of attorney granted under section 16(1) of the 2000 Act.

NOTES
[1] As amended by the Act of Sederunt (Summary Applications, Statutory Applications and Appeals etc. Rules) Amendment (No.3) (Adults with Incapacity) 2002 (SSI 2002/146), r.2(2).
[2] As amended by the the Mental Health (Care and Treatment) (Scotland) Act 2003 (Modification of Subordinate Legislation) Order 2005 (SSI 2005/445) (effective October 5, 2005).
[3] Inserted by the the Mental Health (Care and Treatment) (Scotland) Act 2003 (Modification of Subordinate Legislation) Order 2005 (SSI 2005/445) (effective October 5, 2005).
[4] As substituted by the Act of Sederunt (Summary Applications, Statutory Applications and Appeals etc. Rules) Amendment (Adult Support and Protection (Scotland) Act 2007) 2008 (SSI 2008/111) r.3(1) (effective April 1, 2008).
[5] As inserted by the Act of Sederunt (Summary Applications, Statutory Applications and Appeals etc. Rules) Amendment (Adult Support and Protection (Scotland) Act 2007) 2008 (SSI 2008/111) r.2(1) (effective April 1, 2008).

Appointment of hearing

3.16.2 On an application or other proceedings being submitted under or in pursuance of the 2000 Act the sheriff shall—

    (a) fix a hearing;

    (b) order answers to be lodged (where he considers it appropriate to do so) within a period that he shall specify; and

    (c) appoint service and intimation of the application or other proceedings.

Place, and privacy, of any hearing

[1] **3.16.3** The sheriff may, where he considers it appropriate in all the circumstances, appoint that the hearing of an application or other proceedings shall take place—

    (a) in a hospital, or any other place than the court building;

    (b) in private.

NOTE

[1] As substituted by the Act of Sederunt (Ordinary Cause, Summary Application and Small Claim Rules) Amendment (Miscellaneous) 2004 (SSI 2004/197) para.3(7) (effective May 21, 2004).

Service of application

3.16.4—(1) Service of the application or other proceedings shall be made in Form 20 on—

    (a) the adult;

    (b) the nearest relative of the adult;

    (c) the primary carer of the adult (if any);

[2] (ca) the named person of the adult (if any);

    (d) any guardian, continuing attorney or welfare attorney of the adult who has any power relating to the application or proceedings;

    (e) the Public Guardian;

[1] (ea) where appropriate, the Mental Welfare Commission;

[1] (eb) where appropriate, the local authority;

    (f) any other person directed by the sheriff.

(2) Where the applicant is an individual person without legal representation service shall be effected by the sheriff clerk.

(3) Where the adult is in an authorised establishment the person effecting service shall not serve Form 20 on the adult under paragraph (1)(a) but shall instead serve Forms 20 and 21, together with Form 22, on the managers of that authorised establishment by—

    (a) first class recorded delivery post; or

    (b) personal service by a sheriff officer.

(4) On receipt of Forms 20 and 21 in terms of paragraph (3) the managers of the authorised establishment shall, subject to rule 3.16.5—

    (a) deliver the notice in Form 20 to the adult; and

    (b) as soon as practicable thereafter complete and return to the sheriff clerk a certificate of such delivery in Form 22.

(5) Where the application or other proceeding follows on a remit under rule 3.16.9 the order for service of the application shall include an order for service on the Public Guardian or other party concerned.

[1] (6) Where the application is for an intervention order or a guardianship order, copies of the reports lodged in accordance with section 57(3) of the 2000 Act (reports to be lodged in court along with application) shall be served along with Forms 20, 21 and 22 as the case may be.

NOTES

[1] As amended by the Act of Sederunt (Summary Applications, Statutory Applications and Appeals etc. Rules) Amendment (No.3) (Adults with Incapacity) 2002 (SSI 2002/146), r.2(2).

[2] As inserted by the Act of Sederunt (Summary Applications, Statutory Applications and Appeals etc. Rules) Amendment (Adult Support and Protection (Scotland) Act 2007) 2008 (SSI 2008/111) r.2(2) (effective April 1, 2008).

Dispensing with service on adult

3.16.5—(1) Where, in relation to any application or proceeding under or in pursuance of the 2000 Act, two medical certificates are produced stating that intimation of the application or other proceeding, or notification of any interlocutor relating to such application or other proceeding, would be likely to pose a serious risk to the health of the adult the sheriff may dispense with such intimation or notification.

(2) Any medical certificates produced under paragraph (1) shall be prepared by medical practitioners independent of each other.

[1] (3) In any case where the incapacity of the adult is by reason of mental disorder, one of the two medical practitioners must be a medical practitioner approved for the purposes of section 22(4) of the 2003 Act as having special experience in the diagnosis or treatment of mental disorder.

NOTE

[1] As amended by the the Mental Health (Care and Treatment) (Scotland) Act 2003 (Modification of Subordinate Legislation) Order (SSI 2005/445) (effective October 5, 2005).

Hearing

3.16.6—[1] (1) A hearing to determine any application or other proceeding shall take place within 28 days of the interlocutor fixing the hearing under rule 3.16.2 unless any person upon whom the application is to be served is outside Europe.

(2) At the hearing referred to in paragraph (1) the sheriff may determine the application or other proceeding or may order such further procedure as he thinks fit.

NOTE

[1] As amended by the Act of Sederunt (Summary Applications, Statutory Applications and Appeals etc. Rules) Amendment (No.3) (Adults with Incapacity) 2002 (SSI 2002/146), r.2(2) (effective April 1, 2002).

Prescribed forms of application

3.16.7—(1) An application submitted to the sheriff under or in pursuance of the 2000 Act, other than an appeal or remitted matter, shall be in Form 23.

(2) An appeal to the sheriff under or in pursuance of the 2000 Act shall be in Form 24.

Subsequent applications

3.16.8—[1](1) Unless otherwise prescribed in the Part or under the 2000 Act, any application or proceedings subsequent to an initial application or proceeding considered by the sheriff including an application to renew an existing order, shall take the form of a minute lodged in the process.

[1] (1A) Except where the sheriff otherwise directs, any such minute shall be lodged in accordance with, and regulated by, Chapter 14 of the Ordinary Cause Rules.

(2) Where any subsequent application or proceedings under paragraph (1) above are made to a court in another sheriffdom the sheriff clerk shall transmit the court process to the court dealing with the current application or proceeding.

(3) Transmission of the process in terms of paragraph (2) shall be made within 4 days of it being requested by the sheriff clerk of the court in which the current application or proceedings have been raised.

[1] (4) Where the application is for renewal of a guardianship order, a copy of any report lodged under section 60 of the 2000 Act shall be served along with the minute.

[2] (5) Where the application is for renewal of a guardianship order, a copy shall be served on the local authority and, where it relates to the adult's

personal welfare where incapacity is by reason of mental disorder, on the Mental Welfare Commission.

NOTES

[1] As amended the Act of Sederunt (Summary Applications, Statutory Applications and Appeals etc. Rules) Amendment (No.3) (Adults with Incapacity) 2002 (SSI 2002/146), r.2(2) and the Act of Sederunt (Summary Applications, Statutory Applications and Appeals etc. Rules) Amendment (Adult Support and Protection (Scotland) Act 2007) 2008 (SSI 2008/111) r.3(2)(a) (effective April 1, 2008).

[2] As inserted by the Act of Sederunt (Summary Applications, Statutory Applications and Appeals etc. Rules) Amendment (Adult Support and Protection (Scotland) Act 2007) 2008 (SSI 2008/111) r.3(2)(b) (effective April 1, 2008).

Remit of applications by the Public Guardian etc.

3.16.9 Where an application is remitted to the sheriff by the Public Guardian or by any other party authorised to do so under the 2000 Act the party remitting the application shall, within 4 days of the decision to remit, transmit the papers relating to the application to the sheriff clerk of the court where the application is to be considered.

[3] *Caution and other security*

[1] **3.16.10**—(1) Where the sheriff requires a person authorised under an intervention order or any variation of an intervention order, or appointed as a guardian, to find caution he shall specify the amount and period within which caution is to be found in the interlocutor authorising or appointing the person or varying the order (as the case may be).

[2] (1A) The amount of caution specified by the sheriff in paragraph (1) may be calculated and expressed as a percentage of the value of the adult's estate.

(2) The sheriff may, on application made by motion before the expiry of the period for finding caution and on cause shown, allow further time for finding caution in accordance with paragraph (1).

(3) Caution shall be lodged with the Public Guardian.

(4) Where caution has been lodged to the satisfaction of the Public Guardian he shall notify the sheriff clerk.

(5) The sheriff may at any time while a requirement to find caution is in force—

    (a) increase the amount of, or require the person to find new, caution; or

    (b) authorise the amount of caution to be decreased.

[2] (6) Where the sheriff requires the person referred to in paragraph (1) to give security other than caution, the rules of Chapter 27 of the Ordinary Cause Rules shall apply with the necessary modifications.

NOTES

[1] As inserted by the Act of Sederunt (Summary Applications, Statutory Applications and Appeals etc. Rules) Amendment (No.3) (Adults with Incapacity) 2002 (SSI 2002/146), r.2(2).

[2] As inserted by the Act of Sederunt (Summary Applications, Statutory Applications and Appeals etc. Rules) Amendment (Adult Support and Protection (Scotland) Act 2007) 2008 (SSI 2008/111) r.4 (effective April 1, 2008).

[3] As amended by the Act of Sederunt (Summary Applications, Statutory Applications and Appeals etc. Rules) Amendment (Adult Support and Protection (Scotland) Act 2007) 2008 (SSI 2008/111) r.4 (effective April 1, 2008).

Appointment of interim guardian

[1] **3.16.11** An application under section 57(5) of the 2000 Act (appointment of interim guardian) may be made in the crave of the application for a guardianship order to which it relates or, if made after the submission of the application for a guardianship order, by motion in the process of that application.

NOTE
[1] As inserted by the Act of Sederunt (Summary Applications, Statutory Applications and Appeals etc. Rules) Amendment (No.3) (Adults with Incapacity) 2000 (SSI 2002/146), r.2(2) (effective April 1, 2002).

Registration of intervention order or guardianship order relating to heritable property

[1] **3.16.12** Where an application for an intervention order or a guardianship order seeks to vest in the person authorised under the order, or the guardian, as the case may be, any right to deal with, convey or manage any interest in heritable property which is recorded or capable of being recorded in the General Register of Sasines or is registered or capable of being registered in the Land Register of Scotland, the applicant must specify the necessary details of the property in the application to enable it to be identified in the Register of Sasines or the Land Register of Scotland, as the case may be.

NOTE
[1] As inserted by the Act of Sederunt (Summary Applications, Statutory Applications and Appeals etc. Rules) Amendment (No.3) (Adults with Incapacity) 2002 (SSI 2002/146), r.2(2) (effective April 1, 2002).

Non-compliance with decisions of guardians with welfare powers

[1] **3.16.13**—(1) Where the court is required under section 70(3) of the 2000 Act to intimate an application for an order or warrant in relation to non-compliance with the decision of a guardian with welfare powers, the sheriff clerk shall effect intimation in Form 20 in accordance with paragraphs (2) and (3).

(2) Intimation shall be effected—

(a) where the person is within Scotland, by first class recorded delivery post, or, in the event that intimation by first class recorded delivery post is unsuccessful, by personal service by a sheriff officer; or

(b) where the person is furth of Scotland, in accordance with rule 2.12 (service on persons furth of Scotland).

(3) Such intimation shall include notice of the period within which any objection to the application shall be lodged.

NOTE
[1] As inserted by the Act of Sederunt (Summary Applications, Statutory Applications and Appeals etc. Rules) Amendment (No.3) (Adults with Incapacity) 2002 (SSI 2002/146), r.2(2) (effective April 1, 2002).

[1] PART XVII

ANTI-TERRORISM, CRIME AND SECURITY ACT 2001

NOTE
[1] As inserted by the Act of Sederunt (Summary Applications, Statutory Applications and Appeals etc. Rules) Amendment (Detention and Forfeiture of Terrorist Cash) 2002 (SSI 2002/129), para.2(2) (effective March 8, 2002).

Interpretation

3.17.1 In this Part, any reference to a specified paragraph shall be construed as a reference to the paragraph bearing that number in Schedule 1 to the Anti-terrorism, Crime and Security Act 2001.

Applications for extended detention of cash

3.17.2—(1) An application to the sheriff for an order under paragraph 3(2) (extended detention of seized cash) shall be made by summary application.

(2) An application for any further order for the detention of cash under paragraph 3(2) shall be made by minute in the original process and shall be proceeded with in accordance with sub-paragraph (3) below.

(3) On the lodging of an application for any further order the sheriff shall—

    (a) fix a date for determination of the application; and

    (b) order service of the application together with notice of such date for determination on any persons whom he considers may be affected.

Applications for release of detained cash

3.17.3—(1) An application to the sheriff under paragraph 5(2) (application for release of detained cash) or under paragraph 9(1) (application by person who claims that cash belongs to him) shall, where the court has made an order under paragraph 3(2), be made by minute in the original process of the application for that order, and in any other case shall be made by summary application.

(2) On the lodging of such an application the sheriff shall—

    (a) fix a date for a hearing; and

    (b) order service of the application together with notice of such hearing on the procurator fiscal and any other person whom he considers may be affected by the granting of such an application.

Applications for forfeiture of detained cash

3.17.4—(1) An application to the sheriff under paragraph 6(1) (application for forfeiture of detained cash) shall, where the court has made an order under paragraph 3(2), be made by minute in the original process of the application for that order, and in any other case shall be made by summary application.

(2) On the lodging of such an application the sheriff shall—

    (a) fix a date for a hearing; and

    (b) order service of the application together with notice of such hearing on any person whom he considers may be affected by the granting of such an application.

Applications for compensation

3.17.5—(1) An application to the sheriff under paragraph 10(1) (application for compensation) shall, where the court has made an order under paragraph 3(2), be made by minute in the original process of the application for that order, and in any other case shall be made by summary application.

(2) On the lodging of such an application the sheriff shall—

    (a) fix a date for a hearing; and

    (b) order service of the application together with notice of such hearing on any person whom he considers may be affected by the granting of such an application.

[1] PART XVIII

LOCAL GOVERNMENT (SCOTLAND) ACT 1973

NOTE

[1] As inserted by the Act of Sederunt (Summary Applications, Statutory Applications and Appeals etc. Rules) Amendment (No.2) (Local Government (Scotland) Act 1973) 2002 (SSI 2002/130), r.2(3) (effective March 8, 2002).

Application

3.18.1—This Part applies to appeals to the sheriff principal under section 103J of the Local Government (Scotland) Act 1973 (appeals from the Accounts Commission for Scotland).

Appeals

3.18.2—(1) An appeal under this Part shall be made by summary application.

(2) A summary application made under paragraph (1) shall include grounds of appeal stating—

(a) the finding or sanction or suspension being appealed;

(b) reasons why the appeal should be allowed; and

(c) the date of sending of the finding or imposition of the sanction or suspension concerned,

and shall be accompanied by a copy of such finding, sanction or suspension.

Warrant and form of citation

3.18.3—(1) A warrant for citation in an appeal under this Part shall be in Form 2A and shall state—

(a) the date by which answers should be lodged; and

(b) the date and time when the appeal will call.

(2) Citation in respect of a warrant granted under paragraph (1) shall be in Form 3A.

(3) Where a party on whom service has been made lodges answers under paragraph (1)(a) that party shall, at the same time, send a copy to the applicant.

(4) In Schedule 1 (forms)—

(a) after Form 2 insert Form 2A; and

(b) after Form 3 insert Form 3A,

as set out in the Schedule to this Act of Sederunt.

[1] PART XIX

PROCEEDS OF CRIME ACT 2002

NOTE
[1] As inserted by the Act of Sederunt (Summary Applications, Statutory Applications and Appeals etc. Rules) Amendment (No.5) (Proceeds of Crime Act 2002) 2002 (SSI 2002/563), r.2(2) (effective December 30, 2002).

General

Interpretation and application

[1] **3.19.1.**—(1) In this Part—

"the Act" means the Proceeds of Crime Act 2002;

references to an administrator are to an administrator appointed under section 125(1) or 128(3);

a reference to a specified section is a reference to the section bearing that number in the Act; and any reference to a specified paragraph in a specified Schedule is a reference to the paragraph bearing that number in the Schedule of that number in the Act.

(2) This Part applies to applications to the sheriff under Parts 3, 5 and 8 of the Act; but it only applies to applications under Part 8 in relation to property that is the subject of a civil recovery investigation.

NOTE
[1] As substituted by the Act of Sederunt (Summary Applications, Statutory Applications and Appeals etc. Rules) Amendment (No.6) (Proceeds of Crime Act 2002) 2003 (SSI 2003/98), r.2(2)(a) (effective February 24, 2003 for provisions specified in SSI 2003/98 para.1(1)(b)(ii); March 24, 2003 otherwise).

Recovery of cash in summary proceedings

Applications for extended detention of cash

3.19.2.—(1) An application to the sheriff for an order under sections

295(2) and (7) (extended detention of seized cash) shall be made by summary application.

(2) An application for any further order for the detention of cash under section 295(2) shall be made by minute in the process of the original application for extended detention of seized cash and shall be proceeded with in accordance with sub-paragraph (3) below.

(3) On the lodging of an application for any further order the sheriff shall—

(a) fix a date for determination of the application; and
(b) order service of the application together with notice of such date for determination on any persons whom he considers may be affected.

Applications for release of detained cash

3.19.3.—(1) An application to the sheriff under section 297(3) (application for release of detained cash) or under section 301(1) (application by person who claims that cash belongs to him) shall, where the court has made an order under section 295(2), be made by minute in the process of the application for that order, and in any other case shall be made by summary application in the course of the proceedings or at any other time.

(2) On the lodging of such an application the sheriff shall—

(a) fix a date for a hearing; and
(b) order service of the application together with notice of such hearing on the procurator fiscal and any other person whom he considers may be affected by the granting of such an application.

Applications for forfeiture of detained cash

3.19.4.—(1) An application to the sheriff under section 298(1)(b) (application by the Scottish Ministers for forfeiture of detained cash) shall, where the court has made an order under section 295(2), be made by minute in the process of the application for that order, and in any other case shall be made by summary application.

(2) On the lodging of such an application the sheriff shall—

(a) fix a date for a hearing; and
(b) order service of the application together with notice of such hearing on any person whom he considers may be affected by the granting of such an application.

Applications for compensation

3.19.5.—(1) An application to the sheriff under section 302(1) (application for compensation) shall, where the court has made an order under section 295(2), be made by minute in the process of the application for that order, and in any other case shall be made by summary application.

(2) On the lodging of such an application the sheriff shall—

(a) fix a date for a hearing; and
(b) order service of the application together with notice of such hearing on any person whom he considers may be affected by the granting of such an application.

[1] *Restraint and administration orders*

NOTE
[1] Inserted by the Act of Sederunt (Summary Applications, Statutory Applications and Appeals etc. Rules) Amendment (No.6) (Proceeds of Crime Act 2002) 2003 (SSI 2003/98), r.2(2)(b) (effective February 24, 2003 for provisions specified in SSI 2003/98 para.1(1)(b)(ii); March 24, 2003 otherwise).

Service of restraint orders

3.19.6. The intimation to be made by the prosecutor under section 121(3) shall be made by serving a copy of the interlocutor granting a restraint order on every person named in the interlocutor as restrained by the order.

Recall or variation of restraint orders
3.19.7. An application to the sheriff under section 121(5) (variation or recall of restraint order) shall be made by minute in the process of the application for the restraint order.

Appeals to the Court of Session
3.19.8.—(1) An appeal against an interlocutor of the sheriff refusing, varying or recalling or refusing to vary or recall a restraint order shall be marked within 14 days after the date of the interlocutor concerned.

(2) Such an appeal shall be marked by writing a note of appeal on the interlocutor sheet, or other written record containing the interlocutor appealed against, or on a separate sheet lodged with the sheriff clerk, in the following terms—
"The applicant appeals to the Court of Session.".

(3) The note of appeal shall—
(a) be signed by the appellant;
(b) bear the date on which it is signed; and
(c) where the appellant is represented, specify the name and address of the solicitor or other agent who will be acting for him in the appeal.

(4) The sheriff clerk will transmit the process within 4 days after the appeal is marked to the Deputy Principal Clerk of Session.

(5) Within the period specified in paragraph (4), the sheriff clerk shall—
(a) send written notice of the appeal to every other party; and
(b) certify on the interlocutor sheet that he has done so.

(6) Failure of the sheriff clerk to comply with paragraph (5) shall not invalidate the appeal.

Applications in relation to arrestment
3.19.9.—(1) An application to the sheriff under section 124(1) (arrestment of property affected by restraint order) by the prosecutor for warrant for arrestment may be made—
(a) in the application made under section 121(2) (application for restraint order); or
(b) if made after a restraint order has been applied for, by minute in the process of the application for that order.

(2) An application to the sheriff under section 124(3) (recalling, loosing or restricting arrestment) or under section 124(6) (recall or restriction of arrestment) shall be made by minute in the process of the application for the restraint order.

Applications for appointment of administrators
3.19.10.—(1) An application to the sheriff under section 125(1) (appointment of management administrator) shall be made by minute in the process of the application for the restraint order.

(2) An application to the sheriff under section 128(2) (appointment of enforcement administrator) shall be made—
(a) where made after a restraint order has been made, by minute in the process of the application for that order; or
(b) in any other case, by summary application.

(3) The notification to be made by the sheriff clerk under section 125(3) or 128(8) (as the case may be) shall be made by intimation of a copy of the interlocutor to the accused and the persons subject to the order.

Incidental applications in relation to an administration
3.19.11. An application to the sheriff subsequent to the appointment of an administrator relating to any matter incidental to that appointment shall be

made by minute in the process of the application in which the administrator was appointed.

Documents for Accountant of Court
3.19.12.—(1) A person who has lodged any document in the process of an application for the appointment of an administrator shall forthwith send a copy of that document to the Accountant of Court.

(2) The sheriff clerk shall transmit to the Accountant of Court any part of the process as the Accountant of Court may request in relation to an administration which is in dependence before the sheriff unless such part of the process is, at the time of request, required by the sheriff.

Procedure for fixing and finding caution
3.19.13.—(1) The Accountant of Court shall forthwith, on receiving intimation of an application for the appointment of an administrator, fix the caution to be found in the event of appointment being made and shall notify the amount to the sheriff clerk and the applicant.

(2) During the subsistence of the appointment of the administrator, the Accountant of Court may, at any time—
 (a) require the administrator to increase the amount of or find new or additional caution; or
 (b) authorise the administrator to decrease the amount of existing caution.

Time for finding caution
3.19.14.—(1) Where the time within which caution is to be found is not stipulated in the interlocutor appointing the administrator, the time allowed for finding caution shall be, subject to paragraph (2) of this rule, limited to one calendar month from the date of the interlocutor.

(2) The sheriff may, on application made before the expiry of the period for finding caution, and, on cause shown, allow further time for finding caution.

Procedure on finding caution
3.19.15.—(1) Caution shall be lodged with the Accountant of Court.

(2) Where caution has been found to the satisfaction of the Accountant of Court, he shall notify the sheriff clerk.

Issue of certified copy interlocutor
3.19.16.—(1) A certified copy interlocutor of appointment of an administrator shall not be issued by the sheriff clerk until he receives notification from the Accountant of Court in accordance with rule 3.19.15(2).

Administrator's title to act
3.19.17. An administrator shall not be entitled to act until he has obtained a certified copy of the interlocutor appointing him.

Accounts
3.19.18.—(1) An administrator shall maintain accounts of his intromissions with the property in his charge and shall, subject to paragraph (2)—
 (a) within six months after the date of his appointment; and
 (b) at six monthly intervals after the first account during the subsistence of his appointment,
lodge with the Accountant of Court an account of his intromissions in such form, with such supporting vouchers and other documents, as the Accountant of Court may require.

(2) The Accountant of Court may waive the lodging of an account where

the administrator certifies that there have been no intromissions during a particular accounting period.

Application for discharge of administrator
3.19.19. An application to the sheriff for discharge of an administrator shall be made by minute in the process of the application in which the administrator was appointed.

Appeals against determination of outlays and remuneration
3.19.20. An appeal to the sheriff under paragraph 9(1) of Schedule 3 (appeal against a determination by the Accountant of Court) shall be made by minute in the process of the application in which the administrator was appointed.

[1] *Civil recovery investigations*

NOTE
[1] As inserted by the Act of Sederunt (Summary Applications, Statutory Applications and Appeals etc. Rules) Amendment (No.6) (Proceeds of Crime Act 2002) 2003 (SSI 2003/98), r.2(2)(b) (effective February 24, 2003 for provisions specified in SSI 2003/98 para.1(1)(b)(ii); March 24, 2003 otherwise).

Production orders
3.19.21.—(1) An application to the sheriff under section 382(2) (order to grant entry to premises) may be made—
  (a) in the application for the production order; or
  (b) if made after the production order has been made, by minute in the process of the application for that order.
(2) A report to the sheriff under section 385(4) (report of failure to bring production order made in relation to an authorised government department to the attention of the officer concerned) shall take the form of a letter to the sheriff clerk.
(3) An application to the sheriff under section 386(4) (discharge or variation of a production order or an order to grant entry) shall be made by minute in the process of the application for the production order.

Search warrants
3.19.22. An application to the sheriff under section 387(1) (search warrant) shall be in the form of a summary application.

Customer information orders
3.19.23. An application under section 403(4) (discharge or variation of a customer information order) shall be made by minute in the process of the application for the customer information order.

Account monitoring orders
3.19.24. An application under section 408(4) (discharge or variation of an account monitoring order) shall be made by minute in the process of the application for the account monitoring order.

[1] PART XX

INTERNATIONAL CRIMINAL COURT (SCOTLAND) ACT 2001

NOTE
[1] As inserted by the Act of Sederunt (Summary Applications, Statutory Applications and Appeals etc. Rules) Amendment (International Criminal Court) 2003 (SSI 2003/27), r.2(2) (effective January 24, 2003).

General

Interpretation and application

3.20.1.—(1) In this Part—

"the Act" means the International Criminal Court (Scotland) Act 2001;

"ICC crime" has the same meaning as in section 28(1) of the Act; and a reference to a specified section is a reference to the section bearing that number in the Act, and any reference to a specified paragraph in a specified schedule is a reference to the paragraph bearing that number in the schedule of that number to the Act.

(2) This Part applies to applications to the sheriff under Parts 1 and 2 of schedule 5 to the Act.

Investigations of proceeds of ICC crime

Production or access orders

3.20.2.—(1) An order under Part 1 of schedule 5 to the Act may be made by the sheriff on a summary application by a person authorised for the purpose under section 19 of the Act.

(2) Any such application may be made on an ex parte application to a sheriff in chambers.

(3) Any such application must set out reasonable grounds for suspecting—

    (a) that a specified person has benefited from an ICC crime; and

    (b) that the material to which the application relates is likely to be of substantial value (whether by itself or together with other material) to the investigation for the purposes of which the application is made.

(4) Any application for variation or discharge of an order under Part 1 of schedule 5 to the Act shall be made by minute.

Search warrants

3.20.3.—(1) On a summary application by a person authorised under section 19 of the Act to the sheriff sitting as a court of civil jurisdiction, the sheriff may issue a warrant under Part 2 of the Act.

(2) Any such application must set out grounds sufficient to satisfy the sheriff—

    (a) that a production or access order made in relation to material on the premises has not been complied with;

    (b) that—

        (i) there are reasonable grounds for suspecting that a specified person has benefited from an ICC crime;

        (ii) there are grounds for making a production and access order in relation to material on the premises; and

        (iii) it would not be appropriate to make a production and access order in relation to the material for any of the reasons specified in paragraph 10(4) of schedule 5 to the Act; or

    (c) that—

        (i) there are reasonable grounds for suspecting that a specified person has benefited from an ICC crime;

        (ii) there are reasonable grounds for suspecting that there is material on the premises which cannot be particularised at the time of the application, but which—

            (aa) relates to the specified person, or to the question of whether that person has benefited from an ICC crime, or to any question as to the extent or whereabouts of the proceeds of an ICC crime; and

            (bb) is likely to be of substantial value (whether by itself or

together with other material) to the investigation for the purposes of which the application is made; and
  (iii) any of the circumstances specified in paragraph 10(6) of schedule 5 to the Act applies.

[1] PART XXI

IMMIGRATION AND ASYLUM ACT 1999

NOTE
[1] As inserted by the Act of Sederunt (Summary Applications, Statutory Applications and Appeals etc. Rules) Amendment (Immigration and Asylum) 2003 (SSI 2003/261), r.2(2) (effective May 24, 2003).

Interpretation
3.21.1. In this Part—
"the Act" means the Immigration and Asylum Act 1999; and
"an appeal" means an appeal to the sheriff under section 35A(1) or section 40B(1) of the Act.

Appeals
3.21.2.—(1) A person making an appeal against a decision by the Secretary of State to impose a penalty under section 32 or a charge under section 40 of the Act must, subject to paragraph (2), bring an appeal within 21 days after receiving the penalty notice or charge notice.
  (2) Where the appellant has given notice of objection to the Secretary of State under section 35(4) or section 40A(3) of the Act within the time prescribed for doing so, he must bring an appeal within 21 days after receiving notice of the Secretary of State's decision under section 35(7) or section 40A(6) respectively of the Act in response to the notice of objection.

[1] PART XXII

CRIME AND DISORDER ACT 1998

[*Revoked by the Act of Sederunt (Summary Applications, Statutory Applications and Appeals etc. Rules) Amendment (Antisocial Behaviour etc. (Scotland) Act 2004) 2004 (SSI 2004/455) r.2(2) (effective October 28, 2004: repeal has effect subject to transitional provisions specified in SSI 2004/ 455 r.2(3)).*]

[1] PART XXIII

ETHICAL STANDARDS IN PUBLIC LIFE ETC. (SCOTLAND) ACT 2000

NOTE
[1] As inserted by the Act of Sederunt (Summary Applications, Statutory Applications and Appeals etc. Rules) Amendment (Standards Commission for Scotland) 2003 (SSI 2003/346), r.2(2) (effective July 4, 2003).

Application
3.23.1. This Part applies to appeals to the sheriff principal under sections 22 (appeals from commission) or 26 (appeals by water industry commissioner) of the Ethical Standards in Public Life etc. (Scotland) Act 2000.

Appeals
3.23.2.—(1) An appeal under this Part shall be made by summary application.

(2) A summary application made under paragraph (1) shall include grounds of appeal stating—

(a) which of the findings of, or sanction or suspension imposed by, the Standards Commission for Scotland is being appealed;

(b) reasons why the appeal should be allowed; and

(c) the date of the sending of that finding, or imposition of that sanction or suspension,

and shall be accompanied by a copy of that finding, sanction or suspension.

Warrant and form of citation

3.23.3.—(1) A warrant for citation in an appeal under this Part shall be in Form 2A, or a form as near thereto as circumstances permit, and shall state—

(a) the date by which answers should be lodged; and

(b) the date and time when the appeal will call.

(2) Citation in respect of a warrant granted under paragraph (1) shall be in Form 3A, or a form as near thereto as circumstances permit.

(3) Where a party on whom service has been made lodges answers under paragraph (1)(a) that party shall, at the same time, send a copy to the appellant.

[1] Part XXIV

International Protection of Adults

NOTE

[1] As inserted by the Act of Sederunt (Summary Applications, Statutory Applications and Appeals etc. Rules) Amendment (International Protection of Adults) 2003 (SSI 2003/556), r.2(2) (effective November 14, 2003).

Interpretation

3.24.1. In this Part—

"the Act" means the Adults with Incapacity (Scotland) Act 2000;

"the Convention" means the Hague Convention of 13th January 2000 on the International Protection of Adults;

"international measure" means any measure taken under the law of a country other than Scotland for the personal welfare, or the protection of property, of an adult with incapacity, where—

(a) jurisdiction in the other country was based on the adult's habitual residence there; or

(b) the other country and the United Kingdom were when that measure was taken parties to the Convention, and jurisdiction in that other country was based on a ground of jurisdiction in the Convention; and

"Public Guardian" shall be construed in accordance with section 6 (the public guardian and his functions) of the Act.

Application

3.24.2—(1) An application to register an international measure under paragraph 8(1) of schedule 3 to the Act shall be by summary application made under this Part.

(2) The original document making the international measure, or a copy of that document duly certified as such by an officer of the issuing or a requesting body, shall be lodged with an application under paragraph (1), together with (as necessary) an English translation of that document and that certificate.

(3) Any translation under paragraph (2) must be certified as a correct translation by the person making it, and the certificate must contain the full name, address and qualifications of the translator.

Intimation of application

3.24.3.—(1) The sheriff shall order intimation of an application to register an international measure—

(a) except where the sheriff is satisfied that the person to whom the international measure relates had an opportunity to be heard in the country where that measure was taken, to that person;

(b) which if registered would have the effect of placing the adult to whom the international measure relates in an establishment in Scotland, to the—
  (i) Scottish Central Authority; and
  (ii) Mental Welfare Commission;

(c) to the Public Guardian; and

(d) to any other person whom the sheriff considers appropriate.

(2) In this rule—

(a) "Scottish Central Authority" means an authority—
  (i) designated under Article 28 of the Convention for the purposes of acting as such; or
  (ii) appointed by the Scottish Ministers for the purposes of carrying out the functions to be carried out under schedule 3 of the Act by the Scottish Central Authority, where no authority is designated for the purposes of sub paragraph (i); and

[1] (b) "Mental Welfare Commission" means the Mental Welfare Commission for Scotland continued in being by section 4 of the Mental Health (Care and Treatment) (Scotland) Act 2003.

NOTE

[1] As amended by the Mental Health (Care and Treatment) (Scotland) Act 2003 (Modification of Subordinate Legislation) Order 2005 (SSI 2005/445) Sch.1 para.29(1)(b) (effective October 5, 2005).

Notice to the Public Guardian

3.24.4. The sheriff clerk shall within 7 days after the date of an order registering an international measure, provide the Public Guardian with—

(a) a copy of that order; and

(b) a copy of the international measure, and of any translation.

Register of recognised foreign measures

3.24.5.—(1) There shall be a register of international measures ("the register") registered by order under this Part.

(2) The register shall include—

(a) the nature of the international measure;

(b) the date of the international measure;

(c) the date of the order under this Part granting recognition of the international measure;

(d) the name and address of—
  (i) the person who applied for recognition of the international measure under this Part;
  (ii) the person in respect of whom the international measure was taken; and
  (iii) if applicable, the person on whom any power is conferred by the international measure; and

(e) a copy of the international measure, and of any translation.

(3) The Public Guardian shall maintain the register, and make it available during normal office hours for inspection by members of the public.

(4) The Public Guardian shall if requested by any person certify that an international measure registered under this Part has been entered in the register.

[1] PART XXV

SEXUAL OFFENCES ACT 2003

NOTE
[1] As inserted by the Act of Sederunt (Summary Applications, Statutory Applications and Appeals etc. Rules) Amendment (Sexual Offences Act 2003) 2004 (SSI 2004/222) r.2(2) (effective May 21, 2004).

Interpretation
3.25.1. In this Part—
"the Act" means the Sexual Offences Act 2003;
[1] "main application" has the same meaning as in section 109(1) of the Act,
and words and expressions used in this Part and in the Act shall have the meanings given in the Act.

NOTE
[1] As inserted by the Act of Sederunt (Summary Applications, Statutory Applications and Appeals etc. Rules) Amendment (Protection of Children and Prevention of Sexual Offences (Scotland) Act 2005) 2005 (SSI 2005/473) r.2(2)(a) (effective October 7, 2005).

Time limit for service of a notice under section 99(3)
3.25.2. If the person in respect of whom a notification order is sought wishes to serve on the applicant a notice under section 99(3) of the Act, that person must do so no later than 3 working days before the hearing date for the application for the relevant notification order.

Time limit for service of a notice under section 106(11)
3.25.3. If the person in respect of whom a sexual offences prevention order is sought wishes to serve on the applicant a notice under section 106(11) of the Act, that person must do so no later than 3 working days before the hearing date for the application for the relevant sexual offences prevention order.

Time limit for service of a notice under section 116(6)
3.25.4. If the person in respect of whom a foreign travel order is sought wishes to serve on the applicant a notice under section 116(6) of the Act, that person must do so no later than 3 working days before the hearing date for the application for the relevant foreign travel order.

Variation, renewal or discharge of SOPOs
[1] **3.25.5.**—(1) Where an application under section 108(1) of the Act for an order varying, renewing or discharging a sexual offences prevention order is made in a sheriff court other than the sheriff court in which the process relating to the sexual offences prevention order is held—
  (a) the initial writ containing the application shall contain averments as to the sheriff court in which the process relating to the sexual offences prevention order is held;
  (b) the sheriff clerk with whom the application is lodged shall notify the sheriff clerk of the sheriff court in which the process relating to the sexual offences prevention order is held; and
  (c) the sheriff clerk of the sheriff court in which the process relating to the sexual offences prevention order is held shall, not later than 4 days after receipt of such notification, transfer the process relating to the sexual offences prevention order to the sheriff clerk of the sheriff court in which the application is made.
(2) For the purposes of paragraph (1), the sheriff court in which the process relating to the order is held is the sheriff court in which the sexual offences prevention order was granted or, where the process has been

transferred under that paragraph, the last sheriff court to which the process has been transferred.

(3) A failure of the sheriff clerk to comply with paragraph (1) shall not invalidate the application.

NOTE
[1] As substituted by the Act of Sederunt (Summary Applications, Statutory Applications and Appeals etc. Rules) Amendment (Protection of Children and Prevention of Sexual Offences (Scotland) Act 2005) 2005 (SSI 2005/473) r.2(2)(b) (effective October 7, 2005).

Variation, renewal or discharge of FTOs
[1] **3.25.6.**—(1) Subject to paragraph (2), an application under section 118 of the Act for an order varying, renewing or discharging a foreign travel order shall be made by minute in the process relating to the foreign travel order.

(2) Where an application under section 118(1) of the Act for an order varying, renewing or discharging a foreign travel order is made in a sheriff court other than the sheriff court in which the process relating to the foreign travel order is held—

   (a) the application shall be made by summary application;

   (b) the initial writ containing the application shall contain averments as to the sheriff court in which the process relating to the foreign travel order is held;

   (c) the sheriff clerk with whom the application is lodged shall notify the sheriff clerk of the sheriff court in which the process relating to the foreign travel order is held; and

   (d) the sheriff clerk of the sheriff court in which the process relating to the foreign travel order is held shall, not later than 4 days after receipt of such notification, transfer the process relating to the foreign travel order to the sheriff clerk of the sheriff court in which the application is made.

(3) For the purposes of paragraph (2), the sheriff court in which the process relating to the foreign travel order is held is the sheriff court in which the foreign travel order was granted or, where the process has been transferred under that paragraph, the last sheriff court to which the process has been transferred.

(4) A minute under paragraph (1) shall be made in accordance with and regulated by Chapter 14 of the Ordinary Cause Rules.

(5) A failure of the sheriff clerk to comply with paragraph (2) shall not invalidate the application.

NOTE
[1] As substituted by the Act of Sederunt (Summary Applications, Statutory Applications and Appeals etc. Rules) Amendment (Protection of Children and Prevention of Sexual Offences (Scotland) Act 2005) 2005 (SSI 2005/473) r.2(2)(b) (effective October 7, 2005).

Interim SOPOs
[1] **3.25.7.**—(1) Subject to paragraph (2), an application under section 109(2) of the Act for an interim sexual offences prevention order shall—

   (a) be made by crave in the initial writ containing the main application; and

   (b) once craved, be moved by motion to that effect.

(2) Where an application under section 109(2) of the Act for an interim sexual offences prevention order is made in a sheriff court other than the sheriff court in which the main application was lodged, the application for an interim sexual offences prevention order shall be made by summary application.

(3) The initial writ in a summary application under paragraph (2) shall

contain averments as to the sheriff court in which the main application was lodged.

(4) On receipt of a summary application under paragraph (2), the sheriff clerk shall notify the sheriff clerk of the sheriff court in which the main application was lodged.

(5) There shall be produced with a summary application under paragraph (2) copies of the following documents, certified as correct by the applicant's solicitor or the sheriff clerk—

   (a) the initial writ containing the main application;

   (b) any answers to the main application; and

   (c) any interlocutors pronounced in the main application.

(6) The sheriff clerk shall send a certified copy of any interlocutor disposing of a summary application under paragraph (2) to the sheriff clerk of the sheriff court in which the main application was lodged.

(7) A failure of the sheriff clerk to comply with paragraph (4) or (6) shall not invalidate the main application or the summary application under paragraph (2).

(8) Paragraphs (3) to (7) shall apply to an application for the variation, renewal or discharge of an interim sexual offences prevention order subject to the following modifications—

   (a) for references to a summary application under paragraph (2) there shall be substituted references to a summary application for the variation, renewal or discharge of an interim sexual offences prevention order;

   (b) references to the main application shall include references to any application for an interim sexual offences prevention order and any previous application for the variation, renewal or discharge of such an order; and

   (c) references to any interlocutors pronounced in the main application shall include any interlocutors pronounced in an application for an interim sexual offences prevention order or previous application for the variation, renewal or discharge of an interim sexual offences prevention order.".

NOTE

[1] As inserted by the Act of Sederunt (Summary Applications, Statutory Applications and Appeals etc. Rules) Amendment (Protection of Children and Prevention of Sexual Offences (Scotland) Act 2005) 2005 (SSI 2005/473) r.2(2)(b) (effective October 7, 2005).

[1] PART XXVI

PROTECTION OF CHILDREN (SCOTLAND) ACT 2003

NOTE

[1] As inserted by the Act of Sederunt (Summary Applications, Statutory Applications and Appeals etc. Rules) Amendment (Protection of Children (Scotland) Act 2003) 2004 (SSI 2004/334), r.2(2) (effective July 30, 2004) and renumbered by the Act of Sederunt (Ordinary Cause, Summary Application, Summary Cause and Small Claim Rules) Amendment (Miscellaneous) 2005 (SSI 2005/648), r.3(3) (effective January 2, 2006).

Interpretation

3.26.1. In this Part—

"the Act" means the Protection of Children (Scotland) Act 2003; and

"the list" means the list of individuals considered unsuitable to work with children kept by the Scottish Ministers under section 1(1) of the Act, and cognate expressions shall be construed accordingly.

Application

3.26.2. An application under section 7(6) or 14(1) or an appeal under section 15(1) of the Act shall be made by summary application.

Provisional inclusion in the list
3.26.3. The sheriff may consider and dispose of an application by the Scottish Ministers under section 7(6) of the Act without intimation to, or representation by, any other person.

Applications for removal from the list
3.26.4.—(1) A listed individual shall combine in a single application—
  (a) a request for leave to make an application under section 14(1) of the Act;
  (b) the grounds on which that individual considers that the sheriff should grant leave; and
  (c) the grounds on which that individual considers that the sheriff should grant such an application.
  (2) An application under paragraph (1) shall be intimated to the Scottish Ministers.
  (3) The sheriff shall consider and dispose of at a preliminary hearing that part of an application relating to the request for leave under paragraph (1)(a).

Appeal: inclusion in lists under section 5 or 6 of the Act
3.26.5. An appeal under section 15(1) of the Act against inclusion in the list in terms of section 5 or 6 of the Act shall be intimated to the Scottish Ministers.

Appeals: to the sheriff principal or to the Inner House of the Court of Session
3.26.6. An appeal under section 15(4) of the Act to the sheriff principal or an appeal under section 15(6)(a) of the Act to the Inner House of the Court of Session shall be intimated to the Scottish Ministers.

[1] PART XXVII

ANTISOCIAL BEHAVIOUR ETC. (SCOTLAND) ACT 2004

NOTE
[1] As inserted by the Act of Sederunt (Summary Applications, Statutory Applications and Appeals etc. Rules) Amendment (Antisocial Behaviour etc. (Scotland) Act 2004) 2004 (SSI 2004/455) r.2(4) (effective January 31, 2005 in relation to the provisions specified in SSI 2004/455 r.1(2)(a); April 4, 2005 in relation to the provisions specified in SSI 2004/455 r.1(2)(b); November 15, 2005 in relation to the provisions specified in SSI 2004/455 r.1(2)(c); October 28, 2004 otherwise).

Interpretation
3.27.1.—(1) In this Part—
    "the Act" means the Antisocial Behaviour etc. (Scotland) Act 2004;
    "ASBO" means an antisocial behaviour order under section 4(1) of the Act;
    "interim ASBO" means an interim ASBO under section 7(2) of the Act;
    "parenting order" means a parenting order under section 13 or 102 of the Act; and
    "the Principal Reporter" means the Principal Reporter appointed under section 127 of the Local Government etc. (Scotland) Act 1994.
  (2) Any reference to a section shall, unless the context otherwise requires, be a reference to a section of the Act.

Applications for variation or revocation of ASBOs to be made by minute in the original process
3.27.2.—(1) An application under section 5 (variation and revocation of antisocial behaviour orders) shall be made by minute in the original process

of the application for the ASBO in relation to which the variation or revocation is sought.

(2) Where the person subject to the ASBO is a child, a written statement containing the views of the Principal Reporter on the application referred to in rule 3.27.2(1) shall, where practicable, be lodged with that application.

Application for an interim ASBO
3.27.3.—(1) An application for an interim ASBO shall be made by crave in the initial writ in which an ASBO is sought.

(2) An application for an interim ASBO once craved shall be moved by motion to that effect.

(3) The sheriff shall not consider an application for an interim ASBO until after the initial writ has been intimated to the person in respect of whom that application is made and, where that person is a child, a written statement containing the views of the Principal Reporter on that application has been lodged.

Notification of making etc. of ASBOs and interim ASBOs
3.27.4. [*Repealed by the Act of Sederunt (Ordinary Cause and Summary Application Rules) Amendment (Miscellaneous) 2006 (SSI 2006/410) r.3(2) (effective August 18, 2006).*]

Parenting orders
3.27.5.—(1) Where a sheriff is considering making a parenting order under section 13 (sheriff's power to make parenting order), the sheriff shall order the applicant for the ASBO to—
  (a) intimate to any parent in respect of whom the parenting order is being considered—
    (i) that the court is considering making a parenting order in respect of that parent;
    (ii) that if that parent wishes to oppose the making of such a parenting order, he or she may attend or be represented at the hearing at which the sheriff considers the making of the parenting order;
    (iii) the place, date and time of the hearing set out in sub-paragraph (a)(ii) above; and
    (iv) that if that parent fails to appear and is not represented at the hearing, a parenting order may be made in respect of the parent; and
  (b) serve on any parent in respect of whom the parenting order is being considered a copy of the initial writ in which the ASBO is sought.

(2) Any parent in respect of whom a parenting order under section 13 is being considered may be sisted as a party to the action on their own motion, on the motion of either party or by the sheriff of his own motion.

Closure notice
3.27.6.—(1) A closure notice served under section 27 (service etc.) shall be in the form of Form 25 and shall (in addition to the requirements set out in section 27(5))—
  (a) state that it has been authorised by a senior police officer;
  (b) specify the date, time and place of the hearing of the application for a closure order under section 28; and
  (c) state that any person living on or having control of, responsibility for or an interest in the premises to which the closure notice relates who wishes to oppose the application should attend or be represented.

(2) Certification of service of a copy of the closure notice to all persons identified in accordance with section 27(2)(b) shall be in the form of Form 26.

Application for closure orders
3.27.7. An application to the sheriff for a closure order under section 28 shall be in the form of Form 27.

Application for extension of closure orders
3.27.8. An application to the sheriff for an extension of a closure order under section 32 shall be by minute in the form of Form 28 lodged in the original process of the application for the closure order in relation to which the extension is sought and shall be lodged not less than 21 days before the closure order to which it relates is due to expire.

Application for revocation of closure order
3.27.9. An application to the sheriff for revocation of a closure order under section 33 shall be by minute in the form of Form 29 lodged in the original process of the application for the closure order in relation to which the revocation is sought.

Application for access to premises
3.27.10. An application to the sheriff for an order for access to premises under section 34 shall be by minute in the form of Form 30 lodged in the original process of the application for the closure order in relation to which the access order is sought.

Applications by summary application
3.27.11. An application under section 35 (Reimbursement of expenditure), 63 (Appeal against graffiti removal notice) or 64 (Appeal against notice under section 61(4)) shall be by summary application.

3.27.12. An application under section 71 (Failure to comply with notice: order as to rental income), 74 (Failure to comply with notice: management control order) or 97 (Appeals against notice under section 94) shall be by summary application.

Revocation and suspension of order as to rental income
3.27.13. An application under section 73(2) for the revocation or suspension of an order relating to rental income shall be by minute lodged in the original process of the application for the order relating to rental income in relation to which the order for revocation or suspension is sought.

Revocation of management control order
3.27.14. An application under section 76(1) for the revocation of a management control order shall be by minute lodged in the original process of the application for the management control order in relation to which the order for revocation is sought.

Review of parenting order
3.27.15.—(1) An application under section 105(1) for revocation or variation of a parenting order shall be by minute lodged in the original process of the application for the parenting order in relation to which the order for revocation or variation is sought.

(2) Where the court that made a parenting order makes an order under section 105(5) that court shall within 4 days transmit the original process relating to the parenting order to the court specified in that order.

Procedural requirements relating to parenting orders
3.27.16. Where the sheriff is considering making a parenting order, or a revocation or variation of a parenting order, and it is practicable, having regard to the age and maturity of the child to—

(a) give the child an opportunity to indicate whether the child wishes to express views; and

(b) if the child so wishes, give the child an opportunity to express those views,

the sheriff shall order intimation in the form of Form 31 to the child in respect of whom the order was or is proposed to be made.

3.27.17. Where the sheriff is considering making a parenting order or revoking or varying a parenting order and does not already have sufficient information about the child, the sheriff shall order intimation in the form of Form 32 to the local authority for the area in which the child resides.

Enforcement of local authorities' duties under section 71 of the Children (Scotland) Act 1995

3.27.18. An application under section 71A(2) of the Children (Scotland) Act 1995 by the Principal Reporter shall be by summary application to the sheriff principal of the Sheriffdom in which the principal office of the local authority is situated.

¹ PART XXVIII

LAND REFORM (SCOTLAND) ACT 2003

NOTE
¹ As inserted by the Act of Sederunt (Summary Applications, Statutory Applications and Appeals, etc. Rules) Amendment (Land Reform) (Scotland) Act 2005 (SSI 2005/61), r.2(2) (effective February 9, 2005).

Interpretation
3.28.1. In this Part—
"the Act" means the Land Reform (Scotland) Act 2003.

Public notice of appeal against section 14(2) remedial notice
3.28.2. Where an owner of land appeals by summary application under section 14(4) of the Act against a notice served on him under section 14(2) of the Act, the owner must at the same time as, or as closely in time as practicable to, the lodging of the application, advertise by publication of an advertisement in a newspaper circulating in the area of the land details of the application including details of the notice appealed against.

Restriction on number of persons being party to section 14(4) application
3.28.3. Persons interested in the exercise of access rights over the land to which a summary application under section 14(2) of the Act relates, and persons or bodies representative of such persons, may be parties to the summary application proceedings, but the court may order that any one or more of the persons or bodies who have the same interests and no others, may take an active part in the proceedings.

Public notice and restriction on number of parties to section 15 application
3.28.4. The provisions in rules 3.28.2 and 3.28.3 above apply with necessary modifications to a summary application appealing against a notice served under section 15(2) of the Act.

Public notice and restriction on number of parties to section 28 application
3.28.5.—(1) The provisions in rules 3.28.2 and 3.28.3 above apply with necessary modifications to a summary application for a declaration under section 28(1) or (2) of the Act.

(2) A summary application under section 28(1) or (2) of the Act may be made at any time.

PART XXIX

Risk of Sexual Harm Orders

NOTE
¹ As inserted by Act of Sederunt (Summary Applications, Statutory Applications and Appeals etc. Rules) Amendment (Protection of Children and Prevention of Sexual Offences (Scotland) Act 2005) 2005 (SSI 2005/473) r.2(3) (effective October 7, 2005).

Interpretation
3.29.1. In this Part—
"the Act" means the Protection of Children and Prevention of Sexual Offences (Scotland) Act 2005[5];
"main application" has the same meaning as in section 5 of the Act, and words and expressions used in this Part and in the Act shall have the meanings given in the Act.

Variation, renewal or discharge of RSHOs
3.29.2.—(1) Subject to paragraph (2), an application under section 4(1) of the Act for an order varying, renewing or discharging a risk of sexual harm order shall be made by minute in the process relating to the risk of sexual harm order.
(2) Where an application under section 4(1) of the Act for an order varying, renewing or discharging a risk of sexual harm order is made in a sheriff court other than the sheriff court in which the process relating to the risk of sexual harm order is held—
  (a) the application shall be made by summary application;
  (b) the initial writ containing the application shall contain averments as to the sheriff court in which the process relating to the risk of sexual harm order is held;
  (c) the sheriff clerk with whom the application is lodged shall notify the sheriff clerk of the sheriff court in which the process relating to the risk of sexual harm order is held; and
  (d) the sheriff clerk of the sheriff court in which the process relating to the risk of sexual harm order is held shall, not later than 4 days after receipt of such notification, transfer the process relating to the risk of sexual harm order to the sheriff clerk of the sheriff court in which the application is made.
(3) For the purposes of paragraph (2), the sheriff court in which the process relating to the risk of sexual harm order is held is the sheriff court in which the risk of sexual harm order was granted or, where the process has been transferred under that paragraph, the last sheriff court to which the process has been transferred.
(4) A minute under paragraph (1) shall be made in accordance with and regulated by Chapter 14 of the Ordinary Cause Rules.
(5) A failure of the sheriff clerk to comply with paragraph (2) shall not invalidate the application.

Interim RSHOs
3.29.3.—(1) Subject to paragraph (2), an application under section 5(2) of the Act for an interim risk of sexual harm order shall—
  (a) be made by crave in the initial writ containing the main application; and
  (b) once craved, be moved by motion to that effect.
(2) Where an application under section 5(2) of the Act for an interim risk of sexual harm order is made in a sheriff court other than the sheriff court in which the main application was lodged, the application for an interim risk of sexual harm order shall be made by summary application.
(3) The initial writ in a summary application under paragraph (2) shall

contain averments as to the sheriff court in which the main application was lodged.

(4) On receipt of a summary application under paragraph (2), the sheriff clerk shall notify the sheriff clerk of the sheriff court in which the main application was lodged.

(5) There shall be produced with a summary application under paragraph (2) copies of the following documents, certified as correct by the applicant's solicitor or the sheriff clerk:–

    (a) the initial writ containing the main application;

    (b) any answers to the main application; and

    (c) any interlocutors pronounced in the main application.

(6) The sheriff clerk shall send a certified copy of any interlocutor disposing of a summary application under paragraph (2) to the sheriff clerk of the sheriff court in which the main application was lodged.

(7) Rule 3.29.2 (variation, renewal or discharge of RSHOs) shall apply to an application for an order under section 5(6) of the Act for variation, renewal or discharge of an interim risk of sexual harm order subject to the following modifications:–

    (a) for references to section 4(1) of the Act there shall be substituted references to section 5(6) of the Act; and

    (b) for references to a risk of sexual harm order there shall be substituted references to an interim risk of sexual harm order.

(8) A failure of the sheriff clerk to comply with paragraph (4) or (6) shall not invalidate the main application or the summary application under paragraph (2).

Service of RSHOs

3.29.4.—(1) This rule applies to—

    (a) a risk of sexual harm order;

    (b) an interim risk of sexual harm order; and

    (c) an order varying or renewing an order mentioned in sub-paragraph (a) or (b).

[1] (2) The sheriff clerk shall serve a copy of the order on the person against whom it has effect.

[1] (3) For the purposes of paragraph (2), the copy of the order is served–

    (a) where the person against whom the order has effect is present in court when the order is made–

        (i) by giving it to the person and obtaining a receipt therefor;

        (ii) by sending it to the person by recorded delivery or registered post; or

        (iii) by causing it to be served by sheriff officer; or

    (b) where the person against whom the order has effect is not present in court when the order is made–

        (i) by sending it to the person by recorded delivery or registered post; or

        (ii) by causing it to be served by sheriff officer.

(4) A failure by the sheriff clerk to comply with this rule shall not invalidate the order.

NOTE

[1] As substituted by the Act of Sederunt (Ordinary Cause and Summary Application Rules) Amendment (Miscellaneous) 2006 (SSI 2006/410) r.3(3) (effective August 18, 2006).

[1] Part XXX

Mental Health (Care and Treatment) (Scotland) Act 2003

NOTE

[1] As inserted by Act of Sederunt (Summary Applications, Statutory Applications and

Appeals etc. Rules) Amendment (Mental Health (Care and Treatment) (Scotland) Act 2003) 2005 (SSI 2005/504) r.2(2) (effective October 6, 2005).

Interpretation
3.30.1. In this Part "the Act" means the Mental Health (Care and Treatment) (Scotland) Act 2003.

Applications for removal orders
3.30.2.—(1) An application under section 293 of the Act (removal order to place of safety) shall be lodged with the sheriff clerk who shall fix a date for hearing the application.

(2) An order fixing a hearing shall be intimated in such manner and within such timescales as may be prescribed by the sheriff.

Applications for recall or variation of removal orders
3.30.3.—(1) An application under section 295 of the Act (recall or variation of removal order) shall be lodged with the sheriff clerk who shall fix a date for hearing the application.

(2) An order fixing a hearing shall be intimated by the sheriff clerk in such manner and within such timescales as may be prescribed by the sheriff.

Remit to Court of Session
3.30.4.—(1) Where the sheriff principal to whom an appeal is made remits the appeal to the Court of Session under section 320 of the Act (appeals), the sheriff clerk shall, within four days after the sheriff principal has pronounced the interlocutor remitting the appeal to the Court of Session, transmit the process to the Deputy Principal Clerk of Session.

(2) On transmitting the process under paragraph (1), the sheriff clerk shall—
(a) send written notice of the remit and transmission of the process to each party; and
(b) certify on the interlocutor sheet that he has done so.

[1] PART XXXI

FOOTBALL BANNING ORDERS

NOTE
[1] As inserted by the Act of Sederunt (Summary Applications, Statutory Applications and Appeals etc. (Rules) Amendment (Miscellaneous) 2006 (SSI 2006/437) r.2(2) (effective September 1, 2006).

Interpretation
3.31.1. In this Part—
"the Act" means the Police, Public Order and Criminal Justice (Scotland) Act 2006;
"football banning order" means an order made under section 52(4) of the Act.

Applications for variation or termination of a football banning order
3.31.2.—(1) An application under—
(a) section 57(1) of the Act for variation of a football banning order; or
(b) section 58(1) of the Act for termination of a football banning order,
shall be made by minute in the process relating to the football banning order.

(2) A minute under paragraph (1) shall be made in accordance with and regulated by Chapter 14 of the Ordinary Cause Rules.

[1] PART XXXII

ANIMAL HEALTH AND WELFARE

NOTE
[1] As inserted by the Act of Sederunt (Summary Applications, Statutory Applications and Appeals etc. Rules) Amendment (Miscellaneous) 2006 (SSI 2006/437) r.2(2) (effective September 1, 2006).

Interpretation
3.32.1. In this Part—
  "the 1981 Act" means the Animal Health Act 1981; and
  "the 2006 Act" means the Animal Health and Welfare (Scotland) Act
    2006.

Interim orders
3.32.2.—(1) An application for an interim order under–
  (a) section 28G(10) of the 1981 Act; or
  (b) section 41(9) of the 2006 Act, or
[1] (c) section 48(9) of the Animal Welfare Act 2006,
shall be made by crave in the initial writ in which a seizure order is sought.
  (2) An application for an interim order once craved shall be moved by motion to that effect.

NOTE
[1] As inserted by the Act of Sederunt (Summary Applications, Statutory Applications and Appeals etc. Rules) Amendment (Animal Welfare Act 2006) 2007 (SSI 2007/233) r.2(2) (effective March 26, 2007).

Interim orders pending appeal
3.32.3. An application for an interim order under—
  (a) section 28H(2) of the 1981 Act; or
  (b) section 43(5) of the 2006 Act, or
[1] (c) section 49(5) of the Animal Welfare Act 2006,
where a seizure order is suspended or inexecutable shall be made by motion.

NOTE
[1] As inserted by the Act of Sederunt (Summary Applications, Statutory Applications and Appeals etc. Rules) Amendment (Animal Welfare Act 2006) 2007 (SSI 2007/233) r.2(3) (effective March 26, 2007).

[1] PART XXXIII

EQUALITY ENACTMENTS

NOTE
[1] As inserted by the Act of Sederunt (Ordinary Cause, Summary Application, Summary Cause and Small Claim Rules) Amendment (Equality Act 2006 etc.) 2006 (SSI 2006/509), (effective November 3, 2006).

Application and interpretation
3.33.1.—(1) Subject to paragraph (3), this Part applies to applications under the equality enactments.
  (2) In this Chapter, "the equality enactments" means any of the following enactments—
  (a) Sex Discrimination Act 1975;
  (b) Race Relations Act 1976;
  (c) Disability Discrimination Act 1995;
  (d) Equality Act 2006;
[1] (e) The Equality Act (Sexual Orientation) Regulations 2007.

(3) This rule does not affect any provision of the equality enactments which provides for a claim to be the subject of proceedings in like manner as any claim in reparation for breach of statutory duty.

[2] (4) In this Part "the Commission" means the Commission for Equality and Human Rights.

NOTES
[1] As inserted by the Act of Sederunt (Ordinary Cause, Summary Application, Summary Cause and Small Claim Rules) Amendment (Equality Act (Sexual Orientation) Regulations 2007) (SSI 2007/339) r.3(2) (effective July 20, 2007).
[2] As inserted by the Act of Sederunt (Sheriff Court Rules) (Miscellaneous Amendments) 2008 (SSI 2008/223) r.5(3)(a) (effective July 1, 2008).

Intimation to Commission
[1]3.33.2. The applicant shall, except where the applicant is the Commission, send a copy of the initial writ to the Commission by registered or recorded delivery post.

NOTE
[1] As inserted by the Act of Sederunt (Sheriff Court Rules) (Miscellaneous Amendments) 2008 (SSI 2008/223) r.5(3)(b) (effective July 1, 2008).

Assessor
3.33.3.—(1) The sheriff may, of his own motion or on the motion of any party, appoint an assessor.
(2) The assessor shall be a person who the sheriff considers has special qualifications to be of assistance in determining the cause.

Taxation of Commission expenses
3.33.4. [*Omitted by the Act of Sederunt (Sheriff Court Rules) (Miscellaneous Amendments) 2008 (SSI 2008/223) r.5(3)(c) (effective July 1, 2008).*]

National security
3.33.5.—(1) This rule applies to—
  (a) proceedings in respect of alleged discrimination contrary to the Disability Discrimination Act 1995 (including anything treated by virtue of that Act as amounting to discrimination contrary to that Act); and
  (b) proceedings brought under the Race Relations Act 1976.
(2) Where, on a motion under paragraph (4) or of his own motion, the sheriff considers it expedient in the interests of national security, he may—
  (a) exclude from all or part of the proceedings—
    (i) the pursuer;
    (ii) the pursuer's representatives;
    (iii) any assessors;
  (b) permit a pursuer or representative who has been excluded to make a statement to the court before the commencement of the proceedings or the part of the proceedings, from which he is excluded;
  (c) take steps to keep secret all or part of the reasons for his decision in the proceedings.
(3) The sheriff clerk shall, on the making of an order under paragraph (2) excluding the pursuer or his representatives, notify the Advocate General for Scotland of that order.
(4) A party may apply by motion for an order under paragraph (2).
(5) The steps referred to in paragraph (2)(c) may include the following—
  (a) directions to the sheriff clerk; and

(b) orders requiring any person appointed to represent the interests of the pursuer in proceedings from which the pursuer or his representatives are excluded not to communicate (directly or indirectly) with any persons (including the excluded pursuer)—
    (i) on any matter discussed or referred to;
    (ii) with regard to any material disclosed,
during or with reference to any part of the proceedings from which the pursuer or his representatives are excluded.

(6) Where the sheriff has made an order under paragraph (5)(b), the person appointed to represent the interests of the pursuer may apply by motion for authority to seek instructions from or otherwise communicate with an excluded person.

[1] PART XXXIV

LICENSING (SCOTLAND) ACT 2005

NOTE
[1] As inserted by the Act of Sederunt (Summary Applications, Statutory Applications and Appeals etc. Rules) Amendment (Licensing (Scotland) Act 2005) 2008 (SSI 2008/9) r.2(2) (effective February 1, 2008).

Interpretation
3.34.1. In this Part, "the Act" means the Licensing (Scotland) Act 2005.

Application for stated case
3.34.2.—(1) An appeal under section 131 of the Act—
(a) must be by note of appeal in Form 33;
(b) must state the grounds of appeal; and
(c) must be lodged with the sheriff clerk of the sheriff court district in which the principal office of the Licensing Board is situated not later than 14 days after the relevant date.

(2) The appellant must, at the same time as lodging the note of appeal, intimate a copy of it to—
(a) the clerk to the Licensing Board; and
(b) all parties who appeared at the hearing before the Licensing Board.

(3) Intimation under paragraph (2) and under paragraph (4) of rule 3.34.3 may be given by—
(a) any of the methods of service provided for in Part II of Chapter 2 of this Act of Sederunt; or
(b) where intimation is to a party represented by a solicitor, by—
    (i) personal delivery;
    (ii) facsimile transmission;
    (iii) first class ordinary post;
    (iv) delivery to a document exchange,
to that solicitor.

(4) In this rule the "relevant date" means—
(a) the date of the decision of the Licensing Board; or
(b) where a statement of reasons has been required under section 51(2) of the Act, the date of issue of the statement of reasons.

Adjustment of stated case
3.34.3.—(1) The Licensing Board must, within 28 days of the lodging of a note of appeal, issue a draft case containing—
(a) findings in fact and law or, where appropriate, a narrative of the proceedings before them;
(b) appropriate questions of law;
(c) a note stating the reasons for their decision with particular reference to the grounds of appeal; and
(d) in an appeal where questions of admissibility or sufficiency of

evidence have arisen, a description of the evidence led before them to which these questions relate.

(2) The clerk to the Licensing Board must send a copy of the draft stated case to the parties.

(3) Within 14 days of the issue of the draft stated case—

(a) a party may lodge with the clerk to the Licensing Board a note of any adjustments which he seeks to make; and

(b) a respondent may state any point of law which he wishes to raise in the appeal.

(4) Any party—

(a) lodging a note of adjustments; or

(b) stating a point of law,

under paragraph (3) must at the same time intimate it to every other party.

(5) The Licensing Board—

(a) may, on the motion of a party or of their own accord; and

(b) must, where they propose to reject any proposed adjustment,

allow a hearing on the adjustments.

(6) A hearing under paragraph (5) must be held not later than 28 days after the expiry of the period mentioned in paragraph (3).

(7) The Licensing Board may provide for such further procedure prior to the lodging of the stated case under rule 3.34.4 as they think fit.

(8) The Licensing Board must, within 14 days after—

(a) the latest date on which a note of adjustments has been or may be lodged; or

(b) any hearing on adjustments,

state the case.

(9) The stated case must include questions of law, framed by the Licensing Board, arising from the grounds of appeal and points of law stated by the parties and such other questions of law as they may consider appropriate.

(10) Where the Licensing Board does not accept any adjustment sought under paragraph (3) they shall append to the case—

(a) the terms of the adjustment and a note of any evidence rejected by them which is alleged to support that adjustment;

(b) their reasons for rejecting that adjustment and evidence; and

(c) a note of the evidence upon which they base any finding in fact challenged by a party at any hearing under paragraph (5) on the basis that it is unsupported by the evidence.

(11) On cause shown the sheriff principal or, as the case may be, the sheriff may extend any period specified in paragraph (1), (3), (6) or (8) for such period or periods as he considers reasonable.

Lodging of stated case

3.34.4. The clerk of the Licensing Board must within 4 days of the case being stated by the Licensing Board—

(a) authenticate the case;

(b) lodge the case and all other documents and productions in the case with the sheriff clerk; and

(c) send a copy of the case to the parties.

Appointment of hearing

3.34.5. On a stated case being lodged under rule 3.34.4 the sheriff clerk shall fix a hearing and intimate the date, time and place of that hearing to the parties.

Effect of and abandonment of appeal

3.34.6.—(1) When a note of appeal has been lodged, it may be insisted on by all other parties although they may not have lodged separate appeals.

(2) After a note of appeal has been lodged, the appellant shall not be at liberty to withdraw it except—

(a) with the consent of the other parties, which may be incorporated in a joint minute; or

(b) by leave of the sheriff principal or, as the case may be, the sheriff and on such terms as to expenses or otherwise as to him seem proper.

Hearing of appeal

3.34.7.—(1) Subject to section 132(2) of the Act, the sheriff principal or, as the case may be, the sheriff shall hear the parties or their solicitors or counsel orally on all matters connected with the appeal including liability for expenses, but if any party moves that the question of liability for expenses be heard after the sheriff principal or, as the case may be, the sheriff has given his decision the sheriff principal or, as the case may be, the sheriff may grant that motion.

(2) In the hearing of an appeal, a party shall not be allowed to raise questions of law of which notice has not been given except on cause shown and subject to such conditions as to expenses or otherwise as the sheriff principal or, as the case may be, the sheriff may consider appropriate.

(3) The sheriff principal or, as the case may be, the sheriff may permit a party to amend any question of law or to add any new question of law in accordance with paragraph (2).

Recall of suspension or revocation

3.34.8. An application under section 132(8) of the Act for recall of suspension or revocation of a premises licence shall be made by crave in the note of appeal and shall be heard and determined by the sheriff principal or sheriff, as the case may be, after such procedure as he may direct.

[1] PART XXXV

ADULT SUPPORT AND PROTECTION (SCOTLAND) ACT 2007

NOTE

[1] As inserted by the Act of Sederunt (Summary Applications, Statutory Applications and Appeals etc. Rules) Amendment (Adult Support and Protection (Scotland) Act 2007) (No.2) 2008 (SSI 2008/335) r.2(2) (effective October 29, 2008).

Interpretation

3.35.1. In this Part—

"the Act" means the Adult Support and Protection (Scotland) Act 2007;

"the adult at risk" has the same meaning as in section 3 of the Act.

Variation or recall of removal order

3.35.2.—(1) An application under section 17 of the Act (variation or recall of removal order) for variation or recall of a removal order shall be made by minute in the process relating to the removal order.

(2) A minute under paragraph (1) shall be made in accordance with and regulated by Chapter 14 of the Ordinary Cause Rules.

Applications—banning orders and temporary banning orders

3.35.3.—(1) Where in an application under subsection (1) of section 19 of the Act (banning orders) an order is sought under subsection (2)(a) or (b) of that section there shall, where appropriate and unless the sheriff otherwise directs, be lodged a plan which clearly identifies the area specified in the application.

(2) An application under section 21 of the Act (temporary banning orders) shall—

(a) be made by crave in the application for the banning order concerned; and

(b) once craved, be moved by motion to that effect.

(3) Where a temporary banning order is granted, the related application for a banning order shall be determined within 6 months of the date of the lodging of that application.

(4) An application under section 24(1)(a) of the Act (variation or recall of banning order) shall be made by minute in the process relating to the banning order.

(5) An application under section 24(1)(b) of the Act (variation or recall of temporary banning order) shall be moved by motion to that effect in the process relating to the application for the banning order concerned.

(6) A minute under paragraph (4) shall be made in accordance with and regulated by Chapter 14 of the Ordinary Cause Rules.

Attachment of power of arrest
3.35.4.—(1) The following documents shall be served under section 25(2) of the Act (powers of arrest) along with a power of arrest—
   (a) a copy of the application for the order;
   (b) a copy of the interlocutor granting the order and the power of arrest; and
   (c) where the application to attach the power of arrest was made after the order was granted, a copy of the certificate of service of the order.

(2) The following documents shall be delivered to the chief constable in accordance with section 27(1) of the Act (notification to police)—
   (a) a copy of the application for the order;
   (b) a copy of the interlocutor granting the order;
   (c) a copy of the certificate of service of the order; and
   (d) where the application to attach the power of arrest was made after the order was granted—
      (i) where applicable, a copy of the application for the power of arrest;
      (ii) a copy of the interlocutor granting it; and
      (iii) a copy of the certificate of service of the power of arrest and the documents that required to be served along with it in accordance with section 25(2).

(3) [*Revoked by the Act of Sederunt (Summary Applications, Statutory Applications and Appeals etc. Rules) Amendment (Adult Support and Protection (Scotland) Act 2007) (No.3) 2008 (SSI 2008/375) r.2(2) (effective November 20, 2008).*]

Notification to adult at risk etc.
[1] **3.35.5.** Where section 26(1)(b) of the Act (notification to the adult at risk etc. on the variation or recall of a banning order or temporary banning order) applies, the person prescribed for the purposes of section 26(2) is the sheriff clerk.

NOTE
[1] As substituted by the Act of Sederunt (Summary Applications, Statutory Applications and Appeals etc. Rules) Amendment (Adult Support and Protection (Scotland) Act 2007) (No.3) 2008 (SSI 2008/375) r.2(3) (effective November 20, 2008).

Certificate of delivery of documents
[1] **3.35.6.** Where a person is in any circumstances required to comply with section 26(2), 27(1) or 27(2) of the Act he shall, after such compliance, lodge in process a certificate of delivery in Form 34.

NOTE
[1] As substituted by the Act of Sederunt (Summary Applications, Statutory Applications and Appeals etc. Rules) Amendment (Adult Support and Protection (Scotland) Act 2007) (No.3) 2008 (SSI 2008/375) r.2(4) (effective November 20, 2008).

Warrants for entry

3.35.7.—(1) An application for a warrant for entry under section 38(2) of the Act (criteria for granting warrants of entry under section 7) shall be in Form 35.

(2) The application may be granted without a hearing.

Form of appeal to the sheriff principal

3.35.8.—(1) An appeal under section 51(2) of the Act (appeals) against an interlocutor of the sheriff granting, or refusing to grant, a banning order shall be lodged within 14 days after the date of the interlocutor concerned.

(2) An application for leave to appeal against an interlocutor of the sheriff granting, or refusing to grant, a temporary banning order under section 51(2) of the Act shall be made within 7 days after the date of the interlocutor concerned.

(3) An appeal against an interlocutor referred to in paragraph (2) shall be lodged within 7 days after the date of the interlocutor granting leave to appeal.

Privacy of any hearing

3.35.9. The sheriff may, where he considers it appropriate in all the circumstances, appoint that the hearing of an application or other proceedings under this Part shall take place in private.

[1] PART XXXVI

UK BORDERS ACT 2007

NOTE

[1] As inserted by the Act of Sederunt (Sheriff Court Rules) (Miscellaneous Amendments) (No.2) 2008 (SSI 2008/365) r.6 (effective November 25, 2006).

Interpretation

3.36.1. In this Part—

"the Act" means the UK Borders Act 2007; and

"an appeal" means an appeal to the sheriff under section 11(1) of the Act.

Appeals

3.36.2.—(1) Subject to paragraph (2), an appeal must be lodged with the sheriff clerk not later than 21 days after the date the penalty notice was received by the appellant.

(2) Where the appellant has given notice of objection under section 10(1) of the Act, an appeal must be lodged with the sheriff clerk not later than 21 days after the date that notice of the Secretary of State's decision under section 10(4) of the Act was received by the appellant.

[1] PART XXXVII

EMPLOYMENT TRIBUNALS ACT 1996

NOTE

[1] As inserted by the Act of Sederunt (Summary Applications, Statutory Applications and Appeals etc. Rules) Amendment (Employment Tribunals Act 1996) 2009 (SSI 2009/109) r.2 (effective April 1, 2009).

Conciliation: recovery of sums payable under compromises

3.37.1.—(1) An application to the sheriff for a declaration under section 19A(4) of the Employment Tribunals Act 1996 shall be made not later than

42 days from the date of issue of the certificate stating that a compromise has been reached.

(2) An application to the sheriff for a declaration under section 19A(4) of that Act is pending for the purposes of subsection (7) of that section from the date on which it is lodged with the sheriff clerk until the date upon which final judgment on the application has been extracted.

[1] PART XXXVIII

COUNTER-TERRORISM ACT 2008

NOTE
[1] As inserted by the Act of Sederunt (Sheriff Court Rules) (Miscellaneous Amendments) 2009 (SSI 2009/294) r.18 (effective October 1, 2009).

Variation, renewal or discharge of foreign travel restriction order
3.38.—(1) Where an application under paragraph 9 of Schedule 5 to the Counter-Terrorism Act 2008 for an order varying, renewing or discharging a foreign travel restriction order is made in a sheriff court other than the sheriff court in which the process relating to the foreign travel restriction order is held—
  (a) the initial writ containing the application shall contain averments as to the sheriff court in which the process relating to the foreign travel restriction order is held;
  (b) the sheriff clerk with whom the application is lodged shall notify the sheriff clerk of the sheriff court in which the process relating to the foreign travel restriction order is held; and
  (c) the sheriff clerk of the sheriff court in which the process relating to the foreign travel restriction order is held shall, not later than 4 days after receipt of such notification, transfer the process relating to the foreign travel restriction order to the sheriff clerk of the sheriff court in which the application is made.

(2) For the purposes of paragraph (1), the sheriff court in which the process relating to the order is held is the sheriff court in which the foreign travel restriction order was granted or, where the process has been transferred under that paragraph, the last sheriff court to which the process has been transferred.

(3) A failure of the sheriff clerk to comply with paragraph (1) shall not invalidate the application.

[1] PART XXXIX

PUBLIC HEALTH ETC. (SCOTLAND) ACT 2008

NOTE
[1] As inserted by the Act of Sederunt (Summary Applications, Statutory Applications and Appeals etc. Rules) Amendment (Public Health etc. (Scotland) Act 2008) 2009 (SSI 2009/320) r.2 (effective October 1, 2009).

Interpretation
3.39.1. In this Part—
  "the Act" means the Public Health etc. (Scotland) Act 2008;
  "an investigator" means a person appointed under section 21 of the Act;
  "health board competent person" has the same meaning as in section 124 of the Act, and words and expressions used in this Part and in the Act shall have the same meaning given in the Act.

Application for a public health investigation warrant

3.39.2.—(1) An application made by an investigator for a warrant under section 27(2) of the Act (public health investigation warrants) shall be in Form 36.

(2) Where such a warrant is granted by the sheriff it shall be in Form 37.

Application for an order for medical examination

3.39.3.—(1) An application made by a health board for an order under section 34(1) of the Act (order for medical examination) shall be in Form 38.

(2) On receipt of an application mentioned in paragraph (1), the sheriff may order intimation of the application to such persons, within such a timescale and by such method as he sees fit.

(3) Where an order for a medical examination is granted by the sheriff it shall be in Form 39.

(4) Subject to the requirements of section 34(6)(b)(i) and (ii) of the Act, where an order for a medical examination is granted, the sheriff may direct that the order be notified to such persons, within such a timescale and by such method as he sees fit.

(5) For the avoidance of doubt, the method of intimation or notification referred to in paragraphs (2) and (4) may include intimation or notification by telephone, email or facsimile transmission.

Application for a quarantine order

3.39.4.—(1) An application made by a health board for a quarantine order under section 40(1) of the Act (quarantine orders) shall be in Form 40.

(2) On receipt of an application mentioned in paragraph (1), the sheriff may order intimation of the application to such persons, within such a timescale and by such method as he sees fit.

(3) Where a quarantine order is granted by the sheriff it shall be in Form 41.

(4) Subject to the requirements of section 40(6)(b)(i) and (ii) of the Act, where a quarantine order is granted, the sheriff may direct that the order be notified to such persons, within such a timescale and by such method as he sees fit.

(5) For the avoidance of doubt, the method of intimation or notification referred to in paragraphs (2) and (4) may include intimation or notification by telephone, email or facsimile transmission.

Application for a short term detention order

3.39.5.—(1) An application made by a health board for a short term detention order under section 42(1) of the Act (order for removal to and detention in hospital) shall be in Form 42.

(2) An application made by a health board for a short term detention order under section 43(1) of the Act (order for detention in hospital) shall be in Form 44.

(3) On receipt of an application mentioned in paragraph (1) or (2), the sheriff may order intimation of the application to such persons, within such a timescale and by such method as he sees fit.

(4) Where a short term detention order is granted by the sheriff under section 42(1) of the Act it shall be in Form 43.

(5) Where a short term detention order is granted by the sheriff under section 43(1) of the Act it shall be in Form 45.

(6) Subject to the requirements of sections 42(4)(b)(i) and (ii) and 43(4)(b)(i) and (ii) of the Act, where a short term detention order is granted under section 42(1) or 43(1) of the Act, the sheriff may direct that the order be notified to such persons, within such a timescale and by such method as he sees fit.

(7) For the avoidance of doubt, the method of intimation or notification

referred to in paragraphs (3) and (6) may include intimation or notification by telephone, email or facsimile transmission.

Application for an exceptional detention order
   3.39.6.—(1) An application made by a health board for an exceptional detention order under section 45(1) of the Act (exceptional detention order) shall be in Form 46.
   (2) On receipt of an application mentioned in paragraph (1), the sheriff may order intimation of the application to such persons, within such a timescale and by such method as he sees fit.
   (3) Where an exceptional detention order is granted by the sheriff it shall be in Form 47.
   (4) Subject to the requirements of section 45(4)(b)(i) and (ii) of the Act, where an exceptional detention order is granted, the sheriff may direct that the order be notified to such persons, within such a timescale and by such method as he sees fit.
   (5) For the avoidance of doubt, the method of intimation or notification referred to in paragraphs (2) and (4) may include intimation or notification by telephone, email or facsimile transmission.

Application for extension of a quarantine order, short term detention order or
   exceptional detention order
   3.39.7.—(1) An application made by a health board for an extension to a quarantine order, a short term detention order or an exceptional detention order under section 49(5) of the Act (extension of quarantine and hospital detention orders) shall be in Form 48.
   (2) On receipt of an application mentioned in paragraph (1), the sheriff may order intimation of the application to such persons, within such a timescale and by such method as he sees fit.
   (3) Where an order extending a quarantine order, a short term detention order or an exceptional detention order is granted by the sheriff it shall be in Form 49.
   (4) Subject to the requirements of section 49(10)(b)(i) and (ii) of the Act, where an order mentioned in paragraph (3) is granted, the sheriff may direct that the order be notified to such persons, within such a timescale and by such method as he sees fit.
   (5) For the avoidance of doubt, the method of intimation or notification referred to in paragraphs (2) and (4) may include intimation or notification by telephone, email or facsimile transmission.

Application for modification of a quarantine order, short term detention order
   or exceptional detention order
   3.39.8.—(1) An application made by a health board for an order modifying a quarantine order, a short term detention order or an exceptional detention order under section 51(1) of the Act (variation of quarantine and hospital detention orders) shall be in Form 50.
   (2) On receipt of an application mentioned in paragraph (1), the sheriff may order intimation of the application to such persons, within such a timescale and by such method as he sees fit.
   (3) Where an order modifying a quarantine order, a short term detention order or an exceptional detention order is granted by the sheriff it shall be in Form 51.
   (4) Subject to the requirements of section 51(5)(b)(i) and (ii) of the Act, where an order mentioned in paragraph (3) is granted, the sheriff may direct that the order be notified to such persons, within such a timescale and by such method as he sees fit.
   (5) For the avoidance of doubt, the method of intimation or notification referred to in paragraphs (2) and (4) may include intimation or notification by telephone, email or facsimile transmission.

Application for recall of an order granted in the absence of the person to whom it relates

3.39.9.—(1) An application for recall of a quarantine order, a short term detention order or an exceptional detention order under section 59 of the Act (recall of orders granted in absence of persons to whom application relates) shall be in Form 52.

(2) Subject to section 59(6) of the Act, on receipt of an application mentioned in paragraph (1), the sheriff may order intimation of the application to such persons, within such a timescale and by such method as he sees fit.

(3) Where an order recalling a quarantine order, a short term detention order or an exceptional detention order is granted by the sheriff it shall be in Form 53.

(4) Where an order mentioned in paragraph (3) is granted, the sheriff may direct that the order be notified to such persons, within such a timescale and by such method as he sees fit.

(5) For the avoidance of doubt, the method of intimation or notification referred to in paragraphs (2) and (4) may include intimation or notification by telephone, email or facsimile transmission.

Intimation of applications in relation to a child

3.39.10.—(1) This rule applies where an application is made under this Part and the person who it is proposed will be subject to the order is under 16.

(2) On receipt of an application mentioned in paragraph (1), the sheriff may, in particular, order intimation of the application to a person who has day-to-day care or control of the person mentioned in paragraph (1).

Intimation of orders on the person to whom they apply

3.39.11. Where a sheriff, in the absence of the person to whom it applies, grants—

  (a) a quarantine order under section 40(1) of the Act;

  (b) a short term detention order under section 42(1) of the Act;

  (c) an exceptional detention order under section 45 of the Act,

and the order is intimated to the person to whom it applies, a copy of Form 52 shall be delivered to that person along with the order.

Appeal to the sheriff against an exclusion order or a restriction order

3.39.12.—(1) An appeal to the sheriff under section 61 of the Act (appeal against exclusion orders and restriction orders) in respect of an exclusion order or a restriction order shall be marked by lodging a note of appeal in Form 54.

(2) On the lodging of a note of appeal, the sheriff clerk shall send a copy of the note of appeal to—

  (a) the health board competent person who made the exclusion order or restriction order; and

  (b) the person in relation to whom the order applies, where that person is not the appellant.

(3) The sheriff shall make such order as he thinks fit in order to dispose of the appeal.

Application for a warrant to enter premises and take steps under Part 5 of the Act

3.39.13.—(1) An application made by a local authority for a warrant under section 78(2) of the Act (warrant to enter and take steps) shall be in Form 55.

(2) Where such a warrant is granted by the sheriff it shall be in Form 56.

Application for an order for disposal of a body

3.39.14.—(1) An application made by a local authority for an order for the disposal of a body under section 93 of the Act (power of sheriff to order removal to mortuary and disposal) shall be in Form 57.

(2) Where such an order is granted by the sheriff it shall be in Form 58.

Application for appointment of a single arbiter to determine a dispute in relation to compensation

3.39.15. An application under sections 30(6), 56(5), 57(3), 58(4) or 82(3) of the Act for the appointment of a single arbiter to determine a dispute in relation to compensation may be made by written application in the form of a letter addressed to the sheriff clerk.

Rule 1.2(3)   SCHEDULE 1

FORMS

Rule 2.4(1)   FORM 1

Form of initial writ

SUMMARY APPLICATION UNDER (*title & section of statute or statutory instrument*)

INITIAL WRIT

SHERIFFDOM OF (*insert name of sheriffdom*)

AT (*insert place of sheriff court*)

[A.B.] (*design and state any special capacity in which the pursuer is suing*) Pursuer

against

[C.D.] (*design and state any special capacity in which the defender is being sued*) Defender

The Pursuer craves the court (*here state the specific decree, warrant or order sought*)

CONDESCENDENCE

(*State in numbered paragraphs the facts which form the ground of action*)

PLEAS-IN-LAW

(*State in numbered sentences*)

Signed
[A.B.], Pursuer
or [X.Y.], solicitor for the Pursuer
(*state designation and business address*)

Rule 2.7(4)(a)   FORM 2

[Form of warrant of citation]

(*Insert place and date*). Grants warrant to cite the defender (*insert name and address*) by serving upon him [*or* her] a copy of the writ and warrant [on a period of notice of (*insert period of notice*) days], [and ordains him [*or* her] to answer within the Sheriff Court House (*insert place of sheriff court*) [in Room No. , or in Chambers, *or otherwise, as the case may be*], on the   day of   at   o'clock   noon] [*or otherwise, as the case may be*] [and grants warrant to arrest on the dependence].

Signed
Sheriff [*or* sheriff clerk]

Rule 3.18.3(1)   [1] FORM 2A

Form of warrant of citation

(*Insert place and date*). Grants warrant to cite (*insert name and address of parties specified by sheriff principal*) by serving upon them a copy of the writ and warrant on a period of notice of 21 days and ordains them if they wish to oppose the application—

   (a) to lodge answers within the period of notice; and

   (b) to be represented within the Sheriff Court House (*insert place and address of sheriff court*) [in Room No.   , *or otherwise, as the case may be*], on the   day of
        at   o'clock   noon [*or otherwise, as the case may be*].

                                        Signed
                                        Sheriff [*or sheriff clerk*]

NOTE
   [1] Inserted by the Act of Sederunt (Summary Applications, Statutory Applications and Appeals etc. Rules) Amendment (No.2) (Local Government (Scotland) Act 1973) 2002 (S.S.I. 2002 No. 130), para. 2(4) and Sched.

Rule 2.7(4)(b)   FORM 3

Form of citation for summary application

CITATION FOR SUMMARY APPLICATION

SHERIFFDOM OF (*insert name of sheriffdom*)

AT (*insert place of sheriff court*)

[A.B.], (*insert designation and address*) Pursuer

against

[C.D.], (*insert designation and address*) Defender

Court ref. no.

(*Insert place and date*). You [C.D.] are hereby served with this copy writ and warrant, and are required to answer it.

IF YOU ARE UNCERTAIN AS TO WHAT ACTION TO TAKE you should consult a solicitor. You may be eligible for legal aid depending on your income, and you can get information about legal aid from a solicitor. You may also obtain advice from any Citizens' Advice Bureau or other advice agency.

PLEASE NOTE THAT IF YOU DO NOTHING IN ANSWER TO THIS DOCUMENT the court may regard you as admitting the claim made against you and the pursuer may obtain decree against you in your absence.

                                        Signed
                                        [PQ.], Sheriff Officer,
                                        or [X.Y] (*add designation and
                                        business address*)
                                        Solicitor for the Pursuer

Rule 3.18.3(2)   [1] FORM 3A

Form of citation for summary application

CITATION FOR SUMMARY APPLICATION

SHERIFFDOM OF *(insert name of sheriffdom)*

AT *(insert place of sheriff court)*

[A.B.], *(insert designation and address)*, Applicant

against

[C.D.], *(insert designation and address)*, Respondent

Court ref. no.

(Insert place and date). You [C.D.] are hereby served with this copy writ and warrant, and are required to answer it.

If you wish to oppose the application, you—

(a) must lodge answers with the sheriff clerk at *(insert place and address of sheriff court)* sheriff court, *(insert address)* not later than *(insert date)*, and at the same time, send a copy of the answers to the Applicant; and

(b) should be represented within the Sheriff Court House *(insert place and address of sheriff court)* [in Room No.   , or otherwise, as the case may be] on the day of   at   o'clock   noon [*or otherwise as the case maybe*].

PLEASE NOTE THAT IF YOU DO NOTHING IN ANSWER TO THIS DOCUMENT the court may regard you as admitting the appeal and the Applicant may obtain decree against you in your absence.

                                        Signed
                                        [P.Q.], Sheriff Officer, or [X.Y.]
                                        (*add designation and business address*)
                                        Solicitor for the Applicant

NOTE
[1] Inserted by the Act of Sederunt (Summary Applications, Statutory Applications and Appeals etc. Rules) Amendment (No.2) (Local Government (Scotland) Act 1973) 2002 (S.S.I. 2002 No. 130), para. 2(4) and Sched.

Rule 2.7(5)   [1] FORM 4

Form of warrant of citation where time to pay direction or time order may be applied for

(Insert place and date). *Grants warrant to cite the defender (insert name and address)* by serving a copy of the writ and warrant, together with Form 5, [on a period of notice of *(insert period of notice)* days] and ordains him [*or her*] if he [*or she*]—

(a) intends to defend the action or make any claim [to answer within the Sheriff Court House *(insert place and address of sheriff court)* [in Room No.   , or in Chambers, *or otherwise, as the case may be*], on the   day of   at   o'clock   noon] [*or otherwise, as the case may be*] or

(b) admits the claim and intends to apply for a time to pay direction or time order (and where appropriate apply for recall or restriction of an arrestment) [either to appear at that diet and make such application or] to lodge the appropriate part of Form 5 duly completed with the sheriff clerk at *(insert place of sheriff court)* at least fourteen days before [the diet *or* the expiry of the period of notice *or otherwise*, as the case may be] [and grants warrant to arrest on the dependence].

                                        Signed
                                        Sheriff [*or sheriff clerk*]

NOTE
[1] As amended by SSI 2007/6 (effective January 29, 2007) and SSI 2009/294 (effective December 1, 2009).

Rule 2.7(6) and 2.22(2)(b)   [1] FORM 5

Form of notice to be served on defender where time to pay direction or time order may be applied for

Rule 2.7(6) and
2.22(2)(b)   ACTION RAISED BY

                         PURSUER   DEFENDER

          AT   SHERIFF COURT

          (Including address)

          COURT REF. NO.

          **THIS SECTION MUST BE COMPLETED BY THE PURSUER
          BEFORE SERVICE**

          (1) Time to pay directions

          The Debtors (Scotland) Act 1987 gives you the right to apply to the
          court for a "time to pay direction" which is an order permitting you to
          pay any sum of money you are ordered to pay to the pursuer (which may
          include interest and court expenses) either by way of instalments or
          deferred lump sum. A deferred lump sum means that you must pay all
          the amount at one time within a period specified by the court.

          When making a time to pay direction the court may recall or restrict an
          arrestment made on your property by the pursuer in connection with the
          action or debt (for example, your bank account may have been frozen).

          (2) Time Orders

          The Consumer Credit Act 1974 allows you to apply to the court for a
          "time order" during a court action, to ask the court to give you more
          time to pay a loan agreement. **A time order is similar to a time to pay
          direction, but can only be applied for where the court action is about a
          credit agreement regulated by the Consumer Credit Act.** The court has
          power to grant a time order in respect of a regulated agreement to
          reschedule payment of the sum owed. This means that a time order can
          change:

          - the amount you have to pay each month
          - how long the loan will last
          - in some cases, the interest rate payable

          A time order can also stop the creditor taking away any item bought by
          you on hire purchase or conditional sale under the regulated agreement,
          so long as you continue to pay the instalments agreed.

HOW TO APPLY FOR A TIME TO PAY DIRECTION OR TIME ORDER WHERE YOU ADMIT THE CLAIM AND YOU DO NOT WANT TO DEFEND THE ACTION

1. The appropriate application forms are attached to this notice. After completing the appropriate form it should be returned to the Sheriff Court at least fourteen days before the date of the first hearing or expiry of the period of notice or otherwise, as the case may be, in the warrant of citation. The address of the court is shown on page 1 of the application. No court fee is payable when lodging the application.

2. Before completing the application please read carefully the notes on how to complete the application. In the event of difficulty you may contact the court's civil department at the address above or any sheriff clerk's office, solicitor, Citizens Advice Bureau or other advice agency. Written guidance can also be obtained from the Scottish Court Service website (www.scotcourts.gov.uk).

WHAT WILL HAPPEN NEXT

If the pursuer objects to your application, a hearing will be fixed and the court will advise you in writing of the date and time.

If the pursuer does not object to your application, a copy of the court order for payment (called an extract decree) will be served on you by the pursuer's solicitor advising when instalment payments should commence or deferred payment be made.

Court ref. no.

APPLICATION FOR A TIME TO PAY DIRECTION UNDER THE DEBTORS (SCOTLAND) ACT 1987

*PART A   By

*(This section must be completed by pursuer before service)

                                                        DEFENDER

                                              In an action raised by

                                                        PURSUER

HOW TO COMPLETE THE APPLICATION

PLEASE WRITE IN INK USING BLOCK CAPITALS

PART A of the application will have been completed in advance by the pursuer and gives details of the pursuer and you as the defender.

PART B If you wish to apply to pay by instalments enter the amount and tick the appropriate box at B3(1). If you wish to apply to pay the full sum due in one deferred payment enter the period of deferment you propose at B3(2).

PART C Give full details of your financial position in the space provided.

PART D If you wish the court, when making the time to pay direction to recall or restrict an arrestment made in connection with the action, enter the appropriate details about what has been arrested and the place and date of the arrestment at D5, and attach the schedule of arrestment or copy.

Sign the application where indicated. Retain the copy initial writ and the form of notice which accompanied this application form as you may need them at a later stage. The application should be returned to the Sheriff Court at least fourteen days before the date of the first hearing or expiry of the period of notice or otherwise, as the case may be, in the warrant of citation. The address of the court is shown on page 1 of the application.

PART B

1. The applicant is a defender in the action brought by the above named pursuer.

2. The defender admits the claim and applies to the court for a time to pay direction.

3. The defender applies

(1) To pay by instalments of £

(Tick one box only)

EACH WEEK   FORTNIGHT   MONTH

OR

(2) To pay the sum ordered in one payment within

WEEKS/MONTHS

Please state in this box why you say a time to pay direction should be made. In doing so, please consider the Note below.

NOTE

Under the 1987 Act, the court is required to make a time to pay direction if satisfied that it is reasonable in the circumstances to do so, and having regard in particular to the following matters—

> **The nature of and reasons for the debt in relation to which decree is granted or the order is sought**
>
> **Any action taken by the creditor to assist the debtor in paying the debt**
>
> **The debtor's financial position**
>
> **The reasonableness of any proposal by the debtor to pay that debt**
>
> **The reasonableness of any refusal or objection by the creditor to any proposal or offer by the debtor to pay the debt.**

PART C

4. Defender's financial position

I am employed /self employed / unemployed

My net income is:	weekly, fortnightly or monthly	**My outgoings are:**	weekly, fortnightly or monthly
Wages	£	Mortgage/rent	£
State benefits	£	Council tax	£
Tax credits	£	Gas/electricity etc	£
Other	£	Food	£
		Credit and loans	£
		Phone	£
		Other	£
Total	£	Total	£

People who rely on your income
(e.g. spouse/civil partner/partner/
children) – how many

Here list all assets (if any) e.g. value of house; amounts in bank or building society accounts; shares or other investments:

Here list any outstanding debts:

PART D

5. The defender seeks to recall or restrict an arrestment of which the details are as follows (*please state, and attach the schedule of arrestment or copy*).

6. This application is made under sections 1(1) and 2(3) of the Debtors (Scotland) Act 1987.

Therefore the defender asks the court

*to make a time to pay direction

*to recall the above arrestment

*to restrict the above arrestment (*in which case state restriction wanted*)

Date (*insert date*)

Signed

Defender

Court ref. no.

APPLICATION FOR A TIME ORDER UNDER THE CONSUMER CREDIT ACT 1974

*PART A

By

*(This section must be completed by pursuer before service)

DEFENDER

In an action raised by

PURSUER

HOW TO COMPLETE THE APPLICATION

PLEASE WRITE IN INK USING BLOCK CAPITALS

PART A of the application will have been completed in advance by the pursuer and gives details of the pursuer and you as the defender.

PART B If you wish to apply to pay by instalments enter the amount and tick the appropriate box at B3. If you wish the court to make any additional orders, please give details at B4. Please give details of the regulated agreement at B5.

PART C Give full details of your financial position in the space provided.

Sign the application where indicated. Retain the copy initial writ and the form of notice which accompanied this application form as you may need them at a later stage. The application should be returned to the Sheriff Court at least fourteen days before the date of the first hearing or expiry of the period of notice or otherwise, as the case may be, in the warrant of citation. The address of the court is shown on page 1 of the application.

PART B

1. The Applicant is a defender in the action brought by the above named pursuer.

I/WE WISH TO APPLY FOR A TIME ORDER under the Consumer Credit Act 1974

2. **Details of order(s) sought**

The defender wishes to apply for a time order under section 129 of the Consumer Credit Act 1974

The defender wishes to apply for an order in terms of section ..... of the Consumer Credit Act 1974

3. **Proposals for payment**

I admit the claim and apply to pay the arrears and future instalments as follows:

By instalments of £ .... per *week/fortnight/month

No time to pay direction or time to pay order has been made in relation to this debt.

4. **Additional orders sought**

The following additional order(s) is (are) sought: (*specify*)

The order(s) sought in addition to the time order is (are) sought for the following reasons:

5. **Details of regulated agreement**

   (a) Date of agreement
   (b) Reference number of agreement

(*Please attach a copy of the agreement*)

   (c) Names and addresses of other parties to agreement
   (d) Name and address of person (if any) who acted as surety (guarantor) to the agreement
   (e) Place where agreement signed (e.g. the shop where agreement signed, including name and address)
   (f) Details of payment arrangements
       i. The agreement is to pay instalments of £ ..... per week/month
      ii. The unpaid balance is £ ..... / I do not know the amount of arrears
     iii. I am £ ..... in arrears / I do not know the amount of arrears

PART C   **Defender's financial position**

I am employed /self employed / unemployed

	My net income is:	weekly, fortnightly or monthly	**My outgoings are:**	weekly, fortnightly or monthly
	Wages	£	Mortgage/rent	£
	State benefits	£	Council tax	£
	Tax credits	£	Gas/electricity etc	£
	Other	£	Food	£
			Credit and loans	£
			Phone	£
			Other	£
	Total	£	Total	£

People who rely on your income
(e.g. spouse/civil partner/partner/
children)—how many

Here list all assets (if any) e.g. value of house; amounts in bank or
building society accounts; shares or other investments:

Here list any outstanding debts:

Therefore the defender asks the court to make a time order

Date   Signed

                                        Defender

NOTE
[1] As amended by SSI 2007/6 (effective January 29, 2007) and substituted by Act of Sederunt (Sheriff Court Rules) (Miscellaneous Amendments) 2009 (SSI 2009/294) r.2 (effective December 1, 2009).

Rule 2.22(4)   [1] FORM 5A

Form of pursuer's response objecting to application for time to pay direction or time order

Court ref no:

SHERIFFDOM OF (*insert name of sheriffdom*)

AT (*insert place of sheriff court*)

PURSUER'S RESPONSE OBJECTING TO APPLICATION FOR TIME TO PAY
DIRECTION OR TIME ORDER

in the cause

[A.B.], (*insert designation and address*), Pursuer

against

[C.D.], (*insert designation and address*), Defender

1.   The pursuer received a copy application for a time to pay direction or time order lodged by the defender on (*date*).

2.   The pursuer does not accept the offer.

3.   The debt is (*please specify the nature of the debt*).

4.   The debt was incurred on (*specify date*) and the pursuer has contacted the defender in relation to the debt on (*specify date(s)*).

*5.   The contractual payments were (*specify amount*).

*6.   (*Specify any action taken by the pursuer to assist the defender to pay the debt*).

*7.   The defender has made payment(s) towards the debt of (*specify amount(s)*) on (*specify date(s)*).

*8.   The debtor has made offers to pay (*specify amount(s)*) on (*specify date(s)*) which offer(s) was [were] accepted [*or* rejected] and (*specify amount*) was paid on (*specify date(s)*).

9.   (*Here set out any information you consider relevant to the court's determination of the application*).

*delete as appropriate

(Signed)
Pursuer *or* Solicitor for pursuer

(Date)

NOTE
[1] As inserted by the Act of Sederunt (Sheriff Court Rules) (Miscellaneous Amendments) 2009 (SSI 2009/294) r.2 (effective December 1, 2009).

Rule 2.7(7)   [1] FORM 6

Form of citation where time to pay direction or time order may be applied for in summary application

SHERIFFDOM OF (*insert name of sheriffdom*)

AT (*insert place of sheriff court*)

[A.B.], (*insert designation and address*) Pursuer

against

[C.D.], (*insert designation and address*) Defender

Court ref. no.

(*Insert place and date*). You [C.D.], are hereby served with this copy writ and warrant, together with Form 5 (application for time to pay direction in summary application).

Form 5 is served on you because it is considered that you may be entitled to apply for a time to pay direction or time order [and for the recall or restriction of an arrestment used on the dependence of the action or in security of the debt referred to in the copy writ]. See Form 5 for further details.

IF YOU ADMIT THE CLAIM AND WISH TO APPLY FOR A TIME TO PAY DIRECTION OR TIME ORDER, you must complete Form 5 and return it to the sheriff clerk at the above address at least 7 days before the hearing or the expiry of the period of notice or otherwise, as the case may be, in the warrant of citation.

IF YOU ADMIT THE CLAIM AND WISH TO AVOID A COURT ORDER BEING MADE AGAINST YOU, the whole sum claimed including interest and any expenses due should be paid to the pursuer or his solicitor by the court date.

IF YOU ARE UNCERTAIN AS TO WHAT ACTION TO TAKE you should consult a solicitor. You may be eligible for legal aid depending on your income, and you can get information about legal aid from a solicitor. You may also obtain advice from any Citizens' Advice Bureau, or other advice agency.

PLEASE NOTE THAT IF YOU DO NOTHING IN ANSWER TO THIS DOCUMENT the court may regard you as admitting the claim made against you and the pursuer may obtain decree against you in your absence.

Signed
[P.Q.], Sheriff Officer,
or [X.Y.] (*add designation and business address*)
Solicitor for the Pursuer

NOTE
[1] As amended by the Act of Sederunt (Ordinary Cause, Summary Application, Summary Cause and Small Claim Rules) Amendment (Miscellaneous) 2007 (SSI 2007/6), para.3(6) (effective January 29, 2007).

Rule 2.7(7A)(a) [1] FORM 6A

Form of warrant of citation in an application to which rule 2.7(7A) applies

(*Insert place and date*). Grants warrant to cite the defender (*insert name and address*) by serving a copy of the writ and warrant together with Form 6B [on a period of notice of (*insert period of notice*) days] and ordains him [*or* her] if he [*or* she]—

    (a) intends to defend the action or make any claim to answer within the Sheriff Court House (*insert place and address of sheriff court*) [in Room No , *or in chambers, or otherwise, as the case may be*] on the day of at o'clock noon] [*or otherwise, as the case may be*]; or

    (b) intends to apply for an order under section 2 of the Mortgage Rights (Scotland) Act 2001 to be present or represented at that diet.

NOTE
[1] As inserted by the Act of Sederunt (Amendment of Ordinary Cause Rules and Summary Applications, Statutory Applications and Appeals etc. Rules) (Applications under the Mortgage Rights (Scotland) Act 2001) 2002 (SSI 2002/7), (effective January 17, 2002).

Rule 2.7(7A)(b) [1] FORM 6B

Form of citation in an application to which rule 2.7(7A) applies

SHERIFFDOM OF (*insert name of sheriffdom*)

AT (*insert place of sheriff court*)

[A.B.], (*insert designation and address*) Pursuer

against

[C.D.], (*insert designation and address*) Defender

Court ref. no:

(Insert place and date). You [C.D.], are hereby served with this copy writ and warrant, and you are required to answer it.

IF YOU WISH TO MAKE AN APPLICATION FOR AN ORDER UNDER SECTION 2 OF THE MORTGAGE RIGHTS (SCOTLAND) ACT 2001 you should be present or represented at the diet on (*insert date and time*) within (*insert name and address of sheriff court*)

IF YOU ARE UNCERTAIN AS TO WHAT ACTION TO TAKE you should consult a solicitor. You may be eligible for legal aid depending on your income, and you can get information about legal aid from a solicitor. You may also obtain advice from any Citizens' Advice Bureau, or other advice agency.

PLEASE NOTE THAT IF YOU DO NOTHING IN ANSWER TO THIS DOCUMENT the court may regard you as admitting the claim made against you and the pursuer may obtain decree against you in your absence.

                                                   Signed
                                                   [P.Q.], Sheriff Officer,
                                                   or [X.Y.] (*add designation and business address*)
                                                   Solicitor for the Applicant

NOTE
[1] As inserted by the Act of Sederunt (Amendment of Ordinary Cause Rules and Summary Applications, Statutory Applications and Appeals etc. Rules) (Applications under the Mortgage Rights (Scotland) Act 2001) 2002 (SSI 2002/7), (effective January 17, 2002).

Rule 2.7(8) [1,2] FORM 7

Form of certificate of citation

CERTIFICATE OF CITATION

(Insert place and date) I, hereby certify that upon the day of I duly cited [C.D.], Defender, to answer the foregoing writ. I did this by (*state method of service; [if by officer and not by post, add*: in the presence of [L.M.], (*insert designation*), witness hereto with me subscribing;] *and where service executed by post state whether by registered post or the first class recorded delivery service*).

(*In actions in which a time to pay direction or time order may be applied for, state whether Form 4 and Form 5 were sent in accordance with rule 2.7(5) and (6).*)

(*In actions in which an order under section 2 of the Mortgage Rights (Scotland) Act 2001 may be applied for, state whether Form 6B was sent in accordance with rule 2.7(7A)(b).*)

> Signed
> [P.Q.], Sheriff Officer
> [L.M.], witness
> or [X.Y.] (*add designation and business address*)
> Solicitor for the Pursuer

NOTE
[1] Inserted by the Act of Sederunt (Amendment of Ordinary Cause Rules and Summary Applications, Statutory Applications and Appeals etc. Rules) Applications under the Mortgage Rights (Scotland) Act 2001) 2002 (SSI 2002/7), para.3(4) and Sch.2.
[2] As amended by the Act of Sederunt (Ordinary Cause, Summary Application, Summary Cause and Small Claim Rules) Amendment (Miscellaneous) 2007 (SSI 2007/6), para.3(6) (effective January 29, 2007).

Rule 2.9(1) FORM 8

Form of caveat

[*Omitted by Act of Sederunt (Sheriff Court Caveat Rules) 2006 (SI 2006/198), effective April 28, 2006*]

Rule 2.13(1)(a) FORM 9

Form of advertisement

NOTICE TO [C.D.]

Court ref. no.

An action has been raised in   Sheriff Court by [A.B.], Pursuer calling as a Defender [C.D.], whose last known address was (*insert last known address of defender*).

If [C.D.] wishes to defend the action he [*or* she] should immediately contact the sheriff clerk (*insert address*) from whom the service copy initial writ may be obtained. If he [*or* she] fails to do so decree may pass against him [*or* her] [when the case calls in court on (*date*) or on the expiry of the period of notice *or otherwise, as the case may be* in the warrant of citation].

> Signed
> [X.Y.], (*add designation and business address*)
> Solicitor for the Pursuer
> or [P.Q.] (*add business address*)

Rule 2.13(1)(b)   FORM 10

Form of notice for walls of court

NOTICE TO [C.D.]

Court ref. no.

An action has been raised in   Sheriff Court by [A.B.], Pursuer calling as a Defender
[C.D.], whose last known address was (*insert last known address of defender*).

If [C.D.] wishes to defend the action he [*or* she] should immediately contact the sheriff clerk at
(*insert address*) from whom the service copy initial writ may be obtained. If he [*or* she] fails to do
so decree may pass against him [*or* her] [when the case calls in court on (*date*) *or* on the expiry of
the period of notice *or otherwise, as the case may be in the warrant of citation*].

Date (*insert date*)   Signed
                                                Sheriff clerk (*depute*)
                                                Telephone no. (*insert telephone number
                                                of sheriff clerk's office*)

Rule 2.18A   [1] FORM 10A

Form of schedule of arrestment on the dependence

SCHEDULE OF ARRESTMENT ON THE DEPENDENCE

Date: (*date of execution*)

Time: (*time arrestment executed*)

To: (*name and address of arrestee*)

IN HER MAJESTY'S NAME AND AUTHORITY AND IN NAME AND AUTHORITY
OF THE SHERIFF, I, (*name*), Sheriff Officer, by virtue of:

- an initial writ containing warrant which has been granted for arrestment on the
  dependence of the action at the instance of (*name and address of pursuer*) against (*name
  and address of defender*) and dated (*date*);

- a counterclaim containing a warrant which has been granted for arrestment on the
  dependence of the claim by (*name and address of creditor*) against (*name and address of
  debtor*) and dated (*date of warrant*);

- an order of the Sheriff at (*place*) dated (*date of order*) granting warrant [for arrestment
  on the dependence of the action raised at the instance of (*name and address of pursuer*)
  against (*name and address of defender*)] [*or* for arrestment on the dependence of the
  claim in the counterclaim [*or* third party notice] by (*name and address of creditor*)
  against (*name and address or debtor*)],

arrest in your hands (i) the sum of (*amount*), in excess of the Protected Minimum Balance, where
applicable (*see Note 1*), more or less, due by you to (*defender's name*) [*or name and address of
common debtor if common debtor is not the defender*] or to any other person on his [*or* her] [*or* its]
[*or* their] behalf; and (ii) all moveable things in your hands belonging or pertaining to the said
(*name of common debtor*), to remain in your hands under arrestment until they are made
forthcoming to (*name of pursuer*) [*or name and address of creditor if he is not the pursuer*] or until
further order of the court.

This I do in the presence of (*name, occupation and address of witness*).

                                                (*Signed*)
                                                Sheriff Officer
                                                (*Address*)

NOTE

1. This Schedule arrests in your hands (i) funds due by you to (*name of common debtor*) and (ii) goods or other moveables held by you for him. **You should not pay any funds to him or hand over any goods or other moveables to him without taking legal advice**.

2. This Schedule may be used to arrest a ship or cargo. If it is, you should consult your legal adviser about the effect of it.

3. The Protected Minimum Balance is the sum referred to in section 73F(4) of the Debtors (Scotland) Act 1987. This sum is currently set at [*insert current sum*]. The Protected Minimum Balance applies where the arrestment attaches funds standing to the credit of a debtor in an account held by a bank or other financial institution and the debtor is an individual. The Protected Minimum Balance does not apply where the account is held in the name of a company, a limited liability partnership, a partnership or an unincorporated association or where the account is operated by the debtor as a trading account.

4. Under section 73G of the Debtors (Scotland) Act 1987 you must also, within the period of 3 weeks beginning with the day on which the arrestment is executed, disclose to the creditor the nature and value of the funds and/or moveable property which have been attached. This disclosure must be in the form set out in Schedule 8 to the Diligence (Scotland) Regulations 2009. Failure to comply may lead to a financial penalty under section 73G of the Debtors (Scotland) Act 1987 and may also be dealt with as a contempt of court. You must, at the same time, send a copy of the disclosure to the debtor and to any person known to you who owns (or claims to own) attached property and to any person to whom attached funds are (or are claimed to be due), solely or in common with the debtor.

IF YOU WISH FURTHER ADVICE CONTACT ANY CITIZENS ADVICE BUREAU/LOCAL ADVICE CENTRE/SHERIFF CLERK OR SOLICITOR

NOTE
[1] As inserted by the Act of Sederunt (Sheriff Court Rules Amendment) (Diligence) 2009 (SSI 2009/107) (effective April 22, 2009).

Rule 2.18A   [1] FORM 10B

Form of certificate of execution of arrestment on the dependence

CERTIFICATE OF EXECUTION

I, (*name*), Sheriff Officer, certify that I executed an arrestment on the dependence, by virtue of an interlocutor of the Sheriff at (*place*) on (*date*) obtained at the instance of (*name and address of party arresting*) against (*name and address of defender*) on (*name of arrestee*)–

* by delivering the schedule of arrestment to (*name of arrestee or other person*) at (*place*) personally on (*date*).

* by leaving the schedule of arrestment with (*name and occupation of person with whom left*) at (*place*) on (*date*) [and by posting a copy of the schedule to the arrestee by registered post or first class recorded delivery to the address specified on the receipt annexed to this certificate].

* by depositing the schedule of arrestment in (*place*) on (*date*). (*Specify that enquiry made and reasonable grounds exist for believing that the person on whom service is to be made resides at the place but is not available*) [and by posting a copy of the schedule to the arrestee by registered post or first class recorded delivery to the address specified on the receipt annexed to this certificate].

* by affixing the schedule of arrestment to the door at (*place*) on *(date)*. (*Specify that enquiry made and that reasonable grounds exist for believing that the person on whom service is to be made resides at the place but is not available*) [and by posting a copy of the schedule to the arrestee by registered post or first class recorded delivery to the address specified on the receipt annexed to this certificate].

* by leaving the schedule of arrestment with (*name and occupation of person with whom left*) at

(*place of business*) on (*date*) [and by posting a copy of the schedule to the arrestee by registered post or first class recorded delivery to the address specified on the receipt annexed to this certificate].

* by depositing the schedule of arrestment at (*place of business*) on (*date*). (*Specify that enquiry made and that reasonable grounds exist for believing that the person on whom service is to be made carries on business at that place.*) [and by posting a copy of the schedule to the arrestee by registered post or first class recorded delivery to the address specified on the receipt annexed to this certificate].

* by affixing the schedule of arrestment to the door at (*place of business*) on (*date*). (*Specify that enquiry made and that reasonable grounds exist for believing that the person on whom service is to be made carries on business at that place.*) [and by posting a copy of the schedule to the arrestee by registered post or first class recorded delivery to the address specified on the receipt annexed to this certificate].

* by leaving the schedule of arrestment at (*registered office*) on (*date*), in the hands of (*name of person*) [and by posting a copy of the schedule to the arrestee by registered post or first class recorded delivery to the address specified on the receipt annexed to this certificate].

* by depositing the schedule of arrestment at (*registered office*) on (*date*) [and by posting a copy of the schedule to the arrestee by registered post or first class recorded delivery to the address specified on the receipt annexed to this certificate].

* by affixing the schedule of arrestment to the door at (*registered office*) on (*date*) [and by posting a copy of the schedule to the arrestee by registered post or first class recorded delivery to the address specified on the receipt annexed to this certificate].

I did this in the presence of (*name, occupation and address of witness*).

> (*Signed*)
> Sheriff Officer
> (*Address*)
>
> (*Signed*)
> (Witness)

*Delete where not applicable

NOTE

A copy of the Schedule of arrestment on the dependence is to be attached to this certificate.

NOTE

[1] As inserted by the Act of Sederunt (Sheriff Court Rules Amendment) (Diligence) 2009 (SSI 2009/107) (effective April 22, 2009).

Rule 2.26   FORM 11

Form of extract decree

EXTRACT DECREE

Sheriff Court   Court Ref. No.

Date of decree   *In absence

Pursuer(s)   Defender(s)

The Sheriff

and granted decree against the   for payment of expenses of £

This extract is warrant for all lawful execution hereon.

Date (*insert date*)   Sheriff clerk (*depute*)

*Delete as appropriate

Rule 2.37(3)   ¹FORM 11AA

Form of minute of intervention by the Commission for Equality and Human Rights

SHERIFFDOM OF *(insert name of sheriffdom)*...Court ref. no.

AT *(insert place of sheriff court)*

APPLICATION FOR LEAVE TO INTERVENE BY THE COMMISSION FOR EQUALITY AND HUMAN RIGHTS

in the cause

[A.B.] *(designation and address)*, Pursuer

against

[C.D.] *(designation and address)*, Defender

[*Here set out briefly:*
  (a) *the Commission's reasons for believing that the proceedings are relevant to a matter in connection with which the Commission has a function;*
  (b) *the issue in the proceedings which the Commission wishes to address; and*
  (c) *the propositions to be advanced by the Commission and the Commission's reasons for believing that they are relevant to the proceedings and that they will assist the court.*]

NOTE
¹As inserted by the Act of Sederunt (Sheriff Court Rules) (Miscellaneous Amendments) 2008 (SSI 2008/223) para.5(4) (effective July 1, 2008).

Rule 2.39(2)   ¹FORM 11AB

Form of minute of intervention by the Scottish Commission for Human Rights

SHERIFFDOM OF *(insert name of sheriffdom)*...Court ref. no.

AT *(insert place of sheriff court)*

APPLICATION FOR LEAVE TO INTERVENE BY THE SCOTTISH COMMISSION FOR HUMAN RIGHTS

in the cause

[A.B.] *(designation and address)*, Pursuer

against

[C.D.] *(designation and address)*, Defender

[*Here set out briefly:*
  (a) *the issue in the proceedings which the Commission intends to address;*
  (b) *a summary of the submission the Commission intends to make.*]

NOTE
¹As inserted by the Act of Sederunt (Sheriff Court Rules) (Miscellaneous Amendments) 2008 (SSI 2008/223) para.5(4) (effective July 1, 2008).

Rule 2.40(1)   ¹FORM 11AC

Invitation to the Scottish Commission for Human Rights to intervene

SHERIFFDOM OF *(insert name of sheriffdom)*...Court ref. no.

AT *(insert place of sheriff court)*

INVITATION TO THE SCOTTISH COMMISSION FOR HUMAN RIGHTS TO INTERVENE

in the cause

[A.B.] (*designation and address*), Pursuer

against

[C.D.] (*designation and address*), Defender

[*Here set out briefly:*
   (a) the facts, procedural history and issues in the proceedings;
   (b) the issue in the proceedings on which the court seeks a submission.*]*

NOTE
[1] As inserted by the Act of Sederunt (Sheriff Court Rules) (Miscellaneous Amendments) 2008 (SSI 2008/223) para.5(4) (effective July 1, 2008).

Rule 3.1.6   FORM 11A

Form of order for recovery of documents etc. under Part I of Chapter 3 of Act of Sederunt (Summary Applications, Statutory Applications and Appeals etc. Rules) 1999

SHERIFFDOM OF (*insert name of sheriffdom*)

AT (*insert place of sheriff court*)

in the Summary Application

of

[A.B.] (*designation and address*)

Applicant

against

[C.D.] (*designation and address*)

Respondent

Date: (*date of interlocutor*)

To: (*name and address of party or parties or named third party haver, from whom the documents and other property are sought to be recovered*)

THE SHERIFF having heard the applicant and being satisfied that it is appropriate to make an order under section 1 of the Administration of Justice (Scotland) Act 1972:

ORDERS the Summary Application to be served upon the person(s) named and designed therein;

APPOINTS (*name and designation of Commissioner*) to be Commissioner of the court;

GRANTS commission and diligence;

ORDERS the Commissioner to explain to the haver on executing the order—
   (1) the meaning and effect of the order;
   (2) that the haver may be entitled to claim that certain of the documents and other property are confidential or privileged; and
   (3) that the haver has a right to seek legal or other professional advice of his choice,
and to give to the haver a copy of the Notice in Form 11B of Schedule 1 to the Act of Sederunt (Summary Applications, Statutory Applications and Appeals etc. Rules) 1999.

GRANTS warrant to and authorises the said Commissioner, whether the haver has allowed entry or not—
   (1) to enter, between the hours of 9am and 5pm on Monday to Friday, (*or, where the court has*

found cause shown under rule 3.1.11(1), otherwise specify the time and day) the premises at (*address of premises*) and any other place in Scotland owned or occupied by the haver at which it appears to the Commissioner that any of the items set out in the statement of facts in the application to the court (the "listed items") may be located; and

(2) unless the haver is taking legal or other professional advice on the question of having the order varied—

(a) to search for and take all other steps which he considers necessary to take possession of or preserve (*specify the listed items*); and

(b) to take possession of and to preserve all or any of the listed items and to consign them with the Sheriff Clerk at (*enter name and address of sheriff court*) to be held by him pending the further order of the sheriff,

and for that purpose,

ORDERS the haver or his servants or agents to allow the Commissioner, any person whom the Commissioner considers necessary to assist him, and the Applicant's representatives to enter the premises named in the order and, unless the haver has sought legal or other professional advice on the question of having the order varied, to allow them—

(1) to search for the listed items and take such other steps as the Commissioner considers it is reasonable to take to execute the order;

(2) to provide access to information stored on any computer owned or used by him by supplying or providing the means to overcome any and all security mechanisms inhibiting access thereto;

(3) to allow the Commissioner, any person whom the Commissioner considers necessary to assist him, and the Applicant's representatives to remain in the premises until such time as the search is complete, including allowing them to continue the search on subsequent days if necessary;

(4) to inform the Commissioner immediately of the whereabouts of the listed items; and

(5) to provide the Commissioner with a list of the names and addresses of everyone who has supplied him with any of the listed items and of the names and addresses of everyone to whom he has given any of the listed items,

and not to destroy, conceal or tamper with any of the listed items except in accordance with the terms of this order;

FURTHER AUTHORISES (*specify the representatives*) to be the sole representatives of the Applicant to accompany the Commissioner for the purpose of identification of the said documents and other property.

SCHEDULE TO THE ORDER

Undertakings given by Applicant

The Applicant has given the following undertakings:—

1. That he will comply with any order of the court as to payment of compensation if it is subsequently discovered that the order, or the implementation of the order, has caused loss to the respondent or, where the respondent is not the haver, to the haver.

2. That he will bring within a reasonable time of the execution of the order any proceedings which he decides to bring.

3. That he will not, without leave of the court, use any information, documents or other property obtained as a result of the order, except for the purpose of any proceedings which he decides to bring and to which the order relates.

(*or as modified under rule 3.1.4*)

Rule 3.1.9(a)   FORM 11B

Notice to accompany order in Form 11A when served by Commissioner

IMPORTANT
NOTICE TO PERSON ON WHOM THIS ORDER IS SERVED

1. This order orders you to allow the person appointed and named in the order as Commissioner to enter your premises to search for, examine and remove or copy the items mentioned in the order.

2. It also allows entry to the premises to any person appointed and named in the order as a representative of the person who has been granted the order and to any person accompanying the Commissioner to assist him.

3. No one else is given authority to enter the premises.

4. You should read the order immediately.

5. You have the right to seek legal or other professional advice of your choice and you are advised to do so as soon as possible.

6. Consultation under paragraph 5 will not prevent the Commissioner from entering your premises for the purposes mentioned in paragraph 1 but if the purpose of your seeking advice is to help you to decide if you should ask the court to vary the order he will not be able to search the premises.

7. The Commissioner is obliged to explain the meaning and effect of the order to you.

8. He is also obliged to explain to you that you are entitled to claim that the items, or some of them, are protected as confidential or privileged.

9. You are entitled to ask the court to vary the order provided that—
you take steps to do so at once; and
you allow the Commissioner, any person appointed as a representative of the person who has been granted the order and any person accompanying the Commissioner to assist him, to enter the premises—but not to start the search—meantime.

10. The Commissioner and the people mentioned as representatives or assistants have a right to enter the premises even if you refuse to allow them to do so, unless—
you are female and alone in the premises and there is no female with the Commissioner (where the Commissioner is not female), in which case they have no right to enter the premises;
the Commissioner serves the order before 9am or after 5pm on a weekday or at any time on a Saturday or Sunday (except where the court has specifically allowed this, which will be stated in the order);
in which cases you should refuse to allow entry.

11. You are entitled to insist that there is no one (*or* no one other than*insert name of person*) present who could gain commercially from anything which might be read or seen on your premises.

12. You are required to hand over to the Commissioner any of the items mentioned in the order which are in your possession.

13. You may be found liable for contempt of court if you refuse to comply with the order.

Rule 3.8.3(1)   FORM 12

FORM OF NOTICE TO BE SERVED ON PERSON WHO IS SUBJECT OF HOSPITAL ORDER, GUARDIANSHIP ORDER OR COMMUNITY CARE ORDER PROCEEDINGS.

To [*name and address of patient*]
Attached to this notice is a copy of—

*an application to the managers of [*name of hospital*] for your admission to that hospital in accordance with section 21 of the Mental Health (Scotland) Act 1984.

*an application to the sheriff at [*name of Sheriff Court*] for a Community Care Order in accordance with section 35A of the Mental Health (Scotland) Act 1984.

*an application to the [*name of local authority*] for your reception into guardianship in accordance with Section 40 of the Mental Health (Scotland) Act 1984.

The hearing will be held at [*place*]   **on** [*date*]   **at** [*time*].

You may appear personally at the hearing of this application unless the court decides otherwise on medical recommendations.

In any event, if you are unable or do not wish to appear personally you may request any person to appear on your behalf.

If you do not appear personally or by representative, the sheriff will consider the application in the absence of you or your representative.

[Signed]
Sheriff Clerk

[Place and date]
**delete as appropriate*

Rule 3.8.3(3)   FORM 13

FORM OF NOTICE TO RESPONSIBLE MEDICAL OFFICER

To [*name and address of responsible medical officer*]

In accordance with the Mental Health (Scotland) Act 1984, a copy of the application and notice of hearing is sent with this notice.

1. You are requested to deliver it personally to [*name of patient*] and to explain the contents of it to him.

2. You are also required to arrange if the patient so wishes, for the attendance of [*name of patient*] at the hearing at [*place of hearing*] on [*date*] so that he may appear and be heard in person.

3. You are further requested to complete and return to me in the enclosed envelope the certificate appended hereto before the date of the hearing.

4. If in your opinion it would be prejudicial to the patient's health or treatment for him to appear and be heard personally you may so recommend in writing, with reasons on the certificate.

[Signed]
Sheriff Clerk

[Place and date]

Rule 3.8.4(1)(b) and   FORM 14
3.8.4(2)(a)

FORM OF CERTIFICATE OF DELIVERY BY RESPONSIBLE MEDICAL OFFICER

I, [*name and designation*], certify that—

1. I have on the   day of   personally delivered to [*name of patient*] a copy of the application and the intimation of the hearing; and have explained the contents or purport to him [*or* her].

2. The patient does [not] wish to attend the hearing.

3. The patient does [not] wish to be represented at the hearing [and has nominated [*name and address of representative*] to represent him].

4. I shall arrange for the attendance of the patient at the hearing [*or* in my view it would be prejudicial to the patient's health or treatment for him [*or* her] to appear and be heard in person for the following reasons [*give reasons*]].

[*Signature and designation*]

[*Address and date*]

Rule 3.8.11   FORM 15

FORM OF APPEAL FOR REVOCATION OF A COMMUNITY CARE ORDER UNDER SECTION 35F OF THE MENTAL HEALTH (SCOTLAND) ACT 1984

SHERIFFDOM OF (*insert name of sheriffdom*)

AT (*insert name of Sheriff Court*)

I, [*insert name and address of applicant*],

appeal to the sheriff for revocation of a community care order made on [*insert date of order*] on the following grounds:—

[*State grounds on which appeal is to proceed*]

The community care order was renewed under section 35C(5) of the Mental Health (Scotland) Act 1984 on [*insert date of renewal*] and is still in force.

The special medical officer specified in the community care order is [*insert name and address of special medical officer*].

[*Signed*]
Applicant
[*or* Solicitor for Applicant]
[*Insert designation and address*]

Rule 3.9.9(b)   FORM 16

FORM OF NOTICE TO PERSON WITH INTEREST IN PROPERTY SUBJECT TO AN APPLICATION FOR AN ORDER UNDER PARAGRAPH 12 OF SCHEDULE 1 TO THE PROCEEDS OF CRIME (SCOTLAND) ACT 1995

IN THE SHERIFF COURT

in the

PETITION [*or* NOTE]

of

[A.B.] (*name and address*)

for an order under paragraph 12 of Schedule 1 to the
Proceeds of Crime (Scotland) Act 1995

in respect of the estates of [C.D.] (*name and address*)

Court Ref No.

Date: (*date of posting or other method of service*)

To: (name and address of person on whom notice is to be served)

This Notice—
- (a) gives you warning that an application has been made to the sheriff court for an order which may affect your interest in property; and
- (b) informs you that you have an opportunity to appear and make representations to the court before the application is determined.

TAKE NOTICE

1. That on (*date*) in the sheriff court at (*place*) a confiscation order was made under section 1 of the Proceeds of Crime (Scotland) Act 1995 in respect of [C.D.] (*name and address*).

2. That on (*date*) the administrator appointed under paragraph 1(1)(a) of Schedule 1 to the Proceeds of Crime (Scotland) Act 1995 on (*date*) was empowered to realise property belonging to [C.D.].

or

2. That on (*date*) the administrator was appointed under paragraph 1 (1)(b) of Schedule 1 to the Proceeds of Crime (Scotland) Act 1995 on (*date*) to realise property belonging to [C.D.].

3. That application has been made by petition [or note] for an order under paragraph 12 of Schedule 1 to the Proceeds of Crime (Scotland) Act 1995 (*here set out briefly the nature of the order sought*). A copy of the petition [or note] is attached.

4. That you have the right to appear before the court in person or by counsel or other person having a right of audience and make such representations as you may have in respect of the order applied for. The court has fixed (*insert day and date fixed for hearing the application*), at (*insert time and place fixed for hearing*) as the time when you should appear to do this.

5. That if you do not appear or are not represented on the above date, the order applied for may be made in your absence.

IF YOU ARE UNCERTAIN ABOUT THE EFFECT OF THIS NOTICE, you should consult a Solicitor, Citizen's Advice Bureau or other local advice agency or adviser immediately.

(*Signed*)
Sheriff Officer
[*or* Solicitor [*or* Agent] for petitioner
[*or* noter]]
(*Address*)

Rule 3.11.14(1)   FORM 17

Representation of the People Act 1983

In the petition questioning the election for the   of   , in which   is petitioner and   is respondent.

The petitioner desires to withdraw his petition on the following grounds [*state grounds*], and craves that a diet may be appointed for hearing his application. He has, in compliance, with rule 3.11.14 of the Act of Sederunt (Summary Applications, Statutory Applications and Appeals etc. Rules) 1999, given the written notice of his intention to present this application to the respondent, to the Lord Advocate, and to the returning officer.

[To be signed by the petitioner or his solicitor.]

Rule 3.11.14(4)   FORM 18

Representation of the People Act 1983

In the petition questioning the election for the   of   , in which   is the petitioner and   is respondent.

Notice is hereby given that the above petitioner has applied for leave to withdraw his petition, and that the sheriff principal has, by interlocutor dated the   day of   ,

assigned the   day of   at   o'clock   noon within
the   as a diet for hearing the application.

Notice is further given that under the Act any person who might have been a petitioner in respect of the said election may at the above diet apply to the sheriff principal to be substituted as a petitioner.

[To be signed by the petitioner or his solicitor.]

Rule 3.11.15(1)   FORM 19

Representation of the People Act 1983

In the petition questioning the election for the   of   , in which   was the petitioner [*or* last surviving petitioner] and   is the respondent.

Notice is hereby given that the above petition stands abated by the death of the petitioner [*or* last surviving petitioner], and that any person who might have been a petitioner in respect of the said election and who desires to be substituted as a petitioner must, within 21 days from this date, lodge with the undersigned sheriff clerk of [*name sheriff court district*], a minute craving to be so substituted.

Date (*insert date*)

[To be signed by the sheriff clerk]

Rule 3.16.4(1)   [1] FORM 20

FORM OF NOTICE OF AN APPLICATION UNDER THE ADULTS WITH INCAPACITY (SCOTLAND) ACT 2000

To *(insert name and address)*

Attached to this notice is a copy of an application for *(insert type of application)* under the Adults with Incapacity (Scotland) Act 2000.

The hearing will be held at (insert place) on (insert date) at (insert time)

You may appear personally at the hearing of this application.

In any event, if you are unable or do not wish to appear personally you may appoint a legal representative to appear on your behalf.

If you are uncertain as to what action to take you should consult a solicitor. You may be eligible for legal aid, and you can obtain information about legal aid from any solicitor. You may also obtain information from any Citizens Advice Bureau or other advice agency.

If you do not appear personally or by legal representative, the sheriff may consider the application in the absence of you or your legal representative.

(insert place and date)   (*signed*)
                                 Sheriff Clerk
                                 or
                                 [P.Q.] Sheriff Officer
                                 or
                                 [X.Y.],Solicitor

NOTE
[1] As inserted by the Act of Sederunt (Summary Applications, Statutory Applications and Appeals etc. Rules) Amendment (Adults with Incapacity) 2001 (SSI 2001/142), (effective April 2, 2001).

Rule 3.16.4(3)   [1] FORM 21

FORM OF NOTICE TO MANAGERS

To *(insert name and address of manager)*

A copy of an application made under the Adults with Incapacity (Scotland) Act 2000 and notice of hearing is sent with this notice.

1. You are requested to deliver it personally to (name of adult) and to explain the contents of it to him or her.

2. You are further requested to complete and return to the sheriff clerk in the enclosed envelope the certificate (Form 22) appended hereto before the date of the hearing.

(insert place and date)

(*signed*)
Sheriff Clerk
or
[P.Q.], Sheriff Officer
or
[X.Y.], Solicitor

NOTE
[1] As inserted by the Act of Sederunt (Summary Applications, Statutory Applications and Appeals etc. Rules) Amendment (Adults with Incapacity) 2001 (SSI 2001/142), (effective April 2, 2001).

Rule 3.16.4(4)   [1] FORM 22

FORM OF CERTIFICATE OF DELIVERY BY MANAGER

I, *(insert name and designation)*, certify that—

I have on *(insert date)* personally delivered to (name of adult) a copy of the application and the intimation of the hearing and have explained the contents to him/her.

Date *(insert date)*

(*signed*)
Manager
(add designation and address)

NOTE
[1] As inserted by the Act of Sederunt (Summary Applications, Statutory Applications and Appeals etc. Rules) Amendment (Adults with Incapacity) 2001 (SSI 2001/142), (effective April 2, 2001).

Rule 3.16.7(1)   [1] FORM 23

SUMMARY APPLICATION UNDER THE ADULTS WITH INCAPACITY (SCOTLAND) ACT 2000

SHERIFFDOM OF *(insert name of sheriffdom)*

AT *(insert place of Sheriff Court)*

[A.B.] *(design and state capacity in which the application is made)*, Pursuer

The applicant craves the court *(state here the specific order(s) sought by reference to the provisions in the Adults with Incapacity (Scotland) Act 2000.)*

STATEMENTS OF FACT

(State in numbered paragraphs the facts on which the application is made, including:

1. *The designation of the adult concerned (if other than the applicant).*

  (a)   *the adult's nearest relative;*
  (b)   *the adult's primary carer;*
  (ba) *the adult's named person;*
  (c)   *any guardian, continuing attorney or welfare attorney of the adult; and*
  (d)   *any other person who may have an interest in the application.*

3. *The adult's place of habitual residence and/or the location of the property which is the subject of the application.)*

(insert place and date)

(*signed*)
[A.B.], Pursuer or
[X.Y.], *(state designation and business address)*
Solicitor for the Pursuer

Note. This Form should not be used for appeals to the Sheriff. Appeals should be made in Form 24.

NOTE

[1] As inserted by the Act of Sederunt (Summary Applications, Statutory Applications and Appeals etc. Rules) Amendment (Adults with Incapacity) 2001 (SSI 2001/142), (effective April 2, 2001) and amended by the Act of Sederunt (Summary Applications, Statutory Applications and Appeals etc. Rules) Amendment (Adult Support and Protection (Scotland) Act 2007) (SSI 2008/111) r.2(3) (effective April 1, 2008).

Rule 3.16.7(2)   [1] **FORM 24**

APPEAL TO THE SHERIFF UNDER THE ADULTS WITH INCAPACITY
(SCOTLAND) ACT 2000

SHERIFFDOM OF *(insert name of sheriffdom)*

AT *(insert place of Sheriff Court)*

[A.B.] *(design and state capacity in which the appeal is being made),* Pursuer

This appeal is made in respect of *(state here the decision concerned, the date on which it was intimated to the pursuer, and refer to the relevant provisions in the Adults with Incapacity (Scotland) Act 2000).*

(State here, in numbered paragraphs:

1. *The designation of the adult concerned (if other than the applicant).*

2. *The designation of:*

    (a) *the adult's nearest relative;*
    (b) *the adult's primary carer;*
  (ba) *the adult's named person;*
    (c) *any guardian, continuing attorney or welfare attorney of the adult; and*
    (d) *any other person who may have an interest in the application.*

3. *The adult's place of habitual residence and/or the location of the property which is the subject of the application.)*

The pursuer appeals against the decision on the following grounds *(state here in separate paragraphs the grounds on which the appeal is made).*

The pursuer craves the court *(state here orders sought in respect of appeal).*

(insert place and date)   *(signed)*
                                        [A.B.], Pursuer
                                        or
                                        [X.Y.], *(state designation and*
                                        business address)
                                        Solicitor for the Pursuer

NOTE

[1] Inserted by the Act of Sederunt (Summary Applications, Statutory Applications and Appeals etc. Rules) Amendment (Adults with Incapacity) 2001 (SSI 2001/142), r.3(3) and Sch. and amended by the Act of Sederunt (Summary Applications, Statutory Applications and Appeals etc. Rules) Amendment (Adult Support and Protection (Scotland) Act 2007) (SSI 2008/111) r.2(3) (effective April 1, 2008).

Rule 3.27.6(1) [1]FORM 25

ANTISOCIAL BEHAVIOUR ETC. (SCOTLAND) ACT 2004

CLOSURE NOTICE

Section 27

1. The service of this closure notice is authorised by a senior police officer under section 26(1) of the Antisocial Behaviour etc. (Scotland) Act 2004 ("the Act").

2. The premises to which this closure notice relates are: *(specify premises)*.

3. Access to those premises by any person other than—
    (a) a person who habitually resides in the premises; or
    (b) the owner of the premises,
is prohibited.

4. Failure to comply with this notice is an offence which may result in a fine of up to £2,500 or imprisonment for a term of up to 3 months (or both). The penalties may be higher for repeated failure to comply with this (or any other) closure notice.

5. An application for the closure of these premises will be made under section 28 of the Act and will be considered at *(insert place including Room No. if appropriate)* on the   day of   at am/pm.

6. On such an application as set out in paragraph 5 being made, the sheriff may make a closure order under section 29 of the Act in respect of these premises.

7. The effect of the Closure Order in respect of these premises would be to close the premises to all persons (other than any person expressly authorised access by the sheriff in terms of section 29(3) of the Act) for such period not exceeding 3 months as is specified in the order. Measures may be taken to ensure that the premises are securely closed against entry by any person.

8. If you live on or have control of, responsibility for or an interest in the premises to which this closure notice relates and wish to oppose the application for a closure order, you should attend or be represented at the hearing mentioned in paragraph 5 of this notice.

9. If you would like further information or advice about housing or legal matters you can contact—

(specify at least two persons or organisations (including name and means of contacting) based in the locality of the promises who or which will be able to provide advice about housing and legal matters). You also have a legal right to advice from your local authority should you be threatened with possible homelessness.

NOTE
  [1] Inserted by SSI 2004/455, para 5 and Sch. (effective October 28, 2004).

Rule 3.27.6(2) [1]FORM 26

ANTISOCIAL BEHAVIOUR ETC. (SCOTLAND) ACT 2004

CERTIFICATION OF SERVICE

Section 27
I *(insert designation, including address and rank, of police officer)* certify that a copy of the closure notice which was authorised by *(insert designation of senior police officer)* on *(insert date on which closure notice was authorised)* in respect of *(insert details of the premises to which closure notice relates)* was served on: *(insert name and address of each person to whom a copy of the notice was given, including date)*

_____

_____

_____

_____

_____

by *(insert designation, including address and rank, of police officer who served the copy or copies of the closure notice and, if more than one, indicate which police officer served a copy of the notice on which of the persons listed above).*

_____

Signed

(insert designation, including rank, of police officer)

NOTE
[1] Inserted by SSI 2004/455, para 5 and Sch. (effective October 28, 2004).

Rule 3.27.7   [1] FORM 27

ANTISOCIAL BEHAVIOUR ETC. (SCOTLAND) ACT 2004

Section 28

Sheriff Court . . . . 20. . . . .

(Court Ref No.)

PART A

APPLICATION FOR CLOSURE ORDER IN RESPECT OF PREMISES AT:

_____

_____

_____

("the Premises")

PART B

1. This application is made [by/on behalf of] *(delete as appropriate) (insert name and rank of senior police officer)* of *(insert details of police force).*

2. Service of a closure notice on the Premises was authorised by *(insert details of senior police officer)* on the   day of   . A copy of [the authorisation/written confirmation of such authorisation] *(delete as appropriate)* is attached.

3. A copy of the closure notice was, on the   day of   ,—
    (a) fixed to:
        (insert details of all locations in, or used as part of, the Premises, to which a copy of the notice was fixed)

_____

_____

_____

_____

(b) given to:
(insert name and address of each person to whom a copy of the notice was given)

4. Certification in the prescribed form of service of the closure notice to the persons described at paragraph 3(b) above is attached.

5. This application is made on the following grounds:

(insert reasons for making application)

6. The following evidence is [attached/supplied] *(delete as appropriate)* in respect of this application *(insert short details of supporting evidence)*.

PART C

7. The applicant asks the court to—
    (a) assign the hearing for the   day of   at   am/pm; and
    (b) make a closure order in respect of the Premises.

. . . . Signed

Senior Police Officer for [Police Force] (Applicant)

or [X.Y.] Solicitor for Senior Police Officer

(add designation and business address)

FORM OF INTERLOCUTOR

Sheriff Court . . . . 20. . . . .

(Court Ref No.)

The sheriff having considered this application assigns . . . . at . . . . within . . . . as a hearing, this date having been previously intimated to known interested persons and published in the closure notice.

. . . . Signed

Sheriff

FORM OF INTERLOCUTOR

Sheriff Court . . . . 20 . . . .

(Court Ref No.)

The sheriff having heard *(insert details of parties who attended the hearing)* and having considered the application [, being satisfied that the conditions mentioned in section 30(2) of the Antisocial Behaviour etc. (Scotland) Act 2004 are met] *(delete as appropriate)* and having regard to the matters mentioned in section 30(3) of the Antisocial Behaviour etc. (Scotland) Act 2004 ("the Act"),

*1. makes an order under section 29(1) of the Act that the premises at *(insert details of premises)* are closed to all persons for a period of *(insert period)*.

*2. directs intimation of this interlocutor to *(insert details of all known interested persons)* and by posting a copy thereof at prominent places on the premises at *(indicate where copies have been posted)*.

*3. refuses to make a closure order in respect of the premises at *(insert details of premises)*.

*4. postpones the determination of the application until *(insert date)* at *(insert time)* within *(insert location)*.

*delete as appropriate

. . . . Signed

Sheriff

NOTE
[1] Inserted by SSI 2004/455, para 5 and Sch. (effective October 28, 2004).

Rule 3.27.8   [1] FORM 28

ANTISOCIAL BEHAVIOUR ETC. (SCOTLAND) ACT 2004

Minute

Section 32

Application for extension of closure order

Sheriff Court . . . . :   . . . . 20. . . . .

(Court Ref No.)

PART A

PREMISES IN RESPECT OF WHICH CLOSURE ORDER HAS BEEN MADE:

_____

_____

_____

("the Premises")

PART B

1. This application is made [by/on behalf of] *(delete as appropriate)* *(insert name and rank of senior police officer)* of *(insert details of police force)*.

2. A copy of the closure order made in respect of the Premises is attached. The closure order has effect until *(enter date)*.

3. The applicant believes that it is necessary to extend the period for which the closure order has effect for the purpose of preventing relevant harm, on the following grounds: *(specify reasons for extension)*.

4. *(Insert details of local authority)* has been consulted about the applicant's intention to make this application.

PART C

5. The applicant asks the court to—
   (c) fix a hearing;
   (d) order the applicant to intimate this application and the date of the hearing to such persons as the sheriff considers appropriate; and
   (e) extend the closure order in respect of the Premises for a period of   [months/days] *(delete as appropriate)* or for such period not exceeding 6 months as the court may consider appropriate.

. . . . Signed

Senior Police Officer for [Police Force] (Applicant)

or [X.Y.] Solicitor for Senior Police Officer

(add designation and business address)

FORM OF INTERLOCUTOR

Sheriff Court . . . . 20. . . . .

(Court Ref No.)

The sheriff having considered this minute orders the applicant to intimate this application and interlocutor to . . . ., assigns . . . . at . . . . within . . . . as a hearing and directs any person wishing to oppose the granting of the application to appear or be represented at the hearing to show cause why the application should not be granted.

. . . . Signed

Sheriff

FORM OF INTERLOCUTOR

Sheriff Court . . . . 20. . . . .

(Court Ref No.)

The sheriff having heard *(insert details of parties who attended the hearing)* [and] having considered this minute [and being satisfied that the condition mentioned in section 32(1) of the Antisocial Behaviour etc. (Scotland) Act 2004 is met] *(delete as appropriate)*,

*1. makes an order extending the closure order made under section 29(1) of the Antisocial Behaviour etc. (Scotland) Act 2004 in respect of the premises at *(insert details of premises)* for a period of *(insert period)*.

*2. directs intimation of this interlocutor to *(insert details of persons to whom sheriff considers it to be appropriate to intimate)* and by posting a copy thereof at prominent places on the premises at *(indicate where copies have been posted)*.

*3. refuses to make an order extending the closure order in respect of the premises at *(insert details of premises)*.

*4. postpones the determination of the application until *(insert date)* at *(insert time)* within *(insert location)*.

*delete as appropriate

. . . . Signed

Sheriff

NOTE
  [1] Inserted by SSI 2004/455, para 5 and Sched (effective October 28, 2004).

Rule 3.27.9   [1] FORM 29

ANTISOCIAL BEHAVIOUR ETC. (SCOTLAND) ACT 2004

Minute

Section 33

Application for revocation of closure order

Sheriff Court . . . . 20. . . . .

(Court Ref No.)

PART A

PREMISES IN RESPECT OF WHICH CLOSURE ORDER HAS BEEN MADE:

("the Premises")

The applicant is *(insert name and address of applicant)* who is:

*1. a senior police officer of the police force for the area within which the Premises (or part thereof) are situated.

*2. the local authority for the area within which the Premises or part thereof are situated.

*3. a person on whom a copy of the closure notice relating to the Premises in respect of which the closure order has effect was served under section 27(2)(b) or (3) of the Antisocial Behaviour etc. (Scotland) Act 2004.

*4. a person who has an interest in these premises but on whom the closure notice was not served.

*delete as appropriate.

PART B

1. A copy of the closure order made in respect of the Premises is attached.

2. The applicant believes that a closure order in respect of the Premises is no longer necessary to prevent the occurrence of relevant harm for the following reasons *(specify grounds for application for revocation).*

PART C

3. The applicant asks the court to:
- (a) fix a hearing;
- (b) order the applicant to intimate this application and the date of the hearing to such persons as the sheriff considers appropriate and, where the applicant is not a senior police officer, to such senior police officer as the sheriff considers appropriate; and
- (c) order the revocation of the closure order.

. . . . Signed

Applicant *(include full designation)*

or [X.Y.] Solicitor for Applicant *(include full designation and business address)*

FORM OF INTERLOCUTOR

Sheriff Court . . . . 20. . . . .

(Court Ref No.)

The sheriff having considered this minute orders the applicant to intimate this application and interlocutor to . . . ., assigns . . . . within . . . . as a hearing and directs any person wishing to oppose the granting of the application to appear or be represented at the hearing to show cause why the application should not be granted.

. . . . Signed

Sheriff

FORM OF INTERLOCUTOR

Sheriff Court . . . . 20. . . . .

(Court Ref No.)

The sheriff having heard *(insert details of parties who attended the hearing)* [and] having considered this minute [and being satisfied that a closure order is no longer necessary to prevent the occurrence of relevant harm] *(delete as appropriate)*,

*1. makes an order revoking the closure order made under section 29(1) of the Antisocial Behaviour etc. (Scotland) Act 2004 in respect of the premises at *(insert details of the premises)*.

*2. directs intimation of this interlocutor to *(insert details of persons to whom sheriff considers it to be appropriate to intimate)*.

*3. refuses to make an order revoking the closure order in respect of the premises at *(insert details of the premises)*.

*4. postpones the determination of the application until *(insert date)* at *(insert time)* within *(insert location)*.

*delete as appropriate

. . . . Signed

Sheriff

NOTE
[1] Inserted by SSI 2004/455, para 5 and Sch. (effective October 28, 2004).

ANTISOCIAL BEHAVIOUR ETC. (SCOTLAND) ACT 2004

Minute

Section 34

Application for access to premises in respect of which a closure order is in force

Sheriff Court . . . . 20. . . . .

(Court Ref No.)

PART A

PREMISES IN RESPECT OF WHICH CLOSURE ORDER HAS BEEN MADE:

_____

_____

_____

("the Premises")

PREMISES IN RESPECT OF WHICH APPLICATION FOR ACCESS IS BEING MADE:

_____

_____

_____

PART B

1. A copy of the closure order made in respect of the Premises is attached. The closure order has effect until *(insert date)*.

2. The applicant *(insert details of applicant)* [owns/occupies] *(delete as appropriate)* the following [part of] *(delete as appropriate)* building or structure in which the Premises are situated and in respect of which the closure order does not have effect.

PART C

3. The applicant asks the court to:
   (a) fix a hearing;
   (b) order the applicant to intimate this application and the date of the hearing to such persons as the sheriff considers appropriate and, where the applicant is not a senior police officer, to such senior police officer as the sheriff considers appropriate; and
   (c) make an order allowing access *(detail access provisions requested)*.

. . . . Signed

Applicant *(include full designation)*

or [X.Y.] Solicitor for Applicant *(include full designation and business address)*

FORM OF INTERLOCUTOR

Sheriff Court . . . . 20. . . . .

(Court Ref No.)

The sheriff having considered this minute orders the applicant to intimate this application and interlocutor to . . . ., assigns . . . . at . . . . within . . . . as a hearing and directs any person wishing to oppose the granting of the application to appear or be represented at the hearing to show cause why the application should not be granted.

. . . . Signed

Sheriff

FORM OF INTERLOCUTOR

Sheriff Court . . . . 20. . . . .

(Court Ref No.)

The sheriff having heard *(insert details of parties who attended the hearing)* and having considered this minute,

*1. makes an order an order allowing *(insert name and address)*

_____

_____

_____

access to the following part or parts of the premises at *(insert details of premises)* in relation to which a closure order has been made under section 29(1) of the Antisocial Behaviour etc. (Scotland) Act 2004: *(insert details of parts of premises to which access order is to apply)*

_____

_____

_____

*2. directs intimation of this interlocutor to *(insert details of all known interested persons to whom the sheriff considers it to be appropriate to intimate)*.

*3. refuses to make an access order in respect of the premises at *(insert details of premises)*.

*4. postpones the determination of the application until *(insert date)* at *(insert time)* within *(insert location)*.

*delete as appropriate

. . . . Signed

Sheriff

NOTE
[1] Inserted by SSI 2004/455, para 5 and Sch. (effective October 28, 2004).

Rule 3.27.16   [1] FORM 31

ANTISOCIAL BEHAVIOUR ETC. (SCOTLAND) ACT 2004

Section 13, 102 or 105

Intimation that court may make or revoke or vary a parenting order

Sheriff Court . . . . 20. . . . .

(Court Ref No.)

PART A

This part must be completed by the applicant's solicitor in language a child is capable of understanding

To **(1)**

The Sheriff (the person who has to decide about the parenting order) has been asked by **(2)** to decide:—

(a) **(3)** and **(4)**;
(b) **(5)**;
(c) **(6)**.

If you want to tell the Sheriff what you think about the things **(2)** has asked the Sheriff to decide about your future you should complete Part B of this form and send it to the Sheriff Clerk at **(7)** by **(8)** . An envelope which does not need a postage stamp is enclosed for you to use to return the form.

IF YOU DO NOT UNDERSTAND THIS FORM OR IF YOU WANT HELP TO COMPLETE IT you may get free help from a SOLICITOR or contact the SCOTTISH CHILD LAW CENTRE ON the FREE ADVICE TELEPHONE LINE ON 0800 317 500.

If you return the form it will be given to the Sheriff. The Sheriff may wish to speak with you and may ask you to come and see him or her.

NOTES FOR COMPLETION

(1) Insert name and address of child.	(2) Insert description of party making the application to the court.
(3) Insert appropriate wording for parenting order sought.	(4) Insert appropriate wording, if relevant, for Antisocial Behaviour Order.
(5) Insert appropriate wording for contact.	(6) Insert appropriate wording for any other order sought or determinations to be made by sheriff.
(7) Insert address of sheriff clerk.	(8) Insert the date occurring 21 days after the date on which intimation is given.
(9) Insert court reference number.	(10) Insert name and address of parties to the action.

PART B

IF YOU WISH THE SHERIFF TO KNOW YOUR VIEWS ABOUT THE PARENTING ORDER YOU SHOULD COMPLETE THIS PART OF THE FORM

To the Sheriff Clerk, **(7)**

Court Ref. No. **(9)**

(10) . . . .

QUESTION (1): DO YOU WISH THE SHERIFF TO KNOW WHAT YOUR VIEWS ARE ABOUT THE PARENTING ORDER?

(PLEASE TICK BOX)

YES	
NO	

If you have ticked YES please also answer Question (2) *or* (3)

QUESTION (2): WOULD YOU LIKE A FRIEND, RELATIVE OR OTHER PERSON TO TELL THE SHERIFF YOUR VIEWS ABOUT THE PARENTING ORDER?

(PLEASE TICK BOX)

YES	
NO	

If you have ticked YES please write the name and address of the person you wish to tell the Sheriff your views in Box (A) below. You should also tell that person what your views are about the parenting order.

BOX A:	(NAME)				
	(ADDRESS)				
	Is this person—	A friend?		A relative?	
		A teacher?		Other?	

OR

QUESTION (3): WOULD YOU LIKE TO WRITE TO THE SHERIFF AND TELL HIM WHAT YOUR VIEWS ARE ABOUT THE PARENTING ORDER?

(PLEASE TICK BOX)

YES	
NO	

If you decide that you wish to write to the Sheriff you can write what your views are about the parenting order in Box (B) below or on a separate piece of paper. If you decide to write your views on a separate piece of paper you should send it along with this form to the Sheriff Clerk in the envelope provided.

BOX B:	WHAT I HAVE TO SAY ABOUT THE PARENTING ORDER:—

NAME: . . . .

ADDRESS: . . . .

DATE: . . . .

NOTE
[1] Inserted by SSI 2004/455, para 5 and Sch. (effective October 28, 2004).

ANTISOCIAL BEHAVIOUR ETC. (SCOTLAND) ACT 2004

Section 13, 102 or 105

Form of notice to local authority requesting a report in respect of a child

Sheriff Court . . . . 20. . . . .

(Court Ref No.)

To *(insert name and address)*

1. YOU ARE GIVEN NOTICE that in an action in the Sheriff Court at *(insert address)* an application for [the variation/revocation of] *(delete as appropriate)* a parenting order is being considered in respect of a parent of the child *(insert name of child)*. A copy of the application is enclosed.

2. You are required to submit to the court a report on all the circumstances of the child, including but not limited to:—
- (a) the current or proposed arrangements for the case and upbringing of the child;
- (b) information about the family circumstances of the parent; and
- (c) the likely effect of a parenting order on the family circumstances of the parent and the child.

3. This report should be sent to the Sheriff Court at . . . . on or before . . . . *(insert date)*.

Date *(insert date)*

. . . . Signed:

Applicant *(include full designation)*

or [X.Y.] Solicitor for Applicant *(include full designation and business address)*

or Sheriff Clerk

NOTE
[1] Inserted by SSI 2004/455, para 5 and Sch. (effective October 28, 2004).

Rule 3.34.2   [1] FORM 33

NOTE OF APPEAL UNDER LICENSING (SCOTLAND) ACT 2005

SHERIFFDOM OF *(insert name of sheriffdom)*

AT *(insert place of sheriff court)*

[A.B.] *(design and state address)*, Appellant

The appeal is made in respect of *(state here the decision concerned, the date on which it was made and the Licensing Board which made it with reference to the relevant provisions of the Licensing (Scotland) Act 2005)*

The Licensing Board is requested to state a case.

The appellant appeals against the decision on the following grounds: *(state, in separate, numbered paragraphs the grounds on which the appeal is made with reference to section 131(3) and (4) of the Licensing (Scotland) Act 2005)*.

The appellant craves the court *(state here orders sought in respect of the appeal)*.

(insert place and date)   *(signed)*
                                                                [A.B.], Appellant
                                                                or
                                                                [X.Y.] (state designation and
                                                                business address)

Solicitor for the Appellant

NOTE
[1] As inserted by the Act of Sederunt (Summary Applications, Statutory Applications and Appeals etc. Rules) Amendment (Licensing (Scotland) Act 2005) 2008 (SSI 2008/9), (effective February 1, 2008).

Rule 3.35.6   [1] FORM 34

Form of certificate of delivery of document under section 26(2), 27(1) or 27(2) of the Adult Support and Protection (Scotland) Act 2007

Court ref no:

(Insert place and date) I, *(insert name and designation)*, hereby certify that on *(date)* I duly delivered to *(insert name and address)* *(insert details of the document delivered)*. This I did by *(state method of delivery)*.

                          Signed

                  (add designation and address or business address)

NOTE
[1] As inserted by the Act of Sederunt (Summary Applications, Statutory Applications and Appeals etc. Rules) Amendment (Adult Support and Protection (Scotland) Act 2007) (No.2) 2008 (SSI 2008/335) r.2(3) (effective October 29, 2008) and substituted by the Act of Sederunt (Summary Applications, Statutory Applications and Appeals etc. Rules) Amendment (Adult Support and Protection (Scotland) Act 2007) (No.3) 2008 (SSI 2008/375) para.2(5) (effective November 20, 2008).

[1]FORM 35

FORM OF APPLICATION FOR WARRANT FOR ENTRY UNDER SECTION 38(2) OF THE ADULT SUPPORT AND PROTECTION (SCOTLAND) ACT 2007

SHERIFFDOM OF *(insert name of sheriffdom)*

AT *(insert place of sheriff court)*

[A.B.] *(design and state capacity in which the application is made)*, Applicant

The applicant craves the court to grant a warrant for entry in terms of sections 37 and 38(2) of the Adult Support and Protection (Scotland) Act 2007 to *(state address of specified place to which entry is sought)*.

NOTE
[1] As inserted by the Act of Sederunt (Summary Applications, Statutory Applications and Appeals etc. Rules) Amendment (Adult Support and Protection (Scotland) Act 2007) (No.2) 2008 (SSI 2008/335) r.2(3) (effective October 29, 2008).

FORM OF APPLICATION FOR WARRANT UNDER SECTION 27 OF THE PUBLIC HEALTH ETC. (SCOTLAND) ACT 2008

SHERIFFDOM OF (*insert name of sheriffdom*)

AT (*insert place of sheriff court*)

[A.B.] (*design and state address*), Applicant

Order sought from the court

The applicant applies to the court to grant warrant to him:

1. to enter the premises at (*insert address of premises to which entry is sought*).

2. to take with him any other person he may authorise and, if he has reasonable cause to expect any serious obstruction in obtaining access, a constable.

3. to take with him any equipment or materials required for any purpose for which the power of entry is being exercised.

4. to direct that those premises (or any part of them) are, or any thing in or on them is, to be left undisturbed (whether generally or in particular respects) for so long as he considers appropriate.

5. to exercise any of the powers conferred by sections 23, 24 and 25 of the Public Health etc. (Scotland) Act 2008 ("the Act").

Statement
*Delete as appropriate

1. This application is made pursuant to section 27 of the Act.

2. The applicant is an investigator duly appointed in terms of section 21(2) of the Act to carry out a public health investigation.

3. The said premises are*/are not* a dwellinghouse.

4. The said premises are within the jurisdiction of this court.

5. The applicant considers it necessary for the purpose of, or in connection with, a public health investigation to exercise the powers of entry available to him under section 22 of the Act, the other investigatory powers mentioned in section 23 of the Act, the power to ask questions mentioned in section 24 of the Act and any supplementary power mentioned in section 25 of the Act (*insert here a brief statement of reasons*).

*6. [*If the said premises are a dwellinghouse*] The applicant has in terms of section 26(2) of the Act given 48 hours notice of the proposed entry to a person who appears to be the occupier of the dwellinghouse and the period of notice has expired.

*7. The applicant is an investigator entitled to enter premises under section 22 of the Act and
*the applicant has been refused entry to the said premises, or
*the applicant reasonably anticipates that entry will be refused

OR

*7. The said premises are premises which the applicant is entitled to enter and they are unoccupied.

OR

*7. The said premises are premises which the applicant is entitled to enter and the occupier thereof is temporarily absent and there is urgency because (*here state briefly why there is urgency*).

OR

*7. The applicant is an investigator entitled to exercise a power under section 23 or 24 of the Act and
*has been prevented from exercising that power, or
*reasonably anticipates being prevented from exercising that power.

OR

*7 An application for admission to the said premises would defeat the object of the public health investigation.
8. In the circumstances narrated the applicant is entitled to the warrant sought and it should be granted accordingly.

(*signed*)

[A.B.] Applicant

or [X.Y.] (*add designation and business address*)

Solicitor for applicant

(*insert date*)

NOTE
[1] As inserted by the Act of Sederunt (Summary Applications, Statutory Applications and Appeals etc. Rules) Amendment (Public Health etc. (Scotland) Act 2008) 2009 (SSI 2009/320) r.2 (effective October 1, 2009).

Rule 3.39.2(2)   [1] FORM 37

FORM OF WARRANT FOR A PUBLIC HEALTH INVESTIGATION

Sheriff Court ....

.... 20 ....

(Court Ref. No.)

Delete as appropriate

The sheriff, having considered an application made under section 27 of the Public Health etc. (Scotland) Act 2008 ("the Act") *[and productions lodged therewith] *[and (*where the premises referred to below are a dwellinghouse*) being satisfied that due notice has been given under section 26(2) of the Act and has expired],

Grants warrant to the applicant (*insert name*) as sought and authorises him:

  (a) to enter the premises at (*insert address*),
  (b) on entering the premises referred to at paragraph (a), to take—
       (i)   any other person authorised by him and, if he has reasonable cause to expect any serious obstruction in obtaining access, a constable; and
       (ii) any equipment or materials required for any purpose for which the power of entry is being exercised,
  (c) to direct that—
       (i)   those premises (or any part of them) are; or
       (ii) any thing in or on those premises is,

to be left undisturbed (whether generally or in particular respects) for so long as he considers appropriate.

(d) to exercise any power mentioned in sections 23 to 25 of the Act.

(*signed*)

Sheriff

NOTE
[1] As inserted by the Act of Sederunt (Summary Applications, Statutory Applications and Appeals etc. Rules) Amendment (Public Health etc. (Scotland) Act 2008) 2009 (SSI 2009/320) r.2 (effective October 1, 2009).

Rule 3.39.3(1)   [1] FORM 38

FORM OF APPLICATION FOR MEDICAL EXAMINATION OF A PERSON UNDER SECTION 34 OF THE PUBLIC HEALTH ETC. (SCOTLAND) ACT 2008

SHERIFFDOM OF (*insert name of sheriffdom*)

AT (*insert place of sheriff court*)

[A.B.] (*design health board*), Applicant

Order sought from the court
*Delete as appropriate

The applicant applies to the court to grant an order under section 34(1) of the Public Health etc. (Scotland) Act 2008 ("the Act") authorising the medical examination of (*insert name, address and date of birth of person to be medically examined*) ("the person").

*And (if necessary, request any specialities in connection with the examination, about which the court's additional authority is sought pursuant to section 34(3) of the Act).

Statement
*Delete as appropriate

1. This application is made pursuant to sections 33 and 34 of the Act.

2. The person is present within the applicant's area. The applicant is a health board operating within the jurisdiction of this court. This court accordingly has jurisdiction.

3. *The person is aged 16 years or over.

OR

*The person is under 16. The parent or other person who has day-to-day care or control of the person is (*insert name, address and relationship to the person*).

4. (a) The applicant *knows/*suspects that the person—
      *(i)   has an infectious disease, namely [*insert name of disease*];
      *(ii) has been exposed to an organism which causes an infectious disease [*insert name of disease*];
      *(iii) is contaminated; or
      *(iv) has been exposed to a contaminant,

(*insert here a brief statement indicating the basis upon which these matters are known or suspected by the applicant*)

AND

    (b) It appears to the applicant that as a result—
        (i) there is or may be a significant risk to public health; and
        (ii) it is necessary, to avoid or minimise that risk, for the person to be medically examined.

(*Insert here a brief statement indicating the reason why the applicant considers that there is or may be a significant risk to public health and that it is necessary, to avoid or minimise that risk, for the person to be medically examined*).

5. The applicant proposes that the examination be carried out by (*insert proposed class or classes of health care professional*).

6. The applicant proposes that the examination be (*insert nature of the proposed examination*).

*7. The applicant has explained to the person—

    (a) that there is a significant risk to public health;
    (b) the nature of that risk; and
    (c) why the applicant considers it necessary for the proposed action to be taken in relation to that person.

OR

*7. The applicant states that the person is incapable of understanding any explanation of the matters referred to at section 31(3) of the Act (*state reason*) and has explained to (*insert name and address of a person mentioned in section 31(5)(a) or (b) of the Act and their relationship to the person*)—

    (a) that there is a significant risk to public health;
    (b) the nature of that risk; and
    (c) why the applicant considers it necessary for the proposed action to be taken in relation to that person.

OR

*7. The applicant states that no explanation has been given in relation to this application under section 31(3) or (5) of the Act because (*state why it was not reasonably practicable to do so*).

*8. The applicant states that *a response was made/*representations were made on behalf of the person in the following terms (*insert response or representations made*).

9. The applicant attaches to this application a certificate signed by a health board competent person which indicates that the competent person is satisfied as to the matters mentioned in statement 4 [*and (*in a case where medical examination of a group is sought*) that it is necessary, to avoid or minimise an actual or anticipated significant risk to public health, for all the persons in the group to be medically examined].

10. In the circumstances narrated the applicant is entitled to the order sought and it should be granted accordingly.

(*signed*)

[X.Y.] (*add designation and business address*)

Solicitor for applicant

(*insert date*)

NOTE
  [1] As inserted by the Act of Sederunt (Summary Applications, Statutory Applications and Appeals etc. Rules) Amendment (Public Health etc. (Scotland) Act 2008) 2009 (SSI 2009/320) r.2 (effective October 1, 2009).

Rule 3.39.3(3)   ¹ FORM 39

FORM OF ORDER FOR A MEDICAL EXAMINATION

Sheriff Court ....

.... 20 .... at [*insert time*]

(Court Ref. No.)

The sheriff, having considered an application made under section 33(2) of the Public Health etc. (Scotland) Act 2008 ("the Act") *[and productions lodged therewith], and being satisfied as necessary as to the matters mentioned in section 34(2) of the Act,

1. Makes an order in terms of section 34(1) of the Act authorising the medical examination of (*insert details of the person as given in the application*) and authorises (*insert the class or classes of health care professional by whom the medical examination is to be carried out*) to carry out the examination,

    *And (*add any additional matters to be dealt with in the order in terms of section 34(3) of the Act*).

2. Directs notification of this order (*insert details of method and timing of notice*) to (*the person to whom the order applies*)

    *and (*the name and designation of any person to whom an explanation was given under section 31(5) of the Act*)

    *and (*insert the name and designation of any other person whom the sheriff considers appropriate*).

*Delete as appropriate

(*signed*)

Sheriff

NOTE
¹ As inserted by the Act of Sederunt (Summary Applications, Statutory Applications and Appeals etc. Rules) Amendment (Public Health etc. (Scotland) Act 2008) 2009 (SSI 2009/320) r.2 (effective October 1, 2009).

Rule 3.39.4(1)   ¹ FORM 40

FORM OF APPLICATION FOR QUARANTINE ORDER UNDER SECTION 40 OF THE PUBLIC HEALTH ETC. (SCOTLAND) ACT 2008

SHERIFFDOM OF (*insert name of sheriffdom*)

AT (*insert place of sheriff court*)

[A.B.] (*design health board*), Applicant

Order sought from the court
*Delete as appropriate

The applicant applies to the court for a quarantine order under section 40(1) of the Public Health etc. (Scotland) Act 2008 ("the Act") authorising the quarantining of (*insert name, address and date of birth of person to be quarantined*) ("the person") for a period of (*insert period*).

*and the person's removal to (*insert place of quarantine*) [by (*insert, if sought, the name and designation of a person mentioned in section 40(4)(d) of the Act*)].

*authorising the taking in relation to the person of the following steps, namely *disinfection/ *disinfestation/*decontamination (*specify which steps are sought*)

*and imposing the following conditions in relation to the quarantine (*insert conditions sought*).

Statement
*Delete as appropriate

1. This application is made pursuant to sections 39 and 40 of the Act.

2. The person is present within the applicant's area. The applicant is a health board operating within the jurisdiction of this court. This court accordingly has jurisdiction.

3. *The person is aged 16 years or over.

OR

 *The person is under 16. The parent or other person who has day-to-day care or control of the person is (*insert name, address and relationship to the person*).

4. (a) The applicant *knows/*has reasonable grounds to suspect that the person—
  *(i) has an infectious disease, namely [*insert name of disease*];
  *(ii) has been exposed to an organism which causes an infectious disease [*insert name of disease*];
  *(iii) is contaminated; or
  *(iv) has been exposed to a contaminant,

(*insert here a brief statement indicating the basis upon which these matters are known or suspected by the applicant*)

AND

 (b) that as a result—
  (i) there is or may be a significant risk to public health; and
  (ii) it is necessary, to avoid or minimise that risk, for the person to be quarantined.

(*Insert here a brief statement indicating the reason why the applicant considers that there is or may be a significant risk to public health and that it is necessary, to avoid or minimise that risk, for the person to be quarantined*).

5. The applicant proposes that the person be quarantined at (*insert place and address*) *[and that he should be removed there by (*insert name and designation of person under section 40(4)(d) of the Act*)]. (*Indicate briefly why this is proposed*).

6. The applicant proposes that the person be quarantined for (*insert period of time*).

7. The applicant considers it necessary to *disinfect/*disinfest/*decontaminate the person (*insert details and reasons*).

*8. The applicant considers the conditions sought to be included in the order to be necessary because (*insert reasons*).

*9. The applicant has explained to the person—

 (a) that there is a significant risk to public health;
 (b) the nature of that risk; and
 (c) why the applicant considers it necessary for the proposed action to be taken in relation to that person.

OR

*9. The applicant states that the person is incapable of understanding any explanation of the matters referred to at section 31(3) of the Act (*state reason*) and has explained to (*insert name and address of a person mentioned in section 31(5)(a) or (b) of the Act and their relationship to the person*)—

    (a) that there is a significant risk to public health;
    (b) the nature of that risk; and
    (c) why the applicant considers it necessary for the proposed action to be taken in relation to that person.

OR

*9 The applicant states that no explanation has been given in relation to this application under section 31(3) or (5) of the Act because (*state why it was not reasonably practicable to do so*).

*10. The applicant states that *a response was made/*representations were made on behalf of the person in the following terms (*insert response or representations made*).

11. The applicant attaches to this application a certificate signed by a health board competent person which indicates that the competent person is satisfied as to the matters mentioned in statement 4.

12. In the circumstances narrated the applicant is entitled to the order sought and it should be granted accordingly.

(*signed*)

[X.Y.] (*add designation and business address*)

Solicitor for applicant

(*insert date*)

NOTE
  [1] As inserted by the Act of Sederunt (Summary Applications, Statutory Applications and Appeals etc. Rules) Amendment (Public Health etc. (Scotland) Act 2008) 2009 (SSI 2009/320) r.2 (effective October 1, 2009).

Rule 3.39.4(3)   [1] FORM 41

FORM OF QUARANTINE ORDER

Sheriff Court ....

.... 20 .... at (*insert time*)

(Court Ref. No.)

The sheriff, having considered an application made under section 39(2) of the Public Health etc. (Scotland) Act 2008 ("the Act") *[and productions lodged therewith], and being satisfied as necessary as to the matters mentioned in section 40(2) of the Act,

1. Makes an order in terms of section 40(1) of the Act authorising the quarantining of (*insert details of the person as given in the application*) in (*insert the place in which the person is to be quarantined*) for a period of (*insert the period for which the person is to be quarantined*) and

    Authorising the removal of (*insert name of the person*) to (*insert address at which the person is to be quarantined*)

    Further (*insert any authorisation for disinfection/disinfestation/decontamination*),

    (*Insert any conditions imposed by the order including the name and designation of any person authorised under section 40(4)(d) of the Act to effect a removal*), and

2. Directs notification of this order (*insert details of method and timing of notice*) to (*the person to whom the order applies*)

*and (*the name and designation of any person to whom an explanation was given under section 31(5) of the Act*)

*and (*insert the name and designation of any other person whom the sheriff considers appropriate*).

**Delete as appropriate*

(*signed*)

Sheriff

NOTE
[1] As inserted by the Act of Sederunt (Summary Applications, Statutory Applications and Appeals etc. Rules) Amendment (Public Health etc. (Scotland) Act 2008) 2009 (SSI 2009/320) r.2 (effective October 1, 2009).

Rule 3.39.5(1) [1] FORM 42

FORM OF APPLICATION TO HAVE A PERSON REMOVED TO AND DETAINED IN HOSPITAL UNDER SECTION 42 OF THE PUBLIC HEALTH ETC. (SCOTLAND) ACT 2008

SHERIFFDOM OF (*insert name of sheriffdom*)

AT (*insert place of sheriff court*)

[A.B.] (*design health board*), Applicant

Order sought from the court
**Delete as appropriate*

The applicant applies to the court for a short term detention order under section 42(1) of the Public Health etc. (Scotland) Act 2008 ("the Act") in respect of (*insert name, address and date of birth of person to be subject to the order*) ("the person").

1. authorising the person's removal to hospital *[by (*insert name and designation of a person mentioned in section 42(1)(a) of the Act*)] and the person's detention in hospital for the period of (*insert period*), and

2. authorising the taking in relation to the person of the following steps, namely *disinfection/ *disinfestation/*decontamination (*specify which steps are sought*).

Statement
**Delete as appropriate*

1. This application is made pursuant to sections 41 and 42 of the Act.

2. The person is present within the applicant's area. The applicant is a health board operating within the jurisdiction of this court. This court accordingly has jurisdiction.

3. *The person is aged 16 years or over.

OR

*The person is under 16. The parent or other person who has day-to-day care or control of the person is (*insert name, address and relationship to the person*).

4. (a) The applicant knows that the person—
    *(i) has an infectious disease, namely [*insert name of disease*]; or
    *(ii) is contaminated,

(insert here a brief statement indicating the basis upon which these matters are known to the applicant)

AND

    (b) it appears to the applicant that as a result—
        (i) there is a significant risk to public health; and
        (ii) it is necessary, to avoid or minimise that risk, for the person to be detained in hospital

(Insert here a brief statement indicating the reason why the applicant considers that there is a significant risk to public health and that it is necessary, to avoid or minimise that risk, for the person to be detained in hospital).

5. The applicant proposes that the person be detained at (*insert name and address of hospital*) *[and that he should be removed there by (*insert name and designation of person under section 42(1)(a) of the Act and indicate briefly why this is proposed*)].

6. The applicant proposes that the person be detained for (*insert period of time*).

7. The applicant considers it necessary to *disinfect/*disinfest/*decontaminate the person (*insert details and reasons*).

*8. The applicant has explained to the person—

    (a) that there is a significant risk to public health;
    (b) the nature of that risk; and
    (c) why the applicant considers it necessary for the proposed action to be taken in relation to that person.

OR

*8. The applicant states that the person is incapable of understanding any explanation of the matters referred to at section 31(3) of the Act (*state reason*) and has explained to (*insert name and address of a person mentioned in section 31(5)(a) or (b) of the Act and their relationship to the person*)—

    (a) that there is a significant risk to public health;
    (b) the nature of that risk; and
    (c) why the applicant considers it necessary for the proposed action to be taken in relation to that person.

OR

*8. The applicant states that no explanation has been given in relation to this application under section 31(3) or (5) of the Act because (*state why it was not reasonably practicable to do so*).

*9. The applicant states that *a response was made/*representations were made on behalf of the person in the following terms (*insert response or representations made*).

10. The applicant attaches to this application a certificate signed by a health board competent person which indicates that the competent person is satisfied as to the matters mentioned in statement 4.

11. In the circumstances narrated the applicant is entitled to the order sought and it should be granted accordingly.

(signed)

Solicitor for applicant

[X.Y.] (add designation and business address)

(insert date)

NOTE
[1] As inserted by the Act of Sederunt (Summary Applications, Statutory Applications and Appeals etc. Rules) Amendment (Public Health etc. (Scotland) Act 2008) 2009 (SSI 2009/320) r.2 (effective October 1, 2009).

Rule 3.39.5(4)   [1] FORM 43

FORM OF SHORT TERM DETENTION ORDER—REMOVAL TO AND DETENTION
IN HOSPITAL

Sheriff Court ....

.... 20 .... at (*insert time*)

(Court Ref. No.)

The sheriff, having considered an application made under section 41(2) of the Public Health etc. (Scotland) Act 2008 ("the Act") *[and productions lodged therewith], and being satisfied as necessary as to the matters mentioned in section 42(2) of the Act,

1. Makes an order in terms of section 42(1) of the Act authorising the short term detention in hospital of (*insert details of the person as given in the application*),

    Authorising the removal of that person by (*specify person authorised to carry out removal in terms of section 42(1)(a) of the Act*) to (*specify hospital at which the person is to be detained, including the address*), there to be detained for (*insert period of detention*)

    Further (*insert any authorisation for disinfection/disinfestation/decontamination*), and

2. Directs notification of this order (*insert details of method and timing of notice*) to (*the person to whom the order applies*)

    *and (*the name and designation of any person to whom an explanation was given under section 31(5) of the Act*)

    *and (*insert the name and designation of any other person whom the sheriff considers appropriate*).

Delete as appropriate

(signed)

Sheriff

NOTE
[1] As inserted by the Act of Sederunt (Summary Applications, Statutory Applications and Appeals etc. Rules) Amendment (Public Health etc. (Scotland) Act 2008) 2009 (SSI 2009/320) r.2 (effective October 1, 2009).

Rule 3.39.5(2)   [1] FORM 44

FORM OF APPLICATION FOR A SHORT TERM DETENTION ORDER UNDER
SECTION 43 OF THE PUBLIC HEALTH ETC. (SCOTLAND) ACT 2008

SHERIFFDOM OF (*insert name of sheriffdom*)

AT (*insert place of sheriff court*)

[A.B.] (*design health board*), Applicant

Order sought from the court
Delete as appropriate

The applicant applies to the court for a short term detention order under section 43(1) of the Public Health etc. (Scotland) Act 2008 ("the Act") in respect of *(insert name, address and date of birth of person to be subject to the order)* ("the person").

1. authorising the person's detention in hospital for a period of *(insert period)*, and

2. authorising the taking in relation to the person of the following steps, namely *disinfection/ *disinfestation/*decontamination *(specify which steps are sought).*

Statement
**Delete as appropriate*

1. This application is made pursuant to sections 41 and 43 of the Act.

2. The person is present within the applicant's area. The applicant is a health board operating within the jurisdiction of this court. This court accordingly has jurisdiction.

3. *The person is aged 16 years or over.

OR

   *The person is under 16. The parent or other person who has day-to-day care or control of the person is *(insert name, address and relationship to the person).*

4. (a) The applicant knows that the person—
       *(i) has an infectious disease, namely [*insert name of disease*]; or
       *(ii) is contaminated,

   (insert here a brief statement indicating the basis upon which these matters are known to the applicant)

AND

   (b) it appears to the applicant that as a result—
       (i) there is a significant risk to public health; and
       (ii) it is necessary, to avoid or minimise that risk, for the person to be detained in hospital.

   (Insert here a brief statement indicating the reason why the applicant considers that there is a significant risk to public health and that it is necessary, to avoid or minimise that risk, for the person to be detained in hospital).

5. The person is currently in *(insert name and address of hospital).* The applicant proposes that the person be detained at *(insert name and address of hospital).*

6. The applicant proposes that the person be detained for *(insert period of time).*

7. The applicant considers it necessary to *disinfect/*disinfest/*decontaminate the person *(insert details and reasons).*

*8. The applicant has explained to the person—

   (a) that there is a significant risk to public health;
   (b) the nature of that risk; and
   (c) why the applicant considers it necessary for the proposed action to be taken in relation to that person.

OR

*8. The applicant states that the person is incapable of understanding any explanation of the matters referred to at section 31(3) of the Act *(state reason)* and has explained to *(insert name and address of a person mentioned in section 31(5)(a) or (b) of the Act and their relationship to the person)*—

   (a) that there is a significant risk to public health;

   (b) the nature of that risk; and

   (c) why the applicant considers it necessary for the proposed action to be taken in relation to that person.

OR

*8. The applicant states that no explanation has been given in relation to this application under section 31(3) or (5) of the Act because (*state why it was not reasonably practicable to do so*).

*9. The applicant states that *a response was made/*representations were made on behalf of the person in the following terms (*insert response or representations made*).

10. The applicant attaches to this application a certificate signed by a health board competent person which indicates that the competent person is satisfied as to the matters mentioned in statement 4.

11. In the circumstances narrated the applicant is entitled to the order sought and it should be granted accordingly.

(*signed*)

[X.Y.] (*add designation and business address*)

Solicitor for applicant

(*insert date*)

NOTE
[1] As inserted by the Act of Sederunt (Summary Applications, Statutory Applications and Appeals etc. Rules) Amendment (Public Health etc. (Scotland) Act 2008) 2009 (SSI 2009/320) r.2 (effective October 1, 2009).

Rule 3.39.5(5)   [1] FORM 45

FORM OF SHORT TERM DETENTION ORDER—DETENTION IN HOSPITAL

Sheriff Court ....

.... 20 .... at (*insert time*)

(Court Ref. No.)

The sheriff, having considered an application made under section 41(2) of the Public Health etc. (Scotland) Act 2008 ("the Act") *[and productions lodged therewith], and being satisfied as necessary as to the matters mentioned in section 43(2) of the Act,

1. Makes an order in terms of section 43(1) of the Act authorising the short term detention in hospital of (*insert details of the person as given in the application*) at (*insert name and address of hospital*) for (*insert period of detention*)

   Further (*insert any authorisation for disinfection/disinfestation/decontamination*), and

2. Directs notification of this order (*insert details of method and timing of notice*) to (*the person to whom the order applies*)

   *and (*the name and designation of any person to whom an explanation was given under section 31(5) of the Act*)

   *and (*insert the name and designation of any other person whom the sheriff considers appropriate*).

**Delete as appropriate*

(*signed*)

Sheriff

NOTE
¹ As inserted by the Act of Sederunt (Summary Applications, Statutory Applications and Appeals etc. Rules) Amendment (Public Health etc. (Scotland) Act 2008) 2009 (SSI 2009/320) r.2 (effective October 1, 2009).

¹ FORM 46

Rule 3.39.6(1)

FORM OF APPLICATION FOR EXCEPTIONAL DETENTION ORDER UNDER SECTION 45 OF THE PUBLIC HEALTH ETC. (SCOTLAND) ACT 2008

SHERIFFDOM OF (*insert name of sheriffdom*)

AT (*insert place of sheriff court*)

[A.B.] (*design health board*), Applicant

Order sought from the court
*Delete as appropriate

The applicant applies to the court for an exceptional detention order under section 45(1) of the Public Health etc. (Scotland) Act 2008 ("the Act") in respect of (*insert name, address and date of birth of person to be subject to the order*) ("the person").

1. authorising the person's continued detention in hospital for a period of (*insert period*), and

2. authorising the taking in relation to the person of the following steps, namely *disinfection/ *disinfestation/*decontamination (*specify which steps are sought*).

Statement
*Delete as appropriate

1. This application is made pursuant to sections 44 and 45 of the Act.

2. The person is presently detained in a hospital within the applicant's area by virtue of a short term detention order. The applicant is a health board operating within the jurisdiction of this court and applied for the short term detention order. This court accordingly has jurisdiction.

3. *The person is aged 16 years or over.

OR

*The person is under 16. The parent or other person who has day-to-day care or control of the person is (*insert name, address and relationship to the person*).

4. The applicant is satisfied—

   (a) that the person—
   *(i) has an infectious disease, namely [*insert name of disease*]; or
   *(ii) is contaminated,

AND

   (b) that as a result there is a significant risk to public health,

   (*insert here a brief statement indicating the basis upon which the applicant is satisfied of these matters*)

AND

   (c) that it continues to be necessary, to avoid or minimise that risk, for the person to be detained in hospital (*insert here a brief statement indicating the reason why the applicant considers it necessary for the person to be detained in hospital*),

AND

   (d) that it is necessary, to avoid or minimise that risk, for the person to be detained for a period exceeding the maximum period for which the person could be detained by virtue of the short term detention order were that order to be extended under section 49(5)(a) of the Act (*insert here a brief statement indicating the reason why the applicant considers it necessary for the person to be detained beyond that maximum period*).

5. The person is currently detained in (*insert name and address of hospital*) by virtue of a short term detention order granted on (*insert date*). The said order is extant until [*insert date*]. The applicant proposes that the person be detained at (*insert name and address of hospital*).

6. The applicant applies to the court to order that the person continue to be detained in (*insert name and address of hospital*) for (*insert period of time*) from (*insert date from which the order is to commence*).

7. The applicant considers it necessary to *disinfect/*disinfest/*decontaminate the person (*insert details and reasons*).

*8. The applicant has explained to the person—

   (a) that there is a significant risk to public health;
   (b) the nature of that risk; and
   (c) why the applicant considers it necessary for the proposed action to be taken in relation to that person.

OR

*8. The applicant states that the person is incapable of understanding any explanation of the matters referred to at section 31(3) of the Act (*state reason*) and has explained to (*insert name and address of a person mentioned in section 31(5)(a) or (b) of the Act and their relationship to the person*)—

   (a) that there is a significant risk to public health;

   (b) the nature of that risk; and

   (c) why the applicant considers it necessary for the proposed action to be taken in relation to that person.

OR

*8. The applicant states that no explanation has been given in relation to this application under section 31(3) or (5) of the Act because (*state why it was not reasonably practicable to do so*).

*9. The applicant states that *a response was made/*representations were made on behalf of the person in the following terms (*insert response or representations made*).

10. The applicant attaches to this application a certificate signed by a health board competent person which indicates that the competent person is satisfied as to the matters mentioned in statement 4.

11. In the circumstances narrated the applicant is entitled to the order sought and it should be granted accordingly.

(*signed*)

[X.Y.] (*add designation and business address*)

Solicitor for applicant

(*insert date*)

NOTE
[1] As inserted by the Act of Sederunt (Summary Applications, Statutory Applications and Appeals etc. Rules) Amendment (Public Health etc. (Scotland) Act 2008) 2009 (SSI 2009/320) r.2 (effective October 1, 2009).

[1] FORM 47

Rule 3.39.6(3)

FORM OF EXCEPTIONAL DETENTION ORDER

Sheriff Court ....

.... 20 .... at (*insert time*)

(Court Ref. No.)

The sheriff, having considered an application made under section 44(3) of the Public Health etc. (Scotland) Act 2008 ("the Act") *[and productions lodged therewith], and being satisfied as to the matters mentioned in section 45(2) of the Act,

1. Makes an exceptional detention order in terms of section 45(1) of the Act authorising the continued detention of (*insert details of the person as given in the application*) at (*insert name and address of hospital*) for (*insert period of detention*).

   Further (*insert any authorisation for disinfection/disinfestation/decontamination*), and

2. Directs notification of this order (*insert details of method and timing of notice*) to (*the person to whom the order applies*)

   *and (*the name and designation of any person to whom an explanation was given under section 31(5) of the Act*)

   *and (*insert the name and designation of any other person whom the sheriff considers appropriate*).

Delete as appropriate

(*signed*)

Sheriff

NOTE
[1] As inserted by the Act of Sederunt (Summary Applications, Statutory Applications and Appeals etc. Rules) Amendment (Public Health etc. (Scotland) Act 2008) 2009 (SSI 2009/320) r.2 (effective October 1, 2009).

Rule 3.39.7(1)   [1] FORM 48

FORM OF APPLICATION FOR EXTENSION OF A QUARANTINE ORDER, SHORT TERM DETENTION ORDER OR EXCEPTIONAL DETENTION ORDER UNDER SECTION 49 OF THE PUBLIC HEALTH ETC. (SCOTLAND) ACT 2008

SHERIFFDOM OF (*insert name of sheriffdom*)

AT (*insert place of sheriff court*)

[A.B.] (*design health board*), Applicant

Order sought from the court
Delete as appropriate

The applicant applies to the court to extend for a period of (*insert period*):

*the quarantine order granted on (*insert date*) in respect of (*insert name, address and date of birth of the person in respect of whom the order was granted*) ("the person") OR

*the short term detention order granted on (*insert date*) in respect of (*insert name, address and date of birth of the person*) ("the person") OR

*the exceptional detention order granted on (*insert date*) in respect of (*insert name, address and date of birth of the person*) ("the person").

Statement
*Delete as appropriate

1. This application is made pursuant to section 49 of the Public Health etc. (Scotland) Act 2008.

2. The person is presently *quarantined/*detained in hospital within the applicant's area by virtue of *a quarantine order/*a short term detention order/*an exceptional detention order granted on (*insert date*) which expires on (*insert date*). This court accordingly has jurisdiction.

3. *The person is aged 16 years or over.

OR

   *The person is under 16. The parent or other person who has day-to-day care or control of the person is (*insert name, address and relationship to the person*).

4. The applicant attaches to this application a certificate signed by a health board competent person which indicates that the competent person is satisfied as to the following matters:

   *[*in relation to a proposed extension of a quarantine order*] That it is known, or there are reasonable grounds to suspect, that the person—

      *(i)   has an infectious disease;
      *(ii) has been exposed to an organism which causes an infectious disease;
      *(iii) is contaminated; or
      *(iv) has been exposed to a contaminant,

   AND   that as a result there is or may be significant risk to public health,

   AND   that it is necessary, to avoid or minimise that risk, for the person to continue to be quarantined.

OR

   *[*in relation to a proposed extension of a short term detention order or an exceptional detention order*] That the person—

      *(i) has an infectious disease; or
      *(ii) is contaminated,

   AND   that as a result there is significant risk to public health,

   AND   that it is necessary, to avoid or minimise that risk, for the person to continue to be detained in hospital.

5. The court is asked to extend the order for a period of (*insert period*) from (*insert date from which the order is to commence*).

*6. An extension of the quarantine order, as sought, will not result in the person being quarantined for a continuous period exceeding 12 weeks.

OR

*6 An extension of the short term detention order, as sought, will not result in the person being detained in hospital for a continuous period exceeding 12 weeks.

OR

*6 An extension of the exceptional detention order, as sought, will not result in the person being detained in hospital for a continuous period exceeding 12 months.

7. In the circumstances narrated the applicant is entitled to the order sought and it should be granted accordingly.

(*signed*)

[X.Y.] (*add designation and business address*)

Solicitor for applicant

(*insert date*)

NOTE
[1] As inserted by the Act of Sederunt (Summary Applications, Statutory Applications and Appeals etc. Rules) Amendment (Public Health etc. (Scotland) Act 2008) 2009 (SSI 2009/320) r.2 (effective October 1, 2009).

Rule 3.39.7(3)   [1] FORM 49

FORM OF ORDER EXTENDING A QUARANTINE ORDER, SHORT TERM
DETENTION ORDER OR EXCEPTIONAL DETENTION ORDER

Sheriff Court ....

.... 20 .... at (*insert time*)

(Court Ref. No.)

The sheriff, having considered an application made under section 49(2) of the Public Health etc. (Scotland) Act 2008 ("the Act") and productions lodged therewith, and being satisfied as to the matters mentioned in section 49(6) of the Act,

1. Makes an order in terms of section 49(5) of the Act extending *the quarantine order/*the short term detention order/*the exceptional detention order which was granted in respect of (*insert details of the person as given in the application*) on (*insert date*) for a period of (*insert period*) and

2. Directs notification of this order (*insert details of method and timing of notice*) to (*the person to whom the order applies*)

*and (*the name and designation of any person to whom an explanation was given under section 31(5) of the Act*)

*and (*insert the name and designation of any other person whom the sheriff considers appropriate*).

**Delete as appropriate*

(*signed*)

Sheriff

NOTE
[1] As inserted by the Act of Sederunt (Summary Applications, Statutory Applications and Appeals etc. Rules) Amendment (Public Health etc. (Scotland) Act 2008) 2009 (SSI 2009/320) r.2 (effective October 1, 2009).

[1] FORM 50

Rule 3.39.8(1)

FORM OF APPLICATION FOR MODIFICATION OF A QUARANTINE ORDER,
SHORT TERM DETENTION ORDER OR EXCEPTIONAL DETENTION ORDER
UNDER SECTION 51 OF THE PUBLIC HEALTH ETC. (SCOTLAND) ACT 2008

SHERIFFDOM OF (*insert name of sheriffdom*)

AT (*insert place of sheriff court*)

[A.B.] (*design health board*), Applicant

Order sought from the court
*Delete as appropriate

The applicant applies to the court to modify:

*the quarantine order granted on (*insert date*) in respect of (*insert name, address and date of birth of the person in respect of whom the order was granted*) ("the person") OR

*the short term detention order granted on (*insert date*) in respect of (*insert name, address and date of birth of the person*) ("the person") OR

*the exceptional detention order granted on (*insert date*) in respect of (*insert name, address and date of birth of the person*) ("the person")

by (*specify details of the modification sought*).

Statement
*Delete as appropriate

1. This application is made pursuant to sections 50 and 51 of the Public Health etc. (Scotland) Act 2008.

2. The person is presently *quarantined/*detained in hospital within the applicant's area by virtue of *a quarantine order/*a short term detention order/*an exceptional detention order granted on (*insert date*) which expires on (*insert date*). This court accordingly has jurisdiction.

3. *The person is aged 16 years or over.

OR

    *The person is under 16. The parent or other person who has day-to-day care or control of the person is (*insert name, address and relationship to the person*).

4. The applicant attaches to this application a certificate signed by a health board competent person which indicates that the competent person is satisfied as to the following matters:

    *[*in relation to a proposed modification of a quarantine order*] That it is known, or there are reasonable grounds to suspect, that the person—

        *(i) has an infectious disease;
        *(ii) has been exposed to an organism which causes an infectious disease;
        *(iii) is contaminated; or
        *(iv) has been exposed to a contaminant,

AND   that as a result there is or may be significant risk to public health,

AND   that it is necessary, to avoid or minimise that risk, for the person to continue to be quarantined.

OR

*[*in relation to a proposed modification of a short term detention order or an exceptional detention order*]* That the person—

  *(i) has an infectious disease; or
  *(ii) is contaminated,

AND   that as a result there is significant risk to public health

AND   that it is necessary, to avoid or minimise that risk, for the person to continue to be detained in hospital.

5. The modification is sought for the following reasons (*here insert a brief statement of reasons*).

6. In the circumstances narrated the applicant is entitled to the order sought and it should be granted accordingly.

(*signed*)

[X.Y.] (*add designation and business address*)

Solicitor for applicant

(*insert date*)

NOTE
¹ As inserted by the Act of Sederunt (Summary Applications, Statutory Applications and Appeals etc. Rules) Amendment (Public Health etc. (Scotland) Act 2008) 2009 (SSI 2009/320) r.2 (effective October 1, 2009).

Rule 3.39.8(3)   ¹ FORM 51

FORM OF MODIFICATION OF A QUARANTINE ORDER, SHORT TERM
DETENTION ORDER OR EXCEPTIONAL DETENTION ORDER

Sheriff Court ....

.... 20 .... at [*insert time*]

(Court Ref. No.)

The sheriff, having considered an application made under section 50(2) of the Public Health etc. (Scotland) Act 2008 ("the Act") *[and productions lodged therewith], and being satisfied as to the matters mentioned in section 51(2) of the Act,

1. Makes an order in terms of section 51(1) of the Act modifying *the quarantine order/*the short term detention order/*the exceptional detention order which was granted in respect of (*insert details of the person as given in the application*) on (*insert date*), by

    (*insert details of modification and, if applicable, name and designation of person considered appropriate under section 51(4)(a)(iv) of the Act*).

2. Directs notification of this order (*insert details of method and timing of notice*) to (*the person to whom the order applies*)

    *and (*the name and designation of any person to whom an explanation was given under section 31(5) of the Act*)

    *and (*insert the name and designation of any other person whom the sheriff considers appropriate*).

*Delete as appropriate

(*signed*)

Sheriff

NOTE
[1] As inserted by the Act of Sederunt (Summary Applications, Statutory Applications and Appeals etc. Rules) Amendment (Public Health etc. (Scotland) Act 2008) 2009 (SSI 2009/320) r.2 (effective October 1, 2009).

Rule 3.39.9(1)   [1] FORM 52

Official use only

Court ref:

Date and time of receipt:

FORM OF APPLICATION FOR RECALL OF AN ORDER GRANTED IN THE ABSENCE
OF THE PERSON TO WHOM IT APPLIES UNDER SECTION 59 OF THE PUBLIC
HEALTH ETC. (SCOTLAND) ACT 2008

NOTES

This form should be used if you wish to apply to the sheriff for an order recalling a quarantine order OR a short term detention order OR an exceptional detention order which was made in the absence of the person to whom the order applies.

If you are the person to whom the order applies, you or your solicitor should complete and sign **PART A** and deliver it to the sheriff clerk of the sheriff court at which you wish to make your application.

If you are not the person to whom the order applies but instead are a person who has an interest in the welfare of the person to whom the order applies, you or your solicitor should complete and sign **PART B** and deliver it to the sheriff clerk of the sheriff court at which you wish to make your application.

Your application MUST be received by the sheriff clerk before the expiry of the period of 72 hours beginning with the time at which the order which you wish to be recalled was notified to you (or, as the case may be, the person to whom the order applies).

You should note that, despite the making of your application, the order which you wish recalled will REMAIN IN FORCE unless and until it is revoked by the sheriff.

Before determining your application the sheriff must give you and various other parties (who are specified in section 59(7) of the Act) the opportunity of making representations (whether orally or in writing) and of leading, or producing, evidence.

IF YOU ARE UNCERTAIN WHAT ACTION TO TAKE you should consult a solicitor. You may be entitled to legal aid depending on your financial circumstances, and you can get information about legal aid from a solicitor. You may also obtain advice from any Citizens Advice Bureau or other advice agency.

PART A

Sheriff Court
(*Insert name of court*)

> 1.

Details of applicant
(*Insert full name, address and telephone number and, if available,
e-mail address and fax number*)

> 2.

Type of order you wish the
sheriff to recall
(*Tick as appropriate*)

> 3.   Quarantine Order ☐
>
> Short Term Detention Order ☐
>
> Exceptional Detention Order ☐

Date of order
(*Insert date of order you wish the
sheriff to recall*)

> 4.

Sheriff Court at which the order was
made, if it was not the court
specified in box 1
(*Insert name of court*)

> 5.

If available, a copy of the order which you wish the sheriff to recall should be attached to this
application.

Date and time at which the order
was notified to you
(*Insert date and exact time of day*)

> 6.

I ask the sheriff to recall the order specified in boxes 3 and 4 on the following grounds:

> (*State why you wish the order to be recalled. If necessary, continue on a separate sheet of
> paper*):

Signed:

Date:

(A solicitor should add his or her name and contact details)

PART B

Sheriff Court
(*Insert name of court*)

> 1.

Details of applicant
(*Insert full name, address and telephone number and, if available, e-
mail address and fax number*)

> 2.

Type of order you wish the
sheriff to recall
(*Tick as appropriate*)

> 3. Quarantine Order ☐
>
> Short Term Detention Order ☐
>
> Exceptional Detention Order ☐

Date of order
(*Insert date of order you wish the
sheriff to recall*)

> 4.

Sheriff Court at which the order was
made, if it was not the court
specified in box 1
(*Insert name of court*)

> 5.

Details of person to whom the order
applies
(*Insert name, address and telephone
number and, if available, e-mail
address and fax number*)

> 6.

If available, a copy of the order which you wish the sheriff to recall should be attached to this
application.

Date and time at which the order
was notified to the person named in
box 6
(*Insert date and exact time of day*)

> 7.

I have an interest in the welfare of the person named in box 6 for the following reasons:

> (*State why you have an interest in the welfare of this person. If necessary, continue on a separate
> sheet of paper*):

I ask the sheriff to recall the order specified in boxes 3 and 4 on the following grounds:

(State why you wish the order to be recalled. If necessary, continue on a separate sheet of paper):

Signed:

Date:

(A solicitor should add his or her name and contact details)

NOTE
[1] As inserted by the Act of Sederunt (Summary Applications, Statutory Applications and Appeals etc. Rules) Amendment (Public Health etc. (Scotland) Act 2008) 2009 (SSI 2009/320) r.2 (effective October 1, 2009).

Rule 3.39.9(3) [1] FORM 53

FORM OF ORDER RECALLING A QUARANTINE ORDER, SHORT TERM DETENTION ORDER OR EXCEPTIONAL DETENTION ORDER

Sheriff Court ....

.... 20 ....

(Court Ref. No.)

The sheriff, having considered an application made under section 59(2) of the Public Health etc. (Scotland) Act 2008 for recall of *the quarantine order/*the short term detention order/*the exceptional detention order which was granted in respect of (*insert details of the person as given in the application*) on (*insert date*),

Refuses the application and Confirms the said order

OR

*Grants the application and Revokes the said order,

And Directs notification of this order (*insert details of method and timing of notice*) to *(*enter details of any other person whom the sheriff considers appropriate*).

**Delete as appropriate*

(*signed*)

Sheriff

NOTE
[1] As inserted by the Act of Sederunt (Summary Applications, Statutory Applications and Appeals etc. Rules) Amendment (Public Health etc. (Scotland) Act 2008) 2009 (SSI 2009/320) r.2 (effective October 1, 2009).

Rule 3.39.12(1) [1] FORM 54

Official use only
Court ref:
Date and time of receipt:

FORM OF NOTE OF APPEAL UNDER SECTION 61 OF THE PUBLIC HEALTH ETC. (SCOTLAND) ACT 2008

NOTES

This form should be used if you wish to appeal to the sheriff under section 61 of the Public Health etc. (Scotland) Act 2008 in relation to an exclusion order OR a restriction order. A copy of the section is set out below.

If you are the person to whom the order applies, you or your solicitor should complete and sign **PART A** and deliver it to the sheriff clerk of the sheriff court at which you wish to appeal.

If you are not the person to whom the order applies but instead are a person who has an interest in the welfare of the person to whom the order applies, you or your solicitor should complete and sign **PART B** and deliver it to the sheriff clerk of the sheriff court at which you wish to appeal.

The form MUST be received by the sheriff clerk before the expiry of 14 days beginning with the day on which the order, modification or, as the case may be, decision against which you wish to appeal was made.

IF YOU ARE UNCERTAIN WHAT ACTION TO TAKE you should consult a solicitor. You may be entitled to legal aid depending on your financial circumstances, and you can get information about legal aid from a solicitor. You may also obtain advice from any Citizens Advice Bureau or other advice agency.

61   Appeal against exclusion orders and restriction orders

(1)   This section applies where a person is subject to—

    (a)   an exclusion order; or
    (b)   a restriction order.

(2)   A person mentioned in subsection (3) may appeal to the sheriff against—

    (a)   the making of the order;
    (b)   any conditions imposed by the order;
    (c)   any modification of the order under section 48(2); or
    (d)   a decision of a health board competent person under section 52(4) or 53(3) not to revoke the order.

(3)   The person referred to in subsection (2) is—

    (a)   the person in relation to whom the order applies; or
    (b)   any person who has an interest in the welfare or such a person.

(4)   An appeal under this section must be made before the expiry of the period of 14 days beginning with the day on which the order, modification or, as the case may be, decision appealed against is made.

(5)   On an appeal under this section, the sheriff may—

    (a)   confirm the order appealed against;
    (b)   modify the order;
    (c)   revoke the order;
    (d)   confirm the decision appealed against;
    (e)   quash that decision;
    (f)   make such other order as the sheriff considers appropriate.

(6)   In subsection (5)(b), "modify" is to be construed in accordance with section 48.

PART A

Sheriff Court
(*Insert name of court*)

> 1.

Details of appellant
(*Insert full name, address and telephone number and, if available, e-mail address and fax number*)

> 2.

Type of order
(*Tick as appropriate to indicate what
type of order the appeal is about*)

3.	Exclusion Order	☐
	Restriction Order	☐

Date of order
(*Insert date of order
indicated in box 3*)

4.

Name and address of person who
made the order
(*Insert name and address. You should
find this on the order*)

5.

If available, a copy of the order specified in boxes 3 and 4 should be attached to this application.

I appeal to the sheriff on the following grounds:

(*State here with reasons
(i) what it is about the order that you wish to appeal. You should specify at least one of the
options given in section 61(2).
(ii) what it is that you want the sheriff to do. You should specify one of the options given in
section 61(5). If you choose the option given in section 61(5)(f) you should specify what order
you wish the sheriff to make.
If necessary, continue on a separate sheet of paper*)

Signed:

Date:

(A solicitor should add his or her name and contact details)

PART B

Sheriff Court
(*Insert name of court*)

1.

Details of appellant
(*Insert full name, address and telephone number and, if available, e-mail address and fax number*)

2.

Type of order
(*Tick as appropriate to indicate what type of order the appeal is about*)

3.   Exclusion Order ☐

Restriction Order ☐

Date of order
(*Insert date of order indicated in box 3*)

4.

Name and address of person who made the order
(*Insert name and address. You should find this on the order*)

5.

Details of person to whom the order applies
(*Insert full name, address and telephone number and, if available, e-mail address and fax number*)

6.

If available, a copy of the order specified in boxes 3 and 4 should be attached to this application.

I have an interest in the welfare of the person named in box 6 for the following reasons:

(*State why you have an interest in the welfare of this person. If necessary, continue on a separate sheet of paper*):

I appeal to the sheriff on the following grounds:

(*State here <u>with reasons</u>*
(i) what it is about the order that you wish to appeal. You should specify at least one of the options given in section 61(2).
(ii) what it is that you want the sheriff to do. You should specify one of the options given in section 61(5). If you choose the option given in section 61(5)(f) you should specify what order you wish the sheriff to make.
If necessary, continue on a separate sheet of paper)

Signed:

Date:

(A solicitor should add his or her name and contact details)

NOTE
[1] As inserted by the Act of Sederunt (Summary Applications, Statutory Applications and Appeals etc. Rules) Amendment (Public Health etc. (Scotland) Act 2008) 2009 (SSI 2009/320) r.2 (effective October 1, 2009).

Rule 3.39.13(1)   [1] FORM 55

FORM OF APPLICATION FOR WARRANT TO ENTER PREMISES AND TAKE STEPS UNDER SECTION 78 OF THE PUBLIC HEALTH ETC. (SCOTLAND) ACT 2008

SHERIFFDOM OF (*insert name of sheriffdom*)

AT (*insert place of sheriff court*)

[A.B.] (*design and state address*), Applicant

Order sought from the court

The applicant applies to the court to grant warrant to (*insert name*), an officer of the local authority

1. to enter the premises at (*insert address of premises to which entry is sought*).

2. to take with him any other person he may authorise and, if he has reasonable cause to expect any serious obstruction in obtaining access, a constable.

3. to direct that those premises (or any part of them) are, or any thing in or on them is to be left undisturbed (whether generally or in particular respects) for so long as the officer considers appropriate.

4. to take any step mentioned in section 73(2) of the Public Health etc. (Scotland) Act 2008 ("the Act") or to remove any thing from the premises for the purpose of taking any such step at any other place.

Statement
**Delete as appropriate*

1. This application is made pursuant to section 78 of the Act.

2. The applicant is a local authority and the said officer is an authorised officer within the meaning give in section 73(8) of the Act.

3. The said premises *are/*are not a dwellinghouse within the meaning given in section 26 of the Act.

4. The said premises are within the jurisdiction of this court.

5. The applicant considers it necessary that the authorised officer should exercise the powers of entry and take the other steps mentioned in section 73(2) of the Act (*insert here a brief statement of reasons*).

*6. The authorised officer

*has been refused entry to the said premises, or

*reasonably anticipates that entry will be refused.

OR

*6 The said premises are premises which the authorised officer is entitled to enter and they are unoccupied.

OR

*6 The said premises are premises which the authorised officer is entitled to enter and the occupier thereof is temporarily absent and there is urgency because (*here state briefly why there is urgency*).

OR

*6 The authorised officer

*has been prevented from taking any steps which he is entitled to take under Part 5 of the Act, or

*reasonably anticipates being prevented from taking any steps that he is entitled to take under Part 5 of the Act.

*7 [*If the said premises are a dwellinghouse*] The authorised officer has in terms of section 77(2) of the Act given 48 hours notice of the proposed entry to a person who appears to be the occupier of the dwellinghouse and the period of notice has expired.

8. In the circumstances narrated the applicant is entitled to the warrant sought and it should be granted accordingly.

(*signed*)

[X.Y.[(*add designation and business address*)

Solicitor for applicant

(*insert date*)

Rule 3.39.13(2) [1] FORM 56

FORM OF WARRANT TO ENTER PREMISES AND TAKE STEPS UNDER PART 5
OF THE PUBLIC HEALTH ETC. (SCOTLAND) ACT 2008

Sheriff Court ....

.... 20 ....

(Court Ref. No.)

*Delete as appropriate

The sheriff, having considered an application made under section 78 of the Public Health etc. (Scotland) Act 2008 ("the Act") *[and any productions lodged therewith], [*and (*where the premises referred to below are a dwellinghouse*) being satisfied that due notice has been given under section 77(2) of the Act and has expired],

Grants warrant authorising the authorised person, (*insert name*):

(a) to enter the premises at (*insert address*)
(b) on entering the premises referred to at paragraph (a), to take any other person authorised by

him and, if he has reasonable cause to expect any serious obstruction in obtaining access, a constable; and

(c) to direct that:
  (i) those premises (or any part of them) are; or
  (ii) any thing in or on those premises is,
  to be left undisturbed (whether generally or in particular respects) for so long as he considers appropriate;

(d) to take any steps mentioned in section 73(2) of the Act; and

(e) to remove any thing from the premises for the purpose of taking any such step at any other place.

(*signed*)

Sheriff

NOTE
  [1] As inserted by the Act of Sederunt (Summary Applications, Statutory Applications and Appeals etc. Rules) Amendment (Public Health etc. (Scotland) Act 2008) 2009 (SSI 2009/320) r.2 (effective October 1, 2009).

Rule 3.39.14(1) [1] FORM 57

FORM OF APPLICATION FOR AN ORDER FOR DISPOSAL OF A BODY UNDER SECTION 93 OF THE PUBLIC HEALTH ETC. (SCOTLAND) ACT 2008

SHERIFFDOM OF (*insert name of sheriffdom*)

AT (*insert place of sheriff court*)

[A.B.] (*design local authority*), Applicant

Order sought from the court
*Delete as appropriate

*The applicant applies to the court to make an order authorising the applicant to remove the body of (*insert name and date of birth of deceased person and address of premises in which the body is being retained*) to a mortuary or other similar premises and to dispose of that body before the expiry of (*insert period sought*).

OR

*The applicant applies to the court to make an order authorising the applicant to dispose of the body of (*insert name and date of birth of deceased person and address of premises in which the body is being retained*) as soon as reasonably practicable.

Statement
*Delete as appropriate

1. This application is made pursuant to section 93 of the Public Health etc. (Scotland) Act 2008.

2. The applicant's area falls within the jurisdiction of the court. The court accordingly has jurisdiction.

3. The body of the said (*insert details of deceased person*) is being retained in (*insert name and address of premises*).

4. The applicant is a local authority in whose area the said premises are situated.

5. The applicant considers that the appropriate arrangements have not been made for the disposal of the said body.

6. The applicant is satisfied that as a result there is a significant risk to public health and it is necessary, to avoid or minimise that risk, for the body to be appropriately disposed of.

*7 The applicant considers that the risk to public health is such that it is necessary for the body to be disposed of immediately because (*insert here brief reasons why immediate disposal of the body is sought*).

8. The applicant attaches to this application a certificate signed by a local authority competent person which indicates that the competent person is satisfied as to the matters mentioned in statements 3, 4, 5 and 6.

9. In the circumstances narrated the applicant is entitled to the order sought and it should be granted accordingly.

(*signed*)

[X.Y.] (*add designation and business address*)

Solicitor for applicant

(*insert date*)

NOTE
[1] As inserted by the Act of Sederunt (Summary Applications, Statutory Applications and Appeals etc. Rules) Amendment (Public Health etc. (Scotland) Act 2008) 2009 (SSI 2009/320) r.2 (effective October 1, 2009).

Rule 3.39.14(2)   [1] FORM 58

FORM OF ORDER FOR DISPOSAL OF A BODY

Sheriff Court ....

.... 20 ....

(Court Ref. No.)

**Delete as appropriate*

The sheriff, having considered an application made under section 93 of the Public Health etc. (Scotland) Act 2008 and any productions lodged,

*Being satisfied that there is a significant risk to public health, makes an order authorising the applicant to remove the body of (*insert details of deceased person*) to a mortuary or other similar premises and to dispose of that body before the expiry of (*insert period sought*).

OR

*Being satisfied that the risk to public health is such that it is necessary for the body of (*insert details of deceased person*) to be disposed of immediately, makes an order authorising the applicant to dispose of the body as soon as reasonably practicable.

(*signed*)

Sheriff

NOTE
[1] As inserted by the Act of Sederunt (Summary Applications, Statutory Applications and Appeals etc. Rules) Amendment (Public Health etc. (Scotland) Act 2008) 2009 (SSI 2009/320) r.2 (effective October 1, 2009).

         SCHEDULE 2

REVOCATIONS

(1) Act of Sederunt	(2) Reference	(3) Extent of Revocation
Codifying Act of Sederunt 1913	SR & O 1913/638	Book L, Chapter X (proceedings under the Representation of the People Act 1983)
Codifying Act of Sederunt 1913	SR & O 1913/638	Book L, Chapter XI (appeals to the Court under the Pilotage Act 1913)
Act of Sederunt Regulating Appeals under the Pharmacy and Poisons Act 1933	SR & O 1935/1313	The whole Act of Sederunt
Act of Sederunt (Betting, Gaming and Lotteries Act Appeals) 1965	1965/1168	The whole Act of Sederunt
Act of Sederunt (Housing Appeals) 1966	1966/845	The whole Act of Sederunt
Act of Sederunt (Sheriff Court Procedure under Part IV of the Housing (Scotland) Act 1969) 1970	1970/1508	The whole Act of Sederunt
Act of Sederunt (Proceedings under Sex Discrimination Act 1975) 1976	1976/374	The whole Act of Sederunt
Act of Sederunt (Proceedings under Sex Discrimination Act 1975) No 2 1976	1976/1851	The whole Act of Sederunt
Act of Sederunt (Proceedings under Sex Discrimination Act 1975) 1977	1977/973	The whole Act of Sederunt
Act of Sederunt (Appeals under the Licensing (Scotland) Act 1976) 1977	1977/1622	The whole Act of Sederunt
Act of Sederunt (Betting and Gaming Appeals) 1978	1978/229	The whole Act of Sederunt
Act of Sederunt (Appeals under the Rating (Disabled Persons) Act 1978) 1979	1979/446	The whole Act of Sederunt
Act of Sederunt (Copyright, Deisgns and Patents) 1990	1990/380	The whole Act of Sederunt
Act of Sederunt (Proceedings in the Sheriff Court under the Model Law on International Commercial Arbitration) 1991	1991/2214	The whole Act of Sederunt
Act of Sederunt (Coal Mining Subsidence Act 1991) 1992	1992/798	The whole Act of Sederunt
Act of Sederunt (Applications under Part III of the Criminal Justice (International Co-operation) Act 1990) 1992	1992/1077	The whole Act of Sederunt
Act of Sederunt (Sheriff Court Summary Application Rules) 1993	1993/3240	The whole Act of Sederunt
Act of Sederunt (Mental Health Rules) 1996	1996/2149	The whole Act of Sederunt
Act of Sederunt (Proceeds of Crime Rules) 1996	1996/2446	The whole Act of Sederunt

Act of Sederunt (Proceedings for Determination of Devolution Issues Rules) 1999

(SI 1999/1347)

The Lords of Council and Session, under and by virtue of the powers conferred on them by section 32 of the Sheriff Courts (Scotland) Act 1971, paragraph 37 of Schedule 6 to the Scotland Act 1998, paragraph 38 of Schedule 10 to the Northern Ireland Act 1998 and paragraph 36 of Schedule 8 to the Government of Wales Act 1998 and of all other powers enabling them in that behalf, having approved, draft rules submitted to them by the Sheriff Court Rules Council in accordance with section 34 of the Sheriff Courts (Scotland) Act 1971, do hereby enact and declare:

Citation
   1.—(1) This Act of Sederunt may be cited as the Act of Sederunt (Proceedings for Determination of Devolution Issues Rules) 1999 and shall come into force on 6th May 1999.
   (2) This Act of Sederunt shall be inserted in the Books of Sederunt.

Interpretation
   [1] **2.**—(1) In this Act of Sederunt—
      "Advocate General" means the Advocate General for Scotland;
      "devolution issue" means a devolution issue within the meaning of—
         (a) Schedule 6 to the Scotland Act 1998;
         (b) Schedule 10 to the Northern Ireland Act 1998; or
         (c) Schedule 9 to the Government of Wales Act 2006;
      "initiating document" means the initial writ, summons, petition or other document by which the proceedings are initiated;
      "relevant authority" means the Advocate General and—
         (a) in the case of a devolution issue within the meaning of Schedule 6, the Lord Advocate;
         (b) in the case of a devolution issue within the meaning of Schedule 10, the Attorney General for Northern Ireland, the First Minister and the deputy First Minister;
         (c) in the case of a devolution issue within the meaning of Schedule 9, the Counsel General to the Welsh Assembly Government.
   (2) Any reference in this Act of Sederunt to a numbered Form shall be construed as a reference to the Form so numbered in Schedule 1 to this Act of Sederunt, and any reference to a rule shall be a reference to the rule so numbered in this Act of Sederunt.

NOTE
   [1] As amended by the Act of Sederunt (Proceedings for Determination of Devolution Issues Rules) Amendment 2007 (SSI 2007/362) r.2(2) (effective August 15, 2007) and by the Act of Sederunt (Devolution Issues) (Appeals and References to the Supreme Court) 2009 (SSI 2009/323) (effective October 1, 2009).

Proceedings for determination of a devolution issue
   3. Where the initiating document contains an averment or crave which raises a devolution issue, the initiating document shall include a crave for warrant to intimate it to the relevant authority, unless he is a party to the action.

Time for raising devolution issue
   4. It shall not be competent for a party to any proceedings to raise a

devolution issue after proof is commenced, unless the sheriff, on cause shown, otherwise determines.

Specification of devolution issue
5.—(1) Any party raising a devolution issue shall specify—
(a) where he initiates the action, in the initiating document;
(b) in the written defences or answers; or
(c) in any other case, in Form 1,
the facts and circumstances and contentions of law on the basis of which it is alleged that the devolution issue arises in sufficient detail to enable the sheriff to determine whether such an issue arises in the proceedings.
(2) Where a pay wishes to raise a devolution issue after lodging any writ mentioned in paragraph (1) above he shall do so—
(a) by way of adjustment or minute of amendment; or
(b) in proceedings in which there is no procedure for adjustment or amendment, in Form 1,
so as to provide specification of the matters mentioned in that paragraph.

Intimation of devolution issue
6.—(1) Intimation of a devolution issue shall be given to the relevant authority (unless he is a party to the proceedings) in accordance with this rule.
(2) Where the devolution issue is raised in the initiating document, the sheriff shall order intimation of the devolution issue as craved in the warrant for service.
(3) In any case other than that described in paragraph (2) above, the party raising the devolution issue shall lodge a motion or incidental application, as the case may be, craving a warrant for intimation of the devolution issue on the relevant authority, and on considering the motion or incidental application, where it appears to the sheriff that a devolution issue arises, he shall order such intimation of the devolution issue.
(4) Where intimation is ordered in accordance with paragraphs (2) or (3) above, such intimation shall be in Form 2 and be made in such manner as the sheriff considers appropriate in the circumstances.
(5) The intimation of a devolution issue shall specify 14 days, or such other period as the sheriff thinks fit, as the period within which the relevant authority may enter appearance as a party in the proceedings.
[1] (6) Where, after determination at first instance of any proceedings in which a devolution issue has been raised under this Act of Sederunt, a party to those proceedings marks an appeal under rule 31.3 or 31.4 of the Ordinary Cause Rules 1993 in Schedule 1 to the Sheriff Courts (Scotland) Act 1907, that party shall, unless the relevant authority is already a party to the proceedings, intimate the note of appeal to the relevant authority together with a notice in Form 2A.

NOTE
[1] As inserted by the Act of Sederunt (Proceedings for Determination of Devolution Issues Rules) Amendment 2007 (SSI 2007/362) r.2(3) (effective August 15, 2007).

Response to intimation of devolution issue
7.—(1) This rule applies where the relevant authority receives intimation of a devolution issue.
(2) Where the relevant authority intends to enter an appearance as a party in the proceedings, he shall lodge a minute stating that he intends to do so.
(3) Upon receipt of the minute lodged in accordance with paragraph (2) above, the sheriff shall sist the relevant authority as a party to the action.
(4) Upon the relevant authority being sisted as a party in accordance with paragraph (3) above, the sheriff shall order the relevant authority to lodge a note of his written submissions in respect of the devolution issue specifying

those matters mentioned in rule 5(1) within 7 days, or such other period as the sheriff thinks fit.

(5) A copy of the minute lodged in accordance with paragraph (2) above and a copy of any note lodged in accordance with paragraph (4) above shall, at the same time as lodging the minute or any note, be intimated by the party lodging such to all other parties in the proceedings.

(6) At any time after the note mentioned in paragraph (4) above has been lodged, the sheriff may regulate such further procedure in the proceedings as he thinks fit.

[1] (7) Where a relevant authority does not take part as a party in the proceedings at first instance the court may allow him to take part as a party in any subsequent appeal to the sheriff principal.

NOTE
[1] As inserted by the Act of Sederunt (Proceedings for Determination of Devolution Issues Rules) Amendment 2007 (SSI 2007/362) r.2(4) (effective August 15, 2007).

Intimation under section 102 of the Scotland Act 1998, section 81 of the Northern Ireland Act 1998 or section 153 of the Government of Wales Act 2006
[1] **8.**—(1) This rule applies to orders made under—
  (a) section 102 of the Scotland Act 1998 (powers of courts or tribunals to vary retrospective decisions);
  (b) section 81 of the Northern Ireland Act 1998 (powers of courts or tribunals to vary retrospective decisions); or
  (c) section 153 of the Government of Wales Act 2006 (power to vary retrospective decisions).

(2) Where the sheriff is considering whether to make an order under any of the provisions mentioned in paragraph (1) above, he shall order intimation of that fact to be given to every person to whom intimation is required to be given by that provision.

(3) The intimation mentioned in paragraph (2) above shall—
  (a) be made forthwith by the sheriff clerk in Form 3 by first class recorded delivery post; and
  (b) specify 14 days, or such other period as the sheriff thinks fit, as the period within which a person may enter an appearance as a party in the proceedings so far as they relate to the making of the order.

NOTE
[1] As amended by the Act of Sederunt (Proceedings for Determination of Devolution Issues Rules) Amendment 2007 (SSI 2007/362) r.2(5)–(6) (effective August 15, 2007).

Response to intimation of order under rule 8
9.—(1) This rule applies where a person receives intimation in accordance with rule 8.

(2) Where a person intends to enter an appearance as a party in the proceedings, he shall lodge a minute stating that he intends to do so.

(3) Upon receipt of the minute lodged in accordance with paragraph (2) above, the sheriff shall sist the person as a party to the action.

(4) Upon a person being sisted as a party in accordance with paragraph (3) above, the sheriff shall order the person to lodge a note of his written submissions in respect of the making of the order within 7 days, or such other period as the sheriff thinks fit.

(5) A copy of the minute lodged in accordance with paragraph (2) above and a copy of any note lodged in accordance with paragraph (4) above shall, at the same time as lodging the minute or any note, be intimated by the party lodging such to all other parties in the proceedings.

(6) At any time after the note mentioned in paragraph (4) above has been lodged, the sheriff may regulate such further procedure in the proceedings as he thinks fit.

Reference of devolution issue to Inner House of the Court of Session or Supreme Court

[1] **10.**—(1) This rule applies where—

(a) any reference of a devolution issue is made to the Inner House of the Court of Session; or

(b) the sheriff is required by the relevant authority to refer a devolution issue to the Supreme Court.

(2) Where a reference is made in accordance with paragraph (1) above, the sheriff shall pronounce an interlocutor giving directions about the manner and time in which the reference is to be drafted and adjusted.

(3) When the reference has been drafted and adjusted in accordance with paragraph (2) above, the sheriff shall sign the reference.

(4) The reference shall include such matters as are prescribed in Schedule 2 to this Act of Sederunt, and shall have annexed to it the interlocutor making the reference and any other order of the court in the cause.

(5) The sheriff clerk shall send a copy of the reference by first class recorded delivery post to—

(a) the parties to the proceedings; and

(b) the relevant authority (if he is not already a party) who may have a potential interest in the proceedings,

and shall certify on the back of the principal reference that a copy has been sent and to whom.

NOTE
[1] As amended by the Act of Sederunt (Devolution Issues) (Appeals and References to the Supreme Court) 2009 (SSI 2009/323) (effective October 1, 2009).

Sist of cause on reference to Inner House of the Court of Session or Supreme Court

[1] **11.** On a reference being made in accordance with rule 10, the cause shall, unless the sheriff when making the reference otherwise orders, be sisted until the devolution issue has been determined.

NOTE
[1] As amended by the Act of Sederunt (Devolution Issues) (Appeals and References to the Supreme Court) 2009 (SSI 2009/323) (effective October 1, 2009).

Interim Orders

[1] **12.**—(1) Notwithstanding the reference of a devolution issue to the Inner House of the Court of Session or to the Supreme Court in accordance with rule 10, the sheriff shall have power to make any interim order which a due regard to the interests of the parties may require.

(2) The sheriff may recall a sist made under rule 11 for the purpose of making the interim order mentioned in paragraph (1) above.

NOTE
[1] As amended by the Act of Sederunt (Devolution Issues) (Appeals and References to the Supreme Court) 2009 (SSI 2009/323) (effective October 1, 2009).

Transmission of reference

13.—(1) The sheriff clerk shall forthwith transmit the principal copy of the reference—

(a) to the Deputy Principal Clerk of the Court of Session; or

[1] (b) together with seven copies, to the Registrar of the Supreme Court, as the case may be.

(2) Unless the sheriff otherwise directs, the principal copy of the reference shall not be transmitted in accordance with paragraph (1) above, where an appeal against the making of the reference is pending.

(3) For the purpose of paragraph (2) above, an appeal shall be treated as pending—

(a) until the expiry of the time for making that appeal; or
(b) where an appeal has been made, until that appeal has been determined.

NOTE
[1] As amended by the Act of Sederunt (Devolution Issues) (Appeals and References to the Supreme Court) 2009 (SSI 2009/323) (effective October 1, 2009).

Procedure following determination on reference or appeal
[1] **14.**—(1) This rule applies where either the Inner House of the Court of Session or the Supreme Court have determined—
(a) a devolution issue referred to them in accordance with rule 10; or
(b) an appeal ma to them.
(2) Upon receipt of the determination of the Inner House of the Court of Session or the Supreme Court, as the case may be, the sheriff clerk shall forthwith place before the sheriff a copy of the determination and the court process.
(3) The sheriff may *ex proprio motu* or shall upon the lodging of a motion or incidental application by any of the parties to the proceedings, pronounce an interlocutor ordering such further procedure as may be required.
(4) Where the sheriff *ex proprio motu* pronounces an interlocutor in accordance with paragraph (3) above, the sheriff clerk shall forthwith intimate a copy of the interlocutor to all parties in the proceedings.

NOTE
[1] As amended by the Act of Sederunt (Devolution Issues) (Appeals and References to the Supreme Court) 2009 (SSI 2009/323) (effective October 1, 2009).

Rule 2(2)   SCHEDULE 1

Rules 5(1)(c) and 5(2)(b)   [1] FORM 1

FORM OF SPECIFICATION OF DEVOLUTION ISSUE

SHERIFFDOM OF (*insert name of sheriffdom*)
AT (*insert place of sheriff court*)   Court Ref No.

In the action of

[A.B.] (*designation and address*)

Pursuer

against

[C.D.] (*designation and address*)

Defender

1. The *Pursuer/Defender (*if other please specify*) wishes to raise a devolution issue in the above action.

[*The Pursuer or Defender or other party, as the case may be, should then insert the following information*—

- *the facts and circumstances and contentions of law on the basis of which it is alleged that the devolution issue arises in sufficient detail to enable the sheriff to determine whether such an issue arises in the proceedings;*
- *details of the relevant law including the relevant provisions of the Scotland Act 1998, the Government of Wales Act 2006 or the Northern Ireland Act 1998, as the case may be; and*
- *the reason why the resolution of the devolution issue is considered necessary for the purpose of disposing of the proceedings*].

Date (*insert date*)   (*Signed*)

Solicitor for the *Pursuer/Defender (*if other please specify*)

*Delete as appropriate

NOTE
[1] As amended by the Act of Sederunt (Proceedings for Determination of Devolution Issues Rules) Amendment 2007 (SSI 2007/362) r.2(7)(a) (effective August 15, 2007).

Rule 6(4)   FORM 2

FORM OF INTIMATION TO RELEVANT AUTHORITY OF A DEVOLUTION ISSUE RAISED IN CIVIL PROCEEDINGS IN THE SHERIFF COURT

To (*insert name and address*)   Court Ref No

1. You are given notice that in the Sheriff Court at (*insert address*),

*an action has been raised which includes a crave in respect of a devolution issue;

*a devolution issue has been raised in an action;

A copy of the * initial writ/pleadings in the case (*as adjusted*) is enclosed. A copy of the interlocutor appointing intimation is also enclosed.

2. If you wish to enter appearance as a party to the proceedings, you must lodge with the Sheriff Clerk (*insert name and address*) a notice in writing stating that you intend to appear as a party in the proceedings. The notice must be lodged within 14 days of (*insert date on which intimation was given*).

Date (*insert date*)

                                   (*Signed*)

                                   Solicitor for *Pursuer/Defender

*Delete as appropriate.

Rule 6(6)   [1] FORM 2A

FORM OF INTIMATION TO RELEVANT AUTHORITY OF APPEAL IN PROCEEDINGS IN WHICH A DEVOLUTION ISSUE HAS BEEN RAISED

To: (*name and address of relevant authority*)   Court Ref No:

You are given notice that an appeal has been marked in proceedings in which a devolution issue has been raised. A copy of the note of appeal is enclosed.

Date (*insert date*)   (*Signed*)

                                   Solicitor for the Appellant
                                   (*add designation and business address*)

NOTE
[1] As inserted by the Act of Sederunt (Proceedings for Determination of Devolution Issues Rules) Amendment 2007 (SSI 2007/362) r.2(7)(b) (effective August 15, 2007).

Rule 8(3)   [1] FORM 3

FORM OF INTIMATION UNDER *SECTION 102 OF THE SCOTLAND ACT 1998/ SECTION 81 OF THE NORTHERN IRELAND ACT 1998/SECTION 153 OF THE GOVERNMENT OF WALES ACT 2006

To (*insert name and address*)   Court Ref No

1. You are given notice that in an action raised in the Sheriff Court at (*insert address*), the sheriff has decided

*that an Act/provision of an Act of the Scottish Parliament is not within the legislative competence of the Parliament;

*a member of the Scottish Executive does not have the power to make, confirm or approve a provision of subordinate legislation he has purported to make, confirm or approve;

A copy of the *initial writ/pleadings in the case (*as adjusted*) is enclosed. A copy of the interlocutor appointing intimation is also enclosed.

2. The sheriff is considering whether to make an order under *section 102 of the Scotland Act 1998/section 81 of the Northern Ireland Act 1998/section 153 of the Government of Wales Act 2006 either removing or limiting the retrospective effect of the decision, or suspending the effect of the decision to allow the defect to be corrected.

3. If you wish to enter appearance as a party to the proceedings so far as they relate to the making of the order, you must lodge with the sheriff clerk (*insert name and address*) a notice in writing stating that you intend to appear as a party in the proceedings. The notice must be lodged within 14 days of (*insert date on which intimation was given*).

Date (*insert date*)   (*Signed*)
                                   Sheriff Clerk

*Delete as appropriate

NOTE
[1] As amended by the Act of Sederunt (Proceedings for Determination of Devolution Issues Rules) Amendment 2007 (SSI 2007/362) r.2(7)(c) (effective August 15, 2007).

Rule 10(4)   [1] SCHEDULE 2

DETAILS TO BE INCLUDED WHERE REFERENCE MADE TO *THE INNER HOUSE OF THE COURT OF SESSION/SUPREME COURT

1. The question(s) referred.

2. The addresses of the parties.

3. A concise statement of the background to the matter, including—
  (i)   the facts of the case, including any relevant findings of fact by the referring court; and
  (ii) the main issues in the case and contentions of the parties with regard to them.

4. The relevant law including the relevant provisions of the *Scotland Act 1998/Government of Wales Act 2006/Northern Ireland Act 1998.

5. The reasons why an answer to the question(s) *is/are considered necessary for the purpose of disposing of the proceedings.

Note: A copy of the interlocutor making the reference and a copy of any judgment in the proceedings must be annexed to the reference.

*Delete as appropriate.

NOTE
[1] As amended by the Act of Sederunt (Proceedings for Determination of Devolution Issues Rules) Amendment 2007 (SSI 2007/362) r.2(8) (effective August 15, 2007) and by the Act of Sederunt (Devolution Issues) (Appeals and References to the Supreme Court) 2009 (SSI 2009/323) (effective October 1, 2009).

Act of Sederunt (Summary Cause Rules) 2002

(SSI 2002/132)

The Lords of Council and Session, under and by virtue of the powers conferred by section 32 of the Sheriff Courts (Scotland) Act 1971 (a) and of all other powers enabling them in that behalf, having approved draft rules submitted to them by the Sheriff Court Rules Council in accordance with section 34 of the said Act of 1971, do hereby enact and declare:

Citation and commencement
     1.—(1) This Act of Sederunt may be cited as the Act of Sederunt (Summary Cause Rules) 2002 and shall come into force on 10th June 2002.
     (2) This Act of Sederunt shall be inserted in the Books of Sederunt.

Summary Cause Rules
     2. The provisions of Schedule 1 to this Act of Sederunt shall have effect

for the purpose of providing rules for a summary cause other than a small claim.

Transitional provision

3. Nothing in Schedule 1 to this Act of Sederunt shall apply to a summary cause commenced before 10th June 2002 and any such action shall proceed according to the law and practice in force immediately before that date.

Revocation

4. The Acts of Sederunt mentioned in column (1) of Schedule 2 to this Act of Sederunt are revoked to the extent specified in column (3) of that Schedule except—

    (a) in relation to any summary cause commenced before 10th June 2002; and

    (b) for the purposes of the Act of Sederunt (Small Claim Rules) 1988.

SCHEDULE 1   **Paragraph 2**

SUMMARY CAUSE RULES 2002

ARRANGEMENT OF RULES

Chapter 1

Citation, interpretation and application

1.1. Citation, interpretation and application

Chapter 2

Representation

2.1. Representation

Chapter 3

Relief from failure to comply with rules

3.1. Dispensing power of sheriff

Chapter 4

Commencement of action

Chapter 5

Register of Summary Causes, service and return of the summons

Chapter 18

Recovery of evidence and attendance of witnesses

Chapter 18A

Vulnerable Witnesses (Scotland) Act 2004

Chapter 19

Challenge of documents

Chapter 20

European Court

Chapter 21

Abandonment

Chapter 22

Decree by default

Chapter 23

Decrees, extracts, execution and variation

23.1. Decree
23.2. Final decree
23.3. Expenses
23.4. Correction of interlocutor or note
23.5. Taxes on funds under control of the court
23.6. Extract of decree
23.7. Charge
23.8. Service of charge where address of defender is unknown
23.9. Diligence on decree in actions for delivery
23.10. Applications in same action for variation, etc. of decree

Chapter 24

Recall of decree

24.1. Recall of decree

Chapter 25

Appeals

25.1. Appeals
25.2. Effect of and abandonment of appeal
25.3. Hearing of appeal
25.4. Appeal in relation to a time to pay direction
25.5. Sheriff to regulate interim possession
25.6. Provisions for appeal in actions for recovery of heritable property to which rule 30.2 applies
25.7. Appeal to the Court of Session

Chapter 26

Management of damages payable to persons under legal disability

26.1. Orders for payment and management of money
26.2. Methods of management
26.3. Subsequent orders
26.4. Management of money paid to sheriff clerk
26.5. Management of money payable to children

Chapter 27

Action of multiplepoinding

27.1. Application of chapter
27.2. Application of other rules
27.3. Pursuer in multiplepoinding
27.4. Parties
27.5. Statement of fund or subject *in medio*
27.6. Response to summons
27.7. Procedure where response lodged
27.8. Objections to fund or subject *in medio*
27.9. Claims hearing
27.10. Procedure at claims hearing
27.11. Advertisement
27.12. Consignation and discharge of holder

Chapter 28

Action of furthcoming

28.1. Expenses included in claim

Chapter 36

Equality enactments

36.1 Application and interpretation
36.2 Intimation to Commission
36.3 Assessor
36.4 [Omitted]
36.5 National Security

Chapter 37

Live links

37.1

Appendix 1

Forms

APPENDIX 2

GLOSSARY

CHAPTER 1

CITATION, INTERPRETATION AND APPLICATION

Citation, interpretation and application
   [1] **1.1**—(1) These Rules may be cited as the Summary Cause Rules 2002.
   (2) In these Rules—
   "the 1907 Act" means the Sheriff Courts (Scotland) Act 1907;
   "the 1971 Act" means the Sheriff Courts (Scotland) Act 1971;
   "the 1975 Act" means the Litigants in Person (Costs and Expenses) Act 1975;
   [2] "the 2004 Act" means the Vulnerable Witnesses (Scotland) Act 2004;
   "authorised lay representative" means a person to whom section 32(1) of the Solicitors (Scotland) Act 1980 (offence to prepare writs) does not apply by virtue of section 32(2)(a) of that Act;
   "enactment" includes an enactment comprised in, or in an instrument made under, an Act of the Scottish Parliament;
   "small claim" has the meaning assigned to it by section 35(2) of the 1971 Act;
   "summary cause" has the meaning assigned to it by section 35(1) of the 1971 Act.
   (3) Any reference to a specified Chapter or rule shall be construed as a reference to the Chapter or rule bearing that number in these Rules, and a reference to a specified paragraph, subparagraph or head shall be construed as a reference to the paragraph, sub-paragraph or head so numbered or lettered in the provision in which that reference occurs.

(4) A form referred to by number means the form so numbered in Appendix 1 to these Rules or a form substantially of the same effect with such variation as circumstances may require.

[3] (4A) In these Rules, references to a solicitor include a reference to a member of a body which has made a successful application under section 25 of the Law Reform (Miscellaneous Provisions) (Scotland) Act 1990 but only to the extent that the member is exercising rights acquired by virtue of section 27 of that Act.

(5) The glossary in Appendix 2 to these Rules is a guide to the meaning of certain legal expressions used in these Rules, but is not to be taken as giving those expressions any meaning which they do not have in law generally.

(6) These Rules shall apply to a summary cause other than a small claim.

NOTES

[1] As amended by the Act of Sederunt (Ordinary Cause, Summary Application, Summary Cause and Small Claim Rules) Amendment (Miscellaneous) 2007 (SSI 2007/6) r.4(2) (effective January 29, 2007).

[2] As inserted by the Act of Sederunt (Ordinary Cause, Summary Application, Summary Cause and Small Claim Rules) Amendment (Vulnerable Witnesses (Scotland) Act 2004) 2007 (SSI 2007/463) r.4(2) (effective November 1, 2007).

[3] As inserted by the Act of Sederunt (Sheriff Court Rules Amendment) (Sections 25 to 29 of the Law Reform (Miscellaneous Provisions) (Scotland) Act 1990) 2009 (SSI 2009/164) r.4(2) (effective May 20, 2009).

CHAPTER 2

REPRESENTATION

Representation
[1] **2.1.**—(1) A party may be represented by—
  (a) an advocate;
  (b) a solicitor;
  (c) a person authorised under any enactment to conduct proceedings in the sheriff court, in accordance with the terms of that enactment; and
  (d) subject to paragraphs (2) and (4), an authorised lay representative.

(2) An authorised lay representative shall not appear in court on behalf of a party except at the hearing held in terms of rule 8.2(1) and, unless the sheriff otherwise directs, any subsequent or other calling where the action is not defended on the merits or on the amount of the sum due.

(3) Subject to the provisions of this rule, the persons referred to in paragraph (1)(c) and (d) above may, in representing a party, do everything for the preparation and conduct of an action as may be done by an individual conducting his own action.

(4) If the sheriff finds that the authorised lay representative is—
  (a) not a suitable person to represent the party; or
  (b) not in fact authorised to do so,
that person must cease to represent the party.

(5) A party may be represented by a person other than an advocate or solicitor at any stage of any proceedings under the Debtors (Scotland) Act 1987, other than appeals to the sheriff principal, if the sheriff is satisfied that that person is a suitable person to represent the party at that stage and is authorised to do so.

NOTE

[1] As amended by the Act of Sederunt (Ordinary Cause, Summary Application, Summary Cause and Small Claim Rules) Amendment (Miscellaneous) 2007 (SSI 2007/6) r.4(3) (effective January 29, 2007).

CHAPTER 3

RELIEF FROM FAILURE TO COMPLY WITH RULES

Dispensing power of sheriff
3.1.—(1) The sheriff may relieve any party from the consequences of any failure to comply with the provisions of these Rules which is shown to be due to mistake, oversight or other excusable cause, on such conditions as he thinks fit.

(2) Where the sheriff relieves a party from the consequences of the failure to comply with a provision in these Rules under paragraph (1), he may make such order as he thinks fit to enable the action to proceed as if the failure to comply with the provision had not occurred.

CHAPTER 4

COMMENCEMENT OF ACTION

Form of summons
4.1.—(1) A summary cause action shall be commenced by summons, which shall be in Form 1.
(2) The form of claim in a summons may be in one of Forms 2, 3, 4, 5, 6, 7, 8 or 9.

Statement of claim
4.2. The pursuer must insert a statement of his claim in the summons to give the defender fair notice of the claim; and the statement must include-
(a) details of the basis of the claim including relevant dates; and
(b) if the claim arises from the supply of goods or services, a description of the goods or services and the date or dates on or between which they were supplied and, where relevant, ordered.

Actions relating to regulated agreements
[1] **4.2A.** In an action which relates to a regulated agreement within the meaning given by section 189(1) of the Consumer Credit Act 1974 the statement of claim shall include an averment that such an agreement exists and details of the agreement.

NOTE
[1] As inserted by the Act of Sederunt (Sheriff Court Rules) (Miscellaneous Amendments) 2009 (SSI 2009/294) r.4 (effective December 1, 2009) as substituted by the Act of Sederunt (Amendment of the Act of Sederunt (Sheriff Court Rules) (Miscellaneous Amendments) 2009) 2009 (SSI 2009/402) (effective November 30, 2009).

Defender's copy summons
4.3. A copy summons shall be served on the defender—
(a) where the action is for, or includes a claim for, payment of money—
   (i) in Form 1a where an application for a time to pay direction under the Debtors (Scotland) Act 1987 or time order under the Consumer Credit Act 1974 may be applied for; or
   (ii) in Form 1b in every other case;
(b) where the action is not for, and does not include a claim for, payment of money, in Form 1c; or
(c) in an action of multiplepoinding, in Form 1d.

Authentication and effect of summons
4.4.—(1) A summons shall be authenticated by the sheriff clerk in some appropriate manner except where—
(a) he refuses to do so for any reason;
(b) the defender's address is unknown; or
(c) a party seeks to alter the normal period of notice specified in rule 4.5(2); or
[1](d) a warrant for arrestment on the dependence, or to found jurisdiction, is sought.
(2) If any of paragraphs (1)(a) to (d) applies, the summons shall be authenticated by the sheriff, if he thinks it appropriate.
(3) The authenticated summons shall be warrant for—
(a) service on the defender; and
(b) where the appropriate warrant has been sought in the summons—
   (i) arrestment on the dependence; or
   (ii) arrestment to found jurisdiction,
as the case may be.
[1,2](4) Where a warrant for arrestment to found jurisdiction, is sought, averments to justify that warrant must be included in the statement of claim.

NOTES
[1] As inserted by the Act of Sederunt (Ordinary Cause, Summary Application and Small Claim Rules) Amendment (Miscellaneous) (SSI 2004/197) r.4(2) (effective May 21, 2004).
[2] As substituted by the Act of Sederunt (Sheriff Court Rules) (Miscellaneous Amendments) 2009 (SSI 2009/294) r.7 (effective December 1, 2009).

Period of notice

4.5.—(1) An action shall proceed after the appropriate period of notice of the summons has been given to the defender prior to the return day.

(2) The appropriate period of notice shall be—

    (a) 21 days where the defender is resident or has a place of business within Europe; or

    (b) 42 days where the defender is resident or has a place of business outwith Europe.

(3) The sheriff may, on cause shown, shorten or extend the period of notice on such conditions as to the form of service as he may direct, but in any case where the period of notice is reduced at least two days' notice must be given.

(4) If a period of notice expires on a Saturday, Sunday, public or court holiday, the period of notice shall be deemed to expire on the next day on which the sheriff clerk's office is open for civil court business.

(5) Notwithstanding the terms of section 4(2) of the Citation Amendment (Scotland) Act 1882, where service is by post the period of notice shall run from the beginning of the day next following the date of posting.

(6) The sheriff clerk shall insert in the summons—

    (a) the return day, which is the last day on which the defender may return a form of response to the sheriff clerk; and

    (b) the calling date, which is the date set for the action to call in court.

[1] (7) The calling date shall be 14 days after the return day.

NOTE

[1] As amended by the Act of Sederunt (Sheriff Court Rules) (Miscellaneous Amendments) 2009 (SSI 2009/294) r.7 (effective December 1, 2009).

Intimation

4.6. Any provision in these Rules requiring papers to be sent to or any intimation to be made to any party, applicant or claimant shall be construed as if the reference to the party, applicant or claimant included a reference to the solicitor representing that party, applicant or claimant.

CHAPTER 5

REGISTER OF SUMMARY CAUSES, SERVICE AND RETURN OF THE SUMMONS

Register of Summary Causes

5.1.—(1) The sheriff clerk shall keep a register of summary cause actions and incidental applications made in such actions, which shall be known as the Register of Summary Causes.

(2) There shall be entered in the Register of Summary Causes a note of all actions, together with a note of all minutes under rule 24.1(1) (recall of decree) and the entry for each action or minute must contain the following particulars where appropriate:-

    (a) the names, designations and addresses of the parties;

    (b) whether the parties were present or absent at any hearing, including an inspection, and the names of their representatives;

    (c) the nature of the action;

    (d) the amount of any claim;

    (e) the date of issue of the summons;

    (f) the method of service;

    (g) the return day;

    (h) the calling date;

    (i) whether a form of response was lodged and details of it;

    (j) the period of notice if shortened or extended in accordance with rule 4.5(3);

    (k) details of any minute by the pursuer regarding an application for a time to pay direction or time order, or minute by the pursuer requesting decree or other order;

    (l) details of any interlocutors issued;

    (m) details of the final decree and the date of it; and

    (n) details of any variation or recall of a decree.

(3) There shall be entered in the Register of Summary Causes in the entry for the action to which they relate details of incidental applications including, where appropriate—

    (a) whether parties are present or absent at the hearing of the application, and the names of their representatives;

    (b) the nature of the application; and

    (c) the interlocutor issued or order made.

(4) The Register of Summary Causes must be—

(a) authenticated in some appropriate manner by the sheriff in respect of each day any order is made or application determined in an action; and

(b) open for inspection during normal business hours to all concerned without fee.

(5) The Register of Summary Causes may be kept in electronic or documentary form.

Persons carrying on business under trading or descriptive name

5.2.—(1) A person carrying on a business under a trading or descriptive name may sue or be sued in such trading or descriptive name alone.

(2) An extract of—

(a) a decree pronounced in an action; or

(b) a decree proceeding upon any deed, decree arbitral, bond, protest of a bill, promissory note or banker's note or upon any other obligation or document on which execution may proceed, recorded in the sheriff court books, against such person under such trading or descriptive name shall be a valid warrant for diligence against such person.

(3) A summons, decree, charge or other document following upon such summons or decree in an action in which a person carrying on business under a trading or descriptive name sues or is sued in that name may be served—

(a) at any place of business or office at which such business is carried on within the sheriffdom of the sheriff court in which the action is brought; or

(b) if there is no place of business within that sheriffdom, at any place where such business is carried on (including the place of business or office of the clerk or secretary of any company, corporation or association or firm).

Form of service and certificate thereof

5.3.—(1) Subject to rule 5.5 (service where address of defender is unknown), a form of service in Form 11 must be enclosed with the defender's copy summons.

(2) After service has been effected a certificate of execution of service in Form 12 must be prepared and signed by the person effecting service.

(3) When service is by a sheriff officer, the certificate of execution of service must—

(a) be signed by him; and

(b) specify whether the service was personal or, if otherwise, the mode of service and the name of any person to whom the defender's copy summons was delivered.

(4) If service is effected in accordance with rule 5.4(2), the certificate must also contain a statement of—

(a) the mode of service previously attempted; and

(b) the circumstances which prevented such service from being effected.

Service within Scotland by sheriff officer

5.4.—(1) A sheriff officer may validly serve any summons, decree, charge or other document following upon such summons or decree issued in an action by—

(a) personal service; or

(b) leaving it in the hands of—

(i) an inmate at the person's dwelling place; or

(ii) an employee at the person's place of business.

(2) If a sheriff officer has been unsuccessful in effecting service in accordance with paragraph (1), he may, after making diligent inquiries, serve the document—

(a) by depositing it in the person's dwelling place or place of business by means of a letter box or by other lawful means; or

(b) by affixing it to the door of the person's dwelling place or place of business.

(3) Subject to the requirements of rule 6.1 (service of schedule of arrestment), if service is effected in accordance with paragraph (2), the sheriff officer must thereafter send by ordinary post to the address at which he thinks it most likely that the person may be found a letter containing a copy of the document.

(4) In proceedings in or following on an action, it shall be necessary for any sheriff officer to be accompanied by a witness except where service, citation or intimation is to be made by post.

(5) Where the firm which employs the sheriff officer has in its possession—

(a) the document or a copy of it certified as correct by the pursuer's solicitor, the sheriff officer may serve the document upon the defender without having the document or certified copy in his possession (in which case he shall if required to do so by the person on whom service is executed and within a reasonable time of being so required, show the document or certified copy to the person); or

(b) a certified copy of the interlocutor pronounced allowing service of the document, the sheriff officer may serve the document without having in his possession the certified copy interlocutor if he has in his possession a facsimile copy of the certified copy interlocutor (which he shall show, if required, to the person on whom service is executed).

Service on persons whose address is unknown

5.5.—[1] (A1) Subject to rule 6.A7, this rule applies to service where the address of a person is not known.

(1) If the defender's address is unknown to the pursuer and cannot reasonably be ascertained by him, the sheriff may grant warrant to serve the summons—

    (a) by the publication of an advertisement in Form 13 in a newspaper circulating in the area of the defender's last known address; or

    (b) by displaying on the walls of court a notice in Form 14.

(2) Where a summons is served in accordance with paragraph (1), the period of notice, which must be fixed by the sheriff, shall run from the date of publication of the advertisement or display on the walls of court, as the case may be.

(3) If service is to be effected under paragraph (1), the pursuer must lodge a service copy of the summons with the sheriff clerk.

(4) The defender may uplift from the sheriff clerk the service copy of the summons lodged in accordance with paragraph (3).

(5) If display on the walls of court is required under paragraph (1)(b), the pursuer must supply to the sheriff clerk for that purpose a completed copy of Form 14.

(6) In every case where advertisement in a newspaper is required for the purpose of service, a copy of the newspaper containing said advertisement must be lodged with the sheriff clerk.

(7) If service has been made under this rule and thereafter the defender's address becomes known, the sheriff may allow the summons to be amended and, if appropriate, grant warrant for reservice subject to such conditions as he thinks fit.

NOTE

[1] As inserted by the Act of Sederunt (Sheriff Court Rules) (Miscellaneous Amendments) 2009 (SSI 2009/294) r.11 (effective October 1, 2009).

Service by post

5.6.—(A1) [*Repealed by the Act of Sederunt (Sheriff Court Rules) (Miscellaneous Amendments) 2009 (SSI 2009/294) r.11 (effective October 1, 2009).*]

(1) If it is competent to serve or intimate any document or to cite any person by recorded delivery, such service, intimation or citation, must be made by the first class recorded delivery service.

(2) On the face of the envelope used for postal service under this rule, there must be written or printed a notice in Form 15.

(3) The certificate of execution of postal service must have annexed to it any relevant postal receipt.

Service on persons outwith Scotland

5.7.—(1) If any summons, decree, charge or other document following upon such summons or decree, or any charge or warrant, requires to be served outwith Scotland on any person, it must be served in accordance with this rule.

(2) If the person has a known home or place of business in—

    (a) England and Wales, Northern Ireland, the Isle of Man or the Channel Islands; or

    (b) any country with which the United Kingdom does not have a convention providing for service of writs in that country,

the document must be served either—

    (i) by posting in Scotland a copy of the document in question in a registered letter addressed to the person at his residence or place of business; or

    (ii) in accordance with the rules for personal service under the domestic law of the place in which the document is to be served.

(3) Subject to paragraph (4), if the document requires to be served in a country which is a party to the Hague Convention on the Service Abroad of Judicial and Extra-Judicial Documents in Civil or Commercial Matters dated 15th November 1965 or the European Convention on Jurisdiction and Enforcement of Judgments in Civil and Commercial Matters as set out in Schedule 1 or 3C to the Civil Jurisdiction and Judgments Act 1982, it must be served—

    (a) by a method prescribed by the internal law of the country where service is to be effected for the service of documents in domestic actions upon persons who are within its territory;

    (b) by or through a British consular authority at the request of the Secretary of State for Foreign and Commonwealth Affairs;

    (c) by or through a central authority in the country where service is to be effected at the request of the Secretary of State for Foreign and Commonwealth Affairs;

    (d) where the law of the country in which the person resides permits, by posting in

Scotland a copy of the document in a registered letter addressed to the person at his residence; or

(e) where the law of the country in which service is to be effected permits, service by an *huissier*, other judicial officer or competent official of the country where service is to be made.

[1] (4) If the document requires to be served in a country to which the EC Service Regulation applies, service—

(a) may be effected by the methods prescribed in paragraph (3)(b) or (c) only in exceptional circumstances; and

(b) is effected only if the receiving agency has informed the person that acceptance of service may be refused on the ground that the document has not been translated in accordance with paragraph (12).

(5) If the document requires to be served in a country with which the United Kingdom has a convention on the service of writs in that country other than the conventions specified in paragraph (3) or the regulation specified in paragraph (4), it must be served by one of the methods approved in the relevant convention.

(6) Subject to paragraph (9), a document which requires to be posted in Scotland for the purposes of this rule must be posted by a solicitor or a sheriff officer, and the form of service and certificate of execution of service must be in Forms 11 and 12 respectively.

(7) On the face of the envelope used for postal service under this rule there must be written or printed a notice in Form 15.

(8) Where service is effected by a method specified in paragraph (3)(b) or (c), the pursuer must—

(a) send a copy of the summons and warrant for service with form of service attached, or other document, with a request for service to be effected by the method indicated in the request to the Secretary of State for Foreign and Commonwealth Affairs; and

(b) lodge in process a certificate of execution of service signed by the authority which has effected service.

(9) If service is effected by the method specified in paragraph (3)(e), the pursuer must—

(a) send to the official in the country in which service is to be effected a copy of the summons and warrant for service, with citation attached, or other document, with a request for service to be effected by delivery to the defender or his residence; and

(b) lodge in process a certificate of execution of service by the official who has effected service.

(10) Where service is executed in accordance with paragraph (2)(b)(ii) or (3)(a) other than on another party in—

(a) the United Kingdom;

(b) the Isle of Man; or

(c) the Channel Islands, the party executing service must lodge a certificate stating that the form of service employed is in accordance with the law of the place where the service was executed.

(11) A certificate lodged in accordance with paragraph (10) shall be given by a person who is conversant with the law of the country concerned and who—

(a) practises or has practised law in that country; or

(b) is a duly accredited representative of the government of that country.

[2] (12) Every summons or document and every citation and notice on the face of the envelope referred to in paragraph (7) must be accompanied by a translation in an official language of the country in which service is to be executed, unless English is—

(a) an official language of the country in which service is to be executed; or

(b) in a country to which the EC Service Regulation applies, a language of the member state of transmission that is understood by the person on whom service is being executed.

(13) A translation referred to in paragraph (12) must be certified as a correct translation by the person making it and the certificate must contain the full name, address and qualifications of the translator and be lodged along with the execution of such service.

[3] (14) In this rule "the Council Regulation" means Council Regulation (EC) No. 1348/2000 of 29 May 2000 on service in the Member States of judicial and extrajudicial documents in civil or commercial matters as amended from time to time and as applied by the Agreement of 19 October 2005 between the European Community and the Kingdom of Denmark on the service of judicial and extrajudicial documents in civil or commercial matters.

NOTES

[1] As substituted by Act of Sederunt (Ordinary Cause, Summary Application, Summary Cause and Small Claim Rules) Amendment (Miscellaneous) 2004 (SSI 2004/197) r.4(3)(a) (effective May 21, 2004) and amended by the Act of Sederunt (Sheriff Court Rules) (Miscellaneous Amendments) (No.2) 2008 (SSI 2008/365) r.9(a) (effective November 13, 2008).

² As substituted for existing text by the Act of Sederunt (Ordinary Cause, Summary Application, Summary Cause and Small Claim Rules) Amendment (Miscellaneous) 2004 (SSI 2004/197) r.4(3)(b) (effective May 21, 2004) and by the Act of Sederunt (Sheriff Court Rules) (Miscellaneous Amendments) (No.2) 2008 (SSI 2008/365) r.9(a) (effective November 13, 2008).
³ As substituted by the Act of Sederunt (Sheriff Court Rules) (Miscellaneous Amendments) (No.2) 2008 (SSI 2008/365) r.9(b) (effective November 13, 2008).

Endorsation by sheriff clerk of defender's residence not necessary
5.8. Any summons, decree, charge or other document following upon a summons or decree may be served, enforced or otherwise lawfully executed in Scotland without endorsation by a sheriff clerk and, if executed by a sheriff officer, may be so executed by a sheriff officer of the court which granted the summons, or by a sheriff officer of the sheriff court district in which it is to be executed.

Contents of envelope containing defender's copy summons
5.9. Nothing must be included in the envelope containing a defender's copy summons except—
    (a) the copy summons;
    (b) a response or other notice in accordance with these Rules; and
    (c) any other document approved by the sheriff principal.

Re-service
5.10.—(1) If it appears to the sheriff that there has been any failure or irregularity in service upon a defender, the sheriff may order the pursuer to re-serve the summons on such conditions as he thinks fit.
(2) If re-service has been ordered in accordance with paragraph (1) or rule 5.5(7) the action shall proceed thereafter as if it were a new action.

Defender appearing barred from objecting to service
5.11.—(1) A person who appears in an action shall not be entitled to state any objection to the regularity of the execution of service or intimation on him and his appearance shall remedy any defect in such service or intimation.
(2) Nothing in paragraph (1) shall preclude a party pleading that the court has no jurisdiction.

Return of summons
5.12.—(1) If any appearance in court is required on the calling date in respect of any party—
    (a) the summons; and
    (b) the relevant certificate of execution of service, shall be returned to the sheriff clerk not later than two days before the calling date.
(2) If no appearance by any party is required on the calling date, only the certificate of execution of service need be returned to the sheriff clerk, not later than two days before the calling date.
(3) If the pursuer fails to proceed in accordance with paragraph (1) or (2) as appropriate, the sheriff may dismiss the action.

CHAPTER 6

INTERIM DILIGENCE

NOTE
¹ Chapter renamed and rr.6.A1–6.A7 inserted by the Act of Sederunt (Sheriff Court Rules Amendment) (Diligence) 2008 (SSI 2008/121) r.6 (effective April 1, 2008).

Interpretation
6.A1. In this Chapter—
    "the 1987 Act" means the Debtors (Scotland) Act 1987; and
    "the 2002 Act" means the Debt Arrangement and Attachment (Scotland) Act 2002.

Application for interim diligence
6.A2.—(1) The following shall be made by incidental application—
    (a) an application under section 15D(1) of the 1987 Act for warrant for diligence by arrestment or inhibition on the dependence of an action or warrant for arrestment on the dependence of an admiralty action;

(b) an application under section 9C of the 2002 Act for warrant for interim attachment.

(2) Such an application must be accompanied by a statement in Form 15a.

(3) A certified copy of an interlocutor granting an application under paragraph (1) shall be sufficient authority for execution of the diligence concerned.

Effect of authority for inhibition on the dependence

6.A3.—(1) Where a person has been granted authority for inhibition on the dependence of an action, a certified copy of the interlocutor granting the application may be registered with a certificate of execution in the Register of Inhibitions and Adjudications.

[1] (2) A notice of a certified copy of an interlocutor granting authority for inhibition under rule 6.A2 may be registered in the Register of Inhibitions and Adjudications; and such registration is to have the same effect as registration of a notice of inhibition under section 155(2) of the Titles to Land Consolidation (Scotland) Act 1868.

NOTE

[1] As substituted by the Act of Sederunt (Sheriff Court Rules Amendment) (Diligence) 2009 (SSI 2009/107) r.5 (effective April 22, 2009).

Recall etc of arrestment or inhibition

6.A4.—(1) An application by any person having an interest—
(a) to loose, restrict, vary or recall an arrestment or an interim attachment; or
(b) to recall, in whole or in part, or vary, an inhibition,
shall be made by incidental application.

(2) Paragraph (1) does not apply to an application made orally at a hearing under section 15Kthat has been fixed under section 15E(4) of the Act of 1987.

Incidental applications in relation to interim diligence, etc.

6.A5. An application under Part 1A of the 1987 Act[4] or Part 1A of the 2002 Act other than mentioned above shall be made by incidental application.

Form of schedule of inhibition on the dependence

6.A6. [*Revoked by the Act of Sederunt (Sheriff Court Rules Amendment) (Diligence) 2009 (SSI 2009/107) r.5 (effective April 22, 2009).*]

Service of inhibition on the dependence where address of defender not known

6.A7.—(1) Where the address of a defender is not known to the pursuer, an inhibition shall be deemed to have been served on the defender if the schedule of inhibition is left with or deposited at the office of the sheriff clerk of the sheriff court district where the defender's last known address is located.

(2) Where service of an inhibition on the dependence is executed under paragraph (1), a copy of the schedule of inhibition shall be sent by the sheriff officer by first class post to the defender's last known address.

Form of schedule of arrestment on the dependence

[1] **6.A8.**—(1) An arrestment on the dependence shall be served by serving the schedule of arrestment on the arrestee in Form 15b.

(2) A certificate of execution shall be lodged with the sheriff clerk in Form 15c.

NOTE

[1] As inserted by the Act of Sederunt (Sheriff Court Rules Amendment) (Diligence) 2009 (SSI 2009/107) r.5 (effective April 22, 2009).

Service of schedule of arrestment

6.1. If a schedule of arrestment has not been personally served on an arrestee, the arrestment shall have effect only if a copy of the schedule is also sent by registered post or the first class recorded delivery service to—
(a) the last known place of residence of the arrestee; or
(b) if such place of residence is not known, or if the arrestee is a firm or corporation, to the arrestee's principal place of business if known, or, if not known, to any known place of business of the arrestee,
and the sheriff officer must, on the certificate of execution, certify that this has been done and specify the address to which the copy of the schedule was sent.

Arrestment before service

6.2.—[1] (1) An arrestment to found jurisdiction used prior to service shall cease to have effect, unless the summons is served within 21 days from the date of execution of the arrestment.

(2) When such an arrestment as is referred to in paragraph (1) has been executed, the party using it must forthwith report the execution to the sheriff clerk.

NOTE

[1] As amended by the Act of Sederunt (Sheriff Court Rules Amendment) (Diligence) 2008 (SSI 2008/121) r.6(5) (effective April 1, 2008).

Recall and restriction of arrestment

6.3—(1) The sheriff may order that an arrestment on the dependence of an action or counterclaim shall cease to have effect if the party whose funds or property are arrested—

    (a) pays into court; or

    (b) finds caution to the satisfaction of the sheriff clerk in respect of, the sum claimed together with the sum of £50 in respect of expenses.

(2) Without prejudice to paragraph (1), a party whose funds or property are arrested may at any time apply to the sheriff to exercise his powers to recall or restrict an arrestment on the dependence of an action or counterclaim, with or without consignation or caution.

(3) An application made under paragraph (2) must be intimated by the applicant to the party who instructed the arrestment.

(4) On payment into court in accordance with paragraph (1), or if the sheriff recalls or restricts an arrestment on the dependence of an action in accordance with paragraph (2) and any condition imposed by the sheriff has been complied with, the sheriff clerk must—

    (a) issue to the party whose funds or property are arrested a certificate in Form 16 authorising the release of any sum or property arrested to the extent ordered by the sheriff; and

    (b) send a copy of the certificate to—

        (i) the party who instructed the arrestment; and

        (ii) the party who has possession of the funds or property that are arrested.

CHAPTER 7

UNDEFENDED ACTION

Undefended action

7.1.—(1) Subject to paragraphs (4), (5) and (6), where the defender has not lodged a form of response on or before the return day—

    (a) the action shall not require to call in court on the calling date; and

    (b) the pursuer must lodge a minute in Form 17 before the sheriff clerk's office closes for business on the second day before the calling date.

(2) If the pursuer does not lodge a minute in terms of paragraph (1), the sheriff must dismiss the action.

(3) If the sheriff is not prepared to grant the order requested in Form 17, the sheriff clerk must—

    (a) fix a date, time and place for the pursuer to be heard; and

    (b) inform the pursuer of—

        (i) that date, time and place; and

        (ii) the reasons for the sheriff wishing to hear him.

(4) Where no form of response has been lodged in an action—

    (a) for recovery of possession of heritable property; or

    (b) of sequestration for rent, the action shall call in court on the calling date and the sheriff shall determine the action as he thinks fit.

(5) Where no form of response has been lodged in an action of multiplepoinding the action shall proceed in accordance with rule 27.9(1)(a).

(6) Where no form of response has been lodged in an action of count, reckoning and payment the action shall proceed in accordance with rule 29.2.

(7) If the defender does not lodge a form of response in time or if the sheriff is satisfied that he does not intend to defend the action on the merits or on the amount of the sum due, the sheriff may grant decree with expenses against him.

Application for time to pay direction or time order

7.2.—(1) If the defender admits the claim, he may, where competent—

    (a) make an application for a time to pay direction (including, where appropriate, an application for recall or restriction of an arrestment) or a time order by completing the appropriate part of the form of response contained in the defender's copy summons and lodging it with the sheriff clerk on or before the return day; or

(b) lodge a form of response indicating that he admits the claim and intends to apply orally for a time to pay direction (including, where appropriate, an application for recall or restriction of an arrestment) or time order.

[1] (1A) The sheriff clerk must on receipt forthwith intimate to the pursuer a copy of any response lodged under paragraph (1).

[2] (2) Where the defender has lodged an application in terms of paragraph (1)(a), the pursuer may intimate that he does not object to the application by lodging a minute in Form 18 before the time the sheriff clerk's office closes for business on the day occurring 9 days before the calling date stating that he does not object to the defender's application and seeking decree.

(3) If the pursuer intimates in accordance with paragraph (2) that he does not object to the application—

(a) the sheriff may grant decree on the calling date;
(b) the parties need not attend; and
(c) the action will not call in court.

[2] (4) If the pursuer wishes to oppose the application for a time to pay direction or time order made in accordance with paragraph (1)(a) he must before the time the sheriff clerk's office closes for business on the day occurring 9 days before the calling date—

(a) lodge a minute in Form 19; and
(b) send a copy of that minute to the defender.

(5) Where the pursuer objects to an application in terms of paragraph (1)(a) or the defender has lodged a form of response in accordance with paragraph (1)(b), the action shall call on the calling date when the parties may appear and the sheriff must decide the application and grant decree accordingly.

(6) The sheriff shall decide an application in accordance with paragraph (5) whether or not any of the parties appear.

(7) Where the defender has lodged an application in terms of paragraph (1)(a) and the pursuer fails to proceed in accordance with either of paragraphs (2) or (4) the sheriff may dismiss the claim.

NOTES
[1] As inserted by the Act of Sederunt (Sheriff Court Rules) (Miscellaneous Amendments) 2009 (SSI 2009/294) r.4 (effective December 1, 2009).
[2] As substituted by the Act of Sederunt (Sheriff Court Rules) (Miscellaneous Amendments) 2009 (SSI 2009/294) r.4 (effective December 1, 2009).

Decree in actions to which the Hague Convention or Civil Jurisdiction and Judgements Act 1982 apply
7.3.—(1) If the summons has been served in a country to which the Hague Convention on the Service Abroad of Judicial and Extra-Judicial Documents in Civil or Commercial Matters dated 15th November 1965 applies, decree must not be granted until it is established to the satisfaction of the sheriff that the requirements of Article 15 of that Convention have been complied with.

(2) Where a defender is domiciled in another part of the United Kingdom or in another Contracting State, the sheriff shall not grant decree until it has been shown that the defender has been able to receive the summons in sufficient time to arrange his defence or that all necessary steps have been taken to that end.

(3) For the purposes of paragraph (2)—

(a) the question whether a person is domiciled in another part of the United Kingdom shall be determined in accordance with sections 41 and 42 of the Civil Jurisdiction and Judgments Act 1982;
(b) the question whether a person is domiciled in another Contracting State shall be determined in accordance with Article 52 of the Convention in Schedule 1 or 3C to that Act; and
(c) the term "Contracting State" has the meaning assigned in section 1 of that Act.

CHAPTER 8

DEFENDED ACTION

Response to summons
8.1.—(1) If the defender intends—

(a) to challenge the jurisdiction of the court or the competency of the action;
(b) to defend the action (whether as regards the amount claimed or otherwise); or

(c) state a counterclaim,

he must complete and lodge with the sheriff clerk on or before the return day the form of response contained in the defender's copy summons including a statement of his response which gives fair notice to the pursuer.

(2) The sheriff clerk must upon receipt intimate to the pursuer a copy of any response lodged under paragraph (1).

Procedure in defended action

8.2.—(1) Where the defender has lodged a form of response in accordance with rule 8.1(1) the action will call in court for a hearing.

(2) The hearing shall be held on the calling date.

(3) The sheriff may continue the hearing to such other date as he considers appropriate.

(4) The defender must either be present or be represented at the hearing.

(5) Where the defender—

  (a) does not appear or is not represented; and

  (b) the pursuer is present or is represented,

decree may be granted against the defender in terms of the summons.

(6) Where at the hearing—

  (a) the pursuer does not appear or is not represented; and

  (b) the defender is present or represented, the sheriff shall dismiss the action and may grant decree in terms of any counterclaim.

(7) If all parties fail to appear at the hearing, the sheriff shall, unless sufficient reason appears to the contrary, dismiss the action and any counterclaim.

Purpose of hearing

8.3.—(1) If, at the hearing, the sheriff is satisfied that the action is incompetent or that there is a patent defect of jurisdiction, he must grant decree of dismissal in favour of the defender or, if appropriate, transfer the action in terms of rule 16.1(2).

(2) At the hearing, the sheriff shall—

  (a) ascertain the factual basis of the action and any defence, and the legal basis on which the action and defence are proceeding; and

  (b) seek to negotiate and secure settlement of the action between the parties.

(3) If the sheriff cannot secure settlement of the action between the parties, he shall—

  (a) identify and note on the summons the issues of fact and law which are in dispute;

  (b) note on the summons any facts which are agreed;

  (c) where it appears that the claim as stated or any defence stated in response to it is not soundly based in law in whole or in part, hear parties forthwith on that matter and may grant decree in favour of any party; and

  (d) if satisfied that the claim and any defence have or may have a sound basis in law and that the dispute between the parties depends upon resolution of disputed issues of fact, fix a diet of proof or, alternatively, if satisfied that the claim and any defence have a sound basis in law and that the facts of the case are sufficiently agreed, hear parties forthwith on the merits of the action and may grant decree in whole or in part in favour of any party.

  [1] (e) enquire whether there is or is likely to be a vulnerable witness within the meaning of section 11(1) of the 2004 Act who is to give evidence at any proof or hearing, consider any child witness notice or vulnerable witness application that has been lodged where no order has been made and consider whether any order under section 12(1) of the 2004 Act requires to be made.

(4) Where the sheriff fixes a proof, the sheriff clerk shall make up a folder for the case papers.

NOTE

[1] As inserted by the Act of Sederunt (Ordinary Cause, Summary Application, Summary Cause and Small Claim Rules) Amendment (Vulnerable Witnesses (Scotland) Act 2004) 2007 (SSI 2007/463) r.4(3) (effective November 1, 2007).

Remit to person of skill

8.4.—(1) The sheriff may, on an incidental application by any party or on a joint application, remit to any person of skill, or other person, to report on any matter of fact.

(2) If a remit under paragraph (1) is made by joint application or of consent of all parties, the report of such person shall be final and conclusive with respect to the matter of fact which is the subject of the remit.

(3) If a remit under paragraph (1) is made—

  (a) on the application of one of the parties, the expenses of its execution must, in the first instance, be met by that party; or

(b) on a joint application or of consent of all parties, the expenses must, in the first instance, be met by the parties equally, unless the sheriff otherwise orders.

Inspection and recovery of documents
8.5.—(1) Each party shall, within 28 days after the date of the fixing of a proof, intimate to every other party, and lodge with the sheriff clerk, a list of documents, which are or have been in his possession or control which he intends to use or put in evidence at the proof, including the whereabouts of those documents.

(2) A party who has received a list of documents from another party under paragraph (1) may inspect those documents which are in the possession or control of the party intimating the list at a time and place fixed by that party which is reasonable to both parties.

(3) Nothing in this rule shall affect—
(a) the law relating, or the right of a party to object, to the inspection of a document on the ground of privilege or confidentiality; or
(b) the right of a party to apply under rule 18.1 for a commission and diligence for recovery of documents or under rule 18.3 for an order under section 1 of the Administration of Justice (Scotland) Act 1972.

Exchange of lists of witnesses
8.6.—(1) Within 28 days after the date of the fixing of a proof, each party shall intimate to every other party, and lodge with the sheriff clerk, a list of witnesses, including any skilled witnesses, whom he intends to call to give evidence.

(2) A party who seeks to call as a witness a person not on his list intimated and lodged under paragraph (1) shall, if any other party objects to such a witness being called, seek leave of the sheriff to call that person as a witness; and such leave may be granted on such conditions, if any, as the sheriff thinks fit.

[1] (3) The list of witnesses intimated under paragraph (1) shall include the name, occupation (where known) and address of each intended witness and indicate whether the witness is considered to be a vulnerable witness within the meaning of section 11(1) of the 2004 Act and whether any child witness notice or vulnerable witness application has been lodged in respect of that witness.

NOTE
[1] As amended by the Act of Sederunt (Ordinary Cause, Summary Application, Summary Cause and Small Claim Rules) Amendment (Vulnerable Witnesses (Scotland) Act 2004) 2007 (SSI 2007/463) r.4(4) (effective November 1, 2007).

Exchange of reports of skilled witnesses
8.7.—(1) Not less than 28 days before the diet of proof, a party shall—
(a) disclose to every other party in the form of a written report the substance of the evidence of any skilled person whom he intends to call as a witness; and
(b) lodge a copy of that report in process.

(2) Except on special cause shown, a party may only call as a skilled witness any person the substance of whose evidence has been disclosed in accordance with paragraph (1).

Evidence generally
8.8. Where possible, the parties shall agree photographs, sketch plans, and any statement or document not in dispute.

Notices to admit and notices of non-admission
[1] **8.8A.**—(1) At any time after a form of response has been lodged, a party may intimate to any other party a notice or notices calling on him or her to admit for the purposes of that cause only—
(a) such facts relating to an issue averred in the statement of claim or form of response as may be specified in the notice;
(b) that a particular document lodged with the sheriff clerk and specified in the notice is—
(i) an original and properly authenticated document; or
(ii) a true copy of an original and properly authenticated document.

(2) Where a party on whom a notice is intimated under paragraph (1)—
(a) does not admit a fact specified in the notice, or
(b) does not admit, or seeks to challenge, the authenticity of a document specified in the notice,
he or she must, within 21 days after the date of intimation of the notice under paragraph (1), intimate a notice of non-admission to the party intimating the notice to him or her under paragraph (1) stating that he or she does not admit the fact or document specified.

(3) A party who fails to intimate a notice of non-admission under paragraph (2) will be

deemed to have admitted the fact or document specified in the notice intimated to him or her under paragraph (1); and such fact or document may be used in evidence at a proof if otherwise admissible in evidence, unless the sheriff, on special cause shown, otherwise directs.

(4) The party serving a notice under paragraph (1) or (2) must lodge a copy of it with the sheriff clerk.

(5) A deemed admission under paragraph (3) must not be used—

    (a) against the party by whom it was deemed to be made other than in the cause for the purpose for which it was deemed to be made; or

    (b) in favour of any person other than the party by whom the notice was given under paragraph (1).

(6) The sheriff may, at any time, allow a party to amend or withdraw an admission made by him or her on such conditions, if any, as the sheriff thinks fit.

(7) A party may, at any time, withdraw in whole or in part a notice of non-admission by intimating a notice of withdrawal.

NOTE

[1] As inserted by the Act of Sederunt (Sheriff Court Rules) (Miscellaneous Amendments) 2010 (SSI 2010/279) para.6 (effective July 29, 2010).

Hearing parts of action separately

8.9.—(1) In any action which includes a claim for payment of money, the sheriff may—

    (a) of his own accord; or

    (b) on the incidental application of any party,

order that proof on liability or any specified issue be heard separately from proof on any other issue and determine the order in which the proofs shall be heard.

(2) The sheriff shall pronounce such interlocutor as he thinks fit at the conclusion of the first proof of any action ordered to be heard in separate parts under paragraph (1).

Returning borrowed parts of process before proof

8.10. All parts of process which have been borrowed must be returned to process not later than noon on the day preceding the proof.

Conduct of proof

8.11 The pursuer must lead in the proof unless the sheriff, on the incidental application of any of the parties which has been intimated to the other parties not less than seven days before the diet of proof, directs otherwise.

Administration of oath or affirmation to witness

8.12. The sheriff must administer the oath to a witness in Form 20 or, where the witness elects to affirm, the affirmation in Form 21.

Noting of evidence, etc.

8.13.—(1) The sheriff who presides at the proof may make a note of any facts agreed by the parties since the hearing held in terms of rule 8.2(1).

(2) The parties may, and must if required by the sheriff, lodge a joint minute of admissions of the facts upon which they have reached agreement.

(3) The sheriff must—

    (a) make for his own use notes of the evidence led at the proof, including any evidence the admissibility of which is objected to, and of the nature of any such objection; and

    (b) retain these notes until after any appeal has been disposed of.

Parties to be heard at close of proof

8.14.—(1) After all the evidence has been led relevant to the particular proof, the sheriff must hear parties on the evidence.

(2) At the conclusion of that hearing, the sheriff may—

    (a) pronounce his decision; or

    (b) reserve judgment.

Objections to admissibility of evidence

8.15. If in the course of a proof an objection is made to the admissibility of any evidence and that line of evidence is not abandoned by the party pursuing it, the sheriff must except where—

    (a) he is of the opinion that the evidence is clearly irrelevant or scandalous; or

    (b) it is an objection falling within rule 8.16(1),

note the terms of the objection and allow the evidence to be led reserving the question of its admissibility to be decided by him at the close of the proof.

Incidental appeal against rulings on confidentiality of evidence and production of documents

8.16.—(1) Where a party or any other person objects to the admissibility of oral or documentary evidence on the ground of confidentiality or to the production of a document on any ground, he may, if dissatisfied with the ruling of the sheriff on the objection, express immediately his formal dissatisfaction with the ruling and, with leave of the sheriff, appeal to the sheriff principal.

(2) The sheriff principal shall dispose of an appeal under paragraph (1) with the least possible delay.

(3) Except as provided in paragraph (1), no appeal may be made during a proof against any decision of the sheriff as to the admissibility of evidence or the production of documents.

(4) The appeal referred to in paragraph (1) shall not remove the action from the sheriff who may proceed with the action in relation to any issue which is not dependent on the ruling appealed against.

Application for time to pay direction or a time order in defended action

8.17. A defender in an action which proceeds as defended may, where it is competent to do so, make a incidental application or apply orally at any hearing, at any time before decree is granted, for a time to pay direction (including where appropriate, an order recalling or restricting an arrestment on the dependence) or time order.

Pronouncement of decision

8.18.—(1) If the sheriff pronounces his decision at the end of the hearing held in terms of rule 8.2(1) or any proof, he must state briefly the grounds of his decision, including the reasons for his decision on any question of law or of admissibility of evidence.

(2) If the sheriff pronounces his decision after reserving judgement, he must give to the sheriff clerk within 28 days—

    (a) a statement of his decision; and

    (b) a brief note of the matters mentioned in paragraph (1).

(3) The sheriff clerk must send copies of the documents mentioned in paragraphs (2)(a) and (b) to each of the parties.

CHAPTER 9

INCIDENTAL APPLICATIONS AND SISTS

General

9.1.—(1) Except where otherwise provided, any incidental application in an action may be made—

    (a) orally with the leave of the sheriff during any hearing of the action; or

    (b) by lodging the application in written form with the sheriff clerk.

(2) An application lodged in accordance with paragraph (1)(b) may only be heard after not less than two days' notice has been given to the other party.

(3) Where the party receiving notice of an incidental application lodged in accordance with paragraph (1)(b) intimates to the sheriff clerk and the party making the application that the application is not opposed, the application shall not require to call in court unless the sheriff so directs.

(4) Any intimation made under paragraph (3) shall be made not later than noon on the day before the application is due to be heard.

Application to sist action

9.2.—(1) Where an incidental application to sist an action is made, the reason for the sist—

    (a) shall be stated by the party seeking the sist; and

    (b) shall be recorded in the Register of Summary Causes and on the summons.

(2) Where an action has been sisted, the sheriff may, after giving parties an opportunity to be heard, recall the sist.

CHAPTER 10

COUNTERCLAIM

Counterclaim

10.1.—(1) If a pursuer intends to oppose a counterclaim, he must lodge answers within seven days of the lodging of the form of response.

(2) The pursuer must at the same time as lodging answers intimate a copy of any answers to every other party.

[1] (3) The defender may apply for warrant for interim diligence in respect of a counterclaim.

(4)–(5) [*Repealed by the Act of Sederunt (Sheriff Court Rules) (Miscellaneous Amendments) 2009 (SSI 2009/294) r.11 (effective October 1, 2009).*]

NOTE

[1] As amended by the Act of Sederunt (Sheriff Court Rules) (Miscellaneous Amendments) 2009 (SSI 2009/294) r.11 (effective October 1, 2009).

CHAPTER 11

THIRD PARTY PROCEDURE

Application for third party notice

11.1.—(1) Where in an action a defender claims that—

(a) he has in respect of the subject matter of the action a right of contribution, relief or indemnity against any person who is not a party to the action; or

(b) a person whom the pursuer is not bound to call as a defender should be made a party to the action along with the defender in respect that such person is—

   (i) solely liable, or jointly or jointly and severally liable with the defender to the pursuer in respect of the subject matter of the action; or

   (ii) liable to the defender in respect of the claim arising from or in connection with the liability, if any, of the defender to the pursuer,

he may apply by incidental application for an order for service of a third party notice upon that other person.

(2) An application for service of a third party notice shall be made at the time when the defender lodges a form of response, unless the sheriff on cause shown shall permit a later application.

(3) Where—

(a) a pursuer against whom a counterclaim is made; or

(b) a third party convened in the action,

seeks, in relation to the claim against him, to make against a person who is not a party, a claim mentioned in paragraph (1) as a claim which could be made by a defender against a third party, he shall apply by incidental application for an order for service of a third party notice; and rules 11.2 and 11.3 shall, with the necessary modifications, apply to such a claim as they apply in relation to a counterclaim by a defender.

Procedure

11.2.—(1) If an application in terms of rule 11.1 is granted, the sheriff shall—

(a) fix a date on which he will regulate further procedure; and

(b) grant warrant to serve on the third party—

   (i) a copy of the summons;

   (ii) a copy of the grounds upon which it is claimed that the third party is liable; and

   (iii) a notice in Form 22 and a copy of Form 23.

(2) A copy of the third party notice, and any certificate of execution of service, shall be lodged by the defender before the hearing fixed under paragraph (1)(a).

(3) A third party seeking to answer the claim against him shall complete and lodge the form of response no later than seven days before the hearing fixed under paragraph (1)(a).

(4) The sheriff clerk must upon receipt intimate to the other parties a copy of any response lodged under paragraph (3).

Warrants for diligence on third party notice

11.3.—[2] (1) A defender who applies for an order for service of a third party notice may apply for—

(a) a warrant for arrestment to found jurisdiction;

(b) a warrant for interim diligence,

which would have been permitted had the warrant been sought in an initial writ in a separate action.

[1] (1A) On an application under paragraph (1)(a) being made—

(a) the sheriff may grant the application if he thinks it appropriate; and

(b) the sheriff shall not grant the application unless averments to justify the warrant sought have been made.

(2) A certified copy of the interlocutor granting warrant for diligence shall be sufficient authority for execution of the diligence.

NOTES

[1] As inserted by the Act of Sederunt (Ordinary Cause, Summary Application, Summary Cause and Small Claim Rules) Amendment (Miscellaneous) 2004 (SSI 2004/197) r.4(5) (effective May 21, 2004) and amended by the Act of Sederunt (Sheriff Court Rules) (Miscellaneous Amendments) 2009 (SSI 2009/294) r.11 (effective October 1, 2009).

[2] As substituted by the Act of Sederunt (Sheriff Court Rules) (Miscellaneous Amendments) 2009 (SSI 2009/294) r.11 (effective October 1, 2009).

CHAPTER 12

SUMMARY DECREE

Application of chapter

12.1. This chapter applies to any action other than an action of multiplepoinding.

Application for summary decree

12.2.—(1) A pursuer may at any time after a defender has lodged a form of response apply by incidental application for summary decree against any defender on the ground that there is no defence to the action or any part of it.

(2) In applying for summary decree the pursuer may ask the sheriff to dispose of the whole or part of the subject matter of the action.

(3) The pursuer shall intimate an application under paragraph (1) by registered or recorded delivery post to every other party not less than seven days before the date fixed for the hearing of the application.

(4) On an application under paragraph (1), the sheriff may ordain any party, or a partner, director, officer or office-bearer of any party—

    (a) to produce any relevant document or article; or

    (b) to lodge an affidavit in support of any assertion of fact made in the action or at the hearing of the incidental application.

(5) Notwithstanding the refusal of an application for summary decree, a subsequent application may be made on a change of circumstances.

Summary decree in a counterclaim etc.

12.3. Rule 12.2 shall apply with the necessary modifications to an application by any other party for summary decree.

CHAPTER 13

ALTERATION OF SUMMONS ETC.

Alteration of summons etc.

13.1.—(1) The sheriff may, on the incidental application of a party, allow amendment of the summons, form of response, counterclaim or answers to a counterclaim and adjust the note of disputed issues at any time before final judgment is pronounced on the merits.

(2) In an undefended action, the sheriff may order the amended summons to be re-served on the defender on such period of notice as he thinks fit.

(3) Paragraph (1) includes amendment for the following purposes:-

    (a) increasing or reducing the sum claimed;

    (b) seeking a different remedy from that originally sought;

    (c) correcting or supplementing the designation of a party;

    (d) enabling a party to sue or be sued in a representative capacity; and

    (e) sisting a party in substitution for, or in addition to, the original party.

(4) Where an amendment sists an additional or substitute defender to the action the sheriff shall order such service and regulate further procedure as he thinks fit.

CHAPTER 14

ADDITIONAL DEFENDER

Additional defender

14.1—(1) Any person who has not been called as a defender may apply by incidental application to the sheriff for leave to enter an action as a defender, and to state a defence.

(2) An application under this rule must specify—

    (a) the applicant's title and interest to enter the action; and

    (b) the grounds of the defence which he proposes to state.

(3) On the lodging of an application under this rule—

    (a) the sheriff must appoint a date for hearing the application; and

    (b) the applicant must forthwith serve a copy of the application and of the order for a hearing on the parties to the action.

(4) After hearing the applicant and any party to the action the sheriff may, if he is satisfied that the applicant has shown title and interest to enter the action, grant the application.

(5) Where an application is granted under paragraph (4)—

    (a) the applicant shall be treated as a defender; and

    (b) the sheriff must forthwith consider whether any decision already taken in the action on the issues in dispute between the parties requires to be reconsidered in light of the terms of the application.

[1] CHAPTER 14A

INTERVENTIONS BY THE COMMISSION FOR EQUALITY AND HUMAN RIGHTS

NOTE

  [1] As inserted by the Act of Sederunt (Sheriff Court Rules) (Miscellaneous Amendments) 2008 (SSI 2008/223) r.6(2) (effective July 1, 2008). Originally named Chapter 13B Interventions by the Scottish Commission for Human Rights in a possible drafting error.

Interpretation

14A.1. In this Chapter "the CEHR" means the Commission for Equality and Human Rights.

Interventions by the CEHR

14A.2.—(1) The CEHR may apply to the sheriff for leave to intervene in any summary cause action in accordance with this Chapter.

(2) This Chapter is without prejudice to any other entitlement of the CEHR by virtue of having title and interest in relation to the subject matter of any proceedings by virtue of section 30(2) of the Equality Act 2006 or any other enactment to seek to be sisted as a party in those proceedings.

(3) Nothing in this Chapter shall affect the power of the sheriff to make such other direction as he considers appropriate in the interests of justice.

(4) Any decision of the sheriff in proceedings under this Chapter shall be final and not subject to appeal.

Applications to intervene

14A.3.—(1) An application for leave to intervene shall be by way of minute of intervention in Form 23A and the CEHR shall—

    (a) send a copy of it to all the parties; and

    (b) lodge it in process, certifying that subparagraph (a) has been complied with.

(2) A minute of intervention shall set out briefly—

    (a) the CEHR's reasons for believing that the proceedings are relevant to a matter in connection with which the CEHR has a function;

    (b) the issue in the proceedings which the CEHR wishes to address; and

    (c) the propositions to be advanced by the CEHR and the CEHR's reasons for believing that they are relevant to the proceedings and that they will assist the sheriff.

(3) The sheriff may—

    (a) refuse leave without a hearing;

    (b) grant leave without a hearing unless a hearing is requested under paragraph (4);

    (c) refuse or grant leave after such a hearing.

(4) A hearing, at which the applicant and the parties may address the court on the matters referred to in paragraph (6)(c) may be held if, within 14 days of the minute of intervention being lodged, any of the parties lodges a request for a hearing.

(5) Any diet in pursuance of paragraph (4) shall be fixed by the sheriff clerk who shall give written intimation of the diet to the CEHR and all the parties.

(6) The sheriff may grant leave only if satisfied that—

    (a) the proceedings are relevant to a matter in connection with which the CEHR has a function;

    (b) the propositions to be advanced by the CEHR are relevant to the proceedings and are likely to assist him; and

    (c) the intervention will not unduly delay or otherwise prejudice the rights of the parties, including their potential liability for expenses.

(7) In granting leave the sheriff may impose such terms and conditions as he considers desirable in the interests of justice, including making provision in respect of any additional expenses incurred by the parties as a result of the intervention.

(8) The sheriff clerk shall give written intimation of a grant or refusal of leave to the CEHR and all the parties.

Form of intervention
14A.4.—(1) An intervention shall be by way of a written submission which (including any appendices) shall not exceed 5000 words.

(2) The CEHR shall lodge the submission and send a copy of it to all the parties by such time as the sheriff may direct.

(3) The sheriff may in exceptional circumstances—
  (a) allow a longer written submission to be made;
  (b) direct that an oral submission is to be made.

(4) Any diet in pursuance of paragraph (3)(b) shall be fixed by the sheriff clerk who shall give written intimation of the diet to the CEHR and all the parties.

[1] CHAPTER 14B

INTERVENTIONS BY THE SCOTTISH COMMISSION FOR HUMAN RIGHTS

NOTE
[1] As inserted by the Act of Sederunt (Sheriff Court Rules) (Miscellaneous Amendments) 2008 (SSI 2008/223) r.6(2) (effective July 1, 2008).

Interpretation
14B.1. In this Chapter—
  "the Act of 2006" means the Scottish Commission for Human Rights Act 2006; and
  "the SCHR" means the Scottish Commission for Human Rights.

Applications to intervene
14B.2.—(1) An application for leave to intervene shall be by way of minute of intervention in Form 23B and the SCHR shall—
  (a) send a copy of it to all the parties; and
  (b) lodge it in process, certifying that subparagraph (a) has been complied with.

(2) In granting leave the sheriff may impose such terms and conditions as he considers desirable in the interests of justice, including making provision in respect of any additional expenses incurred by the parties as a result of the intervention.

(3) The sheriff clerk shall give written intimation of a grant or refusal of leave to the SCHR and all the parties.

(4) Any decision of the sheriff in proceedings under this Chapter shall be final and not subject to appeal.

Invitations to intervene
14B.3.—(1) An invitation to intervene under section 14(2)(b) of the Act of 2006 shall be in Form 23C and the sheriff clerk shall send a copy of it to the SCHR and all the parties.

(2) An invitation under paragraph (1) shall be accompanied by—
  (a) a copy of the pleadings in the proceedings; and
  (b) such other documents relating to those proceedings as the sheriff thinks relevant.

(3) In issuing an invitation under section 14(2)(b) of the Act of 2006, the sheriff may impose such terms and conditions as he considers desirable in the interests of justice, including making provision in respect of any additional expenses incurred by the parties as a result of the intervention.

Form of intervention
14B.4.—(1) An intervention shall be by way of a written submission which (including any appendices) shall not exceed 5000 words.

(2) The SCHR shall lodge the submission and send a copy of it to all the parties by such time as the sheriff may direct.

(3) The sheriff may in exceptional circumstances—
  (a) allow a longer written submission to be made;
  (b) direct that an oral submission is to be made.

(4) Any diet in pursuance of paragraph (3)(b) shall be fixed by the sheriff clerk who shall give written intimation of the diet to the SCHR and all the parties.

APPLICATION FOR SIST OF PARTY AND TRANSFERENCE

Application for sist of party and transference

15.1.—(1) If a party dies or becomes legally incapacitated while an action is depending, any person claiming to represent that party or his estate may apply by incidental application to be sisted as a party to the action.

(2) If a party dies or becomes legally incapacitated while an action is depending and the provisions of paragraph (1) are not invoked, any other party may apply by incidental application to have the action transferred in favour of or against, as the case may be, any person who represents that party or his estate.

CHAPTER 16

TRANSFER AND REMIT OF ACTIONS

Transfer to another court

16.1.—(1) The sheriff may transfer an action to any other sheriff court, whether in the same sheriffdom or not, if the sheriff considers it expedient to do so.

(2) If the sheriff is satisfied that the court has no jurisdiction, he may transfer the action to any sheriff court in which it appears to the sheriff that it ought to have been brought.

(3) An action so transferred shall proceed in all respects as if it had been brought originally in the court to which it is transferred.

Remit between procedures

16.2.—(1) If the sheriff makes a drection that an action is to be treated as an ordinary cause, he must, at the time of making that direction—

(a) direct the pursuer to lodge an initial writ, and intimate it to every other party, within 14 days of the date of the direction;

(b) direct the defender to lodge defences within 28 days of the date of the direction; and

(c) fix a date and time for an Options Hearing and that date shall be the first suitable court day occurring not sooner than ten weeks, or such lesser period as he considers appropriate, after the last date for lodging the initial writ.

(2) If the sheriff directs that an ordinary cause or small claim is to be treated as an action under these rules—

(a) he must specify the next step of procedure to be followed in the action; and

(b) in the case of an ordinary cause, the initial writ shall be deemed to be a summary cause summons.

Remit from Court of Session

16.3. On receipt of the process in an action which has been remitted from the Court of Session under section 14 of the Law Reform (Miscellaneous Provisions) (Scotland) Act 1985, the sheriff clerk must—

(a) record the date of receipt in the Register of Summary Causes;

(b) fix a hearing to determine further procedure on the first court day occurring not earlier than 14 days after the date of receipt of the process; and

(c) forthwith send written notice of the date of the hearing fixed under paragraph (b) to each party.

CHAPTER 17

PRODUCTIONS AND DOCUMENTS

Lodging of productions

17.1.—(1) A party who intends to rely at a proof upon any documents or articles in his possession, which are reasonably capable of being lodged with the court, must—

(a) lodge them with the sheriff clerk together with a list detailing the items no later than 14 days before the proof; and

(b) at the same time send a copy of the list to the other party.

(2) The documents referred to in paragraph (1) include any affidavit or other written statement admissible under section 2 (1) of the Civil Evidence (Scotland) Act 1988.

(3) A party lodging a document under this rule must send a copy of it to every other party, unless it is not practicable to do so.

(4) Subject to paragraph (5), only documents or articles produced—

(a) in accordance with paragraph (1) (and, if it was a document to which rule 8.5 (1) applies, was on the list lodged in accordance with that rule);

(b) at a hearing under rule 8.2; or

(c) under rule 18.2 (2) or (3), may be used or put in evidence.

(5) Documents other than those mentioned in paragraph (4) may be used or put in evidence only with the—

(a) consent of the parties; or

(b) permission of the sheriff on cause shown, and on such terms as to expenses or otherwise as to him seem proper.

Copy productions

17.2.—(1) A copy of every production, marked with the appropriate number of process of the principal production, must be lodged for the use of the sheriff at a proof not later than 48 hours before the diet of proof.

(2) Each copy production consisting of more than one sheet must be securely fastened together by the party lodging it.

Borrowing of productions

17.3.—(1) Any productions borrowed must be returned not later than noon on the day preceding the date of the proof.

(2) A receipt for any production borrowed must be entered in the list of productions and that list must be retained by the sheriff clerk.

(3) Subject to paragraph (4), productions may be borrowed only by—

(a) a solicitor; or

(b) his authorised clerk for whom he shall be responsible.

(4) A party litigant or an authorised lay representative may borrow a production only with permission of the sheriff and subject to such conditions as the sheriff may impose.

(5) Productions may be inspected within the office of the sheriff clerk during normal business hours, and copies may be obtained by a party litigant, where practicable, from the sheriff clerk.

Penalty for failure to return productions

17.4.—(1) If a solicitor has borrowed a production and fails to return it for any diet at which it is required, the sheriff may impose upon such solicitor a fine not exceeding £50.

(2) A fine imposed under paragraph (1) shall—

(a) be payable to the sheriff clerk; and

(b) be recoverable by civil diligence.

(3) An order imposing a fine under this rule shall not be subject to review except that the sheriff who granted it may, on cause shown, recall it.

Documents lost or destroyed

17.5.—(1) This rule applies to any—

(a) summons;

(b) form of response;

(c) answers to a counterclaim;

(d) third party notice or answers to a third party notice;

(d) Register of Summary Causes; or

(e) other document lodged with the sheriff clerk in connection with an action.

(2) Where any document mentioned in paragraph (1) is—

(a) lost; or

(b) destroyed,

a copy of it, authenticated in such manner as the sheriff may require, may be substituted and shall, for the purposes of the action including the use of diligence, be equivalent to the original.

Documents and productions to be retained in custody of sheriff clerk

17.6.—(1) This rule applies to all documents or other productions which have at any time been lodged or referred to during a hearing or proof.

(2) The sheriff clerk must retain in his custody any document or other production mentioned in paragraph (1) until—

(a) after the expiry of the period during which an appeal is competent; and

(b) any appeal lodged has been disposed of.

(3) Each party who has lodged productions in an action shall—

(a) after the final determination of the claim, where no appeal has been lodged, within 14 days after the appeal period has expired; or

(b) within 14 days after the disposal of any appeal lodged on the final determination of the action, uplift the productions from the sheriff clerk.

(4) Where any production has not been uplifted as required by paragraph (3), the sheriff clerk shall intimate to—

(a) the solicitor who lodged the production; or
(b) where no solicitor is acting, the party himself or such other party as seems appropriate, that if he fails to uplift the production within 28 days after the date of such intimation, it will be disposed of in such manner as the sheriff directs.

CHAPTER 18

RECOVERY OF EVIDENCE AND ATTENDANCE OF WITNESSES

Diligence for recovery of documents

18.1.—(1) At any time after a summons has been served, a party may make an incidental application in writing to the sheriff to grant commission and diligence to recover documents.

(2) A party who makes an application in accordance with paragraph (1) must list in the application the documents which he wishes to recover.

(3) A copy of the incidental application made under paragraph (1) must be intimated by the applicant to—

(a) every other party; and
(b) where necessary, the Advocate General for Scotland or the Lord Advocate (and if there is any doubt, both).

(4) The Advocate General for Scotland and the Lord Advocate may appear at the hearing of any incidental application under paragraph (1).

(5) The sheriff may grant commission and diligence to recover those documents in the list mentioned in paragraph (2) which he considers relevant to the action.

Optional procedure before executing commission and diligence

18.2.—(1) Any party who has obtained a commission and diligence for the recovery of documents may, at any time before executing it, serve by first class recorded delivery post on the person from whom the documents are sought to be recovered (or on his known solicitor or solicitors) an order with certificate attached in Form 24.

(2) Documents recovered in response to an order under paragraph (1) must be sent to, and retained by, the sheriff clerk who shall, on receiving them, advise the parties that the documents are in his possession and may be examined within his office during normal business hours.

(3) If the party who served the order is not satisfied that full production has been made under the specification, or that adequate reasons for non-production have been given, he may execute the commission and diligence in normal form, notwithstanding his adoption in the first instance of the foregoing procedure by order.

(4) At the commission, the commissioner shall—

(a) administer the appropriate oath or affirmation to any clerk and any shorthand writer appointed for the commission; and
(b) administer to the haver the oath in Form 20, or where the haver elects to affirm, the affirmation in Form 21.

(5) Documents recovered under this rule may be tendered as evidence at any hearing or proof without further formality, and rules 18.4(2), (3) and (4) shall apply to such documents.

Applications for orders under section 1 of the Administration of Justice (Scotland) Act 1972

18.3—(1) An application by a party for an order under section 1 of the Administration of Justice (Scotland) Act 1972, must be made by incidental application in writing.

(2) At the time of lodging an incidental application under paragraph (1), a specification of—

(a) the document or other property sought to be inspected, photographed, preserved, taken into custody, detained, produced, recovered, sampled or experimented with or upon, as the case may be; or
(b) the matter in respect of which information is sought as to the identity of a person who might be a witness or a defender, must be lodged in process.

(3) A copy of the specification lodged under paragraph (2) and the incidental application made under paragraph (1) must be intimated by the applicant to—

(a) every other party;
(b) any third party haver; and
(c) where necessary, the Advocate General for Scotland or the Lord Advocate (and if there is any doubt, both).

(4) If the sheriff grants an incidental application under paragraph (1) in whole or in part, he may order the applicant to find such caution or give such other security as he thinks fit.

(5) The Advocate General for Scotland and the Lord Advocate may appear at the hearing of any incidental application under paragraph (1).

Confidentiality
18.4—(1) Confidentiality may be claimed for any evidence sought to be recovered under rule 18.2 or 18.3.

(2) Where confidentiality is claimed under paragraph (1), the documents or property in respect of which confidentiality is claimed shall be enclosed in a separate, sealed packet.

(3) A sealed packet referred to in paragraph (2) shall not be opened except by authority of the sheriff obtained on the incidental application of the party who sought the commission and diligence or order.

(4) The incidental application made under paragraph (3) must be intimated by the applicant to the party or parties from whose possession the documents specified in the commission and diligence or order were obtained.

(5) Any party received intimation under paragraph (4) may appear at the hearing of the application.

Preservation and obtaining of evidence
18.5—(1) Evidence in danger of being lost may be taken to be retained until required and, if satisfied that it is desirable so to do, the sheriff may, upon the application of any party at any time, either take it himself or grant authority to a commissioner to take it.

(2) The interlocutor granting such a commission shall be sufficient authority for citing the witness to appear before the commission.

(3) The evidence of any witness who—
    (a) is resident beyond the sheriffdom;
    (b) although resident within the sheriffdom, resides at some place remote from the court in which the proof is to be held; or
    (c) is by reason of illness, age, infirmity or other sufficient cause unable to attend the proof, may be taken in the same manner as is provided in paragraph (1).

(4) On special cause shown, evidence may be taken from any witness or haver on a ground other than one mentioned in paragraph (1) or (3).

(5) Evidence taken under paragraph (1), (3) or (4) may be taken down by—
    (a) the sheriff;
    (b) the commissioner; or
    (c) a clerk or shorthand writer nominated by the sheriff or commissioner, and such evidence may be recorded in narrative form or by question and answer as the sheriff or commissioner shall direct and the extended notes of such evidence certified by such clerk or shorthand writer shall be the notes of such oral evidence.

(6) At the commission, the commissioner shall or where the sheriff takes evidence himself, the sheriff shall—
    (a) administer the appropriate oath or affirmation to any clerk and any shorthand writer appointed for the commission; and
    (b) administer to the witness the oath in Form 20, or where the witness elects to affirm, the affirmation in Form 21.

Warrants for production of original documents from public records
18.6—(1) If a party seeks to obtain from the keeper of any public record production of the original of any register or deed in his custody for the purposes of an action, he must apply to the sheriff by incidental application.

(2) Intimation of an incidental application under paragraph (1) must be given to the keeper of the public record concerned at least seven days before the incidental application is lodged.

(3) In relation to a public record kept by the Keeper of the Registers of Scotland or the Keeper of the Records of Scotland—
    (a) where it appears to the sheriff that it is necessary for the ends of justice that an incidental application under this rule should be granted, he must pronounce an interlocutor containing a certificate to that effect; and
    (b) the party applying for production may apply by letter (enclosing a copy of the interlocutor duly certified by the sheriff clerk) addressed to the Deputy Principal Clerk of Session, for an order from the Court of Session authorising the Keeper of the Registers or the Keeper of the Records, as the case may be, to exhibit the original of any register or deed to the sheriff.

(4) The Deputy Principal Clerk of Session must submit the application sent to him under paragraph (3) to the Lord Ordinary in chambers who, if satisfied, shall grant a warrant for production or exhibition of the original register or deed sought.

(5) A certified copy of the warrant granted under paragraph (4) must be served on the keeper of the public record concerned.

(6) The expense of the production or exhibition of such an original register or deed must be met, in the first instance, by the party who applied by incidental application under paragraph (1).

Letter of request

18.7—[1] (1) Subject to paragraph (7), this rule applies to an application for a letter of request to a court or tribunal outside Scotland to obtain evidence of the kind specified in paragraph (2), being evidence obtainable within the jurisdiction of that court or tribunal, for the purpose of an action depending before the sheriff.

(2) An application to which paragraph (1) applies may be made in relation to a request—
- (a) for the examination of a witness;
- (b) for the inspection, photographing, preservation, custody, detention, production or recovery of, or the taking of samples of, or the carrying out of any experiment on or with, a document or other property, as the case may be;
- (c) for the medical examination of any person;
- (d) for the taking and testing of samples of blood from any person; or
- (e) for any other order for obtaining evidence, for which an order could be obtained from the sheriff.

(3) Such an application must be made by minute in Form 25 together with a proposed letter of request in Form 25a.

(4) It shall be a condition of granting a letter of request that any solicitor for the applicant, or a party litigant, as the case may be, is to be personally liable, in the first instance, for the whole expenses which may become due and payable in respect of the letter of request to the court or tribunal obtaining the evidence and to any witness who may be examined for the purpose; and he must consign into court such sum in respect of such expenses as the sheriff thinks fit.

(5) Unless the court or tribunal to which a letter of request is addressed is a court or tribunal in a country or territory—
- (a) where English is an official language; or
- (b) in relation to which the sheriff clerk certifies that no translation is required, then the applicant must, before the issue of the letter of request, lodge in process a translation of that letter and any interrogatories and cross-interrogatories into the official language of that court or tribunal.

(6) The letter of request when issued, any interrogatories and cross-interrogatories and the translations (if any) must be forwarded by the sheriff clerk to the Foreign and Commonwealth Office or to such person and in such manner as the sheriff may direct.

[2] (7) This rule does not apply to any request for the taking of evidence under Council Regulation (EC) No. 1206/2001 of 28th May 2001 on cooperation between the courts of the Member States in the taking of evidence in civil or commercial matters.

NOTES

[1] As amended by the Act of Sederunt (Taking of Evidence in the European Community) 2003 (SSI 2003/601) r.5(2) (effective January 1, 2004).

[2] As inserted by the Act of Sederunt (Taking of Evidence in the European Community) 2003 (SSI 2003/601) r.5(2) (effective January 1, 2004).

Taking of evidence in the European Community

[1] **18.7A.**—(1) This rule applies to any request—
- (a) for the competent court of another Member State to take evidence under Article 1.1(a) of the Council Regulation; or
- (b) that the court shall take evidence directly in another Member State under Article 1.1(b) of the Council Regulation.

(2) An application for a request under paragraph (1) shall be made by minute in Form 25B, together with the proposed request in form A or I (as the case may be) in the Annex to the Council Regulation.

(3) In this rule, "the Council Regulation" means Council Regulation (EC) No. 1206/2001 of 28th May 2001 on cooperation between the courts of the Member States in the taking of evidence in civil or commercial matters.

NOTE

[1] As inserted by the Act of Sederunt (Taking of Evidence in the European Community) 2003 (SSI 2003/601) r.5(3) (effective January 1, 2004).

Citation of witnesses

18.8.—(1) The citation of a witness or haver must be in Form 26 and the certificate of it must be in Form 26a.

(2) A party shall be responsible for securing the attendance of his witnesses or havers at a hearing and shall be personally liable for their expenses.

(3) The summons or the copy served on the defender shall be sufficient warrant for the citation of witnesses and havers.

(4) The period of notice given to witnesses or havers cited in terms of paragraph (3) must be not less than seven days.

(5) A witness or haver shall be cited—
  (a) by registered post or the first class recorded delivery service by the solicitor for the party on whose behalf he is cited; or
  (b) by a sheriff officer—
    (i) personally;
    (ii) by a citation being left with a resident at the person's dwelling place or an employee at his place of business;
    (iii) by depositing it in that person's dwelling place or place of business;
    (iv) by affixing it to the door of that person's dwelling place or place of business; or
    (v) by registered post or the first class recorded delivery service.

(6) Where service is effected under paragraph (5) (b) (iii) or (iv), the sheriff officer shall, as soon as possible after such service, send by ordinary post to the address at which he thinks it most likely that the person may be found, a letter containing a copy of the citation.

Citation of witnesses by party litigants
  18.9.—(1) Where a party to an action is a party litigant he shall—
  (a) not later than 28 days before the diet of proof apply to the sheriff by incidental application to fix caution for expenses in such sum as the sheriff considers reasonable having regard to the number of witnesses he proposes to cite and the period for which they may be required to attend court; and
  (b) before instructing a solicitor or a sheriff officer to cite a witness, find caution in the sum fixed in accordance with paragraph (1).

(2) A party litigant who does not intend to cite all the witnesses referred to in his application under paragraph 1(a), may apply by incidental application for variation of the amount of caution.

Witnesses failing to attend
  18.10.—(1) A hearing must not be adjourned solely on account of the failure of a witness to appear unless the sheriff, on cause shown, so directs.

(2) A witness or haver who fails without reasonable excuse to answer a citation after having been properly cited and offered his travelling expenses if he has asked for them may be ordered by the sheriff to pay a penalty not exceeding £250.

(3) The sheriff may grant decree for payment of a penalty imposed under paragraph (2) above in favour of the party on whose behalf the witness or haver was cited.

(4) The sheriff may grant warrant for the apprehension of the witness or haver and for bringing him to court.

(5) A warrant mentioned in paragraph (4) shall be effective in any sheriffdom without endorsation and the expenses of it may be awarded against the witness or haver.

[1] CHAPTER 18A

VULNERABLE WITNESSES (SCOTLAND) ACT 2004

NOTE
[1] As inserted by the Act of Sederunt (Ordinary Cause, Summary Application, Summary Cause and Small Claim Rules) Amendment (Vulnerable Witnesses (Scotland) Act 2004) 2007 (SSI 2007/463) r.4(5) (effective November 1, 2007).

Interpretation
  18A.1. In this Chapter—
    "child witness notice" has the meaning given in section 12(2) of the 2004 Act;
    "review application" means an application for review of arrangements for vulnerable witnesses pursuant to section 13 of the 2004 Act;
    "vulnerable witness application" has the meaning given in section 12(6) of the 2004 Act.

Child Witness Notice
  18A.2. A child witness notice lodged in accordance with section 12(2) of the 2004 Act shall be in Form 26B.

Vulnerable Witness Application

18A.3. A vulnerable witness application lodged in accordance with section 12(6) of the 2004 Act shall be in Form 26C.

Intimation

18A.4.—(1) The party lodging a child witness notice or vulnerable witness application shall intimate a copy of the child witness notice or vulnerable witness application to all the other parties to the proceedings and complete a certificate of intimation.

(2) A certificate of intimation referred to in paragraph (1) shall be in Form 26D and shall be lodged with the child witness notice or vulnerable witness application.

Procedure on lodging child witness notice or vulnerable witness application

18A.5.—(1) On receipt of a child witness notice or vulnerable witness application, the sheriff may—

(a) make an order under section 12(1) or (6) of the 2004 Act without holding a hearing;

(b) require further information from any of the parties before making any further order;

(c) fix a date for a hearing of the child witness notice or vulnerable witness application.

(2) The sheriff may, subject to any statutory time limits, make an order altering the date of the proof or other hearing at which the child or vulnerable witness is to give evidence and make such provision for intimation of such alteration to all parties concerned as he deems appropriate.

(3) An order fixing a hearing for a child witness notice or vulnerable witness application shall be intimated by the sheriff clerk—

(a) on the day the order is made; and

(b) in such manner as may be prescribed by the sheriff,

to all parties to the proceedings and such other persons as are named in the order where such parties or persons are not present at the time the order is made.

Review of arrangements for vulnerable witnesses

18A.6.—(1) A review application shall be in Form 26E.

(2) Where the review application is made orally, the sheriff may dispense with the requirements of paragraph (1).

Intimation of review application

18A.7.—(1) Where a review application is lodged, the applicant shall intimate a copy of the review application to all other parties to the proceedings and complete a certificate of intimation.

(2) A certificate of intimation referred to in paragraph (1) shall be in Form 26F and shall be lodged together with the review application.

Procedure on lodging a review application

18A.8.—(1) On receipt of a review application, the sheriff may—

(a) if he is satisfied that he may properly do so, make an order under section 13(2) of the 2004 Act without holding a hearing or, if he is not so satisfied, make such an order after giving the parties an opportunity to be heard;

(b) require of any of the parties further information before making any further order;

(c) fix a date for a hearing of the review application.

(2) The sheriff may, subject to any statutory time limits, make an order altering the date of the proof or other hearing at which the child or vulnerable witness is to give evidence and such provision for intimation of such alteration to all parties concerned as he deems appropriate.

(3) An order fixing a hearing for a review application shall be intimated by the sheriff clerk—

(a) on the day the order is made; and

(b) in such manner as may be prescribed by the sheriff,

to all parties to the proceedings and such other persons as are named in the order where such parties or persons are not present at the time the order is made.

Determination of special measures

18A.9. When making an order under section 12(1) or (6) or 13(2) of the 2004 Act the sheriff may, in light thereof, make such further orders as he deems appropriate in all the circumstances.

Intimation of an order under section 12(1) or (6) or 13(2)

18A.10. An order under section 12(1) or (6) or 13(2) of the 2004 Act shall be intimated by the sheriff clerk—

(a) on the day the order is made; and

(b) in such manner as may be prescribed by the sheriff,

to all parties to the proceedings and such other persons as are named in the order where such parties or persons are not present at the time the order is made.

Taking of evidence by commissioner
18A.11.—(1) An interlocutor authorising the special measure of taking evidence by a commissioner shall be sufficient authority for the citing the witness to appear before the commissioner.
(2) At the commission the commissioner shall—
 (a) administer the oath *de fideli administratione* to any clerk appointed for the commission; and
 (b) administer to the witness the oath in Form 20, or where the witness elects to affirm, the affirmation in Form 21.
(3) The commission shall proceed without interrogatories unless, on cause shown, the sheriff otherwise directs.

Commission on interrogatories
18A.12.—(1) Where interrogatories have not been dispensed with, the party citing or intending to cite the vulnerable witness shall lodge draft interrogatories in process.
(2) Any other party may lodge cross-interrogatories.
(3) The interrogatories and cross-interrogatories, when adjusted, shall be extended and returned to the sheriff clerk for approval and the settlement of any dispute as to their contents by the sheriff.
(4) The party who cited the vulnerable witness shall—
 (a) provide the commissioner with a copy of the pleadings (including any adjustments and amendments), the approved interrogatories and any cross-interrogatories and a certified copy of the interlocutor of his appointment;
 (b) instruct the clerk; and
 (c) be responsible in the first instance for the fee of the commissioner and his clerk.
(5) The commissioner shall, in consultation with the parties, fix a diet for the execution of the commission to examine the witness.

Commission without interrogatories
18A.13. Where interrogatories have been dispensed with, the party citing or intending to cite the vulnerable witness shall—
 (a) provide the commissioner with a copy of the pleadings (including any adjustments and amendments) and a certified copy of the interlocutor of his appointment;
 (b) fix a diet for the execution of the commission in consultation with the commissioner and every other party;
 (c) instruct the clerk; and
 (d) be responsible in the first instance for the fees of the commissioner and his clerk.

Lodging of video record and documents
18A.14.—(1) Where evidence is taken on commission pursuant to an order made under section 12(1) or (6) or 13(2) of the 2004 Act the commissioner shall lodge the video record of the commission and relevant documents with the sheriff clerk.
(2) On the video record and any documents being lodged the sheriff clerk shall—
 (a) note—
  (i) the documents lodged;
  (ii) by whom they were lodged; and
  (iii) the date on which they were lodged, and
 (b) intimate what he has noted to all parties concerned.

Custody of video record and documents
18A.15.—(1) The video record and documents referred to in rule 18A.14 shall, subject to paragraph (2), be kept in the custody of the sheriff clerk.
(2) Where the video record of the evidence of a witness is in the custody of the sheriff clerk under this rule and where intimation has been given to that effect under rule 18A.14(2), the name and address of that witness and the record of his evidence shall be treated as being in the knowledge of the parties; and no party shall be required, notwithstanding any enactment to the contrary—
 (a) to include the name of that witness in any list of witnesses; or
 (b) to include the record of his evidence in any list of productions.

Application for leave for party to be present at the commission

18A.16. An application for leave for a party to be present in the room where the commission proceedings are taking place shall be by incidental application..

(2) In rule 37.1(2) (live links) at the end of the definition of "witness" there shall be inserted the following—

", except a vulnerable witness within the meaning of section 11(1) of the 2004 Act.".

(3) In Appendix 1—

  (a) for Form 26 there shall be substituted the form in Part 1 of Schedule 2 to this Act of Sederunt; and

  (b) after Form 26A there shall be inserted the forms set out in Part 2 of Schedule 2 to this Act of Sederunt.

CHAPTER 19

CHALLENGE OF DOCUMENTS

Challenge of documents

19.1.—(1) If a party relies on a deed or other document to support his case, any other party may object to the deed or document without having to bring an action of reduction.

(2) If an objection is made, the sheriff may order the objector, if an action of reduction would otherwise have been competent, to find caution or to consign with the sheriff clerk a sum of money as security.

CHAPTER 20

EUROPEAN COURT

Interpretation of rules 20.2 to 20.5

20.1.—(1) In rules 20.2 to 20.5—

"the European Court" means the Court of Justice of the European Communities;

"reference" means a reference to the European Court for—

  (a) a preliminary ruling under Article 234 of the E.E.C. Treaty, Article 150 of the Euratom Treaty or Article 41 of the E.C.S.C. Treaty; or

  (b) a ruling on the interpretation of the Conventions, as defined in section 1(1) of the Civil Jurisdiction and Judgments Act 1982, under Article 3 of Schedule 2 to that Act.

(2) The expressions "E.E.C. Treaty", "Euratom Treaty" and "E.C.S.C. Treaty" have the meanings assigned respectively in Schedule 1 to the European Communities Act 1972.

Application for reference

20.2.—(1) The sheriff may, on the application of a party or of his own accord make a reference.

(2) A reference must be made in the form of a request for a preliminary ruling of the European Court in Form 27.

Preparation of case for reference

20.3.—(1) If the sheriff decides that a reference shall be made, he must within four weeks draft a reference.

(2) On the reference being drafted, the sheriff clerk must send a copy to each party.

(3) Within four weeks after the date on which copies of the draft have been sent to parties, each party may—

  (a) lodge with the sheriff clerk; and

  (b) send to every other party, a note of any adjustments he seeks to have made in the draft reference.

(4) Within 14 days after the date on which any such note of adjustments may be lodged, the sheriff, after considering any such adjustments, must make and sign the reference.

(5) The sheriff clerk must forthwith intimate the making of the reference to each party.

Sist of action

20.4.—(1) Subject to paragraph (2), on a reference being made, the action must, unless the sheriff when making the reference otherwise orders, be sisted until the European Court has given a preliminary ruling on the question referred to it.

(2) The sheriff may recall a sist made under paragraph (1) for the purpose of making an interim order which a due regard to the interests of the parties may require.

Transmission of reference

20.5. A copy of the reference, certified by the sheriff clerk, must be transmitted by the sheriff clerk to the Registrar of the European Court.

CHAPTER 21

ABANDONMENT

Abandonment of action

21.1.—(1) A pursuer may before an order granting absolvitor or dismissing the action has been pronounced, offer to abandon the action.

(2) Where the pursuer offers to abandon the action in accordance with paragraph (1), the sheriff clerk shall, subject to the approval of the sheriff, fix the amount of the defender's expenses to be paid by the pursuer in accordance with rule 23.3 and the action must be continued to the first appropriate court occurring not sooner than 14 days after the amount has been fixed.

(3) If before the continued diet the pursuer makes payment to the defender of the amount fixed under paragraph (2), the sheriff must dismiss the action unless the pursuer consents to absolvitor.

(4) If before the continued diet the pursuer fails to pay the amount fixed under paragraph (2), the defender shall be entitled to decree of absolvitor with expenses.

CHAPTER 22

DECREE BY DEFAULT

Decree by default

22.1.—(1) If, after a proof has been fixed under rule 8.3(3)(d), a party fails to appear at a hearing where required to do so, the sheriff may grant decree by default.

(2) If all parties fail to appear at a hearing or proof where required to do so, the sheriff must, unless sufficient reason appears to the contrary, dismiss the action and any counterclaim.

(3) If, after a proof has been fixed under rule 8.3(3)(d), a party fails to implement an order of the court, the sheriff may, after giving him an opportunity to be heard, grant decree by default.

(4) The sheriff shall not grant decree by default solely on the ground that a party has failed to appear at the hearing of an incidental application.

[1] CHAPTER 22A

DISMISSAL OF ACTION DUE TO DELAY

NOTE

[1] As inserted by the Act of Sederunt (Sheriff Court Rules) (Miscellaneous Amendments) 2009 (SSI 2009/294) r.15 (effective October 1, 2009).

Dismissal of action due to delay

22A.1.—(1) Any party to an action may, while that action is depending before the court, apply by written incidental application to the court to dismiss the action due to inordinate and inexcusable delay by another party or another party's agent in progressing the action, resulting in unfairness.

[1] (2) An application under paragraph (1) shall include a statement of the grounds on which it is proposed that the application should be allowed.

(3) In determining an application made under this rule, the court may dismiss the action if it appears to the court that—

    (a) there has been an inordinate and inexcusable delay on the part of any party or any party's agent in progressing the action; and

    (b) such delay results in unfairness specific to the factual circumstances, including the procedural circumstances, of that action.

(4) In determining whether or not to dismiss an action under paragraph (3), the court shall take account of the procedural consequences, both for the parties and for the work of the court, of allowing the action to proceed.

(5) Rule 9.1 shall, with the necessary modifications, apply to an application under paragraph (1).

NOTE
[1] As amended by the Act of Sederunt (Sheriff Court Rules) (Miscellaneous Amendments) 2010 (SSI 2010/279) para.7 (effective July 29, 2010).

CHAPTER 23

DECREES, EXTRACTS, EXECUTION AND VARIATION

Decree
23.1. The sheriff must not grant decree against—
   (a) a defender or a third party in respect of a claim; or
   (b) a pursuer in respect of a counterclaim, under any provision of these Rules unless satisfied that a ground of jurisdiction exists.

Final decree
[1] **23.2.** The final decree of the sheriff principal or the sheriff shall be granted, where expenses are awarded, only after expenses have been dealt with in accordance with rules 23.3, 23.3A and 23.3B.

NOTE
[1] As substituted by the Act of Sederunt (Summary Cause Rules) (Amendment) 2002 (SSI 2002/516) r.2(2) (effective January 1, 2003).

Expenses
[1,2] **23.3.**—[3] (1) Subject to rule 23.3A and paragraphs (2) to (4), the sheriff clerk must, with the approval of the sheriff, assess the amount of expenses including the fees and outlays of witnesses awarded in any cause, in accordance with the applicable statutory table of fees.
(2) A party litigant, who is not represented by a solicitor or advocate and who would have been entitled to expenses if he had been so represented, may be awarded any outlays or expenses to which he might be found entitled by virtue of the 1975 Act or any enactment under that Act.
(3) A party who is or has been represented by an authorised lay representative or a person authorised under any enactment to conduct proceedings in the sheriff court and who would have been found entitled to expenses if he had been represented by a solicitor or an advocate may be awarded any outlays or expenses to which a party litigant might be found entitled in accordance with paragraph (2).
(4) A party who is not an individual, and—
     (i) is or has been represented by an authorised lay representative or a person authorised under any enactment to conduct proceedings in the sheriff court;
    (ii) if unrepresented, could not represent itself; and
   (iii) would have been found entitled to expenses if it had been represented by a solicitor or an advocate,
may be awarded any outlays to which a party litigant might be found entitled under the 1975 Act or any enactment made under that Act.
(5) Except where an account of expenses is allowed to be taxed under rule 23.3A, in every case including an appeal where expenses are awarded, the sheriff clerk shall hear the parties or their solicitors on the claims for expenses including fees, if any, and outlays.
(6) Except where the sheriff principal or the sheriff has reserved judgment or where he orders otherwise, the hearing on the claim for expenses must take place immediately upon the decision being pronounced.
(7) When that hearing is not held immediately, the sheriff clerk must—
   (a) fix the date, time and place when he shall hear the parties or their solicitors; and
   (b) give all parties at least 14 days' notice in writing of the hearing so fixed.
(8) The party awarded expenses must—
   (a) lodge his account of expenses in court at least seven days prior to the date of any hearing fixed under paragraph (7); and
   (b) at the same time forward a copy of that account to every other party.
(9) The sheriff clerk must—
   (a) fix the amount of the expenses; and
   (b) report his decision to the sheriff principal or the sheriff in open court for his approval at a diet which the sheriff clerk has intimated to the parties.
(10) The sheriff principal or the sheriff, after hearing parties or their solicitors if objections are stated, must pronounce final decree including decree for payment of expenses as approved by him.

(11) In an appeal, the sheriff may pronounce decree under paragraph (10) on behalf of the sheriff principal.

(12) Failure by—

    (a) any party to comply with any of the foregoing provisions of this rule; or

    (b) the successful party or parties to appear at the hearing on expenses, must be reported by the sheriff clerk to the sheriff principal or the sheriff at a diet which the sheriff clerk has intimated to the parties.

(13) In either of the circumstances mentioned in paragraphs (12)(a) or (b), the sheriff principal or sheriff must, unless sufficient cause be shown, pronounce decree on the merits of the action and find no expenses due to or by any party.

(14) A decree pronounced under paragraph (13) shall be held to be the final decree for the purposes of these Rules.

(15) The sheriff principal or sheriff may, if he thinks fit, on the application of the solicitor of any party to whom expenses may be awarded, made at or before the time of the final decree being pronounced, grant decree in favour of that solicitor for the expenses of the action.

NOTES

  [1] As amended by the Act of Sederunt (Summary Cause Rules) (Amendment) 2002 (SSI 2002/516) r.2(3) (effective January 1, 2003).

  [2] As amended by the Act of Sederunt (Ordinary Cause, Summary Application, Summary Cause and Small Claim Rules) Amendment (Miscellaneous) 2007 (SSI 2007/6) r.4(4) (effective January 29, 2007).

  [3] As amended by the Act of Sederunt (Sheriff Court Rules Amendment) (Sections 25 to 29 of the Law Reform (Miscellaneous Provisions) (Scotland) Act 1990) 2009 (SSI 2009/164) r.4(3) (effective May 20, 2009).

Taxation

  [1] **23.3A.**—(1) Either—

    (a) the sheriff, on his own motion or on the motion of any party; or

    (b) the sheriff clerk on cause shown,

may allow an account of expenses to be taxed by the auditor of court instead of being assessed by the sheriff clerk under rule 23.3.

(2) Where an account of expenses is lodged for taxation, the account and process shall be transmitted by the sheriff clerk to the auditor of court.

(3) The auditor of court shall—

    (a) assign a diet of taxation not earlier than 7 days from the date he receives the account from the sheriff clerk; and

    (b) intimate that diet forthwith from to the party who lodged the account.

(4) The party who lodged the account of expenses shall, on receiving intimation from the auditor of court under paragraph (3)—

    (a) send a copy of the account; and

    (b) intimate the date, time and place of the diet of taxation,

to every other party.

(5) After the account has been taxed, the auditor of court shall transmit the process with the account and his report to the sheriff clerk.

(6) Where the auditor of court has reserved consideration of the account at the date of the taxation, he shall intimate his decision to the parties who attended the taxation.

(7) Where no objections are lodged under rule 23.3B (objections to auditor's report), the sheriff may grant decree for the expenses as taxed.

NOTE

  [1] As inserted by the Act of Sederunt (Summary Cause Rules) (Amendment) 2002 (SSI 2002/516) r.2(4) (effective January 1, 2003).

Objections to auditor's report

  [1] **23.3B.**—(1) A party may lodge a note of objections to an account as taxed only where he attended the diet of taxation.

(2) Such a note shall be lodged within 7 days after—

    (a) the diet of taxation; or

    (b) where the auditor of court reserved consideration of the account under paragraph (6) of rule 23.3A, the date on which the auditor of court intimates his decision under that paragraph.

(3) The sheriff shall dispose of the objection in a summary manner, with or without answers.

NOTE
[1] As inserted by the Act of Sederunt (Summary Cause Rules) (Amendment) 2002 (SSI 2002/516) r.2(4) (effective January 1, 2003).

Correction of interlocutor or note
23.4. At any time before extract, the sheriff may correct any clerical or incidental error in an interlocutor or note attached to it.

Taxes on funds under control of the court
23.5.—(1) Subject to paragraph (2), in an action in which money has been consigned into court under the Sheriff Court Consignations (Scotland) Act 1893, no decree, warrant or order for payment to any person shall be granted until there has been lodged with the sheriff clerk a certificate by an authorised officer of the Inland Revenue stating that all taxes or duties payable to the Commissioners of Inland Revenue have been paid or satisfied.

(2) In an action of multiplepoinding, it shall not be necessary for the grant of a decree, warrant or order for payment under paragraph (1) that all of the taxes or duties payable on the estate of a deceased claimant have been paid or satisfied.

Extract of decree
23.6.—(1) Extract of a decree signed by the sheriff clerk may be issued only after the lapse of 14 days from the granting of the decree unless the sheriff on application orders earlier extract.

(2) In an action (other than an action to which rule 30.2 applies) where an appeal has been lodged, the extract may not be issued until the appeal has been disposed of.

(3) The extract decree—
    (a) may be written on the summons or on a separate paper;
    (b) may be in one of Forms 28 to 28k; and
    (c) shall be warrant for all lawful execution.

Charge
23.7.—(1) The period for payment specified in any charge following on a decree for payment granted in an action shall be—
    (a) 14 days if the person on whom it is served is within the United Kingdom; and
    (b) 28 days if he is outside the United Kingdom or his whereabouts are unknown.

(2) The period in respect of any other form of charge on a decree in an action shall be 14 days.

Service of charge where address of defender is unknown
23.8.—(1) If the address of a defender is not known to the pursuer, a charge shall be deemed to have been served on the defender if it is—
    (a) served on the sheriff clerk of the sheriff court district where the defender's last known address is located; and
    (b) displayed by the sheriff clerk on the walls of court for the period of the charge.

(2) On receipt of such a charge, the sheriff clerk must display it on the walls of court and it must remain displayed for the period of the charge.

(3) The period specified in the charge shall run from the first date on which it was displayed on the walls of court.

(4) On the expiry of the period of charge, the sheriff clerk must endorse a certificate in Form 29 on the charge certifying that it has been displayed in accordance with this rule and must then return it to the sheriff officer by whom service was executed.

Diligence on decree in actions for delivery
23.9.—(1) In an action for delivery, the court may, when granting decree, grant warrant to search for and take possession of goods and to open shut and lockfast places.

(2) A warrant granted under paragraph (1) shall only apply to premises occupied by the defender.

Applications in same action for variation, etc. of decree
23.10.—(1) If by virtue of any enactment the sheriff, without a new action being initiated, may order that—
    (a) a decree granted be varied, discharged or rescinded; or
    (b) the execution of that decree in so far as it has not already been executed be sisted or suspended,
the party requesting the sheriff to make such an order must do so by lodging a minute to that effect, setting out briefly the reasons for the application.

(2) On the lodging of such a minute by the pursuer, the sheriff clerk must grant warrant for service upon the defender (provided that the pursuer has returned the extract decree).

(3) On the lodging of such a minute by the defender, the sheriff clerk must grant warrant for service upon the pursuer ordaining him to return the extract decree and may, where appropriate, grant interim sist of execution of the decree.

(4) Subject to paragraph (5), the minute shall not be heard in court unless seven days' notice of the minute and warrant has been given to the other parties by the party lodging the minute.

(5) The sheriff may, on cause shown, alter the period of seven days referred to in paragraph (4) but may not reduce it to less than two days.

(6) This rule shall not apply to any proceedings under the Debtors (Scotland) Act 1987 or to proceedings which may be subject to the provisions of that Act.

<h2 align="center">CHAPTER 24</h2>

<h3 align="center">RECALL OF DECREE</h3>

Recall of decree

24.1.—(1) A party may apply for recall of a decree granted under rule 7.1 or 8.2(5), (6) or (7) by lodging with the sheriff clerk a minute in Form 30, explaining the party's failure to appear and in the case of—

    (a) a defender; or

    (b) where decree has been granted in respect of a counterclaim, a pursuer, stating, where he has not already done so—

        (i) his proposed defence, in the case of a defender; or

        (ii) his proposed answer, in the case of a pursuer responding to a counterclaim.

(2) A party may apply for recall of a decree in the same action on one occasion only.

(3) Except in relation to an application to which paragraph (4) applies, a minute by a pursuer under paragraph (1) must be lodged within 14 days of the grant of the decree.

(4) A minute lodged by—

    (a) a pursuer in respect of a decree granted in terms of a counterclaim;

    (b) a defender; or

    (c) a third party, shall be lodged—

        (i) if the action was served on the party seeking recall outwith the United Kingdom under rule 5.7, within a reasonable time after he had knowledge of the decree against him or in any event before the expiry of one year from the date of that decree; or

        (ii) in any other case, within 14 days of the execution of a charge or execution of arrestment, whichever first occurs, following on the grant of decree.

(5) On the lodging of a minute for recall of a decree, the sheriff clerk must fix a date, time and place for a hearing of the minute.

(6) If a hearing has been fixed under paragraph (5), the party seeking recall must serve upon the other party not less than seven days before the date fixed for the hearing—

    (a) a copy of the minute in Form 30a; and

    (b) a note of the date, time and place of the hearing.

[1] (7) At a hearing fixed under paragraph (5), the sheriff shall recall the decree so far as not implemented and the hearing shall then proceed as a hearing held under rules 8.2(3) to (7) and 8.3.

(8) A minute for recall of a decree, when lodged and served in terms of this rule, shall have the effect of preventing any further action being taken by the other party to enforce the decree.

(9) On receipt of the copy minute for recall of a decree, any party in possession of an extract decree must return it forthwith to the sheriff clerk.

(10) If it appears to the sheriff that there has been any failure or irregularity in service of the minute for recall of a decree, he may order re-service of the minute on such conditions as he thinks fit.

NOTE

[1] As amended by the Act of Sederunt (Ordinary Cause, Summary Application, Summary Cause and Small Claim Rules) Amendment (Miscellaneous) 2007 (SSI 2007/6) r.4(5) (effective January 29, 2007).

<h2 align="center">CHAPTER 25</h2>

<h3 align="center">APPEALS</h3>

Appeals

25.1.—(1) An appeal to the sheriff principal, other than an appeal to which rule 25.4 applies, must be by note of appeal in Form 31 lodged with the sheriff clerk not later than 14 days after the date of final decree—

    (a) requesting a stated case; and

    (b) specifying the point of law upon which the appeal is to proceed.

(2) The appellant must, at the same time as lodging a note of appeal, intimate a copy of it to every other party.

(3) The sheriff must, within 28 days of the lodging of a note of appeal, issue a draft stated case containing—

    (a) findings in fact and law or, where appropriate, a narrative of the proceedings before him;

    (b) appropriate questions of law; and

    (c) a note stating the reasons for his decisions in law,

and the sheriff clerk must send a copy of the draft stated case to the parties.

(4) In an appeal where questions of admissibility or sufficiency of evidence have arisen, the draft stated case must contain a description of the evidence led at the proof to which these questions relate.

(5) Within 14 days of the issue of the draft stated case—

    (a) a party may lodge with the sheriff clerk a note of any adjustments which he seeks to make;

    (b) a respondent may state any point of law which he wishes to raise in the appeal; and

    (c) the note of adjustment and, where appropriate, point of law must be intimated to every other party.

(6) The sheriff may, on the motion of a party or of his own accord, and must where he proposes to reject any proposed adjustment, allow a hearing on adjustments and may provide for such further procedure under this rule prior to the hearing of the appeal as he thinks fit.

(7) The sheriff must, within 14 days after—

    (a) the latest date on which a note of adjustments has been or may be lodged; or

    (b) where there has been a hearing on adjustments, that hearing, and after considering such note and any representations made to him at the hearing, state and sign the case.

(8) If the sheriff is temporarily absent from duty for any reason, the sheriff principal may extend any period specified in paragraphs (3) or (7) for such period or periods as he considers reasonable.

(9) The stated case signed by the sheriff must include questions of law, framed by him, arising from the points of law stated by the parties and such other questions of law as he may consider appropriate.

(10) After the sheriff has signed the stated case, the sheriff clerk must—

    (a) place before the sheriff principal all documents and productions in the case together with the stated case; and

    (b) send to the parties a copy of the stated case together with a written note of the date, time and place of the hearing of the appeal.

Effect of and abandonment of appeal

25.2.—(1) When a note of appeal has been lodged, it may be insisted on by all other parties in the action although they may not have lodged separate appeals.

(2) After a note of appeal has been lodged, the appellant shall not be at liberty to withdraw it, except—

    (a) with the consent of the other parties which may be incorporated in a joint minute; or

    (b) by leave of the sheriff principal and on such terms as to expenses or otherwise as to him seem proper.

Hearing of appeal

25.3.—(1) The sheriff principal shall hear the parties or their solicitors orally on all matters connected with the appeal including liability for expenses, but if any party moves that the question of liability for expenses be heard after the sheriff principal has given his decision the sheriff principal may grant that motion.

(2) In the hearing of an appeal, a party shall not be allowed to raise questions of law of which notice has not been given except on cause shown and subject to such conditions as to expenses or otherwise as the sheriff principal may consider appropriate.

(3) The sheriff principal may permit a party to amend any question of law or to add any new question in accordance with paragraph (2).

(4) The sheriff principal may—

    (a) adhere to or vary the decree appealed against;

    (b) recall the decree appealed against and substitute another therefor; or

    (c) remit, if he considers it desirable, to the sheriff, for any reason other than to have further evidence led.

(5) At the conclusion of the hearing, the sheriff principal may either pronounce his decision or

reserve judgment in which latter case he must within 28 days thereof give his decision in writing and the sheriff clerk must forthwith intimate it to the parties.

Appeal in relation to a time to pay direction
25.4.—(1) This rule applies to appeals to the sheriff principal or to the Court of Session which relate solely to any application in connection with a time to pay direction.

(2) Rules 25.1, 25.2, 25.3(2) and (3) and 25.7 shall not apply to appeals under this rule.

(3) An application for leave to appeal against a decision in an application for a time to pay direction or any order connected therewith must—
    (a) be made in Form 32 within seven days of that decision, to the sheriff who made the decision; and
    (b) must specify the question of law upon which the appeal is to proceed.

(4) If leave to appeal is granted, the appeal must be lodged in Form 33 and intimated by the appellant to every other party within 14 days of the order granting leave and the sheriff must state in writing his reasons for his original decision.

(5) An appeal under this rule to the sheriff principal shall proceed in accordance with paragraphs (1), (4) and (5) of rule 25.3.

Sheriff to regulate interim possession
25.5—(1) Notwithstanding an appeal, the sheriff shall have power—
    (a) to regulate all matters relating to interim possession;
    (b) to make any order for the preservation of any property to which the action relates or for its sale, if perishable;
    (c) to make any order for the preservation of evidence; or
    (d) to make in his discretion any interim order which a due regard for the interests of the parties may require.

(2) An order under paragraph (1) shall not be subject to review except by the appellate court at the hearing of the appeal.

Provisions for appeal in actions for recovery of heritable property to which rule 30.2 applies
25.6. In an action to which rule 30.2 applies—
    (a) it shall not be competent to shorten or dispense with the period for appeal specified in rule 25.1;
    (b) it shall be competent to appeal within that period for appeal irrespective of the early issue of an extract decree; and
    (c) the lodging of a note of appeal shall not operate so as to suspend diligence unless the sheriff directs otherwise.

Appeal to the Court of Session
25.7.—(1) A certificate that an action is suitable for appeal to the Court of Session may be applied for by completing and lodging an application in Form 34 with the sheriff clerk.

(2) An application made in accordance with paragraph (1) must be lodged within 14 days of the date of the final decree.

(3) The sheriff clerk must put the application before the sheriff principal who, after hearing the parties or their solicitors, shall grant or refuse the certificate.

CHAPTER 26

MANAGEMENT OF DAMAGES PAYABLE TO PERSONS UNDER LEGAL DISABILITY

Orders for payment and management of money
26.1.—(1) In an action of damages in which a sum of money becomes payable, by virtue of a decree or an extra-judicial settlement, to or for the benefit of a person under legal disability (other than a person under the age of 18 years), the sheriff shall make such order regarding the payment and management of that sum for the benefit of that person as he thinks fit.

(2) Any order required under paragraph (1) shall be made on the granting of decree for payment or of absolvitor.

Methods of management
26.2. In making an order under rule 26.1(1), the sheriff may—
    (a) order the money to be paid to—
        (i) the Accountant of Court; or
        (ii) the guardian of the person under legal disability, as trustee, to be applied,

invested or otherwise dealt with and administered under the directions of the sheriff for the benefit of the person under legal disability;

(b) order the money to be paid to the sheriff clerk of the sheriff court district in which the person under legal disability resides, to be applied, invested or otherwise dealt with and administered, under the directions of the sheriff of that district, for the benefit of the person under legal disability; or

(c) order the money to be paid directly to the person under legal disability.

Subsequent orders

26.3.—(1) If the sheriff has made an order under rule 26.1(1), any person having an interest may apply for an order under rule 26.2, or any other order for the payment or management of the money, by incidental application.

(2) An application for directions under rule 26.2(a) or (b) may be made by any person having an interest by incidental application.

Management of money paid to sheriff clerk

26.4.—(1) A receipt in Form 35 by the sheriff clerk shall be a sufficient discharge in respect of the amount paid to him under rules 26.1 to 26.3.

(2) The sheriff clerk shall, at the request of any competent court, accept custody of any sum of money in an action of damages ordered to be paid to, applied, invested or otherwise dealt with by him, for the benefit of a person under legal disability.

(3) Any money paid to the sheriff clerk under rules 26.1 to 26.3 must be paid out, applied, invested or otherwise dealt with by the sheriff clerk only after such intimation, service and enquiry as the sheriff may order.

(4) Any sum of money invested by the sheriff clerk under rules 26.1 to 26.3 must be invested in a manner in which trustees are authorised to invest by virtue of the Trustee Investments Act 1961.

Management of money payable to children

26.5. If the sheriff has made an order under section 13 of the Children (Scotland) Act 1995, an application by a person for an order by virtue of section 11(1)(d) of that Act must be made in writing.

CHAPTER 27

ACTION OF MULTIPLEPOINDING

Application of Chapter

27.1. This Chapter applies to an action of multiplepoinding.

Application of other rules

27.2.—(1) Rule 8.1 shall not apply to an action of multiplepoinding.

(2) Rules 8.2 to 8.17 shall only apply to an action of multiplepoinding in accordance with rule 27.7.

Pursuer in multiplepoinding

27.3. An action of multiplepoinding may be raised by any party holding or having an interest in or claim on the fund or subject *in medio*.

Parties

27.4. The pursuer must call as defenders—

(a) all persons so far as known to him as having an interest in the fund or subject *in medio*; and

(b) where he is not the holder of the fund or subject, the holder of that fund or subject.

Statement of fund or subject in medio

27.5.—(1) Where the pursuer is the holder of the fund or subject *in medio* he shall include a statement of the fund or subject in his statement of claim.

(2) Where the pursuer is not the holder of the fund or subject *in medio*, the holder shall, before the return day—

(a) lodge with the sheriff clerk a statement in Form 5a providing—

(i) a statement of the fund or subject;

(ii) a statement of any claim or lien which he may profess to have on the fund or subject; and

[1] (iii) a list of all persons known to him as having an interest in the fund or subject; and
  (b) intimate the statement in Form 5a to the pursuer, the defenders and all persons listed in the statement as having an interest in the fund or subject.

NOTE
[1] As substituted by SSI 2003/26, r.4(3) (clerical error).

Response to summons
27.6.—(1) If a defender intends to—
  (a) challenge the jurisdiction of the court or the competency of the action;
  (b) object to the extent of the fund or subject *in medio*; or
  (c) make a claim on the fund, he must complete and lodge with the sheriff clerk on or before the return day the form of response contained in the defender's copy summons as appropriate, including a statement of his response which gives fair notice to the pursuer.
  (2) The sheriff clerk must upon receipt intimate to the pursuer a copy of any response lodged under paragraph (1).

Procedure where response lodged
27.7. Where in a form of response a defender states a defence in accordance with rule 27.6(1)(a)—
  (a) the provisions of rules 8.2 to 8.17 shall, with the necessary modifications, apply to the resolution of the issues raised under that sub-paragraph; and
  (b) rules 27.8 to 27.10 shall apply only once those issues have been so dealt with.

Objections to fund or subject in medio
27.8.—(1) If objections to the fund or subject *in medio* have been lodged, the sheriff must, after disposal of any defence—
  (a) fix a hearing; and
  (b) state the order in which the claimants shall be heard at the hearing.
  (2) If no objections to the fund or subject *in medio* have been lodged, or if objections have been lodged and disposed of, the sheriff may approve the fund or subject and if appropriate find the holder liable only in one single payment.

Claims hearing
27.9.—(1) This rule applies where—
  (a) no defence or objection to the extent of the fund or subject *in medio* has been stated;
  (b) any defence stated has been repelled; or
  (c) any such objection stated has been dealt with.
  (2) The sheriff must—
  (a) order claims in Form 5b to be lodged within 14 days; and
  (b) must fix a claims hearing at which all parties may appear or be represented.
  (3) The sheriff clerk must intimate to the parties, the order for claims and the date and time of any claims hearing fixed in terms of paragraph (2).

Procedure at claims hearing
27.10.—(1) If there is no competition between the claimants who appear at the claims hearing, the sheriff may order the holder of the fund or subject *in medio*, or the sheriff clerk if it is consigned with him in terms of rule 27.12, to make it over to the claimants in terms of their claims or otherwise and subject to such provisions as to expenses as he directs.
  (2) If the sheriff is unable at the claims hearing to resolve competing claims, he shall pronounce an order—
  (a) fixing a date, time and place for a further hearing; and
  (b) regulating the nature and scope of the hearing and the procedure to be followed.
  (3) The sheriff may require that evidence be led at the further claims hearing fixed under paragraph (2).
  (4) The sheriff clerk must intimate to all claimants the date, time and place of any hearing fixed under paragraph (2).
  (5) At the conclusion of the claims hearing or the further claims hearing fixed under paragraph (2), the sheriff may either pronounce his decision or reserve judgement in which case he must give his decision in writing within 28 days and the sheriff clerk must forthwith intimate it to the parties.
  (6) In giving his decision under paragraph (5) the sheriff—
  (a) must dispose of the action;
  (b) may order the holder of the fund or subject *in medio*, or the sheriff clerk if it is consigned with him in terms of rule 27.12, to make it over to such claimants and in such quantity or amount as he may determine; and

(c) must deal with all questions of expenses.

Advertisement
27.11. If it appears to the sheriff at any stage in the multiplepoinding that there may be other potential claimants who are not parties to the action, he may order such advertisement or intimation of the order for claims as he thinks proper.

Consignation and discharge of holder
27.12.—(1) At any stage in an action of multiplepoinding the sheriff may order that—
    (a) the fund or subject *in medio* be consigned in the hands of the sheriff clerk; or
    (b) any subject *in medio* be sold and the proceeds of sale consigned in the hands of the sheriff clerk.
(2) After such consignation the holder of the fund or subject may apply for his exoneration and discharge.
(3) The sheriff may allow the holder of the fund or subject, on his exoneration and discharge, his expenses out of the fund as a first charge on the fund.

CHAPTER 28

ACTION OF FURTHCOMING

Expenses included in claim
28.1. The expenses of bringing an action for furthcoming, including the expenses of the arrestment, shall be deemed to be part of the arrestor's claim which may be paid out of the arrested fund or subject.

CHAPTER 29

ACTION OF COUNT, RECKONING AND PAYMENT

Response to summons
29.1. If a defender wishes to admit liability to account in an action for count, reckoning and payment, this must be stated on the form of response.

Accounting hearing
29.2.—(1) This rule applies where in an action of count, reckoning and payment—
    (a) no form of response has been lodged;
    (b) the defender has indicated on the form of response that he admits liability to account; or
    (c) any defence stated has been repelled.
(2) Where paragraph 1(a) or (b) applies, the pursuer must lodge with the sheriff clerk a minute in Form 17 before close of business on the second day before the calling date.
(3) If the pursuer does not lodge a minute in accordance with paragraph (2), the sheriff must dismiss the action.
(4) Where the pursuer has lodged a minute in accordance with paragraph (2), or any defence stated has been repelled, the sheriff shall pronounce an order—
    (a) for the lodging of accounts within 14 days and objections within such further period as the sheriff may direct;
    (b) fixing a date, time and place for an accounting hearing; and
    (c) regulating the nature and scope of the accounting hearing and the procedure to be followed.
(5) The sheriff may require that evidence be led at an accounting hearing fixed under paragraph (4) to prove the accounts and in support of any objection taken.
(6) The sheriff clerk must intimate to all claimants the date, time and place of any hearing fixed under paragraph (4).

CHAPTER 30

RECOVERY OF POSSESSION OF HERITABLE PROPERTY

Action raised under section 38 of the 1907 Act
30.1. An action for the recovery of possession of heritable property made in terms of section 38 of the 1907 Act may be raised by—
    (a) a proprietor;

(b) his factor; or

(c) any other person authorised by law to pursue a process of removing.

Action against persons in possession of heritable property without right or title

30.2.—(1) Subject to paragraph (2), this rule applies only to an action for recovery of possession of heritable property against a person or persons in possession of heritable property without right or title to possess the property.

(2) This rule shall not apply with respect to a person who has or had a title or other right to occupy the heritable property and who has been in continuous occupation since that title or right is alleged to have come to an end.

(3) Where the name of a person in occupation of a heritable property is not known and cannot reasonably be ascertained, the pursuer shall call that person as a defender by naming him as an "occupier".

(4) Where the name of a person in occupation of the heritable property is not known and cannot reasonably be ascertained, the summons shall be served (whether or not it is also served on a named person), unless the sheriff otherwise directs, by an officer of the court—

(a) affixing a copy of the summons and a citation in Form 11 addressed to "the occupiers" to the main door or other conspicuous part of the premises, and if practicable, depositing a copy of each of those documents in the premises; or

(b) in the case of land only, inserting stakes in the ground at conspicuous parts of the occupied land to each of which is attached a sealed transparent envelope containing a copy of the summons and a citation in Form 11 addressed to "the occupiers".

(5) In an action to which this rule applies, the sheriff may in his discretion, and subject to rule 25.6, shorten or dispense with any period of time provided anywhere in these rules.

(6) An application by a party under this rule to shorten or dispense with any period may be made orally and the provisions in rule 9.1 shall not apply, but the sheriff clerk must enter details of any such application in the Register of Summary Causes.

Effect of decree

30.3. When decree for the recovery of possession is granted, it shall have the same force and effect as—

(a) a decree of removing;

(b) a decree of ejection;

(c) a summary warrant of ejection;

(d) a warrant for summary ejection in common form; or

(e) a decree pronounced in a summary application for removing, in terms of sections 36, 37 and 38 respectively of the 1907 Act.

Preservation of defender's goods and effects

[1] **30.4.** When decree is pronounced, the sheriff may give such directions as he deems proper for the preservation of the defender's goods and effects.

NOTE

[1] As amended by the Act of Sederunt (Ordinary Cause, Summary Application, Summary Cause and Small Claim Rules) Amendment (Miscellaneous) 2007 (SSI 2007/6) r.4(6) (effective January 29, 2007).

Action of removing where fixed term of removal

30.5.—(1) Subject to section 21 of the Agricultural Holdings (Scotland) Act 1991—

(a) if the tenant has bound himself to remove by writing, dated and signed—

(i) within 12 months after the term of removal; or

(ii) where there is more than one ish, after the ish first in date to remove, an action of removing may be raised at any time; and

(b) if the tenant has not bound himself, an action of removing may be raised at any time, but—

(i) in the case of a lease of lands exceeding two acres in extent for three years and upwards, an interval of not less than one year nor more than two years must elapse between the date of notice of removal and the term of removal first in date;

(ii) in the case of a lease of lands exceeding two acres in extent, whether written or oral, held from year to year or under tacit relocation, or for any other period less than three years, an interval of not less than six months must elapse between the date of notice of removal and the term of removal first in date; and

(iii) in the case of a house let with or without land attached not exceeding two acres in extent, as also of land not exceeding two acres in extent without houses, as also of mills, fishings, shootings, and all other heritable subjects excepting land exceeding two acres in extent and let for a year or more, 40 days at least must elapse between the date of notice of removal and the term of removal first in date.

(2) In any defended action of removing, the sheriff may order the defender to find caution for violent profits.

Form of notices and letter

30.6.—(1) A notice under section 34, 35 or 36 of the 1907 Act must be in Form 3a.

(2) A notice under section 37 of the 1907 Act must be in Form 3b.

(3) A letter of removal must be in Form 3c.

Giving notice of removal

30.7.—(1) A notice under section 34, 35, 36, 37 or 38 of the 1907 Act may be given by—

  (a) a sheriff officer;

  (b) the person entitled to give such notice; or

  (c) the solicitor or factor of such person,

posting the notice by registered post or the first class recorded delivery service at any post office within the United Kingdom in time for it to be delivered at the address on the notice before the last date on which by law such notice must be given, addressed to the person entitled to receive such notice, and bearing the address of that person at the time, if known, or, if not known, to the last known address of that person.

(2) A sheriff officer may also give notice under any section of the 1907 Act mentioned in paragraph (1) in any manner in which he may serve an initial writ; and, accordingly, rule 5.4 shall, with the necessary modifications, apply to the giving of notice under this paragraph as it applies to service of a summons.

Evidence of notice to remove

30.8.—(1) It shall be sufficient evidence that notice has been given if—

  (a) a certificate of the sending of notice under rule 30.7 dated and endorsed on the lease or an extract of it, or on the letter of removal, is signed by the sheriff officer or the person sending the notice, his solicitor or factor; or

  (b) an acknowledgement of the notice is endorsed on the lease or an extract of it, or on the letter of removal, by the party in possession or his agent.

(2) If there is no lease, a certificate of the sending of such notice must be endorsed on a copy of the notice or letter of removal.

[1] **30.9** Where, in response to a summons for the recovery of heritable property which includes a claim for payment of money, a defender makes a written application about payment, he shall not thereby be taken to be admitting the claim for recovery of possession of the heritable property.

NOTE
[1] As inserted by the Act of Sederunt (Sheriff Court Rules) (Miscellaneous Amendments) 2008 (SSI 2008/223) r.8 (effective July 1, 2008).

CHAPTER 31

Action of sequestration for rent

[*Repealed by the Act of Sederunt (Sheriff Court Rules Amendment) (Diligence) 2008 (SSI 2008/121) r.2(1)(b) (effective April 1, 2008).*]

CHAPTER 32

ACTION FOR ALIMENT

Recall or variation of decree for aliment

32.1.—(1) Applications for the recall or variation of any decree for payment of aliment pronounced in the small debt court under the Small Debt Acts or in a summary cause under the 1971 Act must be made by summons.

(2) The sheriff may make such interim orders in relation to such applications or in relation to actions brought under section 3 of the Sheriff Courts (Civil Jurisdiction and Procedure) (Scotland) Act 1963 as he thinks fit.

(3) In paragraph (1) "the Small Debt Acts" means and includes the Small Debt (Scotland) Acts 1837 to 1889 and Acts explaining or amending the same.

Warrant and forms for intimation

32.2. In the summons in an action brought under section 3 of the Sheriff Courts (Civil Jurisdiction and Procedure) (Scotland) Act 1963, the pursuer must include an application for a warrant for intimation—

    (a) in an action where the address of the defender is not known to the pursuer and cannot reasonably be ascertained, to—

        (i) every child of the marriage between the parties who has reached the age of 16 years; and

        (ii) one of the next-of-kin of the defender who has reached that age,

    unless the address of such a person is not known to the pursuer and cannot reasonably be ascertained, and a notice of intimation in Form 36 must be attached to the copy of the summons intimated to any such person; or

    (b) in an action where the defender is a person who is suffering from a mental disorder, to—

        (i) those persons mentioned in paragraphs (a)(i) and (ii), unless the address of such person is not known to the pursuer and cannot reasonably be ascertained; and

        (ii) the guardian of, the defender, if one has been appointed, and a notice in Form 37 must be attached to the copy of the summons intimated to any such person.

CHAPTER 33

CHILD SUPPORT ACT 1991

Interpretation of rules 33.2 to 33.4

33.1. In rules 33.2 to 33.4 below—

"the 1991 Act" means the Child Support Act 1991;

"child" has the meaning assigned in section 55 of the 1991 Act;

"claim relating to aliment" means a crave for decree of aliment in relation to a child or for recall or variation of such a decree; and

"maintenance calculation" has the meaning assigned in section 54 of the 1991 Act.

Statement of claim

33.2.—(1) Any summons or counterclaim which contains a claim relating to aliment and to which section 8(6), (7), (8) or (10) of the 1991 Act applies must—

    (a) state, where appropriate—

        (i) that a maintenance calculation under section 11 of the 1991 Act (maintenance calculations) is in force;

        (ii) the date of the maintenance calculation;

        (iii) the amount and frequency of periodical payments of child support maintenance fixed by the maintenance calculation; and

        (iv) the grounds on which the sheriff retains jurisdiction under section 8(6), (7), (8) or (10) of the 1991 Act; and

    (b) unless the sheriff on cause shown otherwise directs, be accompanied by any document issued by the Secretary of State to the party intimating the making of the maintenance calculation referred to in sub-paragraph (a).

(2) Any summons or counterclaim which contains a claim relating to aliment and to which section 8(6), (7), (8) or (10) of the 1991 Act does not apply must include a statement—

    (a) that the habitual residence of the absent parent, person with care or qualifying child, within the meaning of section 3 of the 1991 Act, is outwith the United Kingdom; or

    (b) that the child is not a child within the meaning of section 55 of the 1991 Act.

(3) A summons or counterclaim which involves parties in respect of whom a decision has been made in any application, review or appeal under the 1991 Act must—

    (a) include in the statement of claim statements to the effect that such a decision has been made and give details of that decision; and

    (b) unless the sheriff on cause shown otherwise directs, be accompanied by any document issued by the Secretary of State to the parties intimating that decision.

Effect of maintenance calculations

33.3.—(1) On receiving notification that a maintenance calculation has been made, cancelled or has ceased to have effect so as to affect an order of a kind prescribed for the purposes of section 10 of the 1991 Act, the sheriff clerk must enter in the Register of Summary Causes in respect of that order a note to that effect.

(2) The note mentioned in paragraph (1) must state that—

    (a) the order ceases or ceased to have effect from the date two days after the making of the maintenance calculation; or

    (b) the maintenance calculation has been cancelled or has ceased to have effect.

Effect of maintenance calculations on extacts of decrees relating to aliment

33.4—(1) Where a decree relating to aliment is affected by a maintenance calculation, any extract of that decree issued by the sheriff clerk must be endorsed with the following certificate:—

"A maintenance calculation having been made under the Child Support Act 1991 on (*insert date*), this order, in so far as it relates to the making or securing of periodical payments to or for the benefit of (*insert name(s) of child/children*), ceases to have effect from (*insert date two days after the date on which the maintenance calculation was made*).".

(2) Where a decree relating to aliment has ceased to have effect on the making of a maintenance calculation and that maintenance calculation is later cancelled or ceases to have effect, any extract of that order issued by the sheriff clerk must be endorsed also with the following certificate:—

"The jurisdiction of the child support officer under the Child Support Act 1991 having terminated on (*insert date*), this order, in so far as it relates to (*insert name(s) of child/children*), again shall have effect as of (*insert date of termination of child support officer's jurisdiction*).".

CHAPTER 34

ACTION OF DAMAGES FOR PERSONAL INJURY

Application of Chapter and disapplication of certain rules

34.1.—(1) This Chapter applies to an action of damages for personal injuries or the death of a person from personal injuries.

(2) In this Chapter "personal injuries" includes any disease or impairment of physical or mental condition.

(3) The following rules shall not apply to an action of damages for personal injuries or death:—

Rule 4.2, other than the requirement to give fair notice of the claim; and

Rule 8.1.

(4) Rules 8.2 to 8.17 shall only apply to an action of damages for personal injuries or death in accordance with rule 34.3(2).

Form of summons

34.2.—(1) The statement of claim in the summons shall be in Form 10 and shall include—

(a) a concise statement of the grounds of action, and the facts relied upon to establish the claim;

(b) the date of birth and where applicable National Insurance number of the pursuer; and

(c) the names of every medical practitioner from whom, and every hospital, or other institution in which, the pursuer, or in an action in respect of the death of a person, the deceased, received treatment for injuries sustained or for disease suffered by him.

(2) There shall be lodged along with the summons—

(a) all medical reports then available to the pursuer on which he intends, or intends to reserve the right, to rely in the action or a statement that there are no such medical reports; and

(b) a statement of valuation of claim (which shall include a list of supporting documents) in Form 10c.

(3) An application for an order under section 12(2)(a) of the Administration of Justice Act 1982 (provisional damages for personal injuries) shall be made by including in the summons a claim for provisional damages in Form 10a, and where such application is made, a concise statement as to the matters referred to in paragraphs (a) and (b) of section 12(1) of that Act shall be included in the statement of claim.

(4) In paragraph (3) above "provisional damages" means the damages referred to in section 12(4)(a) of the Administration of Justice Act 1982.

(5) A summons may include—

(a) an application for warrants for intimation in so far as permitted under these Rules; and

(b) a specification of documents containing such of the calls in Form 10e as the pursuer considers appropriate.

[1] (6) Where a summons includes a specification of documents in accordance with paragraph (5)(b) it shall be intimated to—

(a) in respect of an application under section 1(1) of the Administration of Justice (Scotland) Act 1972, any third party haver; and

(b) where necessary—

(i) the Advocate General for Scotland (in a case where the document or other property sought is in the possession of either a public authority exercising functions in relation to reserved matters within the meaning of Schedule 5 to the Scotland Act 1998, or a cross-border public authority within the meaning of section 88(5) of that Act); or

(ii) the Lord Advocate (in any other case)

and, if there is any doubt, both.

(7) A copy of Form 10b and a copy of the statement of valuation of claim lodged by the pursuer in Form 10c shall accompany the defender's copy summons when it is served on the defender.

NOTE

[1] As substituted by the Act of Sederunt (Sheriff Court Rules) (Miscellaneous Amendments) (No.2) 2008 (SSI 2008/365) r.5(2) (effective December 1, 2008).

Response to summons

34.3.—(1) A defender wishing to defend the action shall complete and lodge with the sheriff clerk on or before the return day the form of response in Form 10b stating, in a manner which gives the pursuer fair notice, the grounds of fact and law on which the defender intends to resist the claim together with a brief statement of the facts upon which the defender relies in his defence.

(2) Where a defender lodges a form of response in accordance with paragraph (1), the provisions of rules 8.2 to 8.17 shall apply with the necessary modifications.

Inspection and recovery of documents

34.4.—(1) This rule applies where the summons includes a specification of documents in accordance with rule 34.2 (5)(b).

(2) Subject to paragraph (5), where a response in Form 10b is lodged stating a defence to the action, the sheriff clerk shall make an order granting commission and diligence for the production and recovery of the documents mentioned in the specification.

(3) An order under paragraph (2) shall be treated for all purposes as an interlocutor of the court granting commission and diligence signed by the sheriff.

(4) Nothing in this rule shall affect the right of a party to apply under rule 18.1 for a commission and diligence for recovery of documents or under rule 18.3 for an order under section 1 of the Administration of Justice (Scotland) Act 1972 in respect of any document or other property not mentioned in the specification included in the summons.

(5) Where the defender, or where appropriate, the Advocate General for Scotland or the Lord Advocate, objects to the specification of documents, he shall make such objection by incidental application.

(6) An incidental application under paragraph (5) shall be—

(a) lodged on or before the return day; and

(b) determined at the hearing held in terms of rule 8.2(1).

Statement of valuation of claim

34.5.—(1) Each party to an action who is not required elsewhere in these rules to do so shall make a statement of valuation of claim (which shall include a list of supporting documents) in Form 10c in accordance with the following paragraphs of this rule.

(2) A statement of valuation of claim made in terms of paragraph (1) shall be lodged with the sheriff clerk.

(3) Each party on lodging a statement of valuation of claim in terms of paragraph (2), shall give written intimation to every other party of the statement and the list of documents contained in the statement of valuation of claim.

(4) A party who fails to lodge a statement of valuation of claim not later than 28 days before the date fixed for proof shall be liable to any other party for the expenses of proving the quantification of the claim, unless the sheriff, on special cause shown, otherwise directs.

Intimation to connected persons

34.6.—(1) This rule applies to an action of damages in which, following the death of any person from personal injuries, damages are claimed—

(a) by the executor of the deceased, in respect of the injuries from which the deceased died; or

(b) by any relative of the deceased, in respect of the death of the deceased.

(2) In this rule—

"connected person" means a person, not being a party to the action, who has title to sue the defender in respect of the personal injuries from which the deceased died or in respect of his death; and

"relative" has the meaning assigned to it in Schedule 1 to the Damages (Scotland) Act 1976.

(3) The pursuer shall state in the summons, as the case may be—

(a) that there are no connected persons;

(b) that there are connected persons, being the persons specified in the application for warrant for intimation; or

(c) that there are connected persons in respect of whom intimation should be dispensed with on the ground that—

    (i) the names or whereabouts of such persons are not known to, and cannot reasonably be ascertained by, the pursuer; or

    (ii) such persons are unlikely to be awarded more than £200 each.

(4) Where the pursuer makes statements under rule 34.6(3)(b) he shall include an application for warrant in the summons for intimation to any such person.

(5) A notice of intimation in Form 10d shall be attached to the copy of the summons, and a copy of Form 10c shall accompany the summons, where intimation is given on a warrant under paragraph (4).

(6) Where the pursuer makes statements under rule 34.6(3)(c), he shall apply in the summons for an order to dispense with intimation.

(7) In determining an application under paragraph (6), the sheriff shall have regard to—

(a) the desirability of avoiding a multiplicity of actions; and

(b) the expense, inconvenience or difficulty likely to be involved in taking steps to ascertain the name or whereabouts of the connected person.

(8) Where the sheriff is not satisfied that intimation to a connected person should be dispensed with, he may—

(a) order intimation to a connected person whose name and whereabouts are known;

(b) order the pursuer to take such further steps as he may specify in the interlocutor to ascertain the name or whereabouts of any connected person; and

(c) order advertisement in such manner, place and at such times as he may specify in the interlocutor.

(9) Where the name or whereabouts of a person, in respect of whom the sheriff has dispensed with intimation on a ground specified in rule 34.6(3)(c), subsequently becomes known to the pursuer, the pursuer shall apply to the sheriff by incidental application for a warrant for intimation to such a person; and such intimation shall be made in accordance with rule 34.6(5).

(10) A connected person may apply by incidental application to be sisted as an additional pursuer to the action.

(11) Such an incidental application shall also seek leave of the sheriff to adopt the existing grounds of action, and to amend the claim.

(12) The period within which answers to an incidental application under paragraph (10) may be lodged shall be 14 days from the date of intimation of the incidental application.

(13) There shall be lodged along with the incidental application a statement of valuation of claim (which shall include a list of supporting documents) in Form 10c.

(14) The statement of valuation of claim lodged in accordance with paragraph (13) shall be intimated to the other parties at the same time as the incidental application.

(15) Where a connected person to whom intimation is made—

(a) does not apply to be sisted as an additional pursuer to the action;

(b) subsequently raises a separate action against the same defender in respect of the same personal injuries or death; and

(c) would, apart from this rule, be awarded the expenses or part of the expenses of that action,

he shall not be awarded those expenses except on cause shown.

Application for further damages

34.7.—(1) An application for further damages by a pursuer in respect of whom an order under section 12(2)(b) of the Administration of Justice Act 1982 has been made shall be made by lodging a minute with the sheriff clerk in Form 10f, which minute shall include—

(a) a claim for further damages;

(b) a concise statement of the facts supporting that claim;

(c) an application for warrant to serve the minute on—

    (i) every other party; and

    (ii) where such other parties are insured or otherwise indemnified, their insurer or indemnifier, if known to the pursuer; and

(d) a request for the court to fix a hearing on the application.

(2) A notice of intimation in Form 10g shall be attached to every copy of the minute served on a warrant granted under paragraph (1)(c).

(3) At the hearing fixed under paragraph (1)(d) above, the sheriff may determine the application or order such further procedure as he thinks fit.

CHAPTER 35

ELECTRONIC TRANSMISSION OF DOCUMENTS

Extent of provision
35.1.—(1) Any document referred to in these rules which requires to be—
    (a) lodged with the sheriff clerk;
    (b) intimated to a party; or
    (c) sent by the sheriff clerk,
may be in electronic or documentary form, and if in electronic form may be lodged, intimated or sent by e-mail or similar means.

(2) Paragraph (1) does not apply to any certificate of execution of service, citation or arrestment, or to a decree or extract decree of the court.

(3) Where any document is lodged by e-mail or similar means the sheriff may require any principal document to be lodged.

Time of lodgement
35.2. The time of lodgement, intimation or sending shall be the time when the document was sent or transmitted.

[1] CHAPTER 36

EQUALITY ENACTMENTS

NOTE
  [1] As inserted by the Act of Sederunt (Ordinary Cause, Summary Application, Summary Cause and Small Claim Rules) Amendment (Equality Act 2006 etc.) 2006 (SSI 2006/509) r.4(2) (effective November 3, 2006).

Application and interpretation
36.1.—(1) This Chapter applies to claims under the equality enactments.

(2) In this Chapter, "claims under the equality enactments" means proceedings in reparation for breach of statutory duty under any of the following enactments—
    (a) Sex Discrimination Act 1975;
    (b) Race Relations Act 1976;
    (c) Disability Discrimination Act 1995;
    (d) Equality Act 2006;
  [1] (e) The Equality Act (Sexual Orientation) Regulations 2007.
  [2] (3) In this Chapter "the Commission" means the Commission for Equality and Human Rights.

NOTES
  [1] As inserted by the Act of Sederunt (Ordinary Cause, Summary Application, Summary Cause and Small Claim Rules) Amendment (Equality Act (Sexual Orientation) Regulations 2007) 2007 (SSI 2007/339) r.4(2) (effective July 20, 2007).
  [2] As inserted by the Act of Sederunt (Sheriff Court Rules) (Miscellaneous Amendments) 2008 (SSI 2008/223) r.6(3) (effective July 1, 2008).

[1] *Intimation to Commission*
36.2. The pursuer shall send a copy of the summons to the Commission by registered or recorded delivery post.

NOTE
  [1] As substituted by the Act of Sederunt (Sheriff Court Rules) (Miscellaneous Amendments) 2008 (SSI 2008/223) r.6(3)(b) (effective July 1, 2008).

Assessor
36.3. —(1) The sheriff may, of his own motion or on the incidental application of any party, appoint an assessor.

(2) The assessor shall be a person who the sheriff considers has special qualifications to be of assistance in determining the cause.

Taxation of Commission expenses

36.4. [*Repealed by the Act of Sederunt (Sheriff Court Rules) (Miscellaneous Amendments) 2008 (SSI 2008/223) r.6(3)(c) (effective July 1, 2008).*]

National security

36.5.—(1) Where, on an incidental application under paragraph (3) or of his own motion, the sheriff considers it expedient in the interests of national security, he may—

    (a) exclude from all or part of the proceedings—

        (i) the pursuer;

        (ii) the pursuer's representatives;

        (iii) any assessors;

    (b) permit a pursuer or representative who has been excluded to make a statement to the court before the commencement of the proceedings or the part of the proceedings, from which he is excluded;

    (c) take steps to keep secret all or part of the reasons for his decision in the proceedings.

(2) The sheriff clerk shall, on the making of an order under paragraph (1) excluding the pursuer or his representatives, notify the Advocate General for Scotland of that order.

(3) A party may make an incidental application for an order under paragraph (1).

(4) The steps referred to in paragraph (1)(c) may include the following—

    (a) directions to the sheriff clerk; and

    (b) orders requiring any person appointed to represent the interests of the pursuer in proceedings from which the pursuer or his representatives are excluded not to communicate (directly or indirectly) with any persons (including the excluded pursuer)—

        (i) on any matter discussed or referred to;

        (ii) with regard to any material disclosed,

during or with reference to any part of the proceedings from which the pursuer or his representatives are excluded.

(5) Where the sheriff has made an order under paragraph (4)(b), the person appointed to represent the interests of the pursuer may make an incidental application for authority to seek instructions from or otherwise communicate with an excluded person.

(6) The sheriff may, on the application of a party intending to lodge an incidental application in written form, reduce the period of two days specified in rule 9.1(2) or dispense with notice.

(7) An application under paragraph (6) shall be made in the written incidental application, giving reasons for such reduction or dispensation.

[1] CHAPTER 37

LIVE LINKS

NOTE

[1] As inserted by the Act of Sederunt (Ordinary Cause, Summary Application, Summary Cause and Small Claim Rules) Amendment (Miscellaneous) 2007 (SSI 2007/6) r.4(7) (effective January 29, 2007).

37.1.—(1) On cause shown, a party may apply by incidental application for authority for the whole or part of—

    (a) the evidence of a witness or the party to be given; or

    (b) a submission to be made,

through a live link.

(2) in paragraph (1)—

    [1] "witness" means a person who has been or may be cited to appear before the court as a witness except a vulnerable witness within the meaning of section 11(1) of the Act of 2004;

    "submission" means any oral submission which would otherwise be made to the court by the party or his representative in person including an oral submission in support of an incidental application; and

    "live link" means a live television link or such other arrangement as may be specified in the incidental application by which the witness, party or representative, as the case may be, is able to be seen and heard in the proceedings or heard in the proceedings and is able to see and hear or hear the proceedings while at a place which is outside the court room.

NOTE

[1] As amended by the Act of Sederunt (Ordinary Cause, Summary Application, Summary Cause and Small Claim Rules) Amendment (Vulnerable Witnesses (Scotland) Act 2004) 2007 (SSI 2007/463) r.4(6) (effective November 1, 2007).

Rule 1.1(4)

APPENDIX 1

FORMS

Rule 4.1(1)

[1] FORM 1

Summons

FORM 1	OFFICIAL USE ONLY SUMMONS No.

Summary Cause Summons

Action for/of

(state type, e.g. payment of money)

Sheriff Court (name, address, e-mail and telephone no.)	**1**	
Name and address of person raising the action (**pursuer**)	**2**	
Name and address of person against whom action raised (**defender, arrestee, etc.**)	**3**	
Name(s) and address(s) of any interested party (eg. connected person)	**3a**	
Claim (form of decree or other order sought)	**4**	
Name, full address, telephone no, and e-mail address of pursuer's solicitor or representative (if any) acting in the case	**5**	
Fee Details (Enter these only if forms sent electronically to court)	**5a**	

6	**RETURN DAY**	20		
	CALLING DATE	20	**at**	**am.**

*Sheriff Clerk to delete as appropriate	The pursuer is authorised to serve a copy summons in form *1a/1b/1c, on the defender, and give intimation to any interested party, not less than * 21/42 days before the **RETURN DAY** shown in the box above. The summons is warrant for service, and for citation of witnesses to attend court on any future date at which evidence may be led.
Court Authentication	Sheriff clerk depute (name) Date: 20

NOTE: The pursuer should complete boxes 1 to 5a above and box 7 on page 2. The sheriff clerk will complete box 6.

7. **STATE DETAILS OF CLAIM HERE (all cases) and PARTICULARS OF ARRESTMENT (furthcoming actions only)**
(To be completed by the pursuer. If space is insufficient, a separate sheet may be attached)

The details of the claim are:

FOR OFFICIAL USE ONLY

Sheriff's notes as to:

1. Issues of fact and law in dispute
2. Facts agreed
3. Reasons for any final disposal at the hearing held on the calling date.

NOTE
[1] As amended by the Act of Sederunt (Sheriff Court Rules Amendment) (Diligence) 2008 (SSI 2008/121) r.6(6) (effective April 1, 2008).

[1] FORM 1a

Rule 4.3(a)

Defender's copy summons—claim for or including payment of money where time to pay direction or time order may be applied for

> **OFFICIAL USE ONLY**
> **SUMMONS No.**

Summary Cause Summons
Action for/of
(state type, e.g. payment of money)

DEFENDER'S COPY: Claim for or including payment of money (where time to pay direction or time order may be applied for)

Sheriff Court (name, address, e-mail and telephone no.)	**1**	
Name and address of person raising the action (**pursuer**)	**2**	
Name and address of person against whom action raised (**defender, arrestee, etc.**)	**3**	
Name(s) and address(es) of any interested party (e.g. connected person)	**3a**	
Claim (form of decree of other order sought)	**4**	
Name, full address, telephone no., and e-mail address of pursuer's solicitor or representative (if any) acting in the case	**5**	

6	**RETURN DAY**	**20**		
	CALLING DATE	**20**	**at**	**am.**

NOTE: You will find details of claim on page 2.

7.   STATEMENT OF CLAIM
            PARICULARS OF ARRESTMENT (furthcoming actions only)
            (To be completed by the pursuer. If space is insufficient, a separate sheet may be attached)

            The details of the claim are:

8.   **SERVICE ON DEFENDER**

            (Place)   **(Date)**

            To: **(Defender)**

            You are hereby served with a copy of the above summons.

                                             Solicitor / sheriff officer
                                             delete as appropriate

NOTE: The pursuer should complete boxes 1 to 6 on page 1, the statement of claim in box 7 on page 2 and section A on page 6 before service on the defender. The person serving the Summons will complete box 8, above.

WHAT MUST I DO ABOUT THIS SUMMONS?

The RETURN DAY (on page 1 of this summons) is the deadline by which you need to reply to the court. You must send the correct forms back (see below for details) by this date if you want the court to hear your case. If you do not do this, in most cases there will not be a hearing about your case and the court will make a decision in your absence.

The CALLING DAY (on page 1 of this summons) is the date for the court hearing.

Note: If your case is about **recovery of possession of heritable property** (eviction) there will be a hearing even if you do not send back the forms, so you should attend court on the calling date. If you make an application for time to pay in such a case and the court accepts your application, it may still make an order for eviction, so you should attend court if you wish to defend the action for eviction.

You should decide whether you wish to dispute the claim and/or whether you owe any money or not, and how you wish to proceed. Then, look at the 5 options listed below. Find the one that covers your decision and follow the instructions given there.

If you are not sure what you need to do, contact the sheriff clerk's office before the return day. Written guidance can also be obtained from the Scottish Court Service website (www.scot-courts.gov.uk).

OPTIONS

1. **ADMIT LIABILITY FOR THE CLAIM and settle it with the pursuer now.**

   If you wish to avoid the possibility of a court order passing against you, you should settle the claim (including any question of expenses) with the pursuer or his representative **in good time before the return day**. Please do not send any payment direct to the court. Any payment should be made to the pursuer or his representative.

2. **ADMIT LIABILITY FOR THE CLAIM and make written application to pay by instalments or by deferred lump sum.**

   Complete Box 1 of section B on page 6 of this form and return pages 6, 8 and 9 to the court to arrive on or before the return day. You should then contact the court to find out whether or not the pursuer has accepted your offer. If he has not accepted it, the case will then call in court on the calling date, when the court will decide how the amount claimed is to be paid.

   NOTE: If you fail to return pages 6, 8 and 9 as directed, or if, having returned them, you fail to attend or are not represented at the calling date if the case is to call, the court may decide the claim in your absence.

3. **ADMIT LIABILITY FOR THE CLAIM and attend at court to make application to pay by instalments or deferred lump sum.**
   Complete Box 2 on page 6. Return page 6 to the court so that it arrives on or before the return day.

You must attend personally, or be represented, at court on the calling date. Your representative may be a Solicitor, or someone else having your authority. It may be helpful if you or your representative bring pages 1 and 2 of this form to the court.

NOTE: If you fail to return page 6 as directed, or if, having returned it, you fail to attend or are not represented at the calling date, the court may decide the claim in your absence.

4. **DISPUTE THE CLAIM and** <u>attend at court</u> **to do any of the following:**

   - Challenge the jurisdiction of the court or the competency of the action
   - Defend the action (whether as regards the sum claimed or otherwise)
   - State a counterclaim

   Complete Box 3 on page 6. Return page 6 to the court so that it arrives **on or before the return day. You must attend personally, or be represented, at court on the calling date.**

   Your representative may be a solicitor, or someone else having your authority. It may be helpful if you or your representative bring pages 1 and 2 of this form to the court.

   NOTE: If you fail to return page 6 as directed, or if, having returned it, you fail to attend or are not represented at the calling date, the court may decide the claim in your absence.

   WRITTEN NOTE OF PROPOSED DEFENCE

   You must send to the court by the return day a written note of any proposed defence, or intimate that you intend to dispute the sum claimed or wish to dispute the court's jurisdiction. You must also attend or be represented at court on the calling date.

5. **ADMIT LIABILITY FOR THE CLAIM and make** <u>written</u> **application for a time order under the Consumer Credit Act 1974.**

   Complete Box 4 on page 6 and return pages 6 and 10 to 12 to the court to arrive on or before the return day. You should then contact the court to find out whether or not the pursuer has accepted your offer. Where you have been advised that the pursuer has not accepted your offer then the case will call in court on the calling date. You should appear in court on the calling date as the court will decide how the amount claimed is to be paid.

   NOTE: If you fail to return pages 6 and 10 to 12 as directed, or if, having returned them, you fail to attend or are not represented at the calling date if the case is to call, the court may decide the claim in your absence.

<u>PLEASE NOTE</u>

If you do nothing about this summons, the court will almost certainly, where appropriate, grant decree against you and order you to pay the pursuer the sum claimed, including any interest and expenses found due.

YOU ARE ADVISED TO KEEP PAGES 1 AND 2, AS THEY MAY BE USEFUL AT A LATER STAGE OF THE CASE.

Notes:

(1) Time to pay directions

The Debtors (Scotland) Act 1987 gives you the right to apply to the court for a "time to pay direction". This is an order which allows you to pay any sum which the court orders you to pay either in instalments or by deferred lump sum. A "deferred lump sum" means that you will be ordered by the court to pay the whole amount at one time within a period which the court will specify.

If the court makes a time to pay direction it may also recall or restrict any arrestment made on your property by the pursuer in connection with the action or debt (for example, your bank account may have been frozen).

No court fee is payable when making an application for a time to pay direction.

If a time to pay direction is made, a copy of the court order (called an extract decree) will be sent to you by the pursuer telling you when payment should start or when it is you have to pay the lump sum.

If a time to pay direction is not made, and an order for immediate payment is made against you, an order to pay (called a charge) may be served on you if you do not pay.

(2) Determination of application

Under the 1987 Act, the court is required to make a time to pay direction if satisfied that it is reasonable in the circumstances to do so, and having regard in particular to the following matters—

- The nature of and reasons for the debt in relation to which decree is granted
- Any action taken by the creditor to assist the debtor in paying the debt
- The debtor's financial position
- The reasonableness of any proposal by the debtor to pay that debt
- The reasonableness of any refusal or objection by the creditor to any proposal or offer by the debtor to pay the debt.

(3) Time Orders

The Consumer Credit Act 1974 allows you to apply to the court for a "time order" during a court action, to ask the court to give you more time to pay a loan agreement. **A time order is similar to a time to pay direction, but can only be applied for where the court action is about a credit agreement regulated by the Consumer Credit Act**. The court has power to grant a time order in respect of a regulated agreement to reschedule payment of the sum owed. This means that a time order can change:

- the amount you have to pay each month
- how long the loan will last
- in some cases, the interest rate payable

A time order can also stop the creditor taking away any item bought by you on hire purchase or conditional sale under the regulated agreement, so long as you continue to pay the instalments agreed.

No court fee is payable when making an application for a time order.

SECTION A

This section must be
completed before service

Summons No
Return Day
Calling Date

SHERIFF COURT (Including address)

PURSUER'S FULL NAME
AND ADDRESS

DEFENDER'S FULL
NAME AND ADDRESS

SECTION B   DEFENDER'S RESPONSE TO THE SUMMONS
** Delete those boxes which do **not** apply

**Box 1	**ADMIT LIABILITY FOR THE CLAIM and make <u>written</u> application to pay by instalments or by <u>deferred</u> lump sum.**
	I do not intend to defend the case but admit liability for the claim.
	I wish to make a written application about payment.
	I have completed the application form on pages 8 and 9.

**Box 2	**ADMIT LIABILITY FOR THE CLAIM and <u>attend at court</u> to make application to pay by instalments or deferred lump sum.**
	I admit liability for the claim.
	I intend to appear or be represented at court on the calling date.

**Box 3	**DISPUTE THE CLAIM (or the amount due) and attend at court**
	*I intend to challenge the jurisdiction of the court.
	*I intend to challenge the competency of the action.
	*I intend to defend the action.
	*I wish to dispute the amount due only.
	*I apply for warrant to serve a third party notice (see page 14).
	I intend to appear or be represented in court on the calling date.
	―――――――――――――
	*I attach a note of my proposed defence/counterclaim.
	OR
	*I return form 10b (personal injury cases only).
	*delete as necessary

**Box 4	**ADMIT LIABILITY FOR THE CLAIM and apply for a time order under the Consumer Credit Act 1974.**
	I do not intend to defend the case but admit liability for the claim.
	I wish to apply for a time order under the Consumer Credit Act 1974.
	I have completed the application form on pages 10 to 12.

WRITTEN NOTE OF PROPOSE DEFENCE / COUNTERCLAIM
State which facts in the statement of claim are admitted:

State briefly any facts regarding the circumstances of the claim on which you intent to rely:

State details of counterclaim, if any:

PLEASE REMEMBER: You must send your response to the court to **arrive on or before the return day** if you have completed a response in Section B. If you have admitted the claim, please do not send any payment direct to the court. **Any payments you wish to make should be made to the pursuer or his solicitor.**

APPLICATION IN WRITING FOR A TIME TO PAY DIRECTION UNDER THE
DEBTORS (SCOTLAND) ACT 1987

I WISH TO APPLY FOR A TIME TO PAY DIRECTION
I admit the claim and make application to pay as follows:

(1) By instalments of £ _____ per *week / fortnight / month

  OR

(2) In one payment within _____ *weeks / months from the date of the
   court order.

The debt is for (*specify the nature of the debt*) and has arisen (*here set out the reasons the debt
has arisen*)

Please also state why you say a time to pay direction should be made. In doing so, please
consider the Notes (1) and (2) on page 5.

To help the court please provide details of your financial position in the boxes below.

I am employed / self-employed / unemployed
*Please also indicate whether payment/receipts are weekly, fortnightly or monthly

My outgoings are:	*Weekly / fortnightly/ monthly	My net income is	*Weekly / fortnightly/ monthly
Rent/mortgage	£	Wages/pensions	£
Council tax	£	State benefits	£
Gas/electricity etc	£	Tax credits	£
Food	£	Other	£
Loans and credit agreements	£		
Phone	£		
Other	£		
Total	£	Total	£

People who rely on your
income (e.g. spouse/civil
partner/ partner/children)—
how many

Please list details of all capital held, e.g. value of house; amount in savings account, shares or other investments:

I am of the opinion that the payment offer is reasonable for the following reason(s):

Here set out any information you consider relevant to the court's determination of the application. In doing so, please consider Note (2) on page 5.

*APPLICATION FOR RECALL OR RESTRICTION OF AN ARRESTMENT

I seek the recall or restriction of the arrestment of which the details are as follows:

Date:
*Delete if inapplicable

<table>
<tr><td></td><td>

APPLICATION FOR A TIME ORDER UNDER THE CONSUMER CREDIT ACT 1974

</td></tr>
<tr><td></td><td>

By

</td></tr>
<tr><td></td><td>

DEFENDER

</td></tr>
<tr><td></td><td>

In an action raised by

</td></tr>
<tr><td></td><td>

PURSUER

</td></tr>
<tr><td></td><td>

PLEASE WRITE IN INK USING BLOCK CAPITALS

</td></tr>
<tr><td></td><td>

If you wish to apply to pay by instalments enter the amount at box 3. If you wish the court to make any additional orders, please give details at box 4. Please give details of the regulated agreement at box 5 and details of your financial position in the spaces provided below box 5.

Sign and date the application where indicated. You should ensure that your application arrives at the court along with the completed page 6 on or before the return day.

</td></tr>
<tr><td></td><td>

1. The Applicant is a defender in the action brought by the above named pursuer.

I/WE WISH TO APPLY FOR A TIME ORDER under the Consumer Credit Act 1974

</td></tr>
<tr><td></td><td>

2. **Details of order(s) sought**

The defender wishes to apply for a time order under section 129 of the Consumer Credit Act 1974.

The defender wishes to apply for an order in terms of section ..... of the Consumer Credit Act 1974.

</td></tr>
</table>

PAGE 10

	3. Proposals for payment I admit the claim and apply to pay the arrears and future instalments as follows: By instalments of £ .... per *week/fortnight/month No time to pay direction or time to pay order has been made in relation to this debt.
	4. Additional orders sought The following additional order(s) is (are) sought: (*specify*) The order(s) sought in addition to the time order is (are) sought for the following reasons:

	5. Details of regulated agreement
	
	   (a) Date of agreement
	
	   (b) Reference number of agreement
	
	(*Please attach a copy of the agreement*)

	(c) Names and addresses of other parties to agreement
	
	   (d) Name and address of person (if any) who acted as surety (guarantor) to the agreement
	
	   (e) Place where agreement signed (e.g. the shop where agreement signed, including name and address)
	
	   (f) Details of payment arrangements
	       i. The agreement is to pay instalments of £ ..... per week/month
	      ii. The unpaid balance is £ ..... / I do not know the amount of arrears
	     iii. I am £ ..... in arrears / I do not know the amount of arrears

	Defender's financial position
	I am employed /self employed / unemployed

	My net income is:	weekly, fortnightly or monthly	**My outgoings are:**	weekly, fortnightly or monthly
	Wages	£	Mortgage/rent	£
	State benefits	£	Council tax	£
	Tax credits	£	Gas/electricity etc	£
	Other	£	Food	£
			Credit and loans	£
			Phone	£
			Other	£
	Total	£	Total	£

	People who rely on your income (e.g. spouse/civil partner/partner/children)—how many
	Here list all assets (if any) e.g. value of house; amounts in bank or building society accounts; shares or other investments:
	Here list any outstanding debts:
	Therefore the defender asks the court to make a time order
	Date: Signed: Defender:

APPLICATION FOR SERVICE OF A THIRD PARTY NOTICE

NOTE:
You can apply to have another party added to the action if:

(A)   **You think that, as regards the matter which the action is about, that other party has a duty to:**

1.   Indemnify you; or

2.   Make a contribution in respect of the matter; or

3.   Relieve you from any responsibility as regards it.

or

(B)   **You think that other party is:**

1.   Solely liable to the pursuer; or

2.   Liable to the pursuer along with you; or

3.   Has a liability to you as a result of the pursuer's claim against you.

You may apply for warrant to found jurisdiction if you wish to do so.

FORM OF APPLICATION

(TO BE RETURNED TO THE COURT ALONG WITH YOUR RESPONSE)

I request the court to grant warrant for service of a third party notice on the following party:

Name:

Address:

The reason I wish a third party notice to be served on the party mentioned above is as follows:
(Give details below of the reasons why you wish the party to be made a defender in the action.)

*I apply for warrant to found jurisdiction

*delete as appropriate

Date:

NOTE
[1] As amended by the Act of Sederunt (Sheriff Court Rules Amendment) (Diligence) 2008 (SSI 2008/121) r.6(8) (effective April 1, 2008) and substituted by the Act of Sederunt (Sheriff Court Rules) (Miscellaneous Amendments) 2009 (SSI 2009/294) r.4 (effective December 1, 2009).

Rule 4.3(a)

[1] FORM 1b

Defender's copy summons – claim for or including payment of money (where time to pay direction or time order may not be applied for)

FORM 1b

| OFFICIAL USE ONLY |
| SUMMONS No. |

Summary Cause Summons
Action for/of
(state type, e.g. payment of money)

DEFENDER'S COPY: Claim for or including payment of money (where time to pay direction or time order may not be applied for)

Sheriff Court (name, address, e-mail and telephone no.)	**1**	
Name and address of person raising the action (**pursuer**)	**2**	
Name and address of person against whom action raised (**defender, arrestee, etc.**)	**3**	
Name(s) and address(s) of any interested party (e.g. connected person)	**3a**	
Claim (Form of decree or other order sought)	**4**	
Name, full address, telephone no., and e-mail address of pursuer's solicitor or representative (if any)	**5**	

6			
RETURN DAY	20		
CALLING DATE	20	at	am.

NOTE: You will find details of claim on page 2.

---

7. STATEMENT OF CLAIM
PARTICULARS OF ARRESTMENT (furthcoming actions only.)
(To be completed by the pursuer. If space is insufficient, a separate sheet may be attached)

The details of the claim are:

8. SERVICE ON DEFENDER

(Place)   (Date)

To: (defender)

You are hereby served with a copy of the above summons.

Solicitor / sheriff officer
delete as appropriate

NOTE: The pursuer should complete boxes 1 to 6 on page 1, the statement of claim in box 7 on page 2 and section A on page 5 before service on the defender. The person serving the Summons will complete box 8.

WHAT MUST I DO ABOUT THIS SUMMONS?

Decide whether you wish to dispute the claim, or admit any liability for the claim and whether you owe any money or not, and how you wish to proceed. Thereafter, look at the 2 options listed below. Find the one which covers your decision and follow the instructions given there. You will find the RETURN DAY and the CALLING DATE on page one of the summons.

Written guidance on summary cause procedure can be obtained from the sheriff clerk at any sheriff clerk's office. Further advice can also be obtained by contacting any of the following:

> **Citizen's Advice Bureau, Consumer Advice Centre, Trading Standards or Consumer Protection Department or a Solicitor. (Addresses can be found in the guidance booklets)**

OPTIONS

1.   **ADMIT LIABILITY FOR THE CLAIM and settle it with the pursuer now.**

   If you wish to avoid the possibility of a court order passing against you, you should settle the claim (including any question of expenses) with pursuer or his representative **in good time before the return day.** Please do not send any payment direct to the court. Any payment should be made to the pursuer or his representative.

2.   **DISPUTE THE CLAIM and <u>attend at court</u> to do any of the following:**

   - Challenge the jurisdiction of the court or the competency of the action
   - Defend the action
   - Dispute the sum claimed
   - State a counterclaim

   Complete Section B on page 4. Return your response to the court so that it arrives **on or before the return day. You must attend personally, or be represented, at court on the calling date.**

   Your representative may be a solicitor, or someone else having your authority. It may be helpful if you or your representative bring pages 1 and 2 of this form to the court.

   NOTE: If you fail to return your response as directed, or if, having returned it, you fail to attend or are not represented at the calling date, the court will almost certainly decide the claim in your absence.

WRITTEN NOTE OF PROPOSED DEFENCE

You must send to the court by the return day a written note of any proposed defence, or intimate that you intend to dispute the sum claimed or wish to challenge the court's jurisdiction. You must also attend or be represented at court on the calling date.

PLEASE NOTE:

If you do nothing about this summons, the court will almost certainly, where appropriate, grant decree against you and order you to pay the pursuer the sum claimed, including any interest and expenses found due.

YOU ARE ADVISED TO KEEP PAGES 1 AND 2, AS THEY MAY BE USEFUL AT A LATER STAGE OF THE CASE.

SECTION A
This section must
be completed
before service

Summons No
Return Day
Calling Date

SHERIFF COURT (Including address)

PURSUER'S FULL NAME AND ADDRESS

DEFENDER'S FULL NAME AND
ADDRESS

SECTION B   **DEFENDER'S RESPONSE TO THE SUMMONS**

DISPUTE THE CLAIM (or the amount due) and attend at court
* I intend to challenge the jurisdiction of the court.
* I intend to challenge the competency of the action.
* I intend to defend the claim.
* I wish to dispute the amount due only.
* I apply for warrant to serve a third party notice (see page 6).

I intend to appear or be represented in court on the calling date.
----
*I attach a note of my proposed defence/counterclaim (see page 5).
OR
* I return Form 10b (personal injury cases only).

* *delete as necessary*

WRITTEN NOTE OF PROPOSED DEFENCE / COUNTERCLAIM
State which facts in the statement of claim are admitted:

State briefly any facts regarding the circumstances of the claim on which you intend to rely:

State details of counterclaim, if any:

PLEASE REMEMBER: You must send your response to the court to **arrive on or before the return day** if you have completed a response in Section B. If you have admitted the claim, please do not send any payment direct to the court. **Any payments you wish to make should be made to the pursuer or his solicitor.**

APPLICATION FOR SERVICE OF A THIRD PARTY NOTICE

NOTE:
You can apply to have another party added to the action if:

(A)   **You think that, as regards the matter which the action is about, that other party has a duty to:**
1.   Indemnify you; or
2.   Make a contribution in respect of the matter; or
3.   Relieve you from any responsibility as regards it.
                              or
(B)   You think that other party is:
4.   Solely liable to the pursuer; or
5.   Liable to the pursuer along with you; or
6.   Has a liability to you as a result of the pursuer's claim against you.

You may apply for warrant to found jurisdiction if you wish to do so.

FORM OF APPLICATION

     (TO BE RETURNED TO THE COURT ALONG WITH YOUR RESPONSE)

I request the court to grant warrant for service of a third party notice on the following party:
Name   :

Address   :

The reason I wish a third party notice to be served on the party mentioned above is as follows:
(Give details below of the reasons why you wish the party to be made a defender in the action.)

* **I apply for warrant to found jurisdiction**

* delete as appropriate

NOTE
[1] As amended by the Act of Sederunt (Sheriff Court Rules Amendment) (Diligence) 2008 (SSI 2008/121) r.6(8) (effective April 1, 2008).

Rule 4.3(b)

[1] FORM 1c

Defender's copy summons – non monetary claim

FORM 1c

Summary Cause Summons
Action for/of
(state type, e.g. delivery)

OFFICIAL USE ONLY
SUMMONS No.

DEFENDER'S COPY: Non Monetary Claim

Sheriff Court (name, address, e-mail and telephone no.)	**1**	
Name and address of person raising the action (**pursuer**)	**2**	
Name and address of Person against whom Action raised (**defender**)	**3**	
Claim (Form of decree or other order sought)	**4**	
Name, full address, telephone no, and e-mail address of pursuer's solicitor or representative (if any)	**5**	

6	RETURN DAY	20		
	CALLING DATE	20	at	am.

NOTE: You will find details of claim on page 2.

7.   **STATE DETAILS OF CLAIM HERE OR ATTACH A STATEMENT OF CLAIM**
(to be completed by the pursuer. If space is insufficient, a separate sheet may be attached)

The details of the claim are:

8.   **SERVICE ON DEFENDER**

(Place)   (Date)

To: (defender)

You are hereby served with a copy of the above summons.

* Solicitor / sheriff officer
(delete as appropriate)

NOTE: The pursuer should complete boxes 1 to 6 on page 1, the statement of claim in box 7 on page 2 and section A on page 5 before service on the defender. The person serving the Summons will complete box 8.

WHAT MUST I DO ABOUT THIS SUMMONS?

Decide whether you wish to dispute the action and how you wish to proceed. Thereafter, look at the 2 options listed below. Find the one which covers your decision and follow the instructions given there. You will find the RETURN DAY and the CALLING DATE on page one of the summons.

Written guidance on summary cause procedure can be obtained from the sheriff clerk at any sheriff clerk's office. Further advice can also be obtained by contacting any of the following:

Citizen's Advice Bureau, Consumer Advice Centre, Trading Standards or Consumer Protection Department or a Solicitor. (Addresses can be found in the guidance booklets)

OPTIONS

1.   ADMIT LIABILITY FOR THE CLAIM and settle it with the pursuer now.

If you wish to avoid the possibility of a court order passing against you, you should settle the claim (including any liability for expenses) with the pursuer or his representative **in good time before the return day.**

2.   DISPUTE THE CLAIM and <u>attend at court</u> to do any of the following:

- Challenge the jurisdiction of the court or the competency of the action
- Defend the action
- State a counterclaim

Complete Section B on page 4. Return page 4 to the court so that it arrives **on or before the return day. You must attend personally, or be represented, at court on the calling date.**

Your representative may be a solicitor, or someone else having your authority. It may be helpful if you or your representative bring pages 1 and 2 of this form to the court.

NOTE: If you fail to return page 4 as directed, or if, having returned it, you fail to attend or are not represented at the calling date, the court will almost certainly decide the claim in your absence.

WRITTEN NOTE OF PROPOSED DEFENCE

You must send to the court by the return day a written note of any proposed defence, or intimate that you wish to challenge the jurisdiction of the court. You must also attend or be represented at court on the calling date.

PLEASE NOTE

If you do nothing about this summons, the court will almost certainly, where appropriate, grant decree against you, including any interest and expenses found due.

YOU ARE ADVISED TO KEEP PAGES 1 AND 2, AS THEY MAY BE USEFUL AT A LATER STAGE OF THE CASE.

SECTION A

This section must
Be completed
Before service

Summons No
Return Day
Calling Date

SHERIFF COURT (Including address)

PURSUER'S FULL NAME AND ADDRESS

DEFENDER'S FULL NAME AND
ADDRESS

SECTION B   **DEFENDER'S RESPONSE TO THE SUMMONS**

DISPUTE THE CLAIM and attend at court
* I intend to challenge the jurisdiction of the court.
* I intend to challenge the competency of the court.
* I wish to defend the action.
* I apply for warrant to serve a third party notice (see page 6).

I intend to appear or be represented in court on the calling date.
*I attach a note of my proposed defence/counterclaim (see page 5).

delete as necessary

WRITTEN NOTE OF PROPOSED DEFENCE / COUNTERCLAIM
State which facts in the statement of claim are admitted:

State briefly any facts regarding the circumstances of the claim on which you intend to rely:

State details of counterclaim, if any:

PLEASE REMEMBER: You must send your response to the court to **arrive on or before the return day** if you have completed a response in Section B.

APPLICATION FOR SERVICE OF A THIRD PARTY NOTICE

NOTE:
You can apply to have another party added to the action if:

(A) **You think that, as regards the matter which the action is about, that other party has a duty to:**
1. Indemnify you; or
2. Make a contribution in respect of the matter; or
3. Relieve you from any responsibility as regards it.
    or
(B) You think that other party is:
4. Solely liable to the pursuer; or
5. Liable to the pursuer along with you; or
6. Has a liability to you as a result of the pursuer's claim against you.

You may apply for warrant to found jurisdiction if you wish to do so.

FORM OF APPLICATION

(TO BE RETURNED TO THE COURT ALONG WITH YOUR RESPONSE)

I request the court to grant warrant for service of a third party notice on the following party:
Name   :

Address   :

The reason I wish a third party notice to be served on the party mentioned above is as follows:
(Give details below of the reasons why you wish the party to be made a defender in the action.)

* I apply for warrant to found jurisdiction

delete as appropriate

NOTE
[1] As amended by the Act of Sederunt (Sheriff Court Rules Amendment) (Diligence) 2008 (SSI 2008/121) r.6(8) (effective April 1, 2008).

Rule 4.3(c)

FORM 1d

Defender's copy summons - multiplepoinding

FORM 1d

Summary Cause Summons

| OFFICIAL USE ONLY |
| SUMMONS No. |

Action of Multiplepoinding

DEFENDER'S COPY

Sheriff Court
(name, address, e-mail
and telephone no.)

1

Name and address
of person raising
the action (**pursuer**)

2

Name and address of
persons against whom
action raised (**defenders**)

3

Claim (Form of decree or
other order sought – see
Form 5)

4

Name, full address, telephone
no., and e-mail address of
pursuer's solicitor (if any)

5

6

| **RETURN DAY** | 20 | | |
| **CALLING DATE** | 20 | at | am. |

NOTE: You will find details of claim on page 2.

7. **STATE DETAILS OF CLAIM HERE OR ATTACH A STATEMENT OF CLAIM**
(to be completed by the pursuer. If space is insufficient, a separate sheet may be attached)

The details of the claim are:

8. **SERVICE ON DEFENDER**

(Place) (Date)

To: (Defender.)

You are hereby served with the above summons. The pursuer has been authorised by the court to serve it on you.

Solicitor / sheriff officer
(delete as appropriate)

NOTE: The Pursuer should complete boxes 1 to 6 on page 1, the statement of claim in box 7 on page 2 and section A on page 5 before service on the defender. The person serving the Summons will complete box 8.

WHAT MUST I DO ABOUT THIS SUMMONS?

Decide whether you wish to dispute the action and how you wish to proceed. Thereafter, look at the 2 options listed below. Find the one which covers your decision and follow the instructions given there. You will find the RETURN DAY and the CALLING DATE on page one of the summons.

Written guidance on summary cause procedure can be obtained from the sheriff clerk at any sheriff clerk's office. Further advice can also be obtained by contacting any of the following:

Citizen's Advice Bureau, Consumer Advice Centre, Trading Standards or Consumer Protection Department or a solicitor. (Addresses can be found in the guidance booklets)

OPTIONS

1.   **ADMIT LIABILITY FOR THE CLAIM and settle it with the pursuer now.**

If you wish to avoid the possibility of a court order passing against you, you should attempt to settle the claim (including any liability for expenses) with the pursuer or his Solicitor **in good time before the return day.**

2.   **DISPUTE THE CLAIM and <u>attend at court</u> to do any of the following:**

- Challenge the jurisdiction of the court or the competency of the action.
- Object to the extent of the fund or subject detailed in the statement of claim on page 2.
- Make a claim on the fund or subject.

Complete Section B on page 4. Return page 4 to the court so that it arrives **on or before the return day. You must attend personally, or be represented, at court on the calling date.**

Your representative may be a Solicitor, or someone else having your authority. It may be helpful if you or your representative bring pages 1 and 2 of this form to the court.

NOTE: If you fail to return page 4 as directed, or if, having returned it, you fail to attend or are not represented at the calling date, the court will almost certainly deal with the action in your absence.

NOTES:

1.   If you do nothing about this summons, the court will almost certainly deal with the action in your absence.

2.   **IF YOU ARE THE HOLDER OF THE FUND,** you must complete the enclosed form 5a and send it to the sheriff clerk before the return day. You must also, before the return day, send a copy of form 5a to the pursuer, the other defenders in the action and to all the persons you have listed in form 5a as having an interest in the fund or subject.

YOU ARE ADVISED TO KEEP PAGES 1 AND 2, AS THEY MAY BE USEFUL AT A LATER STAGE OF THE CASE.

SECTION A
This section must
be completed
Before service

Summons No
Return Day
Calling Date

SHERIFF COURT (Including address)

PURSUER'S FULL NAME AND ADDRESS

DEFENDER'S FULL NAME AND
ADDRESS

SECTION B   **DEFENDER'S RESPONSE TO THE SUMMONS**

DISPUTE THE CLAIM and attend at court

I intend to:

* (1)   Challenge the jurisdiction of the court or the competency of the action.
* (2)   Object to the extent of the fund or subject detailed in the statement
        of claim.
* (3)   Make a claim on the fund or subject.

I intend to appear or be represented in court on the calling date.

*   *delete as necessary*

**Please give below brief details of your reason(s) for disputing the claim in
accordance with your response to 1, 2 or 3 above:**

Rule 4.1(2)   FORM 2

Form of claim in a summons for payment of money

The pursuer claims from the defender(s) the sum of £   with   interest on that sum
at the rate of   annually from the date of service, together with the expenses of bringing the
action.

Rule 4.1(2)   FORM 3

Form of claim in a summons for recovery of possession of heritable property

The pursuer claims that, in the circumstances described in the statement contained on page 2 of
this copy summons, he is entitled to recover possession of the property at (*address*), and that
you refuse or delay to remove from said property.

The pursuer therefore asks the court to grant a decree against you, removing you, and your
family, sub-tenants and dependants (if any) with your goods and possessions from the said
property.

The pursuer also claims from you the expenses of bringing the action.

Rule 30.6(1)   FORM 3A

Form of notice of removal under sections 34, 35 or 36 of the Sheriff Courts
(Scotland) Act 1907

To: (*name, designation and address of party in possession*)

You are hereby required to remove from (*describe subjects*) at the term of (*or, if different terms,
state them and the subjects to which they apply*), in terms of (*describe lease, terms of letter of
removal or otherwise*).

(date)   *(signature, designation and address)*

Rule 30.6(2)   FORM 3B

Form of notice of removal under section 37 of the Sheriff Courts (Scotland) Act 1907

NOTICE OF REMOVAL UNDER SECTION 37 OF THE SHERIFF COURTS
(SCOTLAND) ACT 1907

To:
(*name, designation and address*)
You are hereby required to remove from (*describe subjects*) at the term of (*Whitsunday or
Martinmas*), (*date*).

(date)   *signature, designation and address)*

Rule 30.6(3)   FORM 3C

Form of letter of removal

To: (*name, designation and address*)
(*place and date*). I am to remove from (describe subjects by usual name or give a short
description sufficient for identification) at the term of (*insert term and date*).

(date)   *(signature, designation and address)*

Rule 4.1(2) FORM 4

Form of claim in a summons of sequestration for rent

[Repealed by the Act of Sederunt (Sheriff Court Rules Amendment) (Diligence) 2008 (SSI 2008/ 121) r.2(1)(b) (effective April 1, 2008).]

Rule 31.2(2) FORM 4A

Notice informing defender of right to apply for certain orders under the Debtors (Scotland) Act 1987

[Repealed by the Act of Sederunt (Sheriff Court Rules Amendment) (Diligence) 2008 (SSI 2008/ 121) r.2(1)(b) (effective April 1, 2008).]

Rule 31.2(2) FORM 4B

Certificate of Sequestration

[Repealed by the Act of Sederunt (Sheriff Court Rules Amendment) (Diligence) 2008 (SSI 2008/ 121) r.2(1)(b) (effective April 1, 2008).]

Rule 4.1(2) FORM 5

Form of claim in a summons of multiplepoinding

The pursuer claims that, in the circumstances described in the statement contained on page 2 of this copy summons, the (*state party*) is the holder of a fund (*or subject*) valued at £   on which competing claims are being made by the defenders.

The pursuer therefore asks the court to grant a decree finding the holder of the said fund or subject liable to make payment of, or to deliver, same to the party found by the court to be entitled thereto.

The pursuer also asks that the expenses of bringing the action be deducted from the value of the said fund or subject before payment is made.

Rule 27.5(2)(a) FORM 5A

Form of statement by holder of fund or subject when not the pursuer

(1) I, (*name, address*), hereby state that the fund or subject in the summary cause summons raised at the instance of AB (*design*) against CD, (*EF and GH*) (*design*) is as follows: (*description and details of fund or subject*).

(2) I have the following claim or lien on said fund or subject (give details, including a reference to any document founded upon in support of the claim).

(3) I am aware that the persons listed below have an interest in the said fund/subject:

(*list names and addresses*)

(4) I certify that I have today intimated a copy of this statement to each of the persons contained in the list at (3) above.

(*date*)

Rule 27.9(2)(a) FORM 5B

Form of claim on the fund or subject in action of multiplepoinding

I, EF, claim to be preferred on the fund in the multiplepoinding raised in the name of AB against CD, EF etc. for the sum of £   by reason of (*state ground of claim, including a reference to any document founded upon in support thereof*) with interest thereon from (*date*).

I also claim any appropriate court expenses which I may incur by appearing in this action.

(*signature*)

Rule 4.1(2)   FORM 6

Form of claim in a summons of furthcoming

The pursuer claims that, in the circumstances described in the statement contained on page 2 of this copy summons, the said (*name of common debtor*) is due to him the sum of £   .

He further claims that he has lawfully arrested in the hands of the said (*name of arrestee*) the goods or money valued at £   and described in the said statement of claim, which ought to be made furthcoming to him.

He therefore asks the court to order that you make furthcoming and deliver to him the said arrested goods or money or so much thereof as will satisfy (*or part satisfy*) the said sum of £   owing to him.

The pursuer also claims from you the expenses of bringing this action. If the value of the arrested funds are insufficient to meet the sum owing to the pursuer plus the expenses of the action, the pursuer claims those expenses from the said (*name of common debtor*).

Rule 4.1(2)   FORM 7

Form of claim in a summons for delivery

The pursuer claims that, in the circumstances described in the statement contained on page 2 of this copy summons, he has right to the possession of the article(s) described therein.

He therefore asks the court to grant a decree ordering you to deliver the said articles to the pursuer.

Alternatively, if you do not deliver said articles, the pursuer asks the court to grant a decree ordering you to pay to him the sum of £   with interest on that sum at the rate of   % annually from (*date*) until payment.

The pursuer also claims from you the expenses of bringing the action.

Rule 4.1(2)   FORM 8

Form of claim in a summons for implement of an obligation

The pursuer claims that, in the circumstances described in the statement contained on page 2 of this copy summons, you are obliged to

He therefore asks the court to grant a decree ordering you to implement the said obligation.

Alternatively, if you do not fulfil the obligation, the pursuer asks the court to grant a decree ordering you to pay to him the sum of £   with interest on that sum at the rate of   % annually from (*date*) until payment.

The pursuer also claims from you the expenses of bringing the action.

Rule 4.1(2)   FORM 9

Form of claim in a summons for count, reckoning and payment

The pursuer claims that, in the circumstances described in the statement contained on page 2 of this copy summons, you have intromitted with (*describe briefly the fund or estate*), in which he has an interest.

He therefore asks the court to grant a decree ordering you to produce a full account of your intromissions therewith, and for payment to him of the sum of £   , or such other sum as appears to the court to be the true balance due by you, with interest thereon at the rate of   % annually from (*date*) until payment.

Alternatively, if you do not produce such an account, the pursuer asks the court to grant a decree ordering you to pay to him the said sum of £   with interest thereon at the rate of   % annually from (*date*) until payment.

The pursuer also claims from you the expenses of bringing the action.

Rule 34.2(1) FORM 10

Form of statement of claim in a summons for damages for personal injury

1.   The pursuer is (*state designation, address, occupation, date of birth and National Insurance number of the pursuer*). (*In an action arising out of the death of a relative state designation of the deceased and relation to the pursuer.*)

2.   The defender is (*state designation, address and occupation of the defender*).

3.   The court has jurisdiction to hear this claim against the defender because (*state briefly ground of jurisdiction*).

4.   (*State briefly the facts necessary to establish the claim*).

5.   (*State briefly the personal injuries suffered and give the names and addresses of medical practitioners and hospitals and other institutions in which the person injured received treatment; and specify every medical practitioner from whom, and hospital and other institution in which the pursuer or the deceased received treatment in respect of injury or disease to which the action relates*).

6.   (*State whether claim based on fault at common law or breach of statutory duty, or other basis of liability; if breach of statute, state provision of enactment*).

*It is not necessary to include in the statement of claim the amount(s) claimed. This should be done by completing a valuation of claim in Form 10c.

Rule 34.2(3) FORM 10A

Form of claim for provisional damages

For payment to the pursuer by the defender of the sum (*amount in words and figures*) as provisional damages.

(*Statements to include risk that pursuer will as result of cause of action develop serious disease or deterioration of condition in future; and that defender public authority or corporation or insured or indemnified in respect of claim*).

Rules 34.2(7) and 34.3(1) FORM 10B

Form of response

SHERIFF COURT OF

(Action for damages: personal injuries)

[AB] (*designation and address*), pursuer

against

[CD] (*designation and address*), defender

RESPONSE TO STATEMENT OF CLAIM

Question	*Response*
1. Is it intended to dispute the description and designation of the pursuer? If so, why?	
2. Is the description and designation of the defender disputed? If so, why?	
3. Is there any dispute that the court has jurisdiction to hear the claim. If so, why?	
4. (a) State which facts in paragraph 4 of the statement of claim are admitted.	
(b) State any facts regarding the circumstances of the claim upon which the defender intends to rely.	

5. (a) State whether the nature and extent of the pursuer's injuries is disputed and whether medical reports can be agreed.
   (b) If the defender has a medical report upon which he intends to rely to contradict the pursuer's report in any way, state the details.
   (c) State whether the claims for other losses are disputed in whole or in part.
   (d) State any other facts in relation to the quantification claim upon which the defender intends to rely.

6. (a) Does the defender accept that <u>the common law duty</u> or duties in the statement of claim were incumbent upon the defender in the circumstances? If not, state why.
   (b) Does the defender accept that the <u>statutory duty or duties alleged</u> in the statement of claim were incumbent upon them in the circumstances? If not, state why.
   (c) State any other provisions or propositions upon which the defender proposes to rely in relation to the question of his liability for the accident including, if appropriate, details of any allegation of contributory negligence.
   (d) Does the defender allege that the accident was caused by any other wrongdoer? If so, give details.
   (e) Does the defender allege that he is entitled to be indemnified or relieved from any liability he might have to the pursuer? If so, give details.

Rules 34.2(2)(b), 34.5(1) and 34.6(13)   FORM 10C

Form of statement of valuation of claim

SHERIFF COURT OF

(Action for damages: personal injuries)

[AB] (*designation and address*), pursuer

against

[CD] (*designation and address*), defender

Head of Claim	Components	Valuation
Solatium	Past	£x
	Future	£x
Interest on past solatium	Percentage applied to past solatium. State percentage rate.	£x
Past wage loss	Date from which wage loss claimed	£x
	(............)	
	Date to which wage loss claimed	
	(............)	
	Rate of net wage loss (per week, per month or per annum)	

Interest on past wage loss	Percentage applied to past wage loss (State percentage rate)	£x
Past services Specify nature, duration, and components of calculation	Total amount claimed (............) Interest	£x
Future losses including wages, disadvantage on the labour market, services or loss of capacity to provide services. Specify which and provide details.		
Other financial losses	Specify	£x
	TOTAL	£x

DEFENDER ONLY.

The defender should adapt the form as appropriate.

Where the defender is unable to state a valuation of any part of the claim because of the absence of information properly and reasonably sought in writing from the pursuer, please explain and produce with this form a copy of the relative request.

Rule 34.6(5)   FORM 10D

Form of intimation to connected persons

Court ref. no.

To: (*insert name and address as in warrant*)

You are hereby given notice that an action has been raised against (*name*), your (*insert relationship, e.g., father, brother or other relative as the case may be*). A copy of the summons is enclosed.

It is believed that you may have a title or interest to sue the said (*name of defender*) in this action, which is based upon (*the injuries from which the late (insert name and designation) died*) (*or the death of the late (name and designation)*). You may therefore be entitled to enter this action as an additional pursuer.

If you wish to appear as a party in the action, or are uncertain about what action to take, you should contact a solicitor. You may, depending on your financial circumstances, be entitled to legal aid, and you can get information about legal aid from a solicitor.

You may also obtain advice from any Citizen's Advice Bureau, other advice agency or any sheriff clerk's office.

Rule 34.6(5)   FORM 10E

Specification of documents

SPECIFICATION OF DOCUMENTS

1. All books, medical records reports, charts, X-rays, notes and other documents of (*specify name of each medical practitioners named in summons in accordance with rule 34.2(1)(c)*), and relating to the pursuer [*or as the case may be the deceased*], in order that excerpts may be taken therefrom at the sight of the Commissioner of all entries showing or tending to show the nature, extent and cause of the pursuer's [*or, as the case may be, the deceased's*] injuries when he attended his doctor on or after (*specify date*) and the treatment received by him since that date.

2. All books, medical records reports, charts, X-rays, notes and other documents of (*specify name of each institution named in summons in accordance with rule 34.2(1)(c)*), and relating to the pursuer [*or, as the case may be, the deceased*], in order that excerpts may be taken therefrom at the sight of the Commissioner of all entries showing or tending to show the nature, extent and cause of all injuries from which the pursuer [*or, as the case may be, the deceased*] was suffering when he was admitted to that institution on or about (*specify date*), the treatment received by him since that date and his certificate of discharge, if any.

3. All wage books, cash books, wage sheets, computer records and other earnings information held by or on behalf of the defenders, for the period (*specify dates*) in order that excerpts may be taken therefrom at the sight of the Commissioner of all entries showing or tending to show (a) the pursuer's [*or, as the case may be, the deceased's*] earnings, both gross and net, over the said period and (b) the earnings of other employees in the same or similar employment over the said period.

4. All accident reports, memoranda or other written communications made to the defenders or anyone on their behalf by an employee of the defenders at or about the time at which the pursuer [*or, as the case may be, the deceased*] sustained the injuries in respect of which the summons in this cause was issued and relevant to the matters contained in the statement of claim.

5. Failing principals, drafts, copies or duplicates of the above or any of them.

Rule 34.7(1) FORM 10F

Form of minute—application for further damages

Court ref. no.:

Sheriff Court at (*insert place of court*)

APPLICATION FOR FURTHER DAMAGES

in the cause

(AB) (*insert designation and address*), pursuer

against

(CD) (*insert designation and address*), defender

The pursuer claims payment from the defender of the sum (*amount in words and figures*) as further damages.

(*Insert concise statement of facts supporting claim for further damages*).

The pursuer requests the court to fix a hearing on this minute and applies for warrant to serve the minute on—

(*Here state names and addresses of other parties to the action; and, where such other parties are insured or otherwise indemnified, their insurers or indemnifiers, if known to the pursuer*).

Rule 34.7(3) FORM 10G

Form of notice of application for further damages

Date:

To:

TAKE NOTICE

(*Pursuer's name and address*), pursuer, raised an action against (*defender's name and address*), defender, in the sheriff court at (*insert place of court*).

In the action, the sheriff on (*date*) made an award of provisional damages in favour of the pursuer against (*you or name of party*). [The sheriff specified that the pursuer may apply for an award of further damages at any time before (*date*)]. The pursuer has applied by minute for an award of further damages against you [or name of party]. A copy of the minute is attached.

A hearing on the minute has been fixed for (*date and time*) at (*place of sheriff court*). If you wish to be heard on the minute, you should attend or be represented at court on that date.

Rule 5.3(1) FORM 11

Form of service

XY, you are hereby served with a copy of the above (or attached) summons.

(*signature of solicitor or sheriff officer*)

Rule 5.3(2) FORM 12

Form of certificate of execution of service

Case name:

Court ref: no:

(*Place and date*)

I, ,hereby certify that on the day of , 20 ,I duly cited XY to answer the foregoing summons. This I did by (*set forth the mode of service*).

(*Signature of solicitor or sheriff officer*)

Rule 5.5(1)(a) FORM 13

Service on person whose address is unknown Form of advertisement

A summary cause action has been raised in the sheriff court at by AB, pursuer against CD, defender, whose last known address was

If the said CD wishes to defend the action he should immediately contact the sheriff clerk's office at the above court.

    Address of court:
    Telephone no:
    Fax no:
    E-mail address:

Rule 5.5(1)(b) FORM 14

Service on person whose address is unknown
Form of notice to be displayed on the walls of court

A summary cause action has been raised in this court by AB, pursuer against CD, defender, whose last known address was

If the said CD wishes to defend the action he should immediately contact the sheriff clerk's office.

(*Date*) Displayed on the walls of court of this date.

Sheriff clerk depute

Rule 5.6(2) FORM 15

Service by post—form of notice

This letter contains a citation to or intimation from the sheriff court at

If delivery cannot be made the letter must be returned immediately to the sheriff clerk at (*insert full address*).

Rule 6.A2(2) [1] FORM 15A

Statement to accompany application for interim diligence

DEBTORS (SCOTLAND) ACT 1987 Section 15D [or DEBT ARRANGEMENT AND ATTACHMENT (SCOTLAND) ACT 2002 Section 9C]

Sheriff Court:........................
In the Cause (Cause Reference No.)
[A.B.] (*designation and address*)

Pursuer

against
[C.D.] (*designation and address*)

Defender

STATEMENT

1. The applicant is the pursuer [*or* defender] in the action by [A.B] *(design)* against [C.D.] *(design)*.

2. [The following persons have an interest [*specify names and addresses*].]

3. The application is [*or* is not] seeking the grant under section 15E(1) of the 1987 Act of warrant for diligence [*or* section 9D(1) of the 2002 Act of interim attachment] in advance of a hearing on the application.

4. [*Here provide such other information as may be prescribed by regulations made by the Scottish Ministers under section 15D(2)(d) of the 1987 Act or 9C(2)(d,) of the 2002 Act*]

(*Signed*)

Solicitor [*or* Agent] for A.B. [*or* C.D.]
(*include full designation*)

NOTE
[1] As inserted by the Act of Sederunt (Sheriff Court Rules Amendment) (Diligence) 2008 (SSI 2008/121) r.6(9) (effective April 1, 2008).

Rule 6.A8 [1] FORM 15B

Form of schedule of arrestment on the dependence

SCHEDULE OF ARRESTMENT ON THE DEPENDENCE

Date: (*date of execution*)

Time: (time arrestment executed)

To: (*name and address of arrestee*)

IN HER MAJESTY'S NAME AND AUTHORITY AND IN NAME AND AUTHORITY OF THE SHERIFF, I, (*name*), Sheriff Officer, by virtue of:

- a summons containing warrant which has been granted for arrestment on the dependence of the action at the instance of (*name and address of pursuer*) against (*name and address of defender*) and dated (*date*);

- a counterclaim containing a warrant which has been granted for arrestment on the dependence of the claim by (*name and address of creditor*) against (*name and address of debtor*) and dated (*date of warrant*);

- an order of the Sheriff at (*place*) dated (*date of order*) granting warrant [for arrestment on the dependence of the action raised at the instance of (*name and address of pursuer*) against (*name and address of defender*)] [*or* for arrestment on the dependence of the claim in the counterclaim [*or* third party notice] by (*name and address of creditor*) against (*name and address or debtor*)],

arrest in your hands (i) the sum of (*amount*), in excess of the Protected Minimum Balance, where applicable (*see Note 1*), more or less, due by you to (*defender's name*) [*or name and address of common debtor if common debtor is not the defender*] or to any other person on his [*or* her] [*or* its] [*or* their] behalf; and (ii) all moveable things in your hands belonging or pertaining to the said (*name of common debtor*), to remain in your hands under arrestment until they are made forthcoming to (*name of pursuer*) [*or name and address of creditor if he is not the pursuer*] or until further order of the court.

This I do in the presence of (*name, occupation and address of witness*).

(*Signed*)
Sheriff Officer
(*Address*)

NOTE

1. This Schedule arrests in your hands (i) funds due by you to (*name of common debtor*) and (ii) goods or other moveables held by you for him. **You should not pay any funds to him or hand over any goods or other moveables to him without taking legal advice.**

2. This Schedule may be used to arrest a ship or cargo. If it is, you should consult your legal adviser about the effect of it.

3. The Protected Minimum Balance is the sum referred to in section 73F(4) of the Debtors (Scotland) Act 1987. This sum is currently set at [*insert current sum*]. The Protected Minimum Balance applies where the arrestment attaches funds standing to the credit of a debtor in an account held by a bank or other financial institution and the debtor is an individual. The Protected Minimum Balance does not apply where the account is held in the name of a company, a limited liability partnership, a partnership or an unincorporated association or where the account is operated by the debtor as a trading account.

4. Under section 73G of the Debtors (Scotland) Act 1987 you must also, within the period of 3 weeks beginning with the day on which the arrestment is executed, disclose to the creditor the nature and value of the funds and/or moveable property which have been attached. This disclosure must be in the form set out in Schedule 8 to the Diligence (Scotland) Regulations 2009. Failure to comply may lead to a financial penalty under section 73G of the Debtors (Scotland) Act 1987 and may also be dealt with as a contempt of court. You must, at the same time, send a copy of the disclosure to the debtor and to any person known to you who owns (or claims to own) attached property and to any person to whom attached funds are (or are claimed to be due), solely or in common with the debtor.

IF YOU WISH FURTHER ADVICE CONTACT ANY CITIZENS ADVICE BUREAU/LOCAL ADVICE CENTRE/SHERIFF CLERK OR SOLICITOR

NOTE
[1] As inserted by the Act of Sederunt (Sheriff Court Rules Amendment) (Diligence) 2008 (SSI 2008/121) r.6(9) (effective April 1, 2008) and substituted by the Act of Sederunt (Sheriff Court Rules Amendment) (Diligence) 2009 (SSI 2009/107) (effective April 22, 2009).

Rule 6.A8   [1] FORM 15C

Form of certificate of execution of arrestment on the dependence

CERTIFICATE OF EXECUTION

I, (*name*), Sheriff Officer, certify that I executed an arrestment on the dependence, by virtue of an interlocutor of the Sheriff at (*place*) on (*date*) obtained at the instance of (*name and address of party arresting*) against (*name and address of defender*) on (*name of arrestee*)—

* by delivering the schedule of arrestment to (*name of arrestee or other person*) at (*place*) personally on (*date*).
* by leaving the schedule of arrestment with (*name and occupation of person with whom left*) at (*place*) on (*date*) [and by posting a copy of the schedule to the arrestee by registered post or first class recorded delivery to the address specified on the receipt annexed to this certificate].
* by depositing the schedule of arrestment in (*place*) on (*date*). (*Specify that enquiry made and reasonable grounds exist for believing that the person on whom service is to be made resides at the place but is not available*) [and by posting a copy of the schedule to the arrestee by registered post or first class recorded delivery to the address specified on the receipt annexed to this certificate].
* by affixing the schedule of arrestment to the door at (*place*) on *(date)*. (*Specify that enquiry made and that reasonable grounds exist for believing that the person on whom service is to be made resides at the place but is not available*) [and by posting a copy of the schedule to the arrestee by registered post or first class recorded delivery to the address specified on the receipt annexed to this certificate].
* by leaving the schedule of arrestment with (*name and occupation of person with whom left*) at (*place of business*) on (*date*).[and by posting a copy of the schedule to the arrestee by registered post or first class recorded delivery to the address specified on the receipt annexed to this certificate].
* by depositing the schedule of arrestment at (*place of business*) on (*date*). (*Specify that enquiry*

made and that reasonable grounds exist for believing that the person on whom service is to be made carries on business at that place.) [and by posting a copy of the schedule to the arrestee by registered post or first class recorded delivery to the address specified on the receipt annexed to this certificate].

* by affixing the schedule of arrestment to the door at (*place of business*) on *(date)*. (*Specify that enquiry made and that reasonable grounds exist for believing that the person on whom service is to be made carries on business at that place.*) [and by posting a copy of the schedule to the arrestee by registered post or first class recorded delivery to the address specified on the receipt annexed to this certificate].

* by leaving the schedule of arrestment at (*registered office*) on *(date)*, in the hands of (*name of person*) [and by posting a copy of the schedule to the arrestee by registered post or first class recorded delivery to the address specified on the receipt annexed to this certificate].

* by depositing the schedule of arrestment at (*registered office*) on (*date*) [and by posting a copy of the schedule to the arrestee by registered post or first class recorded delivery to the address specified on the receipt annexed to this certificate].

* by affixing the schedule of arrestment to the door at (*registered office*) on *(date)*. [and by posting a copy of the schedule to the arrestee by registered post or first class recorded delivery to the address specified on the receipt annexed to this certificate].

I did this in the presence of (*name, occupation and address of witness*).

(*Signed*)

Sheriff Officer

(*Address*)

(*Signed*)

(Witness)

*Delete where not applicable

NOTE

A copy of the Schedule of arrestment on the dependence is to be attached to this certificate

NOTE
[1] As inserted by the Act of Sederunt (Sheriff Court Rules Amendment) (Diligence) 2008 (SSI 2008/121) r.6(9) (effective April 1, 2008) and substituted by the Act of Sederunt (Sheriff Court Rules Amendment) (Diligence) 2009 (SSI 2009/107) (effective April 22, 2009).

Rule 6.3(4)(a) **FORM 16**

Recall or restriction of arrestment
Certificate authorising the release of arrested funds or property

Sheriff court, (*place*)

Court ref. no.:   AB (pursuer) against CD (defender)

I, (*name*), hereby certify that the sheriff on (*date*) authorised the release of the funds or property arrested on the *dependence of the action/counterclaim/third party notice to the following extent:

(*details of sheriff's order*)

(*Date*) Sheriff clerk depute

**delete as appropriate*

Copy to:
      Party instructing arrestment
      Party possessing arrested funds/property

Rule 7.1(1) FORM 17

Form of minute—no form of response lodged by defender

Sheriff court, (*place*)

Calling date:

In respect that the defender(s) has/have failed to lodge a form of response to the summons, the pursuer respectfully craves the court to make the orders specified in the following case(s):

Court ref. No   Name(s) of defender(s)   Minute(s)

Rule 7.1(2) [1] FORM 18

Form of minute—pursuer not objecting to application for a time to pay direction
or time order

Sheriff court, (*place*)

Court ref. no.:

Name(s) of defender(s)

Calling date:

I do not object to the defender's application for

> *a time to pay direction
> *recall or restriction of an arrestment
> *a time order

The pursuer requests the court to grant decree or other order in terms of the following minute(s)

delete as appropriate

NOTE
[1] As amended by the Act of Sederunt (Ordinary Cause, Summary Application, Summary Cause and Small Claim Rules) Amendment (Miscellaneous) 2003 (SSI 2003/26) r.4(4)(b) (effective January 24, 2003).

Rule 7.2(4) [1] FORM 19

Form of minute—pursuer opposing an application for a time to pay direction
or time order

Sheriff court (*place*):

Court ref no:

Name(s) of defender(s):

Calling date:

I oppose the defender's application for

> *a time to pay direction
> *recall or restriction of arrestment
> *a time order

delete as appropriate

1. The debt is (*please specify the nature of the debt*).

2. The debt was incurred on (*specify date*) and the pursuer has contacted the defender in relation to the debt on (*specify date(s)*).

*3. The contractual payments were (*specify amount*).

*4. (*Specify any action taken by the pursuer to assist the defender to pay the debt*).

*5. The defender has made payment(s) towards the debt of (*specify amount(s)*) on (*specify date(s)*).

*6. The debtor has made offers to pay (*specify amount(s)*) on (*specify date(s)*) which offer(s) was [were] accepted] [*or* rejected] and (*specify amount*) was paid on (*specify date(s)*).

7. (*Here set out any information you consider relevant to the court's determination of the application*).

8. The pursuer requests the court to grant decree.

delete as appropriate

(*Signed*)

Pursuer [*or* Solicitor for Pursuer]

(*Date*)

NOTE
[1] As substituted by the Act of Sederunt (Sheriff Court Rules) (Miscellaneous Amendments) 2009 (SSI 2009/294) r.4 (effective December 1, 2009).

Rule 8.12   FORM 20

Form of oath for witnesses

I swear by Almighty God that I will tell the truth, the whole truth and nothing but the truth.

Rule 8.12   FORM 21

Form of affirmation for witnesses

I solemnly, sincerely and truly declare and affirm that I will tell the truth, the whole truth and nothing but the truth.

Rule 11.2(1)(b)(iii)   FORM 22

Form of third party notice

Court ref. no.

SHERIFF COURT, (*place*)

THIRD PARTY NOTICE

in the cause

(AB) (*insert designation and address*), pursuer

against

(CD) (*insert designation and address*), defender

To (EF)

You are given notice by (CD) of an order granted by the sheriff at (*insert place of court*) in which (AB) is the pursuer and (CD) is the defender. A copy of the order is enclosed herewith.

In the action, the pursuer claims from the defender (*insert a brief account of the circumstances of the claim*) as more fully appears in the copy summons enclosed.

The defender claims that,   (*delete as appropriate*).

*if he is liable to the pursuer, you are liable to relieve him wholly/partially of his liability, as more fully appears in the copy grounds upon which the defender relies for this, which are also enclosed.

*he is not liable to the pursuer for the claim made against him. He maintains that any liability to the pursuer in respect of this claim rests solely on you, as more fully appears in the copy grounds upon which the defender relies for this, which are also enclosed.

*if he is liable to the pursuer in respect of this claim, he shares that liability with you, as more fully appears in the copy grounds upon which the defender relies for this, which are also enclosed.

*You are liable to him in respect of the claim, as more fully appears in the copy grounds upon which the defender relies for this, which are also enclosed.

If you wish to resist the claim(s) made by the defender as detailed above, you must—
    (a) return the form of response enclosed to the sheriff clerk at (*address*) by (*date seven days before the date of hearing*); and
    (b) attend or be represented at a hearing on (*date and time*).

(Date)   *(Signature of person serving notice)*

Rule 11.2(1)(b)(iii)   FORM 23

Form of response to third party notice

in the cause

(AB) (*insert designation and address*), pursuer

against

(CD) (*insert designation and address*), defender

I wish to answer the claim made against me by (CD), defender. (*here state briefly the grounds of opposition to the defender's claim.*)

(*date*)

Rule 14A.3(1)   [1] FORM 23A

Form of minute of intervention by the Commission for Equality and Human Rights

SHERIFF COURT, (place)   Court ref. no.

APPLICATION FOR LEAVE TO INTERVENE BY THE COMMISSION FOR EQUALITY AND HUMAN RIGHTS

in the cause

[A.B.] (designation and address), Pursuer

against

[C.D.] (designation and address), Defender

[Here set out briefly:
    (a) the Commission's reasons for believing that the proceedings are relevant to a matter in connection with which the Commission has a function;
    (b) the issue in the proceedings which the Commission wishes to address; and
    (c) the propositions to be advanced by the Commission and the Commission's reasons for believing that they are relevant to the proceedings and that they will assist the court.]

NOTE
[1] As inserted by the Act of Sederunt (Sheriff Court Rules) (Miscellaneous Amendments) 2008 (SSI 2008/223) Sch.3 (effective July 1, 2008).

Rule 14B.2(1) [1] FORM 23B

Form of minute of intervention by the Scottish Commission for Human Rights

SHERIFF COURT, (place)   Court ref. no.

APPLICATION FOR LEAVE TO INTERVENE BY THE SCOTTISH COMMISSION FOR HUMAN RIGHTS

in the cause

[A.B.] (designation and address), Pursuer

against

[C.D.] (designation and address), Defender

[Here set out briefly:

    (a) the issue in the proceedings which the Commission intends to address; and
    (b) a summary of the submission the Commission intends to make.]

NOTE
  [1] As inserted by the Act of Sederunt (Sheriff Court Rules) (Miscellaneous Amendments) 2008 (SSI 2008/223) Sch.3 (effective July 1, 2008).

Rule 14B.3(1) [1] FORM 23C

Invitation to the Scottish Commission for Human Rights to intervene

SHERIFF COURT, (place)   Court ref. no.

INVITATION TO THE SCOTTISH COMMISSION FOR HUMAN RIGHTS TO INTERVENE

in the cause

[A.B.] (designation and address), Pursuer

against

[C.D.] (designation and address), Defender

[Here set out briefly:

    (a) the facts, procedural history and issues in the proceedings;
    (b) the issue in the proceedings on which the court seeks a submission.]

NOTE
  [1] As inserted by the Act of Sederunt (Sheriff Court Rules) (Miscellaneous Amendments) 2008 (SSI 2008/223) Sch.3 (effective July 1, 2008).

Rule 18.2(1)   [1] FORM 24

Order by the court and certificate in optional procedure for recovery of documents

Sheriff Court, (*place and address*)

In the cause (*court ref. no.*)

in which

AB (*design*) is the pursuer

and

CD (*design*) is the defender

To: (*name and designation of party or haver from whom the documents are sought to be recovered.*)

You are required to produce to the sheriff clerk at (*address*) within   days of the service upon you of this order:

(1) This order itself (which must be produced intact);

(2) The certificate marked 'B' attached;

(3) All documents within your possession covered by the specification which is enclosed; and

(4) A list of those documents. You can produce the items listed above either:
    (a) by delivering them to the sheriff clerk at the address shown above; or
    (b) sending them to the sheriff clerk by registered or recorded delivery post.

(*date*)   (*Signature, name, address and designation of person serving order*)

PLEASE NOTE:
If you claim confidentiality for any of the documents produced by you, you must still produce them. However, they may be placed in a separate envelope by themselves, marked "confidential". The court will, if necessary, decide whether the envelope should be opened or not.

Claims for necessary outlays within certain specified limits may be paid. Claims should be made in writing to the person who has obtained an order that you produce the documents.

CERTIFICATE

B

Sheriff Court, (*place and address*)

In the cause (*court ref. no.*)

in which

AB (*design*) is the pursuer

and

CD (*design*) is the defender.

Order for recovery of documents dated.................

With reference to the above order and relative specification of documents, I certify:

* *delete as appropriate*

*that the documents produced herewith and the list signed by me which accompanies them are all the documents in my possession which fall under the specification.

* I have no documents in my possession falling under the specification.

* I believe that there are other documents falling within the specification which are not in my possession. These documents are (*list the documents as described in the specification.*) These documents were last seen by me on (*date*) in the possession of (*name and address of person/ company, if known*).

* I know of no documents falling within the specification which are in the possession of any other person.

(*name*) (*date*)

NOTE

[1] As substituted by Act of Sederunt (Ordinary Cause, Summary Application, Summary Cause and Small Claim Rules) Amendment (Miscellaneous) 2005 (SSI 2005/648) (effective January 2, 2006).

Rule 18.7(3)   FORM 25

Form of minute in an application for letter of request

Sheriff Court, (*place and address*)

MINUTE

for (*designation*)

In the cause (court ref. no.)

in which

AB (*design*) is the pursuer

and

CD (*design*) is the defender.

The minuter states to the court that the evidence specified in the proposed letter of request lodged with this minute is required for the purpose of this cause. The minuter respectfully asks the court to issue a letter of request in terms of the proposed letter of request to (*central authority of the country or territory in which the evidence is to be obtained*) in order to obtain the evidence so specified.

(*designation of minuter*)

Rule 18.7(3)   FORM 25A

Form of letter of request

PART A—items to be included in every letter of request

1.	Sender	(*Identity and address*)...........................
2.	Central authority of the requested state	(*Identity and address*)........................
3.	Persons to whom the executed request is to be returned	(*Identity and address*)........................
4.	The undersigned applicant has the honour to submit the following request:	
5.	a. Requesting Judicial authority	(*Identity and address*)........................
	b. To the competent authority	(*the requested state*)...........................
6.	Names and addresses of the parties and their representatives a. pursuer	....

b. defender ....

c. other parties ....

7. Nature and purpose of the proceedings ....
and summary of the facts ....

8. Evidence to be obtained or other judicial ....
act to be performed ....

PART B—items to be completed where applicable
9. Identity and address of any person to be ....
examined ....

10. Questions to be put to the person to be *(or, see attached list)*...........................
examined, or statement of the subject ....
matter about which they are to be ....
examined ....

11. Documents or other property to be *(specify whether to be produced, copied,*
inspected *valued etc.)*.......................................

12. Any requirement that the evidence be *(in the event that the evidence cannot be*
given on oath or affirmation and any *taken in the manner requested, specify*
special form to be used *whether it is to be taken in such manner*
as provided by local law for the formal
taking of evidence)

13. Special methods or procedure to be ....
followed ....

14. Request for notification of the time and ....
place for the execution of the request and ....
identity and address of any person to be ....
notified ....

15. Request for attendance or participation of ....
judicial personnel of the requesting ....
authority at the execution of the letter of ....
request ....

16. Specification of privilege or duty to refuse ....
to give evidence under the law of the state ....
of origin ....

17. The fees and expenses incurred will be *(identity and address)*...........................
borne by ....

PART C—to be included in every letter of request
18. Date of request, signature and seal of the ....
requesting authority ....

Rule 18.7A(2) [1] FORM 25B

Form of minute in application for taking of evidence in the European Community

Sheriff Court, (*place and address*)

MINUTE

for (*designation*)

In the cause (court ref. no.)

in which

AB (*design*) is the pursuer

and

CD (*design*) is the defender.

The minuter states to the court that the evidence specified in the proposed Form A [or Form I] lodged with this minute is required for the purpose of this cause. The minuter respectfully asks the court to issue that Form to (*specify the applicable court, tribunal, central body or competent authority*) in order to obtain the evidence specified.

Signed (*designation of minuter*)

NOTE
[1] As inserted by the Act of Sederunt (Taking of Evidence in the European Community) 2003 (SI 2003/601).

Rule 18.8(1) [1] FORM 26

Form of citation of witness or haver

(*date*)

CITATION

SHERIFFDOM OF (*insert name of sheriffdom*)

AT (*insert place of sheriff court*)

TO [A.B.] (*design*)

(*Name*) who is pursuing/defending a case against (*name*) [*or* is a (*specify*) in the case of (*name*) against (*name*)] has asked you to be a witness. You must attend the above sheriff court on (*insert date*) at (*insert time*) for that purpose, [and bring with you (*specify documents*)].

If you

- would like to know more about being a witness
- are a child under the age of 16
- think you may be a vulnerable witness within the meaning of section 11(1) of the Vulnerable Witnesses (Scotland) Act 2004 (that is someone the court considers may be less able to give their evidence due to mental disorder or fear or distress connected to giving your evidence at the court hearing).

you should contact (*specify the solicitor acting for the party or the party litigant citing the witness*) for further information.

If you are a vulnerable witness (including a child under the age of 16) then you should be able to use a special measure (such measures include use of a screen, a live TV link or a supporter, or a commissioner) to help you give evidence.

Expenses

You may claim back money which you have had to spend and any earnings you have lost within certain specified limits, because you have to come to court on the above date. These may be paid to you if you claim within specified time limits. Claims should be made to the person who has asked you to attend court. Proof of any loss of earnings should be given to that person.

If you wish your travelling expenses to be paid before you go to court, you should apply for payment to the person who has asked you to attend court.

Failure to attend

It is very important that you attend court and you should note that failure to do so may result in a warrant being granted for your arrest. In addition, if you fail to attend without any good reason, having requested and been paid your travelling expenses, you may be ordered to pay a penalty not exceeding £250.

If you have any questions about anything in this citation, please contact (*specify the solicitor acting for the party or the party litigant citing the witness*) for further information.

Signed

[P.Q.] Sheriff Officer

or [X.Y.], (*add designation and business address*)

Solicitor for the pursuer [*or* defender][*or* (*specify*)]

NOTE
[1] As substituted by the Act of Sederunt (Ordinary Cause, Summary Application, Summary Cause and Small Claim Rules) Amendment (Vulnerable Witnesses (Scotland) Act 2004) 2007 (SSI 2007/463) (effective November 1, 2007).

Rule 18.8(1)   FORM 26A

Form of certificate of witness citation

I certify that on (*date*) I duly cited AB (*design*) to attend at (*name of court*) on (*date*) at (*time*) as a witness for the (*design party*) in the action at the instance of CD (*design*) against EF (*design*) (and I required him to bring with him   ....). This I did by   ....

(*Signature of solicitor or sheriff officer*)

[1] FORM 26B

Form of child witness notice

Rule 18A.2   VULNERABLE WITNESSES (SCOTLAND) ACT 2004 Section 12

Received the   day of   20

(*Date of receipt of this notice*)

.... (*signed*)

Sheriff Clerk

CHILD WITNESS NOTICE

Sheriff Court   20

Court Ref. No.

1. The applicant is the pursuer [*or* defender] in the action by [A.B.] (*design*) against [C.D.] (*design*).

2. The applicant has cited [*or* intends to cite] [E.F.] (*date of birth*) as a witness.

3. [E.F.] is a child witnesses under section 11 of the Vulnerable Witnesses (Scotland) Act 2004 [and was under the age of sixteen on the date of the commencement of proceedings].

4. The applicant considers that the following special measure[s] is [are] the most appropriate for the purpose of taking the evidence of [E.F.][*or* that [E.F.] should give evidence without the benefit of any special measure]:-

(*delete as appropriate and specify any special measure(s) sought*).

5. [(a) The reason[s] this [these] special measure[s] is [are] considered the most appropriate is [are] as follows:-

(*here specify the reason(s) for the special measure(s) sought*)].

OR

[(b) The reason[s] it is considered that [E.F.] should give evidence without the benefit of any special measure is [are]:-

(*here explain why it is felt that no special measures are required*)].

6. [E.F.] and the parent[s] of [*or* person[s] with parental responsibility for] [E.F.] has [have] expressed the following view[s] on the special measure[s] that is [are] considered most appropriate [*or* the appropriateness of [E.F.] giving evidence without the benefit of any special measure]:—

(*delete as appropriate and set out the views(s) expressed and how they were obtained*)

7. Other information considered relevant to this application is as follows:-

(*here set out any other information relevant to the child witness notice*).

8. The applicant asks the court to –

(a) consider this child witness notice;

(b) make an order authorising the special measure[s] sought;
     or

(c) make an order authorising the giving of evidence by [E.F.] without the benefit of special measures.

(*delete as appropriate*)

(*Signed*)

[A.B. *or* C.D.]

[or Representative of A.B. [*or* C.D.]] (*include full designation*)

NOTE: This form should be suitably adapted where section 16 of the Act of 2004 applies.

NOTE
[1] As inserted by the Act of Sederunt (Ordinary Cause, Summary Application, Summary Cause and Small Claim Rules) Amendment (Vulnerable Witnesses (Scotland) Act 2004) 2007 (SSI 2007/463) (effective November 1, 2007).

' FORM 26C

Form of vulnerable witness application

Rule 18A.3

VULNERABLE WITNESSES (SCOTLAND) ACT 2004 Section 12

Received the ....day of ....20............

(Date of receipt of this notice)

................(*signed*)

Sheriff Clerk

VULNERABLE WITNESS APPLICATION

Sheriff Court ....20 ....

Court Ref. No.

1. The applicant is the pursuer [*or* defender] in the action by [A.B] (*design*) against [C.D.] (*design*).

2. The applicant has cited [*or* intends to cite] [E.F.] (*date of birth*) as a witness.

3. The applicant considers that [E.F.] is a vulnerable witness under section 11(1)(b) of the Vulnerable Witnesses (Scotland) Act 2004 for the following reasons:–

(*here specify reasons witness is considered to be a vulnerable witness*).

4. The applicant considers that the following special measure[s] is [are] the most appropriate for the purpose of taking the evidence of [E.F.]:–

(*specify any special measure(s) sought*).

5. The reason[s] this [these] special measure[s] is [are] considered the most appropriate is [are] as follows:–

(*here specify the reason(s) for the special measures(s) sought*).

6. [E.F.] has expressed the following view[s] on the special measure[s] that is [are] considered most appropriate:–

(*set out the views expressed and how they were obtained*).

7. Other information considered relevant to this application is as follows:–

(*here set out any other information relevant to the vulnerable witness application*).

8. The applicant asks the court to–

(a) consider this vulnerable witness application;

(b) make an order authorising the special measure[s] sought.

(*Signed*)

[A.B. *or* C.D.]

[*or* Representative of A.B. [*or* C.D.]] (*include full designation*)

NOTE: This form should be suitably adapted where section 16 of the Act of 2004 applies.

NOTE
[1] As inserted by the Act of Sederunt (Ordinary Cause, Summary Application, Summary Cause and Small Claim Rules) Amendment (Vulnerable Witnesses (Scotland) Act 2004) 2007 (SSI 2007/463) (effective November 1, 2007).

[1] FORM 26D

Form of certificate of intimation

Rule 18A.4(2)

VULNERABLE WITNESSES (SCOTLAND) ACT 2004 Section 12

CERTIFICATE OF INTIMATION

Sheriff Court ....20......

Court Ref. No.

I certify that intimation of the child witness notice [*or* vulnerable witness application] relating to (*insert name of witness*) was made to (*insert names of parties or solicitors for parties, as appropriate*) by (*insert method of intimation; where intimation is by facsimile transmission, insert fax number to which intimation sent*) on (*insert date of intimation*).

Date: ....

(*Signed*)

Solicitor [*or* Sheriff Officer]

(*include full business designation*)

NOTE
[1] As inserted by the Act of Sederunt (Ordinary Cause, Summary Application, Summary Cause and Small Claim Rules) Amendment (Vulnerable Witnesses (Scotland) Act 2004) 2007 (SSI 2007/463) (effective November 1, 2007).

[1] FORM 26E

Form of application for review

Rule 18A.6(1)

VULNERABLE WITNESSES (SCOTLAND) ACT 2004 Section 13

Received the ....day of...................20....

(*date of receipt of this notice*)

....(*signed*)

Sheriff Clerk

APPLICATION FOR REVIEW OF ARRANGEMENTS FOR VULNERABLE WITNESS

Sheriff Court...   ....20...

Court Ref. No.

1. The applicant is the pursuer [*or* defender] in the action by [A.B.] (*design*) against [C.D.] (*design*).

2. A proof [*or* hearing] is fixed for (*date*) at (*time*).

3. [E.F.] is a witness who is to give evidence at, or for the purposes of, the proof [*or* hearing]. [E.F.] is a child witness [*or* vulnerable witness] under section 11 of the Vulnerable Witnesses (Scotland) Act 2004.

4. The current arrangements for taking the evidence of [E.F.] are (*here specify current arrangements*).

5. The current arrangements should be reviewed as (*here specify reasons for review*).

6. [E.F.] [and the parent[s] of [*or* person[s] with parental responsibility for] [E.F.]] has [have] expressed the following view[s] on [the special measure[s] that is [are] considered most appropriate] [*or* the appropriateness of [E.F.] giving evidence without the benefit of any special measure]:–

   (*delete as appropriate and set out the view(s) expressed and how they were obtained*).

7. The applicant seeks (here specify the order sought).

(*Signed*)

[A.B. *or* C.D.]

[*or* Representative of A.B. [*or* C.D.]] (*include full designation*)

NOTE: This form should be suitably adapted where section 16 of the Act of 2004 applies.

NOTE
[1] As inserted by the Act of Sederunt (Ordinary Cause, Summary Application, Summary Cause and Small Claim Rules) Amendment (Vulnerable Witnesses (Scotland) Act 2004) 2007 (SSI 2007/463) (effective November 1, 2007).

[1] FORM 26F

Form of certificate of intimation

Rule 18A.7(2)

VULNERABLE WITNESSES (SCOTLAND) ACT 2004 Section 13

CERTIFICATE OF INTIMATION

Sheriff Court ....20......

                                                 Court Ref. No.

I certify that intimation of the review application relating to (*insert name of witness*) was made to (*insert names of parties or solicitors for parties, as appropriate*) by (*insert method of intimation; where intimation is by facsimile transmission, insert fax number to which intimation sent*) on (*insert date of intimation*).

Date: ....

(*Signed*)

Solicitor [*or* Sheriff Officer]

(*include full business designation*)

NOTE
[1] As inserted by the Act of Sederunt (Ordinary Cause, Summary Application, Summary Cause and Small Claim Rules) Amendment (Vulnerable Witnesses (Scotland) Act 2004) 2007 (SSI 2007/463) (effective November 1, 2007).

Rule 20.2(2)   FORM 27

Form of reference to the European Court

REQUEST

for

PRELIMINARY RULING

of

THE COURT OF JUSTICE OF THE EUROPEAN COMMUNITIES

from

THE SHERIFFDOM OF (*insert name of sheriffdom*) at (*insert place of court*)

In the cause

AB (*insert designation and address*),

                       Pursuer

Against

CD (*insert designation and address*)

                       Defender

(*Here set out a clear and succinct statement of the case giving rise to the request for a ruling of the European Court in order to enable the European Court to consider and understand the issues of Community law raised and to enable governments of Member states and other interested parties to submit observations. The statement of the case should include*:

(*a*) *particulars of the parties*;

(*b*) *the history of the dispute between the parties*;

(*c*) *the history of the proceedings*;

(*d*) *the relevant facts as agreed by the parties or found by the court or, failing such agreement or finding, the contentions of the parties on such facts*;

(*e*) *the nature of the issues of law and fact between the parties*;

(*f*) *the Scots law, so far as relevant*;

(*g*) *the Treaty provisions or other acts, instruments or rules of Community law concerned*;

(*h*) *an explanation of why the reference is being made*).

The preliminary ruling of the Court of Justice of the European Communities is accordingly requested on the following questions:

1,2,etc.   (*Here set out the question(s) on which the ruling is sought, identifying the Treaty provisions or other acts, instruments or rules of Community law concerned.*)

Dated the   day of   20

Rule 23.6(3)   FORM 28

Form of extract decree—basic

Sheriff Court

                       Court ref. no.

Date of decree

                       *in absence

Pursuer(s)

                       Defender(s)

The sheriff

and granted decree against the   for payment of expenses of £   against the (name of party).

This extract is warrant for all lawful execution thereon.

Date

                       Sheriff clerk depute

**delete as appropriate*

Rule 23.6(3) FORM 28A

Form of extract decree—payment

Sheriff Court Court ref. no.

Date of decree *in absence

Pursuer(s) Defender(s)

The sheriff granted decree against the for payment to the the undernoted sums:

(1) Sum(s) decerned for: £

(2) Interest at per cent per year from (*date*) until payment.

(3) Expenses of £ against the (*name of party*).

*A time to pay direction was made under section 1(1) of the Debtors (Scotland) Act 1987.

*A time order was made under section 129(1) of the Consumer Credit Act 1974.

*The amount is payable by instalments of £percommencing within

*days/weeks/months of intimation of this extract decree.

*The amount is payable by lump sum within*days/weeks/months of intimation of this extract decree.

This extract is warrant for all lawful execution thereon.

Date Sheriff clerk depute

delete as appropriate

Rule 23.6(3) FORM 28B

Form of extract decree—recovery of possession of heritable property

Sheriff Court Court ref. no.

Date of decree *in absence

Pursuer(s) Defender(s)

The sheriff

(1) granted warrant for ejecting the defender (and others mentioned in the summons) from the premises at , such ejection being not sooner than (*date*) at 12 noon.

(2) granted decree against the defender for payment to the pursuer of the sum of £ of expenses.

This extract is warrant for all lawful execution thereon.

Date Sheriff clerk depute

Rule 23.6(3) FORM 28C

Form of extract decree and warrant to sell in sequestration for rent and sale

[*Repealed by the Act of Sederunt (Sheriff Court Rules Amendment) (Diligence) 2008 (SSI 2008/ 121) r.2(1)(b) (effective April 1, 2008).*]

Rule 23.6(3) FORM 28D

Form of extract—warrant for ejection and to re-let in sequestration for rent and sale

[*Repealed by the Act of Sederunt (Sheriff Court Rules Amendment) (Diligence) 2008 (SSI 2008/ 121) r.2(1)(b) (effective April 1, 2008).*]

Rule 23.6(3)   FORM 28E

Form of extract decree—furthcoming

Sheriff Court   Court ref. no.

Date of decree   *in absence

Date of original decree

Pursuer(s)

Defender(s)/Arrestee(s)

Common debtor

The sheriff granted decree

(1) against the arrestee(s) for payment of £, or such other sum(s) as may be owing by the arrestee(s) to the common debtor(s) by virtue of the original decree mentioned above in favour of the pursuer(s) against the common debtor(s).

(2) for expenses of £

*payable out of the arrested fund.

*payable by the common debtor.

*delete as appropriate

This extract is warrant for all lawful execution thereon.

Date   Sheriff clerk depute

Rule 23.6(3)   FORM 28F

Form of extract decree—delivery

Sheriff Court   Court ref. no.

Date of decree   *in absence

Pursuer(s)

Defender(s)

The sheriff granted decree against the defender

(1) for delivery to the pursuer of (*specify articles*)

(2) for expenses of £

*Further, the sheriff granted warrant to officers of court to (1) open shut and lockfast places occupied by the defender and (2) search for and take possession of said goods in the possession of the defender.

*delete as appropriate

This extract is warrant for all lawful execution thereon.

Date   Sheriff clerk depute

Rule 23.6(3)   FORM 28G

Form of extract decree—delivery—payment failing delivery

Sheriff Court   Court ref. no.

Date of decree   *in absence

Pursuer(s)

Defender(s)

The sheriff, in respect that the defender has failed to make delivery in accordance with the decree granted in this court on (*date*), granted decree for payment against the defender of the undernoted sums:

(1) Sum(s) decerned for: £ , being the alternative crave claimed.

(2) Interest at per cent per year from (*date*) until payment.

(3) Expenses of £ against the (*name of party*).

*A time to pay direction was made under section 1(1) of the Debtors (Scotland) Act 1987.

*A time order was made under section 129(1) of the Consumer Credit Act 1974.

*The amount is payable by instalments of £ per .commencing within *days/weeks/months of intimation of this extract decree.

*The amount is payable by lump sum within *days/weeks/months of intimation of this extract decree.

delete as appropriate

This extract is warrant for all lawful execution thereon.

Date   Sheriff clerk depute

Rule 23.6(3)   FORM 28H

Form of extract decree—aliment

Sheriff Court   Court ref. no.

Date of decree   *in absence

Pursuer(s)

Defender(s)

The sheriff

Granted decree against the defender for payment to the pursuer of aliment at the rate of £ per *week/month.

delete as appropriate

This extract is warrant for all lawful execution thereon.

Date   Sheriff clerk depute

Rule 23.6(3)   FORM 28I

Form of extract decree—ad factum praestandum

Sheriff Court   Court ref. no.

Date of decree   *in absence

Pursuer(s)

Defender(s)

The sheriff

(1) ordained the defender(s)

(2) granted decree for payment of expenses of £against the defender(s).

delete as appropriate

This extract is warrant for all lawful execution thereon.

Date   Sheriff clerk depute

Rule 23.6(3)   FORM 28J

Form of extract decree—absolvitor

Sheriff Court   Court ref. no.

Date of decree   *in absence

Pursuer(s)

Defender(s)

The sheriff

(1) absolved the defender(s)

(2) granted decree for payment of expenses of £   against the

delete as appropriate

This extract is warrant for all lawful execution thereon.

Date   Sheriff clerk depute

Rule 23.6(3)   FORM 28K

Form of extract decree—dismissal

Sheriff Court   Court ref. no.

Date of decree   *in absence

Pursuer(s)

Defender(s)

The sheriff

(1) dismissed the action against the defender(s)

*(2) granted decree for payment of expenses of £   against the

*(3) found no expenses due to or by either party

delete as appropriate

This extract is warrant for all lawful execution thereon.

Date   Sheriff clerk depute

Rule 23.8(4)   FORM 29

Form of certificate by sheriff clerk
Service of charge where address of defender is unknown

I certify that the foregoing charge was displayed on the walls of court on (*date*) and that it remained so displayed for a period of (*period of charge*) from that date.

(*date*)   Sheriff clerk depute

Rule 24.1(1)   FORM 30

Minute for recall of decree

Sheriff Court: (place)

Court ref. no.:

AB (*pursuer*) against CD (*defender(s)*)

The *(*pursuer/defender*) moves the court to recall the decree pronounced on (*date*) in this case *
and in which execution of a charge/arrestment was effected on (*date*)

Reason for failure to appear or be represented:

Proposed defence/answer:

**delete as appropriate*

Rule 24.1(6)(a)   FORM 30A

Minute for recall of decree—service copy

Sheriff Court: (*place*)

Court ref. no.:

AB (*pursuer*) against CD (*defender(s)*)

The *(*pursuer/defender*) moves the court to recall the decree pronounced on (*date*) in this case *
and in which execution of a charge/arrestment was effected on (*date*)

Reason for failure to appear or be represented:

Proposed defence/answer:

**delete as appropriate*

NOTE: You must return the summons to the sheriff clerk at the court mentioned at the top of
this form by (*insert date 2 days before the date of the hearing.*)

Rule 25.1(1)   FORM 31

Form of note of appeal to the sheriff principal

SHERIFF COURT (*place*)

Court ref. no.   AB (pursuer) against CD (defender)

The pursuer/defender appeals the sheriff's interlocutor of (*date*) to the sheriff principal and
requests the sheriff to state a case.

The point(s) of law upon which the appeal is to proceed is/are: (*give brief statement*)

(*date*)

Rule 25.4(3)(a)   FORM 32

Application for leave to appeal against time to pay direction

SHERIFF COURT (*place*)

Court ref. no.   AB (pursuer) against CD (defender)

The pursuer/defender requests the sheriff to grant leave to appeal the decision made on (*date*) in
respect of the defender's application for a time to pay direction to the sheriff principal/Court of
Session.

The point(s) of law upon which the appeal is to proceed is/are: (*give brief statement*)

(*date*)

Rule 25.4(4) FORM 33

Appeal against time to pay direction

SHERIFF COURT (*place*)

Court ref. no. AB (pursuer) against CD (defender)

The pursuer/defender appeals the decision made on (*date*) in respect of the defender's application for a time to pay direction to the sheriff principal/Court of Session.

(*date*)

Rule 25.7(1) FORM 34

Application for certificate of suitability for appeal to the Court of Session

The pursuer/defender in the summary cause at the instance of AB against CD hereby moves the sheriff principal to certify that the cause is suitable for appeal to the Court of Session.

Rule 26.4(1) FORM 35

Form of receipt for money paid to the sheriff clerk

In the sheriff court of (*name of sheriffdom*) at (*place of sheriff court*).

In the cause (*state names of parties or other appropriate description*)

AB (*designation*) has this day paid into court the sum of £ , being a payment made in terms of rule 26(4)(1) of the Summary Cause Rules 2002.

*Custody of this money has been accepted at the request of (*insert name of court making the request*)

**delete as appropriate*

(Date) Sheriff clerk depute

Rule 32.2(a) FORM 36

Action for aliment
Form of notice of intimation to children and next of kin
where address of defender is unknown

Court ref. no.

To: (*insert name and address as in warrant*)

You are hereby given notice that an action for aliment has been raised against (*name*), your (*insert relationship, e.g, father, brother or other relative as the case may be*). A copy of the summons is enclosed.

If you know of his/her present address, you are requested to inform the sheriff clerk at (*insert full address*) in writing immediately.

If you wish to appear as a party in the action, or are uncertain about what action to take, you should contact a solicitor. You may, depending on your financial circumstances, be entitled to legal aid, and you can get information about legal aid from a solicitor.

You may also obtain advice from any Citizen's Advice Bureau, other advice agency or any sheriff clerk's office.

Rule 32.2(b) FORM 37

Action for aliment
Form of notice of intimation to children, next of kin and guardian where
defender suffers from mental disorder

Court ref. no.

To: (*insert name and address as in warrant*)

You are hereby given notice that an action for aliment has been raised against (*name*), your (*insert relationship, e.g, father or other relative, or ward, as the case may be*). A copy of the summons is enclosed.

If you wish to appear as a party in the action, or are uncertain about what action to take, you should contact a solicitor immediately. You may, depending on your financial circumstances, be entitled to legal aid, and you can get information about legal aid from a solicitor.

You may also obtain advice from any Citizen's Advice Bureau, other advice agency or any sheriff clerk's office.

APPENDIX 2

GLOSSARY

Absolve
To find in favour of and exonerate the defender.

Absolvitor
An order of the court granted in favour of and exonerating the defender which means that the pursuer is not allowed to bring the same matter to court again.

Action of count, reckoning and payment
A legal procedure for requiring someone to account for their dealings with assets under their stewardship. For example, a trustee might be subject to such an action.

Action of furthcoming
A final stage of diligence or enforcement. It results in whatever has been subject to arrestment being made over to the person who is suing. For example, where a bank account has been arrested this results in the appropriate amount being transferred to the pursuer.

Appellant
A person making an appeal against the sheriff's decision. This might be the pursuer or the defender.

Arrestee
A person subject to an arrestment.

Arrestment on the dependence
A court order to freeze the goods or bank account of the defender until the court has heard the case.

Arrestment to found jurisdiction
A court order to used against a person who has goods or other assets in Scotland to give the court jurisdiction to hear a case. This is achieved by preventing anything being done with the goods or assets until the case has been disposed of.

Authorised lay representative
A person other than a lawyer who represents a party to a summary cause.

Calling date
The date on which the case will first be heard in court.

Cause
Another word for case or claim.

Caution (pronounced kay-shun)
A security, usually a sum of money, given to ensure that some obligation will be carried out.

Certificate of execution of service
The document recording that an application to, or order or decree of, the court for service of documents has been effected.

Charge
An order to obey a decree of a court. A common type is one served on the defender by a sheriff officer on behalf of the pursuer who has won a case demanding payment of a sum of money.

Claim
The part of the summons which sets out the legal remedy which the pursuer is seeking.

Commission and diligence
Authorisation by the court for someone to take the evidence of a witness who cannot attend court or to obtain the production of documentary evidence. It is combined with a diligence authorising the person appointed to require the attendance of the witness and the disclosure of documents.

Consignation
The deposit in court, or with a third party, of money or an article in dispute.

Continuation
An order made by the sheriff postponing the completion of a hearing until a later date or dates.

Contribution, Right of
The right of one person who is legally liable to pay money to someone to claim a proportionate share from others who are also liable.

Counterclaim
A claim made by a defender in response to the pursuer's case and which is not necessarily a defence to that case. It is a separate but related case against the pursuer which is dealt with at the same time as the pursuer's case.

Damages
Money compensation payable for a breach of contract or some other legal duty.

Declarator of irritancy of a lease
A decision of a court finding that a tenant has failed to observe a term of a lease which may lead to the termination of the lease.

Decree
An order of the court containing the decision of the case in favour of one of the parties and granting the remedy sought or disposing of the case.

Decree of ejection
A decree ordering someone to leave land or property which they are occupying. For example, it is used to remove tenants in arrears with their rent.

Decree of removing
A court order entitling someone to recover possession of heritable property and ordering a person to leave land which he is occupying. For example, it is used to remove tenants in arrears with their rent.

Defender
Person against whom a summary cause is started.

Deliverance
A decision or order of a court.

Diet
Date for a court hearing.

Diligence
The collective term for the procedures used to enforce a decree of a court. These include arrestment of wages, goods or a bank account.

Dismissal
An order bringing to an end the proceedings in a summary cause. It is usually possible for a new summary cause to be brought if not time barred.

Domicile
The place where a person is normally resident or where, in the case of a company, it has its place of business or registered office.

Execution of service
See *Certificate of execution of service.*

Execution of a charge
The intimation of the requirement to obey a decree or order of a court.

Execution of an arrestment
The carrying out of an order of arrestment.

Expenses
The costs of a court case.

Extract decree
The document containing the order of the court made at the end of the summary cause. For example, it can be used to enforce payment of a sum awarded.

Fund in medio
See *Multiplepoinding.*

Haver
A person who holds documents which are required as evidence in a case.

Heritable property
Land and buildings as opposed to moveable property.

Huissier
An official in France and some other European countries who serves court documents.

Incidental application
An application that can be made during the course of a summary cause for certain orders. Examples are applications for the recovery of documents or to amend the statement of claim.

Interlocutor
The official record of the order or judgment of a court.

Interrogatories
Written questions put to someone in the course of a court case and which must be answered on oath.

Intimation
Giving notice to another party of some step in a summary cause.

Jurisdiction

The authority of a court to hear particular cases.

Ish
The date on which a lease terminates.

Letter of request
A document issued by the sheriff court requesting a foreign court to take evidence from a specified person within its jurisdiction or to serve Scottish court documents on that person.

Messenger at arms
Officers of court who serve documents issued by the Court of Session.

Minute
A document produced in the course of a case in which a party makes an application or sets out his position on some matter.

Minute for recall
A form lodged with the court by one party asking the court to recall a decree.

Multiplepoinding (pronounced "multiple pinding")
A special type of summary cause in which the holder of property, etc. (referred to as the fund*in medio*) requires claimants upon it to appear and settle claims in court. For example, where the police come into possession of a stolen car of which two or more people claim to be owner this procedure could be used.

Options Hearing
A preliminary stage in an ordinary cause action.

Ordinary cause
Another legal procedure for higher value cases available in the sheriff court.

Party litigant
A person who conducts his own case.

Process
The court file containing the collection of documents relating to a case.

Productions
Documents or articles which are used in evidence.

Pursuer
The person who starts a summary cause.

Recall of an arrestment
A court order withdrawing an arrestment.

Restriction of an arrestment
An order releasing part of the money or property arrested.

Recall of a decree
An order revoking a decree which has been granted.

Recovery of documents
The process of obtaining documentary evidence which is not in the possession of the person seeking it (e.g. hospital records necessary to establish the extent of injuries received in a road accident).

Remit between procedures
A decision of the sheriff to transfer the summary cause to another court procedure e.g. small claim or ordinary cause procedure.

Respondent
When a decision of the sheriff is appealed against, the person making the appeal is called the appellant. The other side in the appeal is called the respondent.

Return day
The date by which the defender must send a written reply to the court and, where appropriate, the pursuer must return the summons to court.

Schedule of arrestment
The list of items which may be arrested.

Serve | service
Sending a copy of the summons or other court document to the defender or another party.

Sheriff clerk
The court official responsible for the administration of the sheriff court.

Sheriff officer
A person who serves court documents and enforces court orders.

Sist of action
The temporary suspension of a court case by court order.

Sist as a party
To add another person as a litigant in a case.

Small claim
Another legal procedure in the sheriff court for claims having a lower value than summary cause.

Specification of documents
A list lodged in court of documents for the recovery of which a party seeks a court order.

Stated case
An appeal procedure where the sheriff sets out his findings and the reasons for his decision and states the issues on which the decision of the sheriff principal is requested.

Statement of claim
The part of the summons in which pursuers set out details of their cases against defenders.

Summons
The form which must be filled in to begin a summary cause.

Time to pay direction
A court order for which a defender who is an individual may apply permitting a sum owed to be paid by instalments or by a single payment at a later date.

Time order
A court order which assists debtors who have defaulted on an agreement regulated by the Consumer Credit Act 1974 (c.39) and which may be applied for during a court action.

Warrant for diligence
Authority to carry out one of the diligence procedures.

Writ
A legally significant writing.

Paragraph 4   SCHEDULE 2

REVOCATIONS

(1) *Act of Sederunt*	*(2)* *Reference*	*(3)* *Extent of revocation*
Act of Sederunt (Summary Cause Rules, Sheriff Court) 1976	S.I. 1976/476	The whole Act of Sederunt
Act of Sederunt (Summary Cause Rules, Sheriff Court) (Amendment) 1978	S.I. 1978/112	The whole Act of Sederunt
Act of Sederunt (Summary Cause Rules, Sheriff court) (Amendment no. 2) 1978	S.I. 1978/1805	The whole Act of Sederunt
Act of Sederunt (Summary Cause Rules, Sheriff Court) (Amendment) 1980	S.I. 1980/455	The whole Act of Sederunt
Act of Sederunt (Ordinary Cause Rules, Sheriff Court) 1983	S.I. 983/747	Paragraph 4
Act of Sederunt (Civil Jurisdiction of the Sheriff Court) 1986	S.I. 1986/1946	Paragraph 3
Act of Sederunt (Miscellaneous Amendments) 1986	S.I. 1986/1966	Paragraph 3
Act of Sederunt (Small Claim Rules)1988	S.I. 1988/1976	Paragraph 3
Act of Sederunt (Amendment of Sheriff Court Ordinary Cause, and Summary Cause, Rules) 1988	S.I. 1988/1978	Paragraphs 19 to 35 and Schedule 2
Act of Sederunt (Amendment of Ordinary Cause and Summary Cause Rules) (Written Statements) 1989	S.I. 1989/436	Paragraph 3
Act of Sederunt (Amendment of Sheriff Court Ordinary Cause, Summary Cause and Small Claim, Rules) 1990	S.I. 1990/661	Paragraph 3
Act of Sederunt (Amendment of Sheriff Court Ordinary Cause, Summary Cause and Small Claim, Rules) (No. 2) 1990	S.I. 1990/2105	Paragraph 3
Act of Sederunt (Amendment of Summary Cause and Small Claim Rules) 1991	S.I. 1991/821	The whole Act of Sederunt
Act of Sederunt (Amendment of Ordinary Cause, Summary Cause and Small Claim Rules) 1992	S.I. 1992/249	Paragraph 3
Act of Sederunt (Child Support Act 1991) (Amendment of Ordinary Cause and Summary Cause Rules) 1993	S.I. 1993/919	Paragraph 4
Act of Sederunt (Sheriff Court Ordinary Cause Rules) 1993	S.I. 1993/1956	Paragraph 3

Act of Sederunt (Small Claim Rules) 2002

(SSI 2002/133)

The Lords of Council and Session, under and by virtue of the powers conferred by section 32 of the Sheriff Courts (Scotland) Act 1971 and of all other powers enabling them in that behalf, having approved draft rules submitted to them by the Sheriff Court Rules Council in accordance with section 34 of the said Act of 1971, do hereby enact and declare:

Citation and commencement
1.—(1) This Act of Sederunt may be cited as the Act of Sederunt (Small Claim Rules) 2002 and shall come into force on 10th June 2002.

(2) This Act of Sederunt shall be inserted in the Books of Sederunt.

Small Claim Rules
2. The provisions of Schedule 1 to this Act of Sederunt shall have effect for the purpose of providing rules for the form of summary cause process known as a small claim.

Transitional provision
3. Nothing in Schedule 1 to this Act of Sederunt shall apply to a small claim commenced before 10th June 2002 and any such claim shall proceed according to the law and practice in force immediately before that date.

Revocation
4. The Acts of Sederunt mentioned in column (1) of Schedule 2 to this Act of Sederunt are revoked to the extent specified in column (3) of that Schedule except in relation to any small claim commenced before 10th June 2002.

SCHEDULE 1

SMALL CLAIM RULES 2002

ARRANGEMENT OF RULES

Chapter 1

Citation, interpretation and application

1.1. Citation, interpretation and application

Chapter 2

Representation

2.1. Representation

Chapter 3

Relief from failure to comply with rules

3.1. Dispensing power of sheriff

Chapter 17A

Vulnerable Witnesses (Scotland) Act 2004

Chapter 18

European Court

Chapter 19

Abandonment

Chapter 20

Decree by default

Chapter 21

Decrees, extracts, execution and variation

Chapter 22

Recall of decree

Chapter 23

Appeals

Chapter 24

Management of damages payable to persons under legal disability

Chapter 25

Electronic transmission of documents

Chapter 26

Equality Enactments

Chapter 27

Live Links

APPENDIX 1

FORMS

16　Witness citation
16a　Certificate of execution of witness citation
17　Reference to the European Court
18　Extract decree—(basic)
18a　Extract decree—payment
18b　Extract—delivery
18c　Extract decree—delivery—payment failing delivery
18d　Extract decree—recovery of possession of moveable property
18e　Extract decree—recovery of possession of moveable property—payment failing recovery
18f　Extract decree—*ad factum praestandum*
18g　Extract decree—*ad factum praestandum*—payment upon failure to implement obligation
18h　Extract decree—absolvitor
18i　Extract decree—dismissal
19　Certificate by sheriff clerk—service of charge were address of defender is unknown
20　Minute for recall of decree
20a　Minute for recall of decree—service copy
21　Note of appeal to the sheriff principal
22　Application for leave to appeal against time to pay direction
23　Appeal against time to pay direction
24　Form of receipt for money paid to sheriff clerk

APPENDIX 2

GLOSSARY

CHAPTER 1

CITATION, INTERPRETATION AND APPLICATION

Citation, interpretation and application
[1] **1.1.**—(1) These Rules may be cited as the Small Claim Rules 2002.

(2) In these rules—

"the 1971 Act" means the Sheriff Courts (Scotland) Act 1971;

"the 1975 Act" means the Litigants in Person (Costs and Expenses) Act 1975;

[2] "the 2004 Act" means the Vulnerable Witnesses (Scotland) Act 2004;

"authorised lay representative" means a person to whom section 32(1) of the Solicitors (Scotland) Act 1980 (offence to prepare writs) does not apply by virtue of section 32(2)(a) of that Act;

"enactment" includes an enactment comprised in, or in an instrument made under, an Act of the Scottish Parliament;

"small claim" has the meaning assigned to it by section 35(2) of the 1971 Act;

"summary cause" has the meaning assigned to it by section 35(1) of the 1971 Act.

(3) Any reference in these Rules to a specified rule shall be construed as a reference to the rule bearing that number in these Rules, and a reference to a specified paragraph, sub-paragraph or head shall be construed as a reference to the paragraph, sub-paragraph or head so numbered or lettered in the provision in which that reference occurs.

(4) A form referred to by number in these Rules means the form so numbered in Appendix 1 to these rules or a form substantially of the same effect with such variation as circumstances may require.

[3] (4A) In these Rules, references to a solicitor include a reference to a member of a body which has made a successful application under section 25 of the Law Reform (Miscellaneous Provisions) (Scotland) Act 1990 but only to the extent that the member is exercising rights acquired by virtue of section 27 of that Act.

(5) The glossary in Appendix 2 to these Rules is a guide to the meaning of certain legal expressions used in these Rules, but is not to be taken as giving those expressions any meaning which they do not have in law generally.

(6) These Rules shall apply to a small claim.

NOTES
[1] As amended by the Act of Sederunt (Ordinary Cause, Summary Application, Summary Cause and Small Claim Rules) Amendment (Miscellaneous) 2007 (SSI 2007/6) r.5(a) (effective January 29, 2007).

[2] As inserted by the Act of Sederunt (Ordinary Cause, Summary Application, Summary Cause and Small Claim Rules) Amendment (Vulnerable Witnesses (Scotland) Act 2004) 2007 (SSI 2007/463) r.5(2) (effective November 1, 2007).

[3] As inserted by the Act of Sederunt (Sheriff Court Rules Amendment) (Sections 25 to 29 of the Law Reform (Miscellaneous Provisions) (Scotland) Act 1990) 2009 (SSI 2009/164) r.5(2) (effective May 20, 2009).

CHAPTER 2

REPRESENTATION

Representation
[1] **2.1.**—(1) A party may be represented by—
(a) an advocate;
(b) a solicitor;
(c) a person authorised under any enactment to conduct proceedings in the sheriff court, in accordance with the terms of that enactment; and
(d) subject to paragraph (3), an authorised lay representative.
(2) The persons referred to in paragraph (1)(c) and (d) above may in representing a party do everything for the preparation and conduct of a small claim as may be done by an individual conducting his own claim.
(3) If the sheriff finds that the authorised lay representative is—
(a) not a suitable person to represent the party; or
(b) not in fact authorised to do so,
that person must cease to represent the party.

NOTE
[1] As amended by the Act of Sederunt (Ordinary Cause, Summary Application, Summary Cause and Small Claim Rules) Amendment (Miscellaneous) 2007 (SSI 2007/6) r.5(b) (effective January 29, 2007).

CHAPTER 3

RELIEF FROM FAILURE TO COMPLY WITH RULES

Dispensing power of sheriff
3.1.—(1) The sheriff may relieve any party from the consequences of any failure to comply with the provisions of these Rules which is shown to be due to mistake, oversight or other excusable cause, on such conditions as he thinks fit.
(2) Where the sheriff relieves a party from the consequences of the failure to comply with a provision in these Rules under paragraph (1), he may make such order as he thinks fit to enable the claim to proceed as if the failure to comply with the provision had not occurred.

CHAPTER 4

COMMENCEMENT OF CLAIM

Form of summons
4.1.—(1) A small claim shall be commenced by summons, which shall be in Form 1.
(2) The claim in a small claim summons may be in one of Forms 2 to 4.

Statement of claim
4.2. The pursuer must insert a statement of his claim in the summons to give the defender fair notice of the claim; and the statement must include—
(a) details of the basis of the claim including relevant dates; and
(b) if the claim arises from the supply of goods or services, a description of the goods or services and the date or dates on or between which they were supplied and, where relevant, ordered.

Actions relating to regulated agreements
[1] **4.2A.** In an action which relates to a regulated agreement within the meaning given by section 189(1) of the Consumer Credit Act 1974 the statement of claim shall include an averment that such an agreement exists and details of the agreement.

NOTE
[1] As inserted by the Act of Sederunt (Sheriff Court Rules) (Miscellaneous Amendments) 2009 (SSI 2009/294) r.5 (effective December 1, 2009) as substituted by the Act of Sederunt (Amendment of the Act of Sederunt (Sheriff Court Rules) (Miscellaneous Amendments) 2009) 2009 (SSI 2009/402) (effective November 30, 2009).

Defender's copy summons
4.3. A copy summons shall be served on the defender—
    (a) in Form 1a where—
        (i) the small claim is for, or includes a claim for, payment of money; and
        (ii) an application for a time to pay direction under the Debtors (Scotland) Act 1987 or time order under the Consumer Credit Act 1974 may be applied for;
    or
    (b) in Form 1b in every other case.

Authentication and effect of summons
4.4.—(1) A summons shall be authenticated by the sheriff clerk in some appropriate manner except where—
    (a) he refuses to do so for any reason;
    (b) the defender's address is unknown; or
    (c) a party seeks to alter the normal period of notice specified in rule 4.5(2); or
[1]   (d) a warrant for arrestment on the dependence, or to found jurisdiction, is sought
[2] (2) If any of paragraphs (1)(a) to (d) applies, the summons shall be authenticated by the sheriff, if he thinks it appropriate.
(3) The authenticated summons shall be warrant for—
    (a) service on the defender; and
    (b) where the appropriate warrant has been sought in the summons—
        (i) arrestment on the dependence; or
        (ii) arrestment to found jurisdiction,
as the case may be.
[1] (4) Where a warrant for arrestment to found jurisdiction, is sought, averments to justify that warrant must be included in the statement of claim.

NOTES
[1] As inserted by the Act of Sederunt (Ordinary Cause, Summary Application and Small Claim Rules) Amendment (Miscellaneous) 2004 (SSI 2004/197) r.5(2) (effective May 21, 2004) and amended by the Act of Sederunt (Sheriff Court Rules) (Miscellaneous Amendments) 2009 (SSI 2009/294) r.12 (effective October 1, 2009).
[2] As substituted by the Act of Sederunt (Ordinary Cause, Summary Application, Summary Cause and Small Claim Rules) Amendment (Miscellaneous) 2004 (SSI 2004/197) r.5(2)(b) (effective May 21, 2004).

Period of notice
4.5.—(1) A claim shall proceed after the appropriate period of notice of the summons has been given to the defender prior to the return day.
(2) The appropriate period of notice shall be—
    (a) 21 days where the defender is resident or has a place of business within Europe; or
    (b) 42 days where the defender is resident or has a place of business outwith Europe.
(3) The sheriff may, on cause shown, shorten or extend the period of notice on such conditions as to the form of service as he may direct, but in any case where the period of notice is reduced at least two days' notice must be given.
(4) If a period of notice expires on a Saturday, Sunday, public or court holiday, the period of notice shall be deemed to expire on the next day on which the sheriff clerk's office is open for civil court business.
(5) Notwithstanding the terms of section 4(2) of the Citation Amendment (Scotland) Act 1882, where service is by post the period of notice shall run from the beginning of the day next following the date of posting.
(6) The sheriff clerk shall insert in the summons—
    (a) the return day, which is the last day on which the defender may return a form of response to the sheriff clerk; and
    (b) the hearing date, which is the date set for the hearing of the claim.

Intimation
4.6. Any provision in these Rules requiring papers to be sent to or any intimation to be made to any party or applicant shall be construed as if the reference to the party or applicant included a reference to the solicitor representing that party or applicant.

REGISTER OF SMALL CLAIMS

Register of Small Claims
5.1.—(1) The sheriff clerk shall keep a register of claims and incidental applications made in claims, which shall be known as the Register of Small Claims.

(2) There shall be entered in the Register of Small Claims a note of all claims, together with a note of all minutes under rule 22.1(1) (recall of decree) and the entry for each claim or minute must contain the following particulars where appropriate:-
   (a) the names, designations and addresses of the parties;
   (b) whether the parties were present or absent at any hearing, including an inspection, and the names of their representatives;
   (c) the nature of the claim;
   (d) the amount of any claim;
   (e) the date of issue of the summons;
   (f) the method of service;
   (g) the return day;
   (h) the hearing date;
   (i) whether a form of response was lodged and details of it;
   (j) the period of notice if shortened or extended in accordance with rule 4.5(3);
   (k) details of any minute by the pursuer regarding a time to pay direction or time order, or minute by the pursuer requesting decree or other order;
   (l) details of any interlocutors issued;
   (m) details of the final decree and the date of it; and
   (n) details of any variation or recall of a decree by virtue of the Debtors (Scotland) Act 1987.

(3) There shall be entered in the Register of Small Claims, in the entry for the claim to which they relate, details of incidental applications including, where appropriate—
   (a) whether parties are present or absent at the hearing of the application, and the names of their representatives;
   (b) the nature of the application; and
   (c) the interlocutor issued or order made.

(4) The Register of Small Claims must be—
   (a) authenticated in some appropriate manner by the sheriff in respect of each day any order is made or application determined in a claim; and
   (b) open for inspection during normal business hours to all concerned without fee.

(5) The Register of Small Claims may be kept in electronic or documentary form.

CHAPTER 6

SERVICE AND RETURN OF THE SUMMONS

Persons carrying on business under trading or descriptive name
6.1.—(1) A person carrying on a business under a trading or descriptive name may sue or be sued in such trading or descriptive name alone.

(2) An extract of a decree pronounced in a claim against such person under such trading or descriptive name shall be a valid warrant for diligence against that person.

(3) A summons, decree, charge or other document following upon such summons or decree in a claim in which a person carrying on business under a trading or descriptive name sues or is sued in that name may be served—
   (a) at any place of business or office at which such business is carried on within the sheriffdom of the sheriff court in which the claim is brought; or
   (b) if there is no place of business within that sheriffdom, at any place where such business is carried on (including the place of business or office of the clerk or secretary of any company, corporation or association or firm).

Form of service
6.2.—(1) Subject to rule 6.6 (service where address of defender is unknown), a form of service in Form 5 must be enclosed with the defender's copy summons.

(2) After service has been effected a certificate of execution of service in Form 6 must be prepared and signed by the person effecting service.

(3) When service is effected by a sheriff officer the certificate of execution of service must specify whether the service was personal or, if otherwise, the mode of service and the name of any person to whom the defender's copy summons was delivered.

(4) If service is effected in accordance with rule 6.4(2) (service within Scotland by sheriff officer where personal service etc. unsuccessful) the certificate must also contain a statement of—
  (a) the mode of service previously attempted; and
  (b) the circumstances which prevented the service from being effected.

Service of the summons

6.3.—(1) Subject to rule 6.5 (service on persons outwith Scotland), a copy summons may be served on the defender—
  (a) by the pursuer's solicitor, a sheriff officer or the sheriff clerk sending it by first class recorded delivery post; or
  (b) in accordance with rule 6.4 (service within Scotland by sheriff officer).
(2) On the face of the envelope used for postal service in terms of this rule, there must be printed or written a notice in Form 7.
(3) The certificate of execution of service in the case of postal service must have annexed to it any relevant postal receipt.
(4) If the pursuer requires the sheriff clerk to effect service on his behalf by virtue of section 36A of the 1971 Act (pursuer not being a partnership, body corporate or acting in a representative capacity) under paragraph (1), he may require the sheriff clerk to supply him with a copy of the summons.

Service within Scotland by sheriff officer

6.4.—(1) A sheriff officer may validly serve any summons, decree, charge or other document following upon such summons or decree issued in a claim by—
  (a) personal service; or
  (b) leaving it in the hands of—
    (i) an inmate at the person's dwelling place; or
    (ii) an employee at the person's place of business.
(2) If a sheriff officer has been unsuccessful in effecting service in accordance with paragraph (1), he may, after making diligent inquiries, serve the document—
  (a) by depositing it in the person's dwelling place or place of business by means of a letter box or by other lawful means; or
  (b) by affixing it to the door of the person's dwelling place or place of business.
(3) If service is effected in accordance with paragraph (2), the sheriff officer must thereafter send by ordinary post to the address at which he thinks it most likely that the person may be found a letter containing a copy of the document.
(4) In proceedings in or following on a claim, it shall be necessary for any sheriff officer to be accompanied by a witness except where service, citation or intimation is to be made by post.
(5) Where the firm which employs the sheriff officer has in its possession—
  (a) the document or a copy of it certified as correct by the pursuer's solicitor or the sheriff clerk, the sheriff officer may serve the document upon the defender without having the document or certified copy in his possession (in which case he shall if required to do so by the person on whom service is executed and within a reasonable time of being so required, show the document or certified copy to the person); or
  (b) a certified copy of the interlocutor pronounced allowing service of the document, the sheriff officer may serve the document without having in his possession the certified copy interlocutor if he has in his possession a facsimile copy of the certified copy interlocutor (which he shall show, if required, to the person on whom service is executed).
(6) If the pursuer requires the sheriff clerk to effect service of the summons on his behalf by virtue of section 36A of the 1971 Act, the sheriff clerk may instruct a sheriff officer to effect service in accordance with this rule on payment to the sheriff clerk by the pursuer of the fee prescribed by order of the Scottish Ministers.

Service on persons outwith Scotland

6.5.—(1) If any summons, decree, charge or other document following upon such summons or decree, or any charge or warrant, requires to be served outwith Scotland on any person, it must be served in accordance with this rule.
(2) If the person has a known home or place of business in—
  (a) England and Wales, Northern Ireland, the Isle of Man or the Channel Islands; or
  (b) any country with which the United Kingdom does not have a convention providing for service of writs in that country,
the document must be served either—
    (i) by posting in Scotland a copy of the document in question in a registered letter addressed to the person at his residence or place of business; or

(ii) in accordance with the rules for personal service under the domestic law of the place in which the document is to be served.

(3) Subject to paragraph (4), if the document requires to be served in a country which is a party to the Hague Convention on the Service Abroad of Judicial and Extra-Judicial Documents in Civil or Commercial Matters dated 15th November 1965 or the European Convention on Jurisdiction and Enforcement of Judgments in Civil and Commercial Matters as set out in Schedule 1 or 3C to the Civil Jurisdiction and Judgments Act 1982, it must be served—

   (a) by a method prescribed by the internal law of the country where service is to be effected for the service of documents in domestic actions upon persons who are within its territory;

   (b) by or through a British consular authority at the request of the Secretary of State for Foreign and Commonwealth Affairs;

   (c) by or through a central authority in the country where service is to be effected at the request of the Secretary of State for Foreign and Commonwealth Affairs;

   (d) where the law of the country in which the person resides permits, by posting in Scotland a copy of the document in a registered letter addressed to the person at his residence; or

   (e) where the law of the country in which service is to be effected permits, service by an *huissier*, other judicial officer or competent official of the country where service is to be made.

[1,3] (4) If the document requires to be served in a country to which the EC Service Regulation applies, service—

   (a) may be effected by the methods prescribed in paragraph (3)(b) or (c) only in exceptional circumstances; and

   (b) is effected only if the receiving agency has informed the person that acceptance of service may be refused on the ground that the document has not been translated in accordance with paragraph (12).

(5) If the document requires to be served in a country with which the United Kingdom has a convention on the service of writs in that country other than the conventions specified in paragraph (3) or the regulation specified in paragraph (4), it must be served by one of the methods approved in the relevant convention.

(6) Subject to paragraph (9), a document which requires to be posted in Scotland for the purposes of this rule must be posted by a solicitor, the sheriff clerk or a sheriff officer, and the form for service and the certificate of execution of service must be in Forms 5 and 6 respectively.

(7) On the face of the envelope used for postal service under this rule there must be written or printed a notice in Form 7.

(8) Where service is effected by a method specified in paragraph (3)(b) or (c), the pursuer must—

   (a) send a copy of the summons and warrant for service with form of service attached, or other document, with a request for service to be effected by the method indicated in the request to the Secretary of State for Foreign and Commonwealth Affairs; and

   (b) lodge in process a certificate of execution of service signed by the authority which has effected service.

(9) If service is effected by the method specified in paragraph (3)(e), the pursuer must—

   (a) send to the official in the country in which service is to be effected a copy of the summons and warrant for service, with citation attached, or other document, with a request for service to be effected by delivery to the defender or his residence; and

   (b) lodge in process a certificate of execution of service by the official who has effected service.

(10) Where service is executed in accordance with paragraph (2)(b)(ii) or (3)(a) other than on another party in—

   (a) the United Kingdom;

   (b) the Isle of Man; or

   (c) the Channel Islands,

the party executing service must lodge a certificate stating that the form of service employed is in accordance with the law of the place where the service was executed.

(11) A certificate lodged in accordance with paragraph (10) shall be given by a person who is conversant with the law of the country concerned and who—

   (a) practises or has practised law in that country; or

   (b) is a duly accredited representative of the government of that country.

[1] (12) Every summons or document and every citation and notice on the face of the envelope referred to in paragraph (7) must be accompanied by a translation in—

   (a) an official language of the country in which service is to be executed; or

[3] (b) in a country to which the EC Service Regulation applies, a language of the member

state of transmission that is understood by the person on whom service is being executed.

(13) A translation referred to in paragraph (12) must be certified as a correct translation by the person making it and the certificate must contain the full name, address and qualifications of the translator and be lodged along with the execution of such service.

(14) If the pursuer requires the sheriff clerk to effect service on his behalf under this rule by virtue of section 36A of the 1971 Act (pursuer not a partnership, body corporate or acting in a representative capacity)—

    (a) the cost must be borne by the pursuer;

    (b) no service shall be instructed by the sheriff clerk until such cost has been paid to him by the pursuer; and

    (c) the pursuer may require the sheriff clerk to supply him with a copy of the summons.

[2] (15) In this rule "the EC Service Regulation" means Regulation (EC) No. 1393/2007 of the European Parliament and of the Council of 13th November 2007 on the service in the Member States of judicial and extrajudicial documents in civil or commercial matters (service of documents), and repealing Council Regulation (EC) No. 1348/2000, as amended from time to time.

NOTES

[1] As substituted by the Act of Sederunt (Ordinary Cause, Summary Application, Summary Cause and Small Claim Rules) Amendment (Miscellaneous) 2004 (SSI 2004/197) r.5(3) (effective May 21, 2004).

[2] As inserted by the Act of Sederunt (Ordinary Cause, Summary Application, Summary Cause and Small Claim Rules) Amendment (Miscellaneous) 2004 (SSI 2004/197) r.5(3) (effective May 21, 2004) and substituted by the Act of Sederunt (Sheriff Court Ordinary Cause, Summary Application, Summary Cause and Small Claim Rules) Amendment (Council Regulation (EC) No.1348 of 2000 Extension to Denmark) 2007 (SSI 2007/440) (effective October 9, 2007) and the Act of Sederunt (Sheriff Court Rules) (Miscellaneous Amendments) (No.2) 2008 (SSI 2008/365) r.10(b) (effective November 13, 2008).

[3] As substituted by Act of Sederunt (Sheriff Court Rules) (Miscellaneous Amendments) (No.2) 2008 (SSI 2008/365) r.10(a) (effective November 13, 2008).

Service where address of defender is unknown

6.6.—[1] (A1) Subject to rule 7.A7 this rule applies to service where the address of a person is not known.

(1) If the defender's address is unknown to the pursuer and cannot reasonably be ascertained by him, the sheriff may grant warrant to serve the summons—

    (a) by the publication of an advertisement in Form 8 in a newspaper circulating in the area of the defender's last known address; or

    (b) by displaying on the walls of court a copy of a notice in Form 9.

(2) Where a summons is served in accordance with paragraph (1), the period of notice, which must be fixed by the sheriff, shall run from the date of publication of the advertisement or display on the walls of court, as the case may be.

(3) If service is to be effected under paragraph (1), the pursuer must lodge a defender's copy summons with the sheriff clerk.

(4) The defender may uplift from the sheriff clerk the copy summons lodged in accordance with paragraph (3).

(5) If the pursuer requires the sheriff clerk to effect service on his behalf under paragraph (1) by virtue of section 36A of the 1971 Act (pursuer not a partnership, body corporate or acting in a representative capacity)—

    (a) the cost of any advertisement required under sub-paragraph (a) of that paragraph must be borne by the pursuer;

    (b) no advertisement required under sub-paragraph (a) of that paragraph shall be instructed by the sheriff clerk until such cost has been paid to him by the pursuer; and

    (c) the pursuer may require the sheriff clerk to supply him with a copy of the summons.

(6) A copy of the newspaper containing the advertisement referred to in paragraph (1)(a) must be lodged with the sheriff clerk unless the sheriff clerk instructed such advertisement.

(7) If display on the walls of court is required under paragraph (1)(b), the pursuer must supply to the sheriff clerk for that purpose a completed copy of Form 9.

(8) If service has been made under this rule and thereafter the defender's address becomes known, the sheriff may allow the summons to be amended and, if appropriate, grant warrant for resserve subject to such conditions as he thinks fit.

Small Claim Rules 2002 629

NOTE
¹ As inserted by the Act of Sederunt (Sheriff Court Rules Amendment) (Diligence) 2008 (SSI 2008/121) r.7(2) (effective April 1, 2008).

Endorsation by sheriff clerk of defender's residence not necessary
6.7. Any summons, decree, charge or other document following upon a summons or decree may be served, enforced or otherwise lawfully executed in Scotland without endorsation by a sheriff clerk and, if executed by a sheriff officer, may be so executed by a sheriff officer of the court which granted the summons, or by a sheriff officer of the sheriff court district in which it is to be executed.

Contents of envelope containing defender's copy summons
6.8. Nothing must be included in the envelope containing a defender's copy summons except—
  (a) the copy summons;
  (b) a response or other notice in accordance with these Rules; and
  (c) any other document approved by the sheriff principal.

Re-service
6.9.—(1) If it appears to the sheriff that there has been any failure or irregularity in service upon a defender, the sheriff may order the pursuer to re-serve the summons on such conditions as he thinks fit.
  (2) If re-service has been ordered in accordance with paragraph (1) or rule 6.6(8), the claim shall proceed thereafter as if it were a new claim.

Defender appearing barred from objecting to service
6.10.—(1) A person who appears in any claim shall not be entitled to state any objection to the regularity of the execution of service or intimation on him and his appearance shall remedy any defect in such service or intimation.
  (2) Nothing in paragraph (1) shall preclude a party pleading that the court has no jurisdiction.

Return of summons and execution
6.11.—(1) If—
  (a) someone other than the sheriff clerk has served the summons; and
  (b) the case requires to call in court for any reason on the hearing date, the pursuer must return the summons and the certificate of execution of service to the sheriff clerk at least two days before the hearing date.
  (2) If the case does not require to call in court on the hearing date, the pursuer must return the certificate of execution of service to the sheriff clerk by the date mentioned in paragraph (1) above.
  (3) If the pursuer fails to return the summons or certificate of execution of service in accordance with paragraph (1) or (2) as appropriate, the sheriff may dismiss the claim.

CHAPTER 7

¹ INTERIM DILIGENCE

NOTE
¹ Chapter renamed by the Act of Sederunt (Sheriff Court Rules Amendment) (Diligence) 2008 (SSI 2008/121) r.7(3) (effective April 1, 2008).

Interpretation
¹ **7.A1.** In this Chapter—
  "the 1987 Act" means the Debtors (Scotland) Act 1987; and
  "the 2002 Act" means the Debt Arrangement and Attachment (Scotland) Act 2002.

NOTE
¹ As inserted by the Act of Sederunt (Sheriff Court Rules Amendment) (Diligence) 2008 (SSI 2008/121) r.7(4) (effective April 1, 2008).

Application for interim diligence
¹ **7.A2.**—(1) The following shall be made by incidental application—

(a) an application under section 15D(1) of the 1987 Act for warrant for diligence by arrestment or inhibition on the dependence of an action or warrant for arrestment on the dependence of an admiralty action;

(b) an application under section 9C of the 2002 Act for interim attachment.

(2) Such an application must be accompanied by a statement in Form 9a.

(3) A certified copy of an interlocutor granting an application under paragraph (1) shall be sufficient authority for execution of the diligence concerned.

NOTE

[1] As inserted by the Act of Sederunt (Sheriff Court Rules Amendment) (Diligence) 2008 (SSI 2008/121) r.7(4) (effective April 1, 2008).

Effect of authority for inhibition on the dependence

[1] **7.A3.**—(1) Where a person has been granted authority for inhibition on the dependence of an action, a certified copy of the interlocutor granting the application may be registered with a certificate of execution in the Register of Inhibitions and Adjudications.

[2] (2) A notice of a certified copy of an interlocutor granting authority for inhibition under rule 7.A2 may be registered in the Register of Inhibitions and Adjudications; and such registration is to have the same effect as registration of a notice of inhibition under section 155(2) of the Titles to Land Consolidation (Scotland) Act 1868.

NOTES

[1] As inserted by the Act of Sederunt (Sheriff Court Rules Amendment) (Diligence) 2008 (SSI 2008/121) r.7(4) (effective April 1, 2008).

[2] As substituted by the Act of Sederunt (Sheriff Court Rules Amendment) (Diligence) 2009 (SSI 2009/107) r.6 (effective April 22, 2009).

Recall etc of arrestment or inhibition

[1] **7.A4.**—(1) An application by any person having an interest—

(a) to loose, restrict, vary or recall an arrestment or an interim attachment; or

(b) to recall, in whole or in part, or vary, an inhibition,

shall be made by incidental application.

(2) Paragraph (1) does not apply to an application made orally at a hearing under section 15K that has been fixed under section 15E(4) of the Act of 1987.

NOTE

[1] As inserted by the Act of Sederunt (Sheriff Court Rules Amendment) (Diligence) 2008 (SSI 2008/121) r.7(4) (effective April 1, 2008).

Incidental applications in relation to interim diligence, etc

[1] **7.A5.** An application under Part 1A of the 1987 Act or Part 1A of the 2002 Act other than mentioned above shall be made by incidental application.

NOTE

[1] As inserted by the Act of Sederunt (Sheriff Court Rules Amendment) (Diligence) 2008 (SSI 2008/121) r.7(4) (effective April 1, 2008).

Form of schedule of inhibition on the dependence

7.A6. [*Revoked by the Act of Sederunt (Sheriff Court Rules Amendment) (Diligence) 2009 (SSI 2009/107) r.6 (effective April 22, 2009).*]

Service of inhibition on the dependence where address of defender not known

[1] **7.A7.**—(1) Where the address of a defender is not known to the pursuer, an inhibition shall be deemed to have been served on the defender if the schedule of inhibition is left with or deposited at the office of the sheriff clerk of the sheriff court district where the defender's last known address is located.

(2) Where service of an inhibition on the dependence is executed under paragraph (1), a copy of the schedule of inhibition shall be sent by the sheriff officer by first class post to the defender's last known address.

NOTE

[1] As inserted by the Act of Sederunt (Sheriff Court Rules Amendment) (Diligence) 2008 (SSI 2008/121) r.7(4) (effective April 1, 2008).

Form of schedule of arrestment on the dependence
[1] **7.A8.**—(1) An arrestment on the dependence shall be served by serving the schedule of arrestment on the arrestee in Form 9b.

(2) A certificate of execution shall be lodged with the sheriff clerk in Form 9c.

NOTE
[1] As inserted by the Act of Sederunt (Sheriff Court Rules Amendment) (Diligence) 2009 (SSI 2009/107) r.6 (effective April 22, 2009).

Service of schedule of arrestment
7.1. If a schedule of arrestment has not been personally served on an arrestee, the arrestment shall have effect only if a copy of the schedule is also sent by registered post or the first class recorded delivery service to—
   (a) the last known place of residence of the arrestee; or
   (b) if such place of residence is not known, or if the arrestee is a firm or corporation, to the arrestee's principal place of business if known, or, if not known, to any known place of business of the arrestee,
and the sheriff officer must, on the certificate of execution, certify that this has been done and specify the address to which the copy of the schedule was sent.

Arrestment on dependence before service
[1] **7.2**—(1) An arrestment to found jurisdiction used prior to service shall cease to have effect, unless the summons is served within 21 days from the date of execution of the arrestment.

(2) When such an arrestment as is referred to in paragraph (1) has been executed, the party using it must forthwith report the execution to the sheriff clerk.

NOTE
[1] As amended by the Act of Sederunt (Sheriff Court Rules Amendment) (Diligence) (SSI 2008/121) r.7(5) (effective April 1, 2008). This rule as it applied immediately before April 1, 2008 continues to have effect for the purpose of any application for arrestment on the dependence made before that date.

Recall and restriction of arrestment
7.3.—(1) The sheriff may order that an arrestment on the dependence of a claim or counterclaim shall cease to have effect if the party whose funds or property are arrested—
   (a) pays into court; or
   (b) finds caution to the satisfaction of the sheriff clerk in respect of, the sum claimed together with the sum of £50 in respect of expenses.

(2) Without prejudice to paragraph (1), a party whose funds or property are arrested may at any time apply to the sheriff to exercise his powers to recall or restrict an arrestment on the dependence of a claim or counterclaim, with or without consignation or caution.

(3) An application made under paragraph (3) must be intimated by the applicant to the party who instructed the arrestment.

(4) On payment into court or the finding of caution to the satisfaction of the sheriff clerk in accordance with paragraph (1), or if the sheriff recalls or restricts an arrestment on the dependence of a claim in accordance with paragraph (2) and any condition imposed by the sheriff has been complied with, the sheriff clerk must—
   (a) issue to the party whose funds or property are arrested a certificate in Form 10 authorising the release of any sum or property arrested to the extent ordered by the sheriff; and
   (b) send a copy of the certificate to—
      (i) the party who instructed the arrestment; and
      (ii) the party who has possession of the funds or property that are arrested.

CHAPTER 8

UNDEFENDED CLAIM

Undefended claim
8.1.—(1) Where the defender has not lodged a form of response on or before the return day, the claim shall not require to call in court.

(2) Where paragraph (1) applies, the pursuer must lodge a minute in Form 11 before the sheriff clerk's office closes for business on the second day before the date set for the hearing.

(3) Where the pursuer has lodged a minute in accordance with paragraph (2), the sheriff may grant decree or other competent order sought in terms of that minute.

(4) Where the pursuer has not lodged a minute in accordance with paragraph (2), the sheriff must dismiss the claim.

Application for time to pay direction or time order
8.2.—(1) If the defender admits the claim, he may, where competent—
  (a) make an application for a time to pay direction (including, where appropriate, an application for recall or restriction of an arrestment) or a time order by completing the appropriate parts of the Form 1a and lodging it with the sheriff clerk on or before the return day; or
  (b) lodge a form of response indicating that he admits the claim and intends to apply orally for a time to pay direction (including, where appropriate, an application for recall or restriction of an arrestment) or time order.
  [1] (1A) The sheriff clerk must on receipt forthwith intimate to the pursuer a copy of any response lodged under paragraph (1).
  [2] (2) Where the defender has lodged an application in terms of paragraph (1)(a), the pursuer may intimate that he does not object to the application by lodging a minute in Form 12 before the time the sheriff clerk's office closes for business on the day occurring 9 days before the hearing date stating that he does not object to the defender's application and seeking decree.
  (3) If the pursuer intimates in accordance with paragraph (2) that he does not object to the application—
  (a) the sheriff may grant decree on the hearing date;
  (b) the parties need not attend; and
  (c) the action will not call in court.
  [2] (4) If the pursuer wishes to oppose the application for a time to pay direction or time order made in accordance with paragraph (1)(a) he must before the time the sheriff clerk's office closes for business on the day occurring 9 days before the hearing date—
  (a) lodge a minute in Form 13; and
  (b) send a copy of that minute to the defender.
  (5) Where the pursuer objects to an application in terms of paragraph (1)(a) or the defender has lodged a form of response in accordance with paragraph (1)(b), the action shall call in court on the hearing date when the parties may appear and the sheriff must decide the application and grant decree accordingly.
  (6) The sheriff shall decide an application in accordance with paragraph (5) whether or not any of the parties appear.
  (7) Where the defender has lodged an application in terms of paragraph (1)(a) and the pursuer fails to proceed in accordance with either of paragraphs (2) or (4) the sheriff may dismiss the claim.

NOTES
  [1] As inserted by the Act of Sederunt (Sheriff Court Rules) (Miscellaneous Amendments) 2009 (SSI 2009/294) r.5 (effective December 1, 2009).
  [2] As substituted by the Act of Sederunt (Sheriff Court Rules) (Miscellaneous Amendments) 2009 (SSI 2009/294) r.5 (effective December 1, 2009).

Decree in claims to which the Hague Convention or the Civil Jurisdiction and Judgments Act 1982 apply
8.3.—(1) If the summons has been served in a country to which the Hague Convention on the Service Abroad of Judicial and Extra-Judicial Documents in Civil or Commercial Matters dated 15th November 1965 applies, decree must not be granted until it is established to the satisfaction of the sheriff that the requirements of Article 15 of that Convention have been complied with.
  (2) Where a defender is domiciled in another part of the United Kingdom or in another Contracting State, the sheriff shall not grant decree until it has been shown that the defender has been able to receive the summons in sufficient time to arrange his defence or that all necessary steps have been taken to that end.
  (3) For the purposes of paragraph (2)—
  (a) the question whether a person is domiciled in another part of the United Kingdom shall be determined in accordance with sections 41 and 42 of the Civil Jurisdiction and Judgments Act 1982;
  (b) the question whether a person is domiciled in another Contracting State shall be determined in accordance with Article 52 of the Convention in Schedule 1 or 3C to that Act; and
  (c) the term "Contracting State" has the meaning assigned in section 1 of that Act.

CHAPTER 9

DEFENDED CLAIM

The Hearing
9.1.—(1) Where a defender intends to—
  (a) challenge the jurisdiction of the court;
  (b) state a defence (including, where appropriate, a counterclaim); or
  (c) dispute the amount of the claim, he must complete the form of response part of Form 1a or 1b as appropriate indicating that intention and lodge it with the sheriff clerk on or before the return day.
(2) Where the defender has lodged a form of response in accordance with paragraph (1) the claim will call in court for a hearing ("the Hearing").
[1] (3) The Hearing shall be held on the hearing date which shall be 14 days after the return day.
(4) If the claim is not resolved at the Hearing, the sheriff may continue the Hearing to such other date as he considers to be appropriate.
(5) The defender must attend or be represented at the Hearing and the sheriff shall note any challenge, defence or dispute, as the case may be, on the summons.
(6) Where at the Hearing the defender—
  (a) does not appear or is not represented; and
  (b) the pursuer is present or is represented, decree may be granted against the defender in terms of the summons.
(7) Where at the Hearing—
  (a) the pursuer does not appear or is not represented; and
  (b) the defender is present or represented, the sheriff may grant decree of dismissal.
(8) If all parties fail to appear at the Hearing, the sheriff shall, unless sufficient reason appears to the contrary, dismiss the claim.

NOTE
[1] As substituted by the Act of Sederunt (Sheriff Court Rules) (Miscellaneous Amendments) 2009 (SSI 2009/294) r.7 (effective December 1, 2009).

Purpose of the Hearing
9.2.—(1) If, at the Hearing, the sheriff is satisfied that the claim is incompetent or that there is a patent defect of jurisdiction, he must grant decree of dismissal in favour of the defender or, if appropriate, transfer the claim in terms of rule 15.1(2).
(2) At the Hearing, the sheriff shall—
  (a) ascertain the factual basis of the claim and any defence, and the legal basis on which the claim and defence are proceeding; and
  (b) seek to negotiate and secure settlement of the claim between the parties.
(3) If the sheriff cannot secure settlement of the claim between the parties, he shall—
  (a) identify and note on the summons the issues of fact and law which are in dispute;
  (b) note on the summons any facts which are agreed; and
  (c) if possible reach a decision on the whole dispute on the basis of the information before him.
  [1](d) enquire whether there is or is likely to be a vulnerable witness within the meaning of section 11(1) of the 2004 Act who is to give evidence at any proof or hearing, consider any child witness notice or vulnerable witness application that has been lodged where no order has been made and consider whether any order under section 12(1) of the 2004 Act requires to be made.
(4) Where evidence requires to be led for the purposes of reaching a decision on the dispute, the sheriff shall—
  (a) direct parties to lead evidence on the disputed issues of fact which he has noted on the summons;
  (b) indicate to the parties the matters of fact that require to be proved, and may give guidance on the nature of the evidence to be led; and
  (c) fix a hearing on evidence for a later date for that purpose.

NOTE
[1]As inserted by the Act of Sederunt (Ordinary Cause, Summary Application, Summary Cause and Small Claim Rules) Amendment (Vulnerable Witnesses (Scotland) Act 2004) 2007 (SSI 2007/463) r.5(3) (effective November 1, 2007).

Conduct of hearings

9.3.—(1) Any hearing in a claim shall be conducted in accordance with the following paragraphs of this rule.

(2) A hearing shall be conducted as informally as the circumstances of the claim permit.

(3) The procedure to be adopted at a hearing shall be such as the sheriff considers—
   (a) to be fair;
   (b) best suited to the clarification and determination of the issues before him; and
   (c) gives each party sufficient opportunity to present his case.

(4) Before proceeding to hear evidence, the sheriff shall explain to the parties the form of procedure which he intends to adopt.

(5) Having considered the circumstances of the parties and whether (and to what extent) they are represented, the sheriff—
   (a) may, in order to assist resolution of the disputed issues of fact, put questions to parties and to witnesses; and
   (b) shall (if he considers it necessary for the fair conduct of the hearing) explain any legal terms or expressions which are used.

(6) Evidence will normally be taken on oath or affirmation but the sheriff may dispense with that requirement if it appears reasonable to do so.

Inspection of places and objects

9.4.—(1) If, at any hearing, a disputed issue noted by the sheriff is the quality or condition of an object, the sheriff may inspect the object in the presence of the parties or their representatives in court or, if it is not practicable to bring the object to court, at the place where the object is located.

(2) The sheriff may, if he considers it appropriate, inspect any place that is material to the disputed issues in the presence of the parties or their representatives.

Remit to determine matter of fact

9.5.—(1) The sheriff may, where parties agree, remit to any suitable person to report on any matter of fact.

(2) Where a remit is made under paragraph (1) above, the report of such person shall be final and conclusive with respect to the matter of fact which is the subject of the remit.

(3) A remit shall not be made under paragraph (1) of this rule unless parties have previously agreed the basis upon which the fees, if any, of such person shall be met.

Noting of evidence

9.6. The sheriff must make notes of the evidence at a hearing for his own use and must retain these notes until after any appeal has been disposed of.

Application for time to pay direction or time order in defended claim

9.7. A defender in a claim which proceeds as defended may, where it is competent to do so, make an incidental application or apply orally at any hearing, at any time before decree is granted, for a time to pay direction (including where appropriate, an order recalling or restricting an arrestment on the dependence) or a time order.

Pronouncement of decision

9.8.—(1) The sheriff must, where practicable, give his decision and a brief statement of his reasons at the end of the hearing of a claim, or he may reserve judgment.

(2) If the sheriff reserves judgment, he must, within 28 days of the hearing, give his decision in writing together with a brief note of his reasons, and the sheriff clerk must send a copy to the parties.

(3) After giving his judgment, the sheriff must—
   (a) deal with the question of expenses and, where appropriate, make an award of expenses; and
   (b) grant decree as appropriate

(4) The decree of the sheriff shall be a final decree.

CHAPTER 10

INCIDENTAL APPLICATIONS AND SISTS

General

10.1.—(1) Except where otherwise provided, any incidental application in a claim may be made—

(a) orally with the leave of the sheriff during any hearing of the claim; or

(b) by lodging the application in written form with the sheriff clerk.

(2) An application lodged in accordance with paragraph (1)(b) may only be heard after not less than two days' notice has been given to the other party.

(3) A party who is not—

(a) a partnership or a body corporate; or

(b) acting in a representative capacity, and is not represented by a solicitor, may require the sheriff clerk to intimate to the other party a copy of an incidental application.

(4) Where the party receiving notice of an incidental application lodged in accordance with paragraph (1)(b) intimates to the sheriff clerk and the party making the application that it is not opposed, the application shall not require to call in court unless the sheriff so directs.

(5) Any intimation under paragraph (4) shall be made not later than noon on the day before the application is due to be heard.

Application to sist claim

10.2.—(1) Where an incidental application to sist a claim is made, the reason for the sist—

(a) shall be stated by the party seeking the sist; and

(b) shall be recorded in the Register of Small Claims and on the summons.

(2) Where a claim has been sisted, the sheriff may, after giving parties an opportunity to be heard, recall the sist.

CHAPTER 11

COUNTERCLAIM

Counterclaim

11.1.—(1) If a defender intends to state a counterclaim he must—

(a) indicate that on the form of response; and

(b) state the counterclaim—

(i) in writing on the form of response; or

(ii) orally at the Hearing.

(2) Where a defender states a counterclaim in accordance with paragraph (1)(b)(i) he must at the same time send a copy of the form of response to—

(a) the pursuer; and

(b) any other party.

(3) [*Repealed by the Act of Sederunt (Sheriff Court Rules) (Miscellaneous Amendments) 2009 (SSI 2009/294) r.12 (effective October 1, 2009).*]

(5) Where a defender has indicated in terms of paragraph (1)(a) that he intends to state a counterclaim orally at the Hearing the sheriff may continue the Hearing to allow an answer to the counterclaim to be stated.

(6) The defender may state a counterclaim after—

(a) the Hearing; or

(b) any continuation of the Hearing,

as the case may be, only with the leave of the sheriff.

(7) If a counterclaim has been stated orally at any hearing at which the pursuer fails to appear or be represented the sheriff may continue that hearing after noting the counterclaim and the factual basis of it to allow the pursuer to appear.

(8) Intimation of a continued hearing fixed under paragraph (7) shall be given to the pursuer by the sheriff clerk in Form 14 advising him that if he fails to appear or be represented at the continued hearing decree may be granted in terms of the counterclaim.

CHAPTER 12

ALTERATION OF SUMMONS ETC.

Alteration of summons etc.

12.1.—(1) The sheriff may, on the incidental application of a party allow amendment of the summons, form of response or any counterclaim, and adjust the note of disputed issues at any time before final judgment is pronounced on the merits.

(2) In an undefended claim, the sheriff may order the amended summons to be re-served on the defender on such period of notice as he thinks fit.

ADDITIONAL DEFENDER

Additional defender
13.1.—(1) Any person who has not been called as a defender may apply by incidental application to the sheriff for leave to enter a claim as a defender, and to state a defence.

(2) An application under this rule must specify—
  (a) the applicant's title and interest to enter the claim; and
  (b) the grounds of the defence which he proposes to state.

(3) On the lodging of an application under this rule—
  (a) the sheriff must fix a date for hearing the application; and
  (b) the applicant must forthwith serve a copy of the application and of the order for a hearing on the parties to the claim.

(4) After hearing the applicant and any party to the claim the sheriff may, if he is satisfied that the applicant has shown title and interest to enter the claim, grant the application.

(5) Where an application is granted under paragraph (4)—
  (a) the applicant shall be treated as a defender; and
  (b) the claim shall proceed against him as if was the Hearing in terms of rule 9.2.

[1] CHAPTER 13A

INTERVENTIONS BY THE COMMISSION FOR EQUALITY AND HUMAN RIGHTS

NOTE
[1] As inserted by the Act of Sederunt (Sheriff Court Rules) (Miscellaneous Amendments) 2008 (SSI 2008/223) r.7(2) (effective July 1, 2008).

Interpretation
13A.1. In this Chapter "the CEHR" means the Commission for Equality and Human Rights.

Interventions by the CEHR
13A.2.—(1) The CEHR may apply to the sheriff for leave to intervene in any small claim in accordance with this Chapter.

(2) This Chapter is without prejudice to any other entitlement of the CEHR by virtue of having title and interest in relation to the subject matter of any proceedings by virtue of section 30(2) of the Equality Act 2006 or any other enactment to seek to be sisted as a party in those proceedings.

(3) Nothing in this Chapter shall affect the power of the sheriff to make such other direction as he considers appropriate in the interests of justice.

(4) Any decision of the sheriff in proceedings under this Chapter shall be final and not subject to appeal.

Applications to intervene
13A.3.—(1) An application for leave to intervene shall be by way of minute of intervention in Form 14A and the CEHR shall—
  (a) send a copy of it to all the parties; and
  (b) lodge it in process, certifying that subparagraph (a) has been complied with.

(2) A minute of intervention shall set out briefly—
  (a) the CEHR's reasons for believing that the proceedings are relevant to a matter in connection with which the CEHR has a function;
  (b) the issue in the proceedings which the CEHR wishes to address; and
  (c) the propositions to be advanced by the CEHR and the CEHR's reasons for believing that they are relevant to the proceedings and that they will assist the sheriff.

(3) The sheriff may—
  (a) refuse leave without a hearing;
  (b) grant leave without a hearing unless a hearing is requested under paragraph (4);
  (c) refuse or grant leave after such a hearing.

(4) A hearing, at which the applicant and the parties may address the court on the matters referred to in paragraph (6)(c) may be held if, within 14 days of the minute of intervention being lodged, any of the parties lodges a request for a hearing.

(5) Any diet in pursuance of paragraph (4) shall be fixed by the sheriff clerk who shall give written intimation of the diet to the CEHR and all the parties.

(6) The sheriff may grant leave only if satisfied that—

(a) the proceedings are relevant to a matter in connection with which the CEHR has a function;

(b) the propositions to be advanced by the CEHR are relevant to the proceedings and are likely to assist him; and

(c) the intervention will not unduly delay or otherwise prejudice the rights of the parties, including their potential liability for expenses.

(7) In granting leave the sheriff may impose such terms and conditions as he considers desirable in the interests of justice, including, subject to section 36B of the Sheriff Courts (Scotland) Act 1971, making provision in respect of any additional expenses incurred by the parties as a result of the intervention.

(8) The sheriff clerk shall give written intimation of a grant or refusal of leave to the CEHR and all the parties.

Form of intervention

13A.4.—(1) An intervention shall be by way of a written submission which (including any appendices) shall not exceed 5000 words.

(2) The CEHR shall lodge the submission and send a copy of it to all the parties by such time as the sheriff may direct.

(3) The sheriff may in exceptional circumstances—

(a) allow a longer written submission to be made;

(b) direct that an oral submission is to be made.

(4) Any diet in pursuance of paragraph (3)(b) shall be fixed by the sheriff clerk who shall give written intimation of the diet to the CEHR and all the parties.

¹CHAPTER 13B

INTERVENTIONS BY THE SCOTTISH COMMISSION FOR HUMAN RIGHTS

NOTE
¹ As inserted by the Act of Sederunt (Sheriff Court Rules) (Miscellaneous Amendments) 2008 (SSI 2008/223) r.7(2) (effective July 1, 2008).

Interpretation

13B.1. In this Chapter—

"the Act of 2006" means the Scottish Commission for Human Rights Act 2006; and

"the SCHR" means the Scottish Commission for Human Rights.

Applications to intervene

13B.2.—(1) An application for leave to intervene shall be by way of minute of intervention in Form 14B and the SCHR shall—

(a) send a copy of it to all the parties; and

(b) lodge it in process, certifying that subparagraph (a) has been complied with.

(2) In granting leave the sheriff may impose such terms and conditions as he considers desirable in the interests of justice, including, subject to section 36B of the Sheriff Courts (Scotland) Act 1971, making provision in respect of any additional expenses incurred by the parties as a result of the intervention.

(3) The sheriff clerk shall give written intimation of a grant or refusal of leave to the SCHR and all the parties.

(4) Any decision of the sheriff in proceedings under this Chapter shall be final and not subject to appeal.

Invitations to intervene

13B.3.—(1) An invitation to intervene under section 14(2)(b) of the Act of 2006 shall be in Form 14C and the sheriff clerk shall send a copy of it to the SCHR and all the parties.

(2) An invitation under paragraph (1) shall be accompanied by—

(a) a copy of the pleadings in the proceedings; and

(b) such other documents relating to those proceedings as the sheriff thinks relevant.

(3) In issuing an invitation under section 14(2)(b) of the Act of 2006, the sheriff may impose such terms and conditions as he considers desirable in the interests of justice, including, subject to section 36B of the Sheriff Courts (Scotland) Act 1971, making provision in respect of any additional expenses incurred by the parties as a result of the intervention.

Form of intervention
13B.4.—(1) An intervention shall be by way of a written submission which (including any appendices) shall not exceed 5000 words.

(2) The SCHR shall lodge the submission and send a copy of it to all the parties by such time as the sheriff may direct.

(3) The sheriff may in exceptional circumstances—
 (a) allow a longer written submission to be made;
 (b) direct that an oral submission is to be made.

(4) Any diet in pursuance of paragraph (3)(b) shall be fixed by the sheriff clerk who shall give written intimation of the diet to the SCHR and all the parties.

CHAPTER 14

APPLICATIONS FOR SIST OF PARTY AND TRANSFERENCE

Application for sist of party and transference
14.1.—(1) If a party dies or becomes legally incapacitated while a claim is depending, any person claiming to represent that party or his estate may apply by incidental application to be sisted as a party to the claim.

(2) If a party dies or becomes legally incapacitated while a claim is depending and the provisions of paragraph (1) are not invoked, any other party may apply by incidental application to have the claim transferred in favour of or against, as the case may be, any person who represents that party or his estate.

CHAPTER 15

TRANSFER AND REMIT OF CLAIMS

Transfer to another court
15.1.—(1) The sheriff may transfer a claim to any other sheriff court, whether in the same sheriffdom or not, if the sheriff considers it expedient to do so.

(2) If the sheriff is satisfied that the court has no jurisdiction, he may transfer the claim to any sheriff court in which it appears to the sheriff that it ought to have been brought.

(3) A claim so transferred shall proceed in all respects as if it had been brought originally in the court to which it is transferred.

Remit between procedures
15.2.—(1) If the sheriff makes a direction that a claim is to be treated as an ordinary cause, he must, at the time of making that direction—
 (a) direct the pursuer to lodge an initial writ, and intimate it to every other party, within 14 days of the date of the direction;
 (b) direct the defender to lodge defences within 28 days of the date of the direction; and
 (c) fix a date and time for an Options Hearing and that date shall be the first suitable court day occurring not sooner than ten weeks, or such lesser period as he considers appropriate, after the last date for lodging the initial writ.

(2) If the sheriff directs that a claim is to be treated as a summary cause he must specify the next step of procedure to be followed.

(3) If the sheriff directs that an ordinary cause or a summary cause is to be treated as a claim under these rules it shall call for the Hearing held in terms of rule 9.1(2).

CHAPTER 16

PRODUCTIONS AND DOCUMENTS

Lodging of productions
16.1.—(1) A party who intends to rely at a hearing at which evidence is to be led, upon any documents or articles in his possession, which are reasonably capable of being lodged with the court, must—
 (a) lodge them with the sheriff clerk together with a list detailing the items no later than 14 days before the hearing; and
 (b) at the same time send a copy of the list to the other party.

(2) The documents referred to in paragraph (1) include any affidavit or other written statement admissible under section 2(1) of the Civil Evidence (Scotland) Act 1988.

(3) Subject to paragraph (4), only documents or articles produced—

(a) in accordance with paragraph (1);

(b) at an earlier hearing; or

(c) under rule 17.2(3) or (4), may be used or put in evidence.

(4) Documents other than those mentioned in paragraph (3) may be used or put in evidence only with the—

(a) consent of the parties; or

(b) permission of the sheriff on cause shown, and on such terms as to expenses or otherwise as to him seem proper.

Borrowing of productions

16.2.—(1) Any productions borrowed must be returned not later than noon on the day preceding the date of any hearing.

(2) A receipt for any production borrowed must be entered in the list of productions and that list must be retained by the sheriff clerk.

(3) Subject to paragraph (4), productions may be borrowed only by—

(a) a solicitor; or

(b) his authorised clerk for whom he shall be responsible.

(4) A party litigant or an authorised lay representative may borrow a production only with permission of the sheriff and subject to such conditions as the sheriff may impose.

(5) Productions may be inspected within the office of the sheriff clerk during normal business hours, and copies may be obtained by a party litigant, where practicable, from the sheriff clerk.

Documents lost or destroyed

16.3.—(1) This rule applies to any—

(a) summons;

(b) form of response;

(c) counterclaim;

(d) Register of Small Claims; or

(e) other document lodged with the sheriff clerk in connection with a claim.

(2) Where any document mentioned in paragraph (1) is—

(a) lost; or

(b) destroyed,

a copy of it, authenticated in such manner as the sheriff may require, may be substituted and shall, for the purposes of the claim including the use of diligence, be equivalent to the original.

Documents and productions to be retained in custody of sheriff clerk

16.4.—(1) This rule applies to all documents or other productions which have at any time been lodged or referred to during a hearing.

(2) The sheriff clerk must retain in his custody any document or other production mentioned in paragraph (1) until—

(a) after the expiry of the period during which an appeal is competent; and

(b) any appeal lodged has been disposed of.

(3) Each party who has lodged productions in a claim shall—

(a) after the final determination of the claim, where no appeal has been lodged, within 14 days after the appeal period has expired; or

(b) within 14 days after the disposal of any appeal lodged on the final determination of the claim, uplift the productions from the sheriff clerk.

(4) Where any production has not been uplifted as required by paragraph (3), the sheriff clerk shall intimate to—

(a) the solicitor who lodged the production; or

(b) where no solicitor is acting, the party himself or such other party as seems appropriate, that if he fails to uplift the production within 28 days after the date of such intimation, it will be disposed of in such manner as the sheriff directs.

CHAPTER 17

RECOVERY OF DOCUMENTS AND ATTENDANCE OF WITNESSES

Diligence for recovery of documents

17.1—(1) At any time after a summons has been served, a party may make an incidental application in writing to the sheriff to grant commission and diligence to recover documents.

(2) A party who makes an application in accordance with paragraph (1) must list in the application the documents which he wishes to recover.

(3) The sheriff may grant commission and diligence to recover those documents in the list mentioned in paragraph (2) which he considers relevant to the claim.

Optional procedure before executing commission and diligence

17.2.—(1) Any party who has obtained a commission and diligence for the recovery of documents may, at any time before executing it, serve by first class recorded delivery post on the person from whom the documents are sought to be recovered (or on his known solicitor or solicitors) an order with certificate attached in Form 15.

(2) If in a claim the party in whose favour the commission and diligence has been granted is not—

    (a) a partnership or body corporate; or

    (b) acting in a representative capacity, and is not represented by a solicitor, service under paragraph (1) must be effected by the sheriff clerk posting a copy of the order together with a certificate in Form 15 by first class recorded delivery post or, on payment of the fee prescribed by the Scottish Ministers by order, by sheriff officer.

(3) Documents recovered in response to an order under paragraph (1) must be sent to, and retained by, the sheriff clerk who shall, on receiving them, advise the parties that the documents are in his possession and may be examined within his office during normal business hours.

(4) If the party who served the order is not satisfied that—

    (a) full production has been made under the specification; or

    (b) that adequate reasons for non-production have been given, he may execute the commission and diligence in normal form, notwithstanding his adoption in the first instance of the procedure in paragraph (1) above.

(5) Documents recovered under this rule may be submitted as evidence at any hearing without further formality, and rule 17.3(3) and (4) shall apply to such documents.

Confidentiality of documents

17.3.—(1) In any claim where a party has obtained a commission and diligence to recover documents and the documents have been produced either—

    (a) before the execution of the commission and diligence; or

    (b) following execution of the commission and diligence, confidentiality may be claimed for any document produced.

(2) Where confidentiality is claimed under paragraph (1), the documents in respect of which confidentiality is claimed shall be enclosed in a separate, sealed packet.

(3) A sealed packet referred to in paragraph (2) shall not be opened except by authority of the sheriff obtained on the application of the party who sought the commission and diligence.

(4) Before the sheriff grants an application made in accordance with paragraph (3), he shall offer to hear the party or parties from whose possession the documents specified in the commission and diligence were obtained.

Witnesses

17.4.—(1) A party shall be responsible for securing the attendance of his witnesses or havers at a hearing and shall be personally liable for their expenses.

(2) The summons or the copy served on the defender shall be sufficient warrant for the citation of witnesses or havers.

(3) The citation of a witness or haver must be in Form 16 and the certificate of execution of citation must be in Form 16a.

(4) The period of notice given to witnesses or havers cited in terms of paragraph (3) must be not less than seven days.

(5) A witness or haver shall be cited—

    (a) by registered post or the first class recorded delivery service by the solicitor for the party on whose behalf he is cited;

    (b) by a sheriff officer—

        (i) personally;

        (ii) by a citation being left with a resident at the person's dwelling place or an employee at his place of business;

        (iii) by depositing it in that person's dwelling place or place of business;

        (iv) by affixing it to the door of that person's dwelling place or place of business; or

        (v) by registered post or the first class recorded delivery service.

(6) Where service is effected under paragraph 5(b)(iii) or (iv), the sheriff officer shall, as soon as possible after such service, send by ordinary post to the address at which he thinks it most likely that the person may be found, a letter containing a copy of the citation.

Citation of witnesses by party litigants

17.5.—(1) Where a party to a claim is a party litigant he shall—

(a) not later than 28 days before any hearing on evidence apply to the sheriff to fix caution for expenses in such sum as the sheriff considers reasonable having regard to the number of witnesses he proposes to cite and the period for which they may be required to attend court; and

(b) before instructing a solicitor or a sheriff officer to cite a witness, find the sum fixed in accordance with paragraph (1)(a).

(2) A party litigant who does not intend to cite all the witnesses referred to in his application under paragraph (1)(a) may apply for variation of the amount of caution.

Witnesses failing to attend

17.6.—(1) A hearing must not be adjourned solely on account of the failure of a witness to appear unless the sheriff, on cause shown, so directs.

(2) A witness or haver who fails without reasonable excuse to answer a citation after having been properly cited and offered his travelling expenses if he has asked for them may be ordered by the sheriff to pay a penalty not exceeding £250.

(3) The sheriff may grant decree for payment of a penalty imposed under paragraph (2) above in favour of the party on whose behalf the witness or haver was cited.

(4) The sheriff may grant warrant for the apprehension of the witness or haver and for bringing him to court.

(5) A warrant mentioned in paragraph (4) shall be effective in any sheriffdom without endorsation and the expenses of it may be awarded against the witness or haver.

[1] CHAPTER 17A

VULNERABLE WITNESSES (SCOTLAND) ACT 2004

NOTE
[1] As inserted by the Act of Sederunt (Ordinary Cause, Summary Application, Summary Cause and Small Claim Rules) Amendment (Vulnerable Witnesses (Scotland) Act 2004) 2007 (SSI 2007/463) r.5(5) (effective November 1, 2007).

Interpretation

17A.1. In this Chapter—
"child witness notice" has the meaning given in section 12(2) of the 2004 Act;
"review application" means an application for review of arrangements for vulnerable witnesses pursuant to section 13 of the 2004 Act;
"vulnerable witness application" has the meaning given in section 12(6) of the 2004 Act.

Child Witness Notice

17A.2. A child witness notice lodged in accordance with section 12(2) of the 2004 Act shall be in Form 16B.

Vulnerable Witness Application

17A.3. A vulnerable witness application lodged in accordance with section 12(6) of the 2004 Act shall be in Form 16C.

Intimation

17A.4.—(1) The party lodging a child witness notice or vulnerable witness application shall intimate a copy of the child witness notice or vulnerable witness application to all the other parties to the proceedings and complete a certificate of intimation.

(2) A certificate of intimation referred to in paragraph (1) shall be in Form 16D and shall be lodged with the child witness notice or vulnerable witness application.

Procedure on lodging child witness notice or vulnerable witness application

17A.5.—(1) On receipt of a child witness notice or vulnerable witness application, the sheriff may—
(a) make an order under section 12(1) or (6) of the 2004 Act without holding a hearing;
(b) require further information from any of the parties before making any further order;
(c) fix a date for a hearing of the child witness notice or vulnerable witness application.

(2) The sheriff may, subject to any statutory time limits, make an order altering the date of the proof or other hearing at which the child or vulnerable witness is to give evidence and make such provision for intimation of such alteration to all parties concerned as he deems appropriate.

(3) An order fixing a hearing for a child witness notice or vulnerable witness application shall be intimated by the sheriff clerk—
   (a) on the day the order is made; and
   (b) in such manner as may be prescribed by the sheriff,
to all parties to the proceedings and such other persons as are named in the order where such parties or persons are not present at the time the order is made.

Review of arrangements for vulnerable witnesses
17A.6.—(1) A review application shall be in Form 16E.
(2) Where the review application is made orally, the sheriff may dispense with the requirements of paragraph (1).

Intimation of review application
17A.7.—(1) Where a review application is lodged, the applicant shall intimate a copy of the review application to all other parties to the proceedings and complete a certificate of intimation.
(2) A certificate of intimation referred to in paragraph (1) shall be in Form 16F and shall be lodged together with the review application.

Procedure on lodging a review application
17A.8.—(1) On receipt of a review application, the sheriff may—
   (a) if he is satisfied that he may properly do so, make an order under section 13(2) of the 2004 Act without holding a hearing or, if he is not so satisfied, make such an order after giving the parties an opportunity to be heard;
   (b) require of any of the parties further information before making any further order;
   (c) fix a date for a hearing of the review application.
(2) The sheriff may, subject to any statutory time limits, make an order altering the date of the proof or other hearing at which the child or vulnerable witness is to give evidence and make such provision for intimation of such alteration to all parties concerned as he deems appropriate.
(3) An order fixing a hearing for a review application shall be intimated by the sheriff clerk—
   (a) on the day the order is made; and
   (b) in such manner as may be prescribed by the sheriff,
to all parties to the proceedings and such other persons as are named in the order where such parties or persons are not present at the time the order is made.

Determination of special measures
17A.9. When making an order under section 12(1) or (6) or 13(2) of the 2004 Act the sheriff may, in light thereof, make such further orders as he deems appropriate in all the circumstances.

Intimation of an order under section 12(1) or (6) or 13(2)
17A.10. An order under section 12(1) or (6) or 13(2) of the 2004 Act shall be intimated by the sheriff clerk—
   (a) on the day the order is made; and
   (b) in such manner as may be prescribed by the sheriff,
to all parties to the proceedings and such other persons as are named in the order where such parties or persons are not present at the time the order is made.

Taking of evidence by commissioner
17A.11.—(1) An interlocutor authorising the special measure of taking evidence by a commissioner shall be sufficient authority for the citing the witness to appear before the commissioner.
(2) At the commission the commissioner shall—
   (a) administer the oath *de fideli administratione* to any clerk appointed for the commission; and
   (b) administer to the witness the oath, or where the witness elects to affirm, the affirmation.
(3) The commission shall proceed without interrogatories unless, on cause shown, the sheriff otherwise directs.

Commission on interrogatories
17A.12.—(1) Where interrogatories have not been dispensed with, the party citing or intending to cite the vulnerable witness shall lodge draft interrogatories in process.
(2) Any other party may lodge cross-interrogatories.
(3) The interrogatories and cross-interrogatories, when adjusted, shall be extended and

returned to the sheriff clerk for approval and the settlement of any dispute as to their contents by the sheriff.

(4) The party who cited the vulnerable witness shall–

    (a) provide the commissioner with a copy of the pleadings (including any adjustments and amendments), the approved interrogatories and any cross-interrogatories and a certified copy of the interlocutor of his appointment;

    (b) instruct the clerk; and

    (c) be responsible in the first instance for the fee of the commissioner and his clerk.

(5) The commissioner shall, in consultation with the parties, fix a diet for the execution of the commission to examine the witness.

Commission without interrogatories

17A.13. Where interrogatories have been dispensed with, the party citing or intending to cite the vulnerable witness shall—

    (a) provide the commissioner with a copy of the pleadings (including any adjustments and amendments) and a certified copy of the interlocutor of his appointment;

    (b) fix a diet for the execution of the commission in consultation with the commissioner and every other party;

    (c) instruct the clerk; and

    (d) be responsible in the first instance for the fees of the commissioner and his clerk.

Lodging of video record and documents

17A.14.—(1) Where evidence is taken on commission pursuant to an order made under section 12(1) or (6) or 13(2) of the 2004 Act the commissioner shall lodge the video record of the commission and relevant documents with the sheriff clerk.

(2) On the video record and any documents being lodged the sheriff clerk shall—

    (a) note—

        (i) the documents lodged;

        (ii) by whom they were lodged; and

        (iii) the date on which they were lodged, and

    (b) intimate what he has noted to all parties concerned.

Custody of video record and documents

17A.15.—(1) The video record and documents referred to in rule 17A.14 shall, subject to paragraph (2), be kept in the custody of the sheriff clerk.

(2) Where the video record of the evidence of a witness is in the custody of the sheriff clerk under this rule and where intimation has been given to that effect under rule 17A.14(2), the name and address of that witness and the record of his evidence shall be treated as being in the knowledge of the parties; and no party shall be required, notwithstanding any enactment to the contrary—

    (a) to include the name of that witness in any list of witnesses; or

    (b) to include the record of his evidence in any list of productions.

Application for leave for party to be present at the commission

17A.16. An application for leave for a party to be present in the room where the commission proceedings are taking place shall be by incidental application..

(4) In Appendix 1—

    (a) for Form 16 there shall be set out the form in Part 1 of Schedule 3 to this Act of Sederunt; and

    (b) after Form 16A there shall be inserted the forms set out in Part 2 of Schedule 3 to this Act of Sederunt.

CHAPTER 18

EUROPEAN COURT

Interpretation of rules 18.2 to 18.5

18.1.—(1) In rules 18.2 to 18.5—

"the European Court" means the Court of Justice of the European Communities;

"reference" means a reference to the European Court for—

    (a) a preliminary ruling under Article 234 of the E.E.C. Treaty, Article 150 of the Euratom Treaty or Article 41 of the E.C.S.C. Treaty; or

    (b) a ruling on the interpretation of the Conventions, as defined in section 1(1) of the Civil Jurisdiction and Judgments Act 1982, under Article 3 of Schedule 2 to that Act.

(2) The expressions "E.E.C. Treaty", "Euratom Treaty" and "E.C.S.C. Treaty" have the meanings assigned respectively in Schedule 1 to the European Communities Act 1972.

Application for reference
18.2.—(1) The sheriff may, on the incidental application of a party, or of his own accord, make a reference.
(2) A reference must be made in the form of a request for a preliminary ruling of the European Court in Form 17.

Preparation of case for reference
18.3.—(1) If the sheriff decides that a reference shall be made, he must within four weeks draft a reference.
(2) On the reference being drafted, the sheriff clerk must send a copy to each party.
(3) Within four weeks after the date on which copies of the draft have been sent to parties, each party may—
    (a) lodge with the sheriff clerk; and
    (b) send to every other party, a note of any adjustments he seeks to have made in the draft reference.
(4) Within 14 days after the date on which any such note of adjustments may be lodged, the sheriff, after considering any such adjustments, must make and sign the reference.
(5) The sheriff clerk must forthwith intimate the making of the reference to each party.

Sist of claim
18.4.—(1) Subject to paragraph (2), on a reference being made, the claim must, unless the sheriff when making the reference otherwise orders, be sisted until the European Court has given a preliminary ruling on the question referred to it.
(2) The sheriff may recall a sist made under paragraph (1) for the purpose of making an interim order which a due regard to the interests of the parties may require.

Transmission of reference
18.5. A copy of the reference, certified by the sheriff clerk, must be transmitted by the sheriff clerk to the Registrar of the European Court.

CHAPTER 19

ABANDONMENT

Abandonment of claim
19.1.—(1) At any time prior to decree being granted, the pursuer may offer to abandon the claim.
(2) If the pursuer offers to abandon, the sheriff clerk must assess the expenses payable by the pursuer to the defender on such basis as the sheriff may direct subject to the provisions of section 36B of the 1971 Act and rule 21.6, and the claim must be continued to the first appropriate court occurring not sooner than 14 days thereafter.
(3) If before the continued diet the pursuer makes payment to the defender of the amount fixed under paragraph (2), the sheriff must dismiss the action unless the pursuer consents to absolvitor.
(4) If before the continued diet the pursuer fails to pay the amount fixed under paragraph (2), the defender shall be entitled to decree of absolvitor with expenses.

CHAPTER 20

DECREE BY DEFAULT

Decree by default
20.1.—(1) If, after the sheriff has fixed a hearing on evidence under rule 9.2(4), any party fails to appear or be represented at a hearing, the sheriff may grant decree by default.
(2) If all parties fail to appear or be represented at a hearing referred to at paragraph (1) the sheriff must, unless sufficient reason appears to the contrary, dismiss the claim and any counterclaim.
(3) If, after a defence has been stated, a party fails to implement an order of the court, the sheriff may, after giving him an opportunity to be heard, grant decree by default.
(4) The sheriff shall not grant decree by default solely on the ground that a party has failed to appear at the hearing of an incidental application.

CHAPTER 21

DECREES, EXTRACTS, EXECUTION AND VARIATION

Decree
21.1.—(1) The sheriff must not grant decree against—
(a) a defender in respect of a claim; or
(b) a pursuer in respect of a counterclaim,
under any provision of these Rules unless satisfied that a ground of jurisdiction exists.

Decree for alternative claim for payment
21.2.—(1) If the sheriff has granted decree for—
(a) delivery;
(b) recovery of possession of moveable property; or
(c) implement of an obligation,
and the defender fails to comply with that decree, the pursuer may lodge with the sheriff clerk an incidental application for decree in terms of the alternative claim for payment.
(2) If the pursuer lodges an incidental application in terms of paragraph (1), he must intimate it to the defender at or before the time it is lodged with the sheriff clerk.
(3) The pursuer must appear at the hearing of an incidental application under paragraph (1).

Taxes on funds under control of the court
21.3. In a claim in which money has been consigned into court under the Sheriff Court Consignations (Scotland) Act 1893, no decree, warrant or order for payment to any person shall be granted until there has been lodged with the sheriff clerk a certificate by an authorised officer of the Inland Revenue stating that all taxes or duties payable to the Commissioners of Inland Revenue have been paid or satisfied.

Correction of interlocutor or note
21.4. At any time before extract, the sheriff may correct any clerical or incidental error in an interlocutor or note attached to it.

Extract of decree
21.5.—(1) Unless the sheriff on application authorises earlier extract, extract of a decree signed by the sheriff clerk may be issued only after the lapse of 14 days from the granting of the decree.
(2) An application for early extract shall be made by incidental application.
(3) In a claim where an appeal has been lodged, the extract may not be issued until the appeal has been disposed of.
(4) The extract decree—
(a) may be written on the summons or on a separate paper;
(b) may be in one of Forms 18 to 18i; and
(c) shall be warrant for all lawful execution.

Expenses
21.6.—[1] (1) This rule applies, subject to section 36B of the 1971 Act, to the determination of expenses—
(a) in a claim, where the defender has—
  (i) not stated a defence;
  (ii) having stated a defence, has not proceeded with it; or
  (iii) having stated a defence, has not acted in good faith as to its merits;
(b) in a claim where there has been unreasonable conduct on the part of a party to that claim in relation to the proceedings or the claim; or
(c) in an appeal to the sheriff principal.
[3] (2) Subject to paragraphs (3) to (5), the sheriff clerk must, with the approval of the sheriff, assess the amount of expenses including the fees and outlays of witnesses awarded in any claim, in accordance with the applicable statutory table of fees.
[2] (3) Paragraph (4) applies to a party who—
(a) represents himself;
(b) is represented by an authorised lay representative or a person authorised under any enactment to conduct proceedings in the sheriff court; or
(c) is not an individual and—
  (i) is represented by an authorised lay representative or a person authorised under any enactment to conduct proceedings in the sheriff court; and
  (ii) if unrepresented could not represent itself.
(4) A party mentioned in paragraph (3) who, if he had been represented by a solicitor or

advocate would have been entitled to expenses, may be awarded any outlays or expenses to which he might be found entitled by virtue of the 1975 Act or any enactment under that Act.

(5) In every case including an appeal where expenses are awarded, the sheriff clerk shall hear the parties or their solicitors on the claims for expenses including fees, if any, and outlays.

(6) Except where the sheriff principal or the sheriff has reserved judgment or where he orders otherwise, the hearing on the claim for expenses must take place immediately upon the decision being pronounced.

(7) When that hearing is not held immediately, the sheriff clerk must—

    (a) fix the date, time and place when he shall hear the parties or their solicitors; and

    (b) give all parties at least 14 days' notice in writing of the hearing so fixed.

(8) The party awarded expenses must—

    (a) lodge his account of expenses in court at least seven days prior to the date of any hearing fixed under paragraph (7); and

    (b) at the same time forward a copy of that account to every other party.

(9) The sheriff clerk must—

    (a) fix the amount of the expenses; and

    (b) report his decision to the sheriff principal or the sheriff in open court for his approval at a diet which the sheriff clerk has intimated to the parties.

(10) The sheriff principal or the sheriff, after hearing parties or their solicitors if objections are stated, must pronounce final decree including decree for payment of expenses as approved by him.

(11) In an appeal, the sheriff may pronounce decree under paragraph (10) on behalf of the sheriff principal.

(12) Failure by—

    (a) any party to comply with any of the foregoing provisions of this rule; or

    (b) the successful party or parties to appear at the hearing on expenses, must be reported by the sheriff clerk to the sheriff principal or the sheriff at a diet which the sheriff clerk has intimated to the parties.

(13) In either of the circumstances mentioned in paragraphs (12)(a) or (b), the sheriff principal or sheriff must, unless sufficient cause be shown, pronounce decree on the merits of the claim and find no expenses due to or by any party.

(14) A decree pronounced under paragraph (13) shall be held to be the final decree for the purposes of these Rules.

(15) The sheriff principal or sheriff may, if he thinks fit, on the application of the solicitor of any party to whom expenses may be awarded, made at or before the time of the final decree being pronounced, grant decree in favour of that solicitor for the expenses of the claim.

NOTES

[1] As substituted by Act of Sederunt (Ordinary Cause, Summary Application, Summary Cause and Small Claim Rules) Amendment (Miscellaneous) 2005 (SSI 2005/648) r.5(2) (effective January 2, 2006).

[2] As amended by the Act of Sederunt (Ordinary Cause, Summary Application, Summary Cause and Small Claim Rules) Amendment (Miscellaneous) 2007 (SSI 2007/6) r.5(c) (effective January 29, 2007).

[3] As amended by the Act of Sederunt (Sheriff Court Rules Amendment) (Sections 25 to 29 of the Law Reform (Miscellaneous Provisions) (Scotland) Act 1990) 2009 (SSI 2009/164) r.5(3) (effective May 20, 2009).

Charge

21.7.—(1) The period for payment specified in any charge following on a decree for payment granted in a claim shall be—

    (a) 14 days if the person on whom it is served is within the United Kingdom; and

    (b) 28 days if he is outside the United Kingdom or his whereabouts are unknown.

(2) The period in respect of any other form of charge on a decree granted in a claim shall be 14 days.

Service of charge where address of defender is unknown

21.8.—(1) If the address of a defender is not known to the pursuer, a charge shall be deemed to have been served on the defender if it is—

    (a) served on the sheriff clerk of the sheriff court district where the defender's last known address is located; and

    (b) displayed by the sheriff clerk on the walls of court for the period of the charge.

(2) On receipt of such a charge, the sheriff clerk must display it on the walls of court and it must remain displayed for the period of the charge.

(3) The period specified in the charge shall run from the first date on which it was displayed on the walls of court.

(4) On the expiry of the period of charge, the sheriff clerk must endorse a certificate in Form 19 on the charge certifying that it has been displayed in accordance with this rule and must thereafter return the charge to the sheriff officer by whom service was executed.

Diligence on decree in claim for delivery

21.9.—(1) In a claim for delivery, the court may, when granting decree, grant warrant to search for and take possession of goods and to open shut and lockfast places.

(2) A warrant granted under paragraph (1) shall only apply to premises occupied by the defender.

Applications in same claim for variation, etc. of decree

21.10.—(1) If by virtue of any enactment the sheriff, without a new action being initiated, may order that—

    (a) a decree granted be varied, discharged or rescinded; or

    (b) the execution of that decree in so far as it has not already been executed be sisted or suspended, the party requesting the sheriff to make such an order must do so by lodging a minute to that effect, setting out briefly the reasons for the application.

(2) On the lodging of such a minute by the pursuer, the sheriff clerk must grant warrant for service upon the defender (provided that the pursuer has returned the extract decree).

(3) On the lodging of such a minute by the defender, the sheriff clerk must grant warrant for service upon the pursuer ordaining him to return the extract decree and may, where appropriate, grant interim sist of execution of the decree.

(4) Subject to paragraph (5), the minute shall not be heard in court unless seven days' notice of the minute and warrant has been given to the other parties by the party lodging the minute.

(5) The sheriff may, on cause shown, alter the period of seven days referred to in paragraph (4) but may not reduce it to less than two days.

(6) This rule shall not apply to any proceedings under the Debtors (Scotland) Act 1987 or to proceedings which may be subject to the provisions of that Act.

CHAPTER 22

RECALL OF DECREE

Recall of decree

22.1.—(1) A party may apply for recall of a decree granted under rule 8.1(3), rule 9.1(6), (7) or (8) or rule 11.1(8) by lodging with the sheriff clerk a minute in Form 20, explaining the party's failure to appear and in the case of—

    (a) a defender; or

    (b) where decree has been granted in respect of a counterclaim, a pursuer, stating, where he has not already done so—

        (i) his proposed defence, in the case of a defender; or

        (ii) his proposed answer, in the case of a pursuer responding to a counterclaim.

(2) A party may apply for recall of a decree in the same claim on one occasion only.

(3) Except in relation to an application to which paragraph (4) applies, a minute by a pursuer under paragraph (1) must be lodged within 14 days of the grant of the decree.

(4) A minute lodged by—

    (a) a pursuer in respect of a decree granted in terms of a counterclaim; or

    (b) a defender, shall be lodged—

        (i) if the claim has been served outwith the United Kingdom under rule 6.5, within a reasonable time after he had knowledge of the decree against him or in any event before the expiry of one year from the date of that decree; or

        (ii) in any other case, within 14 days of the execution of a charge or execution of arrestment, whichever first occurs, following on the grant of decree.

(5) On the lodging of a minute for recall of a decree, the sheriff clerk must fix a date, time and place for a hearing of the minute.

(6) If a hearing has been fixed under paragraph (5), the party seeking recall must serve upon the other party not less than seven days before the date fixed for the hearing—

    (a) a copy of the minute in Form 20a; and

    (b) a note of the date, time and place of the hearing.

(7) If the party seeking recall—

    (a) is not a partnership or body corporate;

    (b) is not acting in a representative capacity; and

    (c) is not represented by a solicitor,

the sheriff clerk must assist that party to complete and lodge the minute for recall and must arrange service of it—

    (i) by first class recorded delivery post; or

    (ii) on payment of the fee prescribed by the Scottish Ministers by order, by sheriff officer.

[1] (8) At a hearing fixed under paragraph (5), the sheriff shall recall the decree so far as not implemented and the hearing shall then proceed as a Hearing under rules 9.1(4) to (8) and 9.2.

(9) A minute for recall of a decree, when lodged and served in terms of this rule, shall have the effect of preventing any further action being taken by the other party to enforce the decree.

(10) On receipt of the copy minute for recall of a decree, any party in possession of an extract decree must return it forthwith to the sheriff clerk.

(11) If it appears to the sheriff that there has been any failure or irregularity in service of the minute for recall of a decree, he may order re-service of the minute on such conditions as he thinks fit.

NOTE

[1] As amended by the Act of Sederunt (Ordinary Cause, Summary Application, Summary Cause and Small Claim Rules) Amendment (Miscellaneous) 2007 (SSI 2007/6) r.5(d) (effective January 29, 2007).

CHAPTER 23

APPEALS

Appeals

23.1.—(1) An appeal to the sheriff principal, other than an appeal to which rule 23.4 applies, must be by note of appeal in Form 21 and lodged with the sheriff clerk not later than 14 days after the date of final decree—

    (a) requesting a stated case; and

    (b) specifying the point of law upon which the appeal is to proceed.

(2) The appellant must, at the same time as lodging a note of appeal, intimate a copy of it to every other party.

(3) The sheriff must, within 28 days of the lodging of a note of appeal, issue a draft stated case containing—

    (a) findings in fact and law or, where appropriate, a narrative of the proceedings before him;

    (b) appropriate questions of law; and

    (c) a note stating the reasons for his decisions in law, and the sheriff clerk must send a copy of the draft stated case to the parties.

(4) Within 14 days of the issue of the draft stated case—

    (a) a party may lodge with the sheriff clerk a note of any adjustments which he seeks to make;

    (b) a respondent may state any point of law which he wishes to raise in the appeal; and

    (c) the note of adjustment and, where appropriate, point of law must be intimated to every other party.

(5) The sheriff may, on the motion of a party or of his own accord, and must where he proposes to reject any proposed adjustment, allow a hearing on adjustments and may provide for such further procedure under this rule prior to the hearing of the appeal as he thinks fit.

(6) The sheriff must, within 14 days after—

    (a) the latest date on which a note of adjustments has been or may be lodged; or

    (b) where there has been a hearing on adjustments, that hearing, and after considering such note and any representations made to him at the hearing, state and sign the case.

(7) If the sheriff is temporarily absent from duty for any reason, the sheriff principal may extend any period specified in paragraphs (3) or (6) for such period or periods as he considers reasonable.

(8) The stated case signed by the sheriff must include questions of law, framed by him, arising from the points of law stated by the parties and such other questions of law as he may consider appropriate.

(9) After the sheriff has signed the stated case, the sheriff clerk must—

    (a) place before the sheriff principal all documents and productions in the case together with the stated case; and

    (b) send to the parties a copy of the stated case together with a written note of the date, time and place of the hearing of the appeal.

Effect of and abandonment of appeal

23.2.—(1) When a note of appeal has been lodged, it may be insisted on by all other parties in the claim although they may not have lodged separate appeals.

(2) After a note of appeal has been lodged, the appellant shall not be at liberty to withdraw it, except—

   (a) with the consent of the other parties which may be incorporated in a joint minute; or

   (b) by leave of the sheriff principal and on such terms as to expenses or otherwise at to him seem proper.

Hearing of appeal

23.3.—(1) The sheriff principal shall hear the parties or their solicitors orally on all matters connected with the appeal including liability for expenses, but if any party moves that the question of liability for expenses be heard after the sheriff principal has given his decision the sheriff principal may grant that motion.

(2) In the hearing of an appeal, a party shall not be allowed to raise questions of law of which notice has not been given except on cause shown and subject to such conditions as to expenses or otherwise as the sheriff principal may consider appropriate.

(3) The sheriff principal may permit a party to amend any question of law or to add any new question in accordance with paragraph (2).

(4) The sheriff principal may—

   (a) adhere to or vary the decree appealed against;

   (b) recall the decree appealed against and substitute another therefor; or

   (c) remit, if he considers it desirable, to the sheriff, for any reason other than to have further evidence led.

(5) At the conclusion of the hearing, the sheriff principal may either pronounce his decision or reserve judgment in which case he must give his decision in writing within 28 days and the sheriff clerk must forthwith intimate it to the parties.

Appeal in relation to a time to pay direction

23.4.—(1) This rule applies to appeals to the sheriff principal or to the Court of Session which relate solely to any application in connection with a time to pay direction.

(2) Rules 23.1, 23.2 and 23.3(2) and (3) shall not apply to appeals under this rule.

(3) An application for leave to appeal against a decision in an application for a time to pay direction or any order connected therewith must—

   (a) be made in Form 22, within seven days of that decision, to the sheriff who made the decision; and

   (b) must specify the question of law upon which the appeal is to proceed.

(4) If leave to appeal is granted, the appeal must be lodged in Form 23 and intimated by the appellant to every other party within 14 days of the order granting leave and the sheriff must state in writing his reasons for his original decision.

(5) An appeal under this rule to the sheriff principal shall proceed in accordance with paragraphs (1), (4) and (5) of rule 23.3.

Sheriff to regulate interim possession

23.5.—(1) Notwithstanding an appeal, the sheriff shall have power—

   (a) to regulate all matters relating to interim possession;

   (b) to make any order for the preservation of any property to which the claim relates or for its sale, if perishable;

   (c) to make any order for the preservation of evidence; or

   (d) to make in his discretion any interim order which a due regard for the interests of the parties may require.

(2) An order under paragraph (1) shall not be subject to review except by the appellate court at the hearing of the appeal.

CHAPTER 24

MANAGEMENT OF DAMAGES PAYABLE TO PERSONS UNDER LEGAL DISABILITY

Orders for payment and management of money

24.1.—(1) In a claim of damages in which a sum of money becomes payable, by virtue of a decree or an extra-judicial settlement, to or for the benefit of a person under legal disability (other than a person under the age of 18 years), the sheriff shall make such order regarding the payment and management of that sum for the benefit of that person as he thinks fit.

(2) Any order required under paragraph (1) shall be made on the granting of decree for payment or of absolvitor.

Methods of management

24.2. In making an order under rule 24.1 (1), the sheriff may—

   (a) order the money to be paid to—
      (i) the Accountant of Court, or
     (ii) the guardian of the person under legal disability, as trustee, to be applied, invested or otherwise dealt with and administered under the directions of the sheriff for the benefit of the person under legal disability;
   (b) order the money to be paid to the sheriff clerk of the sheriff court district in which the person under legal disability resides, to be applied, invested or otherwise dealt with and administered, under the directions of the sheriff of that district, for the benefit of the person under legal disability; or
   (c) order the money to be paid directly to the person under legal disability.

Subsequent orders
24.3.—(1) If the sheriff has made an order under rule 24.1(1), any person having an interest may apply for an order under rule 24.2, or any other order for the payment or management of the money, by incidental application.

(2) An application for directions under rule 24.2(a) or (b) may be made by any person having an interest by incidental application.

Management of money paid to sheriff clerk
24.4.—(1) A receipt in Form 24 by the sheriff clerk shall be a sufficient discharge in respect of the amount paid to him under rules 24.1 to 24.3.

(2) The sheriff clerk shall, at the request of any competent court, accept custody of any sum of money in an claim of damages ordered to be paid to, applied, invested or otherwise dealt with by him, for the benefit of a person under legal disability.

(3) Any money paid to the sheriff clerk under rules 24.1 to 24.3 must be paid out, applied, invested or otherwise dealt with by the sheriff clerk only after such intimation, service and enquiry as the sheriff may order.

(4) Any sum of money invested by the sheriff clerk under rules 24.1 to 24.3 must be invested in a manner in which trustees are authorised to invest by virtue of the Trustee Investments Act 1961.

Management of money payable to children
24.5. If the sheriff has made an order under section 13 of the Children (Scotland) Act 1995, an application by a person for an order by virtue of section 11(1)(d) of that Act must be made in writing.

Chapter 25

Electronic transmission of documents

Extent of provision
25.1.—(1) Any document referred to in these rules which requires to be—
   (a) lodged with the sheriff clerk;
   (b) intimated to a party; or
   (c) sent by the sheriff clerk, may be in electronic or documentary form, and if in electronic form may be lodged, intimated or sent by e-mail or similar means.

(2) Paragraph (1) does not apply to any certificate of execution of service, citation or arrestment, or to a decree or extract decree of the court.

(3) Where any document is lodged by e-mail or similar means the sheriff may require any principal document to be lodged.

Time of lodgement
25.2. The time of lodgement, intimation or sending shall be the time when the document was sent or transmitted.

[1] Chapter 26

Equality Enactments

NOTE
[1] As inserted by the Act of Sederunt (Ordinary Cause, Summary Application, Summary Cause and Small Claim Rules) Amendment (Equality Act 2006 etc.) 2006 (SSI 2006/509) r.5(2) (effective November 3, 2006).

Application and interpretation
26.1.—(1) This Chapter applies to claims under the equality enactments.

(2) In this Chapter, "claims under the equality enactments" means proceedings in reparation for breach of statutory duty under any of the following enactments—

  (a) Sex Discrimination Act 1975;
  (b) Race Relations Act 1976;
  (c) Disability Discrimination Act 1995;
  (d) Equality Act 2006;
  [1] (e) The Equality Act (Sexual Orientation) Regulations 2007.
[2] (3) In this Chapter "the Commission" means the Commission for Equality and Human Rights.

NOTES
[1] As inserted by the Act of Sederunt (Ordinary Cause, Summary Application, Summary Cause and Small Claim Rules) Amendment (Equality Act (Sexual Orientation) Regulations 2007) 2007 (SSI 2007/339) r.5(2) (effective July 20, 2007).
[2] As inserted by the Act of Sederunt (Sheriff Court Rules) (Miscellaneous Amendments) 2008 (SSI 2008/223) r.7(3)(a) (effective July 1, 2008).

Intimation to Commission
[1] **26.2.** The pursuer shall send a copy of the summons to the Commission by registered or recorded delivery post.

NOTE
[1] As substituted by the Act of Sederunt (Sheriff Court Rules) (Miscellaneous Amendments) 2008 (SSI 2008/223) r.7(3)(b) (effective July 1, 2008).

Assessor
26.3.—(1) The sheriff may, of his own motion or on the incidental application of any party, appoint an assessor.

(2) The assessor shall be a person who the sheriff considers has special qualifications to be of assistance in determining the cause.

Taxation of Commission expenses
26.4. [*Omitted by the Act of Sederunt (Sheriff Court Rules) (Miscellaneous Amendments) 2008 (SSI 2008/223) para.7(3)(c) (effective July 1, 2008).*]

National security
26.5.—(1) Where, on an incidental application under paragraph (3) or of his own motion, the sheriff considers it expedient in the interests of national security, he may—

  (a) exclude from all or part of the proceedings—
    (i) the pursuer;
    (ii) the pursuer's representatives;
    (iii) any assessors;
  (b) permit a pursuer or representative who has been excluded to make a statement to the court before the commencement of the proceedings or the part of the proceedings, from which he is excluded;
  (c) take steps to keep secret all or part of the reasons for his decision in the proceedings.

(2) The sheriff clerk shall, on the making of an order under paragraph (1) excluding the pursuer or his representatives, notify the Advocate General for Scotland of that order.

(3) A party may make an incidental application for an order under paragraph (1).

(4) The steps referred to in paragraph (1)(c) may include the following—

  (a) directions to the sheriff clerk; and
  (b) orders requiring any person appointed to represent the interests of the pursuer in proceedings from which the pursuer or his representatives are excluded not to communicate (directly or indirectly) with any persons (including the excluded pursuer)–
    (i) on any matter discussed or referred to;
    (ii) with regard to any material disclosed,

during or with reference to any part of the proceedings from which the pursuer or his representatives are excluded.

(5) Where the sheriff has made an order under paragraph (4)(b), the person appointed to represent the interests of the pursuer may make an incidental application for authority to seek instructions from or otherwise communicate with an excluded person.

(6) The sheriff may, on the application of a party intending to lodge an incidental application in written form, reduce the period of two days specified in rule 10.1(2) or dispense with notice.

(7) An application under paragraph (6) shall be made in the written incidental application, giving reasons for such reduction or dispensation.

[1] CHAPTER 27

LIVE LINKS

NOTE

[1] As inserted by the Act of Sederunt (Ordinary Cause, Summary Application, Summary Cause and Small Claim Rules) Amendment (Miscellaneous) (SSI 2007/6) r.5(e) (effective January 29, 2007).

27.1.—(1) On cause shown, a party may apply by incidental application for authority for the whole or part of—
  (a) the evidence of a witness or the party to be given; or
  (b) a submission to be made,
through a live link.
  (2) in paragraph (1)—
    [1] "witness" means a person who has been or may be cited to appear before the court as a witness, except a vulnerable witness within the meaning of section 11(1) of the 2004 Act;
  "submission" means any oral submission which would otherwise be made to the court by the party or his representative in person including an oral submission in support of an incidental application; and
  "live link" means a live television link or such other arrangement as may be specified in the incidental application by which the witness, party or representative, as the case may be, is able to be seen and heard in the proceedings or heard in the proceedings and is able to see and hear or hear the proceedings while at a place which is outside the courtroom.

NOTE

[1] As amended by the Act of Sederunt (Ordinary Cause, Summary Application, Summary Cause and Small Claim Rules) Amendment (Vulnerable Witnesses (Scotland) Act 2004) 2007 (SSI 2007/463) r.5(4) (effective November 1, 2007).

Rule 1.1(4)

APPENDIX 1

FORMS

Rule 4.1(1)

[1] FORM 1

Summons

FORM 1

OFFICIAL USE ONLY
SUMMONS No.

Small Claim Summons

Action for/of

(state type, e.g., payment of money)

Sheriff Court (name, address, e-mail and telephone no.)	**1**	
Name and address of person making the claim (**pursuer**)	**2**	
Name and address of person against whom claim made (**defender**)	**3**	
Claim (form of decree or other order sought)	**4**	
Name, full address, telephone no, and e-mail address of pursuer's solicitor or authorised lay representative (if any) acting in the claim	**5**	
Fee Details (Enter these only if forms sent electronically to court)	**5a**	

6	RETURN DAY	20		
	HEARING DATE	20	at	am.

*Sheriff Clerk to

delete as appropriate

The pursuer is authorised to serve a copy summons in Form *1a/1b, on the defender(s) not less than *21/42 days before the **RETURN DAY** shown in the box above. The summons is warrant for service, and for citation of witnesses to attend court on any future date at which evidence may be led.

Court Authentication

NOTE: The pursuer should complete boxes 1 to 5a, and the statement of claim on page 2. The sheriff clerk will complete box 6.

---

7. **STATE DETAILS OF CLAIM HERE (all cases) and PARTICULARS OF ARRESTMENT**
(furthcoming actions only)
(To be completed by the pursuer. If space is insufficient, a separate sheet may be attached)

The details of the claim are:

FOR OFFICIAL USE ONLY

Sheriff's notes as to:

1. Issues of fact and law in dispute
2. Facts agreed
3. Reasons for any final disposal at the hearing held on the calling date.

NOTE
[1] As amended by the Act of Sederunt (Sheriff Court Rules Amendment) (Diligence) (SSI 2008/121) r.7(6) (effective April 1, 2008). This form as it applied immediately before April 1, 2008 continues to have effect for the purpose of any application for arrestment on the dependence made before that date.

[1] FORM 1a

Defender's copy summons—claim for or including claim for payment of money where time to pay direction or time order may be applied for

> **OFFICIAL USE ONLY**
> **SUMMONS No.**

Small Claim Summons
Action for/of
(state type, e.g. payment of money)

DEFENDER'S COPY: Claim for or including payment of money (where time to pay direction or time order may be applied for)

Sheriff Court 1
(name, address, e-mail and telephone no.)

Name and address of person making 2
the claim (**pursuer**)

Name and address of person against 3
whom claim made (**defender**)

Claim (form of decree or other order 4
sought—*complete as in section 4 of Form 1*)

Name, full address, telephone no., 5
and e-mail address of pursuer's solicitor or authorised lay representative (if any) acting in the claim

6	**RETURN DAY**	**20**		
	HEARING DATE	**20**	at	am.

NOTE: You will find details of claim on page 2.

7.   **STATE DETAILS OF CLAIM HERE OR ATTACH A STATEMENT OF CLAIM**
(To be completed by the pursuer. If space is insufficient, a separate sheet may be attached)

The details of the claim are:

8.   **SERVICE ON DEFENDER**

(Place)   (Date)

To: (Defender)

You are hereby served with a copy of the above summons.

Solicitor / sheriff officer
delete as appropriate

NOTE: The pursuer should complete boxes 1 to 6 on page 1, the statement of claim in box 7 on page 2 and section A on page 7 before service on the defender. The person serving the Summons will complete box 8, above.

WHAT MUST I DO ABOUT THIS SUMMONS?

The RETURN DAY (on page 1 of this summons) is the deadline by which you need to reply to the court. You must send the correct forms back (see below for details) by this date if you want the court to hear your case. If you do not do this, in most cases there will not be a hearing about your case and the court will make a decision in your absence.

The HEARING DATE (on page 1 of this summons) is the date for the court hearing.

You should decide whether you wish to dispute the claim, admit liability for the claim and whether you owe any money or not, and how you wish to proceed. Then, look at the 5 options listed below. Find the one that covers your decision and follow the instructions given there.

If you are not sure what you need to do, contact the sheriff clerk's office before the return day. Written guidance can also be obtained from the Scottish Court Service website (www.scot-courts.gov.uk).

OPTIONS

1. **ADMIT LIABILITY FOR THE CLAIM and settle it with the pursuer now.**

   If you wish to avoid the possibility of a court order passing against you, you should settle the claim (including any question of expenses) with the pursuer or his representative in good time before the return day. Please do not send any payment direct to the court. Any payment should be made to the pursuer or his representative.

2. **ADMIT LIABILITY FOR THE CLAIM and make written application to pay by instalments or by deferred lump sum.**

   Complete Box 1 of section B on page 7 of this form and return pages 7, 9 and 10 to the court **to arrive on or before the return day.** You should then contact the court to find out whether or not the pursuer has accepted your offer. If he has not accepted it, the case will then call in court on the calling date, when the court will decide how the amount claimed is to be paid.

   If your claim is for delivery, or implement of an obligation, and you wish to pay the alternative amount claimed, you may also wish to make an application about the method of payment. If so, follow the instructions in the previous paragraph.

   NOTE: If you fail to return pages 7, 9 and 10 as directed, or if, having returned them, you fail to attend or are not represented at the calling date if the case is to call, the court may decide the claim in your absence.

3. **ADMIT LIABILITY FOR THE CLAIM and attend at court to make application to pay by instalments or deferred lump sum.**

   Complete Box 2 on page 7. Return page 7 to the court so that it arrives **on or before the return day.**

   If the claim for delivery, or implement of an obligation, you may wish to pay the alternative amount claimed and attend at court to make an application about the method of payment.

   You must attend personally, or be represented, at court on the hearing date. Your representative may be a solicitor, or someone else having your authority. It may be helpful if you or your representative bring pages 1 and 2 of this form to the court.

   NOTE: If you fail to return page 7 as directed, or if, having returned it, you fail to attend or are not represented at the hearing date, the court may decide the claim in your absence.

4. DISPUTE THE CLAIM and <u>attend at court</u> to do any of the following:

- Challenge the jurisdiction of the court
- State a defence
- State a counterclaim
- Dispute the amount of the claim

Complete Box 3 on page 7. Return page 7 to the court so that it arrives **on or before the return day. You must attend personally, or be represented, at court on the hearing date.**

Your representative may be a solicitor, or someone else having your authority. It may be helpful if you or your representative bring pages 1 and 2 of this form to the court.

NOTE: If you fail to return page 7 as directed, or if, having returned it, you fail to attend or are not represented at the hearing date, the court may decide the claim in your absence.

WRITTEN NOTE OF PROPOSED COUNTERCLAIM

You must send to the court a written note of any counterclaim. If you do, you should also send a copy to the pursuer. You must also attend or be represented at court on the hearing date.

5. ADMIT LIABILITY FOR THE CLAIM and make <u>written</u> application for a time order under the Consumer Credit Act 1974.

Complete Box 4 on page 8 and return pages 7 and 8 and 11 to 13 to the court to arrive on or before the return day. You should then contact the court to find out whether or not the pursuer has accepted your offer. Where you have been advised that the pursuer has not accepted your offer then the case will call in court on the hearing date. You should appear in court on the hearing date as the court will decide how the amount claimed is to be paid.

NOTE: If you fail to return pages 8 and 9 and 11 to 13 as directed, or if, having returned them, you fail to attend or are not represented at the hearing date, if the case is to call, the court may decide the claim in your absence.

PLEASE NOTE

If you do nothing about this summons, the court will almost certainly, where appropriate, grant decree against you and order you to pay the pursuer the sum claimed, including any interest and expenses found due.

If the summons is for delivery, or implement of an obligation, the court may order you to deliver the article or perform the duty in question within a specified period. If you fail to do so, the court may order you to pay to the pursuer the alternative amount claimed, including interest and expenses.

YOU ARE ADVISED TO KEEP PAGES 1 AND 2, AS THEY MAY BE USEFUL AT A LATER STAGE OF THE CASE.

Notes

(1) Time to pay directions

The Debtors (Scotland) Act 1987 gives you the right to apply to the court for a "time to pay direction". This is an order which allows you to pay any sum which the court orders you to pay either in instalments or by deferred lump sum. A "deferred lump sum" means that you will be ordered by the court to pay the whole amount at one time within a period which the court will specify.

If the court makes a time to pay direction it may also recall or restrict any arrestment made on your property by the pursuer in connection with the action or debt (for example, your bank account may have been frozen).

No court fee is payable when making an application for a time to pay direction.

If a time to pay direction is made, a copy of the court order (called an extract decree) will be sent to you by the pursuer telling you when payment should start or when it is you have to pay the lump sum.

If a time to pay direction is not made, and an order for immediate payment is made against you, an order to pay (called a charge) may be served on you if you do not pay.

(2) Determination of application

Under the 1987 Act, the court is required to make a time to pay direction if satisfied that it is reasonable in the circumstances to do so, and having regard in particular to the following matters—

- The nature of and reasons for the debt in relation to which decree is granted
- Any action taken by the creditor to assist the debtor in paying the debt
- The debtor's financial position
- The reasonableness of any proposal by the debtor to pay that debt
- The reasonableness of any refusal or objection by the creditor to any proposal or offer by the debtor to pay the debt.

(3) Time Orders

The Consumer Credit Act 1974 allows you to apply to the court for a "time order" during a court action, to ask the court to give you more time to pay a loan agreement. **A time order is similar to a time to pay direction, but can only be applied for where the court action is about a credit agreement regulated by the Consumer Credit Act.** The court has power to grant a time order in respect of a regulated agreement to reschedule payment of the sum owed. This means that a time order can change:

- the amount you have to pay each month
- how long the loan will last
- in some cases, the interest rate payable

A time order can also stop the creditor taking away any item bought by you on hire purchase or conditional sale under the regulated agreement, so long as you continue to pay the instalments agreed.

No court fee is payable when making an application for a time order.

SECTION A

This section must be completed before service

| Summons No |
| Return Day |
| Hearing Date |

SHERIFF COURT (Including address)

PURSUER'S FULL NAME AND ADDRESS

DEFENDER'S FULL NAME AND ADDRESS

SECTION B   DEFENDER'S RESPONSE TO THE SUMMONS
                ** Delete those boxes which do not apply

**Box 1

ADMIT LIABILITY FOR THE CLAIM and make written application to pay by instalments or by deferred lump sum.

I do not intend to defend the case but admit liability for the claim and wish to pay the sum of money claimed.

I wish to make a written application about payment.

I have completed the application form on pages 9 and 10.

**Box 2

ADMIT LIABILITY FOR THE CLAIM and attend at court.
I admit liability for the claim.

I wish to make an application to pay the sum claimed by instalments or by deferred lump sum.

I intend to appear or be represented at court.

**Box 3

DISPUTE THE CLAIM (or the amount due) and attend at court
*I wish to dispute the amount due only.
*I intend to challenge the jurisdiction of the court.
*I intend to state a defence.
*I intend to state a counterclaim.

*I intend to appear or be represented in court.

_____

*I attach a note of my proposed counterclaim which has been copied to the pursuer.
delete as necessary

**Box 4

ADMIT LIABILITY FOR THE CLAIM and apply for a time order under the Consumer Credit Act 1974.

I do not intend to defend the case but admit liability for the claim.

I wish to apply for a time order under the Consumer Credit Act 1974.

I have completed the application form on pages 11 to 13.

NOTE: Please remember to send your response to the court to arrive on or before the return day if you have completed any of the responses above.

APPLICATION IN WRITING FOR A TIME TO PAY DIRECTION

I WISH TO APPLY FOR A *TIME TO PAY DIRECTION

I admit the claim and make application to pay as follows:

(1)   by instalments of £ _____ per *week / fortnight / month

OR

(2)   in one payment within _____ *weeks / months from the date of the
court order.

The debt is for (*specify the nature of the debt*) and has arisen (*here set out the reasons the
debt has arisen*)

Please also state why you say a time to pay direction should be made. In doing so, please
consider Notes (1) and (2) on page 5.

To help the court please provide details of your financial position in the boxes below.

I am employed / self-employed / unemployed
*Please also indicate whether payment/receipts are weekly, fortnightly or monthly

My outgoings are:	***Weekly / fortnightly/ monthly**	**My net income is**	***Weekly / fortnightly/ monthly**
Rent/mortgage	£	Wages/pensions	£
Council tax	£	State benefits	£
Gas/electricity etc	£	Tax credits	£
Food	£	Other	£
Loans and credit agreements	£		
Phone	£		
Other	£		
Total	£	Total	£

People who rely on your
income (e.g. spouse/civil
partner/ partner/children)—
how many

Please list details of all capital held, e.g. value of house; amount in savings account, shares or other investments:

I am of the opinion that the payment offer is reasonable for the following reason(s):

Here set out any information you consider relevant to the court's determination of the application. In doing so, please consider Note (2) on page 5.

*APPLICATION FOR RECALL OR RESTRICTION OF AN ARRESTMENT

I seek the recall or restriction of the arrestment of which the details are as follows:

Date:
* Delete if inapplicable

APPLICATION FOR A TIME ORDER UNDER THE CONSUMER CREDIT ACT 1974

By

DEFENDER

In an action raised by

PURSUER

PLEASE WRITE IN INK USING BLOCK CAPITALS

If you wish to apply to pay by instalments enter the amount at box 3. If you wish the court to make any additional orders, please give details at box 4. Please give details of the regulated agreement at box 5 and details of your financial position in the space provided below at box 5.

Sign and date the application where indicated.

You should ensure that your application arrives at the court along with completed pages 7 and 8 on or before the return day.

1. The Applicant is a defender in the action brought by the above named pursuer.

I/WE WISH TO APPLY FOR A TIME ORDER under the Consumer Credit Act 1974

2. **Details of order(s) sought**

The defender wishes to apply for a time order under section 129 of the Consumer Credit Act 1974.

The defender wishes to apply for an order in terms of section ..... of the Consumer Credit Act 1974.

3. **Proposals for payment**

I admit the claim and apply to pay the arrears and future instalments as follows:

By instalments of £ .... per *week/fortnight/month

No time to pay direction or time to pay order has been made in relation to this debt.

4. **Additional orders sought**

The following additional order(s) is (are) sought: (*specify*)

The order(s) sought in addition to the time order is (are) sought for the following reasons:

5. **Details of regulated agreement**

(a) Date of agreement

(b) Reference number of agreement

(*Please attach a copy of the agreement*)

(c) Names and addresses of other parties to agreement

(d) Name and address of person (if any) who acted as surety (guarantor) to the agreement

(e) Place where agreement signed (e.g. the shop where agreement signed, including name and address)

(f) Details of payment arrangements

    i. The agreement is to pay instalments of £ ..... per week/ month

    ii. The unpaid balance is £ ..... / I do not know the amount of arrears

    iii. I am £ ..... in arrears / I do not know the amount of arrears

Defender's financial position

I am employed /self employed / unemployed

Defender's financial position

I am employed /self employed / unemployed

My net income is:	weekly, fortnightly or monthly	My outgoings are:	weekly, fortnightly or monthly
Wages	£	Mortgage/ rent	£
State benefits	£	Council tax	£
Tax credits	£	Gas/electri- city etc	£
Other	£	Food	£
		Credit and loans	£
		Phone	£
		Other	£
Total	£	Total	£

People who rely on your income (e.g. spouse/civil partner/partner/ children)—how many

Here list all assets (if any) e.g. value of house; amounts in bank or building society accounts; shares or other investments:

Here list any outstanding debts:

Therefore the defender asks the court to make a time order

Date: Signed:

                               Defender:

NOTE
[1] As amended by SSI 2008/121 and substituted by the Act of Sederunt (Sheriff Court Rules) (Miscellaneous Amendments) 2009 (SSI 2009/294) r.5 (effective December 1, 2009).

FORM 1b

Defender's copy summons – all other claims

FORM 1b

Small Claim Summons
Action for/of
(state type, e.g., payment of money)

| OFFICIAL USE ONLY |
| SUMMONS No. |

DEFENDER'S COPY: (Claim other than claim for or including payment of money where time to pay direction or time order may be applied for)

Sheriff Court (name, address, e-mail and telephone no.)	**1**	
Name and address of person making the claim (**pursuer**)	**2**	
Name and address of person against whom claim made (**defender**)	**3**	
Claim (Form of decree or other order sought - *complete as in section 4 of Form 1*)	**4**	
Name, full address, telephone no, and e-mail address of pursuer's solicitor or authorised lay representative (if any)	**5**	

| **6** | **RETURN DAY** | 20 | | |
| | **HEARING DATE** | 20 | at | am. |

NOTE: You will find details of claim on page 2.

7.   STATE DETAILS OF CLAIM HERE OR ATTACH A STATEMENT OF CLAIM
   (To be completed by the pursuer. If space is insufficient, a separate sheet may be attached)

   The details of the claim are:

8.   SERVICE ON DEFENDER

   (Place)   (Date)

   To: (defender)

   You are hereby served with a copy of the above summons.

                                        Solicitor / sheriff officer
                                        delete as appropriate

The pursuer should complete boxes 1 to 6 on page 1, the statement of claim in box 7 on page 2 and section A on page 4 before service on the defender. The person serving the summons will complete box 8.

<u>**WHAT MUST I DO ABOUT THIS SUMMONS?**</u>

Decide whether you wish to dispute the claim and/or whether you owe any money or not, and how you wish to proceed. Then, look at the 2 options listed below. Find the one which covers your decision and follow the instructions given there. You will find the RETURN DAY and the HEARING DATE on page one of the summons.

Written guidance on small claims procedure can be obtained from the sheriff clerk at any Sheriff Clerk's office.

Further advice can also be obtained by contacting any of the following:

> **Citizen's Advice Bureau, Consumer Advice Centre, Trading Standards or Consumer Protection Department or a solicitor. (Addresses can be found in the guidance booklets).**

<u>**OPTIONS**</u>

1.   **ADMIT LIABILITY FOR THE CLAIM and settle it with the pursuer now.**

If you wish to avoid the possibility of a court order passing against you, you should settle the claim (including any question of expenses) with pursuer or his representative **in good time before the return day**. Please do not send any payment direct to the court. Any payment should be made to the pursuer or his representative.

2.   **DISPUTE THE CLAIM and <u>attend at court</u> to do any of the following:**

- Challenge the jurisdiction of the court
- State a defence
- State a counterclaim
- Dispute the amount of the claim

Complete Section B on page 4. Return page 4 to the court so that it arrives **on or before the return day. You must attend personally, or be represented, at court on the hearing date.**

Your representative may be a solicitor, or someone else having your authority. It may be helpful if you or your representative bring pages 1 and 2 of this form to the court.

NOTE: If you fail to return page 4 as directed, or if, having returned it, you fail to attend or are not represented at the hearing date, the court will almost certainly decide the claim in your absence.

WRITTEN NOTE OF PROPOSED COUNTERCLAIM

You may send to the court a written note of any counterclaim. If you do, you should also send a copy to the pursuer. You must also attend or be represented at court on the hearing date.

<u>**PLEASE NOTE**</u>

If you do nothing about this summons, the court will almost certainly, where appropriate, grant decree against you and order you to pay to the pursuer the sum claimed, including any interest and expenses found due.

If the summons is for delivery, or implement of an obligation, the court may order you to deliver the article or perform the duty in question within a specified period. If you fail to do so, the court may order you to pay to the pursuer the alternative amount claimed, including interest and expenses.

YOU ARE ADVISED TO KEEP PAGES 1 AND 2, AS THEY MAY BE USEFUL AT A LATER STAGE OF THE CASE.

SECTION A
This section must
be completed
before service

Summons No

Return Day

Hearing Date

SHERIFF COURT (Including address)

PURSUER'S FULL NAME AND ADDRESS

DEFENDER'S FULL NAME AND
ADDRESS

SECTION B   **DEFENDER'S RESPONSE TO THE SUMMONS**

DISPUTE THE CLAIM (or the amount due) and attend at court
* I wish to dispute the amount due only.
* I intend to challenge the jurisdiction of the court.
* I intend to state a defence.
* I intend to state a counterclaim.

I intend to appear or be represented in court.

* I attach a note of my proposed counterclaim which has been copied to the
pursuer.

* delete as necessary

PLEASE REMEMBER: You must send this page to the court **to arrive on or before the return day** if you
have completed Section B above.

If you have admitted the claim, please do not send any payment direct to the court. Any payment should be
made to the pursuer or his solicitor.

Rule 4.1(2)   FORM 2

Form of claim in a summons for payment of money

The pursuer claims from the defender(s) the sum of £   with interest on that sum at the rate of   % annually from the date of service, together with the expenses of bringing the claim.

Rule 4.1(2)   FORM 3

Form of claim in a summons for delivery

The pursuer claims that, in the circumstances described in the statement contained on page 2 of this copy summons, he has right to the possession of the article(s) described therein.

He therefore asks the court to grant a decree ordering you to deliver the said articles to the pursuer.

Alternatively, if you do not deliver said articles, the pursuer asks the court to grant a decree ordering you to pay to him the sum of £   with interest on that sum at the rate of   % annually from   until payment.

The pursuer also claims from you the expenses of bringing the claim.

Rule 4.1(2)   FORM 4

Form of claim in a summons for implement of an obligation

The pursuer claims that, in the circumstances described in the statement contained on page 2 of the summons, you are obliged to

He therefore asks the court to grant a decree ordering you to implement the said obligation.

Alternatively, if you do not fulfil the obligation, the pursuer asks the court to grant a decree ordering you to pay to him the sum of £   with interest on that sum at the rate of   % annually from   until payment.

The pursuer also claims from you the expenses of bringing the claim.

Rule 6.2(1)   FORM 5

Form of service

XY, you are hereby served with a copy of the above (or attached) summons.

           (*signature of solicitor or sheriff officer*)

Rule 6.2(2)   FORM 6

Form of certificate of execution of service

(*place and date*)

I,   , hereby certify that on the   day of   20, I duly cited XY to answer the foregoing summons. This I did by (*set forth the mode of service*)

           (*signature of solicitor or sheriff officer*)

Rule 6.3(2)   FORM 7

Postal service—form of notice

This letter contains a citation to or intimation from the sheriff court at

If delivery cannot be made the letter must be returned immediately to the sheriff clerk at (*insert full address*).

Rule 6.6(1)(a) FORM 8

Service on person whose address is unknown—form of advertisement.

A small claim has been raised in the sheriff court at   , by AB., pursuer, against CD, defender, whose last known address was   .

If the said CD wishes to defend the claim he should immediately contact the sheriff clerk's office at the above court, from whom the defender's copy summons may be obtained.

Address of court:
Telephone no:
Fax no:
E mail address:

Rule 6.6(1)(b) FORM 9

Service on person whose address is unknown

Form of notice to be displayed on the walls of court

A small claim has been raised in this court by AB, pursuer against CD, defender, whose last known address was   .

If the said CD wishes to defend the claim he should immediately contact the sheriff clerk's office, from whom the defender's copy summons may be obtained.

(*date*)Displayed on the walls of court of this date.

Sheriff clerk depute

Rule 7.A2(2) [1] FORM 9A

Statement to accompany application for interim diligence

DEBTORS (SCOTLAND) ACT 1987 Section 15D [or DEBT ARRANGEMENT AND ATTACHMENT (SCOTLAND) ACT 2002 Section 9C]

Sheriff Court ....
In the Cause (Cause Reference No.)
[A.B.] *(designation and address)*

Pursuer

against
[C.D.] *(designation and address)*

Defender

STATEMENT

1. The applicant is the pursuer [*or* defender] in the action by [A.B] *(design)* against [C.D.] *(design)*.

2. [The following persons have an interest [*specify names and addresses*].]

3. The application is [*or* is not] seeking the grant under section 15E(1) of the 1987 Act of warrant for diligence [*or* section 9D(1) of the 2002 Act of interim attachment] in advance of a hearing on the application.

4. [Here provide such other information as may be prescribed by regulations made by the Scottish Ministers under section 15D(2)(d) or 9C(2)(d) of the 1987 Act]

(Signed)

Solicitor [*or* Agent] for A.B. [or C.D.]
(include full designation)

NOTE
¹ As inserted by the Act of Sederunt (Sheriff Court Rules Amendment) (Diligence) 2008 (SSI 2008/121) r.7(8) (effective April 1, 2008).

Rule 7.A8   ¹ FORM 9b

Form of schedule of arrestment on the dependence

SCHEDULE OF ARRESTMENT ON THE DEPENDENCE

Date: (*date of execution*)

Time: (*time arrestment executed*)

To: (*name and address of arrestee*)

IN HER MAJESTY'S NAME AND AUTHORITY AND IN NAME AND AUTHORITY OF THE SHERIFF, I, (*name*), Sheriff Officer, by virtue of:

- a summons containing warrant which has been granted for arrestment on the dependence of the action at the instance of (*name and address of pursuer*) against (*name and address of defender*) and dated (*date*);

- a counterclaim containing a warrant which has been granted for arrestment on the dependence of the claim by (*name and address of creditor*) against (*name and address of debtor*) and dated (*date of warrant*);

- an order of the Sheriff at (*place*) dated (*date of order*) granting warrant [for arrestment on the dependence of the action raised at the instance of (*name and address of pursuer*) against (*name and address of defender*)] [or for arrestment on the dependence of the claim in the counterclaim by (*name and address of creditor*) against (*name and address or debtor*)],

arrest in your hands (i) the sum of (*amount*), in excess of the Protected Minimum Balance, where applicable (*see Note 1*), more or less, due by you to (*defender's name*) [*or name and address of common debtor if common debtor is not the defender*] or to any other person on his [*or* her] [*or* its] [*or* their] behalf; and (ii) all moveable things in your hands belonging or pertaining to the said (*name of common debtor*), to remain in your hands under arrestment until they are made forthcoming to (*name of pursuer*) [*or name and address of creditor if he is not the pursuer*] or until further order of the court.

This I do in the presence of (*name, occupation and address of witness*).

(*Signed*)

Sheriff Officer

(*Address*)

NOTE

1.   This Schedule arrests in your hands (i) funds due by you to (*name of common debtor*) and (ii) goods or other moveables held by you for him. **You should not pay any funds to him or hand over any goods or other moveables to him without taking legal advice.**

2.   This Schedule may be used to arrest a ship or cargo. If it is, you should consult your legal adviser about the effect of it.

3.   The Protected Minimum Balance is the sum referred to in section 73F(4) of the Debtors (Scotland) Act 1987. This sum is currently set at [*insert current sum*]. The Protected Minimum Balance applies where the arrestment attaches funds standing to the credit of a debtor in an account held by a bank or other financial institution and the debtor is an individual. The Protected Minimum Balance does not apply where the account is held in the name of a company, a limited liability partnership, a partnership or an unincorporated association or where the account is operated by the debtor as a trading account.

4.   Under section 73G of the Debtors (Scotland) Act 1987 you must also, within the period of 3 weeks beginning with the day on which the arrestment is executed, disclose to the creditor the nature and value of the funds and/or moveable property which have been attached. This disclosure must be in the form set out in Schedule 8 to the Diligence (Scotland) Regulations 2009. Failure to comply may lead to a financial penalty under section 73G of the Debtors (Scotland) Act 1987 and may also be dealt with as a contempt of court. You must, at the same time, send a copy of the disclosure to the debtor and to any person known to you who owns (or claims to own) attached property and to any person to whom attached funds are (or are claimed to be due), solely or in common with the debtor.

**IF YOU WISH FURTHER ADVICE CONTACT ANY CITIZENS ADVICE BUREAU/
LOCAL ADVICE CENTRE/SHERIFF CLERK OR SOLICITOR**

NOTE
[1] As inserted by the Act of Sederunt (Sheriff Court Rules Amendment) (Diligence) 2008 (SSI 2008/121) r.7(8) (effective April 1, 2008) and substituted by the Act of Sederunt (Sheriff Court Rules Amendment) (Diligence) 2009 (SSI 2009/107) (effective April 22, 2009).

Rule 6.A8   [1] **FORM 9c**

Form of certificate of execution of arrestment on the dependence

CERTIFICATE OF EXECUTION

I, (*name*), Sheriff Officer, certify that I executed an arrestment on the dependence, by virtue of an interlocutor of the Sheriff at (*place*) on (*date*) obtained at the instance of (*name and address of party arresting*) against (*name and address of defender*) on (*name of arrestee*)—

* by delivering the schedule of arrestment to (*name of arrestee or other person*) at (*place*) personally on (*date*).

* by leaving the schedule of arrestment with (*name and occupation of person with whom left*) at (*place*) on (*date*) [and by posting a copy of the schedule to the arrestee by registered post or first class recorded delivery to the address specified on the receipt annexed to this certificate].

* by depositing the schedule of arrestment in (*place*) on (*date*). (*Specify that enquiry made and reasonable grounds exist for believing that the person on whom service is to be made resides at the place but is not available*) [and by posting a copy of the schedule to the arrestee by registered post or first class recorded delivery to the address specified on the receipt annexed to this certificate].

* by affixing the schedule of arrestment to the door at (*place*) on (*date*). (*Specify that enquiry made and that reasonable grounds exist for believing that the person on whom service is to be made resides at the place but is not available*) [and by posting a copy of the schedule to the arrestee by registered post or first class recorded delivery to the address specified on the receipt annexed to this certificate].

* by leaving the schedule of arrestment with (*name and occupation of person with whom left*) at (*place of business*) on (*date*) [and by posting a copy of the schedule to the arrestee by registered post or first class recorded delivery to the address specified on the receipt annexed to this certificate].

* by depositing the schedule of arrestment at (*place of business*) on (*date*). (*Specify that enquiry made and that reasonable grounds exist for believing that the person on whom service is to be made carries on business at that place.*) [and by posting a copy of the schedule to the arrestee by registered post or first class recorded delivery to the address specified on the receipt annexed to this certificate].

* by affixing the schedule of arrestment to the door at (*place of business*) on (*date*). (*Specify that enquiry made and that reasonable grounds exist for believing that the person on whom service is to be made carries on business at that place.*) [and by posting a copy of the schedule to the arrestee by registered post or first class recorded delivery to the address specified on the receipt annexed to this certificate].

* by leaving the schedule of arrestment at (*registered office*) on (*date*), in the hands of (*name of

person) [and by posting a copy of the schedule to the arrestee by registered post or first class recorded delivery to the address specified on the receipt annexed to this certificate].

* by depositing the schedule of arrestment at (*registered office*) on (*date*) [and by posting a copy of the schedule to the arrestee by registered post or first class recorded delivery to the address specified on the receipt annexed to this certificate].

* by affixing the schedule of arrestment to the door at (*registered office*) on *(date)* [and by posting a copy of the schedule to the arrestee by registered post or first class recorded delivery to the address specified on the receipt annexed to this certificate].

I did this in the presence of (*name, occupation and address of witness*).

(*Signed*)

Sheriff Officer

(*Address)*

(*Signed*)

(Witness)

*Delete where not applicable

NOTE

A copy of the Schedule of arrestment on the dependence is to be attached to this certificate

NOTE
: [1] As inserted by the Act of Sederunt (Sheriff Court Rules Amendment) (Diligence) 2008 (SSI 2008/121) r.7(8) (effective April 1, 2008) and substituted by the Act of Sederunt (Sheriff Court Rules Amendment) (Diligence) 2009 (SSI 2009/107) (effective April 22, 2009).

Rule 7.3(4)(a)   FORM 10

Recall or restriction of arrestment Certificate authorising the release of arrested funds or property

Sheriff court at (*place*)

Court ref. no.:

AB (pursuer) against CD (defender)

I, (*name*), hereby certify that the sheriff on (*date*) authorised the release of the funds or property arrested on the *dependence of the action / counterclaim to the following extent:

(*details of sheriff's order*)

(*date*)   Sheriff clerk depute

delete as appropriate

Copy to:
    Party instructing arrestment
    Party possessing arrested funds/property

Rule 8.1(2) FORM 11

Form of minute—no form of response lodged by defender

Sheriff court at (*place*)

Hearing date:

In respect that the defender(s) has/have failed to lodge a form of response to the summons, the pursuer requests the court to make the orders specified in the following case(s):

Court ref. no.: Name(s) of defender(s) Minute(s)

Rule 8.2(2) [1] FORM 12

Form of minute—pursuer not objecting to application for a time to pay direction or time order

Sheriff court at (*place*)

Court ref. no.:

Name(s) of defender(s)

Hearing date:

I do not object to the defender's application for

> *a time to pay direction
> *recall or restriction of an arrestment
> *a time order

The pursuer requests the court to grant decree or other order in terms of the following minute(s)

**delete as appropriate*

NOTE

[1] As amended by the Act of Sederunt (Ordinary Cause, Summary Application, Summary Cause and Small Claim Rules) Amendment (Miscellaneous) 2003 (SSI 2003/26), para.5(2)(b) (effective January 24, 2003).

Rule 8.2(4) [1] FORM 13

Form of minute—pursuer opposing an application for a time to pay direction
or time order

Sheriff court (*place*):

Court ref no:

Name(s) of defender(s):

Hearing date:

I oppose the defender's application for

> *a time to pay direction

> *recall or restriction of arrestment

> *a time order

**delete as appropriate*

1. The debt is (*please specify the nature of the debt and any reason known to the pursuer for the debt*).

2. The debt was incurred on (*specify date*) and the pursuer has contacted the defender in relation to the debt on (*specify date(s)*).

*3. The contractual payments were (*specify amount*).

*4. (*Specify any action taken by the pursuer to assist the defender to pay the debt*).

*5. The defender has made payment(s) towards the debt of (*specify amount(s)*) on (*specify date(s)*).

*6. The debtor has made offers to pay (*specify amount(s)*) on (*specify date(s)*) which offer(s) was [were] accepted] [*or* rejected] and (*specify amount*) was paid on (*specify date(s)*).

7. (*Here set out any information you consider relevant to the court's determination of the application*).

8. The pursuer requests the court to grant decree.

**delete as appropriate*

(*Signed*)

Pursuer [*or* Solicitor for Pursuer]

(*Date*)

NOTE
[1] As substituted by the Act of Sederunt (Sheriff Court Rules) (Miscellaneous Amendments) 2009 (SSI 2009/294) r.5 (effective December 1, 2009).

Rule 11.1(8) FORM 14

Counterclaim—form of intimation by sheriff clerk where pursuer fails to appear

Court ref. no.:

(AB) (*insert address*), pursuer

against

(CD) (*insert address*), defender

When the above case called in court on (*insert date*), the defender appeared (or was represented) and stated a counterclaim to the claim made by you against him.

The court continued the case until (*date*) at (*time*).

Please note that, if you fail to appear or be represented at the continued diet, the court may grant decree against you in terms of the counterclaim.

(*date*) Sheriff clerk depute

Paragraph 7(4)

Rule 13A.3(1) [1]FORM 14A

Form of minute of intervention by the Commission for Equality and Human Rights

Sheriff Court at (*place*) Court ref. no.

APPLICATION FOR LEAVE TO INTERVENE BY THE COMMISSION FOR
EQUALITY AND HUMAN RIGHTS

in the cause

[A.B.] (*designation and address*), Pursuer

against

[C.D.] (*designation and address*), Defender

[*Here set out briefly:*
  (*a*) the Commission's reasons for believing that the proceedings are relevant to a matter in connection with which the Commission has a function;

(b) the issue in the proceedings which the Commission wishes to address; and

(c) the propositions to be advanced by the Commission and the Commission's reasons for believing that they are relevant to the proceedings and that they will assist the court.]

NOTE
[1]As inserted by the Act of Sederunt (Sheriff Court Rules) (Miscellaneous Amendments) 2008 (SSI 2008/223) para.7(4) (effective July 1, 2008).

Rule 13B.2(1)   [1]FORM 14B

Form of minute of intervention by the Scottish Commission for Human Rights

Sheriff Court at (*place*)   Court ref. no.

APPLICATION FOR LEAVE TO INTERVENE BY THE SCOTTISH COMMISSION FOR HUMAN RIGHTS

in the cause

[A.B.] (*designation and address*), Pursuer

against

[C.D.] (*designation and address*), Defender

[*Here set out briefly:*
   (a) the issue in the proceedings which the Commission intends to address;
   (b) a summary of the submission which the Commission intends to make.]

NOTE
[1]As inserted by the Act of Sederunt (Sheriff Court Rules) (Miscellaneous Amendments) 2008 (SSI 2008/223) para.7(4) (effective July 1, 2008).

Rule 13B.3(1)   [1]FORM 14C

Invitation to the Scottish Commission for Human Rights to intervene

SHERIFFDOM OF (*insert name of sheriffdom*)   Court ref. no.

AT (*insert place of sheriff court*)

INVITATION TO THE SCOTTISH COMMISSION FOR HUMAN RIGHTS TO INTERVENE

in the cause

[A.B.] (*designation and address*), Pursuer

against

[C.D.] (*designation and address*), Defender

[*Here set out briefly:*
   (a) the facts, procedural history and issues in the proceedings;
   (b) the issue in the proceedings on which the court seeks a submission.]

NOTE
[1]As inserted by the Act of Sederunt (Sheriff Court Rules) (Miscellaneous Amendments) 2008 (SSI 2008/223) para.7(4) (effective July 1, 2008).

Rule 17.2(1)   [1] FORM 15

Sheriff court at (*place*)

In the claim (*court ref. no.*)

in which

AB (*design*) is the pursuer

and

C.D. (*design*) is the defender

To: (*name and designation of party or haver from whom the documents are sought to be recovered*).

You are hereby required to produce to the sheriff clerk at (*address*) within days of the service upon you of this order:

1. This order itself (which must be produced intact);
2. The certificate marked "B" attached;
3. All documents within your possession covered by the specification which is enclosed; and
4. A list of those documents.

You can produce the items listed above either:

  (a) by delivering them to the sheriff clerk at the address shown above; or

  (b) sending them to the sheriff clerk by registered or recorded delivery post.

(*date*)   (*signature, name, address and designation of person serving order*)

PLEASE NOTE:

If you claim confidentiality for any of the documents produced by you, you must still produce them. However, they may be placed in a separate envelope by themselves, marked "confidential". The court will, if necessary, decide whether the envelope should be opened or not.

Where the person ordering you to produce the document is **not** the sheriff clerk, claims for necessary outlays within certain specified limits may be paid. Claims should be made in writing to the person who has obtained an order that you produce the documents.

CERTIFICATE

B

Sheriff Court at (*place*)

In the claim (*court ref. no.*)

in which

AB (*design*) is the pursuer

and

CD (*design*) is the defender

Order for recovery of documents dated (*insert date*).

With reference to the above order and relative specification of documents, I hereby certify:

* that the documents produced herewith and the list signed by me which accompanies them are all the documents in my possession which fall under the specification.

* I have no documents in my possession falling under the specification.

* I believe that there are other documents falling within the specification which are not in my possession. These documents are (*list the documents as described in the specification.*) These documents were last seen by me on (*date*) in the possession of (*name and address of person/ company, if known*).

* I know of no documents falling within the specification which are in the possession of any other person.

                                       * *delete as appropriate*

(*name*) (*date*)

NOTE
[1] Substituted by Act of Sederunt (Ordinary Cause, Summary Application, Summary Cause and Small Claim Rules) Amendment (Miscellaneous) 2005 (SSI 2005/648) (effective January 2, 2006).

Rule 17.4(3)   [1]FORM 16

Form of citation of witness or haver

(*date*)

CITATION

SHERIFFDOM OF (*insert name of sheriffdom*)

At (*insert place of sheriff court*)

To [A.B.] (*design*)

(*Name*) who is pursuing/defending a case against (*name*) [*or* is a (*specify*) in the case of (*name*) against (*name*)] has asked you to be a witness. You must attend the above sheriff court on (*insert date*) at (*insert time*) for that purpose, [and bring with you (*specify documents*)].

If you

- would like to know more about being a witness
- are a child under the age of 16
- think you may be a vulnerable witness within the meaning of section 11(1) of the Vulnerable Witnesses (Scotland) Act 2004 (that is someone the court considers may be less able to give their evidence due to mental disorder or fear or distress connected to giving your evidence at the court hearing).

you should contact (*specify the solicitor acting for the party or the party litigant citing the witness*) for further information.

If you are a vulnerable witness (including a child under the age of 16) then you should be able to use a special measure (such measures include use of a screen, a live TV link or a supporter, or a commissioner) to help you give evidence.

Expenses

You may claim back money which you have had to spend and any earnings you have lost within certain specified limits, because you have to come to court on the above date. These may be paid to you if you claim within specified time limits. Claims should be made to the person who has asked you to attend court. Proof of any loss of earnings should be given to that person.

If you wish your travelling expenses to be paid before you go to court, you should apply for payment to the person who has asked you to attend court.

Failure to attend

It is very important that you attend court and you should note that failure to do so may result in a warrant being granted for your arrest. In addition, if you fail to attend without any good reason, having requested and been paid your travelling expenses, you may be ordered to pay a penalty not exceeding £250.

If you have any questions about anything in this citation, please contact (*specify the solicitor acting for the party or the party litigant citing the witness*) for further information.

Signed

[P.Q.] Sheriff Officer

or [X.Y.], (*add designation and business address*)

Solicitor for the pursuer [*or* defender][*or* (*specify*)]

NOTE

[1] As substituted by the Act of Sederunt (Ordinary Cause, Summary Application, Summary Cause and Small Claim Rules) Amendment (Vulnerable Witnesses (Scotland) Act 2004) 2007 (SSI 2007/463) (effective November 1, 2007).

Rule 17.4(3)   FORM 16A

Form of certificate of execution of witness citation

I certify that on (*date*) I duly cited AB (*design*) to attend at (*name of court*) on (*date*) at (*time*) as a witness for the (*design party*) in the action at the instance of CD (*design*) against EF (*design*) (*and I required him to bring with him*   ). This I did by

(*signature of solicitor or sheriff officer*)

[1] FORM 16B

Form of child witness notice

Rule 11A.2   VULNERABLE WITNESSES (SCOTLAND) ACT 2004 Section 12

Received the   day of   20

(*Date of receipt of this notice*)

.... (*signed*)

Sheriff Clerk

CHILD WITNESS NOTICE

Sheriff court   20

Court Ref. No.

1.   The applicant is the pursuer [*or* defender] in the action by [A.B.] (*design*) against [C.D.] (*design*).

2.   The applicant has cited [*or* intends to cite] [E.F.] (*date of birth*) as a witness.

3.   [E.F.] is a child witnesses under section 11 of the Vulnerable Witnesses (Scotland) Act 2004 [and was under the age of sixteen on the date of the commencement of proceedings].

4.   The applicant considers that the following special measure[s] is [are] the most appropriate for the purpose of taking the evidence of [E.F.][*or* that [E.F.] should give evidence without the benefit of any special measure]:–

(*delete as appropriate and specify any special measure(s) sought*).

5.   [(a) The reason[s] this [these] special measure[s] is [are] considered the most appropriate is [are] as follows:–

(*here specify the reason(s) for the special measure(s) sought*)].

OR

[(b) The reason[s] it is considered that [E.F.] should give evidence without the benefit of any special measure is [are]:–

(*here explain why it is felt that no special measures are required*)].

6.   [E.F.] and the parent[s] of [*or* person[s] with parental responsibility for] [E.F.] has [have] expressed the following view[s] on the special measure[s] that is [are] considered most appropriate [*or* the appropriateness of [E.F.] giving evidence without the benefit of any special measure]:–

(delete as appropriate and set out the views(s) expressed and how they were obtained)

7.   Other information considered relevant to this application is as follows:–

(here set out any other information relevant to the child witness notice).

8.   The applicant asks the court to–

    (a) consider this child witness notice;

    (b) make an order authorising the special measure[s] sought; *or*

    (c) make an order authorising the giving of evidence by [E.F.] without the benefit of special measures.

    (delete as appropriate)

(Signed)

[A.B. *or* C.D.]

[or Representative of A.B. [*or* C.D.]] *(include full designation)*

NOTE: This form should be suitably adapted where section 16 of the Act of 2004 applies.

NOTE
¹ As inserted by the Act of Sederunt (Ordinary Cause, Summary Application, Summary Cause and Small Claim Rules) Amendment (Vulnerable Witnesses (Scotland) Act 2004) 2007 (SSI 2007/463) (effective November 1, 2007).

¹ FORM 16C

Form of vulnerable witness application

Rule 17A.3

VULNERABLE WITNESSES (SCOTLAND) ACT 2004 Section 12

Received the ....day of ....20...........

(Date of receipt of this notice)

.................*(signed)*

Sheriff Clerk

VULNERABLE WITNESS APPLICATION

Sheriff Court ....20 ....

Court Ref. No.

1. The applicant is the pursuer [*or* defender] in the action by [A.B] *(design)* against [C.D.] *(design)*.

2. The applicant has cited [or intends to cite] [E.F.] *(date of birth)* as a witness.

3. The applicant considers that [E.F.] is a vulnerable witness under section 11(1)(b) of the Vulnerable Witnesses (Scotland) Act 2004 for the following reasons:–

(here specify reasons witness is considered to be a vulnerable witness).

4. The applicant considers that the following special measure[s] is [are] the most appropriate for the purpose of taking the evidence of [E.F.].

(specify any special measure(s) sought)

5. The reason[s] this [these] special measure[s] is [are] considered the most appropriate is [are] as follows:–

    (*here specify the reason(s) for the special measures(s) sought*).

6. [E.F.] has expressed the following view[s] on the special measure[s] that is [are] considered most appropriate:–

    (*set out the views expressed and how they were obtained*).

7. Other information considered relevant to this application is as follows:–

    (*here set out any other information relevant to the vulnerable witness application*).

8. The applicant asks the court to–

    (a) consider this vulnerable witness application;

    (b) make an order authorising the special measure[s] sought.

(*Signed*)

[A.B. *or* C.D.]

[*or* Representative of A.B. [*or* C.D.]] (*include full designation*)

NOTE: *This form should be suitably adapted where section 16 of the Act of 2004 applies.*

NOTE
[1] As inserted by the Act of Sederunt (Ordinary Cause, Summary Application, Summary Cause and Small Claim Rules) Amendment (Vulnerable Witnesses (Scotland) Act 2004) 2007 (SSI 2007/463) (effective November 1, 2007).

[1] FORM 16D

Form of certificate of intimation

Rule 17A.4(2)

VULNERABLE WITNESSES (SCOTLAND) ACT 2004 Section 12

CERTIFICATE OF INTIMATION

Sheriff Court					............20......

Court Ref. No.

I certify that intimation of the child witness notice [*or* vulnerable witness application] relating to (*insert name of witness*) was made to (*insert names of parties or solicitors for parties, as appropriate*) by (*insert method of intimation; where intimation is by facsimile transmission, insert fax number to which intimation sent*) on (*insert date of intimation*).

Date: ....

(*Signed*)

Solicitor [*or* Sheriff Officer]

(*include full business designation*)

NOTE
[1] As inserted by the Act of Sederunt (Ordinary Cause, Summary Application, Summary Cause and Small Claim Rules) Amendment (Vulnerable Witnesses (Scotland) Act 2004) 2007 (SSI 2007/463) (effective November 1, 2007).

[1] FORM 16E

Form of application for review

Rule 17A.6(1)

VULNERABLE WITNESSES (SCOTLAND) ACT 2004 Section 13

Received the ....day of....................20....

(date of receipt of this notice)

....*(signed)*

Sheriff Clerk

APPLICATION FOR REVIEW OF ARRANGEMENTS FOR VULNERABLE WITNESS

Sheriff Court...   ....20...

Court Ref. No.

1. The applicant is the pursuer [*or* defender] in the action by [A.B.] (*design*) against [C.D.] (*design*).

2. A proof [*or* hearing] is fixed for (*date*) at (*time*).

3. [E.F.] is a witness who is to give evidence at, or for the purposes of, the proof [*or* hearing]. [E.F.] is a child witness [*or* vulnerable witness] under section 11 of the Vulnerable Witnesses (Scotland) Act 2004.

4. The current arrangements for taking the evidence of [E.F.] are (*here specify current arrangements*).

5. The current arrangements should be reviewed as (*here specify reasons for review*).

6. [E.F.] [and the parent[s] of [*or* person[s] with parental responsibility for] [E.F.]] has [have] expressed the following view[s] on [the special measure[s] that is [are] considered most appropriate] [*or* the appropriateness of [E.F.] giving evidence without the benefit of any special measure]:–

   (*delete as appropriate and set out the view(s) expressed and how they were obtained*).

7. The applicant seeks (here specify the order sought).

(*Signed*)

[A.B. *or* C.D.]

[*or* Representative of A.B. [*or* C.D.]] (*include full designation*)

NOTE: This form should be suitably adapted where section 16 of the Act of 2004 applies.

NOTE
[1] As inserted by the Act of Sederunt (Ordinary Cause, Summary Application, Summary Cause and Small Claim Rules) Amendment (Vulnerable Witnesses (Scotland) Act 2004) 2007 (SSI 2007/463) (effective November 1, 2007).

¹ FORM 16F

Form of certificate of intimation

Rule 17A.7(2)

VULNERABLE WITNESSES (SCOTLAND) ACT 2004 Section 13

CERTIFICATE OF INTIMATION

Sheriff Court ....20......

Court Ref. No.

I certify that intimation of the review application relating to (*insert name of witness*) was made to (*insert names of parties or solicitors for parties, as appropriate*) by (*insert method of intimation; where intimation is by facsimile transmission, insert fax number to which intimation sent*) on (*insert date of intimation*).

Date: ....

(*Signed*)

Solicitor [*or* Sheriff Officer]

(*include full business designation*)

NOTE
¹ As inserted by the Act of Sederunt (Ordinary Cause, Summary Application, Summary Cause and Small Claim Rules) Amendment (Vulnerable Witnesses (Scotland) Act 2004) 2007 (SSI 2007/463) (effective November 1, 2007).

Rule 18.2(2)   FORM 17

Form of reference to the European Court

REQUEST

for

PRELIMINARY RULING

of

THE COURT OF JUSTICE OR THE EUROPEAN COMMUNITIES

from

THE SHERIFFDOM OF (*insert name of sheriffdom*) at (*insert place of court*)

in the cause

AB (*insert designation and address*), pursuer

against

CD (*insert designation and address*), defender

(*Here set out a clear and succinct statement of the case giving rise to the request for a ruling of the European Court in order to enable the European Court to consider and understand the issues of Community law raised and to enable governments of Member states and other interested parties to submit observations. The statement of the case should include:*
  (a) particulars of the parties;
  (b) the history of the dispute between the parties;
  (c) the history of the proceedings;

(d) the relevant facts as agreed by the parties or found by the court or, failing such agreement
or finding, the contentions of the parties on such facts;
(e) the nature of the issues of law and fact between the parties;
(f) the Scots law, so far as relevant;
(g) the Treaty provisions or other acts, instruments or rules of Community law concerned;
(h) an explanation of why the reference is being made).

The preliminary ruling of the Court of Justice of the European Communities is accordingly
requested on the following questions:

1,2, etc. (*Here set out the question(s) on which the ruling is sought, identifying the Treaty
provisions or other acts, instruments or rules of Community law concerned.*)

Dated the   day of   20

Rule 21.5(4)(b)   FORM 18

Form of extract decree (basic)

Sheriff court   Court ref. no.:

Date of decree   *in absence

Pursuer(s)   Defender(s)

The sheriff

and granted decree against the   for payment of expenses of
£   against the (name of party).

This extract is warrant for all lawful execution thereon.

Date   Sheriff clerk depute

delete as appropriate

Rule 21.5(4)(b)   FORM 18A

Form of extract decree for payment

Sheriff court   Court ref. no.

Date of decree   *in absence

Pursuer(s)   Defender(s)

The sheriff granted decree against the   for payment to
the   of the undernoted sums:

(1) Sum(s) decerned for: £

(2) Interest atper cent per year from (*date*) until payment.

(3) Expenses of £   against the (*name of party*).

*A time to pay direction was made under section 1(1) of the Debtors (Scotland) Act 1987.

*A time order was made under section 129 (1) of the Consumer Credit Act 1974.

*The amount is payable by instalments of £   per   commencing

within   *days/weeks/months of intimation of this extract decree.

*The amount is payable by lump sum within   *days/weeks/months of intimation of this
extract decree.

This extract is warrant for all lawful execution thereon.

Date   Sheriff clerk depute

delete as appropriate

Rule 21.5(4)(b) FORM 18B

Form of extract decree in an action of delivery

Sheriff court Court ref. no.:

Date of decree *in absence

Pursuer(s)

Defender(s)

The sheriff granted decree against the defender

(1) for delivery to the pursuer of (*specify articles*)

(2) for expenses of £

* Further, the sheriff granted warrant to officers of court to (1) open shut and lockfast places occupied by the defender and (2) search for and take possession of said goods in the possession of the defender.

delete as appropriate

This extract is warrant for all lawful execution thereon.

Date Sheriff clerk depute

Rule 21.5(4)(b) FORM 18C

Form of extract decree in an action of delivery—payment failing delivery

Sheriff court Court ref. no.:

Date of decree *in absence

Pursuer(s)

Defender(s)

The sheriff, in respect that the defender has failed to make delivery in accordance with the decree granted in this court on (*date*), granted decree for payment against the defender of the undernoted sums:

(1) Sum(s) decerned for: £ , being the alternative amount claimed.

(2) Interest at per cent per year from (*date*) until payment.

(3) Expenses of £ against the (*name of party*).

*A time to pay direction was made under section 1 (1) of the Debtors (Scotland) Act 1987.

*The amount is payable by instalments of £ per commencing within

*days/weeks/monthsof intimation of this extract decree.

*The amount is payable by lump sum within *days/weeks/months of intimation of this extract decree.

delete as appropriate

This extract is warrant for all lawful execution thereon.

Date Sheriff clerk depute

Rule 21.5(4)(b) FORM 18D

Form of extract decree Recovery of possession of moveable property

Sheriff court Court ref. no.:

Date of decree *in absence

Pursuer(s) Defender(s)

The sheriff granted decree against the defender:

(1) Finding the pursuer entitled to recovery of possession of the article(s) (*specify*)

(2) for expenses of £

* Further, the sheriff granted warrant to officers of court to (1) open shut and lockfast places occupied by the defender and (2) search for and take possession of said goods in the possession of the defender.

**delete as appropriate*

This extract is warrant for all lawful execution thereon.

Date   Sheriff clerk depute

Rule 21.5(4)(b)   FORM 18E

Form of extract decree

Recovery of possession of moveable property—payment failing recovery

Sheriff court   Court ref. no.:

Date of decree   *in absence

Pursuer(s)   Defender(s)

The sheriff, in respect that the defender has failed to recover possession in accordance with the decree granted in this court on (*date*), granted decree for payment against the defender of the undernoted sums:

Sum(s) decerned for: £   , being the alternative amount claimed.

Interest at   per cent per year from (*date*) until payment.

Expenses of £   against the (*name of party*).

*A time to pay direction was made under section 1 (1) of the Debtors (Scotland) Act 1987.

*The amount is payable by instalments of £   per   commencing within

     *days/weeks/monthsof intimation of this extract decree.

*The amount is payable by lump sum within   *days/weeks/months of intimation of this extract decree.

**delete as appropriate*

This extract is warrant for all lawful execution thereon.

Date   Sheriff clerk depute

Rule 21.5(4)(b)   FORM 18F

Form of extract decree ad factum praestandum

Sheriff court   Court ref. no.:

Date of decree   *in absence

Pursuer(s)

Defender(s)

The sheriff

(1) ordained the defender(s)

(2) granted decree for payment of expenses of £   against the defender(s).

This extract is warrant for all lawful execution thereon.

Date   Sheriff clerk depute

Rule 21.5(4)(b) FORM 18G

Form of extract decree ad factum praestandum—payment upon failure to
implement obligation

Sheriff court   Court ref. no.:

Date of decree   *in absence

Pursuer(s)

Defender(s)

The sheriff, in respect that the defender has failed to implement the obligation contained in and
in accordance with the decree granted in this court on (*date*), granted decree for payment
against the defender of the undernoted sums:

(1) Sum(s) decerned for: £   ,being the alternative amount claimed.

(2) Interest at   per cent per year from (*date*) until payment.

(3) Expenses of £   against the (*name of party*).

*A time to pay direction was made under section 1(1) of the Debtors (Scotland) Act 1987.

*The amount is payable by instalments of £   per   commencing within

          *days/weeks/monthsof intimation of this extract decree.

*The amount is payable by lump sum within   *days/weeks/months of intimation of this
extract decree.

**delete as appropriate*

This extract is warrant for all lawful execution thereon.

Date   Sheriff clerk depute

Rule 21.5(4)(b) FORM 18H

Form of extract decree of absolvitor

Sheriff court   Court ref. no.:

Date of decree   *in absence

Pursuer(s)

Defender(s)

The sheriff

(1) absolved the defender(s).

(2) granted decree for payment of expenses of £   against the

This extract is warrant for all lawful execution thereon.

Date   Sheriff clerk depute

Rule 21.5(4)(b) FORM 18I

Form of extract decree of dismissal

Sheriff court   Court ref. no.:

Date of decree   *in absence

Pursuer(s)

Defender(s)

The sheriff

(1) dismissed the action against the defender(s).

(2) granted decree for payment of expenses of £   against the

This extract is warrant for all lawful execution thereon.

Date   Sheriff clerk depute

Rule 21.8(4)   FORM 19

Form of certificate by sheriff clerk
Service of charge where address of defender is unknown

I certify that the foregoing charge was displayed on the walls of court on (*date*) and that it remained so displayed for a period of (*period of charge*) from that date.

(*date*)   Sheriff clerk depute

Rule 21.1(1)   FORM 20

Minute for recall of decree

Sheriff court: (*place*)

Court ref. no.:

AB (*pursuer*) against CD (*defender(s)*)

The *(*pursuer/defender*) moves the court to recall the decree pronounced on (*date*) in this case * and in which execution of a charge/arrestment was effected on (*date*).

Reason for failure to appear or be represented:

Proposed defence/answer:

Date

delete as appropriate

Rule 22.1(6)   FORM 20A

Minute for recall of decree—service copy

Sheriff court: (*place*)

Court ref. no.:

AB (*pursuer*) against CD (*defender(s)*)

The *(*pursuer/defender*) moves the court to recall the decree pronounced on (*date*) in this case * and in which execution of a charge/arrestment was effected on (*date*).

Reason for failure to appear or be represented:

Proposed defence/answer:

Date

delete as appropriate

NOTE: You must return the summons to the sheriff clerk at the court mentioned at the top of this form by (insert date 2 days before the date of the hearing).

Rule 23.1(1) FORM 21

Form of note of appeal to the sheriff principal

Sheriff court (*place*)

Court ref. no:

AB (pursuer) against CD (defender(s))

The pursuer/defender appeals the sheriff's interlocutor of (*date*) to the sheriff principal and requests the sheriff to state a case.

The point(s) of law upon which the appeal is to proceed is/are: (*give brief statement*).

(*date*)

Rule 23.4(3)(a) FORM 22

Application for leave to appeal against time to pay direction

Sheriff court (*place*)

Court ref. no.:

AB (pursuer) against CD (defender(s))

The pursuer/defender requests the sheriff to grant leave to appeal the decision made on (*date*) in respect of the defender's application for a time to pay direction to the sheriff principal/Court of Session.

The point(s) of law upon which the appeal is to proceed is/are: (*give brief statement*).

(*date*)

Rule 23.4(4) FORM 23

Appeal against time to pay direction

Sheriff court (*place*)

Court ref. no.:

AB (pursuer) against CD (defender(s))

The pursuer/defender appeals the decision made on (*date*) in respect of the defender's application for a time to pay direction to the sheriff principal/Court of Session.

(*date*)

Rule 24.4(1) FORM 24

Form of receipt for money paid to sheriff clerk

In the sheriff court of (*name of sheriffdom*) at (*place of sheriff court*).

In the claim (*state names of parties or other appropriate description*)

AB (*designation*) has this day paid into court the sum of £   , being a payment made in terms of Chapter 24 of the Small Claim Rules 2002.

*Custody of this money has been accepted at the request of (*insert name of court making the request*).

**delete as appropriate*

(Date) Sheriff clerk depute

Absolve
To find in favour of and exonerate the defender.

Absolvitor
An order of the court granted in favour of and exonerating the defender which means that the pursuer is not allowed to bring the same matter to court again.

Appellant
A person making an appeal against the sheriff's decision. This might be the pursuer or the defender.

Arrestee
A person subject to an arrestment.

Arrestment on the dependence
A court order to freeze the goods or bank account of the defender until the court has heard the case.

Arrestment to found jurisdiction
A court order used against a person who has goods or other assets in Scotland to give the court jurisdiction to hear a claim. This is achieved by preventing anything being done with the goods or assets until the case has been disposed of.

Authorised lay representative
A person other than a lawyer who represents a party to a small claim.

Cause
Another word for case or claim, used for cases under the summary cause procedure.

Caution (pronounced kay-shun)
A security, usually a sum of money, given to ensure that some obligation will be carried out.

Certificate of execution of service
The document recording that an application to, or order or decree of, the court for service of documents has been effected.

Charge
An order to obey a decree of a court. A common type is one served on the defender by a sheriff officer on behalf of the pursuer who has won a case demanding payment of a sum of money.

Commission and diligence
Authorisation by the court for someone to take the evidence of a witness who cannot attend court or to obtain the production of documentary evidence. It is combined with a diligence authorising the person appointed to require the attendance of the witness and the disclosure of documents.

Consignation
The deposit in court, or with a third party, of money or an article in dispute.

Continuation
An order made by the sheriff postponing the completion of a hearing until a later date or dates.

Counterclaim
A claim made by a defender in response to the pursuer's claim and which is not a defence to that claim. It is a separate but related claim against the pursuer which is dealt with at the same time as the pursuer's claim.

Damages
Money compensation payable for a breach of contract or some other legal duty.

Decree
An order of the court containing the decision of the claim in favour of one of the parties and granting the remedy sought or disposing of the claim.

Defender
Person against whom a claim is made.

Deliverance
A decision or order of a court.

Depending
A case is said to be depending when it is going through a court procedure. Technically, this begins with citation of the defender and ends with any final appeal.

Diet
Date for a court hearing.

Diligence
The collective term for the procedures used to enforce a decree of a court. These include arrestment of wages, goods or a bank account.

Dismissal
An order bringing to an end the proceedings in a claim. It is usually possible for a new claim to be brought if not time barred.

Domicile
The place where a person is normally resident or where, in the case of a company, it has its place of business or registered office.

Execution of service
See *Certificate of execution of service.*

Execution of a charge
The intimation of the requirement to obey a decree or order of a court.

Execution of an arrestment
The carrying out of an order of arrestment.

Expenses
The costs of a court case.

Extra-judicial settlement
An agreement between the parties to a case to settle it themselves rather than to await a decision by the sheriff.

Extract decree
The document containing the order of the court made at the end of the claim. For example, it can be used to enforce payment of a sum awarded.

Haver
A person who holds documents which are required as evidence in a case.

Huissier
An official in France and some other European countries who serves court documents.

Incidental application
An application that can be made during the course of a small claim for certain orders. Examples are applications for the recovery of documents or to amend the statement of claim.

Interlocutor
The official record of the order or judgment of a court.

Intimation
Giving notice to another party of some step in the small claim.

Jurisdiction
The authority of a court to hear particular cases.

Messenger at arms
Officers of court who serve documents issued by the Court of Session.

Minute
A document produced in the course of a case in which a party makes an application or sets out his position on some matter.

Minute for recall
A form lodged with the court by one party asking the court to recall a decree.

Options Hearing
A preliminary stage in an ordinary cause action.

Ordinary cause
Another legal procedure for higher value claims available in the sheriff court.

Party litigant
A person who conducts his own case.

Productions
Documents or articles which are used in evidence.

Pursuer
The person making a claim.

Recall of an arrestment
A court order withdrawing an arrestment.

Restriction of an arrestment
An order releasing part of the money or property arrested.

Recall of a decree
An order revoking a decree which has been granted.

Recovery of documents
The process of obtaining documentary evidence which is not in the possession of the person seeking it (e.g. hospital records necessary to establish the extent of injuries received in a road accident).

Remit between procedures
A decision of the sheriff to transfer the claim to another court procedure e.g. summary cause or ordinary cause procedure.

Respondent
When a decision of the sheriff is appealed against, the person making the appeal is called the appellant. The other side in the appeal is called the respondent.

Return day
The date by which the defender must send a written reply to the court and, where appropriate, the pursuer must return the summons to court.

Schedule of arrestment
The list of items which may be arrested.

Serve/Service
Sending a copy of the summons or other court document to the defender or another party.

Sheriff clerk
The court official responsible for the administration of the sheriff court.

Sheriff officer
A person who serves court documents and enforces court orders.

Sist of action
The temporary suspension of a court case by court order.

Sist as a party
To add another person as a litigant in a case.

Stated case
An appeal procedure where the sheriff sets out his findings and the reasons for his decision and states the issues on which the decision of the sheriff principal is requested.

Statement of claim
The part of the summons in which pursuers set out details of their claims against defenders.

Summary cause
Another legal procedure available in the Sheriff Court. It is used for certain types of claim usually having a higher value than small claims though less than those dealt with as ordinary causes.

Summons
The form which must be filled in to begin a small claim.

Time to pay direction
A court order for which a defender who is an individual may apply permitting a sum owed to be paid by instalments or by a single payment at a later date.

Time order
A court order which assists debtors who have defaulted on an agreement regulated by the Consumer Credit Act 1974 (c.39) and which may be applied for during a court action.

Warrant for diligence
Authority to carry out one of the diligence procedures.

Writ
A legally significant writing.

Paragraph 4   SCHEDULE 2

REVOCATIONS

(1) Act of Sederunt	*(2)* Reference	*(3)* Extent of revocation
Act of Sederunt (Small Claim Rules) 1988	S.I. 1988/1976	The whole Act of Sederunt
Act of Sederunt (Amendment of Sheriff Court Ordinary Cause, Summary Cause and Small Claim, Rules) 1990	S.I. 1990/661	Paragraph 4
Act of Sederunt (Amendment of Sheriff Court Ordinary Cause, Summary Cause and Small Claim, Rules) (No. 2) 1990	S.I. 1990/2105	Paragraph 4
Act of Sederunt (Amendment of Summary Cause and Small Claim Rules) 1991	S.I. 1991/821	Paragraph 3
Act of Sederunt (Amendment of Ordinary Cause, Summary Cause and Small Claim Rules) 1992	S.I. 1992/249	Paragraph 3
Act of Sederunt (Sheriff Court Ordinary Cause Rules) 1993	S.I. 1993/1956	Paragraph 4

Act of Sederunt (Sheriff Court Caveat Rules) 2006

(SI 2006/198)

[April 28, 2006]

The Lords of Council and Session, under and by virtue of the powers conferred by section 32 of the Sheriff Courts (Scotland) Act 1971 and of all other powers enabling them in that behalf, having approved draft rules submitted to them by the Sheriff Court Rules Council in accordance with section 34 of the Sheriff Courts (Scotland) Act 1971, do hereby enact and declare:

Citation and commencement
  1.—(1) This Act of Sederunt may be cited as the Act of Sederunt (Sheriff Court Caveat Rules) 2006 and shall come into force on 28th April 2006.
  (2) This Act of Sederunt shall be inserted into the Books of Sederunt.

Orders against which caveats may be lodged
  2.—(1) Subject to paragraphs (2) and (3), a person may lodge a caveat against only—
  (a) an interim interdict sought against the person in an ordinary cause before the person has lodged a notice of intention to defend;
  (b) an interim order sought against the person in an ordinary cause before the expiry of the period within which the person could lodge a notice of intention to defend;
  (c) an interim order sought against the person in a summary application before service of the initial writ;
  (d) an order for intimation, service and advertisement of a petition to wind up, or appoint an administrator to, a company in which he has an interest;
  (e) an order for intimation, service and advertisement of a petition for his sequestration; and
  (f) the disposal of a commissary application.
  (2) In this rule—
  (a) "interim order" does not include an order under section 1 of the Administration of Justice (Scotland) Act 1972 (orders for inspection of documents and other property etc.); and
  (b) "commissary application" means an application for—
    (i) confirmation;
    (ii) appointment of an executor; or
    (iii) restriction of caution in respect of an executor.
  (3) A person may lodge a caveat against an order mentioned in paragraph (1)(d) only where the person is a company, debenture holder, holder of a floating charge, receiver, shareholder of the company or other person claiming an interest.

Form, lodging and renewal of caveats
  3.—(1) A caveat shall be in the form set out in the Schedule to this Act of Sederunt, or a form substantially to the same effect with such variation as circumstances may require, and shall be lodged with the sheriff clerk.
  (2) A caveat shall remain in force for a period of one year from the date on which it was lodged and may be renewed on its expiry for a further period of one year and yearly thereafter.
  (3) An application for the renewal of a caveat shall be made in writing to the sheriff clerk not less than 7 days before its expiry.
  (4) Where a caveat has been lodged and has not expired, no order in

respect of which the caveat was lodged may be pronounced unless the sheriff is satisfied that all reasonable steps have been taken to afford the person lodging the caveat an opportunity of being heard; and the sheriff may continue the hearing on such an order until he is satisfied that such steps have been taken.

Amendments

4.—(1) Rule 20 of the Act of Sederunt (Sheriff Court Company Insolvency Rules) 1986 shall be omitted.

(2) Chapter 4 of, and Form G2 in Appendix 1 to, the Ordinary Cause Rules 1993 in Schedule 1 to the Sheriff Courts (Scotland) Act 1907 shall be omitted.

(3) Rules 2.8 and 2.9 of, and Form 8 in Schedule 1 to, the Act of Sederunt (Summary Applications, Statutory Applications, and Appeals etc. Rules) 1999 shall be omitted.

Transitional and savings provision

5.—(1) Subject to paragraph (2), nothing in this Act of Sederunt shall affect a caveat lodged prior to 28th April 2006.

(2) A caveat lodged prior to 28th April 2006 may not be renewed unless the caveat complies with the requirements of this Act of Sederunt.

Rule 3(1) SCHEDULE

Form of Caveat

SHERIFFDOM OF (*insert name of sheriffdom*)

AT (*insert place of sheriff court*)

CAVEAT for [A.B.] (*insert designation and address **))

Should any application be made for (*here specify, under reference to sub-paragraphs of rule 2(1), the application(s) to which this caveat is to apply*) [before the lodging of a notice of intention to defend [*or (specify for each application which of the following alternatives is to apply*: the expiry of the period within which a notice of intention to defend may be lodged; before service of the initial writ or petition)]], it is requested that intimation be made to the caveator before any order is pronounced.

Date (*insert date*) Signed

[A.B.]

or [X.Y.] Solicitor for [A.B.]
(*add designation, business address and email address*)

Caveator's telephone and fax number (*insert where caveat is not lodged by solicitors*)

Solicitor (*insert name and address, telephone and fax number and reference*)

Out of hours contacts:

1. (*insert name and telephone number*)
2. (*insert name and telephone number*)

* State whether the caveat is lodged in an individual capacity, or a specified representative capacity (e.g. as a trustee of a named trust) or both. Where appropriate, state the nature of the caveator's interest (e.g. shareholder, debenture holder).

Act of Sederunt (Jurisdiction, Recognition and Enforcement of Judgments in Matrimonial Matters and Matters of Parental Responsibility Rules) 2006

(SSI 2006/397)

[August 1, 2006]

The Lords of Council and Session, under and by virtue of the powers conferred by section 32 of the Sheriff Courts (Scotland) Act 1971, and of all other powers enabling them in that behalf, having approved draft rules submitted to them by the Sheriff Court Rules Council in accordance with section 34 of that Act, do hereby enact and declare:

Citation and commencement

1. This Act of Sederunt may be cited as the Act of Sederunt (Jurisdiction, Recognition and Enforcement of Judgments in Matrimonial Matters and Matters of Parental Responsibility Rules) 2006 and shall come into force on 1st August 2006.

Interpretation

2.—(1) In this Act of Sederunt—
"central authority" means an authority designated under Article 53 of the Council Regulation;
"the Council Regulation" means Council Regulation (EC) No. 2201/ 2003 of 27th November 2003 concerning jurisdiction and the recognition and enforcement of judgments in matrimonial matters and matters of parental responsibility;
"foreign court" means a court in a Member State other than the United Kingdom;
"Member State" has the same meaning as in Article 2(3) of the Council Regulation;
"parental responsibility" has the same meaning as in Article 2(7) of the Council Regulation; and
"these Rules" means the rules set out in this Act of Sederunt.
(2) A form referred to in these Rules by number means the form so numbered in the Schedule to this Act of Sederunt or a form substantially to the same effect, with such variation as circumstances may require.
(3) A reference in these Rules to a numbered Article is a reference to the Article of the Council Regulation so numbered.
(4) Except as provided for in these Rules or any order made by a sheriff hereunder, any action to which these Rules apply shall proceed as an ordinary cause under the First Schedule to the Sheriff Courts (Scotland) Act 1907.

Transfer of case involving matters of parental responsibility to sheriff court

3.—(1) A request to a sheriff court under Article 15(1)(a) (request by parties to transfer case involving parental responsibilities) shall be made by initial writ under these Rules.
(2) Where a sheriff court receives a request from a foreign court under Article 15(1)(b) (request by court to assume jurisdiction)—
(a) the sheriff clerk shall forthwith—
(i) acknowledge receipt of the request to the foreign court;
(ii) intimate the request to the parties to the action, their Scottish agents, if known, and any other party to whom the sheriff considers that intimation should be made; and
(iii) intimate to the parties and, if known, their Scottish agents, the requirement to lodge an initial writ under subparagraph (b)

within the time limit set by the foreign court under Article 15(4) (time limit for seising the court); and

(b) one of the parties shall lodge an initial writ under these Rules.

(3) Where no initial writ has been lodged within the time limit set by the foreign court under Article 15(4), the sheriff clerk shall advise the foreign court that the sheriff court has not been seised under Article 16 (seising of a court).

General provisions for transfer to sheriff court

4.—(1) An initial writ under these Rules shall—

(a) include the following heading printed above the instance—
"ACT OF SEDERUNT (JURISDICTION, RECOGNITION AND ENFORCEMENT OF JUDGMENTS IN MATRIMONIAL MATTERS AND MATTERS OF PARENTAL RESPONSIBILITY RULES) 2006"; and

(b) include averments stating—

(i) the full name, designation, postal address, telephone and facsimile numbers and, where appropriate, e-mail address of each of the parties to the action involving parental responsibilities, including any Scottish agent instructed to represent any of the parties;

(ii) the postal address and telephone and facsimile numbers of the foreign court and the name and, where appropriate, e-mail address of any official of the court to whom any document may be sent by the sheriff clerk;

(iii) the full name, postal address and date of birth of the child;

(iv) the status of the proceedings in the foreign court;

(v) the particular connection the child has with Scotland;

(vi) why it is in the best interests of the child that the case should be heard in the sheriff court;

(vii) the time limit set by the foreign court under Article 15(4);

(2) There shall be lodged with an initial writ under these Rules any document considered by the pursuer to be relevant to the action involving parental responsibilities including any papers forming part of the process of the case in the foreign court.

(3) A warrant for citation in respect of an initial writ under these Rules shall be signed by the sheriff.

(4) The sheriff may make such order as to intimation or service, fixing a hearing to determine jurisdiction or otherwise as he thinks fit.

(5) On the fixing of a date for a hearing to determine jurisdiction the pursuer shall—

(a) intimate to every other party a notice in Form 1;

(b) lodge a certificate of intimation in Form 2,

within any time limit specified by the sheriff.

Acceptance of jurisdiction by sheriff court in matters of parental responsibility

5.—(1) An interlocutor accepting or refusing to accept jurisdiction to hear an action commenced by initial writ under these Rules shall be signed by the sheriff.

(2) After the expiry of the time limit for any appeal the sheriff clerk shall intimate the decision of the sheriff court to the foreign court by sending to the foreign court—

(a) a copy interlocutor by electronic mail or facsimile transmission; and

(b) a certified copy interlocutor by first class recorded delivery or registered post.

Application by sheriff court to foreign court for transfer of case involving matters of parental responsibility

6.—(1) Where in any action a sheriff decides to make an application to a foreign court under Article 15(2)(c) (application for transfer of case involving parental responsibilities to sheriff court) he shall append to the interlocutor a note containing—

(a) the full name, designation and postal address, telephone and facsimile numbers and, where appropriate, e-mail address of all the parties to the case involving parental responsibilities, including any agent instructed to represent the parties in the foreign court;

(b) details of the particular connection the child is considered to have with Scotland; and

(c) such other matters as he considers would be of assistance to the foreign court in deciding whether or not to seek a transfer of the case under Article 15(1) (transfer to a court better placed to hear the case).

(2) The sheriff clerk shall forthwith send to the foreign court—

(a) a copy interlocutor and note under paragraph (1) by electronic mail or by facsimile transmission; and

(b) a certified copy interlocutor and note by first class recorded delivery or registered post.

Application by foreign court to sheriff court for transfer of case involving matters of parental responsibility

7. On receipt of an application by a foreign court under Article 15(2)(c) (application for transfer of case involving parental responsibilities to foreign court) the sheriff clerk shall—

(a) give written intimation of the application and any accompanying documents to each party to the case;

(b) fix a time and date for a hearing to consider the application; and

(c) intimate the hearing to each party to the action.

Transfer by sheriff court of case involving matters of parental responsibility

8.—(1) An interlocutor pronounced by a sheriff sisting a case and inviting parties to make a request to a foreign court under Article 15(1)(a) or requesting a foreign court to assume jurisdiction under Article 15(1)(b) shall—

(a) specify the particular connection the child has to the Member State of the foreign court;

(b) set a time limit within which the foreign court may be seised in terms of Article 15(4);

(c) specify which of sub-paragraphs (a) to (c) of Article 15(2) applies and, where appropriate, which of the parties to the action have accepted the transfer.

(2) The sheriff shall append to the interlocutor a note stating—

(a) the reasons why he considers that it would be in the best interests of the child that the foreign court should hear the case; and

(b) such other matters as he considers would be of assistance to the foreign court in deciding whether or not to accept jurisdiction under Article 15(5) (acceptance of jurisdiction).

(3) Where an interlocutor under Article 15(1)(b) has been pronounced on the sheriff's own motion or on an application from the foreign court, the sheriff clerk shall send a certified copy of the interlocutor and note to each of the parties.

(4) Within seven days of any interlocutor pronounced under Article 15(1)(b) (request by court to assume jurisdiction), the sheriff clerk shall send to the foreign court—

(a) a copy of the interlocutor and note under paragraph (2) by electronic mail or by facsimile transmission;

(b) a certified copy of the interlocutor and note by first class recorded delivery or registered post.

(5) The party who effects seisure of the foreign court shall no later than seven days after the expiry of the time limit specified by the sheriff under

paragraph (1)(b) lodge in process a certificate stating the date on which the seisure was effected.

(6) Within 14 days of the date of the decision of the foreign court whether or not to accept jurisdiction in accordance with Article 15(5), the party who effected seisure of that court shall lodge in process a certified copy of the order of the foreign court or other document confirming its decision.

Translation of documents

9. Where any document received from a foreign court or otherwise under these Rules is in a language other than English, the sheriff may order that there shall be lodged with that document a translation into English certified as correct by the translator; and the certificate shall include his full name, address and qualifications.

Enforcement in another Member State of sheriff court judgments etc.

10.—(1) Where a person seeks to apply under the Council Regulation for recognition or enforcement in another Member State of a judgment given by a sheriff court, he shall apply by letter to the sheriff clerk of that court for—

    (a) a certificate under Article 39 of the Council Regulation (certificates concerning judgments in matrimonial matters or matters of parental responsibility); and

    (b) a certified copy of the judgment (incorporating the sheriff's interlocutor and note).

(2) The sheriff clerk shall not issue a certificate under paragraph (1)(a) unless there is produced to him an execution of service of the judgment on the person against whom it is sought to be enforced.

(3) Where a judgment granting rights of access delivered by the sheriff court acquires a cross-border character after the judgment has been delivered and a party seeks to enforce the judgment in another Member State, he shall apply by letter to the sheriff clerk for—

    (a) a certificate under Article 41 of the Council Regulation (certificate concerning rights of access); and

    (b) a certified copy of the judgment (incorporating the sheriff's interlocutor and note).

Placement of child in another Member State

11. Where the sheriff requires under Article 56 of the Council Regulation to obtain the consent of a competent authority in another Member State to the placement of a child he shall send a request in Form 3 and any other documents he considers to be relevant to the Scottish central authority for transmission to the central authority in the other Member State.

SCHEDULE

Rule 4(5)   FORM 1

Form of notice of intimation of a hearing to determine jurisdiction under Article 15 of Council Regulation (EC) No.2201/2003 of 27th November 2003

Date: (*date of posting or other method of intimation*)

To: (*name and address*)

TAKE NOTICE

(*Name and address of pursuer*) has lodged an initial writ in the Sheriff Court at (*place*) against (*name and address of defender*).

The parties are presently engaged in proceedings involving matters of parental responsibility in (*specify court in other Member State where proceedings have been raised*) and a request has been made to the sheriff court to accept jurisdiction of these proceedings and for the action to be dealt with in the Sheriff Court.

A hearing has been fixed on (*date*) at (*time*) within the Sheriff Court to determine the issue of jurisdiction.

You may appear or be represented by a person having a right of audience before the Sheriff Court at the hearing.

You or your representative will be asked whether you agree to jurisdiction being accepted by the Sheriff Court and the proceedings involving matters of parental responsibility being dealt with in the Sheriff Court.

If you do not appear or are not represented at the hearing the court may decide whether to accept jurisdiction in your absence.

(signed)

Solicitor for pursuer

(add name and business address)

Rule 4(5)   FORM 2

Certificate of Intimation of a hearing to determine jurisdiction under Article 15 of Council Regulation (EC) No.2201/2003 of 27th November 2003

in causa

AB Pursuer

against

CD Defender

I certify that intimation of a hearing to determine jurisdiction under Article 15 of Council Regulation (EC) No.2201/2003 of 27 November 2003 was made to:

Date: (*date of posting or other method of intimation*)

To: (*name and address*)

Date: (*date of posting or other method of intimation*)

To: (*name and address*)

Date: (*date of posting or other method of intimation*)

To: (*name and address*)

Date: (*insert date*)   (*signed*)

Solicitor for pursuer

(*add name and business address*)

Rule 11   FORM 3

Form of request for consent to placement of child under Article 56 of Council Regulation (EC) No.2201/2003 of 27th November 2003

Date: (*date of request*)

To: (*name and address of competent authority in other Member State*)

The Sheriff Court has jurisdiction in matters of parental responsibility under the Council Regulation (EC) No.2201/2003 of 27th November 2003 in respect of (*name and address of child*). The court is contemplating the placement of (*name of child*) in (*name and address of institution*) [*or* with (*name and address of foster family*)] and requests your consent to the placement in accordance with Article 56 of Council Regulation.

(*Signed*)

Sheriff Clerk